Human Resource Management

Human Resource Management

Second edition

Edited by
Sarah Gilmore
Steve Williams

OXFORD
UNIVERSITY PRESS

OXFORD
UNIVERSITY PRESS

Great Clarendon Street, Oxford, OX2 6DP,
United Kingdom

Oxford University Press is a department of the University of Oxford.
It furthers the University's objective of excellence in research, scholarship,
and education by publishing worldwide. Oxford is a registered trade mark of
Oxford University Press in the UK and in certain other countries

British Library Cataloguing in Publication Data

Data available

ISBN 978–0–19–960548–4

Printed in Italy by
L.E.G.O.S.p.A–Lavis TN

Acknowledgements

First of all, we would like to record our thanks to the editorial staff of Oxford University Press, particularly Alex Lazarus-Priestly, Francesca Griffin, and Kirsten Shankland, for their help and support in producing the second edition of this book.

We received very helpful feedback on the first edition and on draft chapters for this edition from the publisher's reviewers. Our thanks go to them.

We also acknowledge the kind permission of the following organizations, individuals, and publishers for permission to use their copyright material.

Sandals Holiday Resorts for material used in Box 3.1.

The Firmdale Hotel Group for material used in the Chapter 2 case study.

The National Theatre for material used in the Chapter 6 case study.

M. Easterby-Smith and I. Mikhailava (2011) for material used in Box 6.11.

Mark Power for the use of his work in the Chapter 11 case study.

Tesco PLC for material from its Code of Business Conduct in Box 14.4.

Pearson PLC for material from *People Resourcing and Talent Planning: HRM in Practice* (4th edn, 2010) by Stephen Pilbeam and Marjorie Corbridge, ISBN 9780273719540, used in Chapter 5 (Box 5.10, Figure 5.1, and Table 5.1) and Chapter 7 (Figure 7.1 and Box 7.8).

Pearson PLC for material from *Organizing and Managing Work* (2002) by Tony Watson used in Chapter 5 (Box 5.10).

Edward Elgar for the material in Box 9.9, adapted from *Globalization and Precarious Forms of Production and Employment: Challenges for Workers and Unions* (2010) edited by C. Thornley, S. Jeffreys, and B. Appay.

Gower Publishing for the material in Box 9.4, adapted by permission of the Publishers, from *Labour and Management Co-operation* by Stewart Johnstone (Farnham: Gower, 2010). Copyright © 2010.

The material in Box 15.8, which is adapted from the chapter 'The role of the international personnel function' in P. Almond and A. Ferner (eds), *American Multinationals in Europe*, is included by permission of Oxford University Press.

How to use this book

There are a number of key learning tools within every chapter of *Human Resource Management* that are designed to help you to both retain and organize information. Many of these features emphasize how theory is applied in real-world organizations while others help you to gain a deeper understanding of how this links to practice. All of this helps you to ground your theoretical understanding of process and policy in the practice of human resource management (HRM).

Learning objectives

The main objectives of this chapter are to:

- Discuss the different meanings of the term 'human resource management'
- Illustrate the diverse work undertaken by the human resources (HR) function
- Analyse the reasons for the growth of HRM, placing its arrival and development wider fluctuating economic and political context.
- Focus on contemporary debates concerning HRM, highlighting the 'prom as the difficulties faced in delivering on the main assurances made if org philosophies and practices associated with this mode of people manage

Learning objectives

Each chapter opens with a bulleted list of the main concepts and ideas it covers. These serve as helpful signposts outlining what you can expect to learn from each chapter and help you check your progress.

Box 1.1 Window on work
Recruiting for staff

These organizations all need to expand their staff, but this will take different for challenges given the nature of the business—as these three illustrations suggest.
Jaguar Land Rover (JLR) is taking on more than 1000 production staff at a plant thus increasing the workforce at the Solihull plant by more than 25 per cent. Eme China and India have been key to its success, which has also seen the organizati neers. Whilst the market for cars in Europe is weak, markets like Russia, China, purchase 'trophy brand' cars like Jaguar and Land Rover (BBC News Online 2011a the announcement, the organization had received 8000 applications for the 1000
Since the launch of the UK government's 'East London Tech City' initiative, profile has expanded considerably and the Shoreditch area of London is now

Window on work

The book is packed with examples which link the topic to real-life organizations to help you gain an understanding of HRM in practice.

Assignment and discussion questio

1 What do you understand by the term 'HRM'?
2 How would you account for the growth of interest in HRM? Which factors do yo to its continued appeal and why?
3 To what extent have wider socio-economic developments impacted on the e practices designed to instigate employee commitment and engagement?
4 What are the main reasons behind the devolution of much HR activity to line ma lenges do you think will have been faced by both line managers and the HR functi organizations overcome them?
5 What are the future challenges for people management?

Assignment and discussion questions

A set of carefully designed questions has been provided to help you assess your comprehension of core themes and may also be used as the basis of seminar discussion and coursework.

Box 1.5 Research in focus
Contrasting approaches towards HRM

'Hard'/'low-road' HRM

Business perspective/time horizon: short term
Emphasis of business strategies: competitive advantage gained through price
Orientation to employees: *Utilitarian instrumentalism*—an expense of doing bu
Contractual bases of employment: non-standard workers—PT working, fixed employees to avoid statutory costs associated with permanent employment
'Numerical flexibility' used to contain costs relative to product/service d

Research in focus

Examples of academic research by key writers in the field provide you with access to seminal contributions to HRM.

Box 1.4 International focus
The implications of offshoring and the rise of rural sou

The practice of 'offshoring' generally involves transfer of business functions and one country to another. Whilst the main rationale for offshoring is usually to through the migration of jobs from higher- to lower-waged economies, it can al reasons. These include entering new markets to tap talent that is currently unav or to overcome regulations that restrict business activity. The bulk of offshored centres, software development, human resource management administration, an Increasingly, higher value-added jobs are being offshored, such as complex finance ogy R&D, and innovation. The major providers of offshore services are China, Ind Philippines, Poland, Russia, and South Africa, with India accounting for the larg

International focus

Examples of international research and case studies offer insight into global HRM practice.

Learning activities

These are short questions and examples which give you the opportunity to relate the topic to your own experience.

Box 1.8 Learning activity
Engaging employees

In small groups brainstorm the various actions organizations might take to ensu employees. Evaluate this list against your collective and individual work exper did employers engage in to make you feel more engaged? Why do you think commonly used? To what extent were differential approaches used depending a full-time permanent member of staff or employed on a part-time basis? If th what were the outcomes for you and for the organization? If your experience secure your engagement and that of your colleagues, how did that make you organization and the kinds of effort you were willing to exert on its behalf?

Practitioner perspectives

These boxes provide you with insight into the questions and considerations that HRM practitioners and line managers face when engaging with HRM issues and putting policies into practice.

Box 1.3 Practitioner perspective
Executive pay

For several years, concern has been expressed over the degree of remunerati figures in the financial services industry, leading, for example, to major pensio cal overhaul of boardroom pay in an effort to curb or end the payouts which of public discontent and negative publicity (Treanor 2012a). However, Richard Asset Resolution (UKAR), the operation that oversees Bradford and Bingley and of Northern Rock, decided to take a 5 per cent cut to his £250,000 fees. In his st report Pym said: 'We are very conscious that we currently owe HM Treasury £46.6bn and it is our expectation and our determination to repay that debt in taxpayer' (Treanor 2012b). The bank admits that they have a significant numb

Online video links

Links to videos hosted on the accompanying Online Resource Centre provide further insight into the workings of HRM in practice.

Box 1.7 Online video link
Investigating human capital

For an exploration of human capital in organizations follow the links provided to video content i Online Resource Centre. Note that they are distinctively different in terms of their focus and orientatio

Summary and further reading

Each chapter section ends with a set of key points that summarize the most important arguments developed within that chapter topic. An annotated list of recommended reading on each subject will help guide you further into the literature on a particular subject area.

Summary and further reading

* Organizations have responded to changes in their business environments in a nur have been influenced by developments in IT and its widespread use as well as a sv semi-skilled work to managerial and professional jobs. Other responses involved working time and changes to contracts. The growth of flexible working has also be techniques such as business process re-engineering, downsizing, and delayering.
* Whilst some commentators argue that Britain has survived this period of heighten good shape, there is also evidence of heightened worker insecurity. However, the results in poor performance outcomes is not clear.
* Such evidence questions the extent to which commitment-based approaches tow utilized. Whilst approaches based in the adoption of more sophisticated and rec

Case studies

A longer case study at the end of each chapter provides an opportunity to apply what you have learnt and analyse a real-life example in detail.

Case study
Business strategy and HRM in boutique h

From their inception in the mid-1980s, boutique hotels appealed to consumer alternatives to traditional forms of hotel accommodation. Now, as guests increas hotel provides an experience in itself and is not just a place to sleep, the boutique 'right' place to stay. Hotels seen as 'boutique' tend to stress a highly personalized ser style in every aspect of their offering, from the hotel's architecture to the design of th generous amenities provided (Lim and Endean 2009). Whilst not all boutique hote generally smaller than their chain counterparts and have between 150 and 200 roo important in terms of creating the sense of intimacy that is also a feature of many
    Yet the boutique hotel is phenomenon not simply built on a designer ethos

Policy examples

Examples of HR policies in action illustrate and contextualize real-world people management strategies.

Box 2.10 Policy example
Shaping the future?

What will truly make the difference for the long-term performance of organizati Institute of Personnel and Development's 'Shaping the Future' (CIPD 2011j) hig emerging as being important in achieving this outcome: alignment, shared purp of engagement, assessment and evaluation, balancing short- and long-term h capability-building. For the CIPD, these themes yield core insights for HRM profe ers as to what will truly make the difference for the long-term performance of include the need for an organization to have an agile response to change, for org to find the human connection, for collaborative rather than directive modes of m revitalizing role that middle management could play in organizational transformat

Skills exercises

In these exercises, imagine how you might apply various concepts in practice yourself, developing transferable skills which will stand you in good stead for life beyond university.

Box 2.3 Skills exercise
Making the strategic case for HRM

In two groups, choose a large organization you are familiar with. Investigate what the organization are—these are often found on the company website. One group of the HRM function and the other should be the organization's strategic decision-developing the company's strategic direction and goals. The HRM group should de to the strategists arguing for their inclusion in the forthcoming strategy process. T consider what arguments and evidence the function needs to make in order for t and formulate questions to pose to the other group as they make their presen debriefing the exercise, decide which were the most important arguments that the to make. To what extent were they made and what was the most compelling evid

How to use the Online Resource Centre

 www.oxfordtextbooks.co.uk/orc/gilmore_williams2e/

For registered adopters of the text

Contemporary HRM debates

- Human capital
  - Labour treated as an asset rather than a cost with investment central to competitive advantage
- Talent management

PowerPoint lecture slides

A suite of PowerPoint slides has been designed by the authors for use in your lecture presentations which highlight the main points from each chapter. These can be easily customized to match your own lecture style.

Test bank in QTI XML format

    Choose this option if your institution uses assessme industry standard of QTI XML.

Test bank in Respondus format

    Choose this option if you have Respondus at your in the test bank into Blackboard, WebCT or another Vir Environment/Course Management System.

Test bank in Word format

    Choose this option if your institution does not have a wish to view the questions available in the test bank.

Test bank

For each chapter a set of questions has been devised by the authors. The test bank is fully automated for quick and convenient use online: automated grading allows you to access your students' progress via your university's Virtual Learning Environment and instant feedback shows your students what they need to work on for revision purposes.

Candidates — **THE RECRUITMENT AND SELECTION SUB-SYSTEM** — Effective employees

Labour market characteristics

Recruitment and selection methods
- Attraction
- Reduction
- Selection
- Transition

Organizational constraints

Figures and tables from the book

All figures and tables from the text have been provided for you to download for lecture presentations, or to include in handouts.

1. What do you understand by the term 'HRM'? Wha different from 'personnel management'?

    The chapter argues that there is no one accept definition which includes everything and anythi management and is therefore not tied towards managerial philosophy. However, the early pro was (and remains) a markedly different approa where long-term competitive advantage being

Guide to assignment and discussion questions

Helpful guides have been provided by the authors to assist instructors in using the discussion and assignment questions from the book within their teaching.

Employee Relations

Introductory brief

The chapter focus on illustrations and discussion of relations (both pluralism and the unitary approach a of pursuing either perspective for both employees a significance of joint regulation of the employment re union membership and impacts on the balance of p

Exercises to accompany DVD material

This text is accompanied by a DVD for adopting lecturers, featuring interviews with HRM practitioners from a variety of organizations. The DVD is referenced within the chapters while exercises to accompany the DVD are supplied online, providing a ready-made multi-media teaching package.

Guide to practitioner interviews

Diversity
Ruth Ovens - HR Director, Wilts
Charlotte Rayner - Professor of HRM, University of Portsm
Sarah Veale - Head of Equality and Employment Rights, TU

Employee Relations
Pam Bader - Chief Executive, Molly Maid UK

To help you navigate the DVD, a breakdown has been created showing the time blocks of the topics within each clip (both by theme and by practitioner).

Suggested seminar activities

Divide the seminar group into smaller groups of three
group a different bundle of employment information f
students will have some familiarity. This information
organizational websites and should include recruitme
conditions of employment, their approach towards be
training and development, as well as material illustra
employment and their employees.

The authors have compiled a range of ready-made activities that may be incorporated into your teaching to expand and develop key themes from the book.

VLE content

An easy way to import all the material available on this Online Resource Centre into your VLE.

For students

Multiple-choice questions

Question 1

In which decade did HRM arrive in the UK?

○ a) 1950s
◉ b) 1970s
○ c) 1980s
○ d) 1990s

Ten multiple-choice questions for each chapter provide a quick and easy way to test your understanding during revision. These self-marking questions give you instant feedback and provide page references to the textbook to help you focus on areas which may need further study.

Web links

www.leeds.ac.uk/esrcfutureofwork/
The ESRC's Future of Work Programme spans the full ran
disciplines and seeks to provide much needed evidence a
enhance public understanding of the critical developments
people's working lives.

www.cipd.co.uk/default.cipd
The CIPD is the professional body for those working in the
as well as training and development.

www.berr.gov.uk/

A series of annotated web links provide direction to key research and useful organizations for further reading and study.

Online video links

For an exploration of human capital in organizations watch
distinctively different in terms of their focus and orientation:

http://www.youtube.com/watch?v=2n_TvsJPLQU&feature
http://www.youtube.com/watch?v=UrJDqDUq8JQ

Video links connect relevant external HRM audiovisual content to themes and chapters from the book.

Interactive glossary of terms

◀ PREVIOUS   FLIP ↻ CARD

Downsizing

Learning the jargon associated with the range of topics in human resource management can be a challenge, so this glossary draws together the key terms in one convenient reference tool.

Contents in brief

Detailed contents

Detailed contents

Detailed contents

Part Five: Human resource management in broader perspective
295

List of tables

List of figures

List of boxes

Abbreviations

ACAS	Advisory, Conciliation, and Arbitration Service
ADR	alternative dispute resolution
BARS	behaviourally anchored rating scales
BBC	British Broadcasting Corporation
BERR	(Department of) Business, Enterprise, and Regulatory Reform
BIS	(Department of) Business, Innovation, and Skills
BPR	business process re-engineering
BRIC	Brazil, Russia, India, and China
CAC	Central Arbitration Committee
CBI	Confederation of British Industry
CEDAW	Convention on the Elimination of all forms of Discrimination Against Women
CEO	Chief Executive Officer
CIA	Central Intelligence Agency
CIPD	Chartered Institute of Personnel and Development
CMI	Chartered Management Institute
CoP	community of practice
CPD	continuing professional development
CPI	Consumer Price Index
CSA	Child Support Agency
CSR	corporate social responsibility
CV	curriculum vitae
DCT	disconnected capitalism thesis
DTI	Department of Trade and Industry
DWP	Department of Work and Pensions
EAP	Employee Assistance Programme
ECF	Essex Competency Framework
EHRC	Equality and Human Rights Commission
EI	employee involvement
EOC	Equal Opportunities Commission
ETI	Ethical Trading Initiative
EU	European Union
FDI	foreign direct investment
FLM	front-line manager
GDP	gross domestic product
GMD	genuine material defence
GNP	gross national product
GOR	genuine occupational requirement
HASAWA	Health and Safety at Work Act 1974
HCM	human capital management
HCN	host country national
HPWP	high-performance work practice
HPWO	high-performance work organization
HPWS	high-performance work system
HR	human resources

HRM	human resource management
HSE	Health and Safety Executive
HtFV	hard-to-fill vacancy
ICE	Information and Communication with Employees
ICT	information and communication technology
IDS	Incomes Data Services
IHRM	international human resource management
IiP	Investors in People
IJV	international joint venture
ILO	International Labour Organization
IMD	international management development
IMF	International Monetary Fund
IPPR	Institute for Public Policy Research
IRS	Industrial Relations Services
IT	information technology
KPI	key performance indicator
KSA	knowledge, skills, and attributes
LA	local authority
LCEGS	low carbon and environmental goods and services
LIFO	last-in, first-out
LSVT	large-scale voluntary transfer
MBO	management by objectives
MHSW	Management of Health and Safety at Work
MNC	multi-national company
MSF	Médicins Sans Frontières
NAO	National Audit Office
NCVO	National Council for Voluntary Organizations
NESS	National Employers' Skills Survey
NGO	non-governmental organization
NHS	National Health Service
NMC	Nursing and Midwifery Council
NMW	National Minimum Wage
NT	National Theatre
NUJ	National Union of Journalists
NVQ	National Vocational Qualification
OCBs	organizational citizenship behaviours
OECD	Organization for Economic Cooperation and Development
PATH	Positive Action on Training in Housing
PCN	parent country national
PHT	Portsmouth Hospitals NHS Trust
PMS	performance management system
PRP	performance-related pay
QCA	Qualifications and Curriculum Authority
QCDA	Qualifications and Curriculum Development Agency
QCF	Qualifications and Curriculum Framework
RBV	resource-based view
RPA	Redundancy Payments Act
RPI	Retail Price Index

RSI	repetitive strain injury
SBU	strategic business unit
SH	social housing
SHRM	strategic human resource management
SIE	self-initiated expatriate
SNVQ	Scottish National Vocational Qualification
SOE	state-owned enterprise
SSC	Sector Skills Council
SSV	skill-shortage vacancy
STC	systematic training cycle
SWOT	strengths, weaknesses, opportunities, threats
TCN	third country national
TNA	training needs analysis
TQM	total quality management
TUC	Trades Union Congress
UKCES	UK Commission for Employment and Skills
VAB	values, attitudes, and behaviour
VET	vocational education and training
WERS	Workplace Employment Relations Survey
WEU	Women and Equality Unit
WWF	World Wildlife Fund
WTO	World Trade Organization

About this book

This new edition of *Human Resource Management*, which has been extensively revised and updated, is designed to serve as an introduction to human resource management (HRM), and is suitable for undergraduate students studying HRM modules as part of a degree in business or a business-related subject. The book is also suitable for Master's-level students who are studying HRM modules for the first time. It is written by a team of writers based mainly at the University of Portsmouth's Business School who are actively engaged in teaching, researching, and undertaking consultancy in aspects of HRM.

The sixteen chapters are organized in five parts. Part One is devoted to the nature of HRM in contemporary organizations. In Chapter 1 the origins, development, and characteristics of HRM are considered. In Chapter 2 the focus is on the role of HRM in a strategic business context, examining the key ways in which writers on HRM have sought to understand the relationship between overall business objectives and the management of human resources.

Part Two of the book is concerned with the contexts in which HRM operates. Chapter 3 pays attention to the external context—the nature of the business environment—highlighting among other things some of the key economic, social, and political influences that influence HRM in organizations. The emphasis in Chapter 4 is on the implications of the internal organizational context, such as the structure and design of organizations and organizational change, for the management of human resources.

Part Three consists of five chapters which are devoted to examining integral elements of HRM in practice—what we term the 'essence' of HRM. Chapter 5 is concerned with the recruitment and selection of staff, and includes an analysis of the most effective means of selecting employees. Chapter 6 is devoted to the topics of training and employee development; among other things it examines the extent to which a greater emphasis on learning is coming to dominate this area of HRM. The focus of Chapter 7 is on the nature of, and key contemporary trends in, pay and reward, while Chapter 8 is concerned with the key elements involved in utilizing human resources, including coverage of talent management and employee well-being. In Chapter 9, the final chapter in Part Three, the important topic of redundancy is examined.

Part Four comprises four chapters which highlight particular challenges and controversies in HRM. In Chapter 10, the implications for HRM of issues relating to equality, diversity, and dignity at work are considered. The issue of managing employee performance effectively, and the related topic of employee absence, are covered in Chapter 11. Chapter 12 is concerned with employment relations, which includes material on the challenges of managing employment relationships, especially in environments where trade unions are present. In Chapter 13 the emphasis is on managing workplace conflict, including material on grievances and disciplinary issues, and ways of attempting to resolve it.

The main purpose of Part Five, the final part of the book, is to introduce a broader perspective to HRM. With this in mind, Chapter 14 is concerned with the ethical dimension of HRM, and applies ethical analysis to some key HRM issues. This broader perspective is sustained in Chapter 15, which focuses on some key elements of the increasingly important international aspect of the HRM subject area. The concluding chapter—Chapter 16—reviews the principal features of HRM in organizations and points to some of the possible directions it may take, and the challenges that it is likely to encounter, over the next few years. It also reflects on some of the key principles underpinning the book, namely the relevance of six underlying themes—which we introduce now.

It is often said, and it is something of a cliché, that people are an organization's most valuable assets. But one of the assumptions that underpin contemporary understandings of HRM is that the way in which people are managed in organizations should be undertaken in a way that helps to realize business goals. Thus HRM, it is argued, is marked by a strategic orientation, concerned with designing policies and practices that support business objectives and overall business strategy. But how significant is this supposed strategic role in practice?

Following on from this, the basis of effective HRM is said to be about enabling, developing, and supporting improvements in the performance of employees, and thus by implication enhancing business performance. Thus HRM in contemporary organizations is concerned with managing people in a way that contributes to better performance. But how does HRM deliver performance improvements in practice, and how effectively does it do so?

One of the key sources of business effectiveness in the twenty-first century concerns the extent to which it is capable of being adaptable, responsive, and fleet of foot, and thus able to achieve success in a rapidly changing environment. Clearly, the flexibility of employees is a key determinant of organizational adaptability and responsiveness—something on which HRM will have a profound influence. In what ways, though, does HRM act to promote such flexibility?

Securing the organizational commitment of employees is often viewed as key to performance improvements and realizing organizational flexibility. How far, then, is HRM in contemporary organizations marked by an emphasis on securing the cooperation and commitment of staff to organizational goals, rather than on ensuring that they comply with organizational rules?

One of the main ways in which organizations seek to promote commitment is by establishing certain values and beliefs that help to guide employee behaviour or, as it is often termed, by instituting particular organizational cultures. Clearly, the way in which people are managed at work, and in particular how effectively they are managed, will have a pronounced influence on the degree to which an effective organizational culture can be developed.

Finally, it is important to bear in mind that the interests of the organization and those of its staff may not always be the same. Therefore, as a vehicle for managing people at work, HRM is also a means of effecting control over employees; for example, managers have to decide the level of pay and reward, something which might not attract the support of staff. In having to make decisions over such issues, managers may have to use their authority in organizations and exercise power. It is important to remember that managing human resources in organizations is not primarily about looking after employees, and seeing that their welfare and interests are upheld, although this is not an unimportant feature in some circumstances; rather, it is largely concerned with ensuring that the organization is populated with people whose behaviour is oriented towards securing its success. Thus an appreciation of power as a feature of HRM, as it is of all managerial activities, is central to developing a more critical appreciation of how people are managed in organizations.

In Chapter 16 the overall relevance of the themes, their importance to HRM in general, what we have learned about them, and how they contribute to a more effective understanding of HRM in organizations are considered. It is anticipated that this will enable you to develop a more reflective questioning understanding of the nature of HRM in contemporary organizations, one that does not take things as they appear for granted.

The book features a number of key learning aids that are designed to enhance your knowledge and understanding of HRM, supplementing the main chapter content. Within each chapter there are regular summaries, which highlight the key points of the previous section, or sections, and also feature suggestions for further reading that are designed to enable you to extend your learning of the material in question. There are also references to illustrative material from the DVD which accompanies this book. At the end of each chapter there is a case study which is designed to enhance your understanding of the practical relevance of the material you have covered. The end-of-chapter case studies come with questions which are designed to encourage you to apply your knowledge of HRM topics to organizational scenarios. There are also assignment and discussion questions at the end of each chapter; you can use these to focus, and reflect, on what you have learned. Towards the end of the book there is a guide to the key concepts that have been used, something which you will find handy for revision purposes.

Another key learning aid is the regular boxes that are featured within each chapter. There are seven types of box. 'Windows on work' consist of particularly interesting small cases, or illustrative material, which relate to the main text; they sometimes include questions for you to think about. The 'Learning activity' boxes include exercises for you to undertake, either individually or in a small group, which are designed to extend your knowledge and understanding of the material in question. There are also 'research in focus' boxes. These summarize a key aspect of relevant academic research, helping to illustrate the material in the main text.

'Policy example' boxes illustrate organizational policy, highlighting some aspect of how businesses, government bodies, and other organizations, such as trade unions, claim to deal with an HRM issue. As their name suggests, the 'International focus' boxes are designed to indicate the international dimension of the material. The 'Practitioner perspective' boxes are concerned with the views of people involved with HRM, such as human resource managers in organizations, on a particular topic. Like all the boxes, this is an effective means of illustrating the material in the main chapter and highlighting its relevance. Finally, the 'Skills exercise' boxes feature activities designed to enable you to develop your specific skills in specific areas of HRM, including performance appraisals, selection interviewing, and redundancy planning.

New to this edition

- The material has been reorganized into a new five-part structure.

- Skills exercise boxes have been added to each of the chapters.

- International focus boxes have been added to each chapter.

- A new chapter on utilizing human resources, which covers the topic of talent management, has been included.

- New material on resolving workplace conflict has been added to Chapter 13.

List of contributors

Iona Byford is a senior lecturer in Employment Relations at the University of Portsmouth Business School

Gill Christy is Head of the Department of Human Resource and Marketing Management and Principal Lecturer in Human Resource Management at the University of Portsmouth Business School

Richard Christy retired from the University of Portsmouth Business School in 2011, where he taught business ethics and marketing

Sarah Gilmore is a principal lecturer in Human Resource Management at the University of Portsmouth Business School

David Hall is a principal lecturer in Human Resource Management at the University of Portsmouth Business School

Liza Howe-Walsh is a senior lecturer in Human Resource Management at the University of Portsmouth Business School

Stephen Pilbeam is Principal Consultant at HR2020 Ltd, and was previously at the University of Portsmouth Business School

David Preece is Professor of Technology Management and Organization Studies, and Director of the Centre for Leadership and Organizational Change, at Teesside University Business School, Teesside University

Charlotte Rayner is Professor of Human Resource Management at the University of Portsmouth Business School

Sally Rumbles is a senior lecturer in Human Resource Management at the University of Portsmouth Business School

Peter Scott is a senior lecturer in Employment Relations at the University of Portsmouth Business School

Rob Thomas is an associate senior lecturer at the University of Portsmouth Business School

Steve Williams is a principal lecturer in Employment Relations at the University of Portsmouth Business School

Photograph acknowledgements

Part One

The nature of human resource management

Introducing human resource management

1

Sarah Gilmore

Learning objectives

The main objectives of this chapter are to:

- Discuss the different meanings of the term 'human resource management' (HRM).
- Illustrate the diverse work undertaken by the human resources (HR) function.
- Analyse the reasons for the growth of HRM, placing its arrival and development within a wider fluctuating economic and political context.
- Focus on contemporary debates concerning HRM, highlighting the 'promise' of HRM as well as the difficulties faced in delivering on the main assurances made if organizations adopt the philosophies and practices associated with this mode of people management.

1.1 Introduction

This book is concerned with human resource management (HRM) and the ways in which organizations manage their employees. This chapter will outline the various meanings of HRM, showing that it can refer to a specific functional role carried out by specialist staff as well as being a particular approach to people management. However, many companies do not have a specialist HRM department and line managers are given responsibility for carrying out people management activities. This means that the term 'HRM' can be wide-ranging in terms of what it involves, who undertakes it, and what it actually means. Section 1.2 highlights some of the activities that the human resources (HR) function carries out, and illustrates the contingent nature of their enactment. Although all organizations engage in certain people management activities, the ways in which they do so will depend significantly on factors such as the organization's size, the nature of the company's business, and the accepted professional and organizational norms as to how this work should be done. Section 1.3 explores the 'promise' of HRM, looking at what HRM as a set of ideas and associated practices pledged to organizations that adopted them, with Section 1.4 focusing on three aspects of contemporary HRM and how these connect to the 'bargain' HRM offers organizations. The context of this 'bargain' is explored in Section 1.5, placing attempts to secure high-performance/high-commitment 'high-road' HRM practices within a broader economic context. What these developments mean for the HR function, and what the future might hold for HRM, is explored in Sections 1.6 and 1.7.

1.2 HRM in practice

There is no one accepted view as to what HRM is. This book uses a loose definition of HRM which includes the policies and practices used to organize work and employ people; it encompasses the management of work and the management of people to do the work (Boxall and Purcell 2011: 3). It is also used in a narrower way to denote a distinctive approach to people management in both theoretical and practitioner terms. Other meanings used within this book will use the phrase 'human resources' to refer to the company's employees, and are one element of resource available to organizations, sitting alongside financial and other assets that facilitate the attainment of business goals. Finally, the expression can also refer to the Human Resources (HR) function or department that is tasked by many, often larger companies, with achieving effective people management.

1.2.1 The main HRM activities

It is virtually impossible to grow an organization without employing people, and HRM is a process that accompanies the expansion of organizations and as such can be seen as a correlate of entrepreneurial success and organizational growth (Boxall and Purcell 2011). HRM involves a wide range of activities, and responsibility for their enactment often lies with a range of staff within an organization. As such, it is rarely the *sole* responsibility of a dedicated department—meaning that the function (where it exists) does not always have control over its own domain. This can have unwelcome ramifications even though the devolution of day-to-day responsibility can allow HR staff to do more strategic, as opposed to operational, work. For those companies without a specialist function, HRM is usually the responsibility of line or functional managers.

The most common HRM activities involve a cycle of interrelated tasks starting with those actions concerned with assessing organizational needs for staff. This can involve determining whether such needs can be resourced internally, or whether the company needs to attract staff from the external labour market. But whilst all organizations engage in recruitment and selection of employees, the ways this activity will be carried out will be highly contingent on and depend on the resources available for this activity, such as staff expertise, time and money, the nature of the post, the size of the organization, and the company's business. These are highlighted in Box 1.1; the issues involved with recruitment and selection are discussed in more detail in Chapter 5. The DVD interview with Pam Bader provides insights as to the challenges faced by a small HRM team working in a franchising operation and shed light on the issues outlined below.

Box 1.1 Window on work
Recruiting for staff

These organizations all need to expand their staff, but this will take different forms and have different challenges given the nature of the business—as these three illustrations suggest.

Jaguar Land Rover (JLR) is taking on more than 1000 production staff at a plant in the West Midlands, thus increasing the workforce at the Solihull plant by more than 25 per cent. Emerging markets such as China and India have been key to its success, which has also seen the organization recruit 1000 engineers. Whilst the market for cars in Europe is weak, markets like Russia, China, and India are keen to purchase 'trophy brand' cars like Jaguar and Land Rover (BBC News Online 2011a). Within seven days of the announcement, the organization had received 8000 applications for the 1000 jobs (Peacock 2011).

Since the launch of the UK government's 'East London Tech City' initiative, Silicon Roundabout's profile has expanded considerably, and the Shoreditch area of London is now seeing an influx of entrepreneurs and technology companies. Most arrivals are small business start-ups who are attracted by the lower rents and shorter-term office leases available in the city (Bradshaw 2011). Recruitment company, Silicon Milkroundabout (www.siliconroundabout.org.uk), is concerned with attracting potential recruits from graduates through to senior level developers to opportunities in the tech sector which they might be unaware of because of the advertising spend made by big corporations when recruiting dwarfs that of the start-ups. More than 100 companies attend the regular Silicon Milkroundabout with an average of 500 jobs being on offer at each event (Solon 2011).

When the Glastonbury Festival is in full flow, it is akin to being in a huge tented city with distinct socio-geographic regions scattered across the site. Although 250,000 revellers will join the festival each year, very few people are directly employed by the festival itself. However, the festival requires large numbers of people to do various jobs in order for the event to take place. Specialist jobs such as stage hands, crew, and lighting technicians are handled by relevant companies who provide services to Glastonbury. However, there are opportunities to work for a ticket via other, less specialist, organizations who also provide volunteers to carry out a range of jobs such as gate stewards, tent stewards, and wardens (www.glastonburyfestivals.co.uk www.glastowatch.co.uk).

1.2.2 Achieving performance

Another focus of HR activity is that of achieving high performance by developing the skills and knowledge of staff, and aligning them to the needs of the organization. These development and training activities are outlined in more detail in Chapter 6. Assessing these needs often depends on data gathered from performance management systems, but the policies and procedures used by HR here will depend on a variety of organizational variables and will be explored in Chapter 11. However, the case illustration in Box 1.2 gives an insight into to how organizations can put this into practice.

1.2.3 Rewarding employees

One of the more challenging aspects of HR work involves pay and determining how staff will be rewarded. People are increasingly being paid in very flexible ways, and in many companies individuals can be employed and remunerated on varying bases. The differing bases on which people are paid and rewarded will often depend on the nature of the job they perform, what the organization can afford, and what each occupational group is worth in the wider employment market. They can also be based on the skills, knowledge, and experience individuals bring to a company, and the ways in which their contribution adds value to it. Some companies offer choices concerning their pay and benefits package, which reflects an acknowledgement that staff have diverse needs. These issues are discussed in more detail in Chapter 7, but Box 1.3 highlights some familiar areas of controversy seen with regard to executive pay.

1.2.4 Locating the organization

Finally, organizations and the HR function need to consider where the company will be based. Whilst some organizations have decided to relocate their entire business overseas to take

Box 1.2 Policy example
Matching training interventions with organizational needs at Infosys

Infosys is one of the fastest growing and most successful IT services companies in the world (www.infosys.com). The aim of the company is to become a provider of business solutions leveraging technology to compete with any consultancy in the world. This goal is built upon the vast talent pool available in India where the company is based, but it also depends on their commitment to maintain, enhance, and update skills at every level. Infosys uses a competency system to determine required skills and knowledge, and every individual must have a competency development plan, based on these competencies, which takes account of individual performance, organizational priorities and, where appropriate, client feedback.

Training interventions are organized in four key areas:

- technology and project management
- leadership and managerial including soft skills training
- domain training (knowledge of specific industry)
- quality processes.

The training department delivers programmes which are usually based away from the job itself and are mainly project specific. In addition, there is an ambitious knowledge management programme in place with rewards and recognition for those staff who submit knowledge ideas which are highly rated by their peers (CIPD 2006d; Anderson 2007).

advantage of lower operating costs in developing economies, others have been more selective as to what functions are offshored in this way (as is seen in Box 1.4). In addition, technological developments have had a profound impact on the ways in which work can be carried out, with greater use of home working, tele-working, and virtual working. All these decisions will have implications for people management. The increasingly international dimension of HRM and its staffing implications will be explored in Chapter 15.

Having considered some of the people management issues that all organizations will face as they grow, it is pertinent to explore HRM within the next two sections as a distinctive approach to the management of people, and then place the development of these ideas against a wider socio-economic context in Section 1.6.

Box 1.3 Practitioner perspective
Executive pay

For several years, concern has been expressed over the degree of remuneration received by senior figures in the financial services industry, leading, for example, to major pension funds urging a radical overhaul of boardroom pay in an effort to curb or end the payouts which have been the subject of public discontent and negative publicity (Treanor 2012a). However, Richard Pym, Chairman of UK Asset Resolution (UKAR), the operation that oversees Bradford and Bingley and the 'bad' banking arm of Northern Rock, decided to take a 5 per cent cut to his £250,000 fees. In his statement in the annual report Pym said: 'We are very conscious that we currently owe HM Treasury directly and indirectly £46.6bn and it is our expectation and our determination to repay that debt in full without loss to the taxpayer' (Treanor 2012b). The bank admits that they have a significant number of customers who are finding it difficult to meet their repayments, making 37,000 'mortgage and account modifications' to help those in trouble with repayments (Treanor 2012b).

- What relationship should exist between bonuses and company performance?
- What role do you think HR has or should have in deciding executive pay?

Box 1.4 International focus
The implications of offshoring and the rise of rural sourcing

The practice of 'offshoring' generally involves transfer of business functions and associated jobs from one country to another. Whilst the main rationale for offshoring is usually to achieve cost savings through the migration of jobs from higher- to lower-waged economies, it can also occur for strategic reasons. These include entering new markets to tap talent that is currently unavailable domestically or to overcome regulations that restrict business activity. The bulk of offshored activities include call centres, software development, human resource management administration, and payroll processing. Increasingly, higher value-added jobs are being offshored, such as complex financial analysis, technology R&D, and innovation. The major providers of offshore services are China, India, Ireland, Israel, the Philippines, Poland, Russia, and South Africa, with India accounting for the largest share of offshored jobs, mainly in IT and IT-enabled services.

However, offshoring has often generated negative publicity for organizations that shift jobs overseas. One option to offshoring is rural sourcing—having work done in domestic locations where salaries and operating expenses are lower (e.g. the Midwest of the USA). This allows companies to use the skills of professionals who choose to live in rural areas and reduces the costs to companies seeking their services because those living in rural areas generally have a lower cost of living. This means that companies can keep their projects in their host country and still reduce their overall spending. It also provides advantages in terms of the general absence of a language barrier and the relatively similar time zones—as opposed to most offshoring operations. For the workers, professionals who choose to live in rural communities for personal reasons are often willing to accept lower salaries than those obtainable in cities.

Whether a company opts to offshore or rural source, there will be HR implications associated with each option. What might they be and how might they differ?

1.3 The 'promise' of HRM

The term 'human resource management' originated in the USA in the early 1980s and offers the promise that the people management function, where it exists, can not only meet the challenges faced by contemporary organizations, such as heightened competitive pressures, industrial restructuring, and changes in the nature of work, but can also embody a heightened strategic role if its philosophies and practices are used coherently (Guest 1987; Storey 1992, 2001). Proponents argue that the HR function needs to design, implement, and manage a range of integrated and sophisticated people management techniques concerned with enhancing worker skills and commitment, with these techniques being aligned to the organization's strategic business goals. The emphasis placed upon establishing a secure fit between employment policies and practices and the organization's business objectives continues to be one of the main ways in which HRM asserts its approach towards people management, seeing long-term competitive advantage lying in the alignment between corporate goals, HRM strategy, and HRM activities (e.g. Fombrun, Tichy, and Devanna 1984; Huselid 1995). This will be explored in more detail in Chapter 2.

This has also been accompanied by the HR profession placing considerable emphasis on organizational culture and values (Deal and Kennedy 1982; Peters and Waterman 1982) in order to enhance employee commitment and discretionary effort: i.e. 'going the extra mile' for the organization; putting in additional effort if sufficiently motivated and conscientious. It involves placing an emphasis on creating the conditions for employees to act on their own initiative and to take more responsibility for their work and workplace behaviour (Wood and Albanese 1995: 216). It is also associated with increased employee autonomy and functional flexibility which are achieved through teamworking, direct communication from management to employees, reduction in hierarchical organizational structures through the removal of tiers of middle management (often referred to as 'delayering'), and an investment in staff through recruitment, job security, and career development. In this way, employees are viewed as being more likely to exert discretionary effort based on an internal desire to do so, rather than because sanctions would be forthcoming or from any other form of external pressure (Guest 1987; Purcell et al. 2003).

If the propositions listed above are combined, then organizational effectiveness should be enhanced, leading to employees being able to respond to unanticipated pressures, to be adaptable, and to move freely between tasks. Thompson (2003) argues that these ideas were underpinned by an assumption that a 'bargain' of sorts was in operation. This was based on the notion that cohesiveness and reciprocity existed between strategic (i.e. an organization's senior management/board), functional/departmental, and workplace levels—that in return for workers engaging with expanded job responsibilities, employers will make investments in staff training, improved career structures, job stability, and performance and skill-based reward measures (Appelbaum et al. 2000). The extent to which this bargain has been implemented will be explored in Sections 1.6 and 1.7.

However, these 'soft'/high-road/high-performance work systems (see Box 1.5) are not always appropriate for all organizations or in all circumstances, although some have argued differently (Pfeffer 1994). They have also been juxtaposed with markedly different approaches towards attaining this strategic fit between the goals of the business and HR approaches and activities (often referred to as 'hard' or 'low-road' HRM).

Box 1.5 Research in focus
Contrasting approaches towards HRM

'Hard'/'low-road' HRM

Business perspective/time horizon: short term

Emphasis of business strategies: competitive advantage gained through price

Orientation to employees: *Utilitarian instrumentalism*—an expense of doing business

Contractual bases of employment: non-standard workers—PT working, fixed-term contracts, casual employees to avoid statutory costs associated with permanent employment

'Numerical flexibility' used to contain costs relative to product/service demand by adjusting the quantity of labour employed

Role of HRM function: operationally focused HR function where it exists

Worker representation/relationships: more likely to see need for union/collective representation as the focus on cost containment through head-count reduction likely to result in worker insecurity and conflict with management

Management/HR strategies based on asserting workforce control: threat of unemployment and limited union protection used to intensify work

Key HRM levers: short-term contracts, little investment in training, low job security, low pay, work intensification

Sources: Lawler et al. 1993; Orlitzky and Frenkel 2005.

'Soft'/'high-road'/'high-commitment' HRM/high-performance work practices (HPWP)

Business perspective/time horizon: long term

Emphasis of business strategies: quality and product differentiation; innovation

Orientation to employees: *developmental humanism*—central to business competitiveness, viewed as investment

Contractual bases of employment: permanent contracts more likely

Role of HRM function: facilitate firm investment in HRM, securing employee commitment

'Functional flexibility' used which develops employee capabilities so that workers perform a wider range of more highly skilled work tasks

Worker representation/relationships: individual rather than collective

Key HRM levers: performance-related pay, individual work contracts, teamwork, harmonization of terms and conditions of employment, increased communication, investment in training and development, focus on organizational learning, management of organizational climate and culture, transformational leadership.

Sources: Walton 1985; Guest 1987; Storey 1992; Huselid 1995; Delery and Doty 1996.

Box 1.6 Skills exercise
HRM approaches

Individually, or in small groups, place yourself in the role of an HR professional. Think of organizations where it would be appropriate to use 'hard' and 'soft' HRM approaches. What kind of organizations are they and are there any similarities between them? If so, what are they? What kinds of HRM approaches towards pay, worker representation, training, and general management would be appropriate in which context and why?

Given these different approaches, it is useful to contemplate how and where they might be used—and in what business circumstances. Box 1.6 offers the opportunity to discuss their use.

Summary and further reading

- The nature of people management is highly contingent and its practice will be strongly dependent on a variety of variables that are under the organization's control, but many are not.

- From its inception, the distinctiveness of HRM lay in its emphasis on the fit between people management policies and practices and the organization's business strategy. Hence HRM can be seen to consist of supportive and interlinked sets of employment practices which, taken together, make an important contribution to business performance, whilst also enhancing the status of the HR function.

- The strategy–performance relationship is arguably central to the ways in which HRM is understood both as a concept and as involving a range of practices designed to achieve business goals. It also shows how approaches towards HRM sometimes seek to enlist employee commitment through the configuration of HRM practices such as recruitment and selection, training and rewards.

Guest (1987) and Storey (2001) provide accounts of the ideas outlined in this section. As a counterbalance, it is instructive to read Keenoy (1990), Legge (1995), and P. Thompson (2003, 2011). They critique many of the underpinning assumptions outlined and expose the contradictions they contain.

1.4 Contemporary HRM debates: human capital, talent management, and employee engagement

Three themes which are based on the promise of HRM outlined previously have emerged as being of importance to the contemporary practitioner: the need for organizations to be able to recruit and retain key people—often referred to as 'talent management' (this is explored in more detail in Chapters 5 and 8); employee engagement (the combination of commitment to the organization and its values as well as a willingness to assist colleagues (CIPD 2011*c*); and the centrality of human capital ideas (the knowledge, skills, abilities, and capacity of employees to develop and innovate) (CIPD 2011*e*). These will be explored and then set against the wider organizational backdrop of developments in the economy over time in Section 1.6.

1.4.1 Human capital

According to the CIPD (2011*e*), it is now widely accepted that the value of an organization is drawn from a mix of assets. Some are tangible and manifest physically (such as buildings, machinery, and land), whereas other phenomena such as the organization's brand, its reputation, and the people who work for it are intangible but hugely important in an economy which is increasingly argued to be knowledge-based. The idea of human capital is not a new one, and generally debates concerning this issue often distinguish between 'specific' human capital (skills and knowledge that are only useful to a single employer or industry) and 'general' human capital which covers skills and knowledge such as numeracy and literacy which are useful to all firms (Becker 1994).

Box 1.7 Online video link
Investigating human capital

For an exploration of human capital in organizations follow the links provided to video content in the Online Resource Centre. Note that they are distinctively different in terms of their focus and orientation.

Soft', 'commitment', or 'high-road' models of HRM, outlined in Box 1.5, are based on the idea that labour needs to be treated as an asset to be invested in rather than as a cost—or at least where the more valuable core employees are concerned. Within these approaches, which stress the mutuality existing between the employer and the employee, commitment to and investment in human capital activities has been seen as central to competitive advantage (Beer et al. 1984; Pfeffer 1994; Applebaum et al. 2000). Running alongside these activities are discourses of commitment and engagement that seek to mobilize discretionary effort with the aim of leveraging the investment made in the human capital of the firm (P. Thompson 2011). The links in Box 1.7 provide some ways of seeing how this might work in practice. It is also useful to watch these clips after having completed the skills activity in Box 1.6 and to assess the parallels that might exist between ideas of human capital and models of HRM.

Alongside ideas of human capital, human capital *reporting* aims to provide qualitative and quantitative data on a range of measures (such as staff turnover or employee engagement levels) to help identify the kinds of HR and management interventions that are needed to drive business in any given organization. In this way, there is a strong link between the activities of human capital and talent management.

1.4.2 Talent management

The concept of talent management is discussed in more detail in Chapter 8; however, it is useful to introduce it here as it has attracted increasing attention from professional bodies, academics, and HR practitioners (Iles et al. 2010). Talent management is argued to be critical to organizational success, as it is able to give a competitive edge through the identification, development, and (re)deployment of talented employees.

Interest in this concept and associated practices have been argued to stem from the consulting company, McKinsey and their so-called 'War for Talent' reports (e.g. Michaels, Handfield-Jones, and Beth 2001) which argued that the 'knowledge economy' was putting a premium on talent (Preece et al. 2011). According to the Society of HRM in the USA, talent management demands 'integrated strategies or systems designed to increase workplace productivity by developing improved processes for attracting, developing, retaining and utilizing people with the required skills and aptitude to meet current and future business needs' (Lockwood 2005:1). A joint Chartered Institute of Management/Ashridge study (Blass 2009: 2) sees talent management as 'the additional management, processes and opportunities that are made available to people in the organization who are considered to be 'talented', and argues that all organizations manage talent in some way, whether implicitly or explicitly.

However, this can result in narrower or wider approaches towards talent management. Where the narrower deployment of talent management practices is concerned, resources are often allocated to those identified as 'talented' or to posts and post-holders whose jobs are seen as requiring 'talent'. This suggests the acceptance of a 'differentiated workforce' in which talent management is based on targeted rather than generalized investment in human capital, leading to an emphasis on 'employee of choice' rather than 'employer of choice' (Becker et al. 2009; P. Thompson 2011).

1.4.3 Employee engagement

As stated previously, employers increasingly seek to hire employees who will do their best and exert discretionary effort on the firm's behalf. Employees, it is argued, want jobs that are worthwhile and satisfying. The idea of employee engagement seems to herald a 'win' for both parties to the

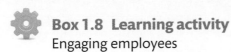

Box 1.8 Learning activity
Engaging employees

In small groups brainstorm the various actions organizations might take to ensure that you are engaged employees. Evaluate this list against your collective and individual work experiences. Which activities did employers engage in to make you feel more engaged? Why do you think that these were more commonly used? To what extent were differential approaches used depending on whether you were a full-time permanent member of staff or employed on a part-time basis? If these differentials existed, what were the outcomes for you and for the organization? If your experiences indicate little effort to secure your engagement and that of your colleagues, how did that make you feel with regard to the organization and the kinds of effort you were willing to exert on its behalf?

employment relationship, and can be seen as a combination of commitment to the organization and its values that goes beyond job satisfaction and motivation. It is something that the employee has to offer and as such it cannot be required as part of the employment contract (CIPD 2011*c*).

Employers are interested in this concept because engaged employees are argued to have a sense of personal attachment to their work and organization; they are motivated and able to give of their best to help it succeed—and from that flows a series of tangible benefits for organization and individual alike (MacLeod and Clarke 2009). This is closely aligned to the promulgation of the concept of the psychological contract, which is based on the belief that when employers deliver on their commitments and fulfil employee expectations they reinforce the employee's sense of fairness and trust in the organization, and generate a positive psychological relationship between employer and employee (CIPD 2011*c*).

The role of the line manager here is critical to securing and sustaining this engagement (Purcell et al. 2003) because employees have choices and can decide what level of engagement to offer the employer. Line managers are crucial to ensuring that engagement occurs. Additionally, employees are aware of the employer's 'brand'. Engaged employees are alleged to be more protective of it and to enhance it through providing good service and productivity. In turn, a good employer brand is now seen as key to attracting and retaining employees; this will be explored further in Chapter 5, but Box 1.8 gives the opportunity to reflect on employee engagement in more detail.

However, Coats (2010) calls into question the extent to which employee engagement is witnessed in UK workplaces, seeing it as a failure of what he terms 'enlightened HRM'—the combination of employee engagement, high-commitment management, and high-performance work systems. Citing the CIPD's own research (CIPD 2006*d*), he highlights key findings: the low level of feedback received by employees from their managers and the lack of proper information as to what is happening in their organization, the lack of trust in senior managers, and that in fact employees are unlikely to be 'engaged' in the sense that their aspirations are aligned with the goals of the business.

If we draw together these three contemporary approaches towards HRM, it is possible to argue that they are mutually reinforcing and are based on shared ideas concerning effective people management, focusing on what are termed 'high-road' HRM practices designed to instigate the discretionary effort that occurs when employees identify with the aims and values of the organization. However, these ideas and attendant practices do not exist in a vacuum and need to be placed within a wider context, one which will test the extent to which these ideas have actually been enacted within contemporary organizations. This follows Thompson (2003) and his disconnected capitalism thesis (DCT) which sought to explore the ways employers struggle and often fail to sustain the 'high-performance' bargains outlined here.

 ## Summary and further reading

- Three issues have emerged as being of central importance to HRM practitioners, their representative organizations, and academics. These pertain to the ideas of human capital, talent management, and employee engagement.

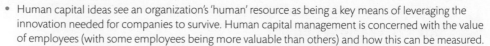

- Human capital ideas see an organization's 'human' resource as being a key means of leveraging the innovation needed for companies to survive. Human capital management is concerned with the value of employees (with some employees being more valuable than others) and how this can be measured.

- Talent management activities are designed to secure much-needed skilled and knowledgeable employees in order to meet the organization's current and future business needs.

- Finally, employee engagement is perceived by many stakeholders, such as government, professional bodies, and academics, as being as a workplace approach designed to ensure that employees are committed to their organization's goals and values, motivated to contribute to organizational success, and at the same time are able to enhance their own sense of well-being.

- It is argued here that these ideas are synergistic and interconnected with roots in high-performance models of HRM and the desire to unlock the discretionary efforts of employees. However, the extent to which these ideas are applied to *all* segments of an organization's workforce is debateable.

The work of Storey and Guest provides an insight into the components of high-commitment HRM. Huselid's (1995) piece is a frequently cited account of high-performance work practices and firm performance. The CIPD's factsheets on human capital, employee engagement, and talent management are a useful and accessible introduction to these ideas. Coats (2010) provides a highly readable critique of the extent to which these ideas and practices have been adopted in the UK.

1.5 Employment restructuring and the changing nature of work

The UK, alongside other economies, has seen a far-reaching industrial restructuring, prompted by changes in the domestic political landscape and significant developments occurring in the external business environment. This section places the contemporary approaches towards HRM outlined previously against these developments in order to help assess the extent to which the 'promise' of HRM has and can be fulfilled.

1.5.1 The challenges facing contemporary organizations

The onset of market and political turbulence experienced in the 1970s saw all Western states experiencing problems with labour productivity as well as unsuccessful economic management (Gamble 1988: 3). Developments such as globalization and the greater integration of Eastern European economies through the auspices of the European Union, the formation of international trading arrangements, and the growth of the BRIC economies (Brazil, Russia, India, and China) continue to confront British companies with significant challenges as well as opportunities for expansion. These involve the need to charge competitive rates for goods and services, whilst simultaneously improving their quality and innovative appeal in the search for new markets and profitability.

This drive for competitiveness has been accompanied by three developments which will be outlined here. First, the increased growth and sophistication of computerized technologies, the rise of knowledge work, and the demand for knowledge workers; secondly, the move away from standard forms of working hours and terms and conditions of employment and a shift towards the implementation of part-time and temporary work, fixed term contracts, and so on; thirdly, the shift towards the 'financialization' of many developed economies. The term 'financialization' refers to a process whereby financial markets, financial institutions, and financial elites gain greater influence over economic policy and economic outcomes and elevate the significance of the financial sector relative to others. The development of financialization is associated with downsizing and delayering as firms seek ways of cutting costs to improve financial performance. As a result of these changes—as well as the experience of three economic downturns—there has been a marked increase in labour market insecurity (Sennett 1998; Burchell et al. 1999). Taken as a whole, it is pertinent to ask whether organizational competitiveness and allied improvements to the state of the British economy have been achieved at some considerable cost to employees, and to question the role of the HR function in these developments.

1.5.2 New technologies and the rise of the knowledge worker

Whilst many of the changes at work involved with the increased use of networks and technologies are very obvious, and are witnessed in routine daily activities, others, like the demand for sophisticated computer skills, higher-level mathematics, and science abilities within the UK's expanding creative industries, are less obvious but are still urgently needed (CBI 2011*b*). Securing competitive advantage is also argued to require the diffusion of complex knowledge and capabilities within organizations. In order to capture and diffuse knowledge across a potentially global business, firms have responded to the idea of competing through the creation of knowledge capture and management programmes designed to preserve the asset value of their own employees' expertise, whilst simultaneously dispersing it throughout the company via the use of intranets or other methods. Thus highlights the need for employees to be able to engage with technologically mediated processes and have relevant skills.

The focus on competition via skills and knowledge has seen continued growth in occupational groups such as managers, professionals, personal service, and customer services. In the EU, almost 40 per cent of the workforce is already employed in higher-level jobs such as management or professional work, with this proportion expected to growth further. As will be outlined in Chapter 6, the main growth in job numbers is expected to be in posts requiring medium and high-level qualifications, and jobs requiring low or no levels of qualifications will steadily reduce (CBI 2009; UKCES 2009; CEDEFOP 2010). This suggests that whilst creative or high-level jobs are being created by new technology or by the application of highly specialized or creative skills and knowledge, some jobs are continuing to be downgraded. For many, the increased use of ICT has coincided with the growth of the services sector, particularly in relation to financial services such as banking and insurance, and the growth of call centres.

Growth in this sector has been underpinned by the creation of jobs that are difficult to define as 'knowledge work' but depend on a 'virtually' structured IT-mediated organization–customer interface where interaction often depends on structured and scripted interactions. These interactions often require 'emotional labour' (Hochschild 1983; Fineman 1993, 1997) to support the 'virtual' interaction with the customer, sustain the smooth flow of service delivery, and ensure customer satisfaction with the interaction as well as the end product. Here, emphasis is placed on the personality of the individual and the extent to which their values and emotions fit the requirements of the job.

Apart from call centre work, in industries such as hospitality and airline travel greater emphasis is placed on the appearance, dress sense, body shape, and manner of the individual employee, with the increased importance of emotional and aesthetic labour contributing to the shifting definition of skill (Tyler and Abbot 1998; Bach 2005*a*). However, within organizations, this kind of emotional labour is often deployed to sustain team cohesion, inter-team competitiveness, and organizational identity—often with the aim of instigating discretionary effort and reducing staff turnover.

1.5.3 Challenges to the knowledge economy

Whilst the ideas outlined above concerning the knowledge economy are widely circulated by a range of government and organizational bodies, and will be explored in more detail in Chapter 6, an alternative argument exists. This suggests that such a high-skills/high-wage strategy for the UK economy is unlikely, given the historically low levels of company investment in research and development as well as in training. Indeed, a low-skill strategy is arguably more important and more likely in many sectors (Boxall et al. 2007) and is often accompanied by what are termed 'low-road' HRM choices—ones that treat employees as a variable input and a cost to be minimized, and are often associated with low-cost business strategies and labour-intensive industries that are not conducive to the high-commitment HRM ideas and practices outlined by Legge (1995). The spread of low-cost competition across the service sector has ramifications for industries which were once relatively protected from competition, and served as sources of relatively high-wage jobs, because they are increasingly subject to tough low-cost competition. If this argument is correct, by implication the relevance of high-performance HRM might soon be confined to a relatively small segment in developed economies such as capital intensive

manufacturing and services that are protected from low-cost competition—for example, where there is a high degree of regulation or there are monopolies which are not subject to international competition.

However, it is argued that, even for organizations which want to compete on the basis of low costs without sacrificing quality, investment in HRM is crucial (Gittell and Bamber 2010) and that the most successful low-cost competitors in the service sector, such as manufacturing, are likely to be those organizations that find ways to achieve the quality standards now demanded by customers whilst also achieving low costs. That is, successful low-cost competition now requires companies to meet quality *and* productivity goals simultaneously. A frequently cited example of this can be seen in low-cost Southwest Airlines whose adoption of high-road pluralistic HRM practices has been accompanied by shareholder profitability. However, it is useful to compare this example with that of Ryanair, whose HR strategy is diametrically opposed to that of Southwest Airlines, where the company become even more profitable than its American counterpart. They have adopted a low-road model which pays little attention to HRM concepts or practices. Rather than focusing on generating and sustaining employee commitment, their approach relies more on worker control and replacing those who depart through burnout (Wallace et al. 2007). But whilst the impact of low-road practices on employees are argued by to be damaging to workers, it is instructive to note that organizations such as Ryanair have their proponents, which suggests that commitment models of HRM with their attendant practices are not necessarily viewed as a requirement by shareholders and wider industry commentators.

1.5.4 The rise of non-standard working and the growth of flexibility

Another development which continues to run alongside the discourses of knowledge management and the implications of networked computerized technologies is the rise of non-standard working and the growth of flexibility. Surveys and other evidence point to ongoing changes to working time and the contractual bases of employment (Cully et al. 1999; Kersely et al. 2006), with the implications of these developments profoundly affecting the employment relationship. In order to understand the implications of these changes, alterations to working time need to be presented next to previous working-time patterns and their regulation.

The work of Beynon et al. (2002) provides helpful illustrations of the changes that have occurred over time. Where their case study companies were concerned, a pattern of regulated working time seemed to be the norm and was based around notions of standard working hours, premium payments for unsocial hours, and in most cases voluntary rather than scheduled extra and unsocial hours working. However, the strength of regulation and the extent to which overtime and unsocial working hours were voluntary varied between the organizations, with trade union presence being an important factor.

Whilst some of their initial starting points differed, all case organizations experienced significant working time change over the five-year period of their investigations. These were seen in three areas: longer opening or operating hours; the rescheduling of work to increase productive hours and to decrease the use of overtime; and the reduction in the distinctions between standard and unsocial hours or standard and extra hours. However, it is important to note that the use of mechanisms such as annual hours contracts, the growth of self-employment, and fixed-term contracts has actually been very limited; and that even the growth of part-time working has been gradual, and evolved over an extended time period.

It is also important to note that, whilst emphasis has been placed on the erosion of established norms as a means of delivering greater flexibility and greater worker intensification, later evidence paints a somewhat different picture. For example, Kersley et al. (2006: 92) found that where multi-skilling and functional flexibility were concerned, fewer workplaces were training substantial proportions of their core employees in this way, and that such a trend had been declining over the past decade. Where multi-skilling and job rotation were more prevalent was in production work and financial services, especially where the workplace produced multiple services or goods. Finally, as issues of work–life integration increasingly come to the fore, debate is shifting and is more concerned with seeing how temporal flexibility can best be used to suit the employee and their circumstances.

1.5.5 Organizational restructuring

One of the ways in which organizations seek to improve profitability is through changing company structures and reducing staff. The shift towards financialization means that the focus of investment activities changes from investing *in* productive enterprises (and by implication an ongoing investment in productive employees) to that of extracting money *from* companies for investment in other domains which yield higher returns. This is particularly true of larger companies who are players in financialized practices via involvement in trading in financial markets or through involvement in successive waves of mergers, acquisitions, and takeovers. This trend has been associated with downsizing (cutting staff numbers) and delayering (removing whole tiers of management or supervisory roles).

Many companies have rationalized, and continue to rationalize, their businesses through tools such as business process re-engineering (Hammer and Champy 1993) or by importing new manufacturing methods such as lean manufacturing (Womack, Jones, and Roos 1990). This has often been accompanied by the kinds of changes to employee terms and conditions of employment described previously as well as by work intensification. For those who became committed to such strategies, the impact on workplace performance and morale was often poor, as illustrated in Box 1.9.

As noted by McGovern et al. (2007), worker insecurity is an outcome of perpetual restructuring and downsizing, but it does not necessarily equate with poor worker performance as there is evidence that employees exert high levels of effort in insecure conditions. As noted in the study of Avatar—an Irish company heralded as 'a great place to work' (Cushen and Thompson 2011)—workers demonstrated very low levels of commitment to the organization as well as hostility to the HR department. However, this did not result in inefficient or poor performance outcomes, but it is uncertain whether this maintenance of performance was due to the employees' professionalism or to compliance with market discipline. This case (and others like it) raises a pertinent question as to whether high performance only results from high commitment or 'enlightened HRM' and whether there are other less fortuitous circumstances in which such outcomes might also be witnessed.

It is also important to note that the developments outlined here have not been restricted to the private sector. Tight budgetary controls, new measurements of 'output', and the generalized introduction of what has been termed 'the new public management' (Dunleavy and Hood 1994) have radically changed many public sector organizations. Consequently, the public–private sector divide has become blurred, and the ways in which people are managed has involved the increased use of flexible employment contracts, reduced opportunities for collective voice among workers, and a potential decline in the public service ethos (Corby and White 1999:

Box 1.9 Research in focus
Downsizing and the serial downsizers

Over the past couple of decades, employee downsizing has become an integral part of organizational life. Global competitive pressures have caused firms to critically examine their cost structures, including those associated with human resources. Once confined primarily to the USA, employee downsizing has, over time, become the norm in many countries. The magnitude of the downsizing activity has been exacerbated by the current recession. The extent of job losses has been staggering (Datta et al. 2010). In the USA alone, more than 6.5 million jobs have been 'downsized' since the economic downturn began in December 2007, with the numbers expected to grow in the foreseeable future. Research concerning the serial use of downsizing found that repeated downsizing led to repeatedly negative consequences in terms of employee satisfaction, workplace conflict, and workplace performance. The organizations sampled over a five-year period in New Zealand did not seem able to shake off the trauma of repeated downsizing, leading the authors to speculate that those serial downsizing organizations were not adjusting future practices to reflect past experiences. Rather than seeing a form of organizational learning taking place, they seemed to witness simple instrumental responses to poor financial performance with a negative impact being an outcome of this strategy (Gilson, Hurd, and Wagar 2004).

15–20). However, privatization did not occur across the whole of the public sector and, even now, 23 per cent of UK employees still work in the public sector (Rogers 2011). But public sector employees continue to see their jobs and conditions of work subject to radical change, especially with regard to increases in workload and centrally imposed targets for service delivery. The economic downturn has also witnessed the occurrence of further changes to the public sector in both the UK and other EU economies, with large-scale redundancies and the further outsourcing of activities to the private and third sectors still being planned.

Finally, these developments, as well as the shift towards financialization, mean that even organizations that develop track records of high performance, creativity, and commitment are finding it harder to sustain the kinds of stable conditions that are needed for high-performance HRM practices (P. Thompson 2011). And if varieties of market discipline can operate as a means of driving performance, to what extent are high-commitment practices—or even HRM itself—required? However, as noted by Godard (2004: 371), it might make good sense for employers to adopt what have traditionally been seen to be good management practices with some alternative work practices grafted onto them. These may not yield the high levels of commitment and discretionary effort promised by the high-performance approach to HRM, but they might be expected to yield reasonable levels of consent and realistic levels of performance.

📖 Summary and further reading

- Organizations have responded to changes in their business environments in a number of ways. These have been influenced by developments in IT and its widespread use as well as a swing away from semi-skilled work to managerial and professional jobs. Other responses involved changing patterns of working time and changes to contracts. The growth of flexible working has also been accompanied by techniques such as business process re-engineering, downsizing, and delayering.

- Whilst some commentators argue that Britain has survived this period of heightened competition in good shape, there is also evidence of heightened worker insecurity. However, the extent to which this results in poor performance outcomes is not clear.

- Such evidence questions the extent to which commitment-based approaches towards HRM were utilized. Whilst approaches based in the adoption of more sophisticated and reconfigured HR practices were advocated, it seems that the organizational preference was for more 'low-road' methods of leveraging strategic advantage in the market with little evidence of personnel specialists being the drivers of change.

P. Thompson (2003, 2011) provides critiques of HRM and places these criticisms within broader considerations of the political economy. Gittell and Bamber (2010) provide an interesting illustration of the deployment/non-deployment of high-road/low-road HRM within the airline industry.

1.6 Reinventing the HR function

At this juncture it is pertinent to assess the developments occurring in relation to the HR function, considering the impact of HRM philosophies and practices on the practitioner role. Since the advent of HRM, there has been no shortage of advice provided to HR practitioners as to how to gain access to the higher echelons of strategic decision-making. Key here has been the work of David Ulrich who argues that the HRM agenda provides opportunities for the HR function to demonstrate 'added value' through a focus on what HR *delivers* rather than on what it does (Ulrich 1997; Ulrich and Brockbank 2005). Gaining added value is achieved by the fulfilment of six key roles (Ulrich et al. 2009: 3–4).

1. **Credible activist.** The HR professional is both credible and active, offering a point of view and challenging assumptions.

2. **Culture and change steward.** The HR professional helps shape a company's culture. They coach managers in how their actions reflect and drive culture, they weave the cultural standards into HR practices and processes, and they help make culture happen via the implementation of relevant activities.

3. **Talent manager/organizational designer.** The HR professional ensures that the company's means of talent management and organizational capabilities are aligned with customer requirements and strategy.

4. **Strategy architect.** The HR professional has a vision of how the organization can compete and thrive, and thus plays an active part in the establishment of the overall strategy. This means recognizing business trends and their impact on the business, forecasting potential obstacles to success, and facilitating the process of gaining strategic clarity.

5. **Operational executor.** The HR professional executes the operational aspects of managing people and organizations, such as policy formation, HR administration, and other operations—often dealt with through technology, shared services, and/or outsourcing.

6. **Business ally.** HR professionals contribute to the success of a business by knowing the setting in which their business operates. They also know who customers are and why they buy the company's products or services, and they have a good understanding of how the parts of the business work together, so that they can help the business organize to ensure profitability.

The strategic architect and business ally roles, and the previous versions of them, have caught the imagination of the organizations representing HR practitioners, such as the Chartered Institute of Personnel and Development (CIPD), and they have been highly influential in defining the strategic business-focused skills and attributes required by contemporary successful HR professionals (Gilmore and Williams 2007). However, over time, this has resulted in a decline of interest in or inclusion of any employee advocate role which, in turn, has led to claims that the function has disappeared from the shop floor (Francis and Keegan 2006). Additionally, the willingness to outsource aspects of HR activity is arguably an instance of the function promoting or being faced with its own marginalization, as not all aspects of outsourced HR work are administrative and non-core.

Additionally, the delivery of HRM has to factor in the critical role played by front-line managers (FLMs). As demonstrated by Purcell and Hutchinson (2007: 16), their evaluation of twelve 'excellent' UK companies showed that in order for FLMs to be effective in the people management role, they needed a good range of HR policies and practices to work with, as well as good leadership skills. The findings showed that employees responded positively to both the HR practices *and* their FLM leadership behaviour. Such findings have interesting implications for the ways in which HRM is conceptualized—seeing it as not only being concerned with the coherent integration of mutually reinforcing policies and practices relating to critical features of employee resourcing, but also as being involved with a wider remit that covers leadership behaviour and organizational climate (Purcell and Hutchinson 2007: 4).

1.7 Assessing change

What have such radical changes meant for the theories and practices of HRM and for its function? The coming of HRM promised change, but it seems to have been a model, in its more 'enlightened' form, that has struggled to meet the dual demands for economic efficiency and improvements to the quality of jobs and working life that it promoted (Coats 2010). In the end, proponents of HRM seriously underestimated the will and ability of managers to instigate the changes to working practices and organizational structures that they deemed necessary to achieve high-performance outcomes. The UK's business system, with its focus on short-term profitability and the dominance of financial capital, was not conducive to the kinds of practices advocated by proponents of high-road HRM. Intensifying competition also failed to drive firms 'up market' in terms of high-skill/high-wage goods and services, and instead arguably encouraged many firms to operate differently and reduce the costs associated with employment where possible (Bach 2005a).

In part, HRM can be seen as a consequence of operating in new territory with new rules governing the employment relationship, especially in relation to the weakening of trade unionism and the rise of a more managerialist perspective (Beardwell 1996). This process of change shows no

signs of abating, and the new work context demands new HRM strategies and practices to meet these challenges, many of which have been caused by the impact of previous 'innovations' and the stresses to working conditions caused by them.

For the HR function, the attempt to shift towards a more strategic role floundered, and harsher economic climates jeopardized the implementation of softer commitment-based models. As focus on these approaches has arguably diminished, and the political and economic context altered; HRM as a term is now used more generically rather than as a particular approach to gaining workforce commitment.

Arguably, greater challenges for the HR function are posed by the shifting organizational boundaries and the permeable 'boundary-less' nature of many companies. The variety of ways in which people are employed and the different contractual bases make it hard to sustain organizational identification, and the rise of the networked enterprise creates tensions in the employment relationship, increasing the complexity of managing and monitoring performance as well as making it harder to sustain commitment. The emphasis on the importance of managing the whole personality of the employee—as witnessed in examples of emotional labour—broadens the scope of HR practice and inevitably spills over into considerations of ethics as well as the boundaries between work and life outside it. More importantly, the emphasis on this form of labour draws attention to the psychological injuries of work and broadens the scope of the HR remit to address issues of bullying, violence, and stress at work (Bach 2005a).

1.8 Conclusion

The arrival of HRM coincided with a period of economic restructuring experienced by many Western economies. But whilst HRM was temporarily identified with a given governmental and organizational 'project' designed to improve business and economic performance, the term is no longer tied to a particular orientation towards people management, managerial philosophy, or style. However, certain ideas still remain influential—if still the object of debate and dispute—and revolve around the performance advantages that are stated to accrue to those organizations who secure alignment between the organization's strategic goals and its HR policies and practices. The promotion of this relationship has allowed those responsible for people management to argue for an increased involvement in the strategic decision-making of the organization, with a consequent enhancement of the HR function. The influential work of authors such as David Ulrich has also provided the HR function with a means by which that leverage might be achieved through the development of core HR roles. But, whilst Ulrich's work remains influential, the strategic role he envisaged for HR is still elusive.

Although the debates concerning HRM occurred at a highly propitious time for the function, the devolution of much HR activity to line managers meant that the clear-cut link between HR practices and organizational performance was less evident; obscured as it was by the involvement of a third party. In addition, organizational responses to competitive pressures have not necessarily involved companies taking the 'high road' in terms of people management practices. Instead of a longer-term investment in worker skills coupled with the provision of more sophisticated managerial styles and abilities, many UK companies adopted a more familiar 'low-road' approach, reducing costs through the increased use of IT systems, the deployment of flexible approaches towards employment, and reductions in headcount.

The process of change shows no sign of abating, and the HR function, together with line managers, needs to develop effective strategies for meeting future challenges. As work continues to be contingent for many, HRM is faced with the enduring challenge of fostering and maintaining commitment to an organization and its goals in an environment where employees might have multiple employers and be employed on a variety of contractual bases. Seeking employee engagement has now gone beyond the ideas of commitment and has been subsumed by an approach that seeks to secure a fit between the values and personality of the employee and the employer 'brand'. But such emotional engagement and labour is being challenged by increased calls for a more effective work–life balance, with HR being required to consider the employee in more holistic ways that spill over the traditional boundaries between work and home.

Assignment and discussion questions

1 What do you understand by the term 'HRM'?

2 How would you account for the growth of interest in HRM? Which factors do you think are central to its continued appeal and why?

3 To what extent have wider socio-economic developments impacted on the enactment of HRM practices designed to instigate employee commitment and engagement?

4 What are the main reasons behind the devolution of much HR activity to line managers? What challenges do you think will have been faced by both line managers and the HR function, and how could organizations overcome them?

5 What are the future challenges for people management?

Online Resource Centre

Test your understanding of this chapter with online questions and answers, keep up to speed with changes to the law through regular updates, and use selected weblinks to quickly access useful resources and further information. Visit the Online Resource Centre at:

www.oxfordtextbooks.co.uk/orc/gilmore_williams2e/

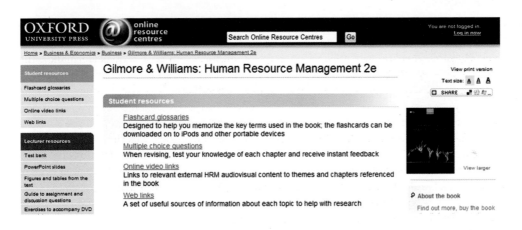

Case study
HRM and elite sports—the case of Team Sky

One of the continuing success stories in UK elite sport is that of the GB Cycling Team (Team GB) who have dominated the road, track, BMX, and MTB disciplines at the World Championships and Olympics over the last decade. Much of the success has been attributed to the work of Dave Brailsford, the Team's Performance Director, and his exceptional 'backroom' staff who support and enhance the work of the cyclists across a range of functions such as bike technology, psychology, and race preparation.

Team Sky was formed in 2009 (www.teamsky.com). Whereas the cycling remit and focus of the Team GB is broadly focused on a range of cycling events, Team Sky focuses mainly, but not exclusively, on competing in the many road races and tournaments taking place on a global basis each year. The most prestigious and best known of these is the Tour de France (TDF). One of the headline aims of Team Sky was to win this coveted road race within five years and to do so with a hub of British cyclists, although the squad of 25 cyclists is highly international. The finances at the disposal of Team Sky also augured well for the fledgling team as they are backed by satellite broadcaster BSkyB via £30 million in sponsorship with the organization until 2013.

However, the formation of Team Sky caused a degree of controversy (Fotheringham 2012). This was due to the employment of Dave Brailsford, who joined the organization's management as Team Principal along with other Team GB staff members such as Head Coach Shane Sutton, Psychiatrist Steve Peters, and Race Coach Rod Ellingworth, with most of these Team Sky personnel still retaining their positions within the Team GB. However, this dual membership and allied experience is fundamental to Team Sky in that they seek to replicate the successful operation founded by the Team GB staff within a road racing context. The relationship between the professional cyclists and their track management team took a while to bed down, with the British Cycling staff having to get used to the demands made by corporate sponsors—who desire a constant flow of success, as opposed to the more sporadic calendar of events and expectations witnessed in track cycling—and a voracious and sometimes intrusive media. Additions were made to the backroom staff, requiring additional work from Brailsford and Peters to ensure that this team was cohesive. Nonetheless, sharp criticisms were made that the track team was affected by Peters' dual role (McRae 2011).

Whilst the 2010 season saw a shaky start for the new team, 2011 saw them enjoy good performances in the Tour Down Unde and the Tours of Qatar and Oman. In the 'classics' season, successes were achieved by Bradley Wiggins and Geraint Thomas, but it was the signing of World Champion and TDF Green Jersey winner, Mark Cavendish, that caught the majority of media attention (Fotheringham 2011), as was the Team's success in the Paris–Nice race in 2012, when the cycling season starts to get serious. In July 2012, and going with form, Bradley Wiggins won the TDF with team mate, Chris Froome, coming second. The final race of the Tour saw Wiggins lead out Team Sky to secure the Champs Elysée stage win for Cavendish. Just over two years into their life as a racing entity, Sky are not merely part of the furniture but one of the strongest squads in the sport.

Questions

1 Although this case is not directly concerned with HRM, what ideas does it prompt as to the links that *might* exist between some of the HR practices mentioned in this chapter and organizational performance?

2 As with many elite sports, there is rarely an HR function tasked with the kinds of activities outlined in this chapter. If you were the newly appointed head of HR at Team Sky, how would you seek to show the value of the function?

3 Team Sky's success seems to depend on attracting and retaining highly experienced and qualified members of staff as well as internationally renowned cyclists. What kinds of HR practices would need to be in place to bring such staff to a *less* prestigious sports organization?

4 How would you suggest that an organization like Team Sky captures, retains, and shares the knowledge and experience possessed by its backroom staff so that they can withstand the loss of valued employees to other teams?

The strategic dimensions of human resource management

2

Sarah Gilmore

Learning objectives

The main objectives of this chapter are:

- to examine the concept of strategy, the variety of ways strategic decisions are made within different organizations, and the implications for HRM;
- to emphasize the importance of viability for companies and the relationship viability has with the firm's human resources;
- to evaluate critically the different approaches to aligning strategy with people management practices.

2.1 Introduction

As the previous chapter showed, the arrival of human resource management (HRM) prompted considerable debate concerning its meaning and its value to organizations. This debate has been accompanied by a growing interest in business strategy, largely caused by the changes occurring in the organizational landscape. These include the impact of information and communications technologies on the world of work and organizational systems, competitive uncertainty, regulatory reform, and the development of an increasingly dynamic free-market *international* economy. As the business environment became, and continues to be, more turbulent and increasingly complex, business leaders across all sectors have sought ways to design and implement strategies that are more likely to ensure organizational profitability and survival (Farnham 2010; Boxall and Purcell 2011).

Early advocates of HRM stated that performance improvements would be achieved if organizations aligned their HRM practices with the firm's business strategy, but this is not a simple process (Kaufman 2010*a*). Part of the problem lies in the ambiguous and diverse nature of HRM practices and the different ways in which organizations engage in strategic management. This leads to difficulties in formulating definitions, concepts, and models when the two components are brought together (Boxall, Purcell, and Wright 2007). However, a number of approaches have been developed which try to do that in order to secure competitive advantage.

This chapter will begin by outlining what is meant by the term 'business strategy' and discuss the different ways organizations develop their business strategies. This will be followed by a consideration of three influential models that seek alignment between strategic goals and people management activities. They are often referred to as the 'best-fit', 'best-practice', and 'resource-based view' (RBV) models. Once these have been outlined and discussed, the chapter will conclude by assessing the evidence as to the extent to which these forms of alignment are evident, evaluating the relationship that such modes of practice have with the HRM function, and discussing what empirical studies suggest is occurring in relation to organizational performance.

2.2 The nature of strategy

In order to show what strategy consists of, how it is formed, and the implications for HRM, it is helpful to start with an organizational illustration, as shown in Box 2.1.

Box 2.1 Window on work
The ongoing saga of Yahoo

Having started life making it easier to search the World Wide Web, Yahoo faces critical questions about its future and whether it has one as an independent company. Although the company fought off a bid from Microsoft in 2008, it is seen by some market analysts as fundamentally wounded. It has lost search engine competitiveness to Google, and although the company linked up with Microsoft's search engine, Bing, this relationship has not resulted in Yahoo establishing itself as a strong search engine alternative. Additionally, Yahoo mail has been highly challenged by Google's gmail and its growing number of additional features, and it has closed its social networking service Yahoo 360. This means that Yahoo cannot leverage its business in one of the fastest-growing online trends. Google, Microsoft, and AOL have emerged as possible players in a takeover. China's Alibaba Group, whose largest shareholder is Yahoo, has also expressed interest, as have several private equity companies (Arthur 2011; Ovide 2011).

What might the HRM implications be if the company is bought by a rival? It is likely that the Yahoo brand and brand name would continue. This might be accompanied by Yahoo retaining its independence from the acquiring organization. The acquiring organization would probably seek an alignment between its HRM practices and those of Yahoo, especially in the areas of succession planning and recruitment. In the short to medium term, the nature of HRM activity will be determined by the targets set for Yahoo in key areas seen to be crucial to securing enhanced performance.

One frequently cited way of viewing strategy sees it as involving the long-term direction of a company which will involve setting goals and the successful allocation of resources in order to achieve them (Chandler 1962). For commentators such as Porter (1985), this process needs to be accompanied by decisions as to how a company's strategy will be different from that of its competitors, deliberately choosing an alternative set of activities to deliver a unique mix of value to the customer. Alternatively, Mintzberg (1994) defines strategy as the pattern evolving in a stream of decisions taken over time, arguing that an organization's strategy might not follow a deliberately chosen logical plan but can emerge in more ad hoc ways.

In contrast, Boxall and Purcell (2011) define strategy by distinguishing between 'strategic problems' that the firm faces in its environment and the characteristic ways in which it tries to cope with them (its 'strategy'). Such a definition, along with that of Mintzberg, inserts a degree of contingency into the ways in which strategy is understood and how it might be formed, because strategic problems and the ways in which they are faced will depend on a number of different issues facing a company at any given time. This will have implications if companies seek to align strategy and HRM policies and practices, because it effectively suggests that there is no one best way of achieving this fit.

Strategic decisions such as the battle for Yahoo are usually determined by the organization's business model, which is concerned with what products or services the organization offers to a market. Such considerations are fundamentally concerned with what the organization should be like and what it should do. They will also be focused on how the company will gain competitive advantage over its rivals and sustain or extend their position within a given market. But where HRM issues are concerned, given that the ownership of Yahoo has been uncertain for several years, it is likely that many talented staff would have departed for more certain, more productive, and more innovative organizations. Whilst research points to talented staff departing following merger or acquisition (Krug 2003), an emerging strand is pointing to a pre-takeover spike in departures, with these employees often possessing key skills and knowledge—thus pointing to a crucial role for HRM in such a scenario in order to retain these core workers (Derbyshire 2010). Proactive HR operatives will typically have an 'at-risk' list regarding valued senior executives who are anticipated to take flight in the face of uncertainty caused by likely changes in organizational direction. Those whom the organization would like to nurture might be persuaded to stay via the deployment of ancillary employment benefits that serve to create loyalty ties. As an example of this practice, during the Alcon acquisition of Novartis, key leaders who might have seen their position threatened were 'chosen' to attend the much coveted Novartis Harvard leadership programme.

2.2.1 Strategy and the scope of company activities

Strategic decisions are also likely to be concerned with the scope of an organization's activities, raising questions as to whether a company should focus on one area of activity or on several. The broadening of activities and the allied need for staff expertise might be important reasons for the purchase of another company. Strategic decisions often involve a process of strategic fit whereby opportunities are identified within the business and its environment, with internal staff resources and competences being adapted so as to take advantage of them. The strategic fit operating in the case of Yahoo is arguably comfortable for all parties to the possible purchase and, where staff capabilities are concerned, these are likely to be in place. But, given comments above, organizations might need to ensure that this is indeed true in key areas, highlighting an important role for the HRM function.

2.2.2 Firm viability

However, simply saying that firms have strategies does not equate with organizational success. The fundamental strategic problem that all organizations face is that of viability. In order to be viable, a firm needs an appropriate set of goals and a relevant set of staff and other resources, as well as systems that will help it survive in its sector.

Such systems also need to be acceptable and 'fit' that sector as well as the society in which it operates (Boxall and Purcell 2011). The case of Saatchi & Saatchi in Box 2.2 shows how the company's viability was restored through a strategy rooted in its staff's capabilities.

Box 2.2 Window on work
Strategic viability and the case of Saatchi & Saatchi

Saatchi & Saatchi is one of the most famous businesses in the global advertising industry, and has been for over thirty years, but rapid expansion in the 1980s saw the company face disaster (Armstrong 2010). This resulted in the organization's founders, the Saatchi brothers being sacked by the board, and, after several failed chief executive appointments, Kevin Roberts was brought in to lead the organization and restore its profitability and reputation. The problem he faced was one of viability.

Roberts focused on restoring the firm's fortunes through a strategic reorientation of Saatchi & Saatchi as an 'ideas company' (Roberts 2005). This involved moving away from its status as an 'advertising agency' to a company that transformed the client's business model, visibility, and reputation through strategically developing the *brand* rather than relying on a simple advertising campaign. This shift was demonstrated in the new ways that Saatchi sought new business. Instead of traditional pitches focusing on advertising campaigns, it broadened its focus to include the client's business strategy. The decision to reorient the organization as an ideas company was also agreeable to the marketing and advertising industries world because the notion of an 'ideas company' was being circulated within these circles. However, the organization was able to gain first-mover advantage through being the first to use it so extensively.

Therefore it could be argued that the success of this strategy rested upon Saatchi & Saatchi being first to market as an ideas company, but the ability to do this depended upon having staff capable of operationalizing it. An important relationship exists between strategy and staff competencies—whilst there is an important need to identify the 'right' strategy that will leverage the organization against its competitors, enacting these plans will depend on the existence, maintenance, or acquisition (at the right price and right number) of staff capable of enacting it. In this case, Saatchi staff were being asked to enact a strategy that lay well within their range of knowledge and skills.

2.2.3 Strategy as process

It is important to understand strategic management as a process whereby strategic decisions and goals are formed and re-formed over time. This process can involve aspects of formal planning and the use of analytical techniques to assess environmental challenges and the organization's ability to exploit them. It can also involve more incremental uncertain processes involving learning from experience until managers find out what works best for them (or their rivals) in practice. Whatever approach is taken, the combination of strategy formation and senior management views as to what it takes to secure viability in their markets will have a powerful impact on HRM. Indeed, it is argued that organizational success will depend heavily upon the ways HRM strategy and staff skills can achieve strategic goals. Therefore it is unsurprising that HRM practitioners want access to strategic decision-making forums because the function ideally possesses information concerning the organization's human capital. In addition, HRM activities will be influenced by the outcomes of these processes—another reason for their desire for inclusion.

 ### Summary and further reading

- There are various definitions as to what strategy is. Usually definitions of the term will refer to the ways in which an organization can secure competitive advantage over time and within competitive markets. Others will see strategy as being the routine ways in which the organization overcomes problems it faces in its environment. Whatever the definition chosen, a degree of contingency exists in terms of the strategies organizations develop because the problems facing companies can change. This will have implications for HRM approaches should an alignment be sought between strategy and people management policies and practices.

- But having a strategy does not mean that a company will be successful. The main challenge facing all organizations is one of viability, and how that is to be secured and maintained. Achieving viability requires that the organization has a set of realistic goals, employees who have appropriate skills and knowledge, and systems that will assist in surviving the various challenges it will experience in its sector.

- Strategy also needs to be seen as a process, and an activity that will have a powerful impact on HRM, with HRM practitioners often seeking access to the forums used to devise it. In turn, it can be argued that successful strategies will fundamentally depend upon the ability of employees to achieve them—as the case of Saatchi & Saatchi demonstrated.

Boxall and Purcell (2011) provide a helpful outline concerning strategy, firm viability, and the relationship of HRM to both.

2.3 Approaches to the strategy-making process

Organizations design their strategic plans in a variety of ways, and these different approaches will have implications for HRM. However, there is often a difference between the reality of strategy formation and the ways in which this is presented. This divergence can have implications for the ways in which we understand how strategy is formed in practice, and therefore how HRM might assert influence in the process and respond to the outcomes.

2.3.1 The rational planning approach

Large complex organizations, especially those that operate in relatively stable environments or have external public accountabilities, such as local authorities, national government departments, or the armed forces, are more likely to follow a rational planning approach to the formation of corporate strategy. These planning processes are usually shown occurring at corporate, strategic business unit, and operational level.

2.3.2 Corporate level strategic planning

Corporate level strategy is concerned with the overall purpose and scope of an organization as well as how value will be added to the business. Issues explored here are likely to include geographical scope, diversity of products and services falling within the remit of the company, acquisitions or divestments, and how resources will be allocated between the different areas of the organization. It is also likely to be concerned with the expectations of owners, shareholders, the stock market, voters, and (where relevant) national government. Being clear about the corporate level strategy is important because this will have profound implications for other strategic decisions and actions. For example, global corporations such as Proctor & Gamble and Unilever have taken decisions to invest in and nurture 'billion dollar brands' that lie within their portfolio (e.g. Ariel, Gillette, Hellmans, and Dove). Taking such strategic decisions will determine where investment will occur—as well as disinvestment, with brands such as Sunny Delight and Pringles being sold by Proctor & Gamble because they did not meet the criteria developed by the organization for continued investment.

At a local level, local government organizations will often set corporate plans for a given time frame, and these will determine priorities for the rest of the organization at departmental and individual levels. However, the parties to the strategic process rarely have a completely free hand here because they will have to consider a range of local needs, and decision-making may involve other organizations who might be central to the strategy's delivery. Additionally, strategic goals will also have to include targets set by national government across a range of local government responsibilities.

Strategic plans are often portrayed as being the outcomes of logical, systematic, and coherent decision-making practices. Sometimes they use analyses of the organization's external and internal environment (outlined in Chapter 3). Such analyses often prompt discussion as to the strategic capabilities of the organization, assessing whether there is an opportunity to exploit, or further exploit, staff resources or core competences of the organization to develop new goods and services, or to enhance existing ones (Prahalad and Hamel 1990; Drejer 2002). This approach provides a route by which HRM can influence and underpin the strategic direction of the organization by ensuring that the organization has the staff required to carry out its strategic goals, now and in the future. In dynamic and competitive organizational environments, this can pose a significant challenge—especially where there is a stiff demand for certain skill sets. In large organizations such as the Daily Mail General Trust (DMGT), the Global Head of

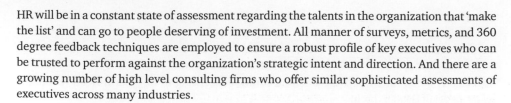

HR will be in a constant state of assessment regarding the talents in the organization that 'make the list' and can go to people deserving of investment. All manner of surveys, metrics, and 360 degree feedback techniques are employed to ensure a robust profile of key executives who can be trusted to perform against the organization's strategic intent and direction. And there are a growing number of high level consulting firms who offer similar sophisticated assessments of executives across many industries.

2.3.3 Business unit level strategic planning

The second level of strategy formation occurs at the level of the business unit—sometimes referred to as the strategic business unit (SBU). In commercial organizations, an SBU is often seen as a part of the organization for which there is a distinct market for goods and services that is different from another SBU. Alternatively, these business units might be stand-alone businesses within a larger corporation—such as Dove which is a stand-alone business owned by Unilever. Business level strategy is often concerned with innovation, the appropriate scale of activities, and the organization's responses to competitors' moves.

For example, Dell sells computer software and hardware to different kinds of customers—large organizations, small and medium-sized companies, the public sector, and home users—so it might choose to organize itself with divisions that serve these different customer bases. These divisions will need different strategies to allow them to compete successfully in those markets and to gain advantage over competitors. So, whereas corporate strategy makes decisions about the organization as a whole, decisions at this level are related to a specific area of business activity.

Within public sector organizations, the SBU equivalent might be found in the service-level business plans devised by local authority departments that deal with distinctively different aspects of their responsibilities such as education, environment and transport, health, housing, and social care. Planning within public sector organizations is generally concerned with how 'business' units should deliver best-value services as well as contributing to the authority's strategic priorities.

Where the organization's approach to managing HRM staff is concerned, a degree of centralization will be needed to ensure commonality of HR policy and practice across the SBUs, and this usually involves a small 'head-office' HRM function. Balanced against that centralization, a degree of operational flexibility at SBU level is also necessary, and this often involves devolution of HRM staff to SBU level as well. Attaining a sense of balance between organizational coherence and SBU level flexibility is difficult, because devolved HRM staff working with the SBU are often pressurized to identify with the SBU over the central HRM function in order to achieve credibility with the managers and staff with whom they work. This can mean that over-arching HRM goals might be sidelined as the local HRM staff become 'captured' by the specific needs of their SBU and place them centre stage. Most certainly, if there is a lack of communication from corporate HR as to key issues, the vacuum will be filled by HR operatives who have to live in the local. This is especially true of corporations that operate across many different countries, reflecting distinct legal systems and idiosyncratic cultural imperatives. In some cases the local environment may even take precedence.

2.3.4 Operational level of strategic planning

The final level of strategy occurs at the operating end of an organization. This is concerned with how the component parts of an organization effectively deliver the corporate and business level strategies in terms of resources, processes, and people.

Where these kinds of plans are concerned, a range of priorities are often formed to ensure that business objectives are met. Each priority usually has time-bounded actions associated with it, and these are linked to various budgets as well as other related plans existing within the organization. This means that there is a vertical fit with corporate goals as well as a horizontal fit with other functions or departments to ensure that appropriate working relationships exist between them to ensure service and product delivery.

However, the impact of the rational approach to strategy formation means that operational practices are separated out and away from higher-level strategic planning. In reality, it is questionable as to whether this separation is helpful, as it is often the case that operational practices

and effective systems of doing business are 'strategic' and might provide sustainable competitive advantage by ensuring that a company is adaptable and can shift with changes in the wider environment (Boxall and Purcell 2011). If this separation of operations and strategic planning is formalized, it could hamper such responsiveness in the longer term. Finally, in an era dominated by the need for knowledge creation, those who often create knowledge are frequently located within the operational activities of the firm. Therefore separating them from influencing and informing the strategy formation process is potentially detrimental in the medium to long term (Whittington 2001). For HRM, it provides a powerful argument for matrix-style structures that allow both central and localized knowledge to occur over time, allowing the HRM function to inform all levels of strategic planning (Box 2.3). In more creative organizations, such as advertising and software, it is not unknown for junior members of the organization to be quickly elevated into high level meetings. For example, at Saatchi & Saatchi Italy a junior assistant was credited with a major insight into an Illy coffee campaign which led to a change in strategic direction for that company. In this case, HR ensured that the junior person found themselves sitting in a meeting with the owner of the company and the worldwide CEO of the agency. Powerful illustrations such as this serve to join up the dots between corporate strategy and operations.

2.3.5 Criticisms of rational planning

Although criticisms are levelled against this approach to strategic planning, it remains influential in terms of the ways in which corporate strategy is depicted and understood. Where some companies are concerned, it is hard to see how they could cope without engaging in these practices, however they are configured (Whittington 2001). For example, it is difficult to see how large multi-divisional firms could survive without using this approach, and there are certain industries, such as construction, where formal planning is essential.

The rational approach to strategy formation will also have significant implications for the ways in which HRM strategy is formed. This is because performance advantage, as seen later in the 'best-fit approach' is believed to occur when HRM strategy and organizational strategies are in alignment. If SBU and organizational strategies are clear and clearly communicated, it is logical to suggest that HRM is more capable of aligning its strategies and practices at these levels so that it can facilitate the achievement of these goals. This is more difficult to achieve in settings where structured approaches to strategy formation do not exist.

2.3.6 The processual approach

In contrast with the rational planned approach of formulating strategy, the strategies of many organizations emerge on a step-by-step basis. This is often true of small businesses, and can be seen in the example of restaurant owners who develop their business from a single well-respected outlet to others—either utilizing the same branding, or diversifying to meet a perceived local need

Box 2.3 Skills exercise
Making the strategic case for HRM

In two groups, choose a large organization you are familiar with. Investigate what the strategic goals of the organization are—these are often found on the company website. One group should take the role of the HRM function and the other should be the organization's strategic decision-makers, charged with developing the company's strategic direction and goals. The HRM group should develop a presentation to the strategists arguing for their inclusion in the forthcoming strategy process. The strategists should consider what arguments and evidence the function needs to make in order for them to be included, and formulate questions to pose to the other group as they make their presentation. Finally, when debriefing the exercise, decide which were the most important arguments that the HRM group needed to make. To what extent were they made and what was the most compelling evidence used to support their assertions?

Box 2.4 Practitioner perspective
Emergent strategy in practice and the case of Macmillan Cancer Support and third-sector organizations

Macmillan Cancer Support's over-arching ambition is to reach and improve the lives of those living with cancer (www.macmillan.org.uk). Their approach towards strategy is to see it as an evolving process because the plans they develop need to be able to adapt to changing circumstances, such as government policy decisions to enhance the role of third-sector organizations. This means that the organization could be asked to increase its work locally at short notice and to sustain and extend it over time. These kinds of external environmental pressures require Macmillan and organizations like it to have flexible strategic processes (Bouverie 2010). Four general processes interact in this organization: the strategic intention devised by those working at the top of the organization, the way the organization responds to its environment, the alignment of action with the organization's strategic intent via performance assessment and other such HRM tools, and the feedback loops by which organizations like Macmillan assess their progress against strategic objectives but also take up and respond to feedback from people at local level (Dowglass 2011). Given that Macmillan seeks to ground its strategy in the things that really matter to people affected by cancer, this is highly important.

or niche in the market. It can also apply to not-for-profit organizations which increasingly witness demands on their services by local users as well as central government who are keen to expand their contribution, as outlined in Box 2.4 and in the DVD interview with Richard Solly, the Head of the Havant Citizens Advice Bureau, who knits strategy development with HR activity. However, the processual approach towards strategy formation is not limited to small and medium-sized businesses but can apply to much larger companies.

The kind of approach taken towards business strategy here is markedly different from that of rational planning and often involves strategies emerging in incremental steps over time, with strategic decisions often occurring in unclear circumstances. It involves an acceptance of the world of markets and organizations as being essentially messy and working with them as they are, abandoning the ideal of a structured process seen in the previous approach and taking the internal complexity of organizations seriously. It also suggests that there are limits to rational action (Mintzberg 1978, 1987), and that organizational decision-makers can only consider a handful of ideas at a time. Such 'bounded rationality' means that there is a reluctance to embark on an extended search for relevant information, as witnessed in the rational planning approach, and a tendency to accept the first satisfactory option rather than insisting on the best. The case of Factory Records in Box 2.5 provides an insight as to how messy and creative this process can be, highlighting that strategic and operational decisions can be based on less than perfect business rationales.

Therefore strategy can become a product of political compromise, as organizational members bargain to arrive at acceptable sets of joint goals (Pettigrew 1973). It can also be seen as a way in which managers try to simplify and order an increasingly complex world. This can sometimes lead to strategy formation taking place incrementally, rather than as an outcome of an extended 'set piece' as seen in the rational planning approach. This implicitly involves experimentation and learning from the organization's experience as well as that of competitors.

Box 2.5 Online video link
The case of Factory Records

Strategic decisions are not always made on the basis of logic and rationality. Visit the link provided to video content in the Online Resource Centre and view the case of Factory Records and the rationale for its founding, as well as the relationships that the record label had with the bands they signed. What does this contribute to our understanding of organizational strategy and HRM?

The HRM implications of such an approach will require flexible and responsive approaches, often stressing cultural acclimatization to suit a potentially fast-paced or evolving organizational environment. Jobs are more likely to have loose task definitions, and employees will be expected to be flexible in their approach to work and prepared to engage in continuous development and training in order to respond quickly and effectively to alterations in strategic orientation and alterations to job content. This poses a particular challenge to HR because investment in people skills and professional development is generally a long-term process, yet ongoing highly changeable conditions frequently require short-term solutions. Under these conditions, the variety and extent of the HRM department's external contacts will be central to the organization's ability to quickly patch in recruits when internal candidates are thin on the ground.

2.3.7 Evolutionary and systemic approaches

Within highly competitive fast-moving markets, it could be argued that, whatever methods managers adopt in developing strategy, only the best performers will survive since markets will choose appropriate strategies in a brutal fashion (Whittington 2001). This approach is often compared to Darwinian theories of natural selection and survival of the fittest, where more individuals of each species are born than can survive, leading to a frequent recurrent struggle for existence. Therefore the use of environmental analyses to select the best strategic choices becomes unnecessary—either because the market is too volatile to make such rational choices, or because the market will determine the ways in which organizations within specific sectors need to compete. The most effective way of developing strategy within markets would be to focus on ensuring operational efficiency through reducing employment costs, whilst also ensuring substantial investment in as many different small initiatives as possible. Over time, the low performers are eliminated and further investment and development of the high performers takes place (Williamson 1991). The learning activity in Box 2.6 offers an illustration of this in practice.

Such a scenario will involve a strong focus on cost reduction—hence the concern with staff overheads—as well as innovation, because there will be a small number of employees whose skills, knowledge, and performance are crucial to the business, and these would need to be identified and retained. This has echoes of the core and peripheral workforce proposed by Atkinson (1984), whereby flexibility of employment and associated costs are managed through a focus of expenditure on those seen as central to the achievement of organizational goals (the core). The remaining employees (the periphery) are managed through various contractual forms aimed at securing employees to suit the needs of the employer. This can involve part-time working, short-term contracts, outsourcing, and other forms of employment that reduce costs whilst also providing staff cover. Training and development opportunities offered to those in the periphery are concerned only with supporting those activities crucial to the attainment of strategic goals. But, as can be

 Box 2.6 Learning activity
The high-street fashion retail market

Primark (www.primark.co.uk) has become a significant player in a fast-moving and highly competitive market, with its success occurring during a time of economic and retail volatility (Press Association 2010; BBC News Online 2012). Whilst some high-street fashion retail companies have seen an upturn in their fortunes, others are increasingly finding themselves squeezed by the competition. Primark, like it rivals Top Shop and H&M, thrives because of its speed at reproducing designs inspired by the catwalk, taking just six weeks for an item to go from concept stage into the shops. As for cost, Primark competes in terms of volume and speed of turnover, allowing it to negotiate cheap prices from its manufacturers in China and Eastern Europe, although it takes a smaller profit margin per item than some other high-street stores. The company's plans for expansion could be seen as just the beginning of Primark's strategy to become a dominant force within the high-street fashion business across Europe.

Look at the Primark website. Access its recruitment area and critically analyse the career paths the company offers. What does this tell you about its competitive strategy and how HRM supports it?

seen in some high street fashion companies, because the strategy has such a strong emphasis on practices associated with 'low-road' HRM, such as low-skill/low-pay jobs that are contractually insecure and unsatisfying in their content, one of the outcomes is high staff turnover, especially at store level, accruing significant costs and disruption associated with recruitment, induction, and lost productivity.

2.3.8 Systemic approaches

Organizational strategy is also influenced by the social system within which it operates, with strategic choices being shaped by the cultural and institutional interests of society. For systemic theorists, firms differ according to the social and economic systems in which they are embedded, as illustrated in Box 2.7.

Differences between countries' social systems and changes occurring here will be important for multinational organizations, and are further explored in Chapter 15. Such differences in institutional setting and allied ways of working can be significant when considering mergers and acquisitions. For example, the merger of Compaq and Digital Equipment fell victim to a culture clash that pitted Compaq's high volume, fast-to-market strategic focus against Digital's lengthier sales cycles. The business challenges created by this difficult merger are now viewed as a reason why Compaq lost its market position to Dell, its long-time competitor. Set against this example, when the French media organization, Publicis Groupe, acquired Saatchi & Saatchi, the new owners took the decision to leave the company unchanged. This approach was arguably an appropriate one, as any attempt to impose the Publicis culture and ways of working could have backfired in an industry dominated by employees whose creative skills would be keenly sought by competitors.

The implications for HRM strategy when considering systemic factors can involve the function understanding the specific legal and cultural complexities involved in constructing strategy and enacting it across national borders. This relies on successful training and development programmes as well as outplacement support for managers engaging in the development of strategic decisions in overseas business units.

 Summary and further reading

- An organization's business strategy is concerned with the direction and scope of the organization over the long term, how it achieves competitive advantage for the organization through its configuration of resources within a changing environment, and ultimately how it fulfils stakeholder expectations.

- Having an organizational strategy does not automatically secure company success or viability. In order to survive, the organization requires appropriate goals and resources, the key resource being the skills, knowledge, and attitudes of its staff—something upon which HRM can exert a substantial influence in terms of its creation and maintenance.

 Box 2.7 Research in focus
HRM in the voluntary sector and the implications for strategy

In their analyses of HRM within the voluntary sector, Parry et al. (2005) and Nickson et al. (2008) note that there are distinctive differences between this sector and its public and private sector counterparts. Organizations in the voluntary sector tend to be strongly values led, and these values may influence the way in which people are managed, with employees often being committed to the relevant cause and forming a moral attachment that is likely to have an impact on the culture of the organization. This may mean that employees are prepared to work for lower extrinsic rewards, such as pay, because of the existence of intrinsic rewards contained in the nature of their work, the higher degree of autonomy they expect and experience in their work, and the more altruistic nature of organization's goals. However, Nickson et al. (2008) highlight that this ethos is accompanied by employee expectations that they will be actively involved in organizational decision-making activities such as strategy formation.

- It is also important to understand strategic management as a process. Whilst the rational approach is still highly influential, for many organizations strategic plans and decisions are often political compromises. Where certain industries are concerned, the dynamism of their environment and the heightened nature of competition have led to approaches that are more akin to natural selection.

- The different methods by which strategy is understood and enacted make it more challenging to influence the process and to align HRM processes and practices to its outcomes. This might mean that the strategy–performance relationship that has been, and continues to be, central to theoretical and practical understandings of HRM is more problematic than it appears. In some settings, an HRM function might be able to leverage influence in terms of guiding business strategy and constructing this alignment. This will depend not only on the existence of the function, but on the credibility it holds within the company. Where the enactment of HRM is devolved with no central function, this process is arguably more difficult to achieve.

For a good introduction to strategy, Johnson, Whittington, and Scholes (2011) provide a comprehensive guide whilst also highlighting the role played by HRM in this area. Where discussions of strategy formation are concerned, Whittington (2001) is much cited and has proved influential in the ways in which this process is understood.

2.4 Strategy, business performance, and human resource strategy

Having investigated how organizations develop their corporate strategies, and the implications and outcomes of the process for HRM, it is now appropriate to investigate the relationship between strategy, HRM, and business performance in more detail. Establishing measurable links between HRM strategy and business performance is hard, and is often termed the 'black box' problem because there is still a lack of clarity as to which HRM inputs lead to which given outputs (Purcell et al. 2003; Boselie, Dietz, and Boon 2005; Gerhart 2005; Purcell and Kinnie 2007). Additionally, whilst investigations into this issue are now occurring in emerging markets and transitional economies, most of the studies examining the relationship between HRM and organizational performance have been conducted in the USA and the UK (Kauhanen 2009). Therefore it remains to be seen how far ideas developed in this particular setting can transfer to others.

However, there is a view that employees provide the primary source of competitive advantage, with the quality of HRM being a critical influence on managing people and firm performance (Boxall and Steeneveld 1999; Gerhart 2007). As argued by Schuler and Jackson (2007), there is an underlying logic permeating the field that human resource activities can lead to the development of a skilled or high-performing workforce—a workforce that engages in functional behaviour for the company, thus forming a source of competitive advantage which in turn leads to higher operating performance, increased profitability, and higher stock market valuations (Becker and Huselid 1998). Boxall and Steeneveld (1999) concluded that successful organizations enact people management practices that enable them to survive as credible members of their industry or sector and also generate some kind of competitive advantage, thereby suggesting that there might be industry-specific institutional rules that might impact on HRM policies and practices in order for the business to be accepted as legitimate. There are a number of approaches that attempt to link strategy, business performance, and HRM policies and practices, but the three best-known general means of doing so are the 'best-fit', 'best-practice', and RBV models.

2.4.1 Best fit

The best-fit approach is based on the view that different types of HRM practices are suitable for different kinds of business conditions. It asserts that there is a link between HRM practices and competitive advantage, but that HRM activity is contingent upon the particular circumstances of each business. This means that companies need to identify the HRM strategies that will 'fit' their organizations in terms of the product market within which the business is competing, the labour market, and the size of the organization, as well as its structure, culture, and so on. This means that what will work for one organization might not necessarily work for another (even within the same sector). Two particular types of best-fit model will be outlined below. One links

HRM choices to the different ways by which the company achieves competitive advantage in a given market. The other relates them to different stages in the firm's business cycle.

2.4.2 Competitive-advantage models

This model sees organizations making strategic choices as to how they attain competitive advantage (Porter 1985). This involves gaining advantage either through cost leadership, asserting differentiation through quality of produce or service, or through focus in a 'niche' market. For example, Primark competes in a highly dynamic market on the basis of cost by selling fashionable clothes at low prices. Companies such as Marks & Spencer compete more on the basis of the quality of their products and customer service. Finally, the haute couture offerings of high-fashion houses, such as Chanel, Armani, and Christian Dior, focus on a much smaller niche market of customers who can afford to buy cutting-edge outfits precisely tailored to themselves.

HRM approaches underpinning such a strategy will be designed to fit these generic strategies of cost reduction, quality, and innovation, with business performance improving when HRM practices mutually reinforce the organization's choice of competitive strategy (Schuler and Jackson 1987). Box 2.8 shows how this would work by using the example of the supermarket chains Lidl and Waitrose, which operate on the basis of cost and differentiation, respectively, comparing them with niche providers of specific foodstuffs such as the Neal's Yard Dairy.

2.4.3 Life-cycle models

Business life-cycle models link HRM policies and practices with the different needs firms have at different stages in their life cycles from start-up through to growth, maturity, and decline, with each stage in an organization's life cycle requiring different HRM approaches (Kochan and Barocci 1985). During the start-up phase, there is an emphasis on flexible HRM practices that will enable the organization to foster entrepreneurialism. But in the growth stage, once the company has moved beyond a certain size, HRM policies and practices will become more formal, with training and development needed to maintain an effective management team through appropriate management development and organizational development activities. As markets mature, margins decrease, and the performance of certain products or services starts to plateau, HRM approaches might start to emphasize cost control or the maintenance of flexibility and the need to update workforce skills. Finally, during the firm's decline, the major challenge for HRM will be downsizing and redundancy issues, with training and development activities focusing on retraining and providing career consulting services to its staff when they face 'outplacement'.

 Box 2.8 Learning activity
Securing competitive advantage in the supermarket business

The German-owned supermarket chain Lidl competes internationally on the basis of low price (www.lidl.co.uk) and the organization stresses the variety of job opportunities available within the company, covering a number of career paths located both within the UK and Europe.

In contrast, Waitrose (www.waitrose.co.uk) operates within the UK on the basis of quality in its foodstuffs and department stores. They offer a wide range of employee benefits and job roles across the partnership and stress career development through engagement in continuous learning and development.

Finally, organizations such as Neal's Yard Dairy compete on the basis of offering high-quality cheeses from a range of small UK cheese providers (www.nealsyarddairy.co.uk). The organization's website is dominated by the creation of an ambience that stresses the nature of the produce on offer as well as the enthusiasm of the staff for cheese.

Think of other organizations that operate on the basis of a specialist service or product. See what information is available on their websites concerning their approaches to people management. If information is forthcoming, to what extent do the organization's policies and practices dovetail with its status in their market and how is this made evident? For example, what kinds of skills, knowledge and attributes are valued by the organization?

An example of this approach can be seen when merging these ideas with the growth–share matrix. It aims to evaluate the products of an organization according to their market share and to their growth prospects. It can also be used to identify the HRM needs the organization faces at each stage, because, as the model implies, no business or market can grow indefinitely and, whilst the profitability of a product depends on its market share, the growth rate of its market, and its position in the product life cycle, that life cycle will have a natural end. This is illustrated in Figure 2.1.

2.4.4 Limitations of the best-fit approach

There are several limitations to this approach. One is that it lacks sophistication in terms of the way it defines competitive strategy. Some successful organizations are good at everything they do, not just cost leadership or differentiation. Companies such as Marks & Spencer and the John Lewis Partnership are examples of organizations that are multi-dimensional in terms of their competitive posture, so that the management of employees there is unlikely to be based on relating HRM practices to being *just* a low-cost leader or a differentiator. This means that linking HRM practices to a position in one of these models would be misleading if variety were needed and the organization wanted to broaden its offering in some way. In such situations where organizational climates have become increasingly competitive, it is desirable to build a management team that can think beyond its current competitive position. This does not invalidate the idea of a fit between competitive strategy and HRM practices, but the fit is not total (Boxall and Purcell 2011).

Another criticism of this approach is that it tends to ignore employee interests in the pursuit of enhanced economic performance, and sometimes fails to recognize the need to align employee interests with the firm. Hence, whilst it is logical to fit HRM to its competitive context because firms need the skills of people who can operate in their chosen markets, employers also need to think about how the company fits the individual employee whose skills are increasingly

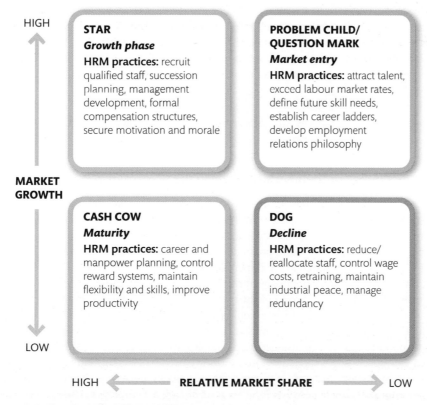

Figure 2.1 The growth–share matrix.
Source: Based on the Boston Consulting Group's Growth–Share Matrix.

important for firm survival. This is particularly important in labour markets requiring skilled employees. Again, this does not undermine the idea of a fit existing between business strategy and HRM, but it does reassert the claim that, whilst HRM supports the attainment of the company's competitive goals, it also has to meet employee needs and comply with social and legal requirements for the management of staff.

Finally, environmental change means that organizational strategy and HRM need to meet the current and *future* strategic needs of the business. This means that companies must ensure that they have the necessary skills base to compete in current and possibly future markets, identifying and building the skills and knowledge required to meet as yet unknowable business challenges.

2.4.5 Best practice

In recent years there has been heightened interest in the idea that performance improvements arise when companies use specific sets of employment practices. One view holds that these are applicable across *all* organizations, *all* sectors, and *all* geographical locations (the universal approach). Another suggests that certain 'bundles' of HRM practices can contribute to improved employee attitudes and behaviours, instigate lower levels of absence and labour turnover, and secure higher levels of productivity. Such 'bundles' are often associated with 'high-performance work systems', or 'high-commitment' or 'high-involvement' HRM.

The universal approach towards best practice is underpinned by a belief that changes in the external business environment have reduced the impact of traditional sources of competitive advantage, such as plant and equipment, and increased the significance of employees who enable an organization to innovate and to adapt. The approach asserts that a certain set of HRM practices is exemplary and applicable to *all* organizations and settings, no matter what their industry, geographical location, or organizational culture (Pfeffer 1998). Whilst Pfeffer's approach has been highly influential in defining the elements of best practice, a number of such lists have emerged stressing different HRM interventions (although there are some similarities running across most of them), which has caused a degree of confusion (Becker and Gerhart 1996: 785).

One development from the universal trend in best-practice HRM is the idea that individual best practices cannot be implemented effectively in isolation from each other, but that the ways in which they are bundled together in a complementary fashion is the crucial factor (MacDuffie 1995). For example, workers might be more likely to welcome teamworking if their efforts are rewarded with performance-related incentives and are accompanied by access to training opportunities. This idea of bundles of integrated HRM practices lies at the heart of thinking on high-performance work practices, an approach that has been promoted in the UK by the Chartered Institute of Personnel and Development (CIPD) and the UK government (DTI 2005; UKCES 2010). This approach differs from the universal trend in that high-performance work practices here are seen as needing to be tailored to the organization's specific context in order to attain maximum performance from them. Therefore these practices have power only if they are aligned and integrated with each other, and if HRM supports key business priorities (Huselid 1995; Boselie, Dietz, and Boon 2005; Becker and Huselid 2006; Combs et al. 2006). This means that powerful connections between relevant interlinked practices need to be identified within the organization.

Supporters of this approach have pointed to the economic benefits to companies who have adopted these integrated systems of high-performance work practice. The DTI and CIPD survey found evidence that the level of high-performance work practices, as measured by the number of practices adopted (out of a total of thirty-five), is linked to organizational performance. Those adopting more of the identified practices had greater employee involvement and greater effectiveness in delivering training provision, motivating staff, managing change, and providing career opportunities. They also had more people earning over £35,000 and fewer earning less than £12,000. Studies carried out in the USA (Huselid 1995; Huselid and Becker 1996) suggest that the quality of a firm's high-performance work practices is associated with changes in company market value of between $15,000 and $60,000 per employee (Huselid 1995: 667).

In the UK, Patterson et al. (1998) cited evidence for HRM as a key contributor to improved organizational performance. The authors argued that 17 per cent of the variation in company profitability could be explained by HRM practices and job design as opposed to just 8 per cent from research and development, and 2 per cent from strategy. More recent studies show similar findings. For example, Flood et al. (2008), using data gathered from 132 organizations in Ireland, found that HPW and partnership are positively associated with labour productivity. In a longitudinal study of 308 UK manufacturing companies focusing on the effects of three specific HPW practices, Birdi et al (2008) found statistically significant positive performance effects for the practices of empowerment and extensive training in particular. Together, empowerment and extensive training accounted for a 9 per cent increase in value added per employee. They also found that the practice of teamworking seems to enhance the effect of all other practices. Finally, research by Tamkin et al (2008) found that a 10 per cent increase in business investment in HRM, training, and management practices equated on average to an increase in profit margins per employee of between 1.19 and 3.66 per cent (i.e. the ratio of profit over sales) as well as a 0.09 per cent increase in sales growth per employee and a 3.1 per cent increase in the probability of achieving sales from new technology.

2.4.6 Limitations of the best-practice approach

Not all studies present positive links between best-practice HRM and organizational performance (Gooderham et al. 2008; Boxall and Macky 2009; Kaufmann 2010*a*,*b*). In particular, the universal application of these approaches and models is contested, with some arguing that differences in institutional settings affect the nature of HRM. Organizations worldwide are confronted with different constraints governing the employment relationship, such as legislation, the existence of national and sectoral cultures, and different employment relations structures. Even within a European setting, there are differences between regional groupings such as the 'Nordic cluster', the 'Germanic cluster', and the 'Latin European' cluster, which have led to a greater emphasis being placed on contextual perspectives where HRM approaches are concerned rather than on the universal, US-based HRM approaches. Those who subscribe to this view suggest that each institutional setting requires its own unique HRM model (Brewster 2004) and that it is wrong to assume that US approaches can simply be transferred to a different setting (Paauwe and Boselie 2007; Boxall and Macky 2009). The case of high-performance work systems in Finland in Box 2.9 is an interesting example of a less than complete transfer of ideas to the national setting thought to be ideal for this approach.

Another concern is that best-practice approaches seem to rest on the assumption that employers take a longer-term perspective of the organization's prospects, but this might be difficult to achieve, especially during periods of economic downturn. It is pertinent to note that the development of these ideas occurred during conditions of economic growth. It is also easier for organizations to engage in high-performance practices when labour costs are low as a proportion of total costs to the business, or where there is a long-term rationale for this investment.

Box 2.9 International focus
High performance working in Finland

The studies by Kalmi and Kauhanen (2008) and Kauhanen (2009) of the incidence of high-performance working systems (HPWS) in Finland found that predictions of the greater use of HPWS in a coordinated market economy such as this were problematic. Concentrating on the key components of HPWS, namely teams having influence opportunities, employer-provided training, and incentive pay, the study found that there was some evidence of bundling taking place, but no dominant pattern emerged. HPWS, consisting of all these key practices, was found to be quite rare in Finland. The findings highlighted that the probability of being in an HPWS is greater for employees with higher socio-economic status (i.e. more complex jobs), on a permanent work contract, on a full-time contract, who use information technology for internal communication in the workplace, who work in foreign-owned firms, and who work in large plants. The authors conclude that the large differences in the probability of participation in HPWS between the socio-economic classes seen in this study are difficult to reconcile with the view that HPWS offers 'good' jobs for blue-collar workers and is a vehicle for 'new partnership' between employers and employees.

When this is not the case and labour costs make up a high proportion of total costs, as in many service sector organizations it is more difficult to make the argument that there are long-term benefits for such investments (Farnham 2006: 49). Hence the growth of individualized employment contracts that exist outside the industry norm has led some to question whether flexible employment is compatible with best-practice HRM, and whether or not it can be applied to all employees irrespective of their occupational status or labour market value. It could be argued that these innovative practices are more likely to occur in an environment where key segments of workers have specific skills and knowledge that are central to the attainment of business goals (Kinnie et al. 2004).

Finally, serious questions have been raised about the relationship between HRM and performance articulated in these studies. Although many of the ideas developed are highly attractive to HRM practitioners, they have not escaped criticism, with much of it being aimed at the ways in which the research was conducted (e.g. Purcell 1999; Marchington and Grugulis 2000; Marchington and Wilkinson 2005a). Whilst the approaches might be intuitively appealing, and have certainly been exploited by practitioner bodies such as the CIPD, the evidence used to support the relationship is less than overwhelming (Kersley et al. 2006; Pfeffer 2007; UKCES 2010). Indeed, the CIPD's Shaping the Future research, as summarized in Box 2.10, arguably marks a 'moving on' from high-performance work practices, potentially acknowledging the findings of the UKCES (2010) that take-up of this approach has failed to appeal to a broad range of UK businesses.

2.4.7 The resource-based view

The approach of companies that use the resource-based view (RBV) is underpinned by a belief that human and technological assets cannot be continually changed to maximize market position (as in the best-fit approach). Instead, organizational strategy is formed by identifying and developing core competencies possessed by the workforce. Therefore the focus is on the personal attributes employees bring into the organization, using them to promote sustained competitive advantage and corporate growth. This heightens the importance of line managers, as they are required to identify, use, and renew these human assets that are so important in terms of securing the long-term competitive future of the organization.

Unlike the best-fit approach, the RBV is an 'inside-out' model, because it focuses on the firm's internal resources and the specific factors enabling the organization to remain viable in the market. But these resources need to be valuable and rare, worth something competitively, very hard to copy or imitate, and therefore irreplaceable. Finally, these internal resources must be capable of proving a superior return to shareholders. Whilst these resource traits will not be

Box 2.10 Policy example
Shaping the future?

What will truly make the difference for the long-term performance of organizations? The Chartered Institute of Personnel and Development's 'Shaping the Future' (CIPD 2011j) highlights eight themes emerging as being important in achieving this outcome: alignment, shared purpose, leadership, locus of engagement, assessment and evaluation, balancing short- and long-term horizons, agility, and capability-building. For the CIPD, these themes yield core insights for HRM professionals and managers as to what will truly make the difference for the long-term performance of organizations. These include the need for an organization to have an agile response to change, for organizational purpose to find the human connection, for collaborative rather than directive modes of management, and the revitalizing role that middle management could play in organizational transformation. This has a degree of resonance with The European Foundation for the Improvement of Living and Working Conditions (Cox, Higgins, and Speckesser 2011). Whilst they stress the centrality of worker training, profit sharing, share ownership, autonomous teamworking, flexible working, and formal employee representation in terms of unlocking employee potential, it could be argued that what both bodies implicitly agree upon is the need for organizations to look at the quality of organizational management/leadership as well as people management efforts that provide workers with the ability to unlock their discretionary effort.

immune to radical breakthroughs or external shocks, such as developments in technology, or natural disasters, many firms will attempt to differentiate themselves in ways that are relatively sustainable in a given competitive situation. The key issue for RBV is one of how management might build valuable firm-specific characteristics and 'barriers to imitation' (Boxall and Purcell 2011). In this way, competitive success comes not only from making choices in the present, but from building up distinctive capabilities over significant periods of time. This means that time and place matter, as does the learning capability of the organization.

Successful companies can become characterized by highly complex patterns of teamwork, cooperation, and coordination, and they possess strong clusters of human and social capital, providing a natural barrier to imitation by rivals. This is sometimes why organizations in some sectors might seek to buy an entire team of employees from a rival. It also means that the organization is potentially vulnerable to the loss of outstanding staff. Mueller (1996) places strong emphasis on socially complex attributes of organizations. He argues that sustained advantage comes from the kinds of hard-to-imitate routines embedded in organizations that are cemented in a firm's 'social architecture'. Thus greater value is more likely to originate from persistent and patient management processes that encourage skill formation and powerful forms of cooperation deep within the firm. It is these processes that generate valuable new combinations of human resources for the company.

2.4.8 Core competencies

As outlined, much of the practical implementation of the RBV lies in the ways the organization defines and manages its competencies. Over the long run, competitive advantage is seen to occur when core competencies are built that are superior to those of competitors. It is the job of senior management within an organization to identify and understand its core competencies, and those that are needed for the future. In this way, the RBV focuses on the development of a knowledge-based, rather than a product-based, view of the firm. This might be a simple distinction to make, but it actually involves a profound change in the way strategic-level managers review company strengths and analyse strategic options.

Where HRM is concerned, it means that companies have the possibility of generating advantage through the careful use of HRM practices. This will involve the recruitment, selection, and retention of outstanding people—people who possess powerful forms of what is termed 'tacit knowledge'. Such knowledge is often intuitive and thus difficult to verbalize, it is difficult to write down, and it is often lost when the individual leaves the company. But, whilst it is possible for managers and the HRM function to develop the HRM dimensions of a knowledge-based and knowledge-creating company (Nonaka and Takeuchi 1995), what are more difficult to create and maintain are the organizational processes that facilitate the development and sharing of tacit knowledge. Both human capital and organizational processes can generate exceptional value for the firm, but are likely to do so when they reinforce each other (Boxall 1996). To put it simply, human resource advantage can be traced to better people employed in organizations with better processes.

2.4.9 Limitations of the resource-based view

A criticism of the RBV is that it downplays the significance of the wider environment. Organizations always exist in environments, and therefore resources are not ends in themselves, but are useful in a business setting only when they create value in their markets. The wider environment will also impact on the ways in which resources can be secured, enhanced, and used. The state, shareholders, and employees themselves will have expectations that resources will be used legitimately. The RBV often fails to consider the wider institutional arrangements that exist in terms of employment relations and HRM at national and industry level. Therefore HRM choices will be fashioned by external forces and not just by line managers (Boxall and Purcell 2011).

There are also questions as to whether RBV relates to the entire workforce existing within a company or just to senior managers, or to a specific segment of employees whose knowledge is more highly prized. Whilst an argument could be made that managers are rarer in quality and also have the ability to exert greater influence over organizational performance, it could also be argued that 'value' is dispersed throughout an organization and that privileging it would be erroneous. It also raises highly pertinent questions as to how RBV and HRM practices could integrate in an organization that relied upon a contingent flexibly employed workforce.

Finally, there needs to be some caution where the issue of differentiation in a given market is concerned. It is easy to exaggerate the differences between companies that operate within the same sector, but all viable organizations in an industry need some *similar* resources in order to establish their identity and secure some legitimacy (Boxall and Purcell 2011). Using the Saatchi & Saatchi example, if traditional ways of working had been completely abandoned in the attempt to secure viability, it is likely that the status of the organization would have been damaged.

Summary and further reading

- For many academics and HRM practitioners, employees are the primary source of competitive advantage. This means that the quality of HRM policies and practices is going to be crucial in terms of securing staff performance, innovation, and organizational longevity. However, a question remains as to which HRM approaches will yield high performance? Many surveys have shown that good people management influences performance, but what is less certain is *how* this occurs.

- Three main approaches have emerged concerning the relationship between HRM and organizational strategy. The best-fit and RBV approaches could be seen as contingency approaches, with HRM policies and practices depending on the organization's place in a market as the best-fit approach advocates, or the creation and maintenance of unique knowledge and skills as suggested by the RBV. For the best-practice model, a universal approach is advocated, or one whereby consistent sets of bundles of practices are carefully selected and enacted within the company, largely ignoring the issue of external fit with the organization's environment.

- Whilst some studies show an association between HRM and corporate performance, the density of evidence is still not overwhelming, but we can certainly expect further debate on this from a variety of interested parties keen to demonstrate the relationship that HRM inputs have with heightened performance.

- This debate focuses on the strategy–performance relationship. However, the successful enactment of the best-practice and RBV approaches often depends on the operation of 'high-road' HRM practices. As illustrated in Chapter 1, this has not been widely evidenced in many sectors of the UK economy, which raises questions as to the willingness of employers to operate such strategies and to develop such strategies.

For those interested in further reading, Boxall and Purcell (2011) provide an account of the three main approaches outlined here. In terms of the approaches themselves, Schuler and Jackson's (2007) adaptation of Porter's model of business strategy for HRM purposes is highly recommended, as is Barney's (1995) account of the resource-based view. Where bundles/high-performance work practices are concerned, Huselid's (1995) paper is the most frequently cited and one of the most influential pieces written on this subject.

2.5 Conclusion

The resurgence of interest in strategy has dovetailed with heightened competition in increasingly global markets as well as the arrival of HRM. Theories and practices of HRM stress the strategic orientation of their contribution more and more, often in tandem with arguments that assert their contribution to organizational performance.

However, as has been illustrated in this chapter, the means by which organizations devise their strategic goals are diverse and frequently reflect the environmental pressures and expectations that companies face. Whilst organizations located in more stable markets for their services might seek to operate formal planning methods, those experiencing dynamism often tend towards more ad hoc emergent forms. Strategy is also a political activity, and the outcome of any planning activity in this area might well be that which suits the needs of key players rather than the best solution.

Whatever process is adopted concerning strategy formation, there are implications for HRM and the policies and practices developed to facilitate the attainment of business goals. Therefore gaining access to the various processes by which strategy is made becomes increasingly important.

This might be more likely if a clearly identified link exists between strategy, HRM, and sustained organizational performance. In their different ways, the best-fit, best-practice, and RBV models seek to provide the leverage that comes with providing an explanation accompanied by empirical research as to how this relationship operates.

The best-fit, best-practice, and RBV approaches are all now of some longevity, but the evidence of their adoption is patchy. Potential reasons for this potentially lies in their reliance on the use of 'high-road' HRM practices (epitomized by highly skilled and highly paid jobs that are safe, secure, and satisfying), which see employees, or at least segments of staff, as long-term recipients of organizational investment because of their centrality to the attainment of organizational goals. This view is not necessarily appealing to institutional investors, especially during an economic downturn, since the costs of such investments are perceived as placing employees' needs ahead of those of shareholders. Additionally, information about the possible benefits of using high-road practices—reduced turnover, higher levels of trust and employee engagement, reduced absenteeism, more discretionary effort—are typically either not measured at all, or not measured and presented in such a way that benefits and costs of high-road and low-road practices can be readily compared (Pfeffer 2007).

Finally, to what extent does low take-up reflect the levels of power wielded by the HRM function, despite the best efforts of those seeking to secure a strategic role? Many human resource functions are being outsourced. In the political dynamics that shape policies, the rise in power of groups not particularly interested in people or human resources and the decline in power of employee advocates provide reasons why the adoption of these models may be retarded.

 ## Assignment and discussion questions

1 What is a business strategy? Why has the issue of strategy become so important to organizations in recent years?

2 Choose an organization you are familiar with and find out how the company formulates its strategy. Why do you think that the organization engages in this method of devising its business strategy and to what extent does it follow the formal, processual, evolutionary, or systemic accounts outlined in this chapter? What information can you find about the kinds of approaches it adopts towards HRM and to what extent do its practices reflect the best-fit, best-practice, or RBV models?

3 Compare and contrast the best-fit and best-practice approaches to HRM.

4 Why do the UK government and the ILO advocate best-practice approaches to HRM?

 ## Online Resource Centre

Test your understanding of this chapter with online questions and answers, keep up to speed with changes to the law through regular updates, and use selected weblinks to quickly access useful resources and further information. Visit the Online Resource Centre at:
www.oxfordtextbooks.co.uk/orc/gilmore_williams2e/

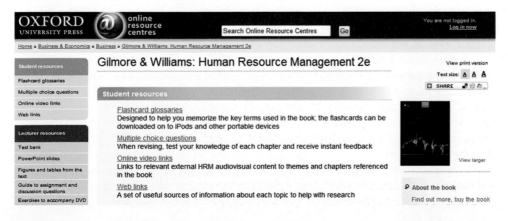

Case study
Business strategy and HRM in boutique hotels

From their inception in the mid-1980s, boutique hotels appealed to consumers who were seeking alternatives to traditional forms of hotel accommodation. Now, as guests increasingly demand that a hotel provides an experience in itself and is not just a place to sleep, the boutique variant is seen as the 'right' place to stay. Hotels seen as 'boutique' tend to stress a highly personalized service and a distinctive style in every aspect of their offering, from the hotel's architecture to the design of the bedrooms and the generous amenities provided (Lim and Endean 2009). Whilst not all boutique hotels are small, they are generally smaller than their chain counterparts and have between 150 and 200 rooms. This seems to be important in terms of creating the sense of intimacy that is also a feature of many boutiques.

Yet the boutique hotel is phenomenon not simply built on a designer ethos with astute marketing. Some industry commentators have calculated that boutique hotels in the UK and USA have been out-performing general hotel trading (Aggett 2007), with research indicating that boutique hotels are the fastest-growing hotel segment in London (Balekjian and Sarheim 2011). This trend is also reflected in international markets such as the Middle East, where designer and branded boutique operations are fuelling growth, and the USA where pioneers of the boutique hotel, such as Ian Schrager, have teamed up with Mariott International in an attempt to bring the boutique phenomenon to a mass market.

In the UK one of the key players in the boutique market is the Firmdale Hotel Group (www.firmdale.com). Founded and owned by Tim and Kit Kemp, it has seven hotels in central London and one in New York. Over the years the group and the individual hotels have won an array of awards, including winning the Queen's Award for Enterprise in 2000, 2006, and 2009 in recognition of its contribution to international trade.

As is typical of a boutique provider, Firmdale places an emphasis on quality, seeing it as a means of attaining competitive advantage through attention to minor details, and believing that, if this is achieved, everything else will follow. One area where this is very evident is in the individual design of the hotel rooms—none of which are replicated elsewhere and all of which contain original works of art. The main aim of the company is to grow—to constantly change and evolve their product so that they are far ahead of their competitors. The Firmdale Group's General Manager has the responsibility to ensure that staff understand their responsibilities and are equipped to carry them out. Unlike the majority of hotels, all services from food and beverages to laundry are owned and run by the company, because they are governed by the view that everything the hotels do and provide are core to the business because they impact on the customer experience. This puts a much greater level of responsibility on employees to provide outstanding customer service. This is even more important when economic conditions are unfavourable and when decisions were taken not to reduce their room rate and other charges (Harmer 2010). Therefore, who the organization hires becomes a strategic decision. In the world of Firmdale, HRM practices are a vital component in maintaining Firmdale's status.

But what is the future for the boutique phenomenon and for Firmdale? How will they maintain and evolve their offering during extended periods of economic growth and downturn? As stated, large hotel chains are now entering the market and these brands have an international reach. Whether or not they will be successful in understanding the boutique hotel and incorporating it remains to be seen. This hotel format is tipped for huge success in London by 2013, but how will Firmdale capitalize on it?

Questions

1 Given that boutique hotels operate a focused strategy of high standards of individualized customer care in a very competitive market, what are the main HRM challenges for organizations like Firmdale?

2 What might Firmdale do in order to maintain its position and reputation? Select the best options and consider the HRM implications for them. Of the options you have developed, which would be the one you would recommend to Firmdale and why?

3 How might the HRM contribution to Firmdale's organizational performance be measured?

4 Consider your answers to the first three questions. To what extent do your suggestions reflect the use of best-fit, best-practice, or resource-based approaches towards HRM?

5 Look at the Firmdale website (www.firmdale.com) and the information given about its graduate recruitment programme and current vacancies. How might Firmdale's employment practices diverge from an industry trend for 'low-road' employment practices, such as low skills, low wages, low commitment, and high turnover? Why might the organization seek to depart from this industry-wide model?

Part Two

The external and internal contexts of human resource management

The business environment of human resource management

3

Rob Thomas

Learning objectives

The main objectives of this chapter are:

- to explain the nature of the external environment of an organization whether it be private for-profit, private not-for-profit, or in the public sector;

- to apply, whilst understanding its limitations, the STEEPLE (or PESTLE) framework to analyse the external environment of an organization;

- to develop critical awareness of the dynamic and complex nature of the external environments that organizations face on a daily basis;

- to explore, using appropriate concepts and frameworks, the ways in which the external environment can affect organizations and be affected by organizational influence.

3.1 Introduction

As has been made explicit in Chapter 2, human resource management does not operate in a void. Decisions and actions by organizations are taken in the contexts of the internal organization (as will be illustrated in Chapter 4) and the external environment. This chapter is concerned with that external environment and the influences on the organization that originate from outside its boundaries. To avoid confusion, the influences that emanate from the natural 'environment', and give rise to so-called 'green' issues, will be termed 'ecological'.

One can immediately think of a myriad of external influences such as employment law, technology, and labour market skills, to name but a few. The aim of this chapter is to provide encouragement and guidance so that you can explore the external influences, actual and potential, that impact on organization. Some may have an immediate impact; others may not seem to have any relevance to the organization until further thought is given to the possibilities. Importantly, it needs to be scrutinized from the perspective of an individual organization because what is crucial for one organization may have little relevance to another.

The link to the previous chapter and its discussion of strategy should be self-evident. Organizations need to be 'ahead of the game' if they are to be successful—this applies to organizations in the private, public, and not-for-profit (or 'third') sectors, although the criteria for success differ. To move ahead involves knowing where the organization is now and the influences, in this case the external factors, impacting and/or likely to impact on its development. Organizations need not be passive, just reacting to changes in their external environment; by identifying forthcoming change, they can be proactive in taking an opportunity, perhaps gaining so-called 'pioneer' or 'first mover advantage' (Kotler and Keller 2012: 334) or blunting a potential threat. As Brooks, Weatherston, and Wilkinson (2011: 11–13) point out, the relationship can be two way: external factors impact on the organization, but organizations can, to some extent, affect their environments.

The above indicates that this chapter is written from the perspective of the organization as a whole rather than directly that of the HR practitioner or line manager. This is because both are expected to understand and contribute to the general management of their organization and not just concentrate on HR issues. Also, many external influences have an indirect impact on HR operations via other parts of the organization, so HR practitioners need to be aware of what is happening—to be 'ahead of the game' and, if possible, to be proactive.

The chapter begins with a consideration of how to 'order' the various influences in the external environment using the STEEPLE (or, in a previous version, PESTLE) framework. Then, working within this framework, the influences are grouped in order to investigate them and thereby emphasize the dynamic interrelations between the individual influences.

3.2 'Scanning' the external environment

That the external environment of an organization is complex is an understatement. Often influences interact. Thus, when employing immigrant labour, managers will need to be aware of the expected demand for the organization's product to determine how many to employ and on what contract duration, and the relevant legislation and required documentation (UK Border Agency n.d.); the skills required will relate to the technology being used to produce the good or service; and there may also be cultural/religious factors, such as prayer times, to take into account.

Putting the words 'changes in' in front of each of the factors introduces the dynamic nature of the external environment. Some changes take a long time, such as the ageing of a population as birth and death rates fall (see Section 3.5.1 for further discussion); others can be very rapid, as was seen in the uprisings of the 'Arab Spring' in Middle East countries in 2011. Whichever, it means that the external environment for all organizations is in a state of flux.

Therefore the ingredients of the melting-pot that is the external environment include complexity and dynamism, to which must be added uncertainty (Johnson, Whittington, and Scholes 2011: 51). The impact of events that have occurred may not be known for some time because of delays in effect, and whilst some future events may be predicable, they may not be predicted with perfect certainty. Then there are the (almost) unpredictable events such as the Japanese earthquake and tsunami.

What is needed is a way of analysing the influences in order to identify and comprehend the possibilities. Costa (1995) identifies two approaches: the 'outside-in' approach which takes a broad view, and the inside-out approach which is more limited in scope in order to relate to the internal organization. The approach adopted in this chapter is the former on the grounds that strategic decision-making should be based on the best information, with 'best' interpreted to include the breadth of potential influences.

3.2.1 STEEPLE analysis

A popular framework that 'orders' the external environment is STEEPLE—an elongated form of PEST and PESTLE (Farnham 2010: 19–27; Kew and Stredwick 2010: 9) Note here that both authors label the second 'E' as environmental, whereas the term used below is 'ecological'.

Social—demographic (population) factors and social behaviour.

Technological—the means by which output is produced and used, and research-generated new products and services.

Economic—the market(s) in which the organization operates, including labour and capital markets, plus conditions in the national and international economy such as inflation and unemployment.

Ecological—impact of the natural world such as climate, resource depletion, flora and fauna.

Political—non-legislated policies and actions of government and of other formal and informal political institutions, including political parties and pressure groups, at local, national, and international levels.

Legal—legislation and the judicial system.

Ethical—social values that affect the perception of how organizations should act, leading to 'corporate social responsibility' (CSR).

The framework is used to scrutinize the external environment of an organization, identifying actual and potential influences, and then sorting them by category. Thus, if the organization believes that a proposed change in the law will affect its operations, this could be listed under 'legal', or if a new competitor is about to enter the product market of the organization, it can be listed under 'economic'. For an example of an organization using the STEEPLE framework, see Hampshire Fire and Rescue Service (2007). Additionally, Box 3.1 offers the opportunity for you to carry out a STEEPLE analysis.

However, the categories are not watertight. The seven categories of STEEPLE overlap, particularly 'political' and 'legal', and 'social', 'ecological', and 'ethical'—the link being a society's culture from which are derived ethical values that change over time on issues such as climate change and the responsibilities of business organizations (Carroll and Buchholtz 2009: 275–7).

Listing every conceivable influence can lead to long lists and the danger of missing the overview. To avoid this, it is necessary to indicate the probability of the influence occurring, the magnitude of the impact on the organization, and whether the organization is able to 'influence the influence'—take action to reduce or change the external factor and/or its effect. However, to raise STEEPLE from a simple listing into a detailed evaluation of factors adds to the time and expertise required (Kew and Stredwick 2010: 15). Many of the techniques available for achieving this are more often applied to SWOT analyses which look at the strengths, weaknesses, opportunities, and threats to the firm (e.g. Jacobs, Shepherd, and Johnson 1998; Panagiotou and van Wijnen 2005).

Even then, organizations can get stuck in their ways of looking at their surroundings. If the environmental scrutiny is always carried out by the same senior managers, they will tend to 'filter' (Brooks, Weatherston, and Wilkinson 2011: 17–19) information in traditional ways that are claimed to benefit the organization, and possibly their position within it. For obvious reasons, the finance director is likely to concentrate on financial factors whilst the HR manager will emphasize workforce aspects. If both are included in the group carrying out the STEEPLE, there will be some balancing of views; if not, then one part of the organization may dominate the thinking. Kew and Stredwick (2010: 15) also suggest using a focus group which includes customers and suppliers.

⚙ Box 3.1 Learning activity
Holiday Sandals

Luxury Included™ is the trademark of Sandals Resorts International which owns and operates a chain of fourteen Sandals outlets, four Beaches holiday centres, and two Grand Pineapple resorts on four Caribbean islands plus The Villas on Fowl Cay.

The brainchild of entrepreneur Gordon 'Butch' Stewart, it began in 1981 with the purchase of an old hotel in Montego Bay, Jamaica. His lack of experience in the industry did not dampen his enthusiasm for developing Sandals based on two particular selling points: all-inclusive, and for couples only. The first 18 months proved expensive and difficult, but eventually the business was turned around and by the mid-1980s, the portfolio of resorts was beginning to expand.

Over the years, in competition with the likes of Club Méditerranée and Kerzner International, Sandals has innovated and redefined its offer: the introduction of WeddingMoons™ with, since 2009, the Martha Stewart weddings packages, butler service, and golf on a course designed by Greg Norman. To cater for families, Beaches Resorts were introduced with the same all-inclusive approach. Numerous travel industry awards bear witness to the company's progress and reputation.

The majority of guests are from North America, with significant numbers from the UK, Germany, and Italy. Repeat business is important, with over 50 per cent of guests having visited before. Online and face-to-face training sessions for agents are offered and lead to 'Certified Sandals Specialist'. Marketing is carefully tailored to the Sandals image and opportunities for positive public relations are sought. However, until 2004, Sandals would not accept same-sex couples; the ban was lifted when the company faced vigorous campaigning, including by the Mayor of London who stopped Sandals from advertising on the London Underground.

In 2009, the Sandals Foundation was established to fund education, community, and environmental projects on the islands. Philanthropy had been part of the Sandals ethos since the beginning, and the company covers the administration costs of the Foundation so that all the proceeds are used to fund the projects. The company employs more than 10,000 staff (Collinder 2011) in the Caribbean and recognizes its importance to the local economies.

Without divulging the figures, Gordon Stewart says that despite the economic recession, 2010 was one of the best years for the company. After 30 years of operations, the company is not slowing: in 2011, father (Gordon, Chairman) and son (Adam, Chief Executive) announced multimillion dollar expansion plans (Collinder 2011).

Carry out a STEEPLE/PESTLE analysis of Sandals Resorts' external environment. The case study contains relevant information, but you should also research the company and the industry. Try and think creatively about recent and potentially relevant international events and influences.

Recognizing these limitations, we will use the STEEPLE framework. However, we will not consider each of the elements in turn; rather, the approach is to group the categories where there is significant overlap in order to demonstrate the potential for interaction between factors—the complexity noted above.

Furthermore, as its metamorphosis from PEST to PESTLE, or PESTEL to STEEPLE, indicates, the framework itself does not prioritize the categories. In what follows, a distinction is made between three types of factors; this approach is related to that proposed by Worthington and Britton (2009: 6), and is similar to the distinction made by Finlay (2000: 193). First, there are those factors that have an immediate and almost continuous influence on the organization because of the frequency of change. In Figure 3.1, where the organization is depicted as a planet, the influences in close orbit are generated by consumers, competitors, suppliers, and labour markets. Secondly, in the outer orbit, are the factors that tend to be of less immediate significance and display less frequent change. Of course, at times, they can become of pressing importance to the organization; changes in the law will be categorized as being 'less immediate' but when the law does change, the impact on organizations can be *very* immediate, as with the change in VAT rates in 2011. Finally, there is the 'sun' of globalization and technology 'radiating light' as over-arching forces interacting with all the STEEPLE categories.

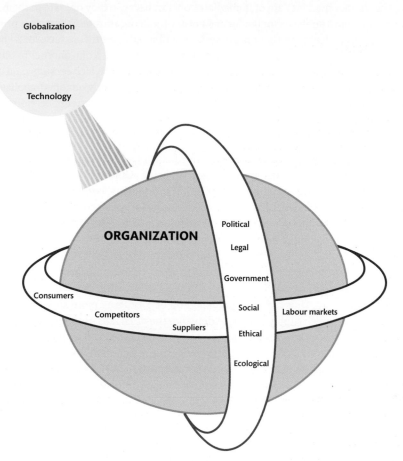

Figure 3.1 The external business context.

Summary and further reading

- The external environment comprises a wide range of actual and potential influences on an organization, be it in the private (for profit), public, or third sectors. For organizations to develop their strategy, the external influences and their impacts need to be identified and understood.

- The external environment is complex and dynamic: influences are often interrelated and changes can be very rapid. The power of these influences varies and their dynamic nature often makes it difficult to forecast the impact on the organization.

- STEEPLE can be used to classify actual and potential external factors. However, in its simplest form it will only provide a listing, and even then a listing that could be biased by the views of the person(s) preparing it. Overcoming these limitations will involve more time and resources as the organization seeks to obtain more information and opinions about the factors, their likely impact, and whether the organization can (pre-emptively) influence the external factors involved. However, such exercises are deemed necessary if the organization is to develop its strategic position.

The first chapters of Farnham (2010) and Kew and Stredwick (2010) relate to the external context to the HR function, whilst those of Worthington and Britton (2009), Harrison (2010), and Brooks, Weatherston, and Wilkinson (2011) provide more general overviews. All are eminently readable.

3.3 Inner orbit: the immediate influences of markets and competition

For organizations in liberal democratic countries such as the UK and other EU member states, markets to which their output is supplied (product markets) and from which they recruit new

employees (labour markets) are of immediate concern because they operate in them on a daily basis. This applies to public sector bodies and not-for-profit organizations as well as private sector firms. Countries with national healthcare systems will supply healthcare services 24 hours a day to people who require (or 'demand') them, charities compete with one another to obtain donations from the public and other sources, and every organization which recruits paid employees must seek them in labour markets, competing to attract relevantly qualified applicants. All of which takes us into the competitive environment and the subject matter of economics.

3.3.1 Product markets

At base level, economics is about scarcity (Harford 2006: 9–11) because we cannot have everything we want. Rather, we must make choices, ignoring what we don't care about but pursuing that which gives us satisfaction (or 'utility', in economists' parlance). As this implies, the assumption is we are motivated by self-interest—be it the satisfaction gained from eating (or 'consuming') a bar of chocolate or the profit to be gained by firms producing and selling the chocolate. There is a conflict involved in this because as consumers we want to pay as little as possible whilst producers, in their pursuit of profit, want to charge as high a price as possible. Markets harness these conflicting self-interests so that a position is achieved with both consumers and producers gaining satisfaction. Put simply, if there is too much demand in relation to supply, the price rises, thus reducing demand and encouraging more supply; in the opposite situation, with too much supply relative to demand, the price falls, thus increasing demand and reducing supply. This is the so-called 'market' or 'price' mechanism' operating via 'market forces' (Sloman and Jones 2011: 31–59). Box 3.2 provides an insight into these competitive forces.

Many product markets operate as just described, although there may be differences in the speed of price change and adjustment (Begg, Fischer, and Dornbusch 2008: 614; Sloman and Wride 2009: 233). The nature of markets also differs according to the types of organization that operate in them.

For a 'takeaway' outlet, the geographical extent of its market might be limited by how quickly the food cools down. This could be a short distance if customers walk, longer if they use a car. At the other extreme, IT companies, such as Microsoft, and car manufacturers, like Toyota and Ford, operate almost worldwide although they do have 'local' offices or agents. In between, the geographical market for an organization may be a town or city, a region within a country, national or international. As with the takeaway, sometimes the geographical area of the market is given; however, in many cases the organization can, to at least some extent, determine the area in which it operates. Advances in transportation and in information and communication technology (ICT) offer the possibility of extending the market area (see the discussion below in Section 3.6). Within the geographical area are two important groups for an organization: the potential buyers, and the competitors; both of which the organization needs to identify if it is to be successful.

To attract buyers, the firm 'stands' in the marketplace and makes its presence known. Some simply rely on 'word of mouth', but many private sector companies employ sophisticated marketing techniques to influence people's decisions as to what to buy and how much they are willing to pay (Kotler and Keller 2012). By using such techniques, the organization is taking action to influence its market size.

Box 3.2 Online video link
India's mobile phone war

As it is the second most populous country in the world and is experiencing rapid economic growth, India offers mobile phone operators a massive potential market. As this report shows, the market has attracted a range of operators and the resultant competition between suppliers is intense. Consumers have benefited from lower call charges (although they always want them even lower). Therefore the competitive pressure has been on the operators to find ways of attracting more users in order to multiply the slim profit margin on each customer into acceptable returns on the large up-front investment. For this example of a competitive market in action, follow the link to the video content provided in the Online Resource Centre. Having viewed the video, think about how the forces of demand and supply have been working in the market to produce lower prices.

Box 3.3 Window on work
Britain's national daily newspapers

Although there are twelve main publishers, more than 80 per cent of the average number of weekday national newspapers circulated in Britain in 2011 were published by News Corporation (33.5 per cent), Daily Mail and General Trust (21.1 per cent), Trinity Mirror (15.2 per cent), and Northern and Shell (13.7 per cent) (Guardian 2011). This highly concentrated market is conventionally divided into three segments:

'popular':	*Daily Mirror, Daily Star, The Sun*
'mid-market':	*Daily Express, Daily Mail*
'quality':	*Daily Telegraph, Financial Times, The Guardian, The Independent, The Times.*

Each segment targets different types of readers and, within the segments, each newspaper tries to differentiate itself from the others; for example, a basic characteristic is the political stance of the paper. The rivalry between the papers has resulted in occasional short-lived 'price wars', but is more evident in non-price actions: competitions, special offers on products (e.g. holidays), free gifts such as CDs and DVDs, celebrity stories, and celebrity writers. A crucial part of the competitive rivalry is the desire for a 'scoop'—being the first to publish a news story.

However, weekday newspaper circulation has been in long-term decline. In the 30 years since 1981, readership has almost halved; between 2006 and 2011, circulation fell 15 per cent and was down nearly 5 per cent between 2010 and 2011. This has had a double financial impact: fewer people buying means not only less revenue from sales but also less advertising revenue, as advertisers seek potential customers via other channels—such as television and the internet (see Thomas 2007).

The long-term changes determining newspaper sales relate to technological and social changes. Television and radio news has been available for a long time but has introduced breakfast news programmes and 'rolling 24-hour' news with live coverage of events—print newspapers take time to reach the reader and so tend to be 'behind the news'. The internet also offers news and comment from around the world, and with the added attraction of access to entertainment and leisure pursuits, this has proved popular with younger age groups. Evidence indicates that older age groups like to buy a daily newspaper, but the declining number of local newsagents in the UK makes it more difficult to just pop out for a paper. To add to the industry's problems, it has been subject to detailed scrutiny of the methods it uses (in particular, voicemail 'hacking') to obtain scoops. One Sunday newspaper (*The News of the World*) was closed as the police investigated the hacking and other charges. The House of Commons Culture, Media, and Sport Select Committee summoned newspaper executives for questioning, and an inquiry under Lord Leveson is tasked with reviewing press conduct.

Newspaper owners have tried to fight back. Investment in production facilities has provided better-quality print, colour, and, amongst the 'quality' papers, changes in paper size. All have also established online versions with free access, though in 2010 News Corporation introduced a 'paywall' for accessing the online content of *The Times* and *The Sunday Times*. So, the days of the paperboy/girl may be numbered as our morning 'newspaper' becomes a mobile phone laid (neatly, of course) on the breakfast table alongside the cereal spoon.

Think about the issues of managing staff in a declining industry but where there is the possibility that some staff can be given different roles in the organization.

For economists, the price of the good or service is an important influence on the amount demanded, but other influences, such as income, tastes and preferences, and the prices of alternative products, are fully recognized (Sloman and Jones 2011: 35–6). Also, in situations where there are few firms supplying the good or service, or an 'oligopoly' as it is called (Brooks, Weatherston, and Wilkinson 2011: 50–4; Sloman and Jones 2011: 128–34), competition may not be via price, but companies turn to other means to secure buyers' attention, as illustrated in Box 3.3.

The identification of competitors can also be tricky because it can depend on how consumers view the product being offered. Branded chocolate bars are in direct competition with one another, although they may try to make their product 'different' by emphasizing the taste. But is the local pizzeria in direct competition with the Chinese takeaway? The answer lies in the extent to which consumers see a takeaway Chinese meal as an alternative or 'substitute' (Sloman and

Jones 2011: 35) product. Therefore competitors are part of the definition of the market of a firm and this includes the geographical extent. Again, firms can influence this by, for example, merging with or acquiring rival companies, although in many countries this may require the agreement of the competition authorities (see Section 3.4.3).

So far the discussion has really been about the markets in which private sector organizations operate. However, similar points can be made with respect to not-for-profit organizations. Small charities may operate in a very limited geographical area, but the larger charities such as Save the Children seek funds internationally, and increasingly use sophisticated marketing techniques (Bennett and Sargeant 2005; Andreasen and Kotler 2008; Sargeant 2009). There is competition for funds: a local zoo competes for membership subscriptions and donations against the World Wildlife Fund (WWF), as does Greenpeace against Friends of the Earth. The role of 'price' can be straightforward where membership is purchased by a subscription and competition can exist between charities offering similar services. However, donations can be made for varying amounts and will reflect the satisfaction a person gets from making the donation.

Public sector organizations, such as a hospitals or local authorities, have 'markets' with defined geographical limits often set by an administrative process. Within the geographical area are the 'customers' who use the good or, more usually, the service provided. The terms 'market' and 'customer' have been placed in quotation marks as they are not used in practice because of two features of the situation. First, in many cases there are few or no competitors—the organization has a monopoly (Sloman and Jones 2011: 121–8) and the service user has no alternative supplier. Secondly, unlike in the private sector, there is often no price at the point of delivery. For example, in many developed countries there are no fees for publicly provided schooling or medical treatment. This can lead to rationing with the development of queues, such as hospital waiting lists. Having said that, recent UK and other Western governments have introduced more market-based approaches, including allowing private sector firms to provide what have been regarded as public services but with payment at the point of delivery, such as toll roads.

The product markets discussed so far have been those where the buyers are the general public. A variant of this is competition between organizations to obtain a supply contract(s) from a separate organization. These are still product markets; the points made above still apply, except that the size of the contracts can be very large. Of particular note are public sector contracts which are often prized by private sector firms, such as defence contracts and the purchase of expensive military equipment.

Decisions and actions in all types of organizations will be subject to changes in their 'market'—be it government decisions, tastes and preferences of buyers perhaps due to migration (see Section 3.5.1), and conditions elsewhere in the world. The constantly changing circumstances will filter through the organization to the HR department. Thus, if another firm in the market becomes more competitive (lower price and/or better quality), your organization will seek increases in productivity from employees via more effort, training, and/or greater flexibility in working; if it does not, your organization could find its sales falling and this can lead to redundancies, or even closure. Another example is in the case study at the end of the chapter, with government deciding to spend more on healthcare leading to increased recruitment of nurses (and other staff). This illustration brings into the discussion one set of markets that directly impinge on HR operations and strategy—labour markets.

3.3.2 Labour markets

As with product markets, there are different markets for different types of labour and they have different geographical dimensions (local, regional, national, international). They can be analysed in a similar way to product markets, but with some important modifications. The nature of demand is different because labour is employed by organizations to produce output and, as indicated in the previous section, the number of employee hours required will depend on the demand for the organization's output (or, in the case of the public and third sectors, how much the organization plans to produce) plus the method used to produce the output (whether it is labour intensive or uses a large amount of equipment and is 'capital' intensive). This is a 'derived' demand and, in labour markets, employing organizations are the demanders. Individuals offering to work (that is, supplying labour) are portrayed as deciding between working (in order to obtain income) and not working, thereby taking time for other activities such as household duties or education—again, self-interest (seeking satisfaction) is the motivation. These changes make the analysis more complex, but the outcome is as expected from the basic market model. Price, or in this case the wage or pay, will rise if there is excess demand for labour and fall if there is an excess supply.

Critics (e.g. Machin and Manning 2004) argue that the employment relationship is too complex and labour markets are too imperfect for the basic market model to provide a satisfactory explanation of pay and employment determination. However, economists counter that market forces operate although full understanding requires the application of further theoretical constructs (Borjas 2010: 2). The situation is made more complicated by the range of remuneration that may be available: pay, incentive pay and bonuses, fringe benefits, and much more, as will be discussed in Chapter 7. The DVD interview with Tony Peers from the National Theatre outlines some of that complexity in more detail, with reference to the diversity of jobs carried out by staff in the organization.

The 'human capital' construct links economics with HRM, viewing labour as an asset rather than a cost. More formally, human capital is 'the qualifications, skills and expertise that contribute to a worker's productivity' (Sloman and Wride 2009: 257). Individuals and organizations, including governments, 'invest' in human capital, i.e. spend now on the acquisition of the skills, broadly defined to include knowledge via education, with the benefits accruing over the years when the skills are used. The different skills and expertise give rise to different markets for different types of labour and, for organizations, there is the question of whether to spend on training or to 'buy in' the skills.

 ## Summary and further reading

- Markets, involving the interaction between the organization and its competitors, consumers, suppliers, and labour, constitute the immediate, or inner, orbit of the organization's external environment because it is in frequent contact with these participants.

- The self-interest of the participants is harnessed in markets via the 'forces' of demand and supply. These market forces operate so that when there is excess demand (supply), price rises (falls) in order to remove the imbalance.

- Demand and supply are influenced by a range of other factors and so can be subject to (at times, rapid) change.

- The market model can be applied to the public and third sectors. In the case of the former, the lack of price at the point of delivery means that the 'market' does not adjust via price and so there is a tendency to 'rationing'.

- The model can be applied to labour markets, although additional theoretical constructs, such as human capital, are needed in order to understand the ways in which market forces operate for different types of labour.

For those who have not studied economics before, Harrison (2010: 25–30) provides a gentle introduction. Heather (2004: 27–49) provides an analysis of stock market adjustment, whilst Levitt and Dubner (2006, 2009), Harford (2006, 2008), and Smith (2003) offer insights into some unusual applications of economic analysis.

3.4 Outer orbit (1): government—politics, the law, and managing the economy

The extent to which government should involve itself in the economy and society of a country, and thereby affect organizations directly and indirectly, became a subject of particular debate following the collapse of communist states in the late 1980s. The current strongly held view (to call it a 'consensus' would be an overstatement—see Farnham 2010: 238–9, 428–31) is to limit the role of government and leave individuals to make their own decisions. This approach attempts to fit together democracy with a market-based economy (Brooks, Weatherston, and Wilkinson 2011: 249), with the role of government being to promote these two basic pillars of society.

A liberal democratic political system, such as that in the UK or USA, is based on 'rights' and 'responsibilities' (Morris, Willey, and Sachdev 2002: 177–8):

* human rights—e.g. right to life, freedom of thought (United Nations 1948)
* political rights—e.g. universal suffrage, secret ballot
* economic rights—e.g. right to work
* social rights—e.g. right to healthcare, right to education
* duties—e.g. compliance with the law.

The government's role is to reflect the values of society in ensuring that rights are protected and that people are responsible in their actions. However, rights and duties can be in conflict. Take, for example, the human right to life and the right for an individual to make their own decisions in respect of their life as seen in the debate on voluntary euthanasia. Or, at what point does the right to freedom of speech stop because what is said is discriminatory? Moreover, a society's values change over time, resulting in more or less government intervention. It is only in the last 45 years that liberal democracies have introduced legislation to prevent many forms of discrimination in employment. These, and many other political and legal changes, impact on organizations and their HR operations. All organizations in a country are part of society, and so these rights and responsibilities apply to them—a topic that arises in Chapter 14 in the context of a discussion of ethics and HRM.

3.4.1 The importance of the political system

Political systems vary in detail between different liberal democratic countries (see CIA (n.d. a) for outlines of political systems in different countries), but some generalizations can be made. A democracy means that almost all adults have the right to influence government policy, including the laws that are passed. Because of the cost and difficulty of millions of people voting on every decision, countries opt for a 'representative democracy' whereby adults elect representatives at different levels of the legislature (e.g. the UK Parliament) and, in some cases, the head of the executive (e.g. the President of the USA). Government usually operates at various geographic levels. Central government is 'at the national level' but in the case of the EU member states, this is blurred by the role of the EU's political system and legislation. Also, a broad definition of 'government' includes international institutions such as the World Trade Organization, as will be discussed in Section 3.6.

Within countries there are further levels of government on a regional/local basis. In the case of the UK, the regional level can be defined as county or metropolitan borough level, although there is the Parliament for Scotland and the Assemblies for Northern Ireland and for Wales. The powers at each level of government are set by the constitution which can change over time. Organizations need to be aware of which 'level' decides what, in order to operate within the system. Thus, in the UK, planning tends to be decided at the local level, but decisions can be overruled at national level (for a basic description, see the UK government website, www.direct.gov.uk). An organization wishing to expand its factory/office space will need to know the local planning regulations (see Dyson (2007) for the consequences of not receiving planning permission). Put simply, an organization may operate globally, but its headquarters and other facilities are based locally (see Morrison (2011: 31–2) for what she calls 'the multilayered environment').

Organizations can try to affect political decisions (another example of how organizations can influence the external environment) by 'lobbying'—communicating with, and thereby trying to influence, politicians and civil servants (or equivalent) at all levels of government (Geiger 2006; Parvin 2007; Spinwatch 2008; Worthington and Britton 2009: 66–7, 339–41). Lobbying is an acceptable part of liberal democracy, with all individuals having the right to communicate with their representatives, but they should not apply undue pressure (threats or bribes). Organizations are normally in a good position to lobby because they represent a group of voters (their employees), have the resources, and can use the media effectively to get their message across. They can hire professional lobbyists who have developed contacts with politicians and can gain access for their clients to communicate with the

Box 3.4 Learning activity
Lobbying

There are many ways in which communicating your views to political decision-makers is an acceptable part of democracy. This exercise requires research to identify the various channels and decide what is acceptable, and what is unacceptable, lobbying by an organization.

Task

The government of a liberal democracy, such as the UK, is reviewing its employment policies. An existing law gives male and female employees the right to take paid leave of up to five working days per year when their child is ill.

Assume that you are the Chief Executive of a large company operating in the country. Because of the costs involved, you wish to see this law changed so that when employees take leave to care for their ill child, the company does not have to pay them.

1 What arguments would you use to persuade the government to change this law?

2 What ways (or 'channels') would you use to persuade the government to change the law?

3 Ethically, and justifying your answers, which ways of trying to persuade government are (a) acceptable and (b) unacceptable?

decision-makers—decision-makers because there are many actions of government that do not require legislation, such as the awarding of government contracts that may be very lucrative for business and lead to recruitment of extra staff if won, but redundancies if lost. For example, see Grainger, Clark, and Asteris (2007) on the potential impact of closing a naval dockyard and Box 3.4 on the skills involved in effective lobbying.

3.4.2 The law: legal changes and organizations

The 'rule of law' is fundamental in liberal democracies (Farnham 2010: 445). Harris (2007: 1–25) notes how the law, and changes in the law, relate to the social, cultural, economic, and political contexts of a country, again illustrating the earlier point in Section 3.2 about complexity of the external environment. There are various classifications of the law (e.g. Brooks, Weatherston, and Wilkinson 2011: 268–70). The one adopted here emphasizes the importance to organizations of legal changes by source: consumer, company, and employment legislation.

Normally, organizations will wish to act within the law, not merely to avoid fines and other penalties but also to ensure that their image is not tarnished by bad publicity. Thus, with consumer law, which seeks to protect the public in its transactions with organizations, a restaurant will not want to fall foul of food safety laws because the consequent loss of trade could far exceed the fine. For the public sector in the UK, there can be 'Crown' immunity from prosecution in some areas but, even then, civil claims can be brought against the organization, again with accompanying bad publicity. Not-for-profit organizations are generally subject to the same consumer legislation as for-profit companies, although some civil disobedience groups may deliberately break the law in order to gain publicity for their cause (e.g. Taylor 2011).

A second group of laws and regulations relate to the way organizations are managed and operated. In the UK this can be seen in the UK Companies Act 2006 and the UK Charities Act 2006. These primarily relate to internal operations such as accounting requirements and practices, but can also include the voting and other rights of shareholders in public limited companies, and members in not-for-profit organizations. An important related piece of recent UK legislation is the Corporate Manslaughter and Corporate Homicide Act 2007 (with Amendment in 2011), by which an organization can be found guilty of causing a person's death.

Finally, and of crucial importance to HR practitioners, there is employment and related legislation. Organizations must comply with the legal requirements or face punishment, but changes in the law could be a catalyst for more far-reaching change as the organization adjusts to a specific piece of legislation, although the evidence suggests that firms do not always make

> ### Box 3.7 Practitioner perspective
> #### BMW's anti-ageing treatment
>
> Germany, like many developed countries, has an ageing population: between 2010 and 2030 its population of working age (15–60 years old) will fall from 60.5 to 50 per cent of the population (United Nations 2011b). As a major employer in Dingolfing, Lower Bavaria, car manufacturer BMW was aware of the issue and in 2007 managers decided to take steps to deal with the problem (Loch et al. 2010; Roth 2010).
>
> Older workers are less productive because of longer periods of illness and declining physical abilities. However, the company did not want to tarnish its reputation as a good employer, so making older workers redundant was not really an option. Instead, it instituted a pilot programme involving 42 employees on the rear-axle gearbox production line. The idea was to have the same age structure as that expected in 2017 when the average age of the workforce would have risen to from 39 to 47 years.
>
> The pilot deliberately involved the employees in the process, getting suggestions from them as to how the workplace should be designed to accommodate older workers. Seventy small changes—including installing wooden floors, stretching exercises, and a new work rotation system—were made to the production line at a total cost for the pilot of about €40,000.
>
> Within a year the productivity of the production line had increased by 7 per cent, the quality target of less than 10 defects per million had been surpassed and stood at zero, and by June 2009 absenteeism was just 2 per cent (below the plant average).
>
> The so-called 'demographic time bomb' is usually portrayed as a threat, but it can be an opportunity.

(Kew and Stredwick 2010: 294). State agencies are also affected by the rise in demand for healthcare and associated provision for the elderly. In the not-for-profit sector, there are a growing number of charities, such as Age Concern in the UK, providing services for the elderly which will want to expand their provision as the number of elderly increases.

In labour markets, the average age of many workforces is rising, with increasing proportions of staff approaching retirement age (as seen in the case study at the end of this chapter), although Bloom, Canning, and Fink (2010) find the changes for some developed countries to be modest rather than catastrophic. Some organizations deliberately recruit and retain staff who are over the retirement age (Craig 2009). The obvious implications of these changes for the HR function in organizations are recruitment and selection, staff retention, and staff retraining. Box 3.7 provides an example of some of the possibilities organizations might want to consider.

Immigration can be a way of closing the gap between demand and supply in labour markets caused at least in part by the ageing of the population. It is not just a matter of numbers; the acquisition of skills can take time during which the demand will not be met unless skilled workers can be recruited from other countries. Such influxes have implications for organizations in all sectors: the increase in demand by ethnic groups for goods and services provided by the private sector that meet their cultural requirements (Sherwood 2007); publicly funded health and education services for ethnic groups (House of Lords 2008); and the role of voluntary organizations in helping immigrants settle and find out about their rights (e.g. Migrants' Rights Network: www.migrantsrights.org.uk/).

Waves of immigration create social and cultural issues that can be portrayed as advantageous, but conflicts can arise and these have implications for the public services and for employing organizations. This is not just a matter of equal treatment and opportunities but also in-house policies to meet the needs of different ethnic groups. These kinds of issues bring external social change into organizations—from changes in class consciousness, through the way people dress in work, to recreational pursuits. All are underpinned by the changing values and social mores of society and thus influence the context of HRM.

3.5.2 Ecological

Changing values have also brought ecological factors into media headlines. These are society-wide issues which impact on organizations of all types. As economies grow they require more

Box 3.8 Research in focus

Green jobs

The UK's Climate Change Act 2008 and subsequent policies are expected to cause significant changes in the structure of the economy. Forecasters see the target of an 80 per cent reduction in greenhouse gases by 2050 relative to 1990 levels (with an interim target of a 34 per cent reduction by 2020) as generating many 'green jobs', although there is also the warning that jobs may be lost in energy consuming industries.

The term 'green jobs' has broadened from its nature/environment beginnings to include employment in '... renewable energy, energy efficiency, low-carbon transport fuels, climate change consultancy and carbon finance' (Bird and Lawton 2009: 14). Even wider definitions are used in some forecasts and, as Bird and Lawton (2009) note, 'workplace greening' could see all jobs becoming green.

The Department for Business Innovation and Skills (BIS 2011b) estimated that in 2009–2010 UK 'low-carbon and environmental goods and services' (LCEGS) sales were close to £177 billion and provided employment for more than 914,000 people. An earlier report commissioned by the government forecast a 45 per cent increase in LCEGS jobs between 2007–2008 and 2014–2015, with over a third of the rise being in manufacturing (Innovas Solutions 2009).

Bird and Lawton (2009) are more cautious, noting the potential political backlash from those whose jobs are threatened (e.g. in coal mining and steel production which is a heavy user of energy). In addition, Hughes (2011) argues that whilst employment may increase in LCEGS, the investment finance needed will have been diverted from other uses and, because green energy is very capital intensive, it may result in fewer jobs being created overall.

Where LCEGS jobs are created, there is the potential for skills shortages. However, Bird and Lawton (2009) did not find any evidence that completely new types of skills will be required. Rather, the need will be for training in particular skills and in 'topping up' existing ones, as well as education and training in more generic green skills.

natural resources to produce the goods and services that people want. Not only are natural resources depleted, but technology often produces goods and services which pollute the environment. Organizations are being, or will be, affected by the changes themselves and motivated to adjust their behaviour by the change in society's values (see Box 3.8). Additionally, those organizations which implemented change early will have gained an advantage. The 'third sector' provides many examples of 'early movers' on social and ecological issues, such as Greenpeace, Friends of the Earth, and the WWF. For private sector firms, the pursuit of profit has not always fitted with ecological actions, but now firms realize that they can reduce costs (e.g. energy bills), as well as raise their reputation and image amongst buyers, by being perceived as 'ecologically aware'.

3.5.3 Ethical

Changing social values are placing pressure on organizations to adopt ethical values and policies (e.g. Box 3.9)—in modern 'management speak', corporate social responsibility (CSR). Kew and Stredwick (2010: 377) argue: '... HR should be the lead department' for CSR because, to be successful, the policies need to affect all activities and, by implication, all employees. This is elaborated in Chapter 14 when HRM's ethical stewardship of organizations is discussed.

  Summary and further reading

- Social and ecological external contexts may tend to change slowly but they can have significant impacts, presenting opportunities and/or threats to organizations.

- An ageing population is a current and future issue for many countries and it permeates many parts of society and economy: from changes in the types of goods and services that are demanded to pressure on the state to provide adequate healthcare and pensions. There are also implications for the labour forces of organizations and of the economy.

Box 3.9 International focus
A holiday for fair trade

Coffee, bananas, and chocolate are probably the best-known products of the fair trade movement in the UK, but late in 2011 the movement added a new dimension—the UK's first fair-trade holiday. Kuoni's 15-day self-drive South Africa Garden Route package included accommodation in lodges and hotels registered with Fair Trade in Tourism South Africa (FTTSA).

Fair trade is a social movement which seeks to ensure that small-scale producers in developing countries are not exploited when selling their products. To be recognized as a fair-trade buyer, an organization must abide by fair terms and conditions of sale, including the payment of a fair price that reflects the work carried out; the buyer should ensure child labour is not used in production, and that there are good working conditions with no discrimination. In addition, the principles include 'respect of the environment' (World Fair Trade Organization 2011).

From its conception in the USA in the 1940s and 1950s, the movement has grown rapidly with the establishment of fair-trade bodies in many developed countries and the introduction of the Fairtrade label. By 2007, worldwide sales of Fairtrade certified products were estimated at £1.6 billion; in the UK estimated sales of fair-trade certified products rose from £32.9 million in 2000 to £799 million in 2009 (Fairtrade Foundation 2011).

The 2009 figures for the UK show more than 70 per cent of fair-trade products are goods such as those listed above plus tea, honey, flowers, wine, and cotton. The importance of the Kuoni initiative for the fair-trade movement in the UK is that it is offering a fair-trade leisure industry service. As with all 'for-profit' business, there are risks, and fair-trade products tend to sell at a higher price—the Kuoni fair-trade holiday in 2011 cost just under £3000, whereas *The Sunday Times* quotes a slightly shorter holiday but with a similar itinerary at £2351 (Sunday Times 2011). Thus, fair-trade products sell because sufficient consumers in countries like the UK are willing to pay extra in order to ensure fairness for the producer.

- Immigration can provide extra labour-market flexibility because it has the potential to fill the gaps in the labour force, especially skill gaps. However, it brings other changes in the economy and in the culture of society and of organizations.

- Society has become much more concerned about climate change and other ecological issues. This is placing pressure on organizations to ensure they reduce waste and do not pollute.

Morrison (2011: 361–422) offers a more extensive and very readable introduction to the issues raised in this section, as do Harrison (2010: 180–203), and Brooks, Weatherston, and Wilkinson (2011: 190–231). More detailed reading on social aspects can be found in Giddens (2009), whilst business ethics are explored by, for example, Fisher and Lovell (2006) and De George (2010).

3.6 Technology and globalization

In many discussions these two topics are treated separately. Here, technology is incorporated as one of the so-called 'drivers' of globalization, with technology defined as 'the application of scientific knowledge to help humans produce goods and services more efficiently' (Farnham 2010: 380), and globalization as 'a mixture of processes by which products, people, companies, money and information are able to move quickly around the world' (Morrison 2011: 43).

Globalization can be viewed as a long-standing process; what proponents argue is new are the speed and scope of the interactions and interconnectedness. Herein lies the role of technology in facilitating the globalization process, offering opportunities for organizations to benefit from involvement in international transactions, political and social as well as economic. Companies such as Microsoft and Google, and other companies, both small and large, have developed alongside the expansion of ICT. They illustrate the role of 'enterprise' whereby, in market-based economies, an individual can start a business and build a multi-billion pound organization by being ahead of competitors and exploiting the external environment as it changes.

Kondratieff cycles (Kew and Stredwick 2010: 319–20) hypothesize that technological revolutions come along every 50–70 years and boost the world economy. It is not just a matter of the invention itself but the ways in which it permeates economies and societies, generating other developments. An early example is seen in the industrial revolution when people were required to move from their rural homes because they had to be physically present in order to carry out their work. Many ICT-based jobs allow people with skills and access to the technology to carry out their work whilst living in rural areas (Ruiz and Walling 2005; Mason, Carter, and Tagg 2011), raising challenges for the management of such employees.

Where work is 'offshored', i.e. moved to another country because of the cost advantages of production, the implications for organizations in the home country are redundancy and/or redeployment (Blinder 2006), although ILO findings (2006) indicate the effect may not be large). China has become a major manufacturing base (Needle 2010: 60–4), but it is not just the ICT-facilitated logistics and lower labour costs that support China's development; with the main markets for China's manufactured goods being thousands of miles away in North America and Europe, lower-cost transportation has also been significant (see Box 3.10).

Globalization affects all the external environment factors identified and discussed above. Arguably, it has increased the interdependence between countries so that economically and politically they are more closely tied together. This can be perceived as a threat to the right of countries to decide their own laws and practices ('sovereignty'). International bodies such as the World Trade Organization (WTO), the International Monetary Fund (IMF), the World Bank, and the United Nations seek to promote the well-being of the international community and resolve

Box 3.10 Window on work
The box that shrank the world

According to Vidal (2006), Christmas that year arrived in the UK in 3000 containers on board the Emma Maersk 3—an overstatement but it made the point. A lot of the goods we buy come to the UK (and other developed countries) by container ship. In 2009, an estimated 1.19 million tons of cargo were transported by sea container; in the 10 years prior to the 2008 recession, world container traffic grew by an average of 10 per cent a year.

This is all because in 1956 a US transport boss, Malcolm McLean, realized that a 'box' would make loading/unloading less time-consuming (Cudahy 2006) and cheaper. In the early 1960s, it was estimated that shipping costs were up to 25 per cent of the value of US exports; by 2006, it cost $10 to ship a $700 TV set and $1 for a $150 vacuum cleaner (Shipping and World Trade n.d.). Of course, not all cargoes can be transported in containers, but when they can be, the advantages are enormous:

- ships are unloaded and loaded more quickly and so spend more time at sea;
- reduced handling costs;
- increased use of inter-modal transport systems;
- less damage and theft.

Therefore the container has changed the costs involved in the economic principle of 'comparative advantage', but not without incurring costs. Vidal (2006) notes that Felixstowe was a little town, but it had a container crane, which meant that a lot of port activity previously undertaken in London and Liverpool moved to Felixstowe, with the resultant loss of jobs in those cities.

Not that it is all plain sailing for the container. Most world trade routes are from China and the Far East to either Europe or North America. Therefore, whilst observers may claim that containers have been an important factor in promoting the economic growth of the likes of China and India, the trade imbalance and competition between the container shipping companies means that freight costs vary greatly according to the route (UNCTAD 2011a: 19).

To accommodate an increasing range of goods, the simple TEU container (20 feet long by 8 feet high with doors at one end) has been adapted in size and form, including 'reefers' for refrigerated goods. Also, bigger and bigger container ships have been built, but the 2008–2009 recession highlighted an oversupply with some being laid up and others broken up (UNCTAD 2011a: 29). In addition, oil price rises adversely affect shipping costs, with some observers talking about the possibility of companies preferring to source production nearer to the main markets (e.g. Mexico for the USA and Central Europe for Western Europe)—or 'globalization lite' as it has been called (Asteris and Thomas 2009).

4.1 Introduction

The overriding concern of this chapter is to explore the ways in which the organizational contexts within which human resource management (HRM) is practised play a part in shaping the nature and orientation of those practices, and vice versa. In other words, we examine how the organizational context influences HR practices and how, at the same time, HR practices play a part in shaping organizations. When we talk about 'organizational contexts' in this chapter, unless we state otherwise, we are referring to the 'inner' or internal contexts of organizations (Pettigrew 1985), i.e. such aspects as organizational structuring, the forms of job design to be found within the organization, and, linked to them, the division of labour, working practices, and organizational culture(s). Chapter 3 focused on the 'outer' or external contexts of organizations, and of course we will not go over this ground again here. However, it is important to bear in mind that these outer contexts will influence the inner contexts and practices and vice versa. Drawing upon Weick (1995), organizational practices 'enact' or influence the nature and shape of the outer contexts in which they operate through 'sense-making' practices.

Section 4.2 addresses the structure and design of organizations, and perspectives on organizational change. The design of jobs and work arrangements is a key issue for managers in all organizations. In Section 4.3 we consider various approaches to managing and organizing work, including teamworking and empowerment initiatives. In Section 4.4 we turn our attention to culture, power, and politics in organizations, before offering a conclusion. When reading this chapter it is important to bear in mind that its primary concern is to enable you to place the management of human resources in an organizational context, and thus the emphasis is upon HRM implications of the material discussed.

4.2 Organizations, organizational change, and HRM

In this section we are primarily concerned with the nature of organizations, the main features of organizational structure and design, and organizational change initiatives.

4.2.1 Organizations and organizing

An initial key task is to review what is commonly understood by the terms 'organization' and 'organizational structure'. Since this is not a book about organizational behaviour, we will not provide much detail on these matters, but will draw on the work of one of the most influential writers in this area, John Child, to highlight some key points. Child (2005) makes a distinction between organizing and organization.

> [Organizing] is the process of arranging collective effort so that it achieves an outcome potentially superior to that of individuals acting or working alone. It almost always involves some division of labour, with different people or groups concentrating on different activities that then have to be integrated (coordinated) to achieve a successful result. Organizing also requires a degree of control, so as to monitor progress against original intentions and to make appropriate adjustments along the way ... a form of hierarchy normally develops such that one or more people take the lead in formulating instructions, providing coordination, and controlling results. These manifestations of organizing, taken together, are commonly termed *organization* ... This term implies that the form of organizing used by a company persists in a recognizable form, at least for a while. (Child 2005: 6)

Child goes on to distinguish between the structural, processual, and boundary-crossing facets of organization. Taking each of these in turn, the first consists of a basic structure and procedures.

> a basic structure distributes responsibilities among the members of a company. Its purpose is to contribute to the successful implementation of objectives by allocating people and resources to necessary tasks and designating responsibility and authority for their control and coordination. This division of labour has both vertical and horizontal aspects. Its vertical aspect provides

for a specialization of discretionary decision-making responsibilities through specifying levels in a *hierarchy*…. The horizontal aspect provides for a *specialization* of tasks according to functional specialty, business focus, or geography. (Child 2005: 6)

Examples of basic structure include organizational charts, job descriptions, codes of conduct, and committees. Procedures focus on influencing behaviour through, for instance, rules and standards that clarify to employees what is expected of them, and attempt to ensure consistency in dealings with staff (e.g. the determination of pay and other forms of reward).

Child (2005) identifies three main organizing processes: integration, control, and reward. Integration focuses upon ensuring that the various complementary activities undertaken by the organization are coordinated in some way (e.g. by meetings). Control is concerned with the setting, implementation, and monitoring of the attainment of organizational goals. As Child (2005: 8) observes: 'there is considerable choice and variation in the broader strategies of control open to management. Some of these strategies require elaborate organizational support, while others rely more on people's "self-control" through their understanding and acceptance of collective objectives.' Reward is concerned with attempts to motivate employees to contribute to the achievement of organizational goals by attracting people with the requisite skills and knowledge, and thereafter gaining their commitment.

Boundary-crossing is focused on achieving internal organizational integration between various organizational roles and units in order to generate creativity and synergy, and the use of inter-organizational (between organizations) arrangements through networking, outsourcing to subcontractors, strategic alliances with other organizations, etc. In summary terms, then, organization is concerned with establishing an internal context within which the processes required for collective activity can proceed.

4.2.2 Principles of organizational design

Having discussed the concepts of organization, organizing, and organizational structure, we now turn to the matter of how organizations are designed. Clearly, the design of organizations will be informed by an attempt to ensure that its goals are realized as efficiently as possible. The most enduring organizational design framework is the bureaucratic form.

In the early twentieth century, the German theorist Max Weber formulated a series of principles that underpinned an 'ideal-type' bureaucracy, distinguishing it from the more general usage of the term to describe any organization that is administered by appointed specialist officials. The main features of Weber's ideal-type bureaucratic organization are as follows.

- The presence of a clear hierarchy of offices.
- The specialization of job roles among the managers and administrators who are the holders of those offices.
- The importance of impersonal considerations in reaching decisions.
- The widespread use of formal rules and procedures to govern the conduct of office holders. The most notable feature of bureaucratic organization concerns the attempt to coordinate and control organizational activities through managerial hierarchies and formal rules (Hales 2002).

Weber considered the ideal or pure type of bureaucracy to be the superior form of organization (Morgan 1997), stating that it is, 'from a purely technical point of view, capable of attaining the highest degree of efficiency and is in this sense formally the most rational known means of carrying out imperative control over human beings' (Weber 1947: 337). What did Weber mean by 'rational'? The concept of rationality that underpins the ideal-type bureaucracy holds that organizations will choose the most logical and efficient means of realizing their goals. This is exemplified by the important role played by formal rules and procedures in providing impersonal and objective criteria for determining organizational action. This was a form of authority based upon rational–legal principles; 'authority' here refers to the way in which people submit to the will of others because they believe that they have the right to give orders because they are according to and within the set rules and regulations.

Bureaucratic principles exert an important influence over the management of people in organizations. The existence of formal rules and procedures for dealing with issues and problems can contribute to the effectiveness with which HRM is undertaken in practice. Organizations use such procedures for, among other things, dealing with the recruitment and selection of staff (see Chapter 5), managing equal opportunities and diversity issues (see Chapter 10), handling grievance and disciplinary issues (see Chapter 13), and determining which staff will be released in a redundancy exercise (see Chapter 9).

The existence of formal bureaucratic procedures for dealing with HRM matters can be advantageous for managers. Using procedures can help to legitimate management decisions by demonstrating that they have been reached in an apparently fair manner. The decision to reject an employee's complaint about his/her treatment at work is more likely to be accepted if it has been arrived at according to the rules and regulations extant in the organization. Procedures provide for consistency in managerial decision-making. The aim of equal opportunities policies and procedures, for example, is to ensure that staff are not subjected to detriment on the basis of some aspect of their social characteristics, such as sex, age, or whether or not they have a disability.

For managers, the main disadvantage of formal procedures can be concerns about the diminution of their flexibility to deal with HRM issues as they see fit. In practice, however, procedures by no means always inhibit managers' actions. For example, in Chapter 13 we see that procedures for dealing with employee grievances and disciplining staff are frequently ignored, or are drawn upon selectively in a way which serves managerial goals, regardless of the substantive merits of the case in question.

An excessive reliance on compliance with rules and regulations can have undesirable consequences (Merton 1940; Gouldner 1954). Some commentators have gone so far as to reject bureaucracy (e.g. Peters and Waterman 1982). However, others defend bureaucracy because of its impartiality, and its promise of equitable and consistent treatment of staff and clients (du Gay 2000).

There is an extensive literature on 'bureaucratic dysfunctionalism'—in other words, how adopting too bureaucratic an approach can subvert organizational goals. For example, goal displacement occurs when managers over-concentrate on complying with procedures to ensure that bureaucratic targets are met, and thus become distracted from taking the important actions necessary for improving the performance of their organizations—the distinction between what Weber (1947) referred to as *formal* rationality (procedures etc.) and *substantive* rationality (focusing upon the goals themselves).

The phenomenon of goal displacement will be familiar to anyone who follows debates about the organization and management of the public services. Hospitals, schools, the police, and so on increasingly have their performance judged according to the extent to which they meet certain specified targets, such as shorter waiting times for operations, examination results, or percentage of crimes solved. However, the trouble with targets is that if they are given too much emphasis, they can give rise to a number of problems. For instance, insufficient attention may be paid to activities that, whilst important, are not the subject of targets. For example, medical staff who prioritize reducing patient waiting times, because there is a target to meet here, may not give matters such as the cleanliness of their wards as much attention, as they do not have targets for this (and, in any event, nowadays this work may be subcontracted out to an external provider).

A key focus of bureaucracy's critics is its alleged inflexibility. How relevant is the bureaucratic form of organization in the twenty-first century, when flexibility, innovation, and creativity are often seen as the main ingredients of organizational success? However, it should be noted that some well-known and successful organizations, such as McDonalds, operate according to classic bureaucratic principles. The fast-food chain, with its rigid set of operating procedures designed to guarantee customers a standardized and predictable product, functions in a way that accords with Weber's ideal type (Ritzer 2004). Yet there are growing pressures on managers to pursue change and innovation as a means of improving the performance of their organizations, and this is linked to an increasing amount of interest in so-called 'post-bureaucratic' organizational forms.

4.2.3 Organizational change

The desirability of operating within a traditional bureaucratic framework has increasingly been called into question, as organizations experience acute pressures to change and pursue innovation as a means of securing business growth in an ever more globally competitive environment (see Chapter 3). Organizational change and talk about change is ubiquitous.

What kinds of change have been occurring in recent years? Common examples include the following.

- Organization-wide restructuring initiatives, such as those arising from mergers or acquisitions between organizations, which are often associated with major job losses.

- Organizational culture interventions, such as attempts to change the dominant beliefs influencing the behaviour of staff (see Section 4.4.1).

- Technological change/innovation, with its associated organizational changes. Examples in recent years include 'cloud computing', enterprise resource planning systems, innovations in healthcare technology, and networking software.

- The reorganization of work, for example through empowerment and/or teamworking initiatives (see Section 4.3.3).

- Attempts to reconfigure/redesign the whole or key parts of the organization in order to improve customer service by becoming more 'customer-focused'. For example, business process re-design is often connected with the trend of business process re-engineering (BPR). Hammer and Champy (1993) argued that organizational efficiency and effectiveness is best achieved by redesigning organizations so that the focus is on having operating processes which add direct value by meeting the needs of customers, 'empowering' employees, and changing the 'mind-sets' of managers.

How has organizational change been theorized? One popular way, especially in managerial/consultant books, is to see it as something which managers can achieve in a rational planned way, and Lewin's (1951) 'force-field analysis' is perhaps the best-known model. He described how managers facing pressures for change can 'unfreeze' the existing way of doing things by altering employee attitudes etc., creating a shift—the change process—from the old pattern to a new one, which is then 'frozen' as the normal state of affairs. Other such models of planned organizational change stress the steps managers need to undertake, generally in a linear sequential fashion, in order to achieve the desired transformation (Collins 1998).

There are a number of problems with such an approach: (i) conflict and resistance to change are given insufficient and inadequate attention; (ii) there is little recognition of the external and internal organizational contexts within which change occurs and the ways in which they impact upon change efforts; and (iii) change in practice is a continuous, messy, political, iterative, and unpredictable process, and never 'freezes' or finishes. For other authors, organizational change is best viewed as 'emergent' rather than planned, where change initiatives develop in unexpected non-sequential ways, influenced by a varying cast of organizational members who all have their own specific interests and agendas. Strongly influenced by Pettigrew (1985), Dawson (2003: 14) argues that organizational change is best viewed as a process rather than an event—'a complex ongoing dynamic in which the politics, substance and context of change all interlock and overlap . . .'.

A processual approach was also adopted by Preece, Steven, and Steven (1999) in their study of a range of organizational change initiatives introduced by the public house retailer Bass Taverns in the 1990s. One example was a change initiative centred upon introducing assessment centres for recruitment and selection, which was designed (in part) to bring in new talent from outside the company. It provided an opportunity to bring women into senior operational roles, and to bring in talented people from other divisions of the company, yet this did not come about. There was considerable resistance from some people within Bass Taverns who saw the proposals as likely to affect their positions adversely; for example, they would be out of a job or demoted. Organizational change from the late 1990s in public house retailing and many other sectors of the economy has been increasingly influenced by the financialization process (see Box 4.1).

Box 4.1 Window on work
Financialization and organizational change

From the late 1990s, public house retailing has been transformed by a process of 'financialization'. This involves, in brief, borrowing money on a short-term basis to acquire pubs, and then (through a process called 'securitization') converting the loans into less costly medium- and longer-term instruments as and when the pub estate confirms its financial projections. These cheaper loans are a result of the perceived lower level of risk which has now been confirmed, such data being required by longer-term lenders in order to securitize the debt. In essence, securitization is a process whereby future cash flows from the organization's asset base (such as rental income) are used as financial backing for investment bonds on international bond markets. As these longer-term debts replace more expensive short-term ones, they help generate additional cash balances for further acquisition and expansion. Thus the possibility arises to move ever 'onwards and upwards' in a pub acquisition spiral. Several pub companies embraced this financial methodology from the late 1990s into the present century (Preece 2008). As Thompson (2003: 367) has observed, financialization strategies have encouraged a movement 'away from internally-oriented, commitment and values-based transformational change, to one that is based on the *financialization* of change in response to the new dynamics of capital markets'. In the UK public house retailing sector, this process led to the emergence of a few large lease-based companies, along with a number of smaller ones. Public houses were acquired because they were excellent generators of cash, from rental payments by the tenant/lessee to sales of beer and other drinks.

Financialization generally worked well as long as global financial institutions were confident that the securitized debts could and would be repaid, and hence continued to provide loans. However, once this confidence dissipated during the world financial crisis of 2007–2008, when banks were no longer willing to lend to each other and some financial institutions failed, with others bailed out by government, this model became highly problematic. To put the matter somewhat simply, it had been built upon weak foundations and unjustified optimism about the future—that this world of expansion built on more and more debt could and would go on indefinitely. Suffice it to say here that as far as public house retailing companies are concerned, times have become much more difficult and challenging for them, and they have found it increasingly difficult to service their debt. There is much turbulence in the sector, compounded by the downturn in the economy, with many pub tenants struggling to pay their rent and meet other bills. Large tranches of the pub companies' estates have been sold off and a number of pubs have closed across the UK.

4.2.4 Towards post-bureaucracy

How far have the extensive changes to organizations described above made the conventional bureaucratic form redundant? There has been an increasing amount of interest in so-called 'post-bureaucratic' organizations, which is really about new or different ways of structuring organizations. Writers on organizations have identified a number of key features of such organizations (e.g. Heckscher 1994; Child and McGrath 2001; Clegg, Kornberger, and Pitsis 2008):

- the emphasis on greater flexibility;
- the decentralization of activities;
- the contraction of hierarchies;
- the importance of horizontal forms of coordination in organizations, such as cross-functional project arrangements;
- the reduced significance of formal command and control structures;
- the erosion of the boundaries between organizations;
- the decline of traditional organizational careers;
- the presence of a participative working environment that gives workers greater influence over decision-making.

The post-bureaucratic paradigm holds that organizations are becoming more 'decentralized, loosely coupled, flexible, non-hierarchical, and fluid' (Alvesson and Thompson 2005: 487).

The search for greater organizational flexibility is one factor held to have undermined conventional bureaucratic arrangements. The principles of bureaucracy, and their manifestation in formal rules and procedures for regulating organizational activities, are no longer seen as being as appropriate and beneficial as they once were. The argument is that an organization's success is influenced much more by its responsiveness, flexibility, and capacity for innovation. This is particularly important given the increasing extent to which the production of goods and services for standardized mass markets has been supplanted by the need to satisfy more specialized and differentiated market niches.

New information and communications technologies (ICTs) have helped organizations secure greater flexibility and reduce bureaucracy by enabling them to decentralize their activities (Ackroyd 2002). As we have seen, the control and coordination of activities in bureaucracies is undertaken through hierarchies of managerial decision-making and by means of formal rules and procedures. However, in post-bureaucratic organizations, such as the fashion retailer Zara, this is achieved through the deployment of sophisticated ICT systems.

What are the implications of post-bureaucracy for the way in which people are managed in organizations? Under conventional bureaucratic arrangements the emphasis is on using formal rules and procedures to circumscribe and control the behaviour of workers. Post-bureaucratic theorists emphasize that managers need to build more informal trust-based relations with their staff. Given the reduced importance accorded to hierarchy, and set against the development of an increasingly knowledge-driven economy (Leadbeater 1999), trust is seen as a particularly effective way of coordinating organizational activities, and also as the source of a more humane and participative working environment (Dale 2001). The DVD interview with Pam Bader highlights some of the HRM issues and challenges in this area with regard to the franchise model of organizing business activity.

A further aspect of managing people in post-bureaucratic organizations concerns the greater emphasis given to the management of culture. Organizational culture consists of the unwritten, tacit, and informal norms, values, and beliefs that influence behaviour in organizations (Clegg, Kornberger, and Pitsis 2008). In contrast with bureaucratic organizations, where managers seek to secure the compliance of their staff by enforcing obedience to formal rules, under post-bureaucracy the emphasis switches to a concern to articulate and secure a shared organizational culture (sometimes referred to as 'corporate culture') which will guide staff in their everyday activities in a more open-ended and flexible way. We deal with the concept of organizational culture more extensively in Section 4.4.1.

Finally, post-bureaucracy is argued to have positive effects on people's working lives. Whereas bureaucratic organizations are marked by an emphasis on internal career ladders, under post-bureaucracy people enjoy greater opportunities to shape their own careers and exercise control over the trajectory of their working lives by following 'boundaryless' or 'portfolio' careers (Arthur and Rousseau 1996; Fraser and Gold 2001), switching between organizations as 'free agents' (Barley and Kunda 2004)—self-employed temporary contractors who sell their services to a range of firms in a way that liberates them from the restrictive 'iron cage' of working as employees in bureaucracies. Under these circumstances, the job of managing human resources focuses on ensuring that the benefits of operating with this more flexible temporary workforce are maximized, and with ensuring that workers' knowledge and skills are deployed in way that adds value to the firm.

Clearly, significant changes have taken place in and to organizations over the years. But have they led to the disappearance of conventional bureaucracies and their replacement by post-bureaucratic organizational forms? Notwithstanding the rhetoric of post-bureaucratic organizations, evidence of their presence is rather thin on the ground (Alvesson and Thompson 2005; Williams 2007; Thompson and McHugh 2009). For example, there is little evidence that workers have embraced 'boundaryless' careers in the manner anticipated by some commentators. In many sectors the durability of bureaucratic forms of organization is apparent. White et al. (2004), in an empirical study in the UK, found that ICT was predominately used not to liberate workers, but rather to monitor and control their activities. The subcontracting and outsourcing of work by both public and private sector organizations has entailed an extensive amount of legally binding and formal specification of the responsibilities of both parties—in short bureaucracy!

It has long been recognized by writers on organizations that bureaucracy can take a variety of forms in practice. Contingency perspectives argue that different forms of organizational structure are appropriate for organizations in different contexts ('best fit', as against 'best practice'), with more flexible 'organic' structures being more appropriate for organizations located in continually changing contexts and bureaucratic structures more appropriate for more stable ones (Burns and Stalker 1961; Pugh and Hickson 1976). At the same time, organizations might have relatively 'tall' or relatively 'flat' hierarchies, but still be structured according to broadly bureaucratic principles. Changes in organization structuring have undoubtedly occurred, often associated with intensified and expanded forms of networking and technological change (Castells 2000), but they have taken place within a design framework that is bureaucratic at heart (Hales 2002). Despite striving for greater flexibility, decentralizing their activities, joining networks, and making more extensive use of ICT, organizations generally continue to deploy bureaucratic features in order to operate efficiently. Bureaucracy has endured for sound managerial reasons. Hierarchical structures and formal rules and procedures continue to be key means of attempting to achieve organizational objectives by coordinating activities, exercising monitoring and control, and effecting compliance (Adler 1999).

Summary and further reading

- It is important to distinguish between 'organization', the components of 'organizational structure', and the process by which 'organizing' occurs.

- The bureaucratic form of organizational design has had an enduring influence on organizations around the world. It is particularly manifest in hierarchy and the formal rules and procedures that govern life in organizations, and is often evident in human resource management practices.

- Organizational change is commonplace. There are a variety of forms of organizational change, and a key contrast is between approaches that see change occurring in a planned strategic way, and those that focus on the emergence of change as a process over time.

- The flexibility and responsiveness required of many organizations in ever more competitive circumstances might appear to have made bureaucratic forms redundant. Post-bureaucratic approaches emphasize, among other things, de-layering, decentralization, and delegation. However, it would be a mistake to write off bureaucracy just yet, as it continues to be widespread and have a significant influence over organizational practices and the ways in which human resources are managed.

See Child (2005) for more on the nature of organizations, the concept of organizational structure, and the process of organizing. Ritzer's study (2004) of 'McDonaldization' captures the way in which conventional bureaucratic approaches are central to the success of the fast-food chain and other companies like it. See Alvesson and Thompson (2005) and Thompson and McHugh (2009) for an assessment of post-bureaucracy. See Box 4.2 for a skills exercise concerning organizational design.

 Box 4.2 Skills exercise
Organizational design

Assume that you work in a medium/large organization which operates in an increasingly competitive global market place producing consumer goods, and which is structured and operated along strict bureaucratic lines. The board of directors is concerned about the financial performance of the company over the last year or so (profits are down, sales are down, etc.), and thinks that one key contributory factor is the extensive degree of bureaucracy to be found in the organization. You are a team of HR specialists, and you have been given a brief by the board (which includes the HR director) to consider the advantages and disadvantages of alternative organization designs, and to come up with a recommendation as to which one should be adopted and why.

4.3 Managing and working in organizations

A key concern for managers is to try to ensure that employees' jobs are designed and their work carried out in such a way as to promise efficiency and effectiveness in their performance, thus helping the organization to achieve its financial goals. Max Weber's ideal type of bureaucracy was, and still is, seen as a key way of achieving this for administrative staff. Around the same time that Weber was writing in the late nineteenth/early twentieth century, Frederick Taylor was advocating a particular way of designing manual or shop floor jobs, so-called 'scientific management', based on his belief that efficiency is paramount, and that the best way of securing it is by dividing up jobs (creating a 'heightened division of labour') and giving workers little discretion over their jobs. 'Taylorism', as scientific management has often been termed, has had an enduring influence on organizational practice across the industrialized world. The 'human relations' approach to employee management emerged a little later (for many writers in the late 1920s); it urges managers and supervisors to recognize that workers have social needs and that jobs should be designed in such a way that they are met (e.g. by creating a degree of involvement in decision-making at the local level). This will help to ensure the achievement of organizational goals. In recent years, some organizations have introduced teamworking and empowerment initiatives in an attempt to create/tap into employee commitment with the same basic goals in mind.

4.3.1 Frederick Taylor and scientific management

Underpinning Taylor's concept of scientific management was his belief that strict organization and control of labour was essential in order to achieve improvements in business performance. Following a series of shop-floor experiments, Taylor elaborated a number of key principles of a 'scientific' approach to management:

- the use of systematic methods for determining the most efficient way of completing a task;
- the 'scientific' selection and training of workers;
- the separation of conception, or knowledge of how to undertake a job, which was to be the exclusive province of managers, from the execution of those tasks, which was to be the responsibility of workers;
- the elaboration of a highly detailed division of labour so that workers concentrate on narrow specialized tasks;
- the use of (unsophisticated) financial incentives to motivate workers to greater effort, particularly arrangements that link pay rates to output in some way.

Taylor's work has influenced management practice in a wide variety of organizations across the world. Famously, motor-car manufacturers like Ford adopted and modified Taylor's ideas when introducing assembly-line technology for the mass production of vehicles (Braverman 1974; Littler 1982) (see Box 4.3). The scientific management approach places a premium on rationality, efficiency, job redesign, and the allocation of tasks amongst jobs in such a way that costs should be minimized and productivity maximized. Taylorism is also concerned with effecting strict control and discipline over staff; people are expected to execute the tasks that they have been allocated according to managerially designed specifications under the strict direction of managers who alone possess the relevant knowledge and expertise to plan work activities effectively. Work, then, is rendered predictable. The everyday job of managing people is concerned

Box 4.3 Online video link
The origins of Taylorism

You can find out more about the origins of Taylorism, and how Taylor's approach was put into practice by the Ford Motor Company in the early twentieth century, in two videos. Go to the Online Resource Centre for the relevant links.

with selecting and training staff for specific tasks as appropriate, ensuring that order is maintained, and dealing with poor performance or misconduct (Thompson and McHugh 2009).

Taylorism is evident in many types of firms today, including call centres, fast-food restaurants, manufacturing companies, and office establishments. Studies of call centres have found that much of the work in such environments is organized in a way that gives workers little control over the pace or content of their jobs; for example, Taylor and Bain (1999) coined the phrase 'assembly line in the head' to describe the Taylorist arrangements that prevailed in the call centres they studied (see also Callaghan and Thompson 2002; Burgess and Connell 2006; Russell and Thite 2008). Many Western companies have established call centres abroad in recent years. Jobs in the fast-food industry are frequently marked by features consistent with Taylor's scientific approach to managing work. The emphasis is on producing standardized products, made according to set procedures, including strict timings over, for example, such things as cooking periods. Jobs are broken down into narrow tasks, with company manuals setting out in some considerable detail how they should be undertaken, how long they should take, and in what order they should be done (Royle 2000). Clearly, the scope for the exercise of worker discretion is very limited in such environments. However, see Box 4.4 for a much more positive view of HRM practices and experiences in McDonald's, and Box 4.5 for details of research findings relating to the experience of work in McDonald's, Australia.

Notwithstanding the enduring influence of Taylorism, it does pose a number of challenges for managers, not least when it comes to having to deal with its adverse effects. Unsurprisingly, people who have Taylorized jobs tend to experience low job satisfaction, have poor morale, and evince limited commitment to their organization. Work, then, far from being a source of pride, is something to be avoided or, where this is not possible, carried out only with grudging minimal commitment. Often the result is a low-trust orientation to work, where workers have little if any motivation to go 'beyond contract' by doing any more than is formally specified (Fox 1974). Further problems can include high rates of sickness absence, recruitment and retention difficulties, low levels of cooperation between managers and workers, and opposition to the exercise of managerial authority. Given these problems, over the years managerialist writers have been keen to identify and propagate a more 'humane' approach to managing people at work, one which is argued to be beneficial for both the organization *and* its staff.

4.3.2 Human relations at work

In contrast with Taylorism, the human relations perspective holds that recognizing that workers have social needs, and encouraging them to feel that they have some influence over decisions that affect them at work, is an effective way of managing people in organizations. The human relations approach originated in the first half of the twentieth century. Research carried out in the 1920s and 1930s at Western Electric's Hawthorne plant near Chicago in

Box 4.4 Practitioner perspective
Refashioning McDonald's as an employer of choice

Fast-food companies like McDonald's have a poor reputation for their employment practices (Royle 2000). However, David Fairhurst, vice-president for people at McDonald's UK, claims that the widely held perception that people who work for his company inhabit dead-end and low-skilled jobs is false. He points to the investment McDonald's has committed to improving the skills of its staff as an example. Fairhurst also emphasizes the opportunities for career progression that exist: most of the company's managers started off as 'crew members', who have been able to work their way up the organization. Although when people start work at McDonald's they tend to see themselves as just doing a job, Fairhurst asserts that 'after three months or so, they become evangelists because of the leadership and community spirit that exists in stores', and that for many 'it's not just a job, but a career' (Thomas 2005; Fairhurst 2008).

Do you think Fairhurst is right when he praises the opportunities offered by working for McDonald's in these terms?

Box 4.5 International focus
Working at McDonald's (Australia)—some redeeming features

In his study of McDonald's in Australia, Gould (2010) found that jobs in the fast-food industry offered workers certain benefits, such as job security and the possibility of career development. Although some workers were either unaware of, or uninterested in, such features, for many they were important aspects of organizational life. It would seem that managers in a company like McDonald's typically take a more benign and developmental view of their workforce than is implied by the negative way in which jobs there are often characterized. Managers generally believed that good work performance should result in promotion and advancement opportunities for staff; for the most part they also supported the view that front-line workers should enjoy some degree of employment continuity. Evidently work in the fast-food industry is not just the expression of a narrow form of Taylorist scientific management.

the United States was particularly influential. Popularized by the writings of Elton Mayo, the purported results of these 'Hawthorne' experiments stimulated considerable interest in the human relations approach to managing people at work (Rose 1975). The Hawthorne studies had two main findings which came to be seen to constitute the basis of the human relations approach. The first concerns the importance of participation—where workers feel that they enjoy influence over decisions that affect them at work, their output is likely to be greater than where they do not. Secondly, workers are not motivated solely by economic concerns. This means that the management of people at work needs to acknowledge, and try to influence as necessary, the social factors, such as group identities, that influence behaviour in organizations. Taylor considered that workers were motivated fundamentally by instrumental considerations, hence the reliance on simple payment systems that linked reward to output.

Although they were marked by some major weaknesses in research, the Hawthorne experiments came to exercise a notable influence over subsequent writing about the management of people in organizations which focused on the desirability of instituting cooperative relations at work, something best achieved, it was argued, by respecting the social needs of the workforce—for example, Maslow (1987) and his 'hierarchy of human needs'. Human relations thinking influenced approaches to the motivation of workers, studies of job satisfaction, and the need to redesign jobs so that people enjoyed more variety and responsibility in their work (Clegg, Kornberger, and Pitsis 2008; Thompson and McHugh 2009).

The human relations approach has several key implications for managing human resources in organizations. Whereas scientific management emphasizes the importance of ensuring that staff comply with organizational rules and decisions, particularly when it comes to undertaking the tasks associated with a job, human relations attaches importance to managers and supervisors addressing the social needs of people at work. Securing the cooperation of staff is seen as a more effective way of managing people at work—for example, ensuring that they are appropriately motivated by having their contribution recognized or by giving them a feeling they have some involvement over how they carry out their jobs. This approach informs the basis of much contemporary HRM practice.

4.3.3 Teamworking and empowerment initiatives

Somewhat more sophisticated approaches to reorganizing work and how it is managed have emerged in recent years, often associated with post-bureaucratic forms of organizing (see Section 4.2.4). Two examples are teamworking and empowerment initiatives. Underpinning both is the assumption that where workers are able to exercise control over their jobs, have more discretion over how they are undertaken, enjoy a wider variety of job tasks, and possess greater knowledge and skills regarding the execution of their jobs, they will be more motivated and committed, and thus more willing and capable of contributing to (improved) organizational performance. Clearly, such an approach marks a departure from Taylorist assumptions about how jobs should be designed in organizations.

Teamworking can be a means of enabling people to participate in, and exercise greater control over, their work activities. While the practice of teamworking varies considerably within and across organizations, the concept typically refers to the way in which workers are allowed to organize and manage aspects of their work collectively—as a team—without direct supervision by managers. In the case of Bass Taverns, where teamworking was introduced within and across its pubs, the majority of pub managers and their staff liked and embraced it, and teamworking had a positive impact on organizational performance (Preece, Steven, and Steven 1999). Therefore a move to teamworking potentially signals a notable change in how people are managed in organizations, perhaps including, for example, the introduction of job-sharing and rotation within the team (and team-based reward and incentives), ensuring that they are appropriately motivated.

In practice, however, teamworking which involves people participating in and exercising greater control over their work activities appears to be the exception; while teams in name are commonplace in organizations, they are often, particularly in the service sector, no more than 'administrative work groups of individual workers under the jurisdiction of one supervisor' (Korczynski 2002: 134). In many cases, teams are more a means of managing and controlling staff, than of promoting the participation of staff (see Procter and Mueller 2000). Some analysts have developed the concept of 'concertive control', drawing our attention to the ways in which organizational priorities can become internalized by employees, not least in teams (Tompkins and Cheney 1985; Barker 1993; Sewell 1998). Barker (1993) studied the introduction of self-managed teams in a small US manufacturing company. He argued that the teams were 'their own masters and their own slaves', and were reluctant to give up control of their working practices, even though they generated a good deal of strain.

With respect to empowerment, as always it is important to define what is meant here, and how far empowerment initiatives have enabled people at work to exercise greater control over, and participation in, the execution of their jobs. Empowerment implies two particular things: (i) that some supervisory tasks which would hitherto have constituted part of the managerial role are delegated to workers; and (ii) that workers are given greater autonomy in their work and therefore, by implication, exercise greater control over how their jobs are undertaken (Cunningham and Hyman 1999).

Being *told* by a manager that you are now empowered and actually *feeling* empowered, or actually *having* more power than before, are not necessarily the same things. This was evident in Bass Taverns, where the organizational changes implied that the local pub managers and their staff would enjoy greater autonomy (see Box 4.6). The pub managers were ambivalent about the company's empowerment concept and the way it had been applied. A substantial proportion did not feel that they had been empowered at all. While there were some areas where pub managers did exercise more influence (e.g. over the appointment of staff), this was not enough to dissipate the senior managerial control culture which permeated the company (see Box 4.7). On the one hand, managers were expected to be flexible and responsive to the needs of their customers, and thus needed to be empowered, whilst at the same time they were told and monitored to run their pubs efficiently (and hence to minimize and save on costs) in order to help meet the corporate objectives of turnover and profitability. There is clearly a basic tension here. Korczynski's (2002: 64) work has much relevance here—he developed the concept of the 'customer-oriented bureaucracy' as a means of conceptualizing front-line service work. It 'captures the requirement for the organization to be both formally rational, to respond to competitive pressures to appeal to customers' wishes for efficiency, and to be formally irrational, to enchant, responding to the customers' desire for pleasure, particularly through the perpetuation of the enchanting myth of customer sovereignty'.

The main criticism of the empowerment concept is the limited evidence for any shift towards a substantially more empowered workforce, suggesting that, on this measure at least, claims about the advance of new forms of work organization need to be treated with a considerable degree of caution. Studies of discretion at work suggest that the level of autonomy and control experienced by workers may have actually declined from a low base (Green 2004; Gallie 2005). The Workplace Employment Relations Survey (WERS) of 2004 found that the extent of autonomy devolved to teams was often limited (Kersley et al. 2006). Managers in organizations seem reluctant to transfer too much power to the staff under their control. Where power

Box 4.6 Policy extract
Empowerment in Bass Taverns

This policy extract concerns the empowerment initiative designed for public house managers in Bass Taverns.

What does 'empowerment' mean?

The word 'empowerment' is increasingly used, but often misunderstood. Quite simply, empowerment is designed to enable LHMs [Licensed House Managers] to 'get the job done' and improve levels of customer service, without always having to seek authority first.

How will lhm empowerment work within bass taverns?

The concept of empowerment has been developed through various brainstorming and validation exercises with LHMs and corporate staff across the country. Areas identified for LHM empowerment and the associated levels of authority and control have been put into a matrix form. This matrix has been given Board approval and will come into effect as the New Retailing Initiative is rolled out.

What benefits am i, as a licensed house manager, going to see?

Historically, regions have varied in terms of the levels of LHM authorization in certain areas. Accordingly, LHMs from different regions will experience different degrees of change when the matrix comes into effect. However, all LHMs will find some positive changes—changes designed to help them to take action more quickly and assist them in running their business more effectively. For the first time, a *national* statement of LHM levels of empowerment and authorization has been put into place. The current matrix represents a starting point; it is hoped that further increases in the levels of LHM empowerment will be able to take place in the future.

Why are there limits to authority within the matrix?

Additional empowerment means additional trust and accountability. However, *everyone* within Bass Taverns, no matter how empowered, has to operate within certain control limits. Without a sensible degree of control, no business can operate profitably. This is a key message. The levels of empowerment given within the matrix represent a carefully considered balance between essential Company controls and the benefits empowerment can bring.

Source: Preece, Steven, and Steven (1999: 160–2).

is shared, it is done so within tightly controlled boundaries. For example, take the experience of staff in the restaurant chain TGI Fridays: while managers encouraged waiting staff to accept customer requests for changes to the standard menu and to rectify any complaints themselves, their discretion was tightly bounded by the need to follow prescribed rules governing service delivery, such as the maximum waiting time between courses (Lashley 2000).

Summary and further reading

- Taylor's scientific management approach has long exercised an important influence over the design of jobs in organizations. Managers operate an extended (technical) division of labour such that workers carry out their jobs within a highly restrictive control-based environment in which they enjoy little power.

- The human relations school of management thought has had some influence over the way in which managers are exhorted to manage people in organizations, although the extent to which this has impacted upon actual practice is another matter, and can be overstated by some writers/management spokespersons. It maintains that organizations will better achieve their objectives where the social needs of the workforce are recognized through, for example, being granted greater autonomy, since this increases organizational commitment.

- In more recent years, teamworking and empowerment initiatives have been advocated and discussed by writers and introduced in many organizations; these are approaches to redesigning work which, in theory at least, give staff more job autonomy. However, the extent to which genuine autonomy has been achieved in practice is open to question.

Box 4.7 Window on work

Experiencing empowerment in Bass Taverns

When we first started with this empowerment thing, we were all a little bit frightened—we're allowed to do it, but we're told we're not, if you understand what I mean. We were all told it's our business now. If, for example, I need new chairs or tables, whereas before it would have taken months, now I can say 'We'll have that'. You're in control of the costs. OK, if you went overboard ... I think most people are not going to do that (but) if you have a function now, you can give everyone a drink. I found it hard at first when we came over to this, because I'd still ask can I do certain things. I don't feel empowered, I don't feel any difference from before. Because we're still employees of the company, we've still got to answer to somebody ... If I'd wanted my own business, I'd have gone and got it.

Why doesn't this manager feel empowered?

Source: Preece, Steven, and Steven (1999: 163–4).

See Burgess and Connell (2006) for a collection of papers which examine call centre practices in a number of countries, and Taylor and Bain (1999) for a study that considers Taylorism and call-centre work. Rose (1975) offers an excellent account of the development of Taylorism and the human relations approach. The concept of the 'customer-oriented bureaucracy' is featured in Korczynski's book (2002) on front-line service work.

4.4 Culture, power, and politics in organizations

In this section we shift our attention away from the structural dimensions of organizations to examine the more intangible aspects of organizational life, which are just as real in their effects and consequences. The focus is upon organizational culture, power, politics, and conflict in organizations.

4.4.1 Organizational culture

What do we mean by organizational culture? Broadly speaking, it refers to the symbols, values, and beliefs that underpin organizational life. In the organizational context, culture has been conceptualized in a variety of ways and no one particular definition has been accepted as definitive (Ogbonna and Wilkinson 2003). Brown (1998: 293) provides a helpful working definition, arguing that organizational culture is 'the pattern of beliefs, values and learned ways of coping with experience that have developed during the course of an organization's history, and which tend to be manifested in its material arrangements and in the behaviours of its members'. Schein (1992), in an influential model, distinguishes between 'governing assumptions' (beliefs about the nature of reality, organization, and its relations to the environment that are taken for granted), 'values and norms' (which prescribe what ought to be done), and the 'artefacts' of organizational culture (such as the contrasting furniture to be found in executive, middle-management, and supervisory offices). This framework facilitates a differentiation between 'deep' and 'shallow' cultural change; for example, it is much easier to change artefacts than values.

What are the implications for the management of people? By managing culture effectively (i.e. in the interests of the organization per se), managers can use it as a means of gaining competitive advantage by winning the 'hearts and minds' of workers (Willmott 1993) and developing/enhancing their commitment to business goals.

There are many examples of organizations which have played with culture as a means of managing staff. The assumption is that 'senior managers can strengthen organizational culture, manipulate it and control it to generate commitment, unity and meaning by organizational symbols' (Gabriel, Fineman, and Sims 2000: 207). Take, for example, supermarket chains, where improved customer service is seen as a source of competitive advantage. Efforts to build stronger corporate cultures in this sector have included recruiting employees who have demonstrated a strong customer orientation at selection, training in, and a promulgation

of, a 'one-team' view of the organization, and communication and training focused upon the importance of the customer. But supermarkets have faced challenges to their attempts at such cultural change. Perhaps what has occurred in many instances is 'surface acting' (Hochschild 1983) or, to put it another way, reflective compliance on the behalf of staff, as they feel obliged to comply to keep their job, rather than changing their values and beliefs (Ogbonna and Wilkinson 1990).

Culture change programmes often constitute a key element of managerial efforts to transform organizations; building a strong corporate culture is viewed as a key contributor to business success. Yet there is little evidence that the messages promulgated by corporate culture change programmes have been internalized by staff (Ackroyd and Thompson 1999; Ogbonna and Wilkinson 2003). Cultural change programmes can be seen as a narrow HR matter, one not really to do with other staff. (Alvesson and Sveningsson 2008).

A further, even more fundamental, problem with corporate culture change programmes concerns their assumption that culture is something that can be altered by managers. Smircich (1983) views culture as a 'root-metaphor' rather than as a variable. In other words, culture is not something an organization *has*, which therefore can be changed by managers, but rather is something an organization *is*. Culture in the latter sense refers to the manifest beliefs, symbols, and values that are created and maintained on an everyday basis by all members of the organization; amongst other considerations, this alerts us to the existence of a number of 'subcultures' in organizations and the possibility of cultural conflict. The implication is that, whilst organizational culture can be described in words, interpreted with words, and analysed through words, it cannot be changed in the basic way that some writers argue. Ogbonna and Wilkinson (2003) identify some middle ground, i.e. a position where there is *some* room for 'cultural manipulation' (i.e. organizational culture as a variable subject to management influence), and yet at the same time (non-organizational) culture exists as a root metaphor. Here, culture change initiatives are 'more likely to influence official as opposed to unofficial versions of an organization' (Hughes 2006: 85). In other words, they are not changing the deep-seated underlying values and assumptions held by people in the organization.

4.4.2 Politics and power in organizations

Our starting point for understanding how politics and power are manifest in organizations is the distinction between the 'rational' and 'political' models of organizational life. The rational model of organizations (illustrated, for example, in the ideal type of bureaucracy (see Section 4.2.2) and scientific management (see Section 4.3.1)) assumes that they pursue logical goals based on relevant evidence and in a consistent fashion. The assumption is that determining an organization's goals and the best means of achieving them are relatively straightforward uncontested processes. All of the actors within an organization will support its goals and agree on the most effective way of realizing them. Much management thought, from its beginnings with Taylorism to the present day, has incorporated, either implicitly or explicitly, these rationalist assumptions. For example, management decision-making is often held up as an area where rationalism prevails (Clegg, Kornberger, and Pitsis 2008).

Yet organizations are political entities. People and groups within them will have different views about what the organization's goals should be and how they should be achieved. Organizational politics becomes particularly evident during periods of change, when uncertainty, and even confusion, can prevail. Actors in organizations strive to maximize their own interests, which are not by any means necessarily the same as the organization's, and to secure their own position relative to others (Buchanan and Badham 2008).

Even if employees do agree with the goals of the organization, *how* they are to be achieved can be another matter entirely, open to all sorts of differences of opinion over resources, tactics, methods, and priorities. We can see politics at work in many aspects of human resource management practice. Take the demand from a departmental manager that an allegedly incompetent worker should be promptly dismissed. An HR practitioner may agree that the worker concerned has a poor record of performance, but is concerned with ensuring that the appropriate procedures are followed before coming to a decision on the worker's fate. While the manager's main objective is to get rid of the worker, the HR practitioner's principal concerns may be with ensuring that the correct procedures are followed and the worker is given a chance to improve, whilst avoiding actions that could result in the organization acting unlawfully and thus being liable to financial penalties.

Political behaviour in organizations is, of course, to do with power. What do we mean by power? Essentially, the exercise of power determines 'who gets what, when, and how' in organizations (Morgan 1997: 170) by determining organizational outcomes, such as how resources are allocated. The possession of power exercises a significant influence over organizational decisions and how it is planned to implement them. Dahl (1957) argued that power is the ability of one organizational actor, such as a manager, to get another actor, say a member of staff, to do something that he/she would otherwise not do. The power a manager has to dismiss a worker for an alleged instance of misconduct is an example of the visible exercise of power in practice. But power is also exercised in less transparent ways, often as a result of *not* making decisions. For example, take the non-promotion of a manager who is perceived to be reluctant to spend additional unpaid time at work during evenings and weekends because of his/her family commitments. No tangible decision has been made, but the exercise of power, in the sense of an ability to secure a particular outcome, is starkly evident.

For Lukes (2005), these one-dimensional (visible decision-making) and two-dimensional (non-decision-making) perspectives on power are inadequate. They neglect the way in which the exercise of power in organizations is underpinned by broader social and economic forces. The majority of work across the world today takes place in capitalist societies. This means that, at least in the majority of private sector organizations, the imperative to generate profits out of the organization takes precedence over everything else. Therefore costs (including labour costs) have to be controlled, and often reduced, and attempts made to maximize revenues through expanding sales/services, all in competition with other organizations in the sector locally, nationally, and internationally which are attempting to do exactly the same. In a market economy, managers enjoy power over their staff because the consequences for the latter of not complying with managerially determined rules could mean putting their jobs and careers at risk and imperilling their livelihoods. Lukes (1974: 23) asks: is it not 'the supreme exercise of power to get another to do what you want them to do by controlling and shaping their wants?' Thus the 'most effective and insidious use of power is to prevent any conflict arising in the first place'.

This three-dimensional perspective on power captures the way in which people in society and organizations are conditioned to accept certain outcomes without seeing them as undesirable and thus contesting them. Managerial initiatives to manage/change corporate culture can be viewed in part as attempts to exercise power over staff by securing their commitment and loyalty to the organization (Willmott 1993). If this is achieved (and it is a big 'if'!), disputes over decisions or non-decisions are rendered irrelevant. Employees (and note, managers are employees too) comply with organizational goals, not because they have to, or because of the adverse consequences for them of not doing so, but from a belief that they are desirable. However, as we see below, the fact that employees often do not behave in ways that accord with managerial edits and expectations indicates that organizations may not be all that successful in exercising power in this way.

From where do managers obtain their power? To address this question we need to distinguish between the concepts of power and authority. Power has already been considered. The possession of authority gives certain people (e.g. managers) the right to issue instructions, and promises that they will be obeyed by those over whom it is legitimate for them to issue those instructions. The basis of this authority, and therefore legitimacy, is that it is 'rational–legal' (Weber 1947), i.e. according to and within the known and accepted rules and regulations of the organization (the other main Weberian sources of legitimacy are charisma and tradition). Thus managers can expect to command the obedience of their subordinates by virtue of the formal position that they hold in the organization; in other words, their authority comes from the legitimate power that is attached to the role that they occupy.

However, other sources of power in organizations have been identified. As discussed above, what about the capacity of an actor to coerce or force another actor to do something he/she would not otherwise have done? Employees join and combine in unions to put pressure on management, for example, to improve their pay and working conditions. The possession of expertise can also be a source of power based, for example, upon professional training and qualifications, which in many countries are a requirement for practice (e.g. accountants). Specialist ICT expertise can be a source of power/influence in organizations for technical staff. Company ownership can be another, and is particularly relevant in the case of smaller enterprises: 'Do as I say because I own this firm'. Power, then, derives from a number of sources, not all of which we have been able to consider here.

Another, in many ways very different, way of conceptualizing power is to draw upon the writings of the Michel Foucault (1972, 1977). Here, as Thompson and McHugh (2009: 129–30) explain, power is 'held to be the central feature of social life from which there is no escape' and is everywhere, rather than in a particular location: 'resistance recreates power, it promotes a ceaseless process of shifting alliances and tensions'. What is more 'power operates not through agencies with specific interests, but through *discourses*: practices of talk, text and argument that continually form that which they speak. Disciplinary practices produce knowledge that is inseparable from power. Language thus becomes a central feature in the discursive production of power, and power/knowledge discourses constitute norms of acceptable conduct, constructing social identities.'

What are the implications of the above for the management of human resources in organizations? One insight that can be drawn from this discussion is that, in situations where managers feel that there is a need to push through unpopular changes—for example, a restructuring initiative likely to result in job losses—the extent to which they are able to do so effectively depends on the respective power resources of the parties involved. For example, if the workforce has a strong trade union to support it, managers will find it more difficult to realize their objectives. It should also be noted that there is the possibility of power being exercised in illegitimate, possibly unlawful, ways in organizations. In Chapter 13, for example, it is suggested that managers sometimes use their power illegitimately, paying little heed to any formal organizational rules and procedures, or indeed employment law, in dealing with disciplinary and grievance issues.

4.4.3 Conflict, resistance, and misbehaviour in organizations

Given that organizational life is marked by the exercise of power relations and power struggles, conflict is inevitable. As Morgan (1997: 167) observes, 'conflict arises whenever interests collide'. There are three broad perspectives we can draw upon to understand conflict in organizations.

The unitary perspective plays down the importance of conflict. It assumes that everyone in the organization shares the same basic interests. Employees recognize, and their behaviour is guided by, the desirability of ensuring that the organization meets its (managerially determined) objectives, which, as we have seen, are usually of an economic and financial nature. If conflict does arise, this is seen as being the result of minor disturbances/disagreements, such as easily resolved personality differences, or as having been brought into the organization by 'disruptive elements' from outside, such as trade unions, particularly those of a more left-wing persuasion.

The pluralist perspective is arguably more realistic, since it is based on the assumption that a diversity, or plurality, of interests exists in organizations. The job of managers is to reconcile these conflicting interests, producing agreements that reduce the scope for disruption. The pluralist perspective, then, puts the onus on managing actual or potential conflictual situations effectively by, for example, ensuring that the proceeds of organizational success are distributed more equitably and/or by developing procedures for handling conflict when it arises, such as dealing with complaints of sexual harassment.

The radical perspective critiques the pluralist assumption that conflict can, or indeed should, be managed effectively in this way. Radical theorists (who, of course, include, but are not restricted to, Marxists) are concerned with how certain people suffer from discrimination, disadvantage, and exploitation as a result of their position in organizations. Many workers (managers and non-managers alike) are put under considerable strain because of intense work pressures; people may not be happy with a pay rise, or a woman, having suffered from sexual harassment, may feel that the organization has not been sufficiently supportive. In such cases, they may

choose to contest, or resist, management actions by trying to change them. This may involve joining, becoming actively involved in, or helping to organize trade unions (see Chapter 12). Thus the radical perspective emphasizes that not only is organizational life marked by conflict, but there are important limits on the extent to which organizations can accommodate it—something which may result in resistance by workers to managerial control. See Box 4.8 for a learning activity about conflict in organizations.

The concept of 'organizational misbehaviour' has been developed as a way of describing and interpreting activities undertaken by people in organizations that do not correspond with managerial edits or expectations (Ackroyd and Thompson 1999: 2). A wide variety of misbehaviour is evident in organizational practice. Gerald Mars, in his book *Cheats at Work*, highlights the wide variety of fiddles that go on in organizations (Mars 1982), including the manipulation of expenses claims by managers and theft from bags by airport baggage handlers. While its extent is often wildly exaggerated, unauthorized absence from work is nonetheless a particularly commonplace aspect of misbehaviour. Call centres, for example, are often marked by the absence of workers who claim that they are ill, when in reality they are fit to attend work but use sickness as an excuse to get some time away from their monotonous, repetitive, and arduous jobs (Mulholland 2004). They also typically suffer from high levels of labour turnover (at least in the UK). Another example of misbehaviour is the use of humour; jokes can be used by workers to promulgate their own distinctive values and belief systems, perhaps in opposition to those laid down by managers (Linstead 1985; Ackroyd and Thompson 1999).

We have discussed the concept of organizational culture in Section 4.4.1, arguing that it is better to interpret culture as something that an organization *is*, rather than something that it *has*. The presence of subcultures and counter-cultures in organizations is further evidence of misbehaviour. 'Subcultures are distinguished by the articulation of value systems within the main value system, whereas counter-cultures are social movements in which there is an active espousal of alternative values' (Ackroyd and Thompson 1999: 106). Research in this tradition has shown how people in organizations produce their own individual and group identities in ways that are separate from, and sometimes come into conflict with, those promulgated by senior managers. This is not to say that managers themselves do not develop their own identities, just that they are usually more consonant with the wider organization's public persona (Collinson 2003; Preece and Iles 2009). However, it is important not to equate misbehaviour with conflict and resistance in organizations, as it can be an expression of frustration or an attempt to secure some respite from an onerous job, not a challenge to the organizational regime per se. Indeed, managers frequently tolerate misbehaviour, particularly if it does not overly disrupt the achievement of organizational goals (Harris and Ogbonna 2002). For one thing, it helps to maintain motivation in what are otherwise fairly mundane and often low-paid jobs; it also enables workers to preserve their sense of identity through this deployment of emotional labour, and it may simply be too much trouble to eradicate. See Box 4.9 for evidence of misbehaviour in a hospitality establishment.

Box 4.9 Research in focus
Organizational misbehaviour in a hospitality establishment

Peacock and Kubler (2001) undertook participant observation research in hotels, restaurants, and bars. One of the establishments was a public house located in central London, where a major refurbishment programme had recently been completed. This included the installation of new IT systems which enabled managers to track employees' activities and customer transactions through the use of surveillance cameras and electronic point-of-sale systems. Despite this, in the first month of trading in its newly refurbished format the pub 'lost' £30,000. It is fairly common knowledge that a fair amount of 'fiddling' or misbehaviour goes on in public houses, but what was interesting about this case was the scale of the theft, despite the sophistication of the systems installed in order to prevent it from occurring. Employee resistance is always possible, whatever the nature of the organizational regime management has established, even in tightly regulated and monitored environments such as here and in call centres.

This discussion points to some important implications for the management of human resources in organizations. Where staff have challenging and interesting jobs, are fairly rewarded, enjoy discretion and autonomy in their work, and have their contribution to the organization appropriately recognized, conflict and misbehaviour may be less likely to occur. Having said this, the author of this chapter has never worked or researched in an organization where conflict and resistance to organizational change are absent.

Summary and further reading

- The concept of organizational culture can be interpreted in a number of ways, but at its heart is a concern with recognizing the tacit symbols, beliefs, and values that govern organizational life. While many organizations have developed culture change programmes, which often have implications for the management of human resources, it remains unclear whether or not something as nebulous as culture can actually be managed in practice.

- A distinction can be made between rational and political approaches to understanding organizations. The political approach, which is arguably much closer to actual organizational practice, holds that the important role of power should be recognized—it undoubtedly influences the realization of organizational goals.

- Organizational life is frequently marked by conflict between actors in organizations, for example between managers and their staff. When it comes to managing human resources, one of the greatest challenges facing organizations is the need to balance the imperative to control with the need to elicit commitment.

See Alvesson and Sveningsson (2008), Clegg, Kornberger, and Pitsis (2008), and Thompson and McHugh (2009) for more detailed treatments of organization culture, power and politics, and conflict and resistance.

4.5 Conclusion

In this chapter we have reviewed the internal organizational context of human resource management. Among other things, we looked at how organizations are structured and designed, organizational change, the way in which work activities are arranged, organizational culture, and the importance of politics, power, and conflict in organizational life. It is clear that these features of organizational life exert an important influence over the management of human resources in practice. The existence in organizations of formal procedures for dealing with matters such as the recruitment and selection of staff, or for handling employee grievances, reflects the influence of a bureaucratic approach to organizational design. Some of the examples we have used, such as from public house retailing, have illustrated how changes in the firm's external environment influence internal structures and processes, including human resource management. All this is relevant to understanding the management of human resources in practice.

Assignment and discussion questions

1 What brings about organizational change? How are organizational change initiatives best understood?

2 What are the implications of scientific management for how human resources are managed in organizations? What are the main advantages and disadvantages of this approach?

3 What is meant by the concept of organizational culture? Why has it become so popular, and what are its implications for how human resources are managed in organizations? How easy is it for managers to change the culture of their organizations?

4 What are the key features of post-bureaucratic organizations? What are the implications for the management of human resources of the post-bureaucratic approach?

5 In what ways does the existence of power relations in organizations affect the way in which human resources are managed within them?

Online Resource Centre

Test your understanding of this chapter with online questions and answers, keep up to speed with changes to the law through regular updates, and use selected weblinks to quickly access useful resources and further information. Visit the Online Resource Centre at:

www.oxfordtextbooks.co.uk/orc/gilmore_williams2e/

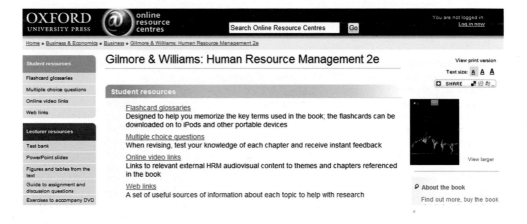

Case study
Change and restructuring in social housing

In recent years, social housing (SH) organizations have experienced extensive change and restructuring, including the creation of over 250 new SH providers, new governance arrangements, and a transformed regulatory regime. This has created organizations which are more business focused, commercial, and entrepreneurial, with a form of service provision which has much in common with private companies, especially as the supply of traditional local authority (LA) provision has declined (Pawson and Mullins 2010: 274). There has been an acceleration of merger activity and other such commercial and strategic developments in the sector (Mullins and Craig 2005; Berg 2006). In the new SH companies, corporate and human resource strategies have been aimed at creating a different type of organization from the model utilized when under LA control and management.

Given that the new SH providers can be privately funded, a core objective is to repay the loans taken out from financial institutions. Senior managers endeavour to change them from a bureaucratic to a performance-related mode of employee management (Cuthbert and Ward 2010), and are introducing new/different roles such as that of housing manager. The sector has also experienced organizational restructuring and downsizing, moves towards a stronger service orientation, and technological change. Bradley (2008: 883) observes that SH organizations have had to become 'market-sensitive' as well as more customer focused. These changing contexts have implications for the (changing) role of managers, which need to be understood in order to design appropriate forms of leadership/management development. The CVC social housing organization was formed as a result of a 'Large Scale Voluntary Transfer' (LSVT) from local authority control in 2002, and has around 550 employees. During 2009–2010, 26 staff participated in a management development programme run by an external provider. What were these employees' views about the changing nature of their work and roles?

It's the first time that I have realised while working for the company that they are empowering us … Working conditions have got better, we have left behind the 'olde worlde council', people's images have changed … public perception has changed.

There was a lot of changes to staffing and quite a few redundancies too … There was too many people and we were perhaps a bit top-heavy. We lost about 50 people from the department.

We are contracting more work out than ever before … everything is a lot more open and there is not the fear factor. More development and training to encompass new knowledge.

I feel one of our biggest changes in the future for the organization is expansion. We are looking at moving into new sorts of fields … Secure some work going forward so we are more commercially oriented for our workforce … Our tradesmen will become multi-skilled.

In talking about the programme and its 'outcomes' the participants found it difficult on occasion, if not impossible, to separate the *management* from the *leadership* development per se. Ward and Preece (2010) referred to what was occurring as *managership* development. This involves a concern with both the day-to-day conduct of work (commercial orientation, using IT, etc.), whilst at the same time looking towards the future and exploring possibilities for new/different ways of working and managing in changing times ('entrepreneurial', marketing orientation, etc.), including consideration of how colleagues might be encouraged to 'embrace the future' and support managerial initiatives. Management's focus was upon developing a collaborative partnership with union representatives and members, with regular communication and monthly meetings all aimed primarily at creating and maintaining a 'positive' pro-organization orientation amongst employees. HR managers and trade union representatives described how they responded to the initiative:

It is just a partnership approach, and I think staff see it as that … it does work and there's more of an emphasis over recent years on the HR department (HR manager).

Because of the culture of the organization, everyone feels they have a voice … we used to be a family culture … [we are] now more professional (HR manager).

The 'them and us' scenario has melted, and not as aggressive as it used to be … it's a cultural change completely (union representative).

We are here to work together as opposed to work against each other … the union-management relationship changed when [there were] changes to management (union representative)

HR specialists have developed, and are likely to continue to develop, policies and procedures and the associated skills and competencies required to deal with the sort of changes and challenges outlined above. The development of the organization's human and social capital seems likely to continue to be high on management's agenda into the future in the competitive and relatively 'alien' market place in which these SH organizations find themselves. It seems likely that merger and takeover activity will continue, and may intensify; organizational downsizing and the resultant redundancies can be anticipated. This will not sit easily with a management emphasis upon staff collaboration, 'employee voice', and a 'one-team' approach to employee relations. It can be anticipated that these 'social businesses' (Collier 2005) will face intensified challenges as 'private sector' exigencies gather momentum.

Question

1 What are the main features of organizational change in the social housing sector?

2 Assess the main implications for managing human resources in this sector.

Part Three

The essence of human resource management

Recruiting and selecting staff in organizations

Sarah Gilmore

5

Learning objectives

The main objectives of this chapter are:

- to place the recruitment and selection process within the wider context of human resource planning and the options organizations have to choose from when vacancies occur;

- to evaluate the main approaches used by organizations when recruiting and selecting employees and to critique the underpinning assumptions made by recruiters that inform their decisions;

- to examine the relationship between recruitment and selection and HRM, appreciating the importance of these activities to business performance and the attainment of organizational goals.

5.1 Introduction

As previous chapters have shown, organizations have to be increasingly responsive to changing business environments. Meeting these challenges depends upon the recruitment and retention of highly capable individuals; hence employing the 'right' people on the right basis is a crucial HR activity. This will require recruitment and selection techniques that can distinguish between candidates to ensure that suitable employees are selected and inappropriate ones rejected. However, this is made more complicated by two factors. First, organizations often have to balance current *and* future workforce attributes when recruiting. Secondly, predicting an individual's ability to prepare for and cope with an uncertain future is very difficult.

Although recruitment and selection are often seen as being two linked elements of a process, they play different roles. Recruitment can be described as the process of attracting people who might make a contribution to the organization in question, with the process usually occurring because an existing employee leaves (Newell and Shackleton 2000: 113). The process of selection involves an evaluation of the candidates who have applied for the job(s) and ultimately making a choice as to whom to appoint. For managers, decisions made here need to be based on informed opinions, and these increasingly rest on systematic and objective assessments. This has led to recruitment and selection processes being dominated by 'psychometric' and other tests that rely upon the systematic evaluation of candidates.

Employers using these tools are usually seeking to develop objective methods in order to match individuals and posts more closely and fairly. Some argue that they assist in establishing a process that reduces the impact of emotion and bias and ensures legal compliance (Pilbeam and Corbridge 2010). However, these methods have been criticized for their failure to take into account the realities of decision-making, illustrating the limitations of the psychometric approach and showing why it can fail, whilst also offering some alternatives (Iles and Salaman 1995; Iles 2001; Newell and Shackleton 2001).

The chapter begins with a discussion of the systematic approach taken to recruitment and selection, before moving on to an outline of the recruitment and selection processes. Once this is complete, we will analyse the psychometric and rational decision-making approaches to this activity, supplementing them with an alternative approach designed to overcome their limitations.

5.2 The systematic approach towards recruitment and selection

The costs involved in recruitment are not insubstantial, with the CIPD proposing an average figure of approximately £7500 for more senior managers and a much lower one for other employees (CIPD 2011h). This means that those involved in recruitment and selection have to adopt cost-effective methods whilst also ensuring that they attract high-quality candidates. Adopting a systematic approach is argued to be helpful in gaining these outcomes from the process.

5.2.1 Workforce planning: reviewing staffing needs

There is a growing awareness that attracting and retaining talented employees can provide organizations with a sustained competitive advantage. The importance of attracting employees, especially in jobs where skills shortages exist, has led to intense competition for the best applicants in a variety of occupations. This has been described as the 'war for talent' (Singh 2001), and we cover this in more detail in Chapter 8. The heightened competition for talented employees has made organizations more aware of the importance of this activity (Carless 2009) and its fundamental importance to achieving business goals now and in the future. Therefore 'owning' and determining the recruitment and selection process is one means by which the HRM function can heighten its status within the organization, especially if it ensures that appropriately skilled staff are employed. However, this is not always easy and success often depends on the kinds of knowledge, skills, and personal attributes being sought, their availability within the firm, the wider labour market, and prevailing economic circumstances.

Over the last 20 years the term 'workforce planning' has fallen out of favour because it became associated with statistical plans that failed to keep pace with fast-paced change in the external environment, but the need for planning has not diminished. Evidence from the CIPD (2011*h*) suggests that one of the potential drivers of sustainable high performance is the organization's ability to develop plans that balance their short- and long-term priorities. Their research found that organizations were engaging in workforce planning not just to acclimatize to changing economic circumstances, but also to have the ability to thrive in the future by making sure that they continue to attract and develop their staff to deal with a range of potential business scenarios.

There is no commonly understood definition of workforce planning. The CIPD (2010*f*: 4) define it as: 'A core process of human resource management that is shaped by the organizational strategy and ensures the right number of people with the right skills, in the right place at the right time to deliver short-and long-term organization objectives'. It typically starts with the organization's business strategy, operations plans, and people management strategies. This implies that organizations engage in the kinds of rational planning activities we outlined in Chapter 2—or at least are in a position to articulate some elements of these strategies in structured coherent ways. Qualitative and quantitative workforce information is then gathered which should assist in providing an understanding of the current situation and what needs to change to meet these strategic requirements in the future. Such information includes the numbers of staff that the organization estimates will be required, their location, and their skill requirements.

The next stage involves data analysis and clarification of the picture. This typically sees HRM and business managers contributing their observations and predictions around resourcing requirements. These discussions should result in agreement about what the plan is trying to achieve, which is then reviewed against available resources. To do this, planners will need to review the supply of labour, internally and externally, assess the potential capability of the workforce to develop any requisite skills, and then identify areas where recruitment will be needed. This approach is advocated by the Advisory, Conciliation, and Arbitration Service (ACAS) (ACAS 2010*d*) who link it to a range of internal activities the organization might undertake in order to meet shifting requirements and to avoid redundancies if possible. An example of this process in action at Siemens, along with the role played by the HR function, is outlined in Box 5.1.

As the example illustrates, whilst the literature concerning workforce planning is dominated by strategic concerns, the success of the process is underpinned by good *relationships* between business and workforce planners at the strategy level and between HR business partners and line managers at the operational level. Achieving a balance between the senior leadership of an organization, which drives the process, and securing line manager input (i.e. those who know locally and operationally whether plans are realistic) can be challenging, especially for

Box 5.1 Window on work
Workforce planning at Siemens

Siemens is a global engineering and technology services company employing over 400,000 employees worldwide with revenues of nearly €73.52 billion in 2010–2011. Business environment analyses identify the markets that are attractive to Siemens, and as the company develops its strategies to take advantage of market opportunities, people implications are identified on either a business unit or a geographic basis. The workforce plan is used to identify not only people resources to deliver business objectives, but also the HR resources needed to support this. The HR business partner engages business unit management teams on the workforce planning implications of their business strategy, examining the type of competence that will be required in the next year and making an assessment of their availability in the marketplace. The HR specialists establish the process for workforce planning, the consistent application of tools and systems across business units, and performance/progress reports over the period of the plan (CBI 2009; CIPD 2010*f*).

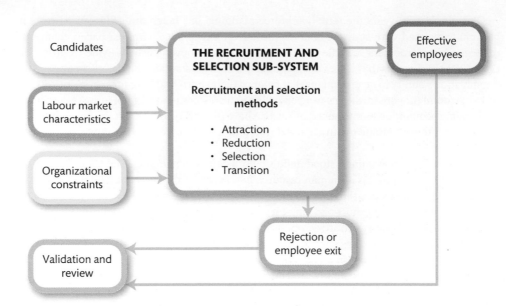

Figure 5.1 The systems approach to recruitment and selection.

geographically dispersed organizations. Given that line managers are usually tasked with the delivery of the workforce plan, they will need to be clear as to the future direction of the organization and how it will impact their team/department. Consequently this will require them to have a vehicle for creating dialogue with managers concerning these micro-needs.

Finally, workforce planning increasingly has to account for wider demographic issues that are beyond the control of the organization. Malik et al. (2010) show that different life stages pose complex work–life challenges for employees which have implications for workforce planning. Where older workers are concerned, Flynn (2010) shows that they possess a range of attitudes towards retirement and planning for it and that a 'one size fits all' approach is not possible. This highlights the tensions organizations face in meeting work–life requirements and operational requirements within existing resource capabilities.

5.2.2 Systematic approaches to recruitment and selection

Pilbeam and Corbridge (2010) have proposed a model of how the recruitment and selection process can be organized in a logical systematic way, as illustrated in Figure 5.1.

Internal and external influences, such as the organization's strategic goals, its operational requirements, the nature of the market, and the demand for the organizations products/services—which will be highly dependent on the wider economic situation—lead to demands for suitably qualified and skilled staff. At times of economic downturn, this demand might be low but, as Ready, Hill, and Conger (2008) and Hewlett and Rashid (2011) indicate, for companies operating in emerging markets such as Brazil, Russia, India, and China (often referred to as BRIC economies), finding talented employees to keep up with the rates of growth they are experiencing is highly challenging as Box 5.2 illustrates. This means that the extent to which candidates for jobs will be available with the requisite knowledge can vary according to region and will depend on specific labour market characteristics.

The recruitment and selection subsystem is composed of four elements: attraction, reduction, selection, and transition. The attraction phase consists of making a case for recruitment—any job analysis needed to determine the nature of the job being offered, and the nature of the labour market. These activities will determine the recruitment methods chosen. Other activities within the subsystem will establish how candidates will be filtered and the choice of selection methods to be used to distinguish between them. Once the choice has been made, the final activity of transition focuses on pre-engagement activities and the induction processes.

Box 5.2 International focus
The talent gap in BRIC countries

Economic activity in emerging economies such as Brazil, Russia, India, and China has led to height-ened competition for employees—employees who, often for the first time in their lives, have numerous options and high expectations.

However, employee surpluses and deficits exist within these countries at four levels: entry, middle management, country leadership, and regional leadership. Brazil, India, and China all have surpluses at entry levels with an over-abundant supply of young people and undergraduates in their workforce. Russia's fast growth, labour shortages, and heavy foreign direct investment means that they have deficits here, and whilst China has an abundance of young workers, its variable education quality at school level means that many young people have inferior preparation or lack language skills.

Brazil, Russia, and China all experience deficits at middle management, country leadership, and regional leadership levels. For China and Russia, the supply of senior talent is limited owing to the legacy of a planned economy (as with Russia) or the Cultural Revolution in China which created a 'missing generation' of talented employees aged 45–55. This means that there is a need for expatriate labour to fill those positions or rapid development of suitable candidates internally. India, however, is notable for exporting talented middle management, country leaders, and regional leaders.

Sources: Ready, Hill, and Conger (2008); Hewlett and Rashid (2011).

The strength of a systems approach such as this lies in its transparency, and this assists in analysing its effectiveness and identifying relevant amendments. It also shows how changes in one area can and will instigate changes elsewhere. So, for example, if the organization experiences a number of staff leaving during the first 18 months of employment—often referred to as the 'induction crisis'—it is possible to return to the recruitment and selection subsystems to analyse the methods and processes being used and to place them against factors such as the labour market demand and organizational constraints such as wages, benefits, and other aspects of the employment contract to see where problems might be occurring and how they can be addressed.

However, this rational process is often influenced by the use of power and micropolitics, as managers will often seek to manipulate the processes to their own advantage (van den Brink, Benschop, and Jansen 2010). Therefore it is common to see recruitment and selection being subject to influence by powerful individuals in order to achieve their goals (Blase 1991) or being swayed by relationships, as we saw in the case of Siemens.

5.2.3 Making recruitment and selection decisions

Whereas the systems approach views recruitment and selection as a set of interlinking elements, the decision-making method looks at how organizational participants make assessment decisions concerning individual candidates, how a choice is made between individuals, and how the 'best' one is selected. This perspective is dominated by the assumption that a rational system will facilitate this activity and assist in eliminating personal bias and the operation of political activity by managers. It involves following a series of steps: understanding the situation and identifying the problem(s); gathering information and materials to solve the problem; generating potential solutions to the problem; systematically evaluating each solution; selecting the 'best' solution; monitoring and evaluating the results; and repeating the process over time in the same ways. This model, as illustrated in Box 5.3, forms the basis for advice given by organizations such as ACAS as to what is permissible, fair, and legal within this area of activity. However, this belief in rationality and order needs to be placed against evidence that organizational decision-making is based on other criteria, as we discussed in Chapter 2 when reviewing approaches towards organizational strategy.

Box 5.3 Policy example
ACAS advice

In its advice to employers concerning good practice in recruitment and selection, ACAS not only high-lights the importance of efficient and effective methods, but also stresses the need for fairness, ensuring that decisions are made on merit alone all the way through the process. This involves:

- ensuring that no unlawful discrimination occurs in the recruitment and selection process on the grounds of sex, race, disability, age, sexual orientation, and religion or belief;
- organizations having the ability to encourage applications from those groups that are under-represented in the organization;
- the consultation of employees and their representatives when new procedures are introduced or existing procedures reviewed;
- compliance with the Disability Discrimination Act 1995, which not only makes it unlawful to discriminate against disabled individuals without justifiable reason, but also requires employers to make reasonable adjustments to the workplace or working arrangements.

Source: ACAS (http://www.acas.org.uk).

Summary and further reading

- The recruitment process needs to be placed within the wider contexts of the organization's need for suitably qualified and skilled staff and the process of human resource planning. Another context concerns the ways in which recruitment and selection processes are conceptualized in terms of rational decision-making or systems approaches. These throw up different, but very real, challenges for those tasked with bringing new employees into the organization—as will be seen again in the following section.

- Although they are part of the same process, there are differences between recruitment and selection. Whereas the former seeks to create a pool of suitably qualified candidates capable of being employed by the organization—and in that sense is a generative activity—selection is concerned with a process of reduction and discrimination between them in order to select the best employee.

Pilbeam and Corbridge (2010) offer an accessible practitioner-oriented view as to the systematic approach towards recruitment and selection. Iles and Salaman (1995), Newell and Shackleton (2000, 2001), and Newell (2006) challenge the ideas of 'scientific recruitment' and 'scientific selection' from allied, but slightly different, perspectives. van den Brink, Benschop, and Jansen (2010) highlight that the protocols that should ensure transparency and accountability in recruitment and selection remain paper tigresses because of the micropolitics and gender practices that are part and parcel of this process.

5.3 The recruitment process

Within the systematic approach towards recruitment and selection, the process of recruitment often follows the cycle of the activities outlined below. These seek to determine the precise nature of the vacancy as well as the options available to the organization by way of filling that gap. If a post needs filling, many organizations will adopt a structured approach to defining the skills and other attributes of the potential post-holder.

5.3.1 Job analysis

Recruitment and selection activities are often, but not exclusively, stimulated by the departure of an employee. Although one response might be to replace that person with a replica, a more systematic approach might be to set this post against the wider context of the organization's staffing requirements before deciding whether a replacement is needed and if it is, on what basis? Answering such questions will provide the context for any job analysis activity and should include those who will be working with the post-holder.

Job analysis consists of the systematic process of collecting information about the tasks and responsibilities of a job. There are several ways to conduct a job analysis, including interviews with incumbents and supervisors, questionnaires (structured, open-ended, or both), observation of staff doing the job or a similar one, or an investigation concerning critical incidents in order to ascertain whether there are additional and specific needs for skills and knowledge. The kinds of information to be collected normally include job objectives and performance measures, accountabilities, responsibilities and organizational relationships, job duties and content, terms of employment and work conditions, and the skills, knowledge and competencies required as well as any other distinctive job characteristics. Once the job analysis process has been completed, the next stage is to develop a job description and person specification—two key tools in the recruitment and selection process.

Managers rarely wish to see reductions in their staff, and the kinds of questions asked above often lead to justifications for employment. Although individuals are recruited to work for a specific company, in reality they are generally working for a department, team, or work group, and that entity is unlikely to admit that it no longer has a need for labour, as that will diminish its power base and reduce capabilities to take on new work. The idea that employee turnover can be used as an opportunity to review the need for staff often ignores these kinds of political realities (Newell 2005).

5.3.2 The job description

A job description is a written statement listing the elements of a particular job or occupation and typically contains the information outlined in the pro forma in Box 5.4. The level of detail seen in a job description will vary according to the complexity of the post or current trends in practice. Generally it will include information as to how the job fits into the organization and its main purpose, as well as any reporting or accountability arrangements. The central element of any job description involves itemizing responsibilities, accountabilities, key objectives, key results areas, or key tasks. Finally, a job description often includes some generalized statements about the values or ethos of the organization or the culture that it tries to foster.

5.3.3 The person specification

The second output from a job analysis is a person specification. This is derived from the job description, and will usually accompany it during the recruitment and selection process since it translates the job activities it outlines into the specific skills and abilities required to perform the job effectively, irrespective of the ways previous job-holders performed it. Whereas the job description focuses on job content, the person specification is concerned with the psychological and behavioural requirements of the post and is worker-oriented. The document should communicate a realistic picture of the job, but it also has a role within the selection process since it will provide a benchmark against which all applicants can be systematically assessed.

Job competencies are another popular approach to designing job descriptions and person specifications. They are concerned with identifying effective individual and collective behaviours, and organizations using them seek to define these, usually in the context of promoting superior organizational performance. An example of such an approach is outlined in Box 5.5.

The advantages of this method are that the criteria relate to job-related behaviour—the things a person can do or needs to be able to do. These kinds of frameworks can also be developed and deployed within an industry on an international basis. For example, the competency framework agreed between the European Chemical Employers Group and the European Mine, Chemical, and Energy Workers' Federation concerning minimum core competences for process operators and first-line supervisors across Europe will improve worker employability and mobility within the industry because the contents of this agreement will now be implemented in each EU country, ensuring the recognition and transferability of these competences across Europe (Carley 2011).

However, in their study of the use of competency frameworks for the selection of judges in the UK, Kirton and Healy (2009) also revealed dangers inherent in competency-based HR

Box 5.4 Window on work
Constructing a job description and person specification

A job description might open with some information about the organization—its history, achievements, and goals—giving an indication as to how the job fits in with the attainment of the wider strategic purpose of the company. This might be followed by a succinct job summary and information about the unit or department. The main body of the job description will provide details of the duties and key result areas/key tasks to be carried out by the successful candidate. These tend to be outlined using the kinds of headings listed below.

Job-specific information:

Title

Department/section

Grade

Salary

Hours

Contract length

Responsible for staff/equipment

Reporting to (reporting relationship)

The person specification will usually refer to the kinds of criteria outlined below with each being defined as either 'desirable' or 'essential' for the job:

Qualifications

Attainments/competencies (list as required)

Previous experience

Special aptitudes (e.g. oral or written skills, manual dexterity, etc.)

Physical abilities, circumstances, but only if justifiable requirement for the job

Source: ACAS (http://www.acas.org.uk).

What other information would you like to see about an organization if you were applying for a job? If you were advertising a post in a less desirable or less well-known location, how might you market the company?

Box 5.5 Window on work
Competency-based approaches to recruitment and selection

Essex County Council employs around 39,000 people, and its Competency Framework (ECF) was developed to reflect the behaviours, skills, and abilities needed to deliver services, and it is directly related to the requirements of jobs within the council. The competency framework itself is shown as a wheel and includes eleven generic headings. Although the framework applies to all employees, not all the competencies and their various measures will apply. It is for the manager who is responsible for drawing together the job profile of a particular role to determine the competencies that are relevant to it.

Each competency is broken down into subdivisions that reflect the skills and behaviour required for the job, and is further supported by a series of measures that inform what is expected of employees.

Job profiles and person specifications are built around competencies and are used as the basis for hiring new recruits and within recruitment advertisements. They are also used in their application form, and all stages of the selection process are designed with close reference to the competencies and measures considered pivotal to the job.

Sources: Skingle (2006); Suff (2006).

practices. These dangers arise from the inescapable fact that human organizational actors (i.e. assessors) are necessarily required to interpret the competencies and evaluate which candidates meet them and which do not. Thus, whatever the rhetoric, there is the potential for bias, prejudice, and discrimination because we cannot take the human element out of assessment.

Summary and further reading

- As part of the recruitment process and to help discriminate between candidates, organizations will often draw up a job description and person specification for the vacant position. Whereas the job description will list the elements of a job and how it fits into the organization, as well as any relevant accountabilities, the person specification will give more detail as to the kinds of skills, knowledge, and personal attributes required to carry it out.

- These documents should provide a realistic job preview, and as such will allow potential candidates to self-select as to whether or not there is a fit between the post and their skills, personal attributes, and career aspirations. They will also provide those involved in the selection process with a benchmark against which applicants can be measured.

Pilbeam and Corbridge (2010) offer a formula for person specifications and outline the reasons why many organizations have used job competencies as a basis for designing job descriptions and person specifications. The CIPD (2011*d*) also issues a factsheet on the design and use of competencies.

5.4 Recruitment methods

Once these processes are complete, the next stage is concerned with how to attract a pool of applicants who meet the job requirements. This section outlines the choices open to employers, the sources of external applicants, and the main recruitment methods used.

5.4.1 Recruitment choices

One key decision is whether to recruit internally or externally. Recruiting internally has several advantages, as existing staff already have an understanding of how the company operates, substantially reducing the need for induction and socialization. Initiatives such as this can motivate existing staff, who can see new opportunities being made available. However, consistent internal recruitment tends to bypass the chance to bring in new talent or experience. It can also be potentially unfair and discriminatory, since it perpetuates an existing workforce and therefore may reinforce existing workforce inequalities. However, it reduces costs because it does away with the need to employ external consultants or pay for advertisements.

The CIPD's Resourcing and Talent Planning Survey (CIPD 2011*h*) found that in the 626 organizations they surveyed, nearly three-quarters (73 per cent) of permanent vacancies were filled with external candidates. Because of the ongoing squeeze on public sector finances, the shedding of jobs in these organizations, and the decline in recruitment, companies that are hiring are more likely to be in the private sector. However, manufacturing and production firms are experiencing greater difficulties in filling technical vacancies internally and therefore are forced to recruit from the wider labour market. This highlights the issue of UK skills shortages, which will be discussed in Chapter 6. Box 5.6 draws attention to the ways in which some

Box 5.6 Online video link
Approaches to recruitment

The links provided in the Online Resource Centre will take you to examples of recruitment videos produced by two of the main global accounting organizations. There are others in a similar mode that you might also like to view. What are the messages being sent by these organizations and to what extent do you find them convincing? How far do they cohere with or depart from the image you have of accountants? You might find it interesting to view some of the comments posted alongside these videos when forming your views.

organizations and their employees challenge dominant views of their work in an attempt to attract potential recruits.

5.4.2 Sources of external applicants

There are four prime reasons why employers use agencies as a source of direct recruits or agency temporary workers (Suff 2011*b*). First, agencies can search through their details of individuals who have registered with them and put forward potential recruits or temporary workers. This can reduce the time-scale of finding a recruit or temporary worker, and give employers access to individuals whom they might not be able to reach through other means, such as recruitment advertising. Linked to the first factor, agencies are used by employers because they can help speed up the time to hire: avoiding or reducing the receipt of large numbers of unsuitable applications that might be submitted were they to advertise openly. Another motivation for using agencies is often based on the premise that agencies know the employer and have a track record of finding suitable staff. However, the scale of outsourcing of recruitment and selection is substantial, with this activity being one of the most commonly outsourced HRM activities (Ordanini and Silvestri 2008).

As noted by Pilbeam and Corbridge (2010), the use of agencies constitutes the externalization of elements of the recruitment and selection process such as administration, candidate attraction activities, and the application of pre-selection criteria to other organizations. Success will depend upon a precise specification by the employer concerning their needs as well as the ability of the agency to attract suitable applicants. Whilst the costs of these kinds of services to the employers can be high, agencies have the potential to fill posts quickly, efficiently, and effectively, making this service a desirable option for many companies. However, survey evidence suggests that employers are seeking to improve the quality of the service they receive from agencies whilst simultaneously reducing their financial outlay, instigating 'preferred-supplier' status, and introducing fixed-price contracts (CIPD 2011*h*).

5.4.3 Recruitment methods

There are a variety of ways in which organizations can increase the pool of applications from which they can select suitable candidates. The CIPD survey (CIPD 2011*h*) identified the four main methods as being the corporate website, recruitment agencies, local press, and employee referral schemes.

The aim of any recruitment method is to achieve a balance between attracting suitable candidates and not incurring an excessive cost. Whilst there is no ideal number of applications, what is sought is quality rather than quantity of candidates. There are a variety of ways of attracting applicants and they can be used exclusively or in combination. The following sections will highlight two of the most frequently used recruitment methods—one that is fairly traditional and one that has increased in use over the past few years.

5.4.4 Press advertising

Local press advertising is still perceived to have a degree of effectiveness in terms of recruiting applicants, but arguably is declining in the face of online media. As with other forms of advertising, budgets, the nature of the job, and the ability to obtain staff locally will determine the kind of press advertising used, and whether local, trade, or national press is needed, but the advertisement has to achieve the objective of attracting a pool of suitable candidates and providing them with a realistic job preview.

Given the increasing importance of how an organization markets what it has to offer potential and existing employees (Balmer and Gray 2004; CIPD 2010*e*, 2011*h*), as well as the costs involved with larger and more expensive forms of advertising, using an advertising agency–whether a local 'shop' or a nationally renowned organization—can be seen as helpful in projecting an accurate picture of the company brand.

5.4.5 Online recruitment

Online recruitment, or e-recruitment, refers to the use of technology to attract candidates. An organization's website is one of the most frequently used recruitment methods and is used

Box 5.7 Window on work
Using social media

Computer games firm Electronic Arts seeks to use social media as a tool to build the brand and recruit for staff in a dynamic market. At the heart of the company's social media strategy, called Inside EA: People, Games and Opportunities, is the InsideEA blog (www.insideea.com). Here, the company showcases simple stories: photos of employees at a team bowling event, a look behind the scenes at the company's offices in Shanghai or San Francisco, insights into how the company puts together learning and development programmes, and so on. The blog also ties in with a number of key social networking sites. New stories on the blog are automatically published to InsideEA's 114,000-plus Facebook fans and 2300-plus Twitter followers. Meanwhile, the InsideEA YouTube channel includes training videos on differing career paths and what the company looks for in job candidates.

across a range of organizational sectors. According to the IRS (2009), the logic for employers' use of their own websites in recruitment seems irrefutable. They believe that these websites provide better-informed candidates at a lower cost than any other recruitment method. Almost nine out of ten (88 per cent) respondents said that using their own website 'increases the likelihood that people who apply for our jobs will know something about us and our work', which also highlights the need for a good employer brand.

However, the nature of online recruitment is changing and there has been a move away from a focus on a one-way communication process based on a static corporate website to a more interactive process facilitated by Web 2.0 and the use of social media by both parties to the recruitment process. For those seeking to use social media, recruiters need to understand the audience that each service, such as Twitter, Facebook, or LinkedIn, attracts in order to target recruitment information to sites that are frequently visited by likely candidates. As the use of social media within recruitment increases, organizations are seeking to move beyond the use of social media to simply advertise vacancies as Box 5.7 illustrates. Nonetheless, set against this picture of the growing popularity of social networking, the CIPD found that most of their respondents in their Annual Survey in Resourcing and Talent Management (CIPD 2010e) did not rate them as being particularly effective for attracting candidates, although professional networking sites, such as LinkedIn, were among the most effective methods for nearly one in five respondents from the private sector. It is also pertinent to note that little is known about applicants to web-based recruitment and selection procedures (Hella and Mol 2009), but nascent research points to these tools as being preferred more by those who are internet savvy. They found that features of the website, perceived efficiency, and user-friendliness were by far the most important determinants of applicant satisfaction, suggesting that organizations will need to take heed of such outcomes in order to utilize this medium effectively.

 ## Summary and further reading

- Once a decision has been take to fill an existing or new post, it is common for companies to devise a job description and person specification that will outline the nature of the job as well as the skills, knowledge, and personal attributes needed to perform it successfully. These documents are generally used within the recruitment and selection process as a means of providing a realistic job preview to prospective candidates, and as a means of assessment when engaging in selection.

- Companies have the choice of recruiting internally and/or externally. Although research currently shows a preference for external recruitment, this is arguably driven by the need for specific kinds of labour. If a decision is taken to hire from the external labour market, a variety of methods exist to assist in attracting a suitable pool of qualified candidates. The choice of approach will depend upon a number of variables, such as the degree of urgency for staff and previous experiences of relevant personnel within the organization, as well as the number of people to be hired and the budget available for it.

In terms of providing an overview of trends in recruitment, the annual surveys of recruitment and selection conducted by the CIPD and IRS provide a good general review of organizational activity in this area.

5.5 The selection process

Research suggests that using best-practice methods concerning selection processes greatly improves an organization's productivity. This 'best practice' is based on three stages: (1) a thorough job analysis to identify selection criteria, as discussed previously; (2) selection tool design; and (3) validation (Carless 2009). In the previous section, recruitment was described as being concerned with attracting qualified candidates to fill job vacancies. The process of selection is involved in whittling down that group and making a hiring decision. A variety of methods are used by organizations (CIPD 2010e), but the top four identified by the CIPD in both 2010 and 2011 surveys on this issue were competency-based interviews, interviews using application form data, structured panel interviews, and tests for specific skills.

At every stage, decisions are being made by employer and candidate as to whether they 'fit'. Therefore, whilst this section is concerned with what the organization does when selecting, it is important to remember that candidates will also be evaluating their potential employer and that they can withdraw their application at any time. Therefore the ways that these processes are handled have an impact on a person's perception of the company and influence their decision as to whether to join the company should a job offer be made.

5.5.1 Assessing candidates

The concepts of validity and reliability help to evaluate the potential and limitations of selection methods. When choosing selection methods, recruiters are usually keen to know which method can predict the job performance of a candidate. This is one of the most challenging aspects of the selection process and should not be underestimated. The validity of a method is concerned with the extent to which it measures what it intends to measure. The predictive validity of selection methods can be compared by using a correlation coefficient to measure the probability that a selection method will predict job performance. A correlation coefficient of 1.0 represents certain prediction, whereas one of 0.5 will approximate to a 50 per cent chance that the method chosen will predict performance. Over the years, studies have attempted to provide a comparison of predictive validity in assessment methods. Table 5.1 shows how they rank in terms of this aspect of validity.

There are limitations to these correlations as they cannot be extended to particular organizational settings or situations, but they are useful in that they urge caution when putting faith in the ability of a given selection method to predict job performance. As illustrated, the interview, which is an extremely popular selection method, is generally a poor performer. But combining it with another selection method might yield a better predictive outcome and it is generally accepted that an appropriate combination of techniques improves predictive validity.

Other forms of validity that need to be considered when choosing selection methods are their face validity and construct validity. A method has face validity if, on the face of it, there appears to be a connection between the selection method and the job. So, for example, a 'cook off' for a chef, where candidates demonstrate their skills practically, would have high face validity. Construct validity is concerned with whether or not a selection method is based on sound evidence or underpinning theory. Hence, whilst biodata (questionnaires that elicit factual and attitudinal information) have a reasonable degree of predictive validity, the underpinning theory that explains why they work is weak.

Another issue that needs to be taken into account when choosing selection methods concerns their reliability—their ability to produce the same candidate result regardless of the people involved in administering or running the process. It is interesting to note that the well-known trio of assessment methods—interviews, references, and application forms—has almost universal popularity, even though there is evidence of low predictive validity and lack of reliability in practice, which suggests that employer preferences—and possibly candidate expectations—prevail despite these concerns.

5.5.2 Selection methods: the application form and candidate information

From the extent of its use in the selection process, organizations clearly see the application form as being important, and many applicants would expect to fill one in or submit a current CV.

Table 5.1 The validity of selection methods

Method	Correlation coefficient
Certain prediction	1.0
	0.9
	0.8
Assessment centres for development	0.7
Skilful and structured interviews	0.6
Ability tests	
Work sampling	0.5
Assessment centres for job performance	0.4
Biodata	
Personality assessment	
Unstructured interviews	0.3
	0.2
References	0.1
Interests	
Years of job experience	
Graphology	0.0
Astrology	
Age	

Note: A correlation coefficient of 1.0 represents certain prediction.
Source: Pilbeam and Corbridge (2010: 189).

Whilst it is usual for application forms to have a dual role of capturing personal information as well as job-related information, tension may occur between these two purposes. Legal developments in areas such as data protection, as well as age discrimination, are constraining the extent to which organizations can legitimately collect and hold personal information on candidates as well as setting parameters as to the kinds of information sought.

In order to assess the degree of 'fit' between prospective employees, the post, and the organization, application forms and requests for CV content can be used to ask extended questions, or to elicit examples of relevant experiences or competencies. However, an application form that operates on this basis is more difficult to complete and might not always be needed. Hence the collection of relevant information about a candidate has to be balanced against the possibility of deterring applicants by requiring them to fill in a lengthy complicated form. Once in receipt of required information, the selection process usually compares candidate information against the requirements of the job description, person specification, or competency profile, if this is being used, in order to reduce personal bias and to avoid the use of arbitrary criteria.

However, organizations are becoming increasingly aware that applicants do not always provide honest content and are prepared to investigate claims made (Schorr Hirsch 2007). A survey of 177 organizations found that over half had exposed discrepancies, inaccuracies, or dishonesty in job applications (Suff 2008), highlighting the need for organizations to thoroughly check the information given by candidates. As noted previously, as people engage more with social media and place increasing amounts of personal information online, recruiters can be tempted to probe into the digital lives being led by potential recruits to their organizations (Matthews 2011) and this has led some organizations into legal difficulties.

5.5.3 The selection interview

The interview is a structured conversation and a social encounter between a candidate and representative(s) of the organization that has multiple roles, one of which being that it personalizes the selection process. Iles (2001: 155–6) states that the social element within the interview ensures its continued use, as it opens up opportunities for bilateral exchanges of views, mutual decision-making, and mutual negotiation. It also communicates information about the job and the organization and therefore gives a realistic job preview to the candidate(s), so that they can make an informed decision concerning acceptance if the job were offered. This is also true for the recruiters and helps form preferences for appointment. The structure of an interview, whilst subject to variations, contains three basic components: introducing the parties to the process, questioning by the interviewer(s) and interviewee, with the closing stage including information as to the next steps and the timeline assigned to each of them.

The practitioner literature strongly advocates the adoption of structured interviews, where the interactions between the interviewer(s) and the candidate are more standardized and the same series of questions is asked of all interviewees, with replies rated on pre-formatted rating scales. However, this process is fraught with difficulty because it is subject to all the problems associated with social and human interaction, such as individual personality differences and perceptual processes. This illustrates the limitations of the rational and systematic processes of recruitment and selection, as Box 5.8 indicates.

These problems can be exacerbated by other issues such as lack of skills or experience in the interviewer(s), the accuracy and clarity of information about the vacancy, the degree to which an interview is clearly structured, and over-reliance on this selection method as an accurate discriminator between candidates. These kinds of factors can impact on the interview's validity and reliability as a predictor, as can perceptual bias and associated problems.

5.5.4 Different forms of interview

There are three common forms of interview: the biographical interview, the competency-based interview, and the situational interview.

The biographical format follows the work history of the candidate, using it as a guide as to whether he/she can take on the responsibilities of the job. Some interviews might focus on relatively recent employment experiences to assess this fit, whereas others might be concerned

Box 5.8 Research in focus

Perceptual problems in interviews

Furnham (2005) argues that the process of making evaluations, judgements, or ratings of people and their performance is subject to a number of perceptual errors. Some of these are particularly problematic in the context of selection and are outlined below.

- **First impressions count** First impressions are formed at a very rapid rate, and interviews can become involved in a search for information that confirms the first impression.

- **The horns and halos effect** This refers to situations where we see a good thing being done by a person (however that is judged) and tend to see any subsequent behaviour by the same person as being good (halo). The horns effect works the opposite way (Thorndike 1920).

- **Like-me judgements** Inevitably, people who possess similar traits to the interviewer are likely to be viewed more positively than those who do not. The fallacy here is that (assuming competence), if a candidate is similar to the interviewer, he/she will also be good at the same job. The reverse also holds true, with poor evaluations being given to people who have qualities or characteristics not possessed by the selector(s).

- **Impression management** Candidates often try to create a certain image of themselves and maintain a particular impression that coincides with what they think the assessors are looking for. However, this can also be true of assessors, in that they want to 'create an impression' in order to attract or retain the best candidates.

Box 5.9 Window on work
Cultural fit

In many organizations, the interview is often used to assess the degree of fit occurring between an applicant and the organization's culture. Companies such as Esso, IBM, and Google all emphasize the importance of cultural fit, often preferring not to hire rather than employ someone who might dilute their culture because they view it as being integral to achieving high staff retention (Phillips 2008a). But there can be a harder edge to this focus on fit. The Equality and Human Rights Commission (EHRC 2011) found that women are generally concentrated in the lower-paid jobs in finance sector firms and significantly under-represented in revenue-generating functions, where both basic and performance-related pay are higher. The recruitment and selection processes which put an emphasis on 'cultural fit' with regard to high-paying jobs were found to perpetuate an industry profile where men dominate the high-earning jobs and women the low-paying jobs. Negative management attitudes to pregnancy and maternity leave make it harder for women to have a 'viable career' because of the sector's 'uniquely young age profile', which means that a very high proportion of employees are in the 25- to 39-year-old age group—the age at which people tend to have children. The inquiry heard 'compelling evidence' of a 'macho' or 'lads' culture, in which women are excluded from networking activities and can suffer adverse effects after taking maternity leave.

with identifying patterns of behaviour that show how candidates respond in certain situations, as well as their technical knowledge. Interviews might also want to ascertain the degree of cultural fit between candidates and the organization, as outlined in Box 5.9.

The competency-based interview will usually ask interviewees to re-enact situations that they have faced to illustrate a given competency—usually ones that are essential or desirable for effective job enactment. Opening questions are often followed by a series of follow-up probes to develop further understanding of the candidate's responses.

The situational interview presents candidates with a series of standard scenarios and asks candidates to explain what they would do. Their answer is scored by comparing it against a 'model' answer. This is seen as a helpful means of assessing candidates when they might have little or no job experience, whilst also offering a realistic job preview.

5.5.5 Multiple- or single-interviewer approaches

As stated, the interview often provides the personal contact with the organization that people desire. Interviews can involve a range of personnel from one-to-one approaches through to panel interviews, where there are a range of interviewers or observers, or group interviews, where a number of applicants can be interviewed simultaneously by one or more interviewers. The approach used will often be based on the number of relevant staff available to conduct the interview(s), the availability of qualified and experienced interviewers, and the nature of the job, as well as other resource constraints such as the extent to which the company has to select staff regularly (Phillips 2008b) or, as in the case of recruiting volunteers for the Olympic Games, recruit in large numbers (*Telegraph* 2011).

5.5.6 Psychometric tests

The term 'psychometric test' refers to the operation of standardized procedures for measuring intelligence, aptitude, or personality. The term is often used interchangeably with 'occupational testing' or 'psychological testing'. The main types of psychometric tests are as follows.

- Ability, aptitude, or trainability tests use similar approaches and are designed to assess specific abilities that are associated with certain professions; they also try to assess whether a person has the potential to train or be educated to do certain types of skilled tasks.

- Specific cognitive ability tests measure verbal reasoning or numerical skills, or such skills as manual dexterity and spatial awareness.

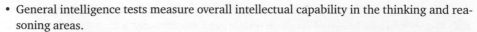

- General intelligence tests measure overall intellectual capability in the thinking and reasoning areas.
- Personality questionnaires aim to uncover relatively enduring individual characteristics and traits as a means of predicting behaviour. These tests produce a profile or description of an individual, and the individual personality information is compared with the profile of a representative sample of an appropriate population, either produced by the questionnaire designer or generated by the user on the basis of the personality characteristics of successful (and less successful) firm performers. They are also the most controversial of the psychometric tests.

Where personality testing is concerned, the widespread availability of testing over the internet has made the process easier and more cost-effective, and has resulted in faster turnaround times for reporting results (Carless 2009). Debate continues as to how far it is possible to measure a quantity as shifting and vague as personality. Where the workplace is concerned, personality assessments tend to measure preferences, and although preferences will shape behaviour, the correlation between the two factors is not always strong and will certainly be moderated by other workplace factors such as management style and the nature of the job (Furnham and Chaudhuri 2001). In addition, critics have argued that such approaches are at odds with the concept of diversity, as evidence highlights the propensity of some tests to produce disparate outcomes on the basis of race or gender.

Despite these criticisms, the use of tests has increased substantially, often at the instigation of HR, with commentators suggesting that this has been associated with the increased professionalism of human resource management (Legge 1995; Caldwell 2001) and their greater involvement in strategic decision-making (Budhwar 2000; Farndale 2005), arguably resulting in the function having more influence in organizations which is turn may have increased test use (Wolf and Jenkins 2006). The experiences of one HR practitioner, illustrated in Box 5.10, highlight the symbolic and political role played by personality tests for senior managers, especially when faced with hiring senior staff whose poor performance could have serious implications for the organization.

Psychometric tests are often used to achieve different objectives within the selection process and are often applied across a range of jobs. For example, companies as diverse as Vodaphone, the NHS, and Waitrose use tests to filter the huge numbers of applications for graduate posts (Suff 2005; Scott 2006; Brockett 2009), National Car Parks use them in order to ascertain whether candidates possess the resilience needed to be a parking warden (People Management 2005), and the Environment Agency uses them to assess how well candidates fit with a public sector culture (Watkins 2003). However, it is important to place the use of psychometric tests into context. Hence, whilst the CIPD's (2008*b*) annual survey found that 56 per cent of

Box 5.10 Practitioner perspective
Personality testing

HR Director Francesca Carbridge explains why she spends time and money on personality testing, something she seems to oppose in principle.

> I decided, after fighting several battles...that it [resisting the use of psychological tests] wasn't worth it. To put it simply, it appears to make a lot of senior managers feel better if they think that something sort of 'scientific' has gone on somewhere within the selection process. I think it plays a sort of symbolic role for a lot of managers—it is a talisman that makes them feel better about the rather chancy thing they are doing when they are making a decision to appoint, say, someone on £50,000 a year whose later underperformance could cause major difficulties. Recruitment and selection...involve a great deal of guesswork. They are very much a gamble, much of the time. And managers are often queasy about this. They feel better if certain procedures have been followed that appear to have something rational or objective about them. I've come to live with this—as long as it does not involve managers denying their responsibility for the decisions they have made...I've therefore become tolerant of the practice of using some personality testing. I'd much prefer to save time and money and drop them though. (Watson 2002: 407)

respondents engaged in forms of personality testing, other forms of testing aimed at assessing skills and general abilities were far more widely used. Additionally, whilst the CIPD's (2011h) Resourcing and Talent Planning Survey found a fairly equal balance between psychometric and other forms of skills testing when selecting employees, the most popular selection method by far was the interview.

5.5.7 Assessment centres

Although the term suggests a place where one goes for assessment, in fact most assessment centres are carried out at an employer's place of business (Suff 2011a). It is an attempt to improve reliability and validity through the integration of multiple assessment methods related to the demands of the vacancy with trained assessors observing candidates' responses and typically scoring them against an objective, predetermined list of job criteria. The range of selection activities designed for an assessment centre usually cover individual and collective activities and typically include work-sample and/or psychometric tests, competency-based interviews, group exercises and presentations—with a focus on how candidates would perform in the role if they are appointed. The example of consulting company KPMG in Box 5.11 illustrates how the process of an assessment centre works in practice.

Because of the time and costs associated with assessment centres, organizations are most likely to use them for high-value roles, such as senior or specialist staff, or when recruiting graduates because they can be envisaged as future leaders within the organization. The 2011 IRS survey concerning the use of assessment centres (Suff 2011a) found that more than half (51.6 per cent) of employers surveyed used them for senior managers, while more than four employers in ten also used them for middle managers, graduates, line managers, and senior specialist and/or technical staff. Because assessment centres are tailored to the specific needs of an organization, it is not possible to be prescriptive in terms of their use. However, if they are properly developed, applied, and validated, the process has the potential to improve the effectiveness and creditability of the selection decision. A key foundation of this is the accuracy of documentation concerning the post, and the provision of good job descriptions and person specifications (CIPD 2011h). The assessment centre must also allocate sufficient time for activities to run and for effective feedback in order for the candidates to demonstrate their abilities and for the process to be perceived as being fair.

Box 5.11 Window on work
Assessment centres at KPMG

KPMG's graduate recruitment process uses a hi-tech assessment centre aimed to create an immersive experience that closely simulates the working environment faced by successful candidates (www.kpmgcareers.co.uk). The centrepiece of this event is an hour-long 'virtual office' exercise which will see applicants, sitting at a computer with headphones, attempt to complete a pre-assigned task while at the same time dealing with incoming e-mails and phone messages. The bespoke software used for the assessment will see animated 3D characters welcome the candidates and also appear during the exercise to give them information or divert them with other tasks. Elsewhere in the day, candidates have two 15-minute role plays with trained actors playing the part of a manager and a client. They also have a report-writing exercise which closely mirrors the real work a graduate trainee would do. The aim of this centre is to move recruitment beyond the traditional numerical and reasoning tests to provide an immersive and interactive experience that will tell the company more about the applicant, and the applicant more about KPMG. Around 2000 candidates are expected to attend the centre, which comes after an initial round of numerical, verbal, and situational judgement tests and a first interview. After the assessment centre, the final round is an interview by a partner or director at the firm. As the organization seeks to recruit about 850 graduates and 250 interns in its next round of recruitment, the new process is designed not only to recruit the most suitable applications, but is also aimed at reducing the time partners need to spend interviewing, hence saving time and money (Brockett 2011).

Assessment centres can also give candidates a realistic job preview because the tasks set should closely match those outlined in the job description and person specification. If it does that effectively, the process is more likely to have face validity because the selection process will test candidate capabilities in relation to typical work-related activities. Attendance at an assessment centre can help candidates assess what is involved in working for the organization and allow them to make an appropriate decision if a job is offered. Furthermore, candidates who attend assessment centres which genuinely reflect the job and the organization are often impressed by the company, even if they are rejected.

As indicated previously, one of the main criticisms levelled against assessment centres concerns their costs. Developing an assessment centre—either using an external provider or developing internal capabilities to do this in-house—can be expensive. Proponents argue that, as with any selection process, these costs need to be set against the potential cost of recruitment error, which can be considerable. More seriously, questions have also been raised as to whether or not assessment centres meet the minimum standards of effectiveness (IRS 2002). Accurately evaluating behaviours can be difficult and therefore requires skilled assessors, so organizations using internal staff in this capacity need to ensure that they are appropriately trained, or use established external providers.

5.5.8 The selection decision

Once the candidates have been assessed, the data from these assessment methods can be evaluated against the person specification, job description, or competency profile. A truly rational decision process would have assessors numerically rate each candidate on each dimension or competency, with specific weightings being given as to the relative importance for the job in question. The candidate who has the highest total score, or is assessed as possessing all or most of the specified essential characteristics and the most desirable ones, should be appointed. In practice, the final decision is often less than clear-cut. The ratings might be numerical, but the evaluations will be made subjectively by assessors, and weightings will sometimes be assigned to justify rather than to make decisions—often in order to select the preferred candidate, who might not necessarily have gained the highest points scored. Once the decision is made, or sometimes prior to the latter stages of selection, references might be sought—often to verify claims made by the candidate. However, as Box 5.12 indicates, this now requires greater attention from those constructing the reference (Rushton 2008).

 ## Summary and further reading

- The selection decision is concerned with issues of fit, and which candidate best fits the demands of the job as well as the organization's culture, ethos, and values. But selection is a two-way process, with candidates also evaluating their prospective employers. The choice of selection method and its implementation will give candidates an insight not only into the organization's rhetorical presentation

 Box 5.12 Learning activity
Job references

Find out the following.

Do employers have to provide a reference? If they choose to do so, what information should be provided or not? What rights do employees have if their company refuses to provide a reference? And what advice would you give someone who was uncomfortable about asking his/her current employer for a reference whilst still being employed by them? Given the case of Jackson v Liverpool Council (Brown 2011), what might constitute a fair or unfair reference? Finally, can you ask to see the reference your employer might have given you?

If you were to draft guidance for a company on this issue, what are the key points you would make and what advice would you give in order to be legally compliant and fair to employees?

but, more importantly, into the ways in which that is represented in action. Hence, in tight labour markets, where skills and knowledge are in high demand, it is the employer who has to engage in 'impression management' just as much as a potential employee.

- The selection methods chosen often depend on a range of variables. Whilst concerns might exist as to the predictive validity and reliability of the selection options and their capability to yield the 'best' candidate, final choices might depend more on organizational preferences and be predicated more on issues of cost, time, the skills of recruiters, and their availability. However, as selection methods increase in sophistication with the use of psychometric tests and assessment centres, concerns still persist as to their appropriate use. To what extent does the normative HR literature mask an abiding preference by managers and recruiters for less structured approaches, as seen in the continuing and widespread use of unstructured interviews? In addition, to what extent are these 'sophisticated' selection approaches applicable across organizations, especially those which might have fewer resources to devote to this activity (Wyatt, Pathak, and Bibarras 2010).

The regular surveys undertaken by the CIPD and Incomes Data Services (IDS) are useful in terms of providing insights into employer's activity in this area, as well as providing evidence over time as to the shifts in selection practice. Where the psychometric approach to selection is concerned, Furnham (2005) provides an assessment of these tests from a psychological perspective, outlining the main problems associated with ensuring their effective use.

5.6 The limitations of the systems and decision-making approaches

One of the main issues connected with the approaches towards recruitment and selection covered in this chapter concerns the assumption that a 'best' person exists for the job and that there is one key decision involved in the process—either to select or to reject the candidate. However, this ignores the fact that successful job performance depends on a number of issues, as an individual job exists within a complex network of structures, processes, and relationships that impact and interact with the employee. This means that a potentially high-performing new hire could be thwarted in terms of performance by a multitude of events, whereas a less competent recruit might perform to a higher standard if exposed to more supportive and benign situations.

This means that it is unhelpful to view the selection decision in isolation from the events that precede and succeed it. Decisions concerning candidates and the company are made by both parties well before the actual advertisement of a job. For example, individuals will form or have impressions of a company based on what they know about its products and services, as well as the ways in which the company presents its brand. These kinds of impressions will influence how or whether potential candidates will surf the company website to search for possible employment or respond to publicized vacancies. Therefore a possibly ideal candidate might not consider the organization if he/she has a negative impression of the firm.

Moreover, processes of socialization and induction occurring after the selection decision will have a considerable impact on the extent to which the employee performs effectively. This suggests that recruitment and selection should be seen as an extended ongoing process of interaction in which the expectations and demands of both parties take place within a process of continuous exchange. The rational model of decision-making often isolates the selection decision from preceding and succeeding actions and decisions, but it is only one episode in the successful integration of the individual into the organization. This is more likely to occur where there are positive expectations, motivation, and commitment from both parties. Thus the more strongly these positive elements are expressed in a decision, the more power that decision exerts as a basis for action (Newell and Shackleton 2001). However, such approaches break all the rules for rational decision-making!

As stated, the selection or development decision is but one decision in many. Successful integration of successful candidates is vital if organizations are to retain new employees. This is more likely to occur if positive expectations, motivation, and commitment exist from both parties. How is this to be achieved?

- Although the rational model assumes that many or all possibilities should be considered, multiple alternatives actually generate uncertainty which in turn reduces commitment

Box 5.13 Skills exercise
Effective recruitment and selection

In pairs or small groups, choose a job that you are all familiar with. Draw up a job description and person specification for this post using the criteria outlined in Box 5.3. Once you have done this, decide how you will recruit this member of staff bearing in mind issues of cost and the need to generate a good-quality field of applicants. Then determine the selection methods you will use. Which will be the most effective and why? Finally, think about how you will introduce your new hire into the organization and show how you will ensure that your new recruit is motivated, made to feel welcome, and treated as having potential—as suggested by Newell and Shackleton (2001).

and motivation. Therefore, where the selection process is concerned, small short lists of candidates might work better in achieving positive outcomes.

• If selectors believe that the appointed candidate is the best, they are more likely to ensure that the person is successful—regardless of whether or not the candidate is the best according to some rational decision criterion (Newell and Shackleton 2001). In turn, if new recruits are treated as having substantial potential, and that message is reinforced, then it is more likely that higher performance will occur.

• Successful job performance depends on motivation and ability. Ability is often enhanced by opportunities for development and training as well as the characteristics of the individual. An 'ideal' person selected for a post, but given no training or development, is more likely to fail than a moderately suitable person who is given those opportunities.

Given these critiques, it is interesting to consider how an awareness of them might prompt changes to the ways we recruit, select, and introduce employees, as suggested in Box 5.13.

Summary and further reading

• This chapter has used the systems and decision-making approaches to illustrate the prevailing attitudes taken towards recruitment and selection. Where the selection decision is concerned, the limitations of these tactics are evident. Whilst selection methods aim to become ever more rational, the assessments are still made by people who are also capable of perceptual bias and distortion. The rational approach to such problems is to impose more rationality—to use multiple methods in order to heighten validity and reliability. However, it is possible to see the selection decision as but one decision taken amongst many in the recruitment and selection process, with positive outcomes being more likely if a more holistic approach is taken with greater consideration being given as to how performance can be achieved once the selected candidate is in post.

• One of the main aims of the recruitment and selection process is not simply to fill a vacant or new post, but to ensure that the person inhabiting the job will be able to demonstrate high degrees of performance and commitment. Those offering a critique of the mainstream practitioner approach rooted in the systems and rational decision-making methods posit a different means by which this might be achieved. This does not invalidate the use of the recruitment and selection methods outlined in this chapter, but will require managers to develop a different perspective on the process, seeing the decision to employ a particular candidate as requiring effective training, socialization, and encouragement in order to ensure that he/she is helped to perform successfully.

Newell and Shackleton (2001) have provided a critique and an alternative to the decision-making approach typically used by many organizations. Newell (2005) also provides a critique of the psychometric approach and suggests that the provision of more accurate information will enhance the psychological contract because a more realistic picture is given.

5.7 Conclusion

As seen in Chapter 1, recruitment and selection have been identified as being critical to meeting the challenges of organizational change. Increasingly, the design of selection systems is being viewed as needing to support the overall organization strategy, with many companies revamping their recruitment, assessment, and selection strategies following strategic realignments and the redefinition of organizational objectives and culture. The industrial restructuring witnessed in the 1980s and 1990s has resulted in companies now demanding employee flexibility and an ability to work in multi-skilled teams within flatter organizations. This means that greater emphasis is now placed on skills and qualities like teamwork, adaptability, tolerance of ambiguity, and a desire to improve, develop, and take responsibility. This has led to the greater use of methods such as structured interviews, assessment centres, and psychometric tests as means of assessing the extent to which individual candidates possess these abilities.

However, there are limitations to the systems and decision-making approaches. One limitation is that these approaches are entirely concerned with improving the efficiency of the process and are not concerned with understanding the wider significance of it. Hence, whilst these methods focus on ensuring that rationality is in charge of the system, there is little evidence that the nature or implications of that rationality are taken into consideration—especially where the candidate is concerned and the impressions he/she might form of the company. Additionally, the relationship between personality preferences and behaviour is a vexed one, with no clear correlation between the two, probably because many factors influence and affect individual and organizational performance. In turn, people change as a result of job experiences and in the course of their career in organizations—these changes will clearly impact on job performance in different and unpredictable ways that are not amenable to testing.

Finally, the jobs people do are increasingly involving negotiation, interaction, and mutual influence. They take place within flexible self-directed work teams. This is perhaps one reason why companies still use the interview as an important selection method, despite all its problems, because it opens up opportunities for an exchange of views, mutual negotiation, and mutual decision-making. In short, these interactive processes acknowledge the usefulness and appropriateness of social processes within the selection procedure and during induction, since high candidate performance depends crucially on a range of other decisions and practices once in post.

 ## Assignment and discussion questions

1 What are the main risks to both the candidate(s) and the organization of poor recruitment and selection processes and how might these be overcome?

2 Given the devolution of much HR activity to line managers, what might organizations need to do to ensure that they can carry out this activity appropriately?

3 Many organizations are now looking to balance cost considerations with securing the best possible candidates for jobs. How is this to be done?

4 Given that organizations seek to engage employee commitment through the recruitment and selection process, how can organizations use e-recruitment and selection methods to generate this connection?

5 How appropriate is it for companies to check a candidate's online presence on social networking sites?

 ## Online Resource Centre

Test your understanding of this chapter with online questions and answers, keep up to speed with changes to the law through regular updates, and use selected weblinks to quickly access useful resources and further information. Visit the Online Resource Centre at:
www.oxfordtextbooks.co.uk/orc/gilmore_williams2e/

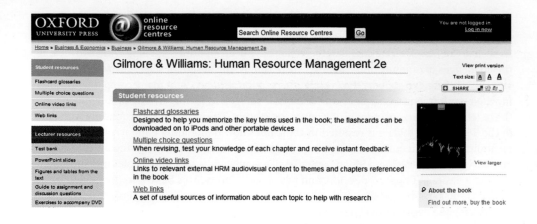

Case study
Recruiting and selecting staff at Médecins Sans Frontières

Médecins Sans Frontières (MSF) is an independent medical humanitarian organization that delivers emergency aid in more than 60 countries to people affected by armed conflict, epidemics, natural or man-made disasters, or exclusion from healthcare.

In emergencies and their aftermath, the organization rehabilitates and runs hospitals and clinics, performs surgery, battles epidemics, carries out vaccination campaigns, operates feeding centres for malnourished children, and offers mental healthcare. The work of MSF is carried out by over 25,000 health professionals, logistics experts, and administrative staff who run projects all around the world.

MSF are very clear as to what they require from their field workers. Most first 'missions' with the organization last a minimum of nine months to a year, with this level of commitment being required in order to maintain organizational continuity, to allow new employees to become acclimatized to a given climate and the degree of responsibility given to the roles. Employees need to be able to live and work as a team because the hours of work can be long and often take place in very inhospitable environments. Hence the ability to be tolerant and get on with others is essential. The work is stressful and situations can change rapidly, requiring flexibility and adaptability from those on the ground. Finally, language skills and experience of volunteering or extensive travel overseas are prerequisites. Information for this case study was taken from the Médecins Sans Frontières website (http://www.msf.org.uk/work) and further details about working for the organization can be found there.

Questions

1 MSF require a variety of highly skilled staff to work in difficult environments for extended periods of time. How would you recruit and assess candidates for this kind of employment? You might like to look at the MSF website (http://www.msf.org.uk/working_overseas_hubpage.aspx) and chose a specific job such as midwife, nurse, medical doctor, anaesthetist or surgeon to help you focus.

2 The organization also recruits interns, volunteers who support permanent staff in places such as London and Dublin. MSF receives a high volume of enquiries in connection with this kind of work, so how would you suggest that they manage this level of interest cost-effectively but succeed in recruiting the best people for the jobs available?

3 How does MSF promote its brand as an employer? How effective are they in positioning themselves as an 'employer of choice' within their field? What more could they do in these areas?

Developing human resources

6

Sarah Gilmore

Learning objectives

The main objectives of this chapter are:

- to locate the demand for skilled workers within a wider context of heightened competition and fluctuating economic conditions, to explore the changing nature of skills, and to outline key government initiatives in this area;

- to explore the ways in which training and development activities are typically structured, enacted, and evaluated using the model of the systematic training cycle, offering a critique of its continued application;

- to assess the extent to which a shift is occurring from training to learning via an exploration of the learning organization, communities of practice, and knowledge management, looking at what the implications might be of such a change in focus for learners and for the training function where it exists;

- to illustrate the relationship that exists between HRM and learning, training, and development activities.

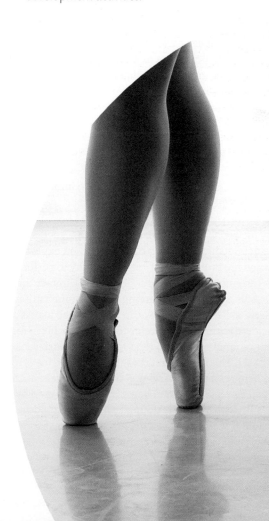

6.1 Introduction

As discussed in Chapter 1, the arrival and growth of human resource management (HRM) have placed an increased emphasis on the importance of employees and the role they play in enhancing organizational performance. Whether the focus is on models of HRM seeking to attain employee commitment to the organization and its goals, or on approaches that treat staff as a 'resource' alongside any other, effective training and development are important because they can help companies improve productivity, performance, and product innovation. In this way, a link is frequently made between investment in effective training and longer-term organizational survival, as well as national prosperity and societal well-being (Wilson 2005; Wang and Swanson 2008).

Developments in technology and the industrial restructuring occurring in many Western economies in the 1980s and 1990s as a response to competitive pressures have resulted in attitudinal change concerning training and development. This has meant that some employers now believe that continued organizational success, adaptability to wider environmental changes, and consumer demands relies upon continuous outlay in this area of their work. Figures released by the European Centre for Development and Vocational Training (CEDEFOP 2010) show that those companies within the EU that train their staff are 2.5 times less likely to go out of business than firms that do not. Such findings support the view that investment here should be supported and encouraged rather than viewed as a cost to be minimized.

Following this introduction, Section 6.2 investigates the changing nature of skills and government responses to organizational and national requirements for competent employees. Section 6.3 shifts the focus from government interventions in the training and skills arena and explores the means by which training and development needs, design, delivery, and evaluation are undertaken in organizations via an explanation and evaluation of the systematic training cycle (STC). This exploration depicts its key stages, culminating in a critique as to its suitability given the length of time it has been operating and the changes witnessed by organizations since its inception 50 years ago. This leads on to an exploration in Section 6.4 of approaches to training and development which emphasize the centrality of learning, especially the ways by which employees, groups, and organizations as a whole can learn from engaging in work, and how organizations are trying to capture and share learning outcomes internationally. The chapter concludes in Section 6.5 with an evaluation of the developments outlined in this chapter.

6.2 The changing nature of skills

When seeking to foster performance improvements, the focus is often on how to improve the knowledge, skills, and attributes (KSA) required by staff to carry out their work both now and in the future. However, given the requirement for workers to be able to move between different kinds of employment, a contemporary focus on skills also looks at ensuring successful job and career transfer over time. 'Skills' are defined here as being capabilities and expertise required to carry out a particular occupation and are often equated with the ability to perform job tasks to a predefined level of competence (Frogner 2002). Basic skills, such as literacy and numeracy, are applicable in most jobs. Other skills, such as teamworking and communication, are often referred to as 'transferable' or 'generic' skills because they can also be used across a large number of different occupations. Specific vocational skills refer to those specific skills needed to work within an occupation or occupational group and tend to be less transferable between occupations (Gibb and Megginson 2001). This means that the labour market needs to be seen not just as one uniform market, but as being composed of several smaller markets, each defined by the skill types and levels demanded by employers and being supplied by employees. It is also pertinent to note that the ways by which 'skill' is defined and understood has undergone a subtle but profound shift in meaning, seeing the growing prioritization of softer social skills, and the possession of generic cognitive skills such as communication, problem-solving, and the ability to use IT over manual dexterity. This trend almost certainly reflects the shift in the occupational structure in many countries—both high-income *and* developing nations—with a common explanation for these developments being skill-biased technological change stemming from progress in information and communication technologies (Kelly 2007; Cörvers and Meriküll 2008).

Governments and employers have always been concerned with the issue of workforce skills because, as stated in the introduction to this chapter, a positive correlation is perceived to exist between the possession of a skilled workforce, higher workplace productivity, and industrial competitiveness. This relationship is clearly stated in the Leitch Review of Skills:

> Productivity is increasingly driven by skills. The ability of firms to succeed in the face of growing international competition depends increasingly on the skilled labour force they can draw from. (Leitch 2006: 13)

This is a view endorsed by the European Commission who state:

> Improving people's skills is a real 'win, win' for all—for the economy, for society, for employers and, of course, for individuals themselves. In every single EU country, unemployment rates systematically vary with qualification levels. The employment rate for those with high skill levels across the EU as a whole is approximately 85%, for medium skill levels 70% and for low skill levels it stands at 50%. (European Commission 2010: 4)

These issues are explored further in Box 6.1.

Thus skills shortages are problematic for government, business owners, and shareholders (not to mention employees and their representatives) because of their potential impact on a range of economic measures such as productivity, GDP growth, employment, and earnings. Therefore it means that securing the requisite skills within the workforce consistently issues a challenge to employers, government, and training providers alike to ensure that these (increasingly higher-order cognitive) needs can be met and sustained over time. For governments, investment in vocational education and skills acquisition involves very substantial sums of money and needs to enhance worker and employer performance. This means that investment in skills must be accurately targeted to areas of demand, and the content of programmes must substantially assist in meeting skills shortages as well as meeting the future needs of companies and workers.

6.2.1 Skills shortages and skills gaps in UK employment

Skills shortages arise when there are more vacancies requiring certain skills than there are people available in the external labour market with those skills. However, these can alter

 Box 6.1 Learning activity
The UK's long-term skills needs

The findings of the Leitch Review of Skills recommended the following headline targets for 2020:

- 95 per cent of adults to achieve the basic skills of functional literacy and numeracy;

- more than 90 per cent of adults to be qualified to at least NVQ level 2;

- an increase of intermediate skills from level 2 to level 3 and an improvement in the esteem, quantity, and quality of intermediate skills;

- an increase of more than 40 per cent of adults qualified to level 4 and above, which was already up from 29 to 40 per cent of adults in 2005, with a commitment to continue progression.

Debates have always raged as to who should be responsible for skills provision, delivery, and accountability between government, employers, and other parties to this debate such as trade unions and the CBI as well as professional groups such as the CIPD. Go to the websites for the TUC (www.tuc.org.uk), CBI (www.cbi.org.uk), and CIPD (www.cipd.co.uk) and view their comments on the Leitch Review and the subsequent reports mentioned above. What do they say on this issue of responsibility, delivery and accountability? To what extent do they share the assessments made in them and to what extent do they have alternative suggestions or strategies to those outlined?

depending on wider national and international economic circumstances. For example, as a result of the economic downturn, the National Employers Skills Survey (NESS 2010) found that the numbers of vacancies, hard-to-fill vacancies (HtFVs), and skill-shortage vacancies (SSVs) were lower than at any time from the start of the NESS series in 2003. However, the study found that where HtFVs are concerned, skill shortages contributed to the difficulties experienced in filling the position. Skills shortages were found to be particularly acute in associate professional, personal services, and skilled trade occupations, with these shortages remaining constant over time. When companies engage in recruitment, the main skills areas where shortages are being found continue to be for technical, practical, and job-specific skills, as well as 'softer' skills such as customer-handling, problem-solving, and teamworking skills, with these findings being replicated across successive surveys. Finally, the proportion of SSVs attributed to poor literacy and numeracy remains a significant issue and an intractable problem over time, with literacy being mentioned in connection with 30 per cent of SSVs and numeracy in connection with 26 per cent.

In addition to skills shortages, skills gaps can also occur. These are deficiencies in the skills of an employer's *existing* workforce, both at the individual level and overall, which prevent the firm from achieving its business objectives. The 2010 NESS indicated that whilst 81 per cent of employers stated that their workforce was fully proficient, 19 per cent (one in five) stated that they employed staff whom they considered not fully proficient. This means that around 1.7 million workers, or 7 per cent of the total workforce in England, were described as having skills gaps. This represents an upward trend on previous surveys which saw skills gaps declining. Sectors experiencing heaviest skills gaps are hotel and catering, education, health and social work, public administration, and defence.

The main continuing reason employers give as to why employees are not fully proficient is that they lack experience, or have recently been recruited. This means that many of these deficiencies may be relatively short term and capable of being bridged over time or by training and development interventions. Other causes of skills gaps are more difficult to overcome and cannot be expected to diminish in the short to medium term because the reason for their existence lies with a lack of employee motivation and inability to keep up with change. NESS (2010) found that approximately 29 per cent of all staff with skills gaps are not fully proficient at least in part because they are not motivated to gain necessary skills, and 25 per cent lack proficiency at least in part because of their inability to adapt to change. But employee culpability needs to be set against a scenario where organizations also lack the ability to train staff appropriately—even when companies engage in training and have training plans. This suggests the importance of continuing to support and develop line-manager abilities, so that they can identify and assist in solving skills needs and play a pivotal role in encouraging skills development as part of longer-term career plans.

6.2.2 Responsibility for skills development

At this point, it is important to raise the question as to where responsibility and accountability for skills lie, as well as who pays for upskilling and who decides the content of skills interventions at national and local level. This is an argument that has been waged by parties to training over time, and therefore it is unsurprising that the Leitch's Review called for a tripartite approach between government, employers, and employees (Leitch 2006).

Leitch links the existence of a skilled workforce to organizational productivity and to national economic health through enhanced competitiveness. The Review projected the prospect of long-term economic decline for UK organizations in global markets because of a lack of skills, with fundamental weaknesses existing in the UK skills base at all levels (basic, intermediary, and higher). It argued that unless these issues were addressed, the UK would drop to near the bottom of the league of European economies by 2020 in terms of economic growth and productivity and would also fall well below the economic growth rates achieved by emerging economies such as China and India. This was echoed by the UK Commission for Employment and Skills (UKCES 2009) which predicted that the country's skills base would be unlikely to improve, let alone become world class by 2020, unless radical action is taken by government, employers, and individuals to increase qualification take-up. However, upskilling will involve engaging more with a working population that has either completed its compulsory education or is coming close to doing so.

Three years later, the Innovation, Universities, Science, and Skills Committee (2009) argued that what was needed was a skills and training strategy that focused more on skills utilization by companies to achieve high-performance outcomes and enhanced productivity. Their alternative suggestion was for the targets in the Leitch Review to be broadened to include re-skilling to help individuals acquire the skills they need to find jobs in a world that is changing because of fluctuating economic circumstances.

When the Leitch Review was published, the UK economy had experienced sustained growth over a 12-year period and had the highest employment rate in the G7 group of leading industrial nations. As economic conditions altered, governments have placed greater emphasis on skills to secure improvements in economic performance and arrest increases in youth unemployment (Stewart 2011). However, concerns with skills and learning also extend more widely. One in three Europeans of working age has few or no formal qualifications, making them 40 per cent less likely to be employed than those with medium-level qualifications. Nearly a third of Europe's population aged 25–64 have no, or only low, formal qualifications and only a quarter have high-level qualifications (CEDEFOP 2010). However, whilst unemployment in the EU rose during the downturn post-2008, the CEDEFOP report found that skilled workers are significantly less likely to be out of work. This focus on upskilling and the perceived relationship between skills and employment can be seen in Box 6.2 and the EU's work in relation to lifelong learning, illustrating the initiatives created across the region and the push for employers and workers to see engagement with lifelong learning as fundamental across all stages of working life (see also European Commission 2010).

6.2.3 National training interventions in the UK

In terms of government approaches to training, successive UK governments have framed their policies around the idea of a market-led system for skills in which demand and supply determine the amount and nature of training provided. As noted by Gold (2007), the demand for skills tends to originate from strategic-level decision-makers in organizations. However, training is not often high on their agenda because of short-term pressures for meeting financial

Box 6.2 Policy example
European Union policy on education and training

Politicians at the European level have recognized that education and training are not just essential to the development of a knowledge-based society and economy, but are fundamental to the attainment of social inclusion and the ability of people to participate fully in society. Key to this occurring on a EU-wide basis is the concept of lifelong learning. EU policies are designed to support national actions and address common challenges such as ageing societies, skills deficits among the workforce, and global competition. These areas demand joint responses as well as sharing of experiences from member states.

The long-term strategic objectives of EU education and training policies are:

- making lifelong learning and mobility a reality;
- improving the quality and efficiency of education and training;
- promoting equity, social cohesion and active citizenship;
- enhancing creativity and innovation, including entrepreneurship, at all levels of education and training.

EU-level activities are being developed to address priority areas in each of the different levels of education and training—early childhood, school, higher, vocational, and adult education—based on these overall aims. These include, for example, expanding opportunities for learning mobility or enhancing partnerships between education and training institutions and the broader society.

Source: http://ec.europa.eu/education

and other performance targets, and even where companies possess a dedicated training and development function, their status and hence their ability to drive a strong agenda here is questionable (Keep 2007). However, the impact of global competition, organizational change, and the impact of changes in technology has seen government agendas widen beyond a focus on the acquisition of technical skills to focus on the 'learning society' and 'high-performance work organizations' where employees can learn all the time as part of their work, and where they can take advantage of the system for performance and innovation (DfEE 1998; Sung and Ashton 2005).

However, whilst government might be keen to stimulate a demand for skills within organizations, they have been reluctant to compel businesses to train their staff. This approach to training—often termed 'voluntarism'—has long been a key feature of governmental attitudes, with this approach being bolstered by governments from the 1980s onwards. Another feature of vocational education and training in the UK has been the tendency of governments to formulate a range of different policies, strategies, and governing and assessment bodies which has resulted in a situation where very little stays the same for very long. However, some systems in the area of vocational education and training (VET) such as the National Vocational Qualifications (NVQs) and Scottish National Vocational Qualifications (SNVQs) and Investors in People (IiP) systems have endured and these are outlined in the following sections.

6.2.4 The competency approach and the NVQ framework

Competence is one of the outcomes of training and development and can be defined as the ability to apply knowledge, skills, and understanding to a work activity; its acquisition is assessed via performance. In this way, competence frameworks focus on what workers are able to *do* in a workplace setting, rather than whether or not they possess the knowledge and understanding that underpin those abilities, although award frameworks have altered to address those concerns. Despite changes in government over time, competency approaches have remained intact. The national framework for NVQs and SNVQs covers most occupations, with qualifications being organized into five levels, as outlined in Table 6.1. Definitions are given for the general requirements for each level of competence and are further refined for specific occupational

Table 6.1 The NVQ and SNVQ framework

Level	Description
Level 1	Competence that involves the application of knowledge in the performance of a range of varied work activities, most of which are routine and predictable.
Level 2	Competence that involves the application of knowledge in a significant range of varied work activities, performed in a variety of contexts. Some of these activities are complex or non-routine, and there is some individual responsibility or autonomy. Collaboration with others, perhaps through membership of a work group or team, is often a requirement.
Level 3	Competence that involves the application of knowledge in a broad range of varied work activities performed in a wide variety of contexts, most of which are complex and non-routine. There is considerable responsibility and autonomy, and control or guidance of others is often required.
Level 4	Competence that involves the application of knowledge in a broad range of complex, technical, or professional work activities performed in a variety of contexts and with a substantial degree of personal responsibility and autonomy. Responsibility for the work of others and the allocation of resources is often present.
Level 5	Competence that involves the application of a range of fundamental principles across a wide and often unpredictable variety of contexts. Very substantial personal autonomy and often significant responsibility for the work of others and for the allocation of substantial resources feature strongly, as do personal accountabilities for analysis, diagnosis, design, planning, execution, and evaluation.

Source: Directgov (2011).

competences based on the required outcomes expected for the performance of a task in a work role, expressed as performance standards with criteria. These outline what competent employees in a particular occupation are expected to be able to do, and it is these that are often referred to as 'competences'.

According to Roe, Wiseman, and Costello (2006), there are now approximately 800 NVQ titles available within the UK. Over a quarter of major employers in the UK offer NVQs to their employees, and about 4.5 million NVQ certificates have been awarded. They are also embedded within government apprenticeship schemes. However, NVQs and SNVQs have been strongly criticized. Oates (2004) argued that occupational competence cannot be adequately described by a series of technical statements, and that when it is so described (as within NVQs) the 'competence' which is thus assured cannot reliably be transferred from one work situation to another. Other critiques focus on the excessive use of jargon and bureaucracy (Swailes and Roodhouse 2003), and the lack of real understanding by employers concerning them. Most damagingly, as noted by Young (2011), despite considerable investment and many changes over a period of over 20 years, researchers and commentators do not see the introduction of NVQs as having led to substantial improvements in skill development or in the work-based training system in the UK. Citing evidence from a number of studies (e.g. James 2006; Cox 2007), he argues that NVQs have not been taken up with any enthusiasm by large numbers of employers for whom it was claimed that they were designed and concludes that the reason for their longevity and their export abroad (usually to former British colonies) has less to do with their addressing the complex problems concerned with the role of skills and knowledge in economic development than with controlling public expenditure in this domain.

Given the longevity of NVQs and SNVQs, it is unsurprising that the qualification is undergoing change and is being progressively replaced with Qualifications and Credit Framework (QCF) awards, certificates, and diplomas. Some awards persist in NVQ format, whilst others have transferred to their new formats. Responsibility for NVQs is now largely overseen by the QCA's replacement agency, QCDA (Qualifications and Curriculum Development Agency), and by OfQual (Office of Qualifications and Examinations Regulation), with industry sector development responsibilities cascading down to industry bodies via the UK Government Department for Business, Innovation, and Skills (BIS), and the Sector Skills Councils (SSCs). Box 6.3 illustrates how one organization has combined NVQs with its own training programme in order to

Box 6.3 Window on work
Closing skills shortages through NVQs

The construction sector has faced many challenges, such as changes in economic circumstances and skills shortages as well as an increased focus on worker safety (Ho and Dzeng 2010). This means that whilst upskilling might be sought, it has to reflect downward pressures on costs as well as greater workforce diversity as companies have recruited overseas for workers with the necessary skills and experience. This is the general background to the Byrne Group's training programmes (www.byrnegroup.co.uk).

The training and development programme they have developed has been made available to all of its 500 staff and 1300 operatives, regardless of their age, nationality, or literacy. Employees can train for NVQs at levels 2 and 3, and for other qualifications in their chosen trade. Areas covered include construction-skills-based training, project management, health and safety, and business administration for non-financial managers. Training and assessment occurs at the workplace and brings together classroom and practical learning. Off-the-job learning or assessment also takes place on site, which enables employees to return to their work subsequently. Because the company's workforce consists of 36 nationalities, training information was translated into English, Polish, Punjabi, Romanian, and Russian so that 90 per cent of the workforce are able to understand it. Visual images and 3D models have also proved successful with those for whom English is not their first language (People Management 2008).

Between October 2006, when the programme started, and October 2008, 555 staff have gained an NVQ level 2 in their chosen subject. The company also met its target of 50 per cent of employees achieving qualifications within a year of the programme starting, and since November 2007, 40 people have been studying on NVQ level 3 programmes.

meet skills shortages. The DVD interview with Clare Fitzgerald from the Hampshire Fire and Rescue Service provides an additional example on NVQs and competencies in action.

6.2.5 Apprenticeships and internships

Apprenticeships are mainly, but not exclusively, aimed at 16- and 17-year-old school leavers. There are three levels of apprenticeship: intermediate, advanced, and higher. Each mode sees apprentices engaging in paid on-the-job training with some off-the-job provision being delivered via local colleges or a local training provider, with these work-based learning qualifications being linked to vocational qualifications or, as with the higher apprenticeship, the process can lead to a knowledge-based qualification such as a Foundation Degree.

There are now over 200 apprenticeships available across more than 80 industry sectors. However, until recently, the scheme has witnessed low completion rates (Fuller and Unwin 2003; DfES 2004), and a study commissioned by the CIPD found that the use of the more advanced apprenticeships by large employers varies considerably (Ryan, Gospel, and Lewis 2007). Fuller and Unwin (2003) argue that as the deployment of this scheme has increased in recent years, the core identity of apprenticeship as a model of learning is in danger of being replaced by a more restrictive form where it is viewed as a policy instrument focused on reducing unemployment figures and thus failing to ensure that it achieves its full potential for the apprentice or the organization.

As youth unemployment has risen because of the economic downturn, 50,000 new apprenticeship places have been funded by the government as a part of pro-growth measures to boost economic growth by stimulating the private sector (Stewart 2011). An example of an aspect of an apprenticeship programme in action is outlined in Box 6.4.

Another initiative aimed largely at university students and graduates is internships, with the government creating the Graduate Talent Pool in 2009 as a partnership between the Department for Business, Innovation, and Skills and employers. The general aim of internships is to gain work experience and to formulate and expand the intern's network of contacts within organizations with the aim of assisting career development and mobility, although the Milburn Report (Milburn 2009) called this into question. As such, there is no standard model of an internship, with some lasting for a few months and others lasting longer. Interns are usually asked to undertake specified pieces of work, to work to deadlines, and to have their performance assessed (Perlin 2011).

Box 6.4 Window on work
Apprenticeship learning at Rolls-Royce

Rolls-Royce is a provider of power systems and services for use on land, at sea, and in the air, and it has a broad customer base comprising airlines, corporate and utility aircraft and helicopter operators, 160 armed forces, more than 2500 marine customers, and energy customers in nearly 120 countries (www.rolls-royce.com). The company has been training apprentices for over 50 years, and its programme has won a series of awards. It has a high retention rate of 98 per cent, and 90 per cent of Rolls-Royce apprentices go on to achieve higher qualifications, half to degree level. Over a third of the company's senior UK managers began their careers as apprentices (www.apprenticeships.org.uk).

An example of the kinds of activities new apprentices can engage in include a five-day residential learning and development course in the Eskdale Fells, which forms part of a three-part modular programme. Apprentices from different sites are brought together to form teams. The teams undertake a number of projects during the week designed to highlight the skills and abilities that they need to operate successfully in the Rolls-Royce work place. These activities allow the apprentices to experience the local environment and take part in challenges in the fells and rivers. The projects are also designed to help the apprentices meet the learning outcomes set by Rolls-Royce. The final task of the week is a presentation to visiting senior managers and their colleagues. For many, this is the hardest task of all. The apprentices are asked to highlight their learning from the course and reflect on how they will transfer that learning back into the workplace (www.outwardbound.org.uk).

The Chartered Institute of Personnel and Development (CIPD 2010*d*) estimated that more than one in five employers planned to hire interns between April and September 2010, which is the equivalent of over 280,000 organizations across the UK potentially offering a quarter of a million internship places over the summer—a phenomenon which the CIPD predicted to increase. However, payment arrangements for interns vary. The CIPD's Learning and Talent Development Survey (CIPD 2010*c*) found that 63 per cent of employers pay their interns at least the national minimum wage (NMW), with 92 per cent of this group of employers paying their interns over and above the NMW out of choice. However, 37 per cent of employers surveyed paid their interns less than the NMW. Such practices have been criticized by the Trades Union Congress (TUC) and unions such as the National Union of Journalists (NUJ), as well as the Institute for Public Policy Research (IPPR) (Lawton and Potter 2010) and intern advocacy groups such as Interns Anonymous, because of their use of interns as sources of unpaid labour, despite their qualifying for the minimum wage. Government legal advice has emerged suggesting that some employers are breaking the law by not following NMW rules. Civil servants advise that internships that do not breach minimum wage laws are likely to exist only in short-term placements, normally classified as work experience. This means that most interns are likely to be defined as 'workers' under NMW laws. This means that they are entitled to the current hourly rate, rather than being classified as 'volunteers' working for a charity or government body (and thus exempted from NMW legislation), and therefore entitled to the NMW and other worker rights (Malik and Ball 2011). The weblinks outlined in Box 6.5 give some insight as to internship experiences and the ongoing debates on their use.

6.2.6 Welfare to work: the Work Programme

Welfare-to-work programmes have long been pursued in European countries, and the so-called Nordic model of active labour market policies served as a role model in the mid-1990s to the rest of Europe (Zaidi 2009). However, UK governments were more influenced by the North American 'Workfare' approach. Welfare-to-work public programmes aim to end what is often described as the 'culture of benefit dependency', where an attribution is made that this dependency occurs because of the design or perceived generosity of the national welfare system where benefits are available with little or no job search requirements needing to be demonstrated on the part of the recipient. In 2011, the UK's welfare-to-work strategy was revised and the Work Programme was introduced, replacing its predecessor, the New Deal.

This scheme's headline aim is to provide tailored support for claimants who need more help to undertake active and effective jobseeking, with the aim of getting more people off benefits and into work than previous schemes had achieved. Participants receive support to overcome barriers that prevent them from finding and staying in work. It is delivered by Department for Work and Pensions (DWP) contracted service providers who have been given complete autonomy to decide how best to support participants while meeting their minimum service delivery standards (DWP 2011*b*). Eighteen different 'prime' providers deliver 40 contracts across 18 areas of the country and are paid on the basis of results. Prime providers are paid according to results over time, and the 'customers' placed who are furthest from the labour market (e.g. someone who has been unemployed for lengthy periods, or who has limited capability for work and has thus been receiving benefits for several years) will secure higher payments for these providers than someone who would be more likely to move into work quickly.

However, the programme has been criticized by the National Audit Office (NAO) (Syal 2012) for overestimating the number of people who will get jobs as a result of attendance on

Box 6.5 Online video link
Internship experiences

Internships are a growing feature of the training and development landscape, but they are proving to be controversial. Follow the link provided in the Online Resource Centre to watch a video discussion concerning this issue.

---

the programme. The DWP expects that 40 per cent of people aged over 25 on the programme will be placed in jobs by providers. The NAO analysis finds that the figures would be closer to 26 per cent, and this could make it much harder for the programme's providers to meet government targets, and hence make it more likely that one or more providers will go under. In turn, this increases the risk that contractors might seek to protect profits by overlooking claimants who are harder to help. It criticized the way in which the government has implemented the programme in a year, compared with four years for previous schemes, and revealed that supporting software is still not operational, thereby leaving the scheme open to fraud.

6.2.7 Investors in People

Whereas the VET initiatives outlined previously focus on the individual learner, IiP operates at the organizational level. It is a national standard which sets out a level of good practice for the development of people in order to enhance performance and achieve an organization's business goals (Investors in People 2011). The IiP framework has three fundamental principles: plan (develop strategies to improve the performance of the organization), do (implement these strategies—taking action to improve the performance of the organization, often through employee training and development), and review (evaluating and adjusting these strategies—looking at and demonstrating the impact they have on the performance of the organization). These three principles are broken down into ten indicators, against which organizations wishing to be recognized as an Investor in People are assessed. To provide greater flexibility and customization of IiP to an employer's priorities and goals, the New Choices approach to IiP was introduced in 2009 and extended progress beyond the IiP Standard to bronze, silver, and gold status, which organizations can achieve by meeting additional evidence requirements from across the broader IiP framework. Responsibility for IiP and the regular review of the IiP standards lies with the UK Commission for Employment and Skills.

According to Bourne et al. (2008) and Martin and Elwes (2008), approximately 48,000 organizations covering nearly a third of the UK workforce are recognized as IiP employers or are working towards achieving recognition. Whilst the findings of these studies and others (e.g. Bourne and Franco-Santos 2010) suggest that adopting IiP has a number of positive outcomes, including improved financial performance, high levels of trust and cooperation, and a more flexible workforce in terms of employee behaviours and skills, these have not necessarily been replicated by other researchers. Studies have warned that companies often let their investment in development slide, only to try and remedy the situation just in time for the re-recognition process (Grugulis and Bevitt 2002; Fernandez, Taylor, and Bell 2005). The take-up and suitability of the programme for small organizations has been questioned (Collins and Smith 2004), and the focus on evidence provision shifts attention away from processes that underpin learning (Bell, Taylor, and Thorpe 2002).

📖 Summary and further reading

- Whilst government and employer rhetoric has increasingly focused on the need for higher-order workforce capabilities, survey data consistently illustrate the need for investment in basic and intermediate skills such as numeracy and literacy.

- Successive governments have implemented a range of initiatives in the skills area. These include NVQs, apprenticeships, and the New Deal, as well as Investors in People. To what extent these programmes will deliver the skills needed for the UK economy to compete will be one important measure of their effectiveness. Another is the extent to which UK companies adopt and engage with them.

- Governmental approaches towards training have a profound concern with employee and individual performance. This is largely due to the argument made connecting national economic performance with the success, innovation, and profitability enjoyed by its organizations. This is based upon the existence of a highly educated and skilled workforce, with employees now being encouraged to view continuous development as a natural and inevitable component of attaining and securing employment over the course of an individual career. The issues of who is responsible for ensuring this, and who pays for it, continue to be discussed.

The Leitch Review of Skills (Leitch 2006) as well as successive NESSs from 2001 onwards have all contributed to providing a full picture of the state of skills in the UK and give an indication as to the challenges faced by government and employers.

6.3 The practice of training

So far, the focus has been on government approaches towards training and the challenges facing employers with regard to skills provision. Therefore it is timely to shift attention to the ways in which organizations engage in training and developing their staff. Whilst some of their interventions might use national training schemes, it is also likely that tailored training and development initiatives will exist that relate directly to business goals. This section will identify the ways organizations engage in these activities, mainly through an exploration and analysis of the stages of the systematic training cycle. Following this coverage, a critique of the training cycle will be offered, noting its influence but questioning its validity in contemporary organizations.

6.3.1 The systematic training cycle

Those tasked with training and developing employees are frequently required to ensure that their interventions support the attainment of strategic business goals. However, whilst those concerns are undoubtedly important (Wilson 2005), there will also be a concern to ensure that activities are effectively designed, delivered, and evaluated. Whilst there are no set procedures or formulas for organizations to follow when planning training and development activities, systematic approaches have been dominant. The main example of this is the systematic training cycle (STC), outlined in Figure 6.1.

The STC emerged in the 1960s and is based on a four-stage process. For some commentators, this model is located in a view of organizations as being essentially stable. Given the increased turbulence that organizations now experience, it is pertinent to ask whether this influential model is still a useful tool in designing and delivering training.

6.3.2 Training needs analysis

The first stage in the STC is the identification of training needs. These can occur at three linked levels: organizational, occupational, and individual (Boydell 1976). At the organizational level, training needs analysis (TNA) usually takes place for strategic reasons: to maintain or extend a strategic position in a given market, or as a response to changes within that market that are due to changes in operating conditions, technology, or legislation. Some companies will engage in organizational TNA because their training and development work has lacked a strategic focus and they are keen to assert a more systematic business-driven approach. This could be linked to an intention to gain IiP status, initiatives such as benchmarking, or the adoption of quality initiatives. Table 6.2 gives an outline of some of the main ways that training needs are analysed at all three levels.

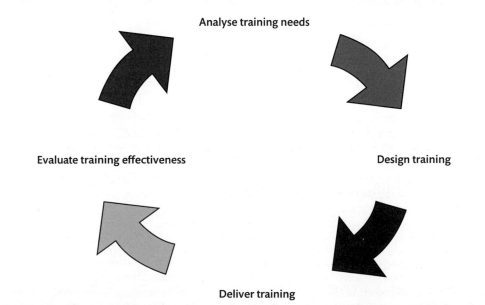

Analyse training needs

Evaluate training effectiveness

Design training

Deliver training

Figure 6.1 The systematic training cycle.

Table 6.2 Analysis of training needs

Organizational level	Job/occupational level	Individual level
'Global' review This involves the analysis of short- and long-term objectives. Each job category is then analysed to ensure it fits with these objectives and identified KSA needs.	**Functional analysis** This process is used to decide on the standards aimed at approval for NVQ use and involves developing statements of competence by analysing employment functions of the job holder.	**Appraisal** The discussion of employee performance will often yield information as to training and development needs.
Competence and performance management approaches Competence standards are developed for all staff by managers. These are used to assess performance and are often linked to NVQs or the organization's own standards.	**Key results analysis** This tool concentrates on the key areas of performance within a job—a useful tool when a job is changing in content and/or can complement a full analysis.	**Assessment/development centres** This assessment identifies strengths or characteristics to be assessed against, using a range of assessment methodologies including some simulation of job tasks to formulate a view of what the candidate needs to do for his/her own development.
Critical incident or priority problem analysis This approach prioritizes training for organizational problems that seem to have a training solution.	**Problem-centred analysis** This analysis focuses on particular aspects of a staff's work and no attempt is made to analyse jobs or key aspects of them.	**Self-assessment** This assessment is often part of the appraisal process, but is being more widely used to encourage workers to take charge of their own learning and to identify their learning needs.
Benchmarking Benchmarking involves a search for best practices leading to high performance (internally and externally) and the identification of performance gaps.	**Critical incident analysis** This method focuses on aspects of the job where the job holder(s) has most difficulty.	**Continuing professional development** This is often needed for certain professions in order to practice (e.g. doctors, lawyers, nurses) or to gain/retain membership of some professional groups. This can be self-generated and/or linked to initiatives instigated by the professional body in order to update knowledge and skills.
	Manual skills analysis This is a tool used to isolate the skills and knowledge employed by experienced workers performing tasks requiring a high degree of manual dexterity.	

Sources: Adapted from Reid, Barrington, and Brown (2004); Buckley and Caple (2009); Mankin (2009).

6.3.3 Designing and delivering training

The TNA process forms the basis for identifying the most significant training needs in more detail, as well as the content. It will also illustrate the most significant elements of any performance gap and should focus training provision onto key areas of need. It also facilitates the formation of performance criterion measures in terms of what effective performance looks like, or what the exhibition of desired attitudes would consist of. These would determine the expected level of performance to be achieved at the end of the training, given some time for learner transfer to occur. In these ways, TNA outcomes should form the basis for training and development objectives.

There are different ways of designing training objectives. Some designers will use structured performance statements which outline specific standards that KSA trainees will be expected to demonstrate as a result of their training as well as the conditions under which performance will occur (Buckley and Caple 2009). It is an approach that coheres effectively with competence and NVQ approaches. However, it is less helpful when what is required of the trainee in terms of specific behaviour or knowledge is ambiguous, or difficult to define or measure. Here, a different way of setting objectives is more useful and involves stating first a general objective, followed by specific behaviours that would be acceptable as evidence of objectives being attained.

Once these objectives are in place, there is a range of choices as to what will constitute the training or development activity and how it can be delivered. These choices will be constrained and informed by a number of factors: the availability of resources (financial, temporal, and physical), the views of the designers and facilitators as to how people learn, previous experiences of training and development activity within the organization, and the status of the function. Decisions here will often be linked to discussions as to whether learning is achieved most profitably through on-the-job activity, off-the-job methods, or a blend of both.

6.3.4 On-the-job training

This approach to training is consistently popular, especially when organizations face straitened economic times (CIPD 2011g). Cannell (1997) has described it as training that is planned and structured, and occurs at the trainee's usual place of work. It can vary in format and complexity, with the most commonly used methods involving observing a skilled worker, learning by doing, mentoring, shadowing, and job rotation, with the aim of teaching a set of skills that have been specified in advance. The process of working with a skilled worker remains a highly popular method, but the success of such an approach usually depends on the correct choice of exemplar and ensuring that they are capable of transmitting the requisite skills and knowledge effectively.

An alternative method of engaging in on-the-job training can be seen in e-learning. This mode of delivery is attractive to organizations and learners because the materials can be accessed at times to suit the individual, with the learner controlling the amount of time devoted to it with easy access to the relevant programmes anywhere in the world. It can encompass the use of CD-ROMs and DVDs as well as materials available through the internet or via company intranets. Whilst the development costs and the accumulation of a stock of e-learning resources can be costly, the method of distribution means that a large number of learners can access learning opportunities over time. Equally, the shelf-life of many e-learning programmes can be extensive as they are relatively easy to update. The example given in Box 6.6 shows the way in which a huge number of employees can access learning modules via this learning mode.

Box 6.6 Window on work
On-the-job training using e-learning

E-learning was set to play a vital part in training about 300,000 emergency services staff for the 'unprecedented demand' created by the London 2012 Olympic and Paralympic Games. An e-learning package had been developed by policing authorities to introduce the key safety and security demands that staff would face. The three-part online training package was used by 250,000 police and 50,000 fire and ambulance personnel. The first 30-minute interactive package included information on the Games' venues and torch relays, plus interviews with athletes and senior people from all three services (Churchard 2011).

Staff had to complete the first e-learning session by a given date, when a second package was released which gave more details on operational planning for the Games, command and control structures, operating procedures, and logistical arrangements. A final session was available prior to the games, and included an operational briefing for the police, ahead of the beginning of Games-related activity, such as the torch relay. Access to the first session was made available to local authorities, partners, volunteer groups, and those working on the Games. The aim of the training was to ensure that the police, fire, and ambulance services could prepare their staff flexibly for the Games in a cost-effective way (www.ufi.com).

6.3.5 Off-the-job training

This usually consists of courses organized by internal or external providers held away from the workplace. It could also include planned organizational experiences in other companies (such as suppliers and competitors). Whilst off-the-job training can provide a learning environment away from immediate work pressures and expose trainees to new ideas, it is commonly perceived to be less than effective if it is not directly related to 'real' organizational issues or perceived challenges in the future. For many organizations, operating on a global basis is a challenge. Box 6.7 illustrates how organizations face the task of developing managers who are able to operate internationally.

6.3.6 Evaluation

The final stage of the STC is evaluation. Whilst it is a key activity, the literature suggests that there is no consensus as to the best way to do it (Anderson 2007). One approach to evaluation adopts quantitative measures to measure the costs and benefits of any intervention, ascertaining whether or not a 'return on investment' can be calculated. Other approaches seek to evaluate at different levels—individual, departmental, or organizational. Different levels of evaluation will use different methods, becoming more complex and involving a wider range of stakeholders (Guerci and Vinante 2011). However, with the advent of more individualistic approaches to training and development and the increasing focus on continuous development, organizations are using different forms of evaluation which are more learner-centric than provider-focused (Edelenbos and van Buuren 2005).

Finally, although evaluation is a vital part of the systematic approach to training, employee development activities usually occur in busy working environments, making extended evaluation difficult (CIPD 2010c). In practice, companies often adopt a pragmatic approach. For example, the Sony Europe senior development programme uses an employee survey as well as a 360 degree feedback process six months after the course has ended to see what is emerging in terms of changed behaviour. However, the ultimate proof of the worth of the programme will be whether Sony is capable of filling key positions more quickly and effectively, and the opinions of its HR and organizational committee (Johnson 2007).

 Box 6.7 International focus
Management development in global companies

The need to develop managers who can deliver results in a globally competitive marketplace has never been more pressing (Tarique and Schuler 2010) (see Chapter 15). Most global organizations still regard international management development (IMD) as a vital way of making sure that they have the right people available to step into top jobs, and many use it to enhance their appeal as employers in a competitive recruitment market. For PricewaterhouseCoopers (PwC), following the corporate scandals and regulatory changes of recent years, internationally integrated management development has significantly increased in importance—one of the reasons why they created Genesis Park, a leadership development initiative, aimed at high-potential staff from across the globe with two to nine years of work experience (www.pwc.com/gx/en/genesis-park). This programme aims to grow future leaders, contribute to the development of PwC's business strategy, drive cultural change and help the firm retain its top performers. Between eight and sixteen individuals at a time go through the five-month programme. Scheduling ensures that intakes overlap with each other so that participants can share their experiences and act as coaches to the next batch. Projects that are either defined by the current group or handed on from an earlier intake form an important element of the programme. These projects revolve around live business issues sponsored by country operations or international functions, and there is also a strong emphasis on team development and individual growth (Pollard 2011). Three full-time coaches and educators help to move the focus towards the development of ideas and assist with the construction of business cases (Dickmann and Harris 2005).

6.3.7 Evaluating the STC

Given the need to plan training policies and activities, the STC helps ensure that training interventions and objectives are appropriate and avoids 'wrong' training occurring because of its focus on TNA, objective setting, and evaluation, thus providing a helpful framework for designers and facilitators.

Where criticisms are made concerning the STC, these tend to focus on the lack of integration between the cycle and business strategy, the changes in responsibility for training delivery from a dedicated function (where it existed) to line managers, and the failure to consider the individual learner (Donnelly 1987; Garavan, Heraty, and Barnicle 1999). Purcell and Hutchinson (2007) show that line-manager input is now highly influential in this area, but this is not reflected in the STC, which still places the professional trainer as the architect and deliverer of training and development with the learner as a passive recipient.

This devolved, strategic form of delivery is more likely to use team-based learning with an emphasis on the need for speedy transfer of knowledge to workplace activity and challenges. Whilst the STC can still be helpful in terms of providing a framework as to how training interventions can be effectively analysed and carried out, it now has to sit alongside other approaches. Box 6.8 provides an opportunity of engaging with one of its stages in practice.

 Summary and further reading

- The provision of any training or development intervention has to meet a perceived or actual need, and these needs should be accurately determined and enacted, increasingly involving learning occuring via engagement in workplace activities.

- All organizational functions face scrutiny as to their effective operation, and training and development activities are also subject to evaluation. In order to make a case for continued investment, there needs to be an ongoing evaluation of the benefits such activities bring to the company. This is not always easy to do; however, it is unlikely that investment will occur on the basis of faith alone.

- Within the STC, power is seen to lie with the designer and instructor, with trainees or learners having little or no power to determine or amend the curriculum or programme. As the training and development agenda has shifted to include notions of continuous development, with responsibility being devolved to the individual learner and their line manager, it could be argued that power and control have shifted away from the function/designer, with them now acting in a different capacity, facilitating learning rather than determining it.

Reid, Barrington, and Brown (2004) and Buckley and Caple (2007) cover the STC in detail. Sloman (2007), on behalf of the CIPD, is challenging the use of the STC.

6.4 Responses to heightened competition: the focus on learning

As illustrated in previous chapters, organizations continue to experience increasingly competitive business environments, often driven and sustained by developments in technology, as well as by customer demands. This has meant that companies face an imperative to innovate and

 Box 6.8 Skills exercise
Training needs analysis in practice

Job training needs analyses to find out the knowledge skills and relevant personal attributes (KSA) staff currently have who do a given job and to compare it against those KSAs believed to be important for good performance. In small groups, decide how you would assess the training needs for waiters and waitresses at a local family-oriented restaurant. What sources of information would you need? What data might you need to collect and how might you go about getting it? Present your findings.

to ensure that new products and services are swiftly delivered to market. These developments have involved many organizations reappraising the need to develop the intellectual capabilities of their employees, often looking at developing capabilities that are hard for competitors to copy in order to secure competitive advantage. Developments here have seen debate and practice shift from a 'learning by acquisition' approach, where the process occurs through more formal approaches, towards training to an engagement with learning via embedding it within routine daily work experiences. It has arguably been accompanied by a reorientation of the training and development function. This is outlined in Box 6.9.

6.4.1 The learning organization

The idea of the learning organization emerged in the 1990s although, as a concept, it has been in existence for much longer. A learning organization is one that seeks to learn from its environment, its employees, and their experiences, and applies what has been learned in terms of improving services and products. They are seen by some to be able to build the capability to adapt and confront change-related issues in order to prevail and excel, and to meet the challenges inherent in an unstable environment (Sackmann, Eggenhofer-Rehart, and Friesl 2009). Senge (1990), Pedler, Burgoyne, and Boydell (1991), and Garvin, Edmonson, and Gino (2008) have identified the characteristics that such an organization needs to possess. These include an organizational learning climate where learning is linked to organizational strategy, and where there is an internal exchange of ideas and knowledge, as well as the provision of self-development opportunities for all staff. However, it is a difficult concept to actualize and sustain (Garavan 1997), and it has been critiqued for its idealized accounts of learning activity (Ashton 1998). However, interest in the learning organization remains (Bui and Baruch 2011). The links outlined in Box 6.10 give an insight as to some key thinkers on the learning organization and their ideas.

Box 6.9 Practitioner perspective
The changing role of the trainer

Where the status of the training and development function is concerned, as noted by Keep (2007), there are two broad approaches to this debate. One argues that the function continues to be a backwater within many organizations with limited influence over the senior management team. The devolution of much training activity and responsibility to line managers might have resulted in a freeing up of specialists to engage in a more strategic role, but in practice this has often generated major problems for managers and trainers (Gibb 2002). Another trend here has been the tendency to outsource activities such as off-the-job training to external consultants and training providers; mirroring developments within the wider HR environment where an increasing volume of 'routine' activity has been contracted out—along with the function.

An alternative approach argues that the role of the trainer has become one of supporting, accelerating, and directing learning interventions which meet organizational needs and are appropriate to the learner and to the organization's context (Sloman 2007). This approach takes the view that the training function is moving from an isolated role to one where learning is seen as relevant to the needs of the business and learners and is integrated in work activities. The move towards a learning culture that this change in roles aims to achieve is seen as an aspiration and one that will take time. The heart of the model requires the roles and relationships of the stakeholders (line manager, employer, individual learner, and trainer/facilitator) to cohere in order to form a continuous integrated learning culture. This requires the employer to express a clear commitment to learning as a business driver, ensuring that sufficient resources are available. In turn, the line manager initiates opportunities for individuals to develop and apply their learning, with the employee taking ownership and responsibility, seeking out learning opportunities and acting upon them. Finally, the trainer/facilitator supports, directs, and accelerates learning interventions that meet organizational needs and are appropriate to the learner.

Box 6.10 Online video link
Learning and creativity at work

The issues of learning and creativity remain of concern to government, employers, managers and employees. The Online Resource Centre contains links to videos which offer some examples of experts talking about these issues. Think about how their ideas might translate into an organizational context.

6.4.2 The knowledge-creating company

Another approach shares similar features to that of the learning organization. Often termed the 'knowledge-creating company', this approach seeks to capture knowledge and experience, to share it, and to develop further learning through such sharing and collaboration (Nonaka 1991). What it adds to the concept and practices of the learning organization is a way of codifying learning and knowledge through an exploration of explicit learning, which is easily defined and capable of being passed on like a computer program, and tacit learning, which is highly personal, difficult to describe, and often associated with craft work or higher-order cognitive abilities.

Learning and knowledge that can be codified and explained is more easily shared. Given that many companies are not necessarily based in one location, the ability to transmit learning and knowledge becomes crucial. Many organizations have attempted to introduce a variety of methods of knowledge management. Knowledge management involves the management of information, knowledge, and experience available to an organization in order that the company's various activities can build on what is already known and extend it further (Mayo 1998). Initiatives here have frequently involved the development of networked software and company intranets to extend and develop the process. The reason for the growth of interest in knowledge management is not difficult to understand. For, if knowledge is a major source of competitive advantage, its capture, storage, and dissemination will form an essential resource for the company's intellectual capital. However, it has been argued that more attention has been paid to the systems and technologies of knowledge management than to exploring how learning occurs within the workplace, and how different kinds of knowledge, gained from a range of settings, require different methods of dissemination (Scarborough and Swan 2001; OECD 2004) as is demonstrated in Box 6.11.

6.4.3 Communities of practice

The more formal perspective on knowledge sharing and development witnessed in the knowledge-management approach to organizational learning has been accompanied by a different approach, which takes a cultural view of learning. This has proved popular, possibly because it focuses on the values, beliefs, and norms that are shared through talk, practices, and stories in a group and often determine the processes by which people learn. Therefore organization learning is concerned with what people do in their local situation and how learning can take place more informally. Crucially, it takes account of the learning context and illustrates how learning is a function of activities occurring at a local level. As shown by Lave and Wenger (1991), these processes often have the ability to transform an unskilled participant or worker, who is located at the periphery of the group, to a skilled involved member of a group or occupation over time. They are rarely associated with the kinds of intervention designed via the STC, and are often described as 'communities of practice' (CoPs).

Within CoPs, learning is strongly related to becoming a skilled practitioner within the group or community, and each CoP will have its own views as to what effective practice consists of. These practices are not easily understood by those outside it (which could include other organizational functions or departments), and it explains how so much insight and learning in an organization can remain hidden. Although they are informal and self-organizing, it is argued that managers can identify potential CoPs and provide an infrastructure of support so that they can

Box 6.11 Research in focus
Communities of practice and knowledge capture

Easterby-Smith and Mikhailava (2011) provide illustrations emphasizing the successes to be obtained by companies placing less reliance on pure IT solutions when engaging in knowledge capture and management. Where organizations have looked at people or social processes in sharing and exchanging knowledge as a natural part of work, and deploying IT to support them, there has been greater success.

Developing communities of practice at ABB

Engineering company ABB made a considerable commitment to developing face-to-face communities among service engineers responsible for maintaining industrial machinery. ABB's attempt was based on an already existing informal network of engineers who regularly communicated with one another seeking advice and support on various daily problems and professional encounters. Wanting to capitalize on this idea, the company decided to turn this informal communication into more organized and systematic initiative of knowledge and expertise sharing. In addition, the senior management also wanted to use this opportunity to increase the engineers' contribution to the business by using interactions with clients to identify where they could offer further services. As a result, based on existing regional divisions, monthly meetings of engineers were introduced. However, during these meeting, engineers ended up spending half the time listening to their line managers delivering company updates, and the other half running through their client visit reports. The new procedure was reviewed after a year as it was found that most of the engineers had stopped filling in visit reports, and the meetings had become a one-way process of information transfer from the managers to the engineers. Proposals for improvements were made by the engineers themselves. They concerned (a) minimizing the reporting requirements, (b) electing the community coordinator from their own number, (c) bottom-up agenda generation, and (d) regional focus and inter-group coordination, suggesting meetings across regions on a regular basis. These suggestions were later accepted by the company management and proved highly successful in terms of improving the quality of knowledge sharing and exchange of ABB's communities of practice.

Capturing knowledge from leavers at Airbus

The departure of highly skilled employees can be damaging to an organization, and aircraft manufacturer Airbus is keen to retain the technical knowledge and (largely tacit) experience of its leaver(s). In order to manage the process, the company uses a 'transfer cell' approach. The transfer begins six months before the scheduled departure of an employee, by establishing the 'cell'. It usually comprises the leaver, the receiver(s) (four or five colleagues related to the departing knowledge-holder), and a skilled knowledge-management facilitator, who manages the process of knowledge transfer between its members. An initial meeting is held to discuss and clarify expectations for the knowledge transfer. This usually leads to a series of one-to-one interviews between the leaver and the facilitator, during which key knowledge (expertise) is identified. To aid the process, mind-mapping is often used along with diaries and logs. The individual meetings result in group discussions that involve all members and aim to agree on a transfer plan. The plan represents series of actions (conversations, observations) that ought to take place to ensure the relocation of knowledge. The facilitator is there to monitor the progress and ensure that all planned actions take place. A final step is a formal closure meeting that reviews and reflects on the process as the whole.

become an important element of their company's success (Wenger and Snyder 2000). However, it should also be noted that these processes of learning are not necessarily amenable to control either by managers or by training and development practitioners. And, whilst they are a site of important learning, it could also be argued that they have the potential to resist change (as well as facilitate it) and close boundaries rather than be amenable to sharing.

6.4.4 Critiques of the learning approach

Although concepts like the learning organization and the knowledge-creating company have a degree of intuitive appeal, there are a number of weaknesses in these approaches. As argued by Garvin (1993), much of the writing and vocabulary surrounding these ideas is inaccessible and lacking in concrete ideas and frameworks for action. Chase's (1997) study of knowledge-creating organizations found that, whilst companies acknowledged the importance of creating, managing, and transferring knowledge, there was a seeming inability to translate this need into organizational strategies. His study also indicated that one of the biggest obstacles to creating a knowledge-creating company lies in organizational culture and the difficulties involved in creating and maintaining an appropriate one.

Some of the recommendations made on the basis of this evidence argue that cultures of trust, openness, and certainty need to be created. However, this is difficult, given that organizational operating environments are often uncertain. These experiences and debates illustrate that there are no easy prescriptions for using learning and knowledge as a strategic lever. It takes time to promote and provoke learning as a means of competitive advantage, which raises additional questions as to how HRM supports such initiatives. Finally, the kinds of learning and development activities used to install and develop learning offer distinctively different challenges to the more stable prescribed approaches embedded in the STC, and consequently require different skills from the function (where it exists) and the development of additional competencies for line managers tasked with developing their staff and fostering learning.

 ## Summary and further reading

- As organizations experience heightened competitive pressures, they have sought to achieve advantage not only through enhancing employees' skills through training, but also from the use of organizational experiences such as learning opportunities and a (re)visiting of the concept of the learning organization.

- Such learning needs to be shared and transmitted. But, whilst much attention has been given to electronic means of knowledge management, these approaches are not always the most fitting method of transmission, especially where forms of tacit learning are concerned.

- Although the concepts of the learning organization and the knowledge-creating company have intuitive appeal, they are difficult to create and maintain. This is largely due to the absence of blueprints for their development and the need for companies to develop their own path towards this ultimate goal.

- Such developments issue challenges for the training and development function. This has seen the trainer role move away from a focus on provision and delivery to one concerned with the identification and development of learning experiences.

- The movement towards learning and development arguably requires a different organizational culture in order for complex learning to occur and be shared. Communities of practice will usually have their own culture, and this will play a crucial role in shaping the ways in which learning occurs and how individuals move from being unskilled, and therefore somewhat peripheral in the community, to a position where they are skilled and established practitioners. Line managers and developers alike will be required to facilitate and nurture these supportive atmospheres, which raises a question as to how they will be equipped with the skills and knowledge to engage in such activities.

Pedler, Burgoyne, and Boydell (1991) developed a framework for organizations interested in becoming learning organizations. Other highly significant texts here include Senge (1990) and Nonaka (1991). Garvin's critique (1993) is also accompanied by suggestions as to how organizations might become learning organizations and has been highly influential because of this practical advice. Finally, where the CoP literature is concerned, Lave and Wenger (1991) provide a range of illustrations of CoPs in practice.

6.5 Conclusion

The inadequacies of training and development and the need for reform of the institutional frameworks in the UK have been a long-running issue within the HRM literature. Governmental reports, such as the Leitch Review of Skills, signal a degree of urgency occurring with reference to skills, highlighting the fact that the ability of organizations to do present and future jobs (which is roughly what training and development are most concerned with) has been, and will continue to be, critically affected by the wider national vocational and education system.

129

These points have been articulated by an increasingly broader band of commentators and policy-makers who, like Leitch, are urging a more general need for greater stress upon skills and knowledge as a source of competitive advantage. One of the arguments often made is that developed countries can no longer compete on the basis of price, but must offer customized tailor-made products and services, with competitive advantage being gained from the ability of organizations to do precisely that. Organizations consistently have to learn new things and to reconfigure the ways that they operate in order to develop and deliver these new products and services. Finally, there is believed to be a sustained shift throughout the developed world towards the knowledge-intensive industries and a rise in demand for knowledge workers.

One response has been to seek a long-term competitive advantage through the full use of employee skills and knowledge. To do this, organizations need to move from systems, processes, and cultures that have been traditionally been aimed at improving individual and group skills to those that support higher levels of collective learning with the aim of achieving competitive advantage. This is often associated with the learning organization and other learning-based approaches such as knowledge-management systems and practices or communities of practice. What underpins them, and their successful implementation, is a focus on the social context within which the learning takes place, as well as a more integrated approach towards training and development. However, it could be argued that these approaches are essentially at odds with the product market strategies of many companies, because they utilize relatively low-skill/ low-pay approaches and operationalize workplace power relations that are at odds with those needed to create the kinds of culture that support complex learning practices.

 ## Assignment and discussion questions

1 Using an organization with which you are familiar, discuss to what extent it uses the STC as a model for structuring training and development activity. Highlight where it is followed and where the organization might depart from it. Discuss the reasons why this adherence and departure might occur.

2 What are some of the implications of the Investors in People award for the HR and training and development functions in an organization?

3 How far should training and development benefit the organization or the individual?

4 What problems might organizations face when they seek to elicit and capture the tacit knowledge that employees possess?

5 Why has such an emphasis been placed on individual and organizational learning over the past two decades? What, if any, might be the pitfalls of such an approach to training and development?

 ## Online Resource Centre

Test your understanding of this chapter with online questions and answers, keep up to speed with changes to the law through regular updates, and use selected weblinks to quickly access useful resources and further information. Visit the Online Resource Centre at:
www.oxfordtextbooks.co.uk/orc/gilmore_williams2e/

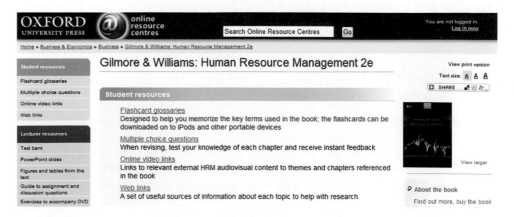

Case study
HRM and employee development at the National Theatre

The National Theatre (NT) is one of the UK's most successful and highly regarded theatres. It presents an eclectic mix of new plays and classics from the world repertoire, with seven or eight productions in repertory at any one time, and shows approximately eighteen new productions each year. Through an extensive programme of associated activities, such as education, research, and development (conducted at the NT Studio), as well as touring and collaborative ventures with a range of innovative theatre companies, it is firmly embedded within the UK's cultural fabric and plays a powerful role in the UK arts scene generally.

The objectives of the NT, as stated in its Annual Report (National Theatre 2011), are:

- to maintain and re-energize the great traditions of the British stage and to expand the horizons of audiences and artists alike;
- to reflect in its repertoire the diversity of British culture;
- to take a particular responsibility for the creation of new work—offering at the NT Studio a space for research and development for the NT's stages and the theatre as a whole;
- through its education programme, Discover, to engage tomorrow's audiences;
- to use its status as the national theatre to foster the health of the wider British theatre through policies of collaboration and touring.

The NT complex houses three theatres, the Olivier, the Lyttelton, and the Cottesloe. It also houses two restaurants and three coffee bars, with several other bars scattered around the complex adjacent to the three theatres; and it hosts a bookshop specializing in theatre, drama, and music. In addition to these functions, and in terms of fulfilling its outreach objectives, the NT also has an Education Department that works with a range of students and teachers as well as a studio facility that is the NT's centre for research and development. At its base on The Cut in Waterloo it provides workspaces where new and established writers, directors, and artists can experiment, develop ideas, and develop their skills. Although it receives some funding each year from the Arts Council, the overwhelming majority of the NT's income comes from ticket sales and commercial sponsorship, as well as from income from its various trading outlets. Therefore, it is evident that the NT is a complex operation spanning the commercial as well as the theatrical worlds.

Managing the NT's HRM activities will have its challenges. The organization employs approximately 1000 staff across its operations and, whilst an efficient and effective delivery of services to a range of stakeholders will be required, it could be argued that this on its own is insufficient because the standards expected of a *national* theatre are much higher than those of its commercial counterparts.

Questions

1 To what extent could government initiatives such as Investors in People and NVQs be used effectively by the NT? Where might they work well and where might they be less effective and why? You might find it helpful to access the NT's website (www.nationaltheatre.org.uk) and assess the range of departments and the nature of their work.

2 How would you construct a TNA for NT staff who work in the various trading outlets such as the box office, bars, or catering outlets? What methods would you use and why?

3 Having completed question 2, design a short session on an issue of your choice that would be relevant to this occupational group. You might like to consider issues such as induction, health and safety, or customer service. How would you deliver such a programme, given that the building and some of the services operate long hours, with staff working full time, part time, and on shifts?

4 How would you evaluate the success of your intervention?

In developing your answers, you might find it helpful to access the practitioner interview with the NT's Head of Personnel.

7 Rewarding people at work

Stephen Pilbeam

Learning objectives

The main objectives of this chapter are:

- to explain the nature of reward strategy and the total reward concept;
- to evaluate the principal characteristics of graded pay, market-related pay, and performance-related pay strategies;
- to identify the role of non-financial and financial benefits within total reward strategies;
- to raise awareness of emerging and declining reward trends, and their location within the wider organizational context.

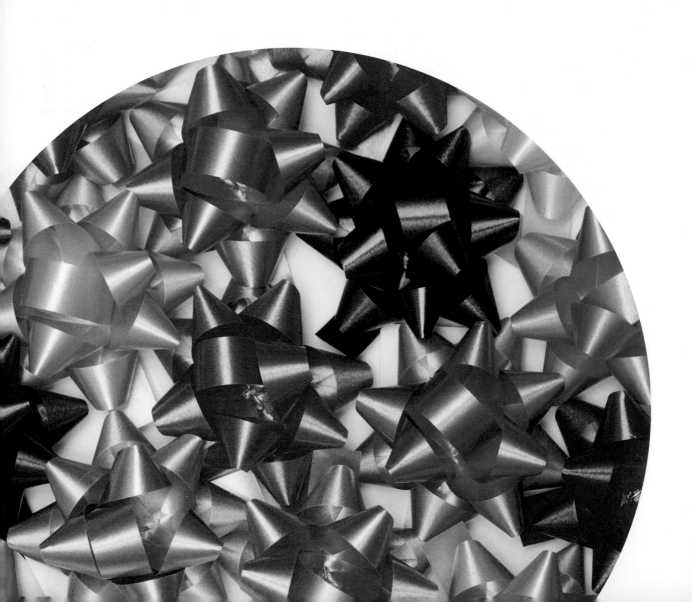

7.1 Introduction to reward management

Reward management is an essential HRM activity because pay and benefits—together with non-financial intrinsic rewards—can have a powerful influence on the recruitment and retention of employees, employee performance, and identification with business goals. Trends in reward are shaped by wider political and economic forces, and the UK has witnessed the promotion of enterprise cultures contributing to the imposition of reward strategies that seek to pay employees for performance rather than time served with the organization.

In the early part of the twenty-first century lower levels of price inflation reduced the significance of pay determination based principally on cost of living pay increases and also provided greater scope for the individualization of pay. During the same period lower levels of unemployment created conditions whereby employers often had to compete for available labour, and this stimulated greater employer interest in pay strategies which aimed to ensure that employers could recruit and retain talented individuals from the available labour market supply. The economic crisis, which commenced in 2008, has created downward pressure on pay and threatened to override the concern with competing for talent with a preoccupation for cost minimization, with consequent reductions in pay increases, pay freezes, and in some cases reductions in pay. Increasing unemployment and higher levels of redundancies all exert a suppressive effect on pay and reduce the power of employees, individually and collectively, to negotiate pay.

In this chapter, the term 'reward' tends to be used in preference to 'pay'. This is because employees increasingly expect more than pay for their efforts. 'Reward', is now being used as a holistic term within a contemporary HRM context, representing a portfolio of managerial practices where financial and non-financial elements are flexibly directed at enabling and rewarding employees who add value in the interests of competitive advantage. It also needs to be recognized that there is no such thing as perfect pay and reward strategies and practices. Organizations have to start from where they are, and typically responses to issues concerning reward strategy involve 'best fit' with contingency approaches usually being adopted (Armstrong 2000, 2005).

Therefore in this context it is necessary to be able to understand the notion of total reward, the concept of new pay, the principal pay strategies, the range of financial benefits, and the important role of non-financial rewards. To achieve this, the chapter is divided into a number of main sections. The strategic approaches taken towards reward will be outlined and discussed before focusing on the principle approaches taken towards the allocation of pay. The chapter will conclude with an exploration of contemporary issues concerning reward, some of which have a degree of longevity.

7.2 Strategic approaches to reward

Reward strategy presents an opportunity for organizations to encourage desirable behaviours and promote objective-based employee performance through the selective deployment of rewards upon their attainment. In this way, rewards are a potentially sophisticated HRM lever that can encourage heightened performance because the rewarding of better performers through better pay has the potential to lead to improved staff retention as well as deliver business-focused objectives. In essence *reward strategy* involves the organization in thinking ahead to set a strategic course which aligns the reward practices with business goals, its culture, and the environment in which it operates (Armstrong and Brown 2001: 83).

There is a need to balance three perspectives: the employer, employee, and cost perspectives. The employer perspective involves achieving a reward strategy which fosters the knowledge, competence, and behaviours necessary for business success, the employee perspective involves ensuring that the reward strategy is attractive, and the cost perspective has to ensure that the reward strategy is affordable and sustainable. In this context the purpose of reward strategy is clear, it is an HRM tool to be used to generate desired employee performance and behaviours in the pursuit of business goals, and the key objective is to achieve alignment with the business strategy to improve employee performance (CIPD 2011i), as illustrated in Figure 7.1.

Business direction—mission and strategy

Internal context

External context

Desired employee competence, performance, and behaviours—the culture

Reward strategy characteristics—integrated with other HR strategies

Labour market characteristics

Reward values, policies, and practices

Affordability dimension

Figure 7.1 Reward strategy—vertically integrated, deterministic, and unitary.

This sequential approach to reward strategy assumes the rational development of business strategy and is, of course, quite deterministic. It fits with a unitary employment relations perspective which extends managerial prerogative to include reward decisions. However, it is possible to challenge this viewpoint. For example, collective representation and the extent to which employees are partners in determining the reward strategy, through some form of co-determination, will influence the reward outcomes. Different interests are being pursued within an organization at any time and they cannot all be subsumed too easily in the pursuit of business goals (White and Druker 2000).

Therefore a reward strategy aims first to ensure that employee rewards are driven by organization needs and not historical practices, secondly, to articulate core principles in relation to what is valued, recognized, and rewarded by management, and, thirdly, to establish responsibilities and accountabilities for reward management. Thus the managerial rationale for having a reward strategy is to clarify organizational values, to provide a coherent sense of purpose, and to promote a consistency between employee results and behaviour and key organizational goals. This is illustrated with some organizational examples in Box 7.1. Survey evidence supports the trend of reward strategy within a contemporary HRM approach being increasingly directed at encouraging employee behaviours and performance which promote and enable the achievement of organizational objectives. This involves the pursuit of the managerial goal of employee engagement with their work, their manager, and the objectives of the organization (CIPD 2011*i*).

7.2.1 Old pay and new pay

'*New pay*' and its juxtaposed stereotypical opposite of '*old pay*' are concepts which are used to distinguish between contemporary and traditional reward practices. Old pay is characterized by bureaucratic salary administration, organizational hierarchy, rigid job evaluation and grading systems, incremental progression, the lack of horizontal integration with other HR activities, and the detachment of pay from the strategic objectives of the organization. In the twenty-first century, old pay, it is alleged, inhibits organizational responsiveness and development in more turbulent organizational environments. New pay can be viewed as a functional adaptation to changes in the external context and increasing competitive pressures. These external influences are demanding flatter, leaner, and more flexible organizational forms, and this includes new forms of reward. The prime characteristics of new pay are first the pursuit of the integration of pay with corporate strategy in order to achieve organizational objectives and commercial imperatives, and, secondly, the use of pay and reward as a sophisticated lever to apply pressure

Box 7.1 Research in focus
Reward strategy examples

Organizations have increasingly taken a more strategic approach to the management of reward issues (Armstrong 2005). For example, the Royal Bank of Scotland articulates the impact of strategic reward as follows:

- expressing what the organization values and being prepared to pay for what it gets from employees;
- providing a sense of purpose and direction;
- integrating with business and HR strategy;
- valuing people according to their contribution;
- being driven by a total reward philosophy.

Glaxo–Wellcome, as a world leader in pharmaceutical research and knowing that long-term investment is needed for survival at the top, has a reward strategy of paying salaries at the upper quartile level to attract, develop, and retain quality research staff. Dow Chemicals has a strategy of recognizing the quality of performance of both employees and the business.

Textron uses rewards to support a strategy of employee flexibility through skills-based pay, while the Whitbread Beer Company and Vauxhall both use rewards to encourage initiative and innovations. Organizations have identified specific competencies, such as customer service, effective communication, teamworking, and a focus of quality, which can differentiate them from their competitors. Volkswagen, Scottish Equitable, Guinness, Royal Bank of Scotland, and ICL have job evaluation schemes based entirely on competencies (Stredwick 2000: 8–9).

to employee performance. New pay fits well with contemporary HRM doctrines by seeking to reward individuals in line with managerial perceptions of their worth to the organization.

Therefore new pay is focused on managing financial reward in order to 'send the right messages' about flexibility, performance, and corporate values to employees. The emphasis is on rewarding contribution rather than seniority or status. New pay incorporates two key reward themes:

- a connection between employee pay and employee performance as a variable incentive linked to corporate objectives through a performance management process;
- a market-related approach to pay and benefits to reflect the commercial worth.

Employees are rewarded for assuming and developing roles, displaying values, exhibiting behaviours (e.g. in relation to flexibility, customer orientation, and product quality), and pursuing performance objectives which are determined by management. One possible source of evidence for these trends is the significant reduction in the number of organizations structuring pay using narrow-graded pay structures (CIPD 2011i). New pay is overtly managerialist, and in the absence of any regulation through employee representation promotes a unitary employment relationship. However, skills or labour market shortages may empower employees to determine reward arrangements, and this contextual factor clearly undermines any prescription in reward approaches.

7.2.2 Pay determination

Pay determination in essence means how pay is determined within a particular organization—basically is it by employers or by employees, or through a process of co-determination? Where trade unions are recognized for collective bargaining purposes, co-determination can be said to exist, and this will constrain managerial prerogative to unilaterally decide pay and other terms and conditions of employment. The existence of arrangements for the co-determination of pay, normally where a trade union is recognized, will introduce a plurality of perspectives regarding the objectives of a reward strategy which will explicitly recognize employee voice, and in this case more traditional types of graded pay strategies will prevail.

This co-determination, which reflects a pluralistic approach to employment relationships, only occurs in around a fifth of organizations. However, the decline in collective bargaining is largely confined to the private sector, where it is present in 11 per cent of organizations. In the public sector, and reflecting higher levels of trade union membership, pay is co-determined in over three-quarters of organizations (Kersley et al. 2006: 182). There remains a higher incidence of 'old pay' approaches with the emphasis on job grades, incremental pay progression, and equity, influenced by the presence of unions who often resist attempts by management to strengthen managerial prerogative through the introduction pay for performance strategies.

Outside the public sector, however, unilateral pay determination by management is by far the most common form of pay-setting arrangement. This reflects the growing trend, associated with contemporary HRM practices and the rise of 'new pay', where managers unilaterally assert the right to manage the pay relationship, reflecting a unitary approach to the employment relationship. In the private sector pay for performance is the managerial mantra and reflects this increased unilateralism in pay, because performance judgements and the selective allocation of pay are principally managerially determined. Performance pay is often referred to as variable pay because worker pay varies according to a managerial judgement of performance or contribution. Basically employee performance is rewarded through increased pay and rewards. Again, we can identify how pay, in being related to employee performance, seeks to achieve the strategic alignment of employee effort and performance with managerially determined organizational objectives. Marsden (2004: 130–1) argues that the employer interest in variable performance-related pay, in preference to co-determination in pay, is motivated by the managerial desire '…to make their organizations more responsive to more competitive and faster changing markets by devolving decision-making and relying more on heavily employee initiative'.

7.2.3 The total reward concept

Total reward is a contemporary HRM term and is exerting considerable influence on approaches to contemporary reward (CIPD 2011i). It describes employers' attempts to combine pay, employment benefits (these are explored later in this chapter), and non-financial rewards in order to improve the recruitment, retention, motivation, and performance of employees. While organizations should not underestimate the power of pay as a means of attracting and retaining staff, non-financial rewards may be more effective at generating long-term commitment and motivation (Armstrong and Brown 2005). The DVD interview with Richard Solly from the Havant Citizens Advice Bureau highlights the importance of these non-financial rewards in the third sector, where organizations do not have the ability to pay exceptional pay rates but compete on other bases.

Total reward approaches recognize that employees have diverse needs and that, whilst pay is important, economic motivation varies in potency (i.e. in its force and strength) between employees. Therefore total reward operates at the top end of Maslow's hierarchy (Maslow 1987) in the areas of self-esteem, the esteem of others, and the self-actualization drive. Non-financial benefits are also described as intangibles and are principally intrinsic to the individual, in contrast with the tangible and more extrinsic rewards of pay and financial benefits.

These intrinsic and intangible benefits are referred to as non-financial because there is not necessarily a direct and quantifiable cost to the organization, as there is with pay and financial benefits, and the motivational potency is derived from within the individual. Clearly there are also linkages with Herzberg's two-factor theory of hygiene and motivation factors (Herzberg 1959). Three non-financial reward clusters can be identified—work–life balance for employees; recognition, development, and self-actualization; and the work environment and the work itself.

Pay and benefits are only part of the reward picture; other aspects that affect the quality of an individual's working life include, for example, learning and development opportunities, a stimulating work environment, effective leadership styles, and employee involvement in decision-making. The conceptual basis for total reward is that of configuration or bundling, so that different reward processes are interrelated, complementary, and mutually reinforcing.

The application of non-financial reward includes:

- redesigning work to provide greater variety, identity, significance, autonomy, discretion, and feedback, together with concern with the health of the physical and psychological work environment;

- providing symbolic rewards where appropriate (e.g. the recognition aspects of 'employee of the month' designation) and creating a managerial culture of positive feedback, praise, and recognition;

- investing in people as a reward through facilitating access to training and development, plus opportunities to engage in new workplace learning experiences;

- providing flexible work patterns, greater time sovereignty for individuals, and wellness activities.

Total reward is an employer reward philosophy which is aims to be responsive to the consumerist world of employment through employer branding and the pursuit of becoming an employer of choice, enhancing the attractiveness of the 'value proposition' to employees—in other words, recognizing that individuals have differing needs and that rewards need to be customised for 'reward consumers'. A total reward approach also fits with promoting employment benefit choice for employees through the deployment of flexible employment benefits as illustrated in Box 7.2.

An advantage of a total reward approach is that it has the potential to enhance the reputation of an organization as an employer of choice, through its capacity to place a value on the non-basic pay and wider non-financial benefits of working for that organization. Employees have traditionally been unaware of the costs to the employer of benefits such as pensions, which can be very substantial. Therefore the use of total reward is associated with the desire to communicate to employees the value of their employment package. Employers are increasingly providing employees with total reward statements that identify the value not only of basic pay but also the wider benefits package. However, the value of intrinsic and non-financial rewards, which will vary between individuals, is more difficult to communicate. Dewhurst, Gutridge, and Mohr (2009) report that the three non-financial rewards of praise from immediate managers,

Box 7.2 Practitioner perspective
Total reward at Eden Trust, Cambridgeshire County Council, and Lands' End

Organizations can achieve success with a total reward approach to make up for an inability to offer high salaries. The Eden Trust has pioneered a range of innovative benefits, including on-site yoga, podiatry, and massages. High-performing employees are nominated for one-off bonuses, vouchers for the shop, or a one-to-one lunch with Eden's chief executive. Workers are also entered into a draw to take an extra week's annual leave. Total reward makes working for Eden rewarding, but not only through the pay packet. This suggests that companies should try new ideas concerning total reward, including a range of intrinsic and extrinsic rewards.

Cambridgeshire County Council has adopted a total reward strategy and overhauled every aspect of pay and benefits, including terms and conditions, childcare vouchers, training, and flexible working. It also communicates the range of rewards on offer, both financial and non-financial, to all employees. Reward and recognition are seen by its HR Director as being part of the Council's strategic approach to managing people—one that has seen average sick absence rates amongst the 18,000 employees fall from ten to six days, employee satisfaction improving, staff turnover for key roles falling, and recruitment for difficult posts becoming easier.

At Lands' End, the mail-order clothing retailer, total reward covers the whole employment relationship from financial rewards to appreciation, challenging work, leader relations, and involvement. With this broad definition, total reward resembles much of contemporary HRM, but places an emphasis on delivery, with a key role for front-line managers.

leadership attention combined with one-to-one contact, and, where there is growth, a chance to lead on tasks may be more effective than financial incentives.

However, total reward poses some challenges. Employers are better at integrating financial aspects of pay and benefits into a total reward approach than the non-financial aspects. If line managers do not support the organization's commitment to total reward, for example over flexible working and providing recognition and development opportunities, the approach is likely to fail. It can also be difficult to meet everyone's requirements—for example, in matters of work space. A further difficulty in developing a total reward package, beyond the challenge of supplying certain rewards, is attempting to measure or weigh their value against one another, particularly if the aim is to include a tangible value in total reward statements distributed to employees.

When organizations experience wider economic difficulties, this curtails their ability to use pay and benefits to reward employees, and this has increased the focus on deploying non-financial rewards to extract employee engagement. But non-financial rewards will not compensate where base pay and benefits are being eroded, so this poses a challenge for advocates of non-financial rewards. Attempts by managers to fall back on the 'you are lucky to have a job' reward may have a consequential impact on the health of the psychological contract between the employer and the employee.

 Summary and further reading

- Contemporary approaches towards reward strategy are increasingly driven by the organization's business needs and seek to achieve an alignment between organizational goals and the ways they are leveraged by the provision of targeted rewards for performance outcomes. In this way, rewards directly and indirectly articulate core management principles, and these are increasingly performance oriented.

- A shift has also occurred in relation to reward strategy, evident in a move away from 'old pay' schemes to 'new pay' approaches. This has involved the rejection of rewards based on seniority, status, longevity of job tenure, and historical practices. 'New pay' strategies now use reward as a lever to apply pressure on performance through its strategic integration with the goals of the company. The advent of 'new pay' has also witnessed a concern with aligning rewards with the labour market in order to reflect the commercial worth of employee performance.

- Employee performance and business strategy are contained within the ambit of reward strategy. This is evident through the alignment being sought between employee performance, organizational goals, and the consequent attainment of rewards. New pay approaches, concerned with sending out the 'right' messages concerning the need for employee flexibility, place a premium on the effective demonstration of this attribute. However, whilst rewards can foster performance-oriented behaviours, they are only one element by which they are attained. Other elements of a reward strategy, such as non-financial rewards, and an employee's experience of the organization will also play a powerful role.

- Finally, new pay approaches are often assessed as being overtly managerialist and determined by the employer, suggesting that the power relationship in this area overwhelmingly favours one party to the employment relationship. In those, largely public sector, organizations where trade unions have collective bargaining agreements, pay co-determination is more likely to exist. This may act as a constraint on the unilateral ability of management to determine pay and conditions.

The CIPD's annual reward surveys are useful illustrations of organizational trends and activities in this area, as are those by the Chartered Management Institute. Perkins and White (2010) are helpful with reference to trends in public sector reward, and Armstrong and Brown (2005) also provide a broad overview which includes the private sector.

7.3 Principal pay strategies (1): graded and labour market pay

The main pay strategies adopted by organizations are outlined in this section and Section 7.4. This section will cover graded and labour market pay approaches; the following section will explore performance-related pay (PRP).

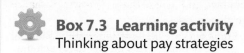

Box 7.3 Learning activity
Thinking about pay strategies

Can you attribute each of the three main pay strategies in to the circles?
Where might tensions and some mixing and matching occur and why?

The pay strategy for a particular organization will be constrained by, first, the existing pay arrangements; secondly, the managerially desired reward strategy values; thirdly, the extent of any co-determination of pay by worker representatives; and, fourthly, affordability. It is important to emphasize that there are few pure pay strategies of each type, and in reality pay strategies are hybridized to achieve the best fit. Nonetheless, it is useful to identify and explore the characteristics of each of the three pay strategies in order to promote understanding. In essence graded pay reflects the *relative worth* of an employee, in other words relative to the importance of the job that an employee does; labour-market-related pay reflects the *commercial worth* of an employee, in relation to the value of the employee in the labour market; and performance-related pay reflects the *individual worth* of an employee, in relation to a managerial assessment of an individual's performance and behaviours. Each of these pay strategies is addressed in turn, but they all, in having different but desirable objectives, produce some tensions and lead to hybridization (mix and match) of pay strategies. These are exposed in the learning activity in Box 7.3.

7.3.1 Graded pay

A graded pay strategy is based on the idea that some jobs are more important to an organization than others and therefore a rank order of relative job importance is established prior to the allocation of rates of pay. A simple example of this is where, in a large office, there might be administrative assistants, administrative officers, and executive administrative officers. The executive officer jobs would have greater responsibility and require a wider range of administrative competencies and consequently would be ranked higher in importance, or relative worth, to the organization than the administrative officers and administrative assistants. Being ranked higher, the executive administrative officers would receive a higher rate of pay.

Within each job grade, there will be a range of pay available and traditionally pay progression within a grade (sometimes referred to, confusingly, as a 'band') depends on length of service. The employee will receive an annual increment each year until the top of the scale is reached. The underlying premise is that the longer an employee spends in a job, the greater their acquisition of skills and knowledge. If the job does not change or the job-holder does not move to a higher-grade job, there is no scope for further pay increases above the annual award. Therefore this approach is consistent with a strategy that rewards experience, loyalty, and commitment to the organization, but is less consistent with a strategy geared towards rewarding performance. Graded pay has traditionally been used within the public sector; however, a hybrid model is gaining popularity. This combines elements of graded incrementalism, as well as elements of performance measurement and market-related supplements in order to achieve multiple pay strategy aims.

Graded-pay structures with incremental progression provide managerial challenges. First, incremental progression based on time served lacks direct motivational potency because each employee receives the annual increment. Secondly, the potential rigidity of narrowly banded structures constrains an organization seeking structural change, a greater emphasis on team-working, or greater work flexibility. The pursuit of reward strategies aligned to business objectives is contributing to a decline in narrow-banded grade structures based on incremental progression. In addition, changes within the public sector, such as the emphasis on customer service and the externalization of services to third-party providers, is generating greater managerial freedom to make changes to existing graded-pay schemes. One change that enables greater flexibility is the broad-banding of graded-pay structures.

139

7.3.2 Broad-banding

Broad-banding means compressing the hierarchy of pay grades into a smaller number of wide bands, typically four or five, thus instigating broader pay bands. This means that each pay band spans the pay opportunities that were previously covered by several pay ranges (CIPD 2006b).

Organizations most suited to the introduction of broad-banding are those that have delayered, and become leaner and flatter. Where organizations have seen declining opportunities for promotion, but simultaneously been faced with the demand for multi-skilling and flexibility, broad-banding has been heralded as a means by which a focus on lateral career movement and development can be attained within the different bands. However, limited opportunities for promotion may mean that employees are resistant to lateral development opportunities if the consequence is a detrimental effect on pay. Broad-banding aligns the reward strategy with other HR strategies which encourage lateral career movement. It also gives the manager greater freedoms by helping to eliminate an obsession with grades and instead encouraging employees to move to jobs where they can develop careers and add value to the organization. The potential benefits of broad-banded pay structures include:

- increasing flexibility in pay management and facilitating greater line management involvement in pay determination;
- rewarding lateral development and continuous improvement;
- clarifying career paths;
- responding to the changing nature of work and employee expectations.

A move from narrow bands to broad bands presents challenges because employees in lower grades may be concerned that promotion opportunities have disappeared, whilst those in the higher grades may perceive that their job has been devalued. However, broad-banding enables lateral job moves to be viewed by the employee as an opportunity for self-development and by the employer as an opportunity to enhance workforce skills.

7.3.3 Job evaluation and graded pay

Job evaluation is a systematic, but not scientific, way of determining the relative worth of jobs within a graded-pay structure by providing the means for ranking jobs in a hierarchy. Fundamental to this process is the fact that it is the job and not the job-holder that is being evaluated. The job-holder is then paid at the rate for the job. The main evaluation methods are as follows.

Job ranking This is the simplest job evaluation method. Whole jobs are compared with one another and ranked on the basis of whether one job is considered to be of more value than another. Job descriptions, or accountability profiles, are produced for all jobs within the organization. Benchmark jobs, which are representative of the range of jobs in the organization, are identified and ranked; other jobs are compared with the benchmark jobs and are inserted into the hierarchy based on the perceived value of the job. The process is subjective and subject to stereotyping, preconceptions, and misconceptions, lacks transparency, and would not provide a defence in an equal pay claim. However, it is a low-cost scheme which can be undertaken quickly, and is perhaps suitable for small employers.

Job classification This is a job evaluation method which measures jobs against predetermined classifications, grade definitions, or role profiles. The three stages in developing and implementing a job classification scheme are:

- the grade definitions or role profiles have to be drawn up and agreed for those jobs being evaluated;
- a job description must be produced for each job to be evaluated;
- each job description is matched to the definition that most closely reflects the duties and responsibilities of the job, and the appropriate grade is assigned.

This method is most commonly used in large bureaucratic organizations with a fairly rigid hierarchy and where there are many jobs of a particular type—for example, teachers, nurses, and civil servants.

Points rating scheme This scheme starts with the definition of a number of factors that are common to all jobs, such as responsibilities, skills, decision-making, and job complexity. The factors are weighted to reflect their importance to the job through different points maxima being available for different factors. Each job is then scored to produce a points score for the job and thereby position the job relative to other jobs. Box 7.4 uses an example taken from the NHS to evaluate a range of jobs, showing the factors and their respective weightings. Each job can be judged against these factors, with the resultant score out of 1000 establishing the rank position.

Each job factor will be accompanied by definitions of what constitutes a low, middle, or high score. Each job is then attributed to a pay grade. To continue with our example, the NHS has nine grades of pay, although grade eight has four subdivisions (and therefore effectively twelve grades). Each NHS grade has a range of pay available, with four to nine incremental steps within the grade. This NHS job evaluation system enables the comparison and ranking of jobs as diverse as nurses, hospital porters, administrators, and senior managers. It establishes a hierarchy of relative worth and allocates a pay grade, as illustrated in Box 7.5. The NHS scheme is also an example of the hybridization of pay strategy in that within the scheme it is possible to pay a recruitment and retention premium for specific positions where labour market pressures would otherwise inhibit the recruitment and retention of staff in sufficient numbers at the normal pay rate for the job. As such, the NHS scheme, although being fundamentally a graded-pay strategy, is also incorporating a labour-market-related strategy.

The generation of a numerical job score gives the impression of accuracy, but job evaluation is neither scientific nor completely accurate as subjective (human) decisions are taken at several stages of the process—at the factor stage, at the factor level stage, and at the weighting stage. Therefore there are several opportunities for bias and stereotyping to occur. However, points rating job evaluation is a systematic and reasonably transparent, and defensible, method (as it is recognized by employment tribunals as an 'analytical' approach) of establishing the relative worth of jobs—a necessary prerequisite to a graded pay strategy.

 Box 7.4 Policy example
Points rating job evaluation factors and weighting in the NHS, 2010

Job factor	Maximum points available
Communication and relationship skills	60
Knowledge, training, and experience	240
Analytical skills and judgement	60
Planning and organization skills	60
Physical skills	60
Responsibility—patient/client care	60
Responsibility—policy and service development	60
Responsibility—financial and physical resources	60
Responsibility—staff/leadership/training	60
Responsibility—information resources	60
Responsibility—research and development	60
Freedom to act	60
Physical effort	25
Mental effort	25
Emotional effort	25
Working conditions	25

Box 7.5 Policy example
Points score and pay bands in the NHS, 2011

Points score for a job	Pay grade	Pay band (£ per annum, 2011)
0–160	1	13,903–14,614
161–215	2	13,903–17,003
216–270	3	15,860–18,827
271–325	4	18,402–21,798
326–395	5	21,176–27,625
396–465	6	25,528–34,189
466–539	7	30,460–40,157
540–584	8a	38,851–46,621
585–629	8b	45,254–55,945
630–674	8c	54,454–67,134
675–720	8d	65,270–80,810
721–765	9	77,079–97,478

7.3.4 Labour-market-related pay

A market-related pay strategy signifies an approach where pay and benefits practice is sharply responsive to the rates of pay in the external labour market. This means that pay rates reflect the market price for labour and incorporates the philosophy of a particular job being 'worth' what the labour market commands at any one time. Market-related pay is based on classical economic theory, where pay decisions are influenced by market supply and demand for labour. Where supply of labour exceeds demand this will tend to suppress levels of pay; conversely, where the demand for work or skills of a particular kind exceeds supply there will be a tendency for upward pressure on pay. In order to secure the quality and quantity of employees required, employers adjust pay and reward packages to reflect the 'going rate'. Therefore market-related pay focuses primarily on external relativities and the 'commercial worth' of employees rather than on establishing the 'relative worth' of jobs within an organization.

This approach enables an employer to compete more effectively for the workers it requires and therefore it is an important consideration in developing reward strategy. However, labour markets are not perfect and employers cannot simply rely on market-related pay to deliver all pay strategy objectives. They also have to consider the impact that such a strategy would have on perceptions of equity and fairness as well as the extent to which the organization has the ability to pay the going rate. Therefore market-related pay is a question of emphasis rather than the sole basis for making reward decisions.

Establishing the market rate is probably best viewed as the identification of a range of pay for a particular type of work, within which decisions can be made about organizational positioning within the range. Therefore identifying the market rate or range serves to inform wider reward decisions within this approach. A prerequisite to establishing and interpreting market rates is the identification of market rates for specified jobs. This is not an exact science because collecting labour market information does not produce a single pay figure which can be relied upon as 'the market rate'—it is only information that can be used to inform reward decisions. However, the tracking of labour market rates of pay is important where the objective is to recognize the external labour market in reward policy.

Comprehensive and accurate information is difficult to acquire, but a number of sources can be used for survey purposes. These include surveys of other organizations that compete in the same labour market, subscriptions to data sources, analysing the pay information in job advertisements, employment agencies, and job centres, and collecting pay data at exit interviews. The raw data are then analysed by calculating the mean average for a given job and the median or mid-point to compensate for extremes in the data set, and establishing upper and

lower quartiles to define the market rate of the in terms of the top 25 per cent and the bottom 25 per cent of the organizations in the survey.

These statistical measures, as well as making comparison easier, will also enable decisions to be made about organization positioning within the market rate range. Market range positioning decisions will be based on beliefs about whether or not paying more for staff buys better performance and the company's financial ability to do so. Prime examples of organizations which place considerable weight on ensuring that pay rates enable them to compete for scarce labour resources are IBM, BT, and Xerox GB. Moreover, public sector organizations increasingly factor local market rates into pay decisions. But however and wherever such schemes are operationalized, market intelligence and general economic conditions are key to employer decisions. Pay is more likely to be suppressed in markets where there are difficult economic conditions and high unemployment; whereas in markets where organizations have to compete for talent, pay rates will tend to rise.

Summary and further reading

This section has examined graded and labour-market pay strategies. Whilst they have been presented as almost 'ideal types' or exemplars, in practice these strategies have been subject to a high degree of hybridization in order to achieve the best fit with the organization or organizational sector to which they are being introduced.

- Each approach uses pay to reward different employee behaviour and structures pay allocation in different ways. Graded pay tends to reward long-term service to the company and is associated with the implicit belief that this will result in employees gaining knowledge and experience. In contrast, broad-banding rewards flexibility, multi-skilling, and lateral, as opposed to traditional vertical, career paths. Through its association with flatter and learner organizational structures, it has provided organizations with a means of responding to the changing nature of work and employee expectations. This has some resonance with labour-market pay approaches where changes in the labour market—especially supply and demand for labour—will impact on the employment and contractual relationship via the mechanism of pay. Under such systems it is the employee's commercial worth in the market that is rewarded, and not the relative worth of his/her job within an organizational setting.

Some useful texts on the issues highlighted in this section include Armstrong's (2012) reward handbook, Perkins and White (2011), and the discussion on pay and reward in Pilbeam and Corbridge (2010).

7.4 Principal pay strategies (2): performance-related pay

Performance-related pay (PRP) describes pay systems where the pay received by the employee is varied according to the work output achieved. PRP is also known as incentive pay or variable pay; the incentive is provided through the carrot of more pay for more output, and the variable dimension reflects the reality that pay may go up or down each pay period according to the measurement of performance. PRP comprises not only what used to be known as payment by results, where work output is measured and pay adjusted accordingly, for example commission payments, which depend on sales achieved or output of garments produced in clothes production factory, but also merit-based approaches in which individual pay is related to a managerial judgement of the individual's worth to the organization. These merit-based approaches have the potential to strengthen the right to manage and align employee performance with organizational objectives. Overall, PRP is principally unitary in perspective and associated with the new pay theme introduced earlier in this chapter.

PRP consists of three sequential stages. First, a form of measurement needs to be established and whilst this may be relatively easy in some jobs such as sales or factory production, it clearly becomes more challenging for jobs with less tangible outputs. How, for example, would you measure the outputs of a surgeon or an HR manager? In order to address this measurement challenge many organizations use one of the following four measures which may be combined:

- performance indicators;
- acquisition or utilization of competencies;

- achievement of job objectives;
- appraisal rating.

Secondly, once the performance measures are established, there needs to be a system of measuring individual employee performance against those measures. This is normally done by the employee's manager which makes the performance evaluation subject to the manager's judgement and is therefore a subjective measurement. Thirdly, organizations will seek to address this subjectivity issue, which may result in inaccurate or misdirected assessments of performance, through articulating employee performance criteria (usually aligned to business goals) and also having a regulatory system of PRP allocation which is not only subject to parameters but also scrutiny by the manager's manager or an HR specialist. Box 7.6 shows how, once employee performance has been measured, a variable pay amount can be allocated.

Box 7.6 Window on work
Performance descriptions used by a blue chip company in the IT sector for determining performance-related pay

Rating	Description	Definition
1	Top performer	Achieves exceptional results and as a top performer clearly stands out from the rest in making a distinctive contribution linked to business objectives and is a role model for the organizations values.
2*	Above average performer	Exceeds job responsibilities in achieving business objectives and in doing so outperforms most peers, and is constantly seeking ways to grow in scope and impact.
2	Consistently solid performer	Consistently achieves business objectives and meets job expectations; is fully reliable and demonstrates a good level of knowledge, skill, effectiveness, and initiative.
3	A lower performer and needs improvement	When compared with solid performers, a lower performer. • Does not fully execute all job responsibilities or executes with lower degree of results *and/or* • Does not demonstrate as high a level of knowledge, skill, effectiveness, or initiative Consecutive ratings at the this level are unacceptable in a high-performance culture and will require improvement to be demonstrated within a 3-month improvement plan period, after which a new rating will be determined.
4	Unsatisfactory performer	Does not demonstrate or utilize knowledge and skill required to execute against job responsibilities. Shows no improvement after consecutive level 3 ratings. Immediate, significant, and sustained improvement to a solid performance level is to be demonstrated to prevent employment being terminated, subject to local legal requirements.

Performance-related pay is an annual bonus in addition to the annual review of salaries.
Managerial discretion to make awards in the following ranges, subject to an overall Business Unit budget:
Rating 2 = 1–4 per cent
Rating 2*= 5–8 per cent
Rating 1 = 9–12 per cent
Ratings 3 and 4 = zero PRP.

7.4.1 PRP and motivation

Although in theory PRP has considerable motivational potential, much research evidence reveals doubts about this in practice. Many managers, employees, and researchers are sceptical and see money as buying just temporary compliance rather than securing motivation. They often have low expectations about the motivational abilities of pay because PRP may actually demotivate average performers receiving small PRP amounts. Evidence suggests that PRP payments may need to be of the order of 10–15 per cent to have any impact on motivation. Therefore average pay awards in single figures do not provide much scope for managers to harness the potency of PRP.

The individual performance focus of PRP has the potential to inhibit teamworking and fragment team behaviour. The greater the individual dependence on other colleagues, the less strong is the motivational potential of PRP because much of the achievement of performance is not within the individual's control. Box 7.7 highlights the problems that might occur if company performance is affected by events outside its control, which will inevitably impact on the amount of money available for PRP—in this case the financial reward is profit-related, rather than related to individual performance, but the principal is the same.

7.4.2 PRP: conflicts and ambiguities

Pilbeam and Corbridge (2010) draw attention to other conflicts and ambiguities associated with PRP. It may discriminate unfairly against women because, in practice, it is primarily male managers who measure performance and they may tend to reward performance characterized by male values, with equal-pay implications. There is concrete, if limited, evidence that the qualities associated with female workers tend to be downgraded in establishing performance criteria for PRP, and the monitoring of performance-related payments by gender is part of addressing the gender pay gap.

Moreover, it is an anathema to many public servants, and others in professional occupations, to suggest that they might be motivated by pay linked to a judgement of their performance, but PRP has penetrated many professional jobs. The injection of enterprise values and governmental concern with organizational performance indicators is being translated into individual performance indicators and PRP. There is tension between the professional ethos

 Box 7.7 Window on work
Rewarding performance in the retail sector

The John Lewis Partnership has a reward strategy of paying the full local market rate and as much above as is justified by individual performance. Its staff are expected to be responsive to customer needs and deliver excellence in customer service and performance, with employees subject to scoring by mystery shoppers. In John Lewis PRP payments are consolidated into pay, rather than paid as one-off bonuses. In addition, as John Lewis is a company owned by its staff, employees share the full distribution of profits after the payment of operational and costs and the costs of future expansion. This results in an annual bonus being paid to staff as a percentage of their pay. In March 2011, the 76,000 staff shared a payout of over £194 million, approximately 18 per cent of their salaries, as profits were up 10 per cent at £431 million. But what happens when the high-street retail sector suffers a downturn?

John Lewis was battered by tough price competition on the high street and slumping consumer confidence leading to profits falling sharply in the first half of 2011, with the Chairman blaming discounting by rivals, increased capital expenditure on new stores, and weak sentiment among hard-pressed consumers for the reverse. The first half-year operating profit at John Lewis stores plunged more than 50 per cent to £15.8 million, and conditions are expected to remain challenging into 2012. The profit margins were squeezed, partly because it was forced to make good on its pledge that it is 'never knowingly undersold' and cut prices when rivals ran promotions. Clearly, this may have implications for the bonus paid to the employees who have come to expect their annual bonus as an integral part of their reward package. What might the implications be for staff rewards and motivation if the tough trading conditions continue?

of self-management and the managerialist approach of PRP. PRP may fail to recognize that, for professionals and public servants, the psychological contract may have primacy over the economic contract; that professionalism and ethics may matter more than money (Pilbeam 1998).

7.4.3 The challenges of measuring and assessing performance

There are fundamental challenges associated with establishing performance criteria and assessing performance effectively. It may be possible to do this where a direct and overt measurement is available, but it is problematic for work which has less tangible and quantifiable outputs, as is likely in non-manual, managerial, and professional occupations. In establishing and assessing performance against performance criteria there can be a tendency to measure what is easy to measure rather than what ought to be measured. An illustration of this is the assessment of police effectiveness by the criteria of the incidence of crimes and of detection rates. In reality, the ability of individual police officers to influence these measures is minimal, as levels of crime are attributable to much wider reasons than police performance. In any case, much police work is symbolic and intangible, so how is this element of performance assessed and measured? In addition to the difficulty of establishing meaningful performance indicators, subjectivity is an inherent feature of PRP assessment, leading to a range of perceptual errors coming into play, as was also witnessed in relation to employee selection processes in Chapter 5.

7.4.4 PRP within a wider performance management system

Although there are conflicts and ambiguities in PRP, it is useful to examine opportunities to contribute to managerial success in PRP. The assumption that PRP can manage performance on its own is misguided, because it is only one dimension of performance management (see Chapter 11). While it is difficult to demonstrate that PRP contributes to the bottom line, it does clarify perceptions about performance and supports a performance culture. It is easier to criticize PRP than it is to perceive it as an effective reward strategy, so here are some of the organizational conditions that may be necessary for PRP to be effective:

- PRP to be integrated with holistic performance management by managers who have the willingness and the skill to manage;
- high levels of trust between the appraising manager and the employee;
- work activity which can be measured together with validity and reliability in the measurement of differences in individual job performance;
- a systematic assessment of performance which is not only fair in practice but is perceived to be fair by managers and employees;
- PRP amounts which are meaningful;
- overall reward structures which are competitive so that PRP is genuinely in addition to 'normal' pay.

 ## Summary and further reading

- PRP is used to describe pay systems where pay is varied according to the work performance achieved. However, as with market-based approaches, the value of those performance outputs will clearly vary according to the organization's needs and to the scarcity (or not) of the performance outputs produced by the employee.

- In practice, PRP relies upon systems of performance measurement and a clear demonstration as to how reward will be allocated. Whilst these are often presented as being transparent and fair, as jobs become more complex, designing measurement becomes increasingly difficult. Also, given that line managers often have responsibility for determining whether individual or collective performance standards have been attained, the success of the PRP system could be undermined by subjective measurements.

- Whilst the linking of pay to desired organizational outcomes could be seen as a beneficial means of promoting improvements in performance, research suggests that the motivational abilities of pay might secure only temporary rather than longer-term outcomes. There are additional concerns about its impact on teamworking and its potential to instigate conflict, since employees will rely on others as well as their own efforts to secure financial rewards. Finally, PRP has been linked to gender discrimination, and there are questions as to how well PRP fits with professional workers whose approach towards work might be dominated by an alternative ethos.

The analysis of the effects of PRP on productivity and employment by Gielen, Kerkhofs, and van Ours (2009)is recommended, as is Dewhurst, Gutridge, and Mohr (2009).

7.5 Contemporary issues in pay and reward

This chapter has taken a contingency approach towards pay and reward, arguing that there are no perfect solutions for all organizations or industries and no quick fixes. However, emerging and declining trends exist, reflecting the contextual as well as the contingent nature of reward and in no way dampening enthusiasm for pursuing 'perfection' in reward systems. Therefore the search continues with some vigour with reward approaches being increasingly characterized by sophistication, complexity, and flexibility of response to employee and employer needs. Managing employee rewards is a crucial element in encouraging flexibility, leveraging performance, and competing for talent in tight labour markets, and also in minimizing costs in difficult economic times

Contingency theory suggests that the business context is crucial in determining reward strategies, and a number of factors are influential. These include whether or not the organization is in the public or private sector, although there is some evidence of convergence in practices towards those witnessed more commonly in the private sector. It also includes the size of the organization, as the more sophisticated strategies are seen in larger companies—arguably because they are better placed to pay for them. Finally, the extent to which the company is expanding or contracting is significant, as is its profitability and success. As with larger organizations, those who are doing better are more likely to offer more attractive rewards as a means of attracting and retaining higher-calibre employees.

However, even within the context of contingency and a need for best fit, a number of trends in pay and reward are evident and these are outlined in Box 7.8. Box 7.9 provides a video link to a discussion about the relationship between inflation and pay increases. Three trends, those concerning developments in the area of employee benefits, occupational pension provision, and the issue of equal pay for work of equal value, will be explored in more detail below. However, the important international dimension of pay and reward also needs to be acknowledged (see Box 7.10).

7.5.1 Employment benefits

Employment benefits include things like occupational pensions, healthcare and well-being initiatives, life insurance cover, financial assistance, company cars, childcare provision, enhanced sick pay, and leave entitlement. Like pay, they are principally a financial reward because there is a direct cost to the employer associated with providing them. Moreover, employment benefits principally result in extrinsic employee satisfaction rather than the more intrinsic satisfaction gained through the non-financial rewards discussed above. The reasons for offering employment benefits are, first, to increase the potency of the total reward package in terms of recruitment, retention, and motivation, although the impact of financial benefits remains more a matter of faith than proven correlation. Secondly, the provision of financial benefits enhances the value proposition and contributes to the employer brand in the pursuit of becoming the employer of choice. Thirdly, employees in the labour market from which the employer recruits may expect a certain range of benefit provision.

With the cost of employee financial benefits averaging 10–20 per cent of total pay costs, and being more than 30 per cent in some cases, there is a compelling employer argument for the active management of the benefits package to ensure that reward strategy objectives are met and value for money is achieved. A significant challenge is that the provision of a standard

Box 7.8 Window on work
Emerging and declining reward trends

Declining reward trends

Incremental graded-pay systems	Viewed as not responsive to the strategic integration of reward or to market pricing
Inflation-linked increases	The low-inflation climate up to 2008 and the subsequent economic crisis are continuing to loosen the link between inflation and employee pay expectations
Annual pay reviews	Annual pay reviews
Collective pay bargaining	Declining because of hostile political environments in the 1980s and 1990s, and with the election of a Conservative–Liberal Democrat coalition government would from 2010, as well as structural changes in employment
Final salary pensions	Escalating costs and the financial risk to the employer
Traditional job evaluation	Inflexibility concerns when nimble reward strategies are needed in organic organizations

Emerging reward trends

Total reward	Pay plus financial and non-financial benefits deployed in pursuit of competitive advantage
New pay	Strategic alignment of rewards with business objectives and the use of pay as a lever on employee performance
Market-driven pay	Labour market responsiveness to meet local conditions
Performance-related pay	The application of individual PRP to reward the exhibition of desired performance and competencies with some interest in team reward
Broad-banding of graded pay	Increased flexibility in delayered organization structures
Money purchase pensions	The escalating costs of final salary schemes and a transfer of the risk to employees
Flexible benefits	To meet the diverse needs of the workforce; to increase the potency of the reward strategy, and to target benefits cost

Box 7.9 Online video link
Current and future trends in pay in relation to inflation

Go to the Online Resource Centre and follow the link provided to view video content about inflation, then reflect on the following.
How is inflation measured?
What are the links between pay rates and inflation?
What are the implications for pay negotiations, individually and collectively, of using the measure of RPI or CPI or average earnings?
Discuss the extent to difficult economic conditions and surplus labour markets impact on the level of pay increases for employees.

Box 7.10 International focus
Pay and reward—the international dimension

When it comes to pay and reward there are two distinct areas of international HRM interest—the management and reward of international assignees from multinationals on the one hand, and HRM and reward practices in specific countries on the other. Much of the literature on international HRM focuses on the employment of international assignees by multinational companies. Debates about pay and reward centre on incentivizing and managing the performance of assignees, as well as managing their reintegration into the home country on the completion of the overseas assignment (see Chapter 15). However, there is much less research published *in English* about pay and reward practices in different countries. The following illustrations provide tasters of some comparative pay and reward issues in order to emphasize the importance of context, culture, and contingency in reward strategies.

China

Reward management continues to be influenced by the legacy of the 'iron rice bowl' welfare package—an employment system where employees are accommodated in company dormitories, fed in company restaurants, cared for by company medical staff, and entertained by company recreational facilities. However, the level of interest in management education is promoting an interest in moving from egalitarianism in pay to a greater propensity to reward employees according to their contribution to the enterprise.

France

French organizations make greater use of incentive pay, despite the stereotypes of the UK as a deregulated economy and France as a social market economy. This greater use of incentive pay is influenced by government tax incentives for profit sharing and the activities of employer organizations. French employers are more active in employer networks and promoted greater urgency than the UK for pay reform in the 1980s, when incentive pay was in HRM vogue. This provided a spur for pooling expertise and collective learning about the operation of incentive pay arrangements.

Southeast Asia

Many Asian countries now recognize that high technology, productivity, and low earnings cannot be combined and sustained over a long period of time and seek to sustain their competitiveness through pay increases which are more related to performance measures to reward and motivate employees. Japan, Singapore, and Korea, for example, have succeeded in moving to high-value-added and technology-based or service activities partly because they invested in skills development and recognized that higher earnings are an essential strategy for entry and survival in the knowledge-based industries. Increases in real earnings have been made possible because investment in education and skills contributed to productivity enhancement which created the capacity to absorb higher earnings.

Australia and New Zealand

The wage determination system in Australia encourages employers and unions to negotiate part of wage increases in the context of productivity-related improvements. The fundamental shift of industrial relations to the enterprise level and the individualization of the employment relationship in New Zealand has provided scope for performance-related pay. Therefore it is increasingly recognized that performance and skills criteria need to be injected into pay determination, that it cannot be achieved through centralized or macro-level pay determination, and that changes need to be negotiated at the enterprise level.

benefits package for all employees makes the assumption that its valence (perceived personal value) is the same for all employees, and this is clearly not the case. This suggests that an element of employee choice in financial benefits will not only recognize diverse needs but also increase the ability of the reward strategy to achieve HR objectives.

7.5.2 Flexible benefits

Flexible, cafeteria, or 'pick and mix' benefits are terms given to benefit arrangements which allow the exercise of employee choice within a total reward package. Adding flexibility to

traditional benefits packages can mean anything from allowing some choice in company car value to having different levels of pension contributions, but a full-blown flexible benefits scheme will allocate a benefits allowance to each employee and allow employees to choose benefits according to preferences and lifestyle needs. In essence, flexible benefits involve the presentation of a menu or portfolio of benefits from which employees can select according to their needs, within manageable guidelines.

Box 7.11 illustrates a flexible benefits menu; within each of the elements there will be further choices available to employees. For example, pensions could be enhanced through increased contributions and a reduction elsewhere in the selected benefits, life cover could be extended to dependents, extra holidays could be bought, or a car benefit could be cashed in or a better model selected. The menu provides a quasi-market where employees spend their benefits allowance. The flexible benefit approach acknowledges diversity of workforce need and circumstances and therefore has managing diversity as well as reward strategy objectives. Other potential advantages to the employer are, first, through targeting the cost and value of employee benefits (and avoiding paying for what individuals do not want) and, secondly, through linking available benefits with particular reward objectives. The key reasons for introducing flexible benefits are staff retention, staff motivation, enhancing recruitment, competitive pressures in the labour market, not paying for benefits that employees do not want, and the ability to recognize diverse individual needs. Therefore flexible benefits provide an imaginative opportunity to integrate reward strategy with other HR strategies, and also with corporate strategy.

Flexible benefits empower employees by enabling them to recognize the value of their benefits and to exercise some control over their own rewards. Flexible benefits are also compatible with moves to individualize the employment relationship, and with personal contracts. Employees have diverse economic, security, and social needs, and several demographic trends have contributed to this. These trends include an increase in female participation in the labour market, an increase in single parents, those with caring responsibilities, and others in the sandwich generation, an ageing workforce with increasing post-employment life expectancies, new career patterns, and dual-career families. Flexible benefits potentially enable organizations to be responsive to the lifestyle needs of a more diverse workforce. The French-owned telecommunications manufacturer Alcatel Telecom introduced flexible benefits for its 600 employees and installed electronic kiosks in the workplace to enable staff to monitor and modify their benefits. Whilst there is interest in flexible benefits as an innovative and business-focused reward initiative, the anticipated costs of implementation and administration, together with 'benefit inertia', are significant barriers to progress.

Box 7.11 Window on work
Illustration of a flexible benefits menu

Enhanced pension benefits	Income protection	Health assessments	Travel insurance	Learning account
Critical illness cover	Personal accident cover	Childcare vouchers	Partner life insurance	Concierge services
Personal computers	Health screening	Enhanced life insurance	Extra holiday purchase	Private medical cover
Hospital cash plan	Retail vouchers	Dental cover	Sports club subsidy	Bicycles or cars

Which benefits would you value now?
Which might you value in 5 years time, or in 10 or 20 years?
Why might these changes occur and what difficulties might such alterations cause HR or those tasked with designing and administering flexible benefits systems?

7.5.3 The occupational pension

The occupational pension is one of the most significant benefits provided by the organization and valued by the employee, but it is an expensive benefit for the employer to provide although it is normal for the employee to make a contribution as well. It is useful to distinguish between final salary and money purchase arrangements. Final salary schemes pay benefits which are determined by taking the number of years of employee service and applying them to final salary on retirement to produce a pension entitlement. Therefore final salary arrangements provide defined benefits. In contrast, money purchase schemes pay benefits which are determined by the value of a pot of money which is accumulated through employee and/or employer contributions and investment decisions. The pot of money is ring-fenced to purchase a pension for the employee. Therefore money purchase arrangements provide defined contributions, but do not provide defined or predictable benefits.

In 2001, British Telecom notably closed its final salary scheme to new employees and offered money purchase arrangements instead. Other high-profile companies such as the Cooperative Group, Marks & Spencer, and British Airways followed. The closing of final salary schemes continues apace because of reduced stock market returns and longer life expectancy predictions. There is a significant trend away from defined benefit schemes linked to final salary and towards money purchase schemes where contributions are defined. Alternatives to closing final salary schemes, while still responding to funding challenges, include raising employer and/or employee contribution rates so that the historical norm of 15 per cent is exceeded, increasing the age at which occupational pensions can be taken, and basing the final salary calculation on average earnings rather than final salary. The CIPD Reward Management Survey (CIPD 2011i) reported that over two-thirds of pension schemes are defined contribution (money purchase) schemes with the majority of defined benefit (final salary) schemes closed or being wound up.

New employer duties in relation to worker pensions came into force in October 2012. Under these duties, employers will have to enrol eligible workers into a qualifying workplace pension arrangement. Employers will need either to make a minimum 3 per cent contribution towards a defined contribution scheme or NEST (the National Employment Savings Trust), or to offer membership of a defined benefit scheme that meets the scheme standard. There will be a minimum contribution of 8 per cent of qualifying earnings (£5035 to £33,540 in 2012), of which the employer must pay a minimum of 3 per cent, the worker will pay 4 per cent, with a further 1 per cent being paid as tax relief by the government. These minimum contribution levels are being phased in between October 2012 and October 2017.

Increases in the state pension age and the abolition of the statutory retirement age also impact on employer decisions regarding occupational pension provision. Employees, particularly in the public sector, are most resistant to degradation of perceived occupational pension entitlements, which impacts significantly on the employment relationship. The wider debate is, of course, whether the whole notion of pensionable retirement is becoming a redundant concept, with workers of the future working as long as humanly possible, albeit with a different career curve.

7.5.4 Equal pay for work of equal value

More than 40 years on from when the Equal Pay Act reached the statute book, women still earn around 20 per cent less per hour than men, combining full-time and part-time earnings (ONS 2011). Depending upon how comparisons are made (see below for pay gap measures) this gender pay gap is around 25 per cent in the private sector and 19 per cent in the public sector.

According to the Chartered Management Institute (CMI 2011) the gap between the pay of male and female managers has widened by £500 to over £10,000. Female managers reported being paid an average of £31,895 per year, compared with £42,441 for men doing the same job. The CMI calculated that, at current rates, parity not be achieved until the twenty-second century. However, for the first time, junior female managers now earn more than males. According to the CMI survey, junior women managers now earn £21,969 on average, £602 more than men at the same level. These are typically recent graduates who are managing projects rather than teams of people (see Chapter 10 for further data).

The causes of the pay gap are complex. In part they are to do with discrimination, in part because women are more likely than men to work in low paid sectors, and in part because women often have to 'trade down' or face other work and pay penalties if they become mothers. This means that the average woman working full-time could lose £330,000 over the course of her working life.

The Equal Pay Act 1970, as amended by the Equal Value Regulations 1983 and now incorporated within the Equality Act 2010, states that men and women are entitled to the same pay for the same work and that it is unlawful to differentiate between the terms and conditions of men and women where they are employed on:

- like work (work which is the same or broadly similar);
- work rated as equivalent under a non-discriminatory job evaluation scheme;
- work of equal value even where the jobs are of a totally different nature (the equal value amendment).

The third of these means that, in addition to similar work and jobs rated as equivalent, an employee (normally a woman) is entitled to equal pay where a higher-paid job being done by a member of the opposite sex is of equal value. Equal value is assessed using criteria such as job demands, skill, effort, responsibility, and decision-making. For an equal pay claim to be legitimate, there must be a job comparator of the opposite sex and the comparator must be employed by the same employer at the same place of work, or at another place of work of the same or an associated employer where common terms and conditions are observed. The comparator can be a current employee, or a predecessor, or a successor. If the employer fails to respond to an equal pay claim, the employee has recourse to an employment tribunal (see Chapter 13). If a tribunal decides that the work is 'like work', or 'equivalent work', or 'work of equal value', and the employer does not have a genuine material defence (see below), the claimant is entitled to equal pay which can be backdated.

In defending an 'equal value' claim an employer will need to demonstrate that the work is not of equal value because of job differences that are of 'practical importance'. A tribunal will consider the size and nature of any differences as well as the frequency with which the differences occur. For example, in the case of physical strength being required for a particular job, the tribunal will take account of the degree of physical strength required and the frequency with which that strength is exercised. If the tribunal decides that the jobs are not equal, the claim will fail. If a tribunal finds that the claimant is employed on like work or work rated as equivalent or work of equal value, it does not necessarily end there as the employer can resist the claim through providing a genuine material defence (GMD) which acknowledges that the jobs are equal, but justifies the inequality in pay by a reason which is not related to sex. Indicative, but unreliable, GMDs include geographical or cost-of-living differences, labour market forces, differences in qualifications, and the value of other contractual terms.

In addition to meeting the legal requirement, there are sound business arguments for ensuring equal pay. According to the Equality and Human Rights Commission (EHRC 2009), pay systems which are transparent and respect the entire workforce send positive messages about an organization's values. Fair and non-discriminatory pay systems represent good management practice and contribute to the efficient achievement of business objectives by encouraging maximum productivity from all employees. The revision of pay strategies in higher education, local government, and the NHS had much to do with promoting an equal pay agenda and avoiding costly and damaging equal pay claims. This has not been entirely successful though; the case of Sheffield City Council in Box 7.12 shows that the gender pay gap remains a hot issue.

7.5.5 Addressing the gender pay gap

The position of the EHRC is that increasing pay transparency is key to addressing the difference between what women and men earn. Greater transparency could also lead to better decision-making on reward, build employee confidence in their employer, and enhance corporate reputation. However, according to research undertaken for the EHRC (2009; Adams, Gore, and Shury 2010), only 9 per cent of employers currently report pay gap information to staff

Box 7.12 Skills exercise
Gender pay gap—the case of Sheffield City Council

A case for unequal pay at Sheffield City Council was brought before an employment tribunal in 2010 by a group of women carers. After a somewhat protracted battle, the courts ruled that the Council's bonus system was sex discriminatory. Male-dominated occupations had been receiving bonus payments for decades, while the mainly female carers received no such incentive pay. The men working as street cleaners and gardeners at the Council received historical productivity bonus payments worth between 33 and 38 per cent more than those for women working in jobs that the local authority agreed were comparable—carers, cleaners, and school catering staff. The Appeal Court described this inequality in pay as tainted by sexism, and ruled that the carers were the victims of indirect sexual discrimination.

In 2011, the council decided not to press ahead with its appeal against the court ruling, and as a result 900 female workers at the Council are in line for equal pay awards in settlement of the long-running legal dispute. The Council is to pay an undisclosed sum to the women involved, and the compensation bill will run into millions. Sheffield Council decided to reach a settlement with the trade union (Unison) because it was more effective than further litigation in terms of both time and cost and incorporated an exhaustive process to reach a positive settlement for all involved. The Council's appeal, had it gone ahead, could have set an important legal precedent for equal pay bids, although the case is still expected to have implications for other councils. It could pave the way for thousands of similar claims from female workers.

To capture the pay and reward gap differences between men and women six measures were identified by the Government Equalities Office (2011: 9–10):

i The difference between the average basic pay and total average earnings of men and women by grade and job type

ii The difference between men's and women's starting salaries

iii Reward components at different levels

iv Full-time gender pay gap

v Part-time gender pay gap

vi Overall gender pay gap

http://www.homeoffice.gov.uk/publications/equalities/womens-equality/gender-equality-reporting/think-act-report-framework?view=Binary

In small groups, discuss each of the six pay gap measures and formulate ideas as to how each might be implemented in practical terms, thus avoiding cases such as that of Sheffield Council.

outside their HR department, while a fifth of employers actively discourage employees from discussing their pay. In 2011, as part of its growth agenda, the UK government made a commitment 'to develop a fairer and more flexible labour market that draws on the talents of all and builds a stronger economy' and set out the principles to encourage a voluntary approach to gender equality reporting available to all private and voluntary sector organizations, but particularly those with 150 or more employees. The objective concerns the importance of promoting gender equality in the workplace as a contribution to securing economic growth. The voluntary approach to gender equality reporting was declared to be an important part of addressing the gender pay gap. Employers were encouraged to take a step-by-step approach, starting by undertaking their own analysis of equality and pay gap issues, where necessary taking action to address them, and in time reporting on gender equality in their organization, including on the gender pay gap. The fundamental concept is that improved knowledge of workforce equality information can drive successful change. Participating organizations were expected to 'Think, Act, and Report'.

- Think about gender equality.
- Take action.
- Report on workforce measures and pay measures.

 Summary and further reading

- This chapter has taken a contingency approach towards the issues of pay and reward, arguing against the idea that a perfect mix exists and promoting the need for best fit with an employer's circumstances. It is possible to identify trends in this area, but the extent to which they are adopted or witnessed is often contingent upon their sector, their size, and the extent to which they are an expanding successful company. Whilst trends might exist and be useful starting points for organizations when reviewing their approaches in this area, the extent of their implementation will, invariably, be contingent.

- Given the estimated costs of employment benefits to the employer, there is a compelling case to be made for their effective management. Increasingly, the provision of these benefits is also being tied to the attainment of reward strategy objectives, and thereby to performance outcomes. The successful management of these rewards will also involve recognizing the diversity of employee needs, and that those needs will alter over time; what is currently valued and perceived as motivating might be less so if an employee's circumstances change.

- Recent developments in pay strategies within large segments of the public sector have been partially driven by the desire to promote an equal pay agenda. However, these changes are arguably even more concerned with the avoidance of costly equal pay and equal value claims being taken by public sector unions with large number of female members.

- Thus far, reward strategies have been largely deployed to secure employee flexibility, as seen in the example of broad-banded pay. However, where employee benefits are concerned, employers may have to be flexible in terms of the benefits they provide, acknowledging the range of employee needs in this area and realizing that what is valued and needed by employees often changes over time as their circumstances alter. Whilst reward strategies and pay determination are increasingly determined by managers, the legal requirement for equity in pay and benefits illustrates one limitation placed on their power.

On the issue of gender pay, the EHRC issues regular surveys, as does the Government Equalities Office. On international pay and reward issues, Sparrow (2009), Perkins and Vartiainen (2010), and Harzing and Pinnington (2011) are helpful. Broader coverage of issues highlighted in this section can be found in Brewster et al. (2003) and Hall, Pilbeam, and Corbridge (2012).

7.6 Conclusions

Reward management is one of the most fundamentally important HRM activities and has been identified as a key lever in all HRM models. Contemporary approaches towards reward increasingly take a strategic approach, acknowledging the important part it plays in determining employee behaviours and seeking to use reward practices to achieve an alignment of behaviour at work with business strategy. Another, central, concept in the reward domain argues for people to be rewarded in accordance with their value to the organization, signalling a shift away from rewarding length of service and seniority to rewarding contribution to business goals and a focus of attention on people, their skills, and their performance (i.e. new pay), rather than on the jobs they hold (old pay).

There has also been an expansion of the way in which reward is understood, shifting away from equating 'reward' with 'pay' and moving instead towards the idea of total reward which combines traditional pay and benefits with other less tangible elements that employees gain from employment, such as flexible working, skills, opportunity, and recognition. In this way, reward becomes more than simply a flexible benefits package or a consideration of the combined value of pay, incentives, and benefits. Although the ways in which such a package is constructed will vary between organizations, the aim of total reward is to construct a package that is tailored to the desires of employees with minimal cost implications for employers.

However, it could be argued that the shift towards a greater individualization of reward not only has an essentially unitary flavour, but also raises questions as to the degree of pay insecurity being faced by employees. For example, the shift towards 'new pay' often involves reducing the element of pay that is fixed and puts a proportion of pay 'at risk' through techniques such as PRP. It could be argued that staff well-being is jeopardized by insecurity and unpredictability, which could lead to behaviours such as overwork which can be damaging both mentally and physically.

Contemporary reward approaches have increased managerial power in this area. It is managers who determine the element of pay that is to be decided by performance and assess the extent to which employees merit that award. This is problematic for two reasons. First, the theory of new pay argues that employees do less well when the organization performs poorly—for example, in terms of its share values. However, shareholders are often better placed to withstand such dips because of their ability to spread the risk of their investments. This is not necessarily an option open to many employees, as they often depend on their salary as their sole source of income. Secondly, managerial decisions with regard to performance are open to the operation of perceptual error (as outlined in Chapter 5). Whilst schemes like PRP might have the appearance of rationality and equity, the conflicts and ambiguities associated with it illustrate its limitations.

Finally, generational expectations and the economic backdrop, together with national government and supranational interventions, provide significant contextual influences on reward practice, and it could be argued that in pay and reward 'context is everything' because it influences the amount of money available and the power relationship between employers and employees. Students of pay and reward will recognize the importance of context and fully embed it in their thinking. This also applies to the international dimensions of pay and reward too.

 ## Assignment and discussion questions

1 Outline the elements of 'total reward' and briefly explain the importance of rewards in managing the performance of employees.

2 Evaluate the aims of broad-banded pay structures in relation to managing employee performance.

3 Discuss the objectives and features of market-driven pay.

4 Discuss two key emerging pay and reward trends.

5 Critically discuss the challenges and ambiguities related to managing employee performance and to gender equality through individual PRP.

 ## Online Resource Centre

Test your understanding of this chapter with online questions and answers, keep up to speed with changes to the law through regular updates, and use selected weblinks to quickly access useful resources and further information. Visit the Online Resource Centre at:
www.oxfordtextbooks.co.uk/orc/gilmore_williams2e/

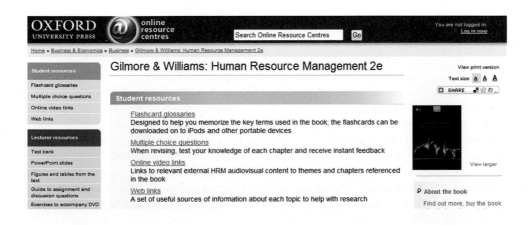

Case study
Is PRP appropriate for university lecturers?

The introduction of increased student fees has resurrected the notion that lecturers should be rewarded in relation to student feedback on their teaching performance. The union view is that linking student feedback forms to individual lecturers' pay will not enhance teaching excellence, but will be a disastrous prospect for students' education and lecturers. They question who will teach the least popular courses and argue that more cynical staff may find ways of working the system—giving out feedback forms before any coursework is marked and suggesting a decent mark for good feedback. The assumption is that students know what a good lecturer is or does, but what does student feedback measure? Is it the subtle use of different theoretical perspectives to shed new light on a subject? The ability to convey complex ideas with clarity and enthusiasm? Or is it the extent to which they are challenged intellectually?

Research shows that students judge lecturing styles and performances over and above content and academic rigour. Whilst the 'customer knows best', are students 'customers' or are they 'learners' with rights and responsibilities? There is potential for a consumer orientation to impact negatively on degrees that attempt to equip students with the critical skills and depth of knowledge to deal with a complex world, and on courses that are difficult and challenge students. To get an upper second or first, students may choose the path of least resistance; less popular courses will simply die, and along with them the skill base for socio-economic stability. Just because languages, civil engineering, and chemistry are all suffering in the popularity stakes does not mean that society needs fewer linguists, engineers, and chemists.

Kline (2006) argued that PRP '...sets team member against team member, corrupts appraisals by linking them directly to pay, is innately prone to discrimination and unfairness, and manages to measure that which doesn't count yet fails to measure that which really does count'.

Back in 2000 the Treasury published a report, *Incentives for Change*, which summarized the research evidence on public service performance-related pay schemes (Makinson 2000). It identified that there was general 'approval of the *principle* and disenchantment with the *practice* of performance pay' and stated that current PRP arrangements were 'ineffective and discredited'. The reaction to incentives can produce negative behaviour in a number of different ways, from the single-minded pursuit of only that which delivers rewards, to the subversion of incentives because people resent the perceived attempt to control them.

Kline points out that most quality targets that could be used for performance ratings are not under the control of individual members of staff. He suggests that the adoption of PRP would force down standards as lecturers are pressurized to pass more and more students, work even longer hours, instantly respond to student emails, and avoid reporting plagiarism for fear that it will dent reputations. Finding motivators that enhance collegiality and improve the quality of teaching and research is a legitimate goal in universities, and therefore performance should be rewarded through an agreed and transparent peer review and research-based approach.

Questions

Is linking student feedback forms to individual lecturers' pay a means of enhancing teaching excellence or a disastrous prospect?

Using the three sequential PRP stages and in relation to lecturers:

1 specify realistic and measurable performance criteria or performance indicators;

2 identify who should measure performance against the criteria/indicators you have specified and how this should be done;

3 specify a pay amount in percentage terms or in annual amounts that should be distributed according to performance differentials between lecturers.

Be prepared to justify the choices you have made above and discuss the PRP challenges and ambiguities you have uncovered in undertaking this task. What does it tell you about linking pay to performance generally?

Utilizing human resources in organizations

Sarah Gilmore and Steve Williams

Learning objectives

The main objectives of this chapter are:

- to identify the ways in which organizations try to benefit from employee flexibility;
- to examine the concept and practices of talent management;
- to analyse the ways in which employers pay attention to the health, safety, and well-being of their staff.

8.1 Introduction

This chapter explores how human resources are utilized in organizations. In doing so we bring together three key issues which individually and collectively have substantial implications for the various parties to the employment relationship. Although they might seem to be discrete areas, we will show how they connect with each other. First, in Section 8.2, our concern is with the characteristic ways in which employers attempt to benefit from flexibility when it comes to managing human resources, and the key issues and implications for workers and employers that relate to this. Secondly, the focus of Section 8.3 is on the organizational arrangements and policies used for the purpose of effective utilization of human resources in organizations, encompassing such matters as the need for organizations to manage and retain 'talented' employees—ensuring arrangements for succession planning so that the organization has the staff it needs both now and in the future. The third key issue, considered in Section 8.4, relates to the importance of employee well-being when considering how human resources are utilized. Whilst this is now the subject of government and health promotion discourses, the extent to which these 'good' practices are observed in practice is questionable. Previous chapters on recruitment and selection of employees (Chapter 5), training and development (Chapter 6), and employee reward (Chapter 7) covered aspects of these issues, this chapter brings elements of them together in order to highlight how human resources are utilized in organizations and why this is a matter of concern for employees, employers, and human resource professionals.

8.2 The 'flexible' utilization of human resources

The question of flexibility is a key element of how human resources are utilized. While employment flexibility can offer organizations greater efficiency and competitive advantage, it also raises certain issues and challenges that need addressing. When it comes to how they utilize their human resources, there are four key issues that face organizations: who are used (contractual flexibility), when they are used (temporal flexibility), where they are used (locational flexibility), and how they are used (functional flexibility).

8.2.1 Contractual flexibility

Here we are concerned with *who* organizations utilize when it comes to the management of human resources. Often referred to as 'numerical flexibility', this type of flexibility enables organizations to be adaptable by giving them greater freedom to adjust the number of workers used in order to respond to fluctuations in demand for a product or service. One way in which organizations often do this is by contracting out certain of their functions, which have previously been operated internally on an 'in-house' basis, to specialist external providers. Haines (2009) distinguishes between two forms of contracting out. The first—subcontracting—applies to situations where organizations contract out work on a project-by-project basis. Such an arrangement is extensively used in some industry sectors, such as construction. The second type of contracting out is outsourcing. This is where organizations contract out certain of their functions, like catering or cleaning, on a longer-term basis. The activity of companies like Compass, for example, which provides business support services, demonstrates the increased popularity of outsourcing. Capita, Amey, and Serco are among the companies which have grown by taking over the running of public sector services previously undertaken by the state; for example, Capita looks after the collection of the BBC licence fee. Contracting out office work, including aspects of the administration of human resources such as payroll work, recruitment and selection, and managing benefits, has become more popular (Haines 2009).

The main benefit for organizations of contracting out supposedly non-core functions is the cost savings that can be realized; specialist providers can supply them more cheaply because of the economies of scale that arise. It also gives organizations greater flexibility over the utilization of human resources; externalization helps to accommodate variations in demand for products or services. Similarly, the use of self-employed workers, who are not directly employed by the organization that hires them to undertake work, can also be an important source of such flexibility and a cheaper means of utilizing human resources, since organizations avoid some of the costs of employing people directly. The use of self-employed contractors is particularly evident in the IT sector, for example (Tremblay and Genin 2010), as well as the media industry (Platman 2004), and can be attractive to both parties. However, despite its supposed advantages, there no great enthusiasm for self-employed status is evident among workers in general, or organizations for that matter (McGovern et al. 2007). The level of self-employment largely remained static during the 2000s, before seeing a marked rise to 14.1 per cent of the workforce in 2011, in the aftermath of the financial and economic crisis. However, this was function of the weak state of the labour market and the absence of alternative employment opportunities, rather than demand from workers for more flexibility, autonomy, and independence (CIPD 2012). Much self-employment is, in fact, disguised employment, as firms save money by passing the costs of employment on to the worker. But why have organizations not been as interested in using self-employed workers as might have been expected? For one thing, other sources of flexibility are often sufficient. Additionally, there are managerial challenges associated with using self-employed workers, such as the potential lack of control over the workforce and the instability this produces.

Another way in which organizations can secure contractual flexibility is by using directly employed staff hired on fixed-term contracts. This can enable managers to hire new staff in order to fill a vacancy, or to meet an anticipated short-term rise in demand, without committing to a long-term relationship. Such arrangements are particularly popular in public services where budget restrictions and uncertainties over funding can make organizations reluctant to employ staff on a permanent contract (Beynon et al. 2002). Overall, though, the take-up of this form of contractual flexibility remains rather modest. While the share of temporary employment rose during the early 1990s, to 7.1 per cent of the workforce in 1994, it fell back to just 5.5 per cent by 2008 before gradually increasing again to 2011 in the context of the economic recession. EU legislation, which obliges employers to treat temporary staff no less favourably than their permanent equivalents when it comes to matters like pay, means that some of the cost benefits associated with using this form of flexible employment have become less important.

A key way in which organizations secure greater flexibility over the use of temporary labour is by using external employment agencies, something which has become more commonplace in certain parts of the economy (Purcell, Purcell, and Tailby 2004; Forde, MacKenzie, and Robinson 2008), especially in sectors where migrant workers comprise a large proportion of the workforce, such as hotels, food processing, cleaning, and social care (James and Lloyd 2008; Knox 2010; McKay and Markova 2010). One estimate suggests that there are between 1.1 and 1.5 million agency workers across the economy (BERR 2008), up to 5 per cent of the overall workforce. Agency labour can be a key source of cost savings and flexibility for organizations, since workers often have lower pay, worse employment conditions, and fewer employment rights than their directly employed counterparts (Forde and Slater 2006). Using agency labour is a relatively efficient way of accommodating short-term fluctuations in demand or even, in some cases, filling vacancies (McKay and Markova 2010). That said, though, there are often well-documented stories of agency workers being highly exploited (e.g. TUC 2007). Whether or not legislation designed to regulate agency working will have any material effect is open to question (see Box 8.1).

The main managerial challenges for organizations wanting to deploy contractual flexibility concern the greater instability of such arrangements, the difficulties of enforcing managerial control, and the limited nature of worker commitment. Balancing the advantages of contractual flexibility with its disadvantages means that such an approach to utilizing human resources is far from straightforward. This is evident when we consider the extent to which the use of contracting out and employment agencies results in the boundaries between different organizations becoming blurred (Marchington et al. 2005). In working environments where more than one employer is present—for example, the client organization and the contractor—effectively managing human resources becomes a more complex affair. The key managerial challenge involves securing organizational commitment and a stable environment in multi-employer situations (Marchington, Cooke, and Hebson 2010). In the health service, employers have responded to the instabilities and uncertainties that often arise from using external suppliers of temporary labour by bringing such arrangements in-house, thus offering greater predictability (Kirkpatrick et al. 2011).

Box 8.1 Policy example
Implementing the Directive on Temporary Agency Work

In 2008 the European Union agreed the Directive on Temporary Agency Work. It provides for equal treatment between agency workers and comparable directly employed workers over certain 'basis working and employment conditions' such as pay and holiday entitlement. The UK government opposed the Directive, on the basis that the additional regulation would restrict the flexibility of employers, raise business costs, and lead to reduced opportunities for temporary working. It dropped its opposition after the Confederation of British Industry (CBI) and Trades Union Congress (TUC) reached an agreement over how the Directive should be implemented, which included provision for a 12-week qualifying period before a worker is entitled to equal treatment (Countouris and Horton 2009). The Department for Business Innovation and Skills (BIS 2011a) provides detailed guidance on the Agency Workers Regulations, which took effect in October 2011, covering such matters as the scope of the legislation and how the 12-week qualifying period is to be calculated in a range of different situations (http://www.bis.gov.uk/assets/biscore/employment-matters/docs/a/11-949-agency-workers-regulations-guidance).

Business groups had expressed concern that the Regulations would impede employers' flexibility, with adverse consequences for competiveness. However, initial evidence suggests that it is unlikely to have a major impact on the temporary job market (Faragher 2011).

8.2.2 Temporal flexibility

A second way in which organizations aim to secure flexibility over how their human resources are utilized concerns *when* work is undertaken, relating to working time—or temporal—flexibility. While many people still work what has come to be known as a 'standard' working week, between the hours of, say, 9.00 a.m. and 5.00 p.m. from Monday to Friday, it is not as commonplace as it once was (Grimshaw and Rubery 2010; Walsh 2010). While some parts of the economy, such as public transport or hospitals, have always been marked by non-standard patterns of working time to ensure adequate service provision, growing numbers of workers operate under 'unsocial hours' arrangements. For example, some 1.3 million workers usually work at night, and 15 per cent of the workforce undertake shift work outside of the standard working day. The importance of temporal flexibility is also illustrated by the persistent growth of part-time employment (McGovern et al. 2007), defined as fewer than 30 hours per week. Between 1984 and 2011 the proportion of part-time jobs in the economy rose from 21 to 27 per cent.

There are three principal reasons for the growing significance of temporal flexibility in the economy. First, the change reflects the broader shift in the economy towards the service sector, where jobs are more likely to be undertaken on a part-time basis. In manufacturing, for example, just one in twenty workers is employed on a part-time basis, whereas over half (53 per cent) of workers in hotels and restaurants are part-timers (Kersley et al. 2006). Secondly, many organizations offer greater consumer choice in accessing their services; for example, call centres operate during the evening when demand for their services is likely to be at its highest. The third factor concerns the need to accommodate staff with caring responsibilities. Some three-quarters (74 per cent) of part-time employees are women (ONS 2012), for whom such work is often desirable because it enables them to combine paid employment with unpaid household labour effectively.

Moreover, the growing number of dual-career households (where both partners are in paid employment) has encouraged organizations to consider instituting more flexible working time arrangements as a means of tackling the work–family conflict that can arise in such circumstances, and which might have adverse consequences for the business such as difficulties with staff retention (Walsh 2010). This was seen in the hotels studied by Doherty (2004) which had put various types of flexible working in place in order retain talented female managers. Many organizations have developed innovative forms of working time flexibility, such as compressed working weeks, where a standard number of working hours is worked over fewer than five full days, or flexi-time arrangements, which give workers some element of discretion over starting and finishing times. These arrangements are generally more common in public sector organizations, or where there

Table 8.1 The availability of flexible working arrangements (percentage of employees)

	2001	2004	2006
Part-time working	49	67	69
Reduced hours for a limited period	56	62	54
Flexitime	32	48	53
Job share	46	41	47
Term-time-only working	22	32	37
Compressed working week	25	30	35
Annualized hours	17	20	24
Regular home working	N/A	20	23

Source: *Third Work–Life Balance Employee Survey* (Hooker et al. 2007).

is a high proportion of female staff (Kersley et al. 2006; Walsh 2010). Nor should it be forgotten that overtime working remains a leading source of working time flexibility (see Section 8.4.1). Table 8.1 shows the increasing proportion of workplaces with certain flexible working practices available, as reported by employees (Hooker et al. 2007). See Box 8.2 for details of flexible working time arrangements across Europe.

Governments have instituted various measures to encourage greater use of flexible working time arrangements, including establishing a legal right of working parents and carers of adults to request them, based on the belief that there are business benefits—reduced absenteeism, easier recruitment, and better retention—from their operation. The coalition government has even expressed its intention to extend this right to all workers, albeit in a way that gives organizations more scope to refuse requests (HM Government 2011). Yet the apparent consensus in favour of flexible working time arrangements masks some important underlying issues and challenges. For one thing, making them available in theory does not necessarily mean that workers are allowed to use them in practice (e.g. Gatrell 2005), something that helps to explain the sluggish pace of take-up (see Hooker et al. 2007). Moreover, the take-up of flexible working time arrangements can stimulate hostility from those who do not have access to them in the form of a 'family-friendly backlash' (Walsh 2010). We also need to be aware of the conflict that can arise from the mismatch between organizational demands for flexibility—centred on the need to respond effectively to fluctuations in demand—and workers' demands for flexibility—predicated on the desire for working time arrangements that enable them to combine paid employment with family life (Hyman, Scholarios, and Baldry 2005).

Box 8.2 International focus
Flexible working time arrangements in Europe

There has been an increase in the availability of flexible working time arrangements in the UK (Hooker et al. 2007). Plantenga and Remery (2010) undertook a study of flexible working time arrangements across 30 European (mainly EU) countries. Their analysis shows that over 60 per cent of employees in Denmark and Sweden make use of flexible working time schedules, such as flexi-time arrangements, compared with around a third of employees in the UK. However, In some countries, such as Spain, Greece, Romania, and Bulgaria, relatively few employees (less than a sixth) make use of such flexibility. When it comes to part-time working arrangements, The Netherlands is out in front, with a quarter of male (24 per cent) employees and three-quarters (76 per cent) of female employees working on a part-time basis. The prevalence of part-time working is also relatively high in countries such as Norway, Denmark, and the UK, all of which are above the EU average. Some East European countries, particularly Romania and Bulgaria, have very low rates of part-time working. The prevalence of part-time working is also low in Portugal and Greece.

8.2.3 Locational flexibility

A third question concerns where organizations utilize their human resources, or 'locational flexibility'. Although some groups of workers, such as sales people, have always worked in a variety of different locations, conventional places of work such as factories, shops, and offices have workers physically located on their employer's premises. However, there are three main ways in which organizations are seeking to benefit from greater locational flexibility when it comes to managing human resources.

The first concerns the physical transformation of work locations, such as the development of collective open-plan offices and so-called 'hot-desking' arrangements, whereby instead of having a dedicated work space of their own, workers use shared facilities (Millward, Haslam, and Postmes 2007; Hirst 2011). The main organizational benefits include more efficient use of building space, reduced operating costs, and better communication and collaboration between workers who operate in greater proximity with one another. However, health and safety issues can arise in open-plan workplaces if they are noisy or badly ventilated, and hot-desking can lead to worker conflicts over preferred workstations (Hirst 2011). Nevertheless, for managers performance improvements associated with this flexibility, seem to outweigh such difficulties; with evidence suggesting these arrangements appeal to younger workers (McElroy and Morrow 2010).

The rise of multi-locational working, working from home or on the move, physically distant from the employer's premises, is a second key element of this kind of flexibility. While people's homes have long been used as work locations, the development of ICT—broadband internet, mobile telephony—has facilitated a greater amount of working from home, sometimes called 'teleworking', especially among professional and managerial occupations. In 2010, some 1.3 million workers worked entirely from home; and there were an additional 3.7 million workers who sometimes worked at home or used their home as a base. Companies like BT and HSBC have been prominent advocates of the business benefits of encouraging staff to work from home, claiming that it leads to productivity improvements and reduces the incidence of sickness absence (BBC News Online 2011b).

Of course, this type of flexibility is not appropriate for all jobs, but even where greater homeworking could be utilized, there seems to be some reluctance to encourage it. Less visible workers might lead to managerial concern regarding their autonomy, obstructing their efforts to exercise control. As a consequence, perhaps, teleworking tends to be associated with highly qualified workers, particularly those in professional and managerial occupations, who tend to be more trusted by their employers (White et al. 2004; Ruiz and Walling 2005). However, a key challenge facing organizations wanting to encourage greater teleworking concerns the possible negative reactions of excluded staff. Workers who remain in the office may feel that they become unfairly burdened and have to cope with the difficulties arising from colleagues who are not present, with adverse consequences for their own job satisfaction (Collins 2005; Golden 2007). See Box 8.3 for a case which illustrates some of the issues and challenges arising from this kind of locational flexibility.

The third type of locational flexibility concerns the process of 'off-shoring' (Blinder 2006). As Chapter 15 demonstrates, multinational companies have taken advantage of the benefits provided by globalization to relocate operations to countries around the world where they can be provided at a much cheaper cost. India has become an important location for off-shored business services like accountancy and publishing. However, perhaps it has become best known as a key site for call centres (Taylor and Bain 2005). These examples show how locational flexibility ties in with another form of flexibility—namely contractual flexibility. The work multinationals off-shore to other countries is generally undertaken by contractor firms which specialize in the relevant business. But the process of off-shoring has produced its own challenges and difficulties, not least efforts by campaign groups and international bodies to regulate labour standards in the supply chains of multinationals more effectively (see Williams et al. 2013: chapter 4).

8.2.4 Functional flexibility

The fourth way in which organizations can secure flexibility in the way that they utilize their human resources concerns *how* workers are used, or 'functional flexibility'. By this we mean

Box 8.3 Research in focus
The challenges of managing locational flexibility

Some of the issues and challenges relating to managing locational flexibility are apparent from the study of a publishing company by Fogarty, Scott, and Williams (2011). The organization had made a major strategic effort to encourage greater locational flexibility, setting up a formal scheme whereby staff were permitted to work at home for up to three days per week. However, a new chief executive effectively reversed the policy, closing access to the home-working scheme to new entrants, although staff already using it were able to continue to do so. Subsequently, though, individual managers permitted employees outside the scheme to work from home on an occasional ad hoc basis. Thus two parallel, but contrasting, flexible working regimes ran alongside one another—one formal and regulated, and the other informal and unregulated. The latter caused particular difficulties because of its unpredictability; unlike employees on the 'formal' scheme, it was not always known when 'informal' home-workers would be available in the office, making it difficult to convene meetings. They might fail to inform colleagues that they were working from home until either the day concerned or even after the event. Senior managers seemed to make the most use of informal home-working, giving rise to perceptions of inconsistent treatment and hypocrisy when it was denied to subordinates. Moreover, the vagaries of informal home-working, whose participants received neither training nor support on how to work properly from home, seems to have tainted employees' perceptions of the formal scheme, causing it to be viewed less positively as a result.

how the balance of work tasks, skills, and job requirements of the workforces can be managed to ensure that workers are more effective in a range of different job roles, and thus more able to contribute to improving organizational performance, part of what White et al. (2004) term 'intelligent flexibility' (see Chapter 12). The teamworking and empowerment initiatives described in Chapter 4 are often viewed as key elements of enhancing this mode of flexibility. However, there is little evidence that functional flexibility is widely used. Instead, there seems to be a preference for attaining flexibility either by getting staff to work harder, rather than smarter, as is apparent from studies which point to rising work pressures (e.g. Green 2006), or by instituting more rigorous control over performance standards, and thus lessening workers' autonomy (McGovern et al. 2007).

8.2.5 Flexible human resources?

Evidently, there is a strong business case for utilizing human resources in a flexible manner, consistent with reducing employment costs, enhancing productivity, and securing better performance outcomes through greater adaptability. Yet there are a number of problems with this view. For one thing, it is far from clear that the way in which human resources are utilized in organizations has been transformed through greater flexibility. Change has either been rather gradual, as in the case of temporal flexibility (McGovern et al. 2007), or, when it comes to trends in contractual, locational, and functional flexibility, far from clear-cut. A further problem concerns the short-term considerations driving flexibility, such as cost-cutting, rather than a fundamental belief in the desirability of long-term transformative change.

Organizations also face a number of challenges: some types of flexibility (e.g. contractual flexibility) imply greater flux, whereas managers generally prefer to operate in more stable and predictable environments. They may also have to deal with the potential conflict that arises from differences between organizational demands for flexibility and the expectations of staff. The rather limited prevalence of 'intelligent flexibility' suggests that conventional methods of enhancing productivity, based on flexibility through work intensification, are viewed as more beneficial. Moreover, flexibility often seems to be a euphemism for treating workers as if they are disposable and expendable commodities, deserving of low pay and limited rights and protection. Although EU legislation means that workers on part-time and fixed-term contracts, and those employed on a temporary basis through agencies, have some rather limited rights to equal treatment, it does not do very much to prevent organizations from benefiting from this kind of flexibility.

Summary and further reading

- Securing flexibility over how workers are utilized is a potentially very important way in which organizations can manage human resources effectively. The principal methods we have considered are contractual flexibility, temporal (working time) flexibility, locational flexibility, and functional flexibility.

- There are a number of issues and challenges facing organizations that want to utilize workers in a flexible manner, consistent with a more purposive and strategic approach to managing human resources, including the propensity to use flexibility as a means of achieving short-term cuts in labour and having to meet the expectations of staff.

See Marchington, Cooke, and Hebson (2010) for a review of the HR issues relating to multi-employer environments. Walsh (2010) provides a good assessment of changes in working time arrangements, including flexibility issues. For a good case study of the issues and challenges involved in operating locational flexibility, see Fogarty, Scott, and Williams (2011).

8.3 Talent management: the challenges of succession planning and employee retention

Another means by which labour can be flexibly deployed within an organization will depend upon the extent to which workers possess the requisite skills and knowledge that the company needs to achieve its strategic objectives—now and in the future. Chapter 5 outlines how organizations might engage in workforce planning, often tying in this process with that of recruitment and selection to ensure that the company employs those who have such desired competences. Chapter 6 highlights the additional contribution here made by training and development activities in equipping organizations with requisite skills and knowledge.

8.3.1 The 'war for talent'

In recent years, the concept and practices of 'talent management' have emerged as an area of interest in its own right, not subsumed by the other categories of workforce planning, succession, training, or development. One of the main reasons for this was stimulated by the *War for Talent* reports produced by the consulting firm McKinsey (e.g. Michaels et al. 2001). They argued that the 'knowledge economy' was placing a premium on talented organizational staff, with globalization making competition for these employees a worldwide issue and not simply a local one. In turn, changing demographics (especially ageing populations) were intensifying this 'war for talent', and changing values were generating less organizational loyalty and commitment, thus making talent retention a growing challenge (Preece, Iles, and Chuai 2011). Therefore maintaining organizational competitiveness and continuity would become increasingly difficult unless organizations were able to compete effectively in securing the necessary number and quality of requisite staff (Stephens 2010).

Although economic circumstances have fluctuated since 2008, the challenge of attracting, developing, and retaining talented employees remains, because even though a large pool of unemployed workers might exist nationally or internationally, there is an acute shortage of talent in key areas (as shown in the discussion of skills shortages in Chapter 6). This means that the competition for talent worldwide will continue to be a significant challenge, which will be exacerbated when economic conditions are more favourable and talented employees are even more in demand. If such challenges are left unmet, this will impact global business strategies in both the short and longer term (Tarique and Schuler 2010). This is outlined in relation to life sciences in Box 8.4.

8.3.2 Talent management perspectives and practices

Although a number of attempts have been made to define the term 'talent management', there is little agreement as to what it *is*. The CIPD (2007d: 2) observed that talent management requires HRM professionals and their clients to understand how they define talent, who they identify as

Box 8.4 Window on work
Talent management shortages in the life sciences

Employers in the life sciences sector—covering the areas of biotechnology, diagnostics, and medical devices—recognize the importance of talent management but too few are putting it into practice effectively. Survey findings of nearly 400 senior executives conducted by recruitment consultancy RSA found that more than 90 per cent of respondents identified talent management as a key priority. However, only 26 per cent of organizations had an active strategy for retaining talent, while 68 per cent had no clear leadership succession plan. Failing to manage and retain top talent means that 71 per cent of the executives questioned stated that filling senior management vacancies takes six months or more. Almost half (43 per cent) of respondents agreed that the life sciences sector does not give adequate consideration to retaining top talent, and one in five admitted that talent management could not be considered a strength of their organization. One of the challenges to the sector will come as the industry emerges from the wider economic downturn and confidence returns in terms of keeping valued people as well as finding new executives.

Sources: Churchard (2010); RSA (2010).

the talented, and what their typical background might be. However, survey evidence (e.g. Uren et al. 2004) suggests that, whilst companies frequently use a consistent definition of 'talent' and 'talent management', these definitions are highly specific to the company and depend on the organization's business strategy, the type of firm, and the overall competitive environment. This suggests an organizational preference for a contingency approach which allows descriptions of talent to be tailored to individual organizations, rather than adopting standardized models.

The CIPD (2009: 2) defines 'talent management' as 'the systematic attraction, identification, development, engagement/retention and deployment of those individuals with high potential who are of particular value to an organization'. It reserves the term for 'high-value' staff, high performers, or those identified as having high potential. So whilst the *pool* of the talented might be quite wide, suggesting a degree of democracy, talent management activities are reserved for the narrowly defined elite. This approach, which is very common, needs to be set against those which are more inclusive, where the 'talent' element of the term 'talent management' is often synonymous with 'staff'. An example of talent management changing focus from the narrow to the broad can be seen in Box 8.5.

The different definitions of and perspectives taken towards talent management are allied to quite different practices and dependent on whether organizations adopt the more open or the restrictive approach (Iles, Chuai, and Preece 2010; Iles, Preece, and Chuai 2010; Preece, Iles, and Chuai 2011). These are subsumed under four headings: exclusive people, exclusive

Box 8.5 Window on work
Extending talent management activities from the 5 per cent

Financial services organization Aviva took the decision to broaden their definition of talent to that it embraces all staff and not just the elite 5 per cent of employees. The company operates in 27 countries and therefore is engaged in a global multi-front need for skilled employees. This has meant that the organization has had to soften its focus on the extremes of the performance bell curve (i.e. the excellent performers and those with limited potential) and to shift attention to those located in the middle section or the 'vital many' (Baker 2009; Phillips 2009). When the organization experiences lower demand, talent management activities can involve job rotation around different departments, offices, and clients, as well as mentoring activities to train partners. Therefore the focus on the elite has not been elided, but the system overall has been supplemented by a much broader perspective and involvement in talent management.

EXCLUSIVE

Key roles/positions	*Key selected people*
TM Focus: managers/leaders	TM Focus: identifying 'A' performers /roles
Talent management job focused	Talent management performer focused
POSITION	**PEOPLE**
Focus: teams, cultures, networks	Focus: all staff have talent
Grow talent internally & retain it	Regular development for all staff
Retain 'stars' grown by company-specific factors	Manage/develop all for high performance

INCLUSIVE

Social capital	*Wide talent pool*

Figure 8.1 Perspectives on talent management.

positions, inclusive people, and social capital. Figure 8.1 illustrates this diagrammatically (Iles et al. 2010: 182).

The 'exclusive-people' perspective invests scarce developmental assignments and resources in the most promising talent, although this should never be at the expense or neglect of other employees (Walker 2002). This perspective implies that talent is neither title nor position related, but is based on segmentation—the division of the workforce into sections to be treated differently. A controversial example of this in action can be seen in General Electronic's segmentation of its employees into categories A–C, with A being the top 10–20 per cent performing staff, B the middle 70 per cent, and Cthe lowest 10–20 per cent who often face stringent examination of their performance. Ledford and Kochanski (2004: 217) argue that this kind of segmentation is crucial to talent management: 'Successful organizations tend to have a dominant talent segment, whilst their weaker peers have a bit of everything. But no company can be all things to all people'.

The 'exclusive positions' perspective also takes a narrow view, but on a different basis. As the CIPD's Learning and Talent Management Survey (CIPD 2011k) indicates, this is a common approach with nearly two-thirds of organizations across all sectors surveyed focusing activities on designated posts, i.e. senior managers. Here, talent management systems are focused on the identification of key positions in the organization and ensuring a perfect match of 'A players' and 'A positions'. This match is then expected to contribute to higher performance outcomes (Huselid, Beatty, and Becker 2005). Those supporting this perspective argue that, given the limited financial and managerial resources available to attract, select, develop, and *retain* top performers, companies cannot afford to have A quality players in all positions. As a response, a portfolio approach is recommended, placing the best employees in strategic positions and good performers in support positions. Those in the C bracket, who do not add value, are to be outsourced or eliminated. As can be seen, this approach shares some common ground with the 'exclusive people' positions in that it emphasizes workforce differentiation, where various players within an organization receive disproportionate attention and development according to the strategic importance of their position to the company.

In contrast with the two exclusive perspectives taken towards talent management, the inclusive approaches take a more humanistic stance that sees potentially all staff having 'talent' and that the task is to manage employees to deliver high performance. According to Stainton (2005), talent management policies and practices should adopt a broad approach and recognize that everyone has the capability and potential to display talent. Hence, all employees, for example, should go through the same talent identification process. Within this element of the model, opportunities are essential as talent requires an opportunity to be displayed so regular

chances to learn grow and develop are needed to ensure that people can fulfil their potential (Ashton and Morton 2005). Not-for-profit organizations are more likely to operate their talent management strategies on this basis than are organizations from other sectors (CIPD 2011*k*).

The social capital perspective argues that the talent management literature fails to take context, social capital, and organizational capital in relation to organizational performance. Put simply, proponents of this view argue that talent management over-emphasizes individual talents and downplays the role of teams, cultures, leadership, and networks in giving talent direction and opportunity. Within this frame, organizations should focus on growing talent internally and retaining emerging stars. But it also sees company-specific factors such as resources, systems, leadership, training, and team membership as facilitating and impacting on the stars' success. Organizations like drilling company KCA Deutag (CIPD 2010*g*) provide an example of a more inclusive form of talent management in a global organization—one which acknowledges the ways that talent management intersects with social, cultural, and communication factors and is also shaped by these issues.

8.3.3 Engagement with talent management

The CIPD's (CIPD 2011*k*) Learning and Talent Management Survey (CIPD 2011*k*) found that increasing numbers of companies surveyed were engaging in talent management, but that this was more prevalent within the private sector—especially with companies that had a training budget—and was more likely to be found in larger companies employing 5000 or more staff than in those organizations with smaller numbers of employees. Larger companies were more concerned with developing high-potential employees and securing managerial/leader succession, whereas smaller employers were tending to use it to attract and retain key staff. Therefore the rationales adopted for the use of talent management schemes also seem to vary according to size.

However, the survey's findings as to their effectiveness suggest that many organizations are finding their talent management activities problematic. Only half of the organizations surveyed with talent management activities rated them as effective and only 3 per cent saw them as very effective. From the employee perspective, whilst being included within a talent management programme is viewed positively by participants, a common cause for complaint was the perceived lack of transparency around the selection process as well as a lack of line manager buy-in to the programme and a lack of management trust in the talent pool, which also undermined the value of the programme for participants. The survey found that that those who were not actively talent managed were less likely to feel that they had a future within the organization, were less able to secure development opportunities, and were less likely to exert a high degree of control over their careers (CIPD 2010*c*). This suggests that the 'exclusive' talent management approaches have a potential 'sting' for the excluded. Box 8.6 offers the opportunity to think through the implications for this group of workers.

8.3.4 Talent management and employee retention

When reviewing the success of talent management strategies, many organizations look at retention figures. According to the CIPD (2011*k*), one of the four most common ways talent management activities are evaluated is via the retention of those identified as 'high potential' and through the ability of the organization to fulfil its succession management plans. The direct costs, work disruption, and losses of organizational memory and seasoned mentors

Box 8.6 Learning activity
Talent management

Much of the talent management literature focuses on those included within talent management initiatives. But how would you respond to those who fall outside these programmes?

associated with turnover are significant issues. Even when economic circumstances are volatile, it is short-sighted to ignore retention management, as there is evidence that high unemployment rates have little impact on the turnover of high-performing employees (Trevor 2001). Additionally, the aggressive recruitment of valuable employees still occurs and the retention of high performers remains critical (Smith 2009). Departing employees often take valuable knowledge, expertise, and relationships with them when they go—and will often use them with their new employer, meaning that the loss of an employee can result in the loss of competitive advantage. Thus, when looking at retaining valued staff, those tasked with responsibility for talent management must understand what is important to employees. As firms find it more challenging to retain their key employees, understanding reasons for turnover might help an organization to achieve a competitive advantage (Allen, Bryant, and Vardaman 2010).

 ## Summary and further reading

- Organizations have always needed to ensure that they have sufficiently skilled employees in order to achieve their strategic business goals. According to the CIPD (2010c), what differentiates 'talent management' initiatives from the familiar range of HRM activities are changes in workforce demography with an increasingly elderly population and declining numbers of younger workers, the persistence of skills shortages in certain areas, the desire for many to have a more equitable work–life balance, and the increasingly competitive global markets within which businesses now operate.

- Talent management represents a far wider-reaching holistic approach which moves towards better 'joining up' of business strategy, HR practices, and individual goals. But it is important to note that talent management is overwhelmingly owned by the organization for its own strategic ends. This does not mean that individuals cannot benefit from talent management activities, but for some organizations inclusion within these programmes can be exclusive, raising questions about the implications for those who fall outside the remit of talent management practices.

- Organizations have adopted a variety of different approaches to talent management, highlighting that each organization will have different resourcing requirements now and in the future and that these are led by organizational strategies—with little or no room for worker agency.

The CIPD surveys provide a good overview over time as to the extent of talent management engagement in the UK and associated practices. Preece, Iles, and Chuai (2011) provide a highly readable account of the background and growth of talent management as well as the main perspectives taken towards this work.

8.4 Managing employee well-being

The ways in which staff are utilized have implications for their health, safety, and overall well-being. Effective management of human resources may offer a link between employee well-being and business performance (Pilbeam and Corbridge 2010) by, for example, reducing the extent of sickness absence or enhancing levels of organizational commitment. Moreover, it can also help organizations to avoid the costs of litigation arising from poor health and safety standards. Perhaps understandably, then, there is an increasing emphasis attached to the importance of 'wellness' at work (MacDonald 2005; Berry, Mirabito, and Baun 2010; Lee and Blake 2010) based on this notion that staff well-being is an integral feature of successful organizations. One of the purposes of this section is to expose this claim to critical scrutiny.

8.4.1 The rationale for management action (1): the business case

Claims are often made that organizations are increasingly taking the health, safety, and well-being of their employees more seriously (e.g. MacDonald 2005; Cartwright and Cooper 2011). Two factors seem to be particularly important when such claims are made. First, a key rationale for management action concerns the business benefits that are said to arise from taking effective action here. Central to this argument is the assumption that if people are managed at work effectively, their commitment to organizational goals and their contribution to business goals

will increase. Hence, it is logical to assume that ensuring the health, safety, and well-being of staff is good for business—especially given the costs of sickness absence for organizations (Coats and Max 2005; CIPD 2008a). The Health and Safety Executive (HSE) calculate that in 2010–2011 some 26.4 million days were not worked as a result of work-related injury or ill-health, and much of this total (10.8 million days) was attributable to work-related stress, depression, or anxiety. As a result, the annual cost to employers of work-related injury and ill-health amounts to more than £3 billion (HSE 2011a).

Yet in a competitive market environment, it is doubtful that by itself the 'business case' for improved employee well-being will necessarily guarantee better health and safety outcomes at work. Nor should one assume that human resource management interventions would necessarily help, because there are circumstances under which it makes business sense for staff to be treated as 'resources', with the minimum of concern given to their welfare. Such a 'sacrificial' approach to managing human resources has been identified in some call centres (Wallace, Eagleson, and Waldersee 2000, cited in Boyd 2003) and has been illustrated by James and Lloyd (2008) in their study of three food processing factories where persistent pressure from supermarkets for reductions in costs and flexibility in ordering led to greater pressures being placed on workers, to the detriment of their well-being.

8.4.2 The rationale for management action (2): legislation

A second rationale for management action concerns the part played by the law in contributing to health and safety improvements in workplaces. The Health and Safety at Work Act 1974 (HASAWA) is the basis of the statutory framework regulating workplace health and safety in the UK, and it sets out the legal responsibilities of all parties when it comes to maintaining healthy and safe workplaces. Importantly, HASAWA was designed as a 'piece of enabling legislation' (Dawson et al. 1988: 14); in other words, it provides a mechanism for the implementation of additional regulations, particularly those emanating from the EU, which have statutory effect.

There are five key elements of the statutory framework relating to health and safety at work that should be noted. First, there is a particular emphasis on self-regulation of health and safety standards by employers and workers themselves. HASAWA does not set out a series of rules that must be followed; rather, it places the onus on people in organizations to effect good practice themselves.

Secondly, related to this there is a standard of 'reasonable practicability' that employers must follow when judging whether or not to deal with a potential risk to workplace health and safety. This is important because it gives employers some flexibility to manage risk in their workplaces appropriately, rather than impose a set of prescriptive rules upon them.

The third element concerns the key role of risk assessment. The Management of Health and Safety at Work (MHSW) Regulations 1999 oblige employers to undertake a risk assessment of all workplaces. In carrying out risk assessments, employers are required to judge whether or not any risk to health and safety can be eradicated entirely; if it cannot, action must be taken to diminish its potential effects.

A fourth key element pertains to the involvement of workers. Where trade unions are recognized, an employer is obliged to permit the appointment and activities of union safety representatives and, where at least two union safety representatives request it, to establish a safety committee. These representatives have the right to time off, to be trained, to carry out investigations and inspections, and to make representations on these matters. While effective independent worker representation has a positive impact on health and safety outcomes, it is often lacking, and there is evidence of a widespread failure of managers to consult with their staff over health and safety issues (Walters et al. 2005; Walters and Nichols 2007).

The final element of the legal framework concerns the role of the HSE. It is responsible for upholding and enforcing health and safety standards by publishing advice and guidance (e.g. on how to manage work-related stress effectively (http://www.hse.gov.uk/stress/standards/)) and through inspection and enforcement activity. For example, in 2010–2011 the HSE initiated 912 prosecutions of employers as a result of inadequate health and safety standards (HSE 2011a).

The HSE increasingly emphasizes the importance of education, advice, and information provision in promoting improved workplace health and safety standards. It also maintains that inspections should be directed at identified problem areas. Such an approach would seem to accord with the legal emphasis on self-regulation. However, without the stick of effective legal sanctions behind it, the carrot of self-regulation loses much of its capacity to change behaviour (Dawson et al. 1988).

Plans by the coalition government for 'very substantial' reductions in inspections, alongside major cuts to the HSE's budget (DWP 2011a: 3), have prompted concerns that workplace health and safety standards could deteriorate. The government has been particularly influenced by complaints from business that systems of health and safety regulation are overly bureaucratic, burdensome, and generate too much frivolous litigation from workers seeking financial compensation (Lord Young 2010). However, a government-commissioned review of the system of health and safety regulation found that there was little wrong with it and that most of the perceived problems arise from a lack of understanding of what the regulations require or their inappropriate application by employers (Löfstedt 2011). Self-regulation already gives managers a considerable amount of discretion concerning health and safety procedures and their design, but many employers do not comply with, or are ignorant of, their statutory obligations (Robinson and Smallman 2006). Weakening a regulatory system which already imposes few obligations on employers to improve employee well-being seems likely to undermine efforts to build healthier and safer workplaces.

8.4.3 Health, safety, and the working environment

It is generally recognized that a large degree of under-reporting means that official health and safety statistics fail to capture the full extent of work-related injuries and ill-health (Nichols 1997; Boyd 2003). For example, there are an estimated 600,000 injuries at work each year, around a third of which lead to absences from work of at least three days. Yet reported injury rates are much lower (HSE 2011a). The most serious incidents involve workplace fatalities; in 2010–2011, 171 workers were killed at work. A high proportion of workplace fatalities occur in two industry sectors—construction (50 deaths) and agriculture (34). The incidence of worker fatalities has declined considerably since the 1980s, partly because of the efforts of the HSE, but more importantly because there has been a substantial decline in the number of people who work in relatively dangerous industries where the proportion of fatal incidents is relatively high. However, the incidence of worker fatalities does not capture the full extent to which jobs are responsible for mortality. For example, about 8000 people die each year as a result of having been exposed to carcinogens at work. In 2009, some 2300 people died from mesothelioma, mainly because they had been exposed to asbestos at work; a slightly lower number (2000) died from asbestos-related lung cancer.

The incidence of non-fatal injuries that occur at work has also fallen since the 1980s, again largely because the number of people employed in dangerous industries has declined. In 2010–2011, there were some 25,000 reported work-related major non-fatal injuries among employees, and a further 90,000 other injuries. Injury rates are relatively high in some parts of the economy, notably the agriculture, construction, transport, and manufacturing sectors. There is also an association between workplace size and injury and illness rates. All things being equal, workers in smaller workplaces are more likely to suffer from a work-related injury than those in larger workplaces (Fenn and Ashby 2004). In addition to being a cause of deaths and injuries, work is also a source of ill-health. See Table 8.2 for the prevalence of work-related ill-health and the number of workplace injuries reported by employers in 2010–2011.

8.4.4 Changes in occupational structure and workplace hazards and injuries

One of the most notable developments in the area of occupational health and safety concerns the changing nature of workplace hazards. For much of the twentieth century, injuries and illnesses sustained in industries such as mining and manufacturing dominated the occupational health and safety agenda. Many workers continue to suffer from injuries or illnesses caused or exacerbated by industrial processes of some kind. Where some jobs are concerned, such as firefighters, it is impossible to make this inherently dangerous work safe. However, the DVD interview with Clare Fitzgerald of the Hampshire Fire and Rescue service outlines their 'safe

Table 8.2 Workplace health and safety in the UK, 2010–2011

Total number of cases of work-related illness in the previous 12 months	1,384,000
Musculoskeletal disorders	508,000
Stress, depression, or anxiety	400,000
Breathing or lung problems	31,000
Hearing problems	22,000
Total number of fatal injuries	171
Total number of employer-reported non-fatal injuries to employees	115,379
Major non-fatal injuries	24,726

Source: HSE (2011*a*).

person' approach; illustrating what this entails and the pressures that resulted in changes to health and safety management systems.

Other changes in the economy and occupational structure have contributed to a large growth in the number of people working in office environments, and an increasing number of people are also employed in the service sector. This has resulted in a shift in the kind of work-related injuries and illnesses being reported (Fenn and Ashby 2004). As a result of this shift in occupational structure, over half a million people suffer from some kind of musculoskeletal disorder that has been caused, or exacerbated, by a job. The most common conditions include back problems and those that affect the upper limbs and neck, with the most well-known musculoskeletal disorder being 'repetitive strain injury' (RSI). This is a condition that causes people to suffer from pain, numbness, muscle weakness, pins and needles, and loss of movement (Canaan 1999: 145), largely in their fingers, hands, and arms. It is a condition which is often linked to the use of new technology by office-based workers. In a study of the Australian public sector, Goldfinch, Gauld, and Baldwin (2011) demonstrate that the prevalence of shoulder and arm pain among workers was related to the use of laptop computers, emails, and handheld technology devices such as smartphones.

Violence at work is an increasingly notable feature of the contemporary service economy and can be costly for businesses because it is often a source of sickness absence (McCarthy and Mayhew 2004). The HSE (2011*b*: 3) defines work-related violence as 'any incident in which a person is abused, threatened, or assaulted in circumstances relating to their work'. In 2010–2011 there were an estimated 313,000 threats of violence against workers and some 341,000 actual physical assaults on workers. Although the number of violent incidents at work seems to have declined during the 2000s, they particularly affect some occupations, including the police, the prison service, and those jobs that are characterized by front-line customer service work. Aspects of violence can be neglected by managers, as witnessed by mainly female workers in the social care sector (Baines and Cunningham 2011). Moreover, much verbal abuse of workers by customers goes unreported, partly because of the perception that managers would not take a complaint seriously, or that it would be interpreted as a sign that the complainant was 'not up to the job' (Boyd 2003: 61).

A further aspect of working life in organizations that has important implications for the well-being of employees concerns the nature of their working time arrangements (MacDonald 2005). These increasingly require a large number of workers to undertake their jobs outside normal working hours. For example, the opening hours of call centres often stretch around the clock in order to meet customer convenience (Deery and Kinnie 2004). By disrupting the natural rhythms of the body, night-shift working can be a source of disrupted sleep patterns, increased accident rates, mental health problems, and an increased risk of cardiovascular disease among the workers concerned (Harrington 2001; HSE 2006; Virtanen et al. 2010).

8.4.5 Stress-related ill-health

Finally, we need to recognize the damaging effects of work-related stress on employee well-being. For an individual to experience stress symptoms, the source of the stress must be negatively perceived, and the individual must have inadequate ability to cope with it. Thus the experience of stress is subjective and dependent on individual differences (Clarke and Cooper

2000: 175). The HSE (2008: 1) defines stress as 'the adverse reaction a person has to excessive pressure or other types of demand placed on them'. In 2010–2011, there were some 400,000 reported cases of work-related stress, anxiety, or depression, and the illness can seriously compromise health and well-being with excessive levels of stress being associated with 'heart disease, back pain, gastrointestinal disturbances, anxiety and depression' (Boyd 2003: 46).

The ways in which many jobs are organized and managed are major sources of stress-related ill-health (Robinson and Smallman 2006). This is evident in two particular respects. First, the limited extent to which people are able to exercise discretion over how their jobs are undertaken has been identified as a stressor (Coats and Max 2005). Secondly, it is widely accepted that there has been a process of work intensification over recent years, linked to organizational demands for more effort, in order to produce improvements in business performance, and the use of technical systems that enable managers to monitor the activities of their staff more closely (Green 2006). Excessive work pressures account for a major proportion of the work-related mental health problems experienced by workers. See Box 8.7 for an example of the kind of work being done by the mental health charity Mind to tackle this problem.

Organizational approaches that are designed to improve employee well-being through tackling stress usually fall into one into one of three categories: primary, secondary, or tertiary (see Table 8.3).

Primary preventative interventions are proactive and are designed to prevent exposure to the occurrence of stress. They address sources of difficulty in the workplace through

Box 8.7 Online video link
Boosting mental well-being at work

Go to the Online Resource Centre for a link to video content about mental health issues in the workplace published by the charity Mind.

Table 8.3 A systems approach to job stress

Intervention level		Intervention targets	Examples
Definition and description	Effectiveness		
Primary Proactive **Goal:** reducing potential risk factors or altering the nature of the stressor before workers experience stress-related symptoms or disease	+++	Dealing with stressors at source; organization of work; working conditions Organization focus	Job redesign, workload reduction, improved communication, conflict management and management style, skills development, changing organizational structures, employee consultation
Secondary Ameliorative **Goal:** to help equip workers with knowledge, skills and resources to cope with stressful conditions	++	Employee response to stressors (perceived stress or strain) Organization–individual interface	Cognitive behavioural therapy, coping classes, anger management, time management, stress management training
Tertiary Reactive Goal: to treat, compensate, and rehabilitate workers with enduring stress-related symptoms or disease	+	Short-term and enduring adverse health effects of job Individual focus	Return to work programmes, occupational therapy, medical intervention

Sources: Clarke and Cooper (2000); LaMontagne et al. (2007: 269).

alterations in physical or psychosocial work environments, or via organizational changes. Common examples of primary interventions include job design, changes in work pacing, and enhancement of social support (LaMontagne et al. 2007).

Secondary interventions modify responses to stressors, targeting the individual with the underlying assumption being that addressing individual responses to stressors should be done in addition to—or sometimes in preference to—removing or reducing them. Examples of interventions include stress management classes, meditation, or other forms of intervention designed to help employees either modify or control their perceptions of stressful situations and to make them less vulnerable to stress (Le Fevre, Kolt, and Matheny 2006).

Finally, tertiary responses are reactive and aim to minimize the effects of stress once they have occurred, through either management or treatment of symptoms or disease. These include counselling as well as other rehabilitation programmes. Problems identified in secondary and tertiary interventions should feed back to stressor-focused primary intervention; however instances of this occurring are rare (LaMontagne et al. 2007).

Reviews of job stress interventions indicate that the strategies used are generally limited to the individual-orientated approach (Noblet and LaMontagne 2006). This has been widely condemned because of the elision of the contribution made by adverse working conditions to diseases such as heart disease and cancer. Overall, the criticism that has been directed at this approach indicates that individually focused stress prevention programmes generally fail to deliver sustainable benefits for the employee and the organization (LaMontagne 2004). However, it is an approach that dovetails with the HRM focus on the *individualization* of the employment relationship, arguably sidelining of the role of the organization in producing unhealthy systems and working conditions and generally failing to involve employees in developing strategies to overcome them (LaMontagne et al. 2007).

8.4.6 Organizational responses to promoting well-being (1): occupational health

Occupational health has been defined as the 'promotion and maintenance of the highest degree of physical, mental and social well-being of workers in all occupations by preventing departures from health, controlling risks and the adaptation of work to people, and people to their jobs' (Alli 2008) and as such reflects a long-standing concern of employers with occupational health arrangements. Occupational health has traditionally been associated with manual work, and the function is more likely to be found in larger organizations in the private and public sectors. The kinds of activities carried out by occupational health workers are highly varied, but traditionally they have included providing advice, information, training, and education, pre-employment and statutory medical assessments, health screening and surveillance, post accident/incident assessment and advice, and sickness absence monitoring. However, occupational health practitioners now have to meet the challenge of dealing with very different workplace health issues, such as work-related stress, as well as the demands of an ageing workforce (Arnold 2008).

The Black (2008) Review of the health of Britain's working population has arguably stimulated a new approach to health and work in Britain based on the prevention of illness, the promotion of health and well-being, and an improvement in the health of those out of work. This approach sought a shift in attitudes from key stakeholders; requiring workplaces to play a central role in the promotion of health and well-being and for employers and employees to recognize the importance of preventing ill-health. It also highlighted the ongoing uncertainty within the business community about the business case for investing in workplace health promotion; suggesting that widespread acceptance of a relationship between workplace health and organizational performance has yet to be achieved. Whilst initiatives following the Black Review, such as the Workplace Well-being Charter, and the Public Health Responsibility Deal, promote the business case, there is a paucity of evaluation of such activities and where evaluations occur—see, for example, the account of Liverpool's Year of Health and Well-being in 2010 (http://www.liv.ac.uk/PublicHealth/obs/publications/other/2010Evaluationsingledocreadable.pdf)—finding conclusive evidence as to their impacts is acknowledged as being difficult.

8.4.7 Organizational responses to promoting well-being (2): employee assistance programmes

Dovetailing with the tendency for organizations to deploy secondary and tertiary methods concerning occupational stress and well-being, there has been an increase in the use of Employee Assistance Programmes (EAPs) as organizations seek ways of dealing with particularly challenging aspects of these issues. The Employee Assistance Professionals Association states that 'EAPs address team and individual performance and well being in the workplace. They are strategic interventions *designed to produce organisational benefit* (a quantifiable outcome measurement) through a systems-led approach and human asset management' (emphasis added) (http://www.eapa.org.uk).

EAPs are now a popular benefit provided by many employers. The 2011 IRS survey on benefits provision found that more than six in ten (69.2 per cent) of the 364 employers surveyed offered a counselling service or an EAP (Welfare 2011), with this benefit overtaking private medical insurance as the most commonly offered health benefit. The CIPD's Absence Management Survey (CIPD 2011*l*) found that for the 592 companies surveyed, EAPs were one of the most commonly provided well-being benefits and that for 46 per cent of respondents used the EAP to identify and assist with workplace stress—the highest cause of long-term absence. An example of a UK EAP in practice is outlined in Box 8.8.

However, the precise take-up of EAPs by employees is difficult to assess, as is any evaluation of published findings (Cascio and Boudreau 2011). In the UK, research survey evidence typically covers only a few hundred organizational respondents, so although it is possible to plot trends across time in terms of such issues as take-up and the range of activities EAPs provide, the evidence obtained is hardly definitive. This is not *necessarily* worrying for organizations, but it might depend on the rationales used by the organization when introducing EAPS and whether those accessing the EAP were doing so for those reasons. The costs of EAPs are variable, with providers calculating the cost of their services according to a fairly low level of use, and range widely from £30 per capita for a group of 200 employees to £10 per capita for a group of 1000, or less than £7 for a group of 3000 (Charlton 2010*a*). Box 8.9 gives the opportunity to consider how an EAP might be evaluated by an organization.

Although a standard EAP model does not exist, many EAPs have common core components such as the provision of confidential assessment, counselling, and therapeutic services for employees who might be experiencing a range of personal, emotional, and psychological problems. This is often accompanied by a telephone helpline for advice on domestic, legal, and financial matters. Some will provide an advice line for line managers to help them handle difficult situations at work, such as interpersonal conflicts and emotional problems that staff might

Box 8.8 Practitioner perspective
EAPs in practice

One example of an organization that has introduced an EAP is Cambridge University Hospitals NHS Foundation Trust (http://www.cuh.org.uk). It has 7000 employees and the EAP offers a range of services, such as face-to-face and telephone counselling, internet and intranet advice, mediation, and critical incident responses. Most people self-refer to the service and annual take-up runs at around 5 per cent of the workforce. The EAP is promoted through a number of routes such as leaflets, posters, quarterly information, and question and answer sessions, and an EAP representative attends departmental and team briefings as well as occupational health meetings. An EAP management information report is produced quarterly, detailing usage and making recommendations about relevant issues as well as promoting the service. Whilst those responsible for the introduction and maintenance of the EAP acknowledge that it is difficult to measure whether there are any quantifiable benefits to the organization, they argue that the EAP is a contributory factor to the very good levels of staff engagement and low labour turnover and sickness figures, seeing the EAP as a contributory factor and also helpful in terms of its dignity at work initiative (Suff 2010*c*; Cambridge University Hospitals NHS Foundation Trust 2011).

Box 8.9 Skills exercise
Evaluating Employee Assistance Programmes (EAPs)

In small groups, look at the kinds of activities provided by EAPs. Try and derive a degree of consensus as to what they generally offer and how they deliver their services. Once you have done this, decide how you would evaluate the effectiveness of an EAP if you were an employer who had purchased one for his/her employees. What criteria would you use? How would you implement these criteria and come to an ultimate assessment of the effectiveness of this programme?

be experiencing. Critical success factors for an EAP will include offering a range of provision and tailoring it to the needs of the organization and the workforce, reaching and supporting staff before crisis, being effectively promoted, and having a clear referral process (Suff 2010c).

Finally, EAPs should provide feedback to the organization about service usage as well as 'hotspot' areas in the organization. This benefit has often been used by HR and occupational health personnel when advocating the adoption of an EAP. However, the extent to which this is provided has been questioned (Rankin 2007). It has been argued that the success of an EAP will be determined by its ability to recognize the ethos and predominant values of the organization and then to install or adjust the EAP provision accordingly (Berridge and Cooper 1994). However, it is important to note that an individual or collective voice by the employee in determining the introduction, focus, or content of any proposed EAP is largely absent; EAPS are usually a managerially instigated and imposed intervention.

Summary and further reading

- The health, safety, and well-being of staff are key aspects of the way in which human resources are managed in organizations. Employee well-being can, in theory, lead to heightened employee commitment and to improvements in organizational performance.

- Although there has been a decline in the incidence of work-related injuries and ill-health linked to occupations based in manufacturing industries, the development of an office-based service economy has directed attention to other types of condition.

- Organizational approaches to managing employee well-being are generally dominated by secondary and tertiary types of intervention. These put the onus on the individual to make any appropriate lifestyle changes, or to undertake procedures that enable them to cope with unhealthy working environments more readily. Despite their effectiveness, primary types of intervention have been effectively sidelined, and there has been a trend to the externalization of occupational health and safety provision, largely in the form of Employee Assistance Programmes (EAPs).

- Effective human resource management has the potential to reconcile the conflict that exists between the pressure to maximize productivity and the need to maintain the health and safety of staff. However, in a competitive market environment, the business case for supporting employee well-being may be insufficient to ensure that it actually takes place.

The Health and Safety Executive (www.hse.gov.uk) and the Institute of Occupational Health and Safety (www.iosh.co.uk) are useful sources of information about news and current developments. LaMontagne (2007) offers a critical assessment of organizational approaches to stress management and Rankin (2007) offers a rare critique of EAPs.

8.5 Conclusion

This chapter has explored the ways in which employees are utilized within contemporary organizations, highlighting the problematic nature of many of these practices. It has illustrated that demands for worker flexibility, for example, can have profound consequences for their well-being. In the so-called 'War for Talent', the concept of the 'talented' worker can be designed in highly inclusive ways whereby the term effectively stands for all staff. However, the balance of rhetoric and practice suggests that organizations utilize a narrower view, with a much smaller range of employees being included within the ranks of the 'talented' with positive implications for investment in training and careers, as well as knock-on effects for an employee's sense of emotional well-being. For those who are not included, the evidence is highly negative in terms of their commitment, morale, and perceptions of their employer; suggesting that there is a potential 'sting' here to exclusive talent management practices.

Finally, as highlighted in Section 8.4, a case is now being argued that a safe and healthy workforce will result in sustained business performance. However, the relationship between well-being interventions and organizational performance is more problematic than generally presented. In some cases, as shown in Sections 8.2 and 8.4, business performance can be contingent upon the use of unhealthy practices and unsafe working environments. But evidence suggests that instead of investing in primary interventions, the onus is being placed upon individualized interventions witnessed in Employment Assistance Programmes, which effectively sideline line managers and the HR function from tackling the issues giving rise to stress or poor working conditions at source.

Improvements to worker well-being and the alleviation of stress could potentially be delivered through effective HRM and the creation of 'healthy' jobs and more inclusive talent management strategies that are argued to be good for employee and employers. But, as this chapter shows, reconciling the conflict between maximizing performance and maintaining a physically and mentally healthy working environment is often undermined by attaining short-term targets linked to cost reductions.

 ## Assignment and discussion questions

1 What are the main risks to the health, safety, and well-being of employees in contemporary workplaces?

2 Critically assess the main features of the statutory framework governing health and safety at work.

3 To what extent can human resource management interventions improve employee well-being while also contributing to improvements in business performance?

4 Some organizations include all staff within their definitions and practices of talent management, whereas others are more restrictive. Drawing on your own experiences of organizations, what is your view on this issue and why?

5 How far do responsibilities for worker well-being lie with the employer or with the employee?

 ## Online Resource Centre

Test your understanding of this chapter with online questions and answers, keep up to speed with changes to the law through regular updates, and use selected weblinks to quickly access useful resources and further information. Visit the Online Resource Centre at:
www.oxfordtextbooks.co.uk/orc/gilmore_williams2e/

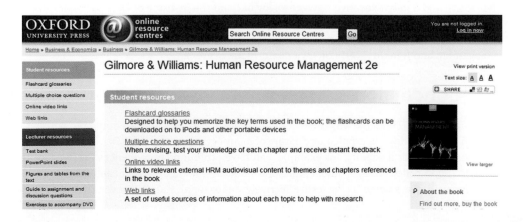

Case study
Obesity at work—challenges for employers?

According to a European Commission report (Godfrey 2011), the UK is the most overweight country in Europe with roughly one in four UK adults being obese and more than half being overweight. If this trend continues at its current rate, nine in ten British men and women of working age will be overweight or obese by 2050 (Smedley 2012). In recent years, governments have attempted to engage businesses on this issue, arguing that tackling obesity needs to involve employers, retailers, the leisure industry, the media, local government, and the voluntary sector (Griffiths 2009). Where employers are concerned, obesity accounts for approximately £1.3–1.6 billion of lost earnings in the UK, or around 16 million days off as a consequence of certified sickness absence.

However, the scientific consensus is that the continuing growth in the levels of obesity is not predominantly a matter of personal choice, but more the result of a so-called 'obesogenic' environment—that the world we live in allows and facilitates obesity—which arguably puts pressure on employers to provide an environment which encourages and facilitates weight loss and a healthy lifestyle. The ways work is designed and carried out in contemporary organizations often exacerbates the problem of obesity and weight gain because of its increasingly sedentary nature, and flexible working patterns can see employees missing out on workplace initiatives designed to promote exercise and healthy living because they fail to cohere with these modes of work. But whilst many employers already offer regular health checks and subsidized gym membership, provide healthier food options, and subsidize regular sporting activity (Hale 2010), evidence suggests that the longer-term use of these strategies by employees is low, and that organizations need to ensure that a longer-term focus occurs in order to sustain lifestyle change (Bevan 2010).

Finally, research indicates that the overweight and obese face discrimination in the workplace. A survey by Personnel Today in 2007 (Dempsey 2007) found that the majority of the 2603 professionals questioned preferred to offer jobs to staff of a 'normal weight' than to obese employees where candidates were identically qualified. More than a quarter felt that obese workers negatively affected their corporate image and almost half believed that obesity had a negative impact on employee productivity. Yet despite recognition of the problem, almost three-quarters of the respondents admitted that their organization was doing nothing substantive to tackle it.

Questions

1 When it is pertinent for organizations—usually via the line manager—to intervene with reference to an obese member of staff?

2 To what extent should organizations engage with government in fighting obesity? How far is it a private issue for the individual employee?

3 Where employees are working long or antisocial hours, they are less likely to make healthy choices or find time to exercise. What would you suggest employers do to amend the workplace environment? What is feasible here for a variety of organizations—from large to medium-sized and small companies with potentially restricted budgets?

4 What would you recommend employers do to ensure the longer-term engagement with health promotion campaigns aimed at dealing with weight and obesity issues? How would you evaluate their success?

9 Redundancy and human resource management

Steve Williams

Learning objectives

The main objectives of this chapter are:

- to examine the concept of redundancy as a feature of human resource management;
- to identify the principal causes of redundancies;
- to consider how managers in organizations handle redundancies;
- to distinguish the main alternatives to making people compulsorily redundant;
- to assess the impact of redundancy exercises on the workers affected, including remaining employees, and the implications for managing human resources.

9.1 Introduction

Redundancy is an essential feature of human resource management in practice. Its relevance is particularly evident during periods of economic recession, when employers may be overly concerned with reducing employment levels. The term 'redundancy' refers to the dismissal of employees by an employer when, because of the need to make cost savings, for example, job cuts are necessary. Redundancy is one of the most challenging aspects of human resource management, since any decision to make job losses will have a profound impact on the affected people's jobs, their careers, and indeed their entire livelihoods. Much of the current interest in the management of redundancies is devoted to how it can be approached and handled with sensitivity through the provision of timely information, for example, or by putting in place arrangements designed to support people made redundant and to help them to find alternative jobs. One of the main issues in this chapter concerns the extent to which such approaches contribute to the maintenance of managerial control when it comes to instituting redundancy programmes. How far are sophisticated HRM interventions necessary, not out of a concern for employee welfare, but because they support the realization of business objectives, in particular the need to reduce staff numbers as smoothly as possible? For the workers concerned, redundancies, no matter how they are handled, are understandably viewed as a threat and, often, something to be challenged.

Following this introduction, in Section 9.2 we examine what is meant by the concept of redundancy, demonstrate its relevance in contemporary organizations, and identify the main causes of redundancies. In Section 9.3 we consider the main alternatives used by organizations to reduce costs, make efficiency savings, and cut jobs without having to make compulsory redundancies, such as early retirement schemes and voluntary redundancy programmes. The focus of Section 9.4 is on the characteristic methods managers in organizations use to handle redundancies, including the typical criteria used to select people for dismissal. In Section 9.5 the emphasis is on the aftermath of redundancy exercises. The importance of dealing appropriately with surviving staff is widely recognized as being of crucial importance to the effective management of human resources following a redundancy exercise. Four key issues that arise from this overview of redundancy are then considered in the concluding Section 9.6.

9.2 The nature and causes of redundancy

This section is devoted to understanding the nature and causes of redundancy as a feature of human resource management. Following a discussion of what is meant by 'redundancy', and the need to distinguish it from the broader concept of 'downsizing', the relevance of redundancies to contemporary human resource management is demonstrated. The main causes of redundancies are then examined, illustrated by some key examples, before four key issues relating to understanding redundancy are considered.

9.2.1 The nature of redundancy

Our first task is to examine what is meant by the term 'redundancy', distinguishing it from other terms that are often used in the HRM vocabulary, such as 'downsizing' and 'delayering'. The concept of 'downsizing' refers to situations where managers in organizations purposefully get rid of hierarchical levels ('delayering'), functions, or job roles in an effort to streamline operations. It can be defined as 'the planned elimination of positions or jobs' (Cascio 1993, cited in Clarke 2005: 245). The main aim of downsizing is to reduce the size of an organization's workforce in order to improve productivity, realize efficiency gains, and thus enhance business performance (Thornhill and Saunders 1998). An employee downsizing programme can be effected in a variety of ways, by encouraging older staff to take early retirement, for example, or by establishing a moratorium on hiring new employees, of which lay-offs and redundancies are just one (Datta et al. 2010). Therefore, while the terms redundancy and downsizing are often used interchangeably, they are by no means synonymous (Cascio 2010).

Redundancy has a more specific meaning, relating to the dismissal of employees as part of a downsizing event, and is one method of realizing a downsizing initiative, albeit a very

important one. It applies to situations where an employer requires fewer employees to undertake a specific set of work activities in a particular area, thus necessitating job losses. In theory it is the position or role filled by an employee that is made redundant, not the employee him/herself, an important distinction that is understandably overlooked, first, because of the tendency of managers to refer to people being made redundant, and, secondly, because of the personal consequences of redundancy for those employees affected by it.

Under UK law, redundancy is a potentially fair reason for dismissing staff. In other words, if employers can demonstrate that a genuine redundancy situation exists, then they should be protected against claims for unfair dismissal from redundant employees. However, see Section 9.4 below for examples of the kinds of action, such as a failure to consult or the use of unlawful criteria for selecting staff for redundancy purposes, that can provoke legal challenges from employees and unions. The key issue is that an employer has to be able to demonstrate that changing business circumstances mean that fewer employees are required, not that there has been a reduction in the amount of work. Thus employers can claim that a redundancy situation arises even when there is no change, or even an increase, in the amount of work to be done, if the needs of the business mean that efficiency savings and staff cutbacks are required.

9.2.2 Redundancy in practice

Redundancy has become an established feature of the human resource management landscape. During the economic recessions of the 1980s and 1990s, for example, millions of workers were made redundant as a result of the closure of coal mines, manufacturing plants, and other sources of industrial employment (Gallie et al. 1998). Yet it is important to recognize the wider significance of redundancy in contemporary human resource management. It is something that is central to the practice of managing human resources in many organizations today since, for an organization faced with pressures to generate cost savings, eliminating jobs through redundancy programmes is often the quickest and easiest way of demonstrating efficiency gains. Organizations frequently resort to redundancies as a means of instituting cost savings because of adverse market conditions or in order to improve competitiveness.

The incidence of redundancies diminished during the late 1990s and 2000s, linked to the growth of the economy. However, during 2008 there was a marked increase in the number of people being made redundant as a result of the economic recession created by the banking crisis. Table 9.1 shows changes in both the level and the rate of redundancies in the UK over the period 2001–2011. The redundancy rate (the number of redundancies per 1000 employees) fluctuated around the 7.5 mark in the early 2000s, before falling to 5.0 in 2007. However, the onset of the recession prompted a rapid rise in the number of redundancies during 2008, with the rate increasing to 9.3 in 2009—in fact it peaked at 11.8 in the first three months of that year—before falling back to 6.2 in 2010, and 4.6 in the first quarter of 2011. However, the redundancy rate began to creep up again during the latter part of 2011 and early 2012, consistent with predictions about the adverse impact of government spending cuts on jobs in public sector organizations such as local government, health, and the police (CIPD 2011f).

It is important to bear in mind that the official redundancy figures do not include other measures used to reduce staff numbers, such as so-called early retirement which may be considered a form of 'disguised' redundancy (Worrall, Cooper, and Campbell 2000). Redundancies are an international phenomenon. In the USA, for example, the economic recession of the late 2000s resulted in the loss of some 6.5 million jobs; and job cuts were also commonplace in many Asian countries, such as South Korea and Taiwan (Datta et al. 2010). See Box 9.1 for details of how Chinese enterprises have had to face the prospect of making considerable redundancies in order to maintain their competitiveness in a fast-changing economic context.

9.2.3 The causes of redundancy

Redundancy, then, is a crucially important feature of human resource management. But what are the principal causes of redundancies? Clearly, the main rationale is economic in nature. Organizations institute redundancies in order to maintain or improve their competitiveness; thus the importance of redundancy lies in its capacity to help employers realize cost savings (Cascio 2010). Yet while managers often justify the need for job losses with reference to vague

Table 9.1 The level and rate of redundancies in the UK, 2001–2011

	Redundancy level*	Redundancy rate**
2001	177,000	7.4
2002	185,000	7.6
2003	158,000	6.4
2004	141,000	5.7
2005	143,000	5.7
2006	138,000	5.5
2007	127,000	5.0
2008	163,000	6.4
2009	234,000	9.3
2010	152,000	6.2
2011	153,000	6.2

*Quarterly averages.
**The number of redundancies per 1000 employees.
Source: Labour Force Survey (www.statistics.gov.uk).

assertions about the need to cut costs and improve efficiency, in fact six main reasons for instituting redundancies can be identified: the structural decline of an industry; the diminution of economic activity; the introduction of new technology and the associated process of work reorganization; organizational restructuring; a requirement for improved financial performance; and business insolvency.

Industrial decline is one reason why organizations institute redundancy exercises. During the 1960s interest in redundancy issues among policy-makers was stimulated by a perceived need to respond to the decline of staple industries and to encourage employees who no longer enjoyed job security to move elsewhere in search of alternative opportunities. The structural decline that affected specific industries was a major cause of redundancies during the 1980s

Box 9.1 International focus
Redundancies in China

Since the 1990s, some 30 million workers have been laid off by state-owned enterprises (SOEs) in China. The development of market forces made many of these organizations, which often employed tens, and even hundreds, of thousands of people, increasingly uncompetitive. One of the key challenges for SOEs was balancing the need to shed labour, often on a large scale, in order to secure efficiency savings, while at the same time avoiding the industrial and political unrest that huge numbers of job losses would produce. Therefore managers spent a considerable amount of time justifying the need for workforce reductions and also persuading workers to leave, for example by emphasizing the opportunities available elsewhere. During 2008, the global economic crisis contributed to job losses in other areas of the Chinese economy. Falling external demand for the goods produced by manufacturing enterprises in China led to hundreds of thousands of lay-offs in the coastal regions, which had hitherto been sites of dynamic growth. One of the challenges facing the authorities in China is the need to stifle the resulting social unrest, or at least to deal with its consequences. Job losses in China have contributed to widespread labour protests, not only because of the termination of employment, but also because of demands for unpaid wages.

Sources: Sheehan, Morris, and Hassard (2000); Friedman and Lee (2010); Pringle (2011).

and 1990s, as jobs were eliminated from coal mining, the docks, and the iron and steel industry in their tens of thousands. This process is still evident in the steel industry (Forde et al. 2009). For example, in May 2011 the Indian company Tata Steel announced plans to cut hundreds of jobs from its plants in the North of England.

Redundancies also occur when firms experience declining demand for their products or services, or decide to rationalize their operations in some way, leading them to institute job losses as a result. In 2011, for example, the multinational drugs company Pfizer announced that it was to close its research and development facility in Sandwich, Southeast England, with the loss of some 2400 jobs. See Box 9.2 for details of the government's response. A particularly notable example of how business rationalization results in redundancies occurred in July 2011 when the media company News International closed its profitable Sunday newspaper, the *News of the World*, with the loss of some 200 jobs. This was in reaction to the scandal which broke out after it emerged that its journalists had been hacking into the phones of celebrities and victims of crime.

The introduction of new technology can be a further source of job losses in organizations, since its effect is often to enable work processes to be rationalized, reducing the need for certain job roles. A notable example of this occurred in the dock industry when technological innovation, in the form of containers for shipping goods at sea, meant that large numbers of dock workers were no longer required for loading and unloading ships. One can see how the process of technological change makes certain jobs redundant when going shopping. More and more retailers now use self-service checkout technology, where the customer is responsible for scanning and paying for their purchases, enabling the stores to reduce costs by employing fewer checkout operators.

Organization-wide restructuring processes frequently cause redundancies. One form of restructuring that has become increasingly commonplace concerns the transfer of organizational functions to locations in countries like India, where staff are much less costly to employ. Such 'offshoring' of jobs, as it is often known, can be an important source of redundancies among the workforce of firms that adopt such an approach. In 2006, for example, the financial services company Aviva announced that hundreds of jobs in its Norwich Union insurance business were to be transferred to India, resulting in redundancies in the UK.

We have already established that redundancies are popular among organizations as a means of realizing efficiency savings, with the aim of improving financial performance. Demands from shareholders for greater profitability, so that the value of their shares rises, mean that managers in publicly quoted companies often come under pressure to institute short-term cost reductions, something that makes redundancy exercises an attractive option. When companies are taken off the stock market and into private ownership, such demands can intensify as the new owners seek to maximize productivity gains. For example. the car breakdown and recovery operator AA made some 3000 job cuts when its operations were rationalized after it was taken over by private equity. Spending cuts linked to the drive to reduce the government's budget deficit seem likely to increase the level of redundancies in the public sector. In July 2011, for example, Her Majesty's Inspector of Constabulary (HMIC) estimated that some 34,000 police jobs would be lost by 2015.

Box 9.2 Online video link
The Pfizer 'task force'

In February 2011, the pharmaceutical company Pfizer announced the closure of its research and development facility in Kent, England. The potential loss of some 2400 jobs, in an area which was already disadvantaged, would clearly have a major adverse impact on the local economy. In response, the government established a task force, comprising politicians, local authority representatives, and members of the business community, which sought to create an 'enterprise zone', combining funds from regional growth initiatives with tax and planning concessions to attract employment to the area. For a report on the first meeting of the task force established to respond to the closure of Pfizer's research and development facility in Sandwich, Kent, go to the Online Resource Centre and follow the relevant link.

Finally, when a business becomes insolvent, redundancies inevitably ensue unless a new buyer can be found quickly. Business failures are a commonplace feature of market economies, especially in a period of economic recession. Between 2008 and 2011, for example, many retail firms ceased trading because of the fall in consumer demand, including Woolworths, music retailer Zavvi, and off licence chain Oddbins. Staff often have little, if any, advance notice of redundancies. In June 2011, for example, the Homeform Group, the owner of Moben Kitchens, Kitchens Direct, and Dolphins Bathrooms, went into administration with some 550 job losses. Moben workers, who claimed that they were given no notice of the intended closure and had not even officially been made redundant, protested outside its Manchester head office demanding unpaid wages.

Redundancy situations may have more than one cause. While business failure was the ultimate reason for the 2005 closure of MG Rover, the last UK-owned volume car manufacturer, with over 5000 redundancies, this has to be seen in the context of the broader structural decline affecting the European car industry. Moreover, the numbers employed had fallen away over a period of many years as MG Rover managers slimmed down the workforce to realize cost savings and introduced new labour-saving technology. See Box 9.3 for a learning activity concerning redundancy.

9.2.4 Understanding redundancy

In order to understand redundancy properly, we need to recognize four important aspects of its nature. First, it is something that has a major impact on the experience of managers and staff. In one in seven UK workplaces, for example, workers will have been either directly or indirectly affected by a redundancy exercise. Moreover, as we have seen, the economic recession of the late 2000s resulted in increased levels of redundancy around the world. Even during periods of economic growth, with rising employment levels, employees' fears of redundancy are seemingly 'well founded' (Turnbull and Wass 2000). The consequences of losing one's job can be profound, since, for most people, it is the principal means of maintaining their livelihoods. Understandably, then, redundancy 'is probably the most evocative and fear inducing form of organizational change for many workers' (Worrall, Cooper, and Campbell 2000: 460).

Secondly, redundancies are commonplace among firms that are operating successfully (Blyton and Turnbull 2004). As we shall see below, the concept of redundancy was originally conceived as applying to firms based in declining sectors of the economy or suffering from adverse business conditions, enabling them to shed labour relatively easily given the diminution in the amount of work required. Yet often redundancies are not so much an effect of organizational poor performance, but rather are used as a means of trying to improve performance.

Box 9.3 Learning activity
Thinking about redundancies

The purpose of this learning activity is to develop your knowledge and understanding of redundancy in practice. Find a recent case where an organization has made redundancies, perhaps by searching the web sites of reputable news organizations like the *Financial Times* or the BBC, and see if you can address the following questions.

1 What were the reasons given for the redundancies?

2 How many redundancies were made?

3 How did the workforce respond to the prospect of being made redundant?

4 Were any alternatives to redundancy considered?

5 Were redundancies avoidable in this case, or were they inevitable?

6 If the organization remains in business, are further redundancies likely, and if they are, why?

7 Overall, how significant are redundancies as a feature of human resource management in practice?

The use of redundancy programmes to institute job losses, and thus realize cost savings, is often viewed by managers as a prime means of improving competitiveness. For an example, see the case of the further education college studied by Hudson (2002). Here, teaching staff employed on permanent contracts were made redundant and re-engaged through an employment agency on a cheaper part-time basis.

Thirdly, following on from this, it is evident that redundancy is a convenient way in which managers can dismiss staff. During the 1960s legislation was enacted (the Redundancy Payments Act (RPA) 1965) which, among other things, gave workers the right to a payment, based on their age and length of service, when they were made redundant by their employer. In part the aim was to encourage workers in declining sectors of the economy (e.g. heavy industry) to move elsewhere in return for an appropriate level of compensation. The government was also concerned to reduce the level of trade union opposition to employers' proposals to dismiss staff. Therefore it is important to view redundancy provisions not just as a form of employee protection, but also as an aid to managers wanting to reduce the size of their workforce (Fryer 1973). Indeed, the concept of redundancy has been used in an increasingly loose fashion, to the extent that it now applies to an employer's decision that fewer employees are needed to undertake a particular area of work without any obligation to demonstrate that the amount of work has in fact diminished (Lewis 1993).

The fourth aspect of redundancy that we need to consider concerns the use of redundancy exercises as a means of maintaining managerial control over human resources in organizations. It 'is a time when new standards can be laid down as the organization gears up to operating in a changed environment' (Lewis 1993: 39). This is evident from the selection criteria used to pick people for redundancy, which can be used to communicate and reinforce managerial priorities (Cascio 2010). For example, the use of attendance records as a selection criterion during a redundancy programme, whereby staff with high absence rates are selected for dismissal first, sends out a message that absence is being taken seriously as a human resource management issue and that less tolerance is to be shown to staff who have poor attendance records. Thus it is important to recognize that redundancy is essentially a managerial process—something that is used by an organization to secure greater flexibility, performance, and competitiveness, and also to maintain control over the attitudes and behaviour of staff (Turnbull 1988).

📖 Summary and further reading

- Redundancy, which can be defined as a process in which the number of employees undertaking a particular set of work activities is deliberately reduced, is a key element of organizational downsizing initiatives.

- Redundancies are a highly relevant aspect of contemporary human resource management, though their incidence varies from sector to sector. The economic recession of the late 2000s led to increased redundancy levels, not just in the UK and the USA, but around the world.

- While the broad rationale for redundancies is concerned with the need to make financial savings, six particular causes can be identified: industrial decline; reductions in economic activity; the introduction of new technology and work reorganization initiatives; organizational restructuring processes; pressures to realize cost savings and improve financial performance; and business insolvency.

- Redundancy is a managerial process. Generally, redundancy exercises in organizations are conceived by managers who then have considerable latitude over how they are executed. Redundancies are increasingly used by organizations as a convenient means of getting rid of employees as a way of boosting short-term performance, even when the amount of work has not declined.

There is a lack of good up-to-date overviews of redundancy in human resource management. The chapter by Cascio (2010) is particularly recommended. The book-length overview of redundancy by Lewis (1993) and the more concise discussion of the key issues surrounding the management of redundancies by Thornhill and Saunders (1998) offer important insights, but are both rather dated now.

9.3 Alternatives to redundancy

The main focus of this section concerns alternatives to compulsory redundancies. These include measures that obviate the need for job cuts at all, such as reductions in working time, policies that reduce the size of the workforce by letting staff numbers fall without the need for redundancies, such as allowing older workers to retire earlier than anticipated, arrangements for redeploying staff from areas under threat to other parts of the organization, and the encouragement given to employees to depart of their own accord, generally with a hefty financial incentive.

9.3.1 Avoiding the need to make redundancies

Managers in organizations may consider alternatives to redundancies when it comes to responding to pressure to cut costs and improve efficiency (e.g. ACAS 2010*a*). One of the most striking features of the economic recession, compared with previous periods of economic difficulty, is that many employers have made more of an effort to mitigate the impact of the recession on their staff by instituting alternative ways of cutting employment costs, eschewing the need for lay-offs. By retaining skilled and experienced staff, employers are better positioned to take advantage of the opportunities that arise when the economy recovers (IDS 2009*b*). The most popular alternatives to redundancies during the recession were imposing a restriction on, or suspending, external recruitment activity, 'natural wastage' (not filling posts when they become vacant, through early retirements for example), reviewing the employment of temporary staff, redeploying workers at risk of redundancy to other parts of the organization, and reducing overtime arrangements (IDS 2009*b*).

In some cases, employers looked to get through the recession by instituting wage cuts. For example, the car manufacturer Honda reached an agreement with the trade union Unite to cut pay by 3 per cent in order to save some 500 jobs. This was in addition to a four-month shutdown, during which the workforce was on half pay, and 1400 voluntary lay-offs. As the economy gradually emerged from recession, firms took measures to ensure that they remained viable while reducing the prospect of job losses. In May 2010, for example, Vauxhall workers represented by Unite agreed a two-year pay freeze in exchange for company guarantees of future investment and job security. The employers' body the Confederation of British Industry (CBI) welcomed the collaborative efforts of employers and employees to ensure that their businesses can survive the downturn. However, the TUC argued that there is nothing new about firms cutting the pay and hours of their workers during a recession. Moreover, by agreeing to take a cut in pay and hours workers do not guarantee that their jobs will be secure. Unlike in the vehicle firms, where agreement over how to achieve cost savings was reached with the trade unions, some employers have taken a more assertive approach, imposing measures on their workforces with adverse consequences. For example, in 2011 Southampton City Council forced through a 5 per cent pay cut, saying that otherwise it would have to make some 400 job losses in order to make £25 million worth of cost savings. However, its staff and their unions responded furiously, and organized a series of disruptive strikes to oppose the changes.

Measures such as reductions in overtime, voluntary cutbacks in working time, pay freezes, or the discharge of workers engaged through temporary agencies may all obviate the need for job losses. Yet this assumes that organizations endeavour to retain their existing staff. This is by no means always the case. Indeed, as we saw in Section 9.2.4 with the example of the further education college, agency staff are sometimes used as replacements for supposedly redundant post-holders because they are cheaper to employ (Hudson 2002). This reminds us that redundancy exercises are an opportunity for managers to demonstrate and reinforce their control over staff (Lewis 1993), as well as a means of reducing the costs of labour to the business.

Where a recognized trade union is present, there may be additional pressure on managers to consider methods other than redundancy when contemplating the need for change. For example, in the case of Wolverhampton Hospitals NHS Trust managers agreed a procedure with the recognized unions designed to ensure that compulsory redundancies were a last resort after all other alternative ways of cutting labour costs had been considered (IDS 2007). See Box 9.4 for an example of a jointly agreed 'framework' to avoid compulsory redundancies from the finance sector. It is also important to bear in mind that in many countries, particularly those in Western Europe, there are strict legal rules which restrict the capacity of employers to institute redundancies. In Germany, for example, agreement must be reached with works councils comprised of elected employee representatives (Cascio 2010).

 Box 9.4 Policy example
NatBank redundancy agreement

'NatBank' is a pseudonym for a major UK-based multinational financial services company which employs around 100,000 people in some 60 countries. It instituted a change initiative, part of which involved relocating, or 'offshoring', a certain number of jobs from the UK to India. The company reached an agreement with the recognized trade union which provides a framework for avoiding compulsory redundancies in such circumstances. Recognizing that some degree of offshoring in the company was inevitable, the union worked to ensure that employees affected by such restructuring not only got the best possible deal when it came to the details of their redundancy arrangements, but were also helped to find alternative employment if necessary, and were treated fairly and with respect. Among the key provisions of this agreement were:

- the establishment of a voluntary redundancy register;
- ongoing sharing of information with staff about job transfer opportunities;
- the greater use of voluntary job matching and redeployment opportunities for some staff;
- the provision of £2000 worth of support for external career retraining;
- the provision of outplacement support by external consultants.

Source: Johnstone (2010: 72–4).

9.3.2 Attrition and early retirement

If the situation demands that fewer posts are required, some form of attrition, or 'natural wastage', is a popular alternative to redundancies. Attrition, which means letting staff numbers fall without the need for direct intervention to cut existing jobs, can encompass a number of methods, principally early retirement schemes, whereby older staff are encouraged to leave before their normal retirement age with the offer of an appropriate financial incentive, and so-called natural wastage, which involves not replacing staff when they voluntarily resign their positions.

What are the advantages of such methods for avoiding the need to make redundancies? Perhaps most importantly they are more likely to secure the support of employees and trade unions. Managers who can find alternatives to redundancy may win the loyalty and commitment of their staff as a result—something that could work to the advantage of their business. Using such methods is relatively risk free and less prone to damaging staff morale. Promoting early retirement can also help to maintain a balanced age structure within an organization, and open up opportunities for promotion to staff who might otherwise have seen their prospects for advancement blocked by the presence of long-serving post-holders (Cascio 2010).

In practice, early retirement is often used as a means of 'disguised' redundancy. In other words, it is used as a convenient way of ensuring that job losses are achieved without the need to institute formal redundancy proceedings. In the case of the steel company Corus, for example, workers perceived that they were forced into early retirement, since it was the only alternative to accepting compulsory lay-offs (Forde et al. 2009).

Moreover, there are some notable problems with the use of early retirement and natural wastage as alternatives to redundancy. For one thing, whether used on their own or together, they are a potentially very slow means of downsizing an organization (Thornhill and Saunders 1998). The benefits of attrition are realized gradually over time, whereas speedier action may be required to restore the organization's financial viability. Moreover, too much of an emphasis on attrition as a means of cutting jobs may damage an organization if the people coming forward for early retirement or resigning their positions voluntarily are based in key roles or functions (Cascio 2010). Managers may find that they need to exercise discretion when determining whether or not a vacant post should be filled.

9.3.3 Redeployment

A further way in which managers can avoid having to make people redundant is by giving staff working in areas that are threatened by job losses the opportunity to move to other parts of the organization—a procedure known as redeployment. Where redeployment occurs, it is often accompanied by retraining of the employees concerned, giving them the skills and knowledge required in their new posts.

Some organizations have put sophisticated redeployment arrangements in place as a means of mitigating the need for redundancies. For example, the telecommunications company BT places a strong emphasis on retraining and redeploying employees in order to retain skilled and experienced staff (IDS 2009*b*). The utility firm EDF Energy operates a sophisticated job-matching scheme and redeployment database. It recognized that its established policy of encouraging staff to leave voluntarily, with attractive financial incentives to tempt them to go, potentially left it bereft of skilled workers. The firm altered its approach so that, wherever possible, alternative opportunities within the firm would be found for staff whose roles had been made redundant, helping to ensure that key skills were retained. Details of an employee's current job are entered onto the database, summarizing his/her skills and experience, thus enabling the firm to match them to vacancies arising elsewhere (IDS 2007).

There are some problems with the use of redeployment as an alternative to redundancy. For one thing, it is not always appropriate; for example, in insolvency cases the failure of the business means that there is no possibility of redeployment. Moreover, it cannot be assumed that organizations necessarily want to retain the employees concerned. The HRM rationale underpinning redeployment is based on the desirability of retaining skilled and talented staff within the organization, rather than letting them go elsewhere. Yet in many cases, where efficiency savings are needed for example, the onus is on reducing the size of the workforce, not redistributing its members around the organization in general.

A second problem with the use of redeployment as an alternative to redundancy is that it can tie the hands of managers, who are obliged to give priority to existing staff under threat of redundancy elsewhere in the organization when looking to fill vacant posts in their own departments (e.g. Beynon et al. 2002: 164). A third problem concerns the degree to which redeployment is a genuine alternative to redundancy for employees. There is sometimes a perception among staff whose posts are at risk of being made redundant that, even when redeployment was supposedly available, there were in reality few genuine opportunities elsewhere in the organization (Clarke 2007; Forde et al. 2009).

9.3.4 Voluntary redundancy

Perhaps the most common method used by organizations wanting to avoid compulsory redundancies is to encourage staff to depart seemingly of their own accord. There are two main features of voluntary redundancy that distinguish it from a compulsory approach (Clarke 2007). First, it ostensibly gives the employees concerned an element of choice over whether or not they leave the organization, although how much choice exists in reality is rather questionable—a theme we come back to below. Secondly, voluntary redundancy is generally accompanied by financial incentives—in the form of an enhanced redundancy payment, for instance—which encourage employees to leave. For example, US car giant Ford has offered compensation packages of anything up to $100,000 in some circumstances (Cascio 2010).

Understandably, managers in organizations have a predilection for voluntary redundancy arrangements as it makes their job easier. For one thing, they are relieved of the obligation to select people for redundancy; instead employees supposedly self-select themselves. Moreover, the carrot of an attractive financial settlement can be an effective means of securing the necessary number of redundancies without causing potentially damaging conflict. From 'a management perspective voluntary redundancy facilitates the downsizing process by making redundancy a more attractive option' (Clarke 2007: 90).

However, the use of voluntary redundancy as a means of generating job losses poses certain difficulties. Perhaps the most notable problem concerns the potential lack of control enjoyed by managers over who stays and who goes. This can result in organizations losing valued members of staff and the knowledge and skills that they hold. If the redundancy decision is genuinely

voluntary, employees with more up-to-date and marketable skills, who may feel more optimistic about securing a position with an alternative employer, are the ones who are most likely to be lost to the organization (Cascio 2010). There are many examples of organizations that have suffered the ill-effects of voluntary redundancy programmes, in particular the loss of valuable highly skilled staff. The pharmaceutical company studied by Beynon et al. (2002: 162) had experienced a 'massive haemorrhage of experience through voluntary redundancy and extensive redeployment exercises', with adverse consequences for business performance. As a result, some firms, such as EDF Energy, have instituted a shift away from emphasizing voluntary redundancy to an approach where the main concern is, as we saw above, to ensure that staff are moved to alternative positions within the company (IDS 2007).

The adverse effects on organizations of ill-thought-out voluntary redundancy initiatives have prompted managers to take greater control over access to such schemes, raising doubts over just how 'voluntary' they are in practice. Managers refuse applications from staff whom they would prefer to retain, especially where they possess 'certain skills, knowledge or capabilities deemed essential to the firm' (Turnbull and Wass 1997: 33). One of the main issues for managers in such circumstances involves dealing with the negative consequences arising from the potential antipathy of those staff who have been denied access to voluntary redundancy opportunities (ACAS 2010a).

In contrast, managers may actively encourage unwanted staff to apply for voluntary redundancy, in some cases to such an extent that the employees concerned are given no real alternative to leaving the organization. One study of redundancies in Scottish manufacturing companies found a number of cases of workers who, having enquired about the possibility of taking voluntary redundancy, were then targeted for compulsory redundancy (Donnelly and Scholarios 1998). For some employees, the only alternative to taking voluntary redundancy is the acceptance of inferior terms and conditions of employment (Hudson 2002). In the UK dock industry, for example, the introduction of new contracts meant that the workers concerned faced substantially more onerous working conditions, giving them little option but to take voluntary redundancy (Turnbull and Wass 1994).

Perhaps we should not use the term 'voluntary' redundancy at all, given the potentially misleading impression it gives that the choice to go lies in the hands of the employees concerned (Turnbull and Wass 1997). Clarke's Australian study (Clarke 2007) demonstrates that voluntary redundancy situations are marked by a considerable amount of variation when it comes to the degree of employee choice and managerial control they exhibit. In some cases, workers felt that they had very little choice about whether or not they were made voluntarily redundant. According to one former employee of a telecommunications company: 'I love the way they've labelled it voluntary redundancy. It just seems to be a nice name to put on the fact that they're booting someone out and they don't really have a choice' (Clarke 2007: 81). Yet most workers offered a more positive account of the voluntary redundancy process, indicating that they had enjoyed a degree of choice over their departure. Some had even pursued the chance to be made redundant. Three factors seem to have been important in encouraging people to choose redundancy: the opportunity to 'escape' increasingly onerous and unappealing jobs; a recognition that redeployment was unlikely; and the prospect of an attractive severance payment.

Voluntary redundancy, then, is best viewed as involving 'constrained choices' (Clarke 2007). People recognized that managers controlled the redundancy process, notwithstanding its supposedly voluntary dimension. Yet, depending on the circumstances of the individual concerned, in most cases they felt that they could exercise some degree of choice over the circumstances of their departure from the organization. In practice, the balance between management control and employee choice will vary from one redundancy situation to another.

Summary and further reading

- Alternatives to compulsory redundancies include measures designed to prevent the need for job losses, such as reductions in working time, particularly where trade unions enjoy a degree of power to influence organizational policy. The economic recession of the late 2000s saw increased interest among employers in cost-saving alternatives to employee lay-offs.

- Encouraging older workers to take early retirement or instituting a freeze on recruitment activity so that departing staff are not replaced are popular, albeit rather slow, methods of reducing the size of the workforce. By reducing the need for redundancies, such approaches help to maintain the loyalty and commitment of staff, even if early retirement can be interpreted as 'disguised redundancy'.

- While the redeployment of staff from areas under threat of job losses to other parts of the organization might obviate the need for redundancies, it is not always a practical proposition, especially where the need for financial savings looms large. Managers often resent having to take on staff redeployed from elsewhere in their organization on the basis that it erodes their discretion over selection decisions.

- Voluntary redundancy ostensibly gives control over the redundancy decision to the workers themselves, who are encouraged to leave of their own accord by the carrot of a financial incentive. In practice, though, managers generally retain considerable power to influence the voluntary redundancy process, limiting the extent of real choice enjoyed by employees.

See the 2009 report by the research organization Incomes Data Services for insights about the alternatives to redundancy being pursued by employers during the recession (IDS 2009*b*). Clarke's (2007) study, undertaken in Australia, offers some sensitive and insightful perspectives on voluntary redundancy.

9.4 Handling redundancies

The material in this section is concerned with the way in which redundancies are handled by managers in organizations. Following an examination of the nature and content of redundancy policies, key issues involving the management of redundancies are considered, including the arrangements for communicating and consulting with affected staff, the amount of financial compensation due in the form of redundancy payments, and the process for selecting employees for redundancy purposes. All this raises the question of how far managers in organizations handle redundancies in a strategic purposive fashion, supporting the interests of the business while maintaining the loyalty and commitment of staff.

9.4.1 Redundancy policy, consultation, and payments

Three broad approaches are taken by organizations when it comes to handling redundancies. They can operate a formal written redundancy policy devised by managers, agree arrangements for making redundancies with a recognized trade union, or deal with the situation in an ad hoc manner, responding to redundancy issues as and when they arise, rather than through a consistent procedure (ACAS 2010*a*). What kinds of things do formal redundancy policies and agreements generally contain? They tend to make some mention of the scope of the policy (i.e. which employees it covers), how news of prospective redundancies is to be communicated to staff, what alternatives to redundancy are to be considered, the methods whereby staff are to be selected for redundancy, and how severance payments are to be calculated (CIPD 2007*c*). Where trade unions are present, they generally try to ensure that the emphasis in redundancy procedures is placed on avoiding job losses wherever possible—for instance, through redeployment arrangements. For example, the financial services company NatBank agreed a procedure for dealing with organizational restructuring with the recognized union which stresses the need to find alternatives to redundancy before job losses are contemplated (Johnstone 2010).

Statutory requirements that employers inform and consult with workers and their representatives in the event of redundancies being proposed are commonplace in many countries. In the UK, for example, where an employer proposes to dismiss 20 or more employees within a 90-day period and a 'collective redundancy' situation arises, at least 30 days before the first dismissals are due (90 days where it is proposed to dismiss 100 or more employees) the employer is obliged to inform and consult with either the representatives of the recognized unions, where they exist, or, in non-union firms, with elected staff representatives of the affected employees. Consultation should be undertaken with the purpose of finding ways of avoiding dismissals, reducing the number of staff to be made redundant, and lessening the impact on staff who lose their jobs. In theory, such consultation should be meaningful and be undertaken with a view to reaching an agreement. Failure to undertake appropriate consultation can lead to employees being awarded up to 90 days' pay in compensation.

ACAS (2010*a*) highlights the advantages of effective consultation during redundancy situations. It can help to promote cooperation, for example, and can enable unions and staff representatives to come up with practical alternatives to the proposed redundancies. ACAS (2010*a*) recommends that, regardless of whether or not a collective redundancy situation exists, employers should seek to inform and consult the affected workforce. It is also important to bear in mind that redundancy is a means of dismissing employees. In the UK, an employer's failure to inform and consult individual employees who are due to be made redundant, and thus dismissed, could render them liable to a successful claim for unfair dismissal from the staff concerned. Therefore employers should use an appropriate procedure to effect any dismissals caused by redundancy, which gives staff the right to be informed and consulted on an individual basis as to the reasons why they have been selected for redundancy (IDS 2009*b*).

There is some evidence that consultation can lead to redundancy proposals being altered. For example, in one case, as the result of a consultation exercise, managers made voluntary redundancy opportunities available to staff, having initially decided to rely solely on compulsory measures (Hall and Edwards 1999). For the most part, though, the obligation on employers to inform and consult union and staff representatives rarely leads to major changes being made to their original proposals (Kersley et al. 2006). Although in theory employers face the prospect of financial penalties if they are found not to have complied with the obligation to inform and consult union and staff representatives, in practice this is rarely much of an obstacle to the management of redundancy (White 1983). Trade union leaders argue that information and consultation rights should be strengthened, bringing the UK into line with some of its European neighbours. However, business groups claim that the current obligations are already too onerous and need relaxing (see Box 9.5).

A further statutory obligation on employers concerns the need to pay financial compensation to staff who are dismissed for reasons of redundancy. In the UK, for example, employees with at least two years of continuous service with an employer are entitled to minimum redundancy payments, depending on the length of time they have been employed, and also which one of three age bands they come under. Redundancy payments are calculated as follows:

- 0.5 week's pay for each full year of service for workers aged under 22;
- 1 week's pay for each full year of service for workers aged from 22 to 40;
- 1.5 weeks' pay for each full year of service for workers aged 41 and over.

Box 9.5 Practitioner perspective
Government, business, and union views on redundancy consultation

This practitioner perspective concerns calls from representatives of the business community for certain redundancy protections to be weakened, on the grounds that employers should have more flexibility in responding to adverse economic conditions. In June 2010 the Confederation of British Industry (CBI) published proposals for reforming employment relations. The report—*Making Britain the Place to Work: an Employment Agenda for the New Government*—emphasized the importance role of flexible labour markets in producing economic competitiveness. One of its more controversial proposals concerned changes to legislation governing redundancy consultation. The CBI proposed reducing the minimum period of consultation in collective redundancy situations from 90 days to 30 days (20–99 employees). In May 2011, the Department for Business, Innovation and Skills (BIS) announced that redundancy consultation was one of the areas it wanted to include as part of its review of employment red tape, with a view to shortening the period for consultation. The then minister for employment relations, Ed Davey, said that removing unnecessary bureaucracy was an important precondition for economic growth, and that the government wants 'to make it easier for businesses to take on staff and grow'. However, Brendan Barber, general secretary of the Trades Union Congress (TUC) criticized the proposal, saying that it would be counterproductive—'making it easier to make people redundant and giving the workforce less time to come up with alternatives to job losses threatens to make unemployment worse'.

There are caps on the number of years' service that count towards the purpose of redundancy payments (20 years) and on the amount of a week's pay that can be taken into account (£400 in 2011–2012). Thus the maximum redundancy payment to which a redundant employee is legally entitled is £12,000 (20 years' service × 1.5 weeks' pay × £400). Given that the direct costs to employers of making employees redundant are rarely onerous (Turnbull 1988), one can see the attractiveness of redundancy to employers as a means of instituting efficiency savings. Nevertheless, some firms make provision for redundancy payments that go beyond the statutory requirement. The financial services company Standard Life, for example, pays redundant staff four weeks' salary for each year of continuous service (IDS 2007).

9.4.2 Selecting for redundancy

Assuming that alternative ways of cutting costs and reducing jobs fail to realize the required efficiency savings, and that compulsory redundancies are necessary, a key issue for managers in organizations concerns the methods used to select staff for redundancy. The first task is to determine those employees whose jobs are at risk, which needs to be justified on objective grounds (i.e. all the jobs in a particular department, or all jobs of a particular type). For many years, the most popular method of selecting staff from within this 'pool' for redundancy, which tended to be supported by the trade unions, was to use the length of an employee's service as the principal selection criterion. Under the principle of 'last-in, first-out' (LIFO), staff with the least experience in the organization are the ones chosen to go first. Such an approach is becoming rarer, however. For one thing, it is a very crude method of selecting for redundancy. From an organizational perspective, LIFO makes very little sense. It values the most recently hired staff the least, when it is likely that these are the ones whose capabilities are more closely matched to those needed by the organization. Under LIFO, experience is accorded a higher value than skills, competence, or performance, and therefore has fallen out of favour. Age discrimination legislation has further discouraged the use of LIFO as a criterion for redundancy selection, since length of service can be a proxy for age. While employers can lawfully continue to use length of service as one of the criteria when selecting for redundancy, they must be able to justify their reasons for doing so on objective grounds, for example as part of a broader approach to managing human resources that rewards employee loyalty (IDS 2009b).

The use of certain criteria for redundancy selection is unlawful—for example, selecting staff based on, among other things, their sex, ethnicity, age, and whether or not they are a trade union member. There is an increasing preference for using ostensibly objective points-scoring arrangements when it comes to selecting people for redundancy. In order to determine who is, and who is not, selected, under points-scoring systems managers give a value to a particular criterion and then rate staff accordingly by assessing them against the criteria and awarding them the appropriate number of points. The criteria used by organizations to select for redundancy may include the attendance, disciplinary, and performance records of individual staff. Komatsu, a manufacturer of mining and construction equipment, operates an arrangement whereby staff are given a rating based on their performance, sickness absence record, timekeeping, reliability and dependability, skills and ability, and length of service. This rating is then used to rank staff in descending order according to their overall score. Depending upon the number of job losses needed, a cut-off point is established, with staff whose ranking falls beneath it being selected for redundancy (IDS 2009b).

While the use of ostensibly rational and objective arrangements for redundancy selection is in part a response to the need of employers to demonstrate that the criteria used are fair and can be justified, it can also enable human resources to be managed more effectively. Redundancy exercises can be used as a means of re-profiling the workforce, enabling organizations to rid themselves of staff who are deemed to be performing relatively poorly, whose attendance record is deemed to be not up to scratch, or whose skills do not match up to changing organizational requirements. Managerial control over the criteria for selecting people for redundancy enables employers to streamline their workforce in a desirable manner through the use of supposedly objective factors, helping to enhance organizational flexibility and competitiveness. The use of point-scoring systems, in particular, demonstrates how organizations use redundancy exercises as a means of securing control over their workforce and of gaining more value from their staff.

While organizational policy might set out the criteria that should be used when selecting for redundancy, in practice managers often prefer to exercise greater discretion and secure greater flexibility over selection decisions. In a study of redundancies in Scotland, Donnelly and Scholarios (1998) observed that in one case, although workers were selected for redundancy ostensibly according to a points score based on their performance, other criteria seemed to influence the selection process. According to one worker: 'The selection method was sick to say the least. I was picked out for one and a half days ill in seven years with the company, the same week I got my assessment sheet and my total points were 28 out of 30' (Donnelly and Scholarios 1998: 332).

9.4.3 Handling redundancies: further issues

A number of other issues when handling redundancies. For example, the importance of effective communications is often attested (e.g. Thornhill and Saunders 1998). Employers are encouraged to ensure that a consistent message concerning the need for redundancies is delivered to staff to make sure that managers are briefed appropriately so that they can deal with the inevitable queries and concerns that arise, and to give managers relevant training so that they are capable of dealing with redundancy issues efficiently and sensitively. For example, Komatsu provides guidance to managers outlining the actions they are required to undertake, according to a pre-arranged timetable, on the day that redundancy announcements are made (IDS 2009b).

However, such methods, emblematic of a more purposive strategic approach to dealing with redundancy by managing it in a way that helps to maintain the morale and organizational commitment of staff, are by no means universal. Famously, one UK firm told its staff that they had lost their jobs by text message (see Box 9.6). In practice, redundancy announcements and other communications issues are often handled in an insensitive manner, with adverse consequences for the morale and commitment of the staff concerned. An element of secrecy often pervades redundancy decisions, with managers reluctant to divulge details of proposed dismissals until it is absolutely necessary. One reason put forward for this is that by withholding information from the workforce managers gain greater control over the redundancy process, enhancing their flexibility over the details of the redundancy exercise (Doherty and Tyson 1993, cited in Donnelly and Scholarios 1998).

Following on from this, it is important to recognize that the process of instituting redundancies does not always operate in the smooth rational manner described in texts devoted to helping employers manage redundancy more effectively. In particular, redundant staff often do not accept their fate calmly. The decision to make redundancies, and also the terms on which those redundancies are then put into effect, can be a source of conflict in the workplace as staff try to resist management objectives. Workers frequently challenge and contest redundancy proposals. For example, during the summer of 2011 journalists at the BBC undertook strike action as part of a campaign to prevent compulsory redundancies. Moreover, workers

 Box 9.6 Window on work
Sacking staff by text message

Notwithstanding the emphasis placed on ensuring that managers communicate redundancy announcements to staff in a sensitive manner, this is not always the case in practice. When in May 2003 the Accident Group, which dealt with personal injury claims, became insolvent and went into administration, the first time most of its 2500 staff learnt that they had lost their jobs was by a text message. They were advised not to attend work and that their salaries could not be paid. Guidance to managers on how to handle redundancies effectively suggests that the use of text messaging to notify staff about redundancies should be avoided (IDS 2009b). Yet in situations where the business has collapsed, it could be argued that this is a quick, convenient, and efficient method of communicating to staff that their jobs no longer exist.

Box 9.7 Window on work
Contesting redundancies in France and the UK

Workers do not necessarily respond to the threat of redundancy passively, but often challenge decisions to institute job losses by engaging in protests and industrial action, including forms of direct action such as occupations (Gall 2011). Some notable cases have occurred in France, for example. In February 2008, Mike Bacon, the British head of BRS, a car parts company, was held captive by the workforce over a weekend after they had learnt that the factory was to be closed and production moved from France to Slovakia where labour costs are lower. During the first few months of 2009, there were further incidents of this 'bossnapping' phenomenon. Senior managers of multinational companies including Sony and Caterpillar were temporarily held captive following the announcement of plant closures or job losses. Although these incidents have not been replicated in the UK, factory closures caused by the economic recession of the late 2000s prompted a number of cases of workers using direct action to try and preserve their jobs, principally by mounting occupations of their factories. In the summer of 2009, for example, Vestas, a company which made wind turbines at its plant on the Isle of Wight, announced the closure of the factory with the loss of over 500 jobs. However, before the shutdown was completed, some of the workers took control of the factory and blockaded themselves inside for over a fortnight (Gall 2010a).

sometimes take direct action to protest against redundancies (see Box 9.7). Therefore the job of managing redundancies can entail having to deal with the conflict that redundancy causes, and not just ensuring that they are carried out in the most effective way for the organization concerned.

 ## Summary and further reading

- There are a number of broad approaches that managers in organizations take when handling redundancies. While some adopt an ad hoc approach, dealing with redundancy situations as and when they occur—something that gives managers greater flexibility over how redundancies are handled—others use formal policies to guide managerial action, which in some cases take the form of agreements when they have been negotiated with a recognized trade union. Redundancy policies generally cover such matters as how any redundancy announcement is to be made, and the arrangements for compensating dismissed staff.

- Managers are encouraged to inform and consult employees and their representatives when a redundancy situation arises on the basis that the process could result in alternative ways of achieving job losses, or realizing efficiency savings, without the need for redundancies or with reductions in the number of redundancies needed. In practice, however, such consultation, even when it is obligatory, rarely results in changes being made to the original redundancy proposals.

- While length of service was traditionally a very popular criterion when selecting staff for compulsory redundancy, it has generally been superseded by other, supposedly more objective, criteria such as attendance and performance records. These form the basis of points-scoring systems which can be used to rate, and then rank, employees. In practice, however, it seems that managers sometimes override such systems, or at least interpret them to their advantage, in order to secure greater flexibility over selection decisions.

- There is an increasing emphasis on how redundancy exercises are undertaken in ways that contribute to an organization's overall strategic objectives. The implication is that redundancies can be handled in a manner that supports the business—for instance, by helping to maintain the loyalty and commitment of the workforce. However, the decision to make redundancies, and also the terms on which those redundancies are then put into effect, can be a source of conflict in the workplace as staff challenge management objectives.

Incomes Data Services is a good source of examples of organizational policy concerning redundancy handling (e.g. IDS 2007, 2009b). See ACAS (2010a) for guidance on how to manage redundancies effectively (www.acas.org.uk/index.aspx?articleid=747). The study of workers' experiences of redundancy by Donnelly and Scholarios (1998) is also recommended.

9.5 Post-redundancy

In order to understand redundancy properly, we need to consider the aftermath of any decision to effect redundancies and its announcement to the affected staff. Therefore the concept of 'post-redundancy' encompasses the support given to redundant employees, their experience of the impact of redundancy, and the impact on those people who remain employed by the organization and are thus said to have 'survived' the redundancy exercise.

9.5.1 In-house support and outplacement services

What kind of support do employers offer their redundant staff? In the UK, they are under a statutory obligation to give employees who are under notice of redundancy a reasonable amount of time off work to look for alternative employment or to make arrangements for training related to future employment. With regard to the support given by employers to redundant staff, we can distinguish between in-house provision, where services are provided by the organization itself, and outplacement, where the employer uses specialist external providers to deliver support services. Typically, in-house support might encompass providing advice on redundancy payments, disseminating information about current vacancies elsewhere, providing job-search training, giving general financial advice, and offering careers guidance (Donnelly and Scholarios 1998). However, the use of outplacement services has become a more common feature of this area of human resource management in practice (IDS 2009b). Such 'services were originally developed in the USA. They involve structured programmes of help for individuals, usually provided by an external consultancy and paid for by the organisation' (Doherty 1997: 345) (see Box 9.8).

What is the purpose of outplacement providers, and what kinds of intervention do they use? Their work is predominantly concerned with helping individual staff cope with the experience of being made redundant, and with strengthening their capacity to secure alternative job and career opportunities. 'The main goals of an outplacement service are to improve employees' job search skills, provide them with some career advice and help them to find a suitable vacancy', through interventions including assistance with CV preparation, improving interview techniques and presentation skills, and financial planning (IDS 2009b: 20). What is the effect of providing such support services? Studies demonstrate that people who use them have positive experiences, citing the practical support offered and the improvements in their confidence and self-esteem that result. For example, workers made redundant by the steel company Corus found that the on-site support offered by external agencies helped them to prepare for re-entering the labour market (Forde et al. 2009: 19). For employers, the use of outplacement support services appears to help ease the process of making people redundant—by getting them to accept their fate more readily, for example—sustains the morale of remaining employees, and maintains a positive external reputation (Doherty 1997).

However, there are a number of problems with both in-house support and outplacement services. With regard to the latter, given their tendency to be targeted mainly at managerial staff, they are simply irrelevant to the experience of many redundant workers. Outplacement interventions may not be all that effective in securing alternative employment for the workers who use them. In many cases, they seem to be operated as a part of a 'damage limitation' exercise (Doherty, Bank, and Vinnicombe 1996)—part of an approach designed to maintain the morale and commitment of surviving staff, who are given the impression that their former colleagues are being treated as sensitively as possible. Some workers interviewed by Donnelly and Scholarios (1998) in their study of Scottish defence-related companies praised the support

---

 Box 9.8 Online video link
Outplacement provision

Outplacement firms sometimes use the internet to advertise their services. Go to the Online Resource Centre where you will find a link to a website where Corinne Mills of Personal Career Management advertises the services provided by her firm.

services provided by their employer, particularly where they had come as part of a voluntary redundancy package. According to one worker: 'As far as I was concerned they were 100 per cent behind me trying to get a job. They brought in outside agencies . . . helping to make CVs, giving talks . . . I thought the company did really well that way' (Donnelly and Scholarios 1998: 332). Nevertheless, a substantial proportion of workers seem to have had less positive experiences, particularly where they had been made redundant compulsorily. The use of in-house support services was sometimes made difficult because the workers had already been formally excluded from the organization's premises.

9.5.2 The effects of redundancy

What happens to workers once they have been made redundant? In this section we are concerned with the effects of redundancy on the workers involved. For many years this was a prominent area of interest among policy-makers and academics. De-industrialization, and the mass job losses that it causes, not only had major implications for the livelihoods of those workers dismissed from employment, but also affected their families and the communities they inhabited. In large parts of the economy, such as South Wales and Northeast England, the collapse of staple industries such as coal mining and the resulting massive reductions in employment contributed to high levels of unemployment, economic decline, and social decay.

Workers who have been made redundant often experience a period of unemployment, or take jobs with worse pay and conditions than those they have left (Harris 1987; Turnbull and Wass 1997). This is demonstrated by the study of workers made redundant by defence-related companies in Scotland undertaken by Donnelly and Scholarios (1998). Many found it difficult to secure re-employment, and those who did generally had to take jobs that offered lower pay, often on a part-time basis. Workers made redundant from MG Rover when it closed in 2005 have generally not found new jobs with similar pay and conditions (see Box 9.9). In the USA, extensive lay-offs have produced a 'society of downwardly mobile, insecure workers', with adverse consequences for the communities affected (Cascio 2010: 344).

A number of factors influence an individual worker's subsequent experience of redundancy, in particular the likelihood of him/her obtaining alternative suitable employment. Perhaps the most important influence is the age of the worker concerned. Studies of the effects of redundancy demonstrate that older workers experience much greater difficulties finding new jobs than younger ones (see e.g. Pinch and Mason 1991), partly because of discriminatory attitudes among employers, and also because higher redundancy payments may reduce their propensity to seek work elsewhere. Younger workers who lack experience may also find it difficult to secure re-employment (Donnelly and Scholarios 1998).

Another important influence on a worker's experience of redundancy appears to be whether or not it was undertaken on a voluntary basis. Workers who have taken voluntary redundancy report more positive experiences than those who have been dismissed against their will. In her

Box 9.9 Research in focus
The post-redundancy experience of MG Rover workers

Three years after the April 2005 closure of the MG Rover car plant at Longbridge, near Birmingham, only 10 per cent of the more than 6000 workers made redundant had not found alternative employment or self-employment opportunities. While on the face of it this seems to be a highly satisfactory state of affairs, further investigation revealed some negative aspects of the employment changes. Perhaps most importantly, on average the former MG Rover workers earned rather less in their new jobs than when they had been employed in the car plant, with a quarter of households encountering financial difficulties as a consequence. Moreover, ex-MG Rover workers also saw a decline in the quality of their employment, as the new jobs offered them less autonomy, were less skilled, and were marked by greater insecurity than the average for the UK as a whole. The experience of former MG Rover workers provides further evidence of the adverse labour market consequences that face many workers after they have been made redundant.

Source: de Ruyter, Bailey, and Mahdon (2010).

195

Australian study, Clarke (2007) discovered that workers who had been made redundant on a voluntary basis were generally financially secure, on account of the enhanced severance payments they had received, reported that their health had improved, the result of escaping from highly pressurized and stressful job situations, and viewed redundancy more as an opportunity to be taken than a threat to be avoided.

9.5.3 Redundancy exercises and remaining staff

There is now a much greater emphasis on the impact of redundancy exercises on 'surviving' staff, and the resulting implications for managing human resources effectively. This has arisen partly because the purported business benefits of redundancies, such as performance improvements, often fail to materialize in practice. But it also has to be seen in the context of the supposedly more strategic role human resource management enjoys in organizations. In this sense, managing redundancies effectively is not just concerned with the process of dismissing the staff affected, following appropriate procedures and meeting any relevant statutory obligations, but is also about handling them in a way that adds value to, and supports the broader business objectives of, the organization. Therefore how to moderate the impact of job losses on remaining staff has become an increasingly important aspect of managing redundancies.

The implementation of redundancy exercises can have major adverse consequences for remaining—'surviving'—staff (Cascio 2010). Their 'reactions to redundancies may include disbelief, confusion, betrayal, anger, animosity, loss of motivation, lower morale, mistrust, uncertainty, insecurity and lower commitment to the organization' (Thornhill and Gibbons 1995: 5). There is plenty of evidence attesting to the negative effects of redundancies on remaining staff. The study of British Telecom (BT) by Doherty, Bank, and Vinnicombe (1996) demonstrates the 'triple blow' for survivors of redundancy exercises. First, the departure of colleagues, even friends, can be distressing for remaining staff; secondly, their own job prospects inevitably seem threatened; and, thirdly, they may be expected to work harder, as a result of having to cover for their departed coworkers, which can be a source of work stress. Studies show that 'survivors' of redundancy exercises exhibit lower work performance, less attachment to the organization, and a greater propensity to leave (e.g. Maertz et al. 2010).

Although redundancy exercises are often justified with reference to the need for efficiency savings, the negative effects they have on remaining staff may undermine the scope for performance improvements. The available evidence concerning the impact of redundancy exercises on organizational performance is mixed; although some studies indicate that there is a relationship between lay-offs and improvements in performance, others evince more scepticism (Cascio 2010; Datta et al. 2010). Understandably, then, securing the loyalty, commitment, and engagement of surviving staff represents a key challenge for employers during and after redundancy exercises. There are now a large number of studies devoted to identifying the characteristics of what has been termed 'survivor syndrome', examining its causes and prescribing ways in which managers can moderate its effects (e.g. Appelbaum et al. 1997; Westman 2007).

What can help to mitigate the impact of survivor syndrome? Appelbaum et al. (1997) recommend a number of interventions, including the use of a detailed plan on how to deal with survivors, and the importance of effective communications which can engender transparency and build trust, and also help negative rumours from spreading. Others highlight the need to address the personal development concerns of remaining employees (Doherty, Bank, and Vinnicombe 1996). Baruch and Hind (2000) looked at a large financial institution where the problem of survivor syndrome failed to materialize, despite large numbers of redundancies having taken place. It seems that following 'best practice' in the management of redundancies, and also the time when they take place, can prevent survivor syndrome from occurring. This includes, among other things, the use of a fair and open approach to handling redundancies, the provision of effective communications, an emphasis on transparency, and an acknowledgement that employee participation is important. See Box 9.10 for a skills exercise relating to the effective management of redundancies.

However, the capacity of managers to moderate the impact of redundancies on remaining staff may be limited in practice—see, for example, the organizational case studies undertaken by Beynon et al. (2002). Waves of job losses had increased the remaining employees' insecurity

Box 9.10 Skills exercise
Role playing redundancy planning

This skills exercise requires you to play the role of managers in an organization which is under pressure to make considerable savings across all its operations. Having already rejected alternative methods of reducing labour costs, your chief executive has decided that out of a total workforce of 1700 people, at least 90 compulsory redundancies are needed in order to ensure the long-term survival of the business. In groups of three or four discuss and come up with a plan to implement the redundancies, including an estimate of the likely costs involved at each stage. In particular, you should consider the following questions.

1 How do you plan to communicate the news of the redundancies?

2 What actions will you take to select staff for compulsory redundancy?

3 How do you propose to consult with employee representatives?

4 How will you calculate redundancy payments?

5 What measures will you put in place to help staff selected for redundancy?

6 What actions will you take to mitigate the effects of redundancies on remaining staff?

and lowered their morale to such a degree that the methods used by organizations to manage redundancies were of little effect. 'It was not only the actual implementation of redundancy, but also the heightened uncertainty over both future employment prospects and the stability of the current organizational and work arrangements that led to feelings of low morale' (Beynon et al. 2002: 167). There was little that managers in the organizations could do to alter this perception, suggesting that, in a more insecure employment climate, attempts to deal with the problem of so-called survivor syndrome may be of little consequence in practice.

Summary and further reading

- Where support for redundant employees is provided, it is offered either on an in-house basis, or by means of external outplacement specialists. Outplacement providers help staff cope with the experience of being made redundant, and offer advice and support with retraining, job searches, and career planning. There is mixed evidence for the effectiveness of in-house support and outplacement services.

- Being made redundant affects the workers concerned in important ways. They are often obliged to take jobs with worse terms and conditions; the experience is particularly fraught for some types of workers—for example, older workers who may have particular difficulties securing alternative employment. However, people who have taken voluntary redundancy may have a more positive experience.

- There has been an increasing amount of interest within organizations concerning how the effects of redundancy exercises on remaining staff can be handled. Attempts to deal with the 'survivor syndrome' problem, whereby the commitment, motivation, and performance of staff kept on after redundancy exercises deteriorate, suggest the development of a more purposive strategic approach to managing redundancies. However, the extent to which this aspect of redundancy is capable of being controlled by managers is questionable.

See Cascio (2010) for an overview of the effects of redundancy exercises. Maertz et al. (2010) examine the implications of redundancies for the 'survivors'.

9.6 Conclusion

Four aspects of redundancy as a feature of human resource management inform this concluding section. First, the relevance of redundancy to human resource management in contemporary organizations should be evident. Redundancies are a common feature of downsizing initiatives, and are frequently turned to when organizations find it necessary to institute cost savings. For managers, the challenges posed by redundancy extend beyond the process of handling redundancies, including such matters as communicating the redundancy decision and selecting the people to be dismissed, to the need to consider the impact on those staff who remain employed by the organization.

A second feature of redundancy that needs to be emphasized concerns the large extent to which it is a process that is under managerial control. Redundancy practice is influenced more by the need to meet the objectives of the organization and to secure appropriate flexibility over the process of making redundancies and their outcomes, than it is with protecting staff made redundant and looking after their interests. Where organizations do consider the effects on the workforce, this is largely to smooth the redundancy process, to retain the commitment of staff, and to prevent unrest, rather than from a concern with employee welfare. Trade unions claim that is too easy for employers to dismiss staff by means of redundancy, and that workers deserve greater protection.

Thirdly, job cuts, and therefore frequently redundancies, are one of the most obvious ways in which organizations can make savings, and thus supposedly improve business efficiency and performance outcomes. In practice, however, redundancy exercises often fail to live up to their promise. The adverse consequences of redundancies for remaining staff, captured by the 'survivor syndrome' concept, mean that performance improvements are often illusory.

Fourthly, while voluntary redundancies are a popular method of instituting job cuts, since they enable organizations to reduce their workforces in a way that decreases the scope for worker resistance and helps to maintain morale, managers are often obliged to restrict access to voluntary redundancy programmes because too many employees, or the wrong kind of employees, want to leave. Thus the assumption that voluntary redundancy gives staff the choice over whether or not to leave the organization must be qualified.

 ## Assignment and discussion questions

1 What is meant by the concept of redundancy in human resource management? What are the main reasons why employers make redundancies?

2 In what ways did the recession of the late 2000s affect redundancies?

3 To what extent do you agree with the claim made by some business leaders that employers face too many constraints when it comes to dismissing staff for the reason of redundancy?

4 Critically evaluate the main alternatives to compulsory redundancies as a means of instituting workforce reductions.

5 What are the main advantages and disadvantages of 'last-in, first-out' as a selection criterion in redundancy exercises?

6 What is meant by the concept of 'survivor syndrome'? To what extent, and in what ways, can managers reduce the problem of survivor syndrome during and after redundancy exercises?

 ## Online Resource Centre

Test your understanding of this chapter with online questions and answers, keep up to speed with changes to the law through regular updates, and use selected weblinks to quickly access useful resources and further information. Visit the Online Resource Centre at:
www.oxfordtextbooks.co.uk/orc/gilmore_williams2e/

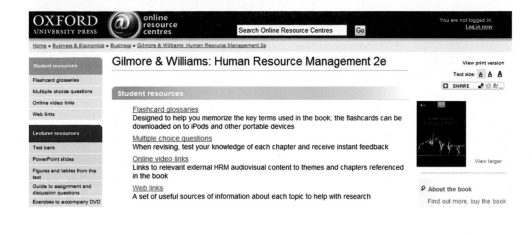

 ## Case study
Handling redundancies at Eastney Cleaning Services Ltd

Eastney Cleaning Services Ltd is a medium-sized manufacturer of cleaning supplies for the hotel and catering industry. From modest beginnings in 1970 it has grown rapidly, such that by 2012 over 350 staff are employed by the company, including some 270 workers directly responsible for a variety of cleaning materials, such as clothing, implements, and specialist cleaning equipment. Many production workers have been employed by the company for a long time, with some having joined it during its initial period of expansion during the 1970s. An increasingly uncertain trading climate, largely the result of greater competition from overseas, meant that in September 2010 Eastney Cleaning Services instituted a 'pay freeze'; workers will not receive a pay rise for at least another two years. The company's chief executive, Gill Tibbs, is already concerned that one of the effects of the pay freeze has been to increase the level of support among the workforce for union representation, and the Cleaning and General Workers Union has asked to be recognized.

However, the latest financial forecasts indicate that on its own the pay freeze will not reduce costs enough, and that up to 25 positions will need to be shed if the company is to survive the current downturn in orders, particularly in the specialist clothing area. With rumours of impending job losses surrounding the plant, the Cleaning and General Workers Union has already hinted that it will vigorously oppose any efforts to make people redundant compulsorily, and will fight attempts to dismiss any of its members.

Therefore Gill asks the human resource manager of Eastney Cleaning Services, Peter Martin, to come up with a plan to eliminate the equivalent of up to 25 jobs in a way that generates as little resistance as possible from the workforce. She requests that he produces a report outlining how the company can best achieve this objective while avoiding having to make compulsory redundancies.

Questions

1 If you were Peter, what would you include in your report to Gill?

2 How would you ensure that any job losses were put into effect in a way that helped to support the performance of Eastney Cleaning Services as a business?

used as a reason to treat people unfairly. Every person has one or more of the protected characteristics, so the Act protects everyone against unfair treatment. The protected characteristics are:

- age
- disability
- gender reassignment
- marriage and civil partnership
- pregnancy and maternity
- race
- religion or belief
- sex
- sexual orientation.

The Act protects people in a variety of situations, not just in employment, and is intended to protect all employees from being discriminated against on grounds that are not relevant to the job. It also affords protection for employees from third-party discrimination and harassment, for example by protecting shop workers from abuse from customers, as well as extending the provisions to cover discrimination by association, primarily aimed at carers of disabled persons. By perception, employees are protected if they are perceived to have a protected characteristic. With the implementation of the Equality Act, the UK is a good exemplar of comprehensive equality legislation.

10.3.4 Positive discrimination, positive action, and quotas

Positive discrimination, also referred to as 'reverse' discrimination, 'preferential treatment', and 'affirmative action', refers to a situation where a less or equally qualified individual who belongs to an under-represented or otherwise disadvantaged group is given precedence over another individual who does not belong to the group in question. Generally, positive discrimination is unlawful in the UK; however, its use is quite widespread in the rest of the world (see Box 10.2).

The purpose of positive discrimination policies is to help redress the balance for disadvantaged groups, and as a result many countries around the world, including Israel, Brazil, and China, all take action to help certain disadvantaged groups. Another example comes from the Northwest Territories in Canada where aboriginal people are given preference for jobs and education. One extension to this concept is the provision of quotas, which are numerical requirements for hiring, promoting, admitting and/or graduating members of a particular group in education or employment. These tend to be gender or racially based. In the USA racial

Box 10.2 International focus
Positive discrimination

Many countries use forms of positive discrimination to help achieve their equality objectives. In Norway, for example, women must comprise at least 40 per cent of the boards of public companies. In the Canadian province of Quebec there is a long tradition of positive discrimination to ensure that the French language is preserved in all aspects of life—including the workplace—as an essential component of its society. In Sweden, positive discrimination is permitted where it is 'part of the drive to achieve equality between men and women', but not generally for other protected groups. One specific example is the Swedish police, who give women and people from minority ethnic backgrounds concessions when it comes to testing for entrance to the police academy. 'Affirmative action' designed to tackle systematic disadvantage among African Americans is legal in the USA; however, there have been numerous court cases challenging affirmative action measures, resulting in separate states developing their own approaches.

quotas have been set in employment, and in Norway a quota of 40 per cent has been set for either gender on all public limited company boards. However, for many people the thought of employing or promoting someone purely based on a protected characteristic and not on merit is unpalatable, so they prefer to enhance diversity through positive action which does not give preferential treatment to certain groups. Positive action or positive measures are steps that employers can take to encourage job applications from people from groups with different needs, or with a past track record of disadvantage or low participation. For example, an employer may consider placing an advertisement in an ethnic minority publication in addition to their normal recruitment methods to attract candidates from this group because they are under-represented in their workforce.

10.3.5 Equal pay

One particular element of discrimination law is that relating to equal pay, particularly between men and women. Prior to the introduction of equal pay legislation men and women were routinely given different rates of pay, which were often negotiated by trade unions. For example, in the UK in 1970 men were paid 37 per cent more than women, although this had dropped to around 18 per cent by 2010 (Fawcett Society 2010). Many jobs were seen as being for a specific gender—for example, men as engineers and women as nurses, teachers, and cleaners. Such a segregated workforce meant that it was sometimes hard to find any men in some professions so as to be able to bring an 'equal pay' claim. Hence, the concept of 'equal pay for work of equal value' was implemented. This makes it unlawful for employers to discriminate between men and women over pay and conditions where they are doing:

- work that is the same or broadly similar;
- work rated as equivalent under a job evaluation study;
- work of equal value in terms of the demands made on them under headings such as effort, skill, and decision-making.

To this day, many gender inequality claims in the UK are made under this aspect of the legislation (see Box 10.3). The majority involve a comparison between existing employees, but comparisons with predecessors and successors can also be made. As with other gender-related legislation, the Act applies to both men and women; hence men can bring cases as well as women. Similar principles apply to bringing equal pay claims in other countries, such as EU member states and the USA.

10.3.6 Equal opportunities achievements

Having described the legislation, we will now look at recent data to review any progress in achieving equality. The position of the 'non-white' population in UK is still less favourable in employment. Racism in employment is still widespread, with the most common complaints

 Box 10.3 Window on work
An equal pay case

Bridget Bodman, a former accountant at manufacturing company API group, received £25,000 after winning an equal pay case in November 2006. Her case was unusual as she used her successor's salary as the basis of the claim as her 'comparator' on higher pay. Ms Bodman's successor was paid £8000 more than her and received an £8640 car allowance and additional benefits. The employment tribunal found that the company had no defence for the differences in salaries. It said: the 'absence of both clear criteria and process for determining pay award and bonus payments creates a climate where pay discrimination on gender grounds can operate, consciously or unconsciously, unsuspected, undetected, and unchallenged' (EOC 2007b)

What are the main implications of this case for organizations wanting to ensure they are compliant with equal opportunity legislation?

being about workplace bullying, lack of career progression, and the inability to get job interviews (Cabinet Office 2003). The rate of unemployment for ethnic minorities is over 11 per cent—twice the overall average. A black person is three times more likely to be out of work than a white person.

With regard to gender equality, there is evidence of positive change, and it is likely that legislation has played a part in this. With regard to pay in the USA, for example, women's median yearly earnings relative to those of men rose rapidly from 1980 to 1990 (from 60.2 to 71.6 per cent), and less rapidly from 1990 to 2000 (from 71.6 to 73.7 per cent) and from 2000 to 2009 (from 73.7 to 77 per cent) (DeNavas-Walt, Proctor, and Smith 2009). In the UK and Europe, the pay gap between men and women has also narrowed, but on average women still earn only around 82 pence for every male pound, compared with 62 pence in 1975. The gender difference is lower in the public sector, where women are paid 13.5 per cent less than men for the same work, compared with 22.5 per cent in the private sector. Whilst women and men may start on the same pay rates, estimates show that after ten years of employment women earn 12 per cent less than a comparable man (Manning 2006); these differentials are even more marked for women from ethnic minority groups. Many women withdraw from the employment market because the low pay for part-time work fails to cover childcare costs (Manning and Petrongolo 2005). See Box 10.4 for a learning activity concerning gender pay inequality.

Male prevalence still persists in many key decision-making roles; for example, just 10 per cent of directors of FTSE 100 companies are women (EOC 2007a).

As legislation concerning sexuality, gender reassignment, disability, religion/belief, and age are relatively new, we would expect few changes to be apparent as yet. Case law is developing; see the CIPD web site for a list of 'key cases' that summarize important verdicts (www.cipd.co.uk).

Summary and further reading

- The scope of discrimination law varies widely from country to country, with more extensive legislation in the more developed countries such as the USA and EU member states. The UK leads the way on

Box 10.4 Learning activity
Understanding the gender pay gap

This learning activity is designed to enable you to develop your knowledge and understanding of gender pay inequality, or the 'gender pay gap' as it is known. In the main text, we present some broad aggregate-level data, but the gender pay gap varies considerably by factors such as employment status and age. In some cases, there is a negative gender pay gap where on average women earn more than men. In 2011, the gender pay gap among full-time employees fell to 9.1 per cent, the lowest recorded level. However, across all employees (part-time and full-time) the overall gender pay gap stood at 19.5 per cent. This reflects the specific pay penalty experienced by part-time workers. Whereas the median hourly earnings in 2011 were £13.11 for full-time male employees and £11.91 for full-time female employees, the figure for part-time female employees was £8.10.

Only 12 per cent of male employees work part-time compared with 42 per cent of female employees. When it comes to just part-time employees, a negative gender pay gap exists; the median hourly earnings of male part-timers are 5.6 per cent less than for females. Interestingly, the gender pay gap seems to widen with age. Among younger workers, the gender pay gap is either very narrow or is negative (i.e. women's earnings outstrip men). Only from the age of 40 onwards does the gender pay gap become such a marked feature of employment (see ONS 2011).

1 Consider the reasons for the persistence of the gender pay gap in the UK.

2 Why has the overall gender pay gap been gradually declining?

3 Why is the gender pay gap wider for some groups of workers than for others?

4 What can organizations do to reduce gender pay inequality?

equality law with the introduction of the 2010 Equality Act which now protects a wide range of individuals from discrimination in the workplace.

- Laws have made a difference to addressing inequalities; however, there is still a considerable challenge for the achievement of equality in work and employment.

It is essential for anyone seeking information on the legal position within this field that they do not 'guess' or use 'old' information. The CIPD web site (www.cipd.co.uk) is very good, with a 'Key Cases' section of recent judgements for cases in equality legislation. It is especially helpful for definitions.

10.4 Key issues in equality and diversity

Legal requirements for organizations on equality have already been outlined, and illustrate continual change. This section will first examine some of the issues associated with the non-achievement of both equality and diversity in our workplaces. In this we invite the reader to consider how we all contribute to maintaining the status quo of inequality by outlining some of the forces at large that act against further shifts in attitude. We will then progress to a summary of actions that organizations can take to monitor their own achievements so that they can identify areas for action.

10.4.1 Stereotyping and segregation

Stereotyping is where we make judgements about a person on the basis of a group to which we see that person belonging, rather than seeing the person as an individual. We all belong to groups, but we want to be judged for ourselves, rather than the group. William Bielby, an American sociologist, contends that white men will inevitably slight women and ethnic minorities because they are not like themselves, terming this 'unconscious bias theory' (cited in Orey 2006). Thus subconscious stereotyping occurs, possibly resulting in discriminatory employment practices. But this is not exclusive to women—President Obama shifted high-profile leadership stereotypes in the USA away from being roles held by white candidates.

Blaine (2007) argues that, because of past inequalities, we apply stereotypes to the world that reinforce the 'old' order. Thus, for example, we expect few women parliamentarians, and that men will receive higher pay for the same job, because it has always been like that. This may deter individuals from complaining or acting in other ways to change existing inequalities.

Geographical segregation in ethnic minority groups (especially in cities) has been a topic of study to understand immigration and the (under-)achievement of minorities of any group. The argument is that ethnic minority groups live in deprived districts as they cannot access employment opportunities. Typically, the schools are poorer in such environments, as are health and childcare opportunities. Hence the 'next-generation' children become disadvantaged and parents are faced with unemployment. In these deprived areas business activity is lower and unemployment is higher; low levels of car ownership and hence restricted mobility may in turn contribute to higher unemployment. This can create a cycle of non-achievement characterized by enduring low employment expectations as generations evolve (see Johnston, Poulsen, and Forrest (2010) for a review and further reading).

Geographical segregation often concerns ethnicity, but occupations can also be segregated by gender. Occupational segregation is prevalent in the many countries where gender-segregated workforces traditionally exist. The expectations held by those in early and mid-careers can help us to understand occupational segregation. The UK Women and Equality Unit (WEU) has suggested that early career choices by women affect how they achieve at later stages in their careers (Women and Work Commission 2006). They found that women are often channelled into 'people jobs'—caring or administrative roles, or roles that enable others—which are seen in many organizations as secondary or support roles (with lower status). For every ten women in employment, six work in just ten occupations, typically those that pay the least. The WEU suggested that underpinning these early career directions are education and socialization influences, which draw on perceptions and stereotypes of what types of work women do—for

example, roles for women are seen as teaching, nursing, and catering. The WEU report considered such pervasive values to be a form of discrimination.

Their findings are mirrored by research into ethnicity. Kamenou and Fearful (2006) found that women from ethnic minority groups thought that they must conform to the existing white-male-dominated culture if they want to advance. Their findings demonstrate the difficulty of changing attitudes and the status quo within the established employment patterns of our workplaces.

10.4.2 Opportunity and choice

Human capital theory and rational choice theories have been combined to form a set of arguments that have been used to explain inequality for both women and ethnic minorities. Human capital is defined as the sum of skill, knowledge, experience, and educational qualifications that a person possesses. Crompton (1997) reports the view initially put forward by the economist Gary Becker that women invest less in their 'human capital' than men because of their domestic and childcaring responsibilities, and thus make a 'rational choice' to choose jobs that are less effort intensive and are generally compatible with their domestic responsibilities. The geographic segregation outlined above for ethnic minorities could result in similar outcomes.

Hakim (2004) has developed Becker's theory and argues that women's choices change over time. She categorized women into three types: career-focused, home-focused, or adaptive. She argues that women can be career-focused and then give it up to have children or vice versa. Women who are career-focused are in the minority, but can, and do, have successful careers in the same way as men. Hakim views women as heterogeneous and argues that 'it is this heterogeneity in itself that has led to women being exploited in the workplace by men, because they are divided in their wants, rather than men collectively exploiting women'. Others suggest that women's choices are far more limited than men's, and the responsibility for children is a complex issue (Fortin 2005). The debate here is that of choice versus opportunity. Hakim suggests that women may have the opportunity for human capital development and high-level jobs, but choose not to exercise it. Many others would suggest that lower-achieving groups lack the opportunity and have no choice.

Avoiding stereotypes is a challenge. Large surveys such as the census are useful in charting broad developments within the population. However, how we use these in our daily life can reinforce stereotypical attitudes, so that we see a middle-aged white male and immediately think that he earns more than his female equivalent, would find it easier to get a job, and undertakes little domestic care. Of course this is incorrect. We are all different. All disabled people are different in their ways of managing their disability. Women might need to make a choice regarding childbirth (if and when they decide to have), but their options and how they evaluate their situation are always different.

10.4.3 The 'glass ceiling'

The term 'glass ceiling' refers to situations where the advancement of a person within the hierarchy of an organization is limited. This limitation is normally based on some form of discrimination, gender being the most commonly studied. Such barriers also exist for ethnic minorities and on the grounds of sexuality (e.g. Frank 2006). Is there evidence that a glass ceiling exists? Arulampalam, Booth, and Bryan (2007) found evidence in Europe of a glass ceiling, particularly with regard to pay. Academics and commentators alike are watching the changes in Norwegian boardrooms (see Section 10.3.4) to evaluate the effect of positive discrimination on changing their glass ceiling. These changes will take several years to work through, but as data become available, they will be reported. See Box 10.5 for a sceptical perspective on the glass ceiling concept as it applies to women.

According to Matthews (2007), excessive working hours and a culture of presenteeism have combined to make women selective about their employer, and discourage them from aspiring to top management. It would appear that women make choices, but, for women at senior level who seek a work–life balance, this is not always in the assumed 'upward-mobility' direction; no doubt the opportunity–choice debate will continue. Recently the notion of a 'glass cliff' has been established (Ryan and Haslam 2007) where women are appointed to senior posts in

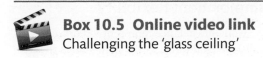

Box 10.5 Online video link
Challenging the 'glass ceiling'

Go to the Online Resource Centre where you will find a link to video content in which businesswoman and star of the TV show Dragons Den, Hilary Devey, talks about women in the workplace. Do you agree with her view that the concept of the 'glass ceiling' is 'rubbish', and that positive discrimination in favour of women is unnecessary?

situations of organizational decline, and are more likely to be blamed later if there is failure. The authors put forward an interesting and persuasive argument, which is likely to apply to other 'minority' groups that are outside traditional appointment patterns. They suggest that women can become 'tea bags' running 'the risk of being dunked in hot water again and again' Ryan and Haslam 2007:8). But also interestingly, they point to some women who nevertheless see this as an opportunity to advance their careers.

10.4.4 Employers' policies and actions to tackle inequality

Whether or not employees choose to take opportunities, it is important that they have the choice. We saw how entrenched values and stereotyping might affect the workplace, which can make it hard for those in power to see the issues clearly through their own—possibly tainted—lens. Many employers have been sparing in their attendance to the spirit of the law (providing equality and discrimination-free working environments), focusing instead on trying to avoid legal action by current or past employees. The Gender Equality Duty is an example of how the emphasis is increasingly on employers (currently only in the public sector) to ensure that their equality practices are robust. This has sparked considerable activity in public sector organizations as they meet this challenge. Many organizations have conducted 'impact assessments' of their policies and practices (note that practice may differ from policy) to evaluate how far they comply with the legislation. It must be added that organizations are being encouraged to look at all equality issues, not just gender, and indeed this is quite practicable.

The process of undertaking impact assessments is changing almost monthly, but it is fundamentally a threefold process. First, the policies need to be assembled, and a careful review of their content and joint coherence undertaken. Policies are often developed at different times, and it is very easy for them to become poorly linked. Employers are finding the policy review helpful in establishing clear pathways for all employees to make decisions. The next stage is to review them for robustness regarding implementation. For example, one might assemble a group of representative employees who examine the policies from different equality perspectives (age, disability, etc.) to see how far they may discriminate and take action to amend them.

The final stage is to examine the evidence of equality achievement, which provides an indicator of equality in practice. Hence a large public sector employer should be employing a profile of staff that reflects the local population. An inner-city local authority will employ more ethnic minority staff than most rural authorities because this reflects local demographics. Demographics also need to be used to assess achievement of various groups within the hierarchy and occupational segments. This will give a 'snapshot' of local practice. Of course, one would expect there to be underachievement. If the reason for this is known, action to ensure that these policies do not discriminate in practice is essential. Sometimes employers do not know why people under-achieve, and here they need to run focus groups or other data-collection exercises to appreciate where their policies may not be effective or where they are failing in practice. Positive action to help under-represented groups is then likely to follow, together with training for managers and awareness-raising for all employees.

Employers are encouraged to take a structured approach to reviewing equal pay in their organizations. They are often shocked to discover the size of the disadvantage, as they believe their policies to be non-discriminatory. Manning (2006) argues that employers should be encouraged rather than compelled to publish the results of these audits, as employers who do well will reap the benefits of being seen as good employers and thus will attract and retain good workers.

10.4.5 Work–life balance and employment flexibility

Employment flexibility and achieving a positive work–life balance represent important issues for employers when making the best use of a diverse workforce, as they are known to affect participation in work. Rigid models of work are driving highly qualified workers into jobs below their skill level in order for them to have a life outside work (EOC 2007b). Unfortunately, the UK distinguishes itself with a 'long-hours culture' or presenteeism (often called face-time in the USA). Research shows that many people work very hard for long hours, and that one in five regularly take work home in the evening, but fewer than one in two workers have any control over their working hours (Doyle and Reeves 2003).

However, the demand for more flexible working is increasing amongst employees. The CIPD (2002) found that 45 per cent of parents had changed jobs in order to work more flexibly, but had downgraded their career ambitions in doing so. The EOC (2007b) found that half the working population want to work more flexibly. It claimed that 6.5 million people in the UK could be using their skills more fully if increased flexible working was available, either by working at the level at which they used to work or by simply returning to the workforce. These pressures on employers will no doubt increase as there are changes in retirement and an overall ageing working population begins to want changes. That said, it is rare to find flexibility on offer to employees by employers, but this probably may develop as skills shortages occur.

 Summary and further reading

- Traditional views and stereotyping exist within and beyond the boundaries of employers, and they extend into education and the way we steer careers for ourselves and others. Early career choices affect employees' levels of achievement, and traditions can be compounded by geographic and occupational segregation.

- Some aspects of work are changing, such as the amount of time that employees work. These in turn are prompting attitude shifts in workers where a good work–life balance and flexibility are desirable facets of employment, and a practical need for some parents. There is debate regarding the level of choice employees actually have.

- Those organizations affected by the Gender Equality Duty are leading the way in undertaking their own assessments to understand their position as regards equality. This involves the examination of policies and practices and the gathering of hard data about employment terms (such as pay and advancement) and comparing these with the relevant demographics.

Bruce Blaine's book *Understanding the Psychology of Diversity* (2007) is very good on stereotyping—the issue that underlies much prejudice. Without doubt, the website of the Equality and Human Rights Commission is the place to find current reports and thinking about contemporary issues (www.equalityhumanrights.com).

10.5 From indignity to decency

10.5.1 Bullying and harassment

For the purposes of this chapter, the experience of harassment and bullying will be treated similarly. As a reminder, 'harassment' is defined as 'unwanted conduct that violates people's dignity or creates an intimidating, hostile, degrading, humiliating or offensive environment' (www.acas.org.uk). What types of behaviour might one be considering? First, the behaviour is interpersonal, and it can be from one or more people. Secondly, the behaviour can be from any direction in the hierarchy and, while the majority of reports in the UK identify a manager as the source, it can also come from peers; there is also 'upwards bullying' from a subordinate (or group of subordinates). Thirdly, the behaviour can take many shapes. For example, it might be overt, such as shouting or highly public criticism. This type of behaviour is dominant in stereotypes of bullying, but actually it is quite rare. A more likely scenario would be exclusion from information required to get the job done, undermining, unrealistic deadlines, malicious gossip, or name-calling. Finally, the pattern of this behaviour can vary enormously, from single major events (again quite rare) to a sequence of apparently small events which, when taken

together, show a pattern of systematic negative treatment. The behaviour has been found to be present within all working communities studied around the world (Rayner and Keashly 2005).

There is law against harassment on the grounds of age, gender, race (etc.) in European countries. There is no law against bullying at work in the UK or the USA, and the situation varies across the world, presenting a far 'messier' picture. Employees who have been bullied can and do make claims against their employers—for example, using harassment law in the equality legislation. If someone has been damaged by bullying, health and safety law can be used as the employer has a duty of care to provide a psychologically safe environment which precludes bullying (Cousins et al. 2004). If someone has been damaged by bullying, he/she can take a private action for personal injury. In these last two instances, people have usually had severe damage, such as a mental breakdown. Pressure exists to create a law that makes employers liable *before* someone has experienced such extreme damage (e.g. Wornham 2003; Yamada 2011).

Defining bullying presents a real problem, since it can take so many forms (Rayner and Keashly 2005; Spence Laschinger et al. 2010). Policies often contain very vague definitions to enable a wide variety of complaints to be considered and dealt with by the employer. This is not helpful to an employee who is trying to work out what is happening and make sense of his/her situation. Hence a recent trend is to have operational (detailed) definitions of what is 'unacceptable behaviour' at a local level. Effective practice is to gather employees together (e.g. worker representatives, HR, and management) in order to articulate a statement. Such definitions are positive for those who are experiencing negative treatment and also for those who are trying to ensure that they do not act as bullies.

What causes bullying? A variety of approaches have characterized this question, ranging from the study of personal individual characteristics to organizational factors. Evidence suggests that the personal characteristics of those involved have little to do with bullying as age, gender, and other demographics fail to correlate with targets or bullies (e.g. Rayner 2009) and also personality studies have failed to find any trends (Glaso, Neilsen, and Einarsen, 2009). Hence the notion that bullying involves a personality clash is in reality unlikely, albeit an attractive option to use as it keeps the problem local and means that one does not have to look further. Instead, it appears that the work climate has a great deal to do with bullying. Within any situation there are enabling factors (such as lack of sanctions or a perception that the behaviour is acceptable), motivating factors (such as high internal competition or targets, or that it is difficult to lay off employees), and precipitating or 'trigger' factors (such as restructuring or change in management) which work together to create a situation where bullying is more likely (Salin 2003).

Some entire working cultures are claimed to be bullying. For example, the 'rough and tumble' dealing rooms in the City of London are profiled as 'tough' environments, as are the uniformed services (e.g. Archer 1999). In such circumstances, bullying may indeed be part of working in a given area, and one is looking for different reasons as to why the behaviour is so pervasive than those described by Salin (2003). Here, one would be concerned that the level of tolerance amongst all levels of the hierarchy provides an environment in which this behaviour is tolerated. While those involved might see developing a thick skin as necessary, the employer needs to be careful that he/she is providing a psychologically safe environment for the average worker. In such situations 'people often burn out' and the employer loses valuable workers (e.g. Farrell 1999).

The costs of bullying are similar to those of stress; indeed, bullying is now the main focus of work being undertaken in stress prevention by the UK Health and Safety Executive (Cousins et al. 2004). Psychological strain for targets of bullying and harassment includes sleepless nights, not wanting to go to work, and other anxiety-related symptoms. They may develop into stress-related physical problems such as back strain and gastric problems. High levels of long-term sick leave are associated with those who have been badly damaged by bullying. Short-term sick leave is not thought to be an indicator, since employees are worried about taking days off for fear of being told they are abusing the sick pay regime (Rayner 1997).

The most stable UK statistic for bullying is that 25 per cent of targets leave their jobs as a means of resolving their situation. Two studies have questioned witnesses of bullying, and it appears that they leave their jobs as a result of witnessing bullying at a rate of about 20 per cent (Rayner 1997, 2009; Hoel and Cooper 2000). The cost of witnesses leaving is likely to be higher

than that of those directly targeted by bullying, as there are more witnesses than targets. Within a large organization, exit rates may be hidden by the organizational internal job market. While exit interviews can and do show bullying 'hot-spots', employers are well advised to examine all leavers, including those going to other jobs within the organization.

Bullying and harassment questions are now part of staff opinion surveys undertaken by organizations, and they are useful indicators of the level of bullying and harassment (e.g. Archer 1999). Employees often use anonymous questionnaires to reveal information about sensitive topics that they would otherwise find difficult to report, especially when their boss is the bully or harasser. See Box 10.6 for survey evidence on bullying in UK National Health Service. There are two ways to ask people whether they have been bullied or harassed. One can ask either if they have been bullied or harassed within a specific time frame (such as the last year) or if they have experienced bullying behaviours (from a provided list) together with the level of frequency within a given period (such as a year). Academic studies have 'counted' the latter as bullying when reported as weekly behaviour. In UK organizations, response rates of between 10 and 15 per cent are common to the question 'Are you being bullied?' Very few people report being bullied without also reporting the experience of negative behaviour (Rayner 2009); hence tackling bullying is about dealing with negative behaviours. Harassment and bullying often have policies associated with them within organizations. Most organizations are moving to calling these 'dignity at work' policies as positive phrasing is seen as more constructive in tone.

10.5.2 Dignity at work

Difficulties about defining bullying and the desire to make positive statements have led to the development of dignity at work initiatives. These programmes address equality, discrimination, harassment, and bullying for all employees. For example, in the UK the Royal Mail decided that it would not design a programme specifically for women since it could not justify doing something exclusively for its female employees. Instead, it decided to change the working culture for everyone, so that it would become a positive and supportive working environment regardless of employee demographics.

Dignity at work initiatives are distinguished by an emphasis on the positive. Hence such organizations generate a positive code of conduct and, for example, promote training on positive behaviour towards one another. It is easier to promote the diversity agenda where one is trying to value difference rather than just ensure equality. This is a very new concept for organizations, and as yet we have no evidence on the effectiveness of such programmes.

One subtlety is worth noting, however. Behaving positively and negatively are not necessarily opposites—sometimes they are different. Getting people to tell the truth (positive behaviour) is not the same as telling people not to lie (preventing negative behaviour). A middle position exists where people are withholding the truth. With regard to dignity initiatives, this becomes a conundrum unless one is careful. Hence a manager can be very good at giving feedback to staff, including them in decisions (strong indicators of providing dignity), but can also engage in some aspects of bullying, such as temper tantrums when things do not go well. Another example

Box 10.6 Research in focus
NHS surveys on bullying

Research studies demonstrate that issues relating to bullying and harassment have become key challenges for organizations (e.g. Rayner 2009). Over the last few years NHS staff surveys have consistently identified staff-on-staff bullying and harassment as a key issue to address. The NHS has taken strong steps to eliminate this kind of behaviour in the workplace, but it is clear that problems persist. The 2007 survey showed that 8 per cent of staff had experienced bullying, harassment, or abuse from their team leader, and 13 per cent had experienced it from colleagues. Just half of those who had experienced incidents of bullying and harassment actually reported it. Fewer than one in ten employees felt that their employer took effective action when it came to cases of bullying and harassment.

Source: http://www.nhsemployers.org/HealthyWorkplaces/StaffHealthAndWell-Being/Pages/
BullyingAndHarassment.aspx

is a manager who is terrific towards some staff and bullying toward others—how would one label this manager? Dignity at work programmes need to ensure that as well as promoting the positive, they are also paying attention to negative behaviour.

If bullying does happen, one needs to have a policy for complaints that works (Rayner and Lewis 2011). However, tackling this early is the key to limiting damage (to the target of bullying, the alleged perpetrator, and those around both), and early mediation can form a helpful intervention (Saam 2010) but this is ineffective if left too late. Saam (2010) provides an interesting study with consultants called in to help with bullying situations and is useful for specialists.

10.5.3 Bringing the strands together

In this chapter we have covered issues to do with equality, diversity, dignity, and bullying and harassment. Clearly they relate to each other, and managers and HRM practitioners can deal with them together. In a practical sense, one is looking to achieve the following through strong HRM practice.

- The organization's policies are compliant regarding equal opportunities.
- All employees understand their rights and obligations under the law covered in this chapter.
- Managers have the confidence and the skills to identify negative situations early on and act appropriately, so that informal resolution can be found quickly and before anyone is damaged.
- A good formal complaints system exists which employees trust so that they can make a complaint.
- Feedback is sought from employees on their experience of the workplace to check actions instituted from above.
- Someone is assigned to track changes in the law and good practice.

To achieve this in practice there is a minimal approach where compliance with the law is sought; here, issues relating to equal opportunities will be the focus. Written policies will need to be reviewed and explicitly comply with the law. HRM specialists might want to be involved in aspects of recruitment, selection, promotion, and reward in order to ensure compliance. Induction and training for all employees will need to be in place to communicate that the organization takes equal opportunities seriously and that bullying and harassment are not tolerated. See Box 10.7 for a skills exercise on designing an appropriate organizational policy. Managers will also need to be trained so that they can identify difficult situations before they occur or, if they do occur, to know what to do to make sure that these situations do not escalate—even if this means simply picking the phone up and asking for help from HRM specialists. Up-to-date information needs to be available for everyone—for example, on a website. If an organization does this, it may be able to provide a reasonable defence in a legal action.

 Box 10.7 Policy example
JD Wetherspoon's 'age positive' approach

Pub company JD Wetherspoon's has put a considerable amount of effort into managing age diversity effectively—to such an extent that its approach has been presented by the government as an exemplar of good practice on this area. Wetherspoon's got rid of its retirement age in 2006, and it claims to recruit trainee managers who are in their fifties and sixties. This approach to age diversity helps to ensure that the composition of the company's workforce matches its broad customer base. Feedback from pubs which employ older workers indicates that they are stable, with low absence, a strong work ethic, and a high level of commitment to the business. According to Mandy Ferries, Head of Personnel and Training for Wetherspoon's, 'employing a diverse workforce of men and women of all ages benefits individual pubs and the company as a whole'. Among the business benefits claimed to arise from the company's age diverse approach are better staff retention, greater work effort from older workers, and lower staff turnover.

Source: http://www.dwp.gov.uk/docs/case-study-jd-wetherspoons.pdf

However, HRM practice should be about more than being able to mount a reasonable defence in court. Preventing and dealing with the negative are only one side of the coin. The other side (positive action, dignity at work programmes, and valuing diversity) can bring great rewards through a well-motivated workforce that trusts its employer, feels valued at work, and gives the extra effort and care that underpins high-performance working (see Box 10.8). As has been outlined elsewhere in this book, finding clear empirical evidence between high performance and any specific initiative is almost impossible. The reality of working life, with the plethora of both internal and external forces impinging on the organization, make such links extremely hard to achieve and very difficult to generalize from one organization to another.

The argument has to be on the negative side. Not providing value and dignity to employees is a recipe for not achieving high-performance working. Evidence connecting innovative problem-solving with genuinely diverse teams continues to grow. For members of a diverse team to feel valued, they all need to have good levels of confidence that their ideas are going to be taken seriously—and this means implementing dignity at work and valuing difference. Hence the message from this chapter is one of encouraging managers to go beyond dealing with the negative, and to use dignity programmes to contribute to the circumstance for high-performance working.

 ## Summary and further reading

- Bullying and harassment damage individuals and organizations by causing stress to individuals, who will often taken sick leave or exit the organization. Neither is positive for any employer who wishes to achieve high-performance working.

- Bullying is difficult to define, and polices need to be flexible so that they can encompass any complaint. Employees need tighter definitions, as do those who seek to ensure that their own behaviour is not bullying.

- Dignity at work programmes provide a positive approach where an organization outlines the positive treatment all employees must give to others and can also expect themselves.

- Employers need to measure the levels of bullying and harassment in their organization as well as making sure that usable complaints systems are in place, so that when the behaviour appears it can be dealt with. Training managers to be strong role models, and to have the skills and confidence to de-escalate conflict quickly, are critical components in tackling bullying and harassment.

A good text for an overall view of workplace bullying is Rayner, Hoel, and Cooper (2002). Another recent book (Bolton 2007) covers bullying, harassment, and the negative side of

 ### Box 10.8 Skills exercise
Designing an organizational policy

This skills exercise needs you to take on the role of managers in a large private sector manufacturing company which does not currently have a formal policy covering equality, diversity, and dignity issues. You have been tasked with designing such a policy and proposing how it should be implemented. Working in small groups, think about and discuss what you believe should go into such a policy, and why. You will then report back on your conclusions to the rest of the class. Among the things you should consider are:

- the scope of the policy (what issues will it cover, and what won't it cover);
- the benefits of adopting the policy;
- how the policy is to be communicated to the workforce;
- any relevant training and development issues relating to the implementation of the policy;
- whether or not anyone will be appointed to champion and take ownership of the policy;
- the responsibility of line managers for implementing the policy;
- the key issues and challenges for the company in operating the policy;
- the likely cost implications of introducing and operating the policy.

organizations very well. It outlines a wide range of descriptions of negative behaviour at work, progresses to issues of reparation, and provides work-based examples throughout.

10.6 Conclusion

Two persuasive arguments encourage employers to engage with equality, diversity, and dignity at work. First, employers do not want fall to foul of the considerable law around equal opportunities. Legal cases are not only expensive in their preparation and defence, but adversely affect reputation, calling into question the moral fibre of those in senior positions. Secondly, the operational costs associated with bullying and harassment (such as sick leave and exit rates for targets and witnesses, and expensive formal complaints and appeal processes) provide an unnecessary drag on the organization. The existence of bullying or harassment (whether labelled or not) is very likely to prevent the organization reporting high performance through the erosion of trust, withdrawal of goodwill, and lowering of motivation and morale, as well as higher exit rates and sickness absence.

To turn such situations around, one needs not only to deal with the bullying and harassment, but also to engage in positive programmes. The process can be lengthy since it involves re-establishing trust and convincing the workforce that their contributions are valued. If an organization is to excel, an equal and fair working community, free from harassment and bullying, is essential to provide the believable basis for the presence of value for employees. The role of managers is pivotal, first through behaving properly themselves, and, secondly, in quickly spotting and resolving situations of conflict.

 ## Assignment and discussion questions

1 What are the main arguments for equality and diversity? If one is trying to achieve both at the same time, what challenges does this present?

2 If an employer introduces a dignity at work policy, how do they make sure that negative behaviours are addressed?

3 What is the link between stereotyping and prejudice?

4 How would international differences affect the interpretation of 'workplace equality'? Would these issues be the same for 'dignity at work'?

5 How does one move an organization beyond the mindset of minimal compliance with the law? Illustrate with examples.

 ## Online Resource Centre

Test your understanding of this chapter with online questions and answers, keep up to speed with changes to the law through regular updates, and use selected weblinks to quickly access useful resources and further information. Visit the Online Resource Centre at:
www.oxfordtextbooks.co.uk/orc/gilmore_williams2e/

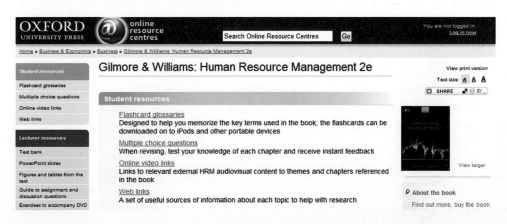

Case study
Managing diversity at InsureCo

InsureCo is a finance company with 11,000 employees. The company is a general insurer, providing house and personal insurance. It is not involved in the car or health insurance market. It also operates several pension fund schemes which other employers and individuals can buy into. Profits are divided equally between the pension and insurance sections. The pension side of the company employs around 3000 people who are generally well paid. The insurance side includes a large call centre based in Birmingham, and employs around 6000 people at various sites who are often less well paid. The remaining staff work for central services where remuneration is based on market rates of pay. This includes a 40-strong HRM department which does little administration. The HRM group operates a 'business partner' model (see Chapter 2).

The Head of HR, Hilary Begum, recently attended a conference on dignity at work for the finance sector and met with several senior HR personnel from similar firms. One speaker spent time asking them to question their formal complaint systems, suggesting that if few complaints were received, then heads of HR should not assume that all was well. Instead, they should check their staff survey data and 'ask around' as to whether people feel able to bring up problems in a formal manner, and if employees did not, where they went for resolution.

On returning to the company, she stops to chat with the car park attendant. He laughs when she asks what he would do if someone were rude to him or treated him in a demeaning way: 'It's a daily occurrence, Mrs Begum. My wife wants to come in and thump some people here for what they say to me—she's fed up with hearing about it. But I say it's just part of the job and the Super (supervisor) says so too. It's a tough world these days'. She then checks the last staff survey on the computer and prints out a more detailed report than the one she usually sees. She is surprised to find that although their average rate for 'bullying and harassment' is 15 per cent, different departments report very different figures. Thus two departments have no instances, but 20 per cent of the firm has over 25 per cent of people saying that they have felt bullied or harassed in the last year.

The next day Begum has a regular meeting with the three HR heads of department—insurance, pensions, and central services. Together they look at their complaint figures and discover that five formal complaints were tabled in the last 12 months. When she comments that this seems low, the heads suggest that most local conflict is sorted out informally. Not reassured by these comments, Begum proposes that they 'ask around', as she had done with the car park attendant.

The meeting moves on to another area of business which is a review of the workforce in terms of demographic diversity. It is clear that they have a segmented workforce with women in lower-paid and lower-status jobs, although now 20 per cent of the managers are women. They employ a good number of non-white staff, mostly of Asian extraction, and only in certain insurance offices. However, about 20 per cent of the firm has no non-white staff in their subdepartments. When Begum asks why not, the heads reply that they do not know, and that they are sure that equal opportunity policies are working in recruitment. She is reminded by them that positive discrimination is illegal.

Driving home, Begum starts to wonder if they might have a problem with the values in the firm, and that possibly they should review what is going on at ground level. She finds it hard to marry the figures she has seen from the staff survey with her own experience of colleagues who work in the departments who had reported high levels of negative behaviour. They don't seem to be aware of anything being wrong. She knows the UK workforce is very segregated, but cannot see why that should occur in the finance sector as the jobs are desk-based, and although experience is needed for many posts, this can be provided internally through staff development. Why should these segregations show up at InsureCo? The more Begum thinks about it, the more she realizes that she doesn't have enough answers. The firm's chief executive had spent time with her recently to explain how InsureCo was slipping in terms of its people costs compared with its competitors—maybe this has something to do with it?

Questions

1 What problems can you identify at InsureCo? What do you think might be going on?

2 What do you think Hilary Begum should do?

3 Which laws might affect her enquiry?

4 How would Hilary know if people feel valued for their difference?

Managing performance and absence

11

David Hall

Learning objectives

The main objectives of this chapter are:

- to describe the relevance and development of performance management;
- to define performance management and describe its application as a management intervention for improving organizational performance;
- to examine how performance management systems operate;
- to critically assess the purpose and effectiveness of performance management arrangements;
- to account for the salience of employee absence as a performance issue and examine how it is managed in organizations.

11.1 Introduction

Managing performance is a workplace phenomenon of the twenty-first century. Following this introduction, in Section 11.2 we examine the growth of performance management, driven by increasing competition in the private and public sectors which affects all employees and has implications for most people. The relationship between HRM and managing performance is explored in Section 11.3, tracing the development and relationship of strategic HRM (SHRM) to performance through the influence of HR policies and high performance work practices. In Section 11.4 our attention turns to how performance management systems operate, including consideration of the main methods which are commonly applied as management interventions, such as performance appraisals. Following on from this, some key issues and challenges relating to performance management are discussed in Section 11.5, before Section 11.6 focuses on an area of performance that is under increasing scrutiny—employee absence.

11.2 Performance management: an organizational phenomenon

Performance management has become firmly established on the management agenda and is a widely practised organizational activity (Pollitt 2006). The prevalence of performance management is reflected in the diversity of organizations from the private, public, and voluntary sectors that have embraced it. This section considers what performance management means, and examines the factors that have led to the spectacular growth of this area of HRM.

11.2.1 What is performance management?

The terms 'managing performance' and 'performance management' are widely used in the literature, raising the important question of whether or not they mean the same thing. 'Managing performance' is typically applied in a wider organizational context, and is used to refer to the broad ways in which organizations plan, coordinate, and utilize their resources to achieve their aims, or 'managing the business' (Mohrman and Mohrman 1995). It is concerned with how individuals, groups, and organizations achieve something that is desirable, or intended as a consequence of their actions, prompting improvements in effectiveness and efficiency. But it is also about how the outcomes are achieved and with what individuals and teams learn from experience to help improve performance in the future.

However, the term 'performance management' tends to be favoured when referring to specific methods, processes, or arrangements for linking people management to organizational goals. It was first used in the 1970s by Beer and Ruh (1976), but did not come into common use until the early 1990s. Beer and Ruh (1976: 59–66) proposed that 'performance was best developed through practical challenges and experiences on the job, with guidance and feedback from superiors'. Their approach emphasizes the experiential—doing and learning—elements of performance management, and highlights the importance of feedback as a management activity in this process. Performance management has been defined as: a 'strategy which relates to every activity of the organisation; set in the context of its human resource policies, culture, style and communication systems. The nature of the strategy depends on the organisational context and can vary from organisation to organisation' (IPM 1992). Coming from an organizational perspective, the strategic and contextual nature of performance management is emphasized here. Thus definition firmly positions performance management within the domain of HRM.

However, Armstrong and Baron (2005) offer an alternative 'people-centred' approach to defining performance management based on the importance of shared understanding. Leadership and development are identified as the means by which organizations will achieve high levels of performance by effectively utilizing their people: performance management, then, is 'a process which contributes to the effective management of individuals and teams in order to achieve high levels of organisational performance. As such, it establishes shared understanding about what is to be achieved and an approach to leading and developing people which will ensure that it is achieved' (Armstrong and Baron 2005: 2).

These definitions provide some important insights into the context, content, and process of managing performance. They also highlight the role of management and the responsibilities it shares with employees to work together to achieve organizational aims, for example by setting objectives, developing understanding and competence, encouraging individual competency and commitment, and contributing to organizational performance.

11.2.2 The growth of performance management

Performance management is now firmly established on the management agenda and has become a widely practised organizational activity (Pollitt 2006). The prevalence of performance management arrangements is reflected by the diversity of organizations from the private, public, and voluntary sectors that have embraced it, including Sony, Luton Borough Council, and the Big Lottery Fund (IDS 2011*b*).

There is nothing new about organizations assessing the performance of employees, particularly managerial staff. Management by objectives (MBO) emphasizes the relevance of goals or objectives in managing performance, and requires the use of performance appraisals to link organizational objectives with employee goals and development (Drucker 1955). The principle of using objectives to manage performance is described by Locke's 'goal theory' (Locke 1968), which states that individuals are motivated and will behave in such a way to achieve goals that are personally desirable. The assertion behind goal theory is that clear goals will enhance an individual's ability to create precise intention and therefore enable them to accurately define (and act out) the behaviour required to achieve the desired goal. MBO was the first systematic approach that attempted to align organizational goals with individual performance and development, involving all levels of management—a feature of performance management systems today. MBO is based on the principles of the management cycle shown in Figure 11.1. The key principles in the practice of MBO are:

- setting objectives (goals) and targets;
- participation of managers in agreeing to objectives and performance criteria;
- continual review and appraisal of results.

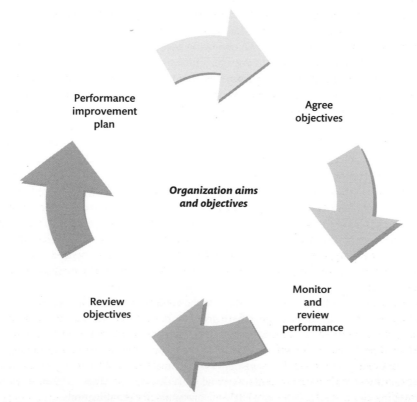

Figure 11.1 Management by objectives.

Several interrelated and interdependent processes are linked within the MBO approach:

- clarification of organizational goals and objectives;
- design of organizational structures and systems to achieve goals and objectives;
- participation of managers to gain acceptance and agreement on objectives, targets, and performance criteria of employees at organizational, group, and individual level;
- agreement to performance improvement plans to enable employees to contribute to achieving individual objectives and targets, and to improving organizational performance;
- monitoring and reviewing employee progress and performance against agreed objectives, through the use of an appraisal process;
- making changes to employees' objectives and targets as a consequence of review;
- review of organizational performance based on outcomes of the MBO cycle of activities.

The key benefits offered by MBO are as follows:

- communicates organizational aims to employees;
- defines work activities based on the aims of the organization;
- enables employees to contribute towards the aims of the organization by working towards their individual goals;
- provides a process for employee and organizational improvement;
- facilitates continuous and systematic management of performance throughout the organization.

An important feature of the MBO approach is communicating information back to employees about their performance; it is an essential element of appraisal because it enables individuals (and groups) to gauge progress against their goals and, ultimately, judge if they are successful. This communication process is known as feedback. Feedback helps individuals to manage their perceptions and intentions to achieve their goals and, if delivered appropriately, can have a positive influence on motivation.

Performance appraisals, where an employee has their performance periodically reviewed in a meeting with their manager, have a long history in organizations. However, on their own performance appraisals can be a rather ineffective way of managing performance. They are often backward-looking, concerned with reviewing past performance rather than facing forwards, and as a result fail to capture the engagement of front-line managers (Armstrong 2006). Performance management, though, operates as a continuous systemic process, with the emphasis more on forward planning and a greater concern with integration with business needs. As a result, 'its value resides in the cycle of integrated activities, which ensure that a systematic link is established between the contribution of each employee and the overall performance of the organization' (Bach 2005b: 291).

The key drivers of performance management in organizations are the greater competitive pressures unleashed by changes in the economic and business context. With pressure to increase competitiveness in the private sector to improve shareholder return on investment, to deliver better value for money to the taxpayer in the public sector, and to meet customer expectations in both, managing performance through improving effectiveness and efficiency has become a strategic activity for many organizations. As global markets have opened up, driven by deregulation, there has been an upsurge in competition as new entrants have poured in and existing businesses searched for growth. As low-cost competitors enter markets, and offer similar or better products at lower prices, established businesses have come under huge pressure to improve their performance. This is particularly evident in the global airline industry, for example.

While much of the increased concern with performance management is linked to questions of competitiveness, there is also an important managing people rationale that needs to be recognized. By setting objectives, and establishing systematic arrangements to ensure that these objectives are met, performance management systems are used to influence employees' expectations, and thus control their standards of behaviour (Edwards and Wajcman 2005). Therefore they are an important tool for effective HRM in contemporary organizations.

11.2.3 Performance management in the public sector

In the same way that global competition fuelled performance management in the private sector, a developing global economy and international competition has resulted in governments across the world turning their attention to the threat presented to national prosperity.

For example, within the UK public sector improvements in the effectiveness and efficiency of public services have been central to government strategies of maintaining and improving national prosperity. Performance management methods, including the use of targets, performance measures, personal development, and so on, typically used as part of performance management systems, are now being widely used within many areas of the public sector. For example, pressure for efficiency savings prompted Luton Borough Council to revamp its performance management system in order to ensure that its staff were performing as well as possible (IDS 2011*b*).

Known as 'the modernization agenda', the Modernizing Government White Paper was published by the UK government in 1999, setting out a 10-year transformational change programme aimed at delivering more responsive high quality public services which can be measured by better results. The modernization agenda called for more of a focus on the user of the services, and employed performance management techniques such as public service agreements between authorities and suppliers which specify clear goals and measures of deliverable performance.

The NHS is probably the most widely publicized example of a UK public service that has undergone 'modernization' and continues to experience significant ongoing change aimed at improving performance. Box 11.1 presents the vision for modernization within NHS Wales.

Organizations in the private and public sectors have embraced the 'promise' of performance management as a means of improving performance, aided by innovations in performance management systems such as the Balanced Scorecard, which is discussed in Section 11.4.5. Such methods have been enthusiastically adopted by companies in the private sector as a means of gaining advantage while facing increasing competition. The public and voluntary sectors are following on the heels of the private sector in looking towards performance management methods to help drive up productivity and provide value for money.

Box 11.1 Policy example
NHS Wales Workforce strategy

The Workforce vision

Designed To Work' supports *Designed for Life*, the plan to achieve world class healthcare for the people of Wales.

It is a strategy for ensuring that we have the right staff with the right skills doing the right jobs in an efficient and managed service.

The challenges facing all of us in NHS Wales are many; in order to deliver services to our patients and public which are efficient, safe, accessible and affordable, we must make major changes.

It is vital that we modernize the way we work and maximize the contribution of staff in improving care and efficiency; this cannot be achieved without the commitment and involvement of all staff.

Services must be reconfigured to concentrate skills and resources where they are most needed; innovative roles must be developed which will necessitate working across traditional boundaries, both professional and organizational.

Workforce planning and education commissioning must adapt to the new requirements of the service to ensure that the skills we need are available when we need them.

Staff must be trained and developed to maximize their contribution, to fully utilize their skill, and to give them the career progression they deserve.

Human resource departments must respond to the demands of the service by ensuring that the necessary strategies are in place and that HR effort is concentrated on achieving change and modernization including the benefits of pay modernization and the electronic staff record.

Source: NHS Wales (2006).

- Performance management is widely used as an intervention for achieving improvement across all sectors of the economy, driven by competitive and stakeholder pressure.
- Performance management is a key part of the government's strategy to manage the performance of the economy, influencing public sector policy aimed at improving the UK's competitive capability.
- Performance management has several definitions which provide a useful insight into the meaning of performance management from a conceptual and practical perspective.

For an introduction and overview of performance management, see Armstrong and Baron (2005). Good insights into the nature of performance management can be gained from Bach (2005b) and Edwards and Wajcman (2005: chapter 5).

11.3 HRM and performance management

The performance of people in organizations has played a major role in shaping HRM for over a century. In the evolution of personnel management from welfare management in the 1940s to human resource management in the 1980s, the management of people and their contribution towards their employers' goals became established as a key responsibility of HR practitioners. That evolution continues today, with strategy and performance underpinning the HR 'Business Partner' concept (Ulrich 1997).

11.3.1 Early HRM models

Managing performance played a significant role in the development of the HRM models of the 1980s, and in response these models described new frameworks for HR policy and practice to facilitate performance management within organizations.

Performance is positioned at the centre of the first HRM model developed by Fombrum, Tichy, and Devanna (1984), who described how employee selection, appraisal, and development influenced performance within the human resource cycle. This early model assumed that managing these HR activities could influence employee performance, but it did not offer any explanation of the processes involved. The Harvard model of HRM (Beer et al. 1984) recognizes that stakeholder interests inform certain areas of HRM policy formulation, and how the implementation of these policies produce outcomes which have long-term consequences, including for organizational effectiveness (performance). Guest's (1989) theory of HRM, with its four HR policy goals of strategic integration, commitment, flexibility, and quality, describes how HR policy implementation can lead to certain organizational outcomes, including job performance, which can affect an organization's performance.

11.3.2 Strategic HRM

The early HRM models acknowledged the increasing demands on organizations and the management of these organizations to effectively manage employee performance. These models were not only a response by HR to a changing business environment, namely increasing competition, return on investment, value for money, and so on, but they also promoted the HR agenda of positioning itself at the centre of managing performance. In adopting such a position, HRM was required to take a more purposive strategic perspective, as opposed to a more routine administrative operational perspective, and align its activities with business strategy, giving rise to the term 'strategic HRM'. The link between strategic HRM and performance is emphasized by Boxall and Purcell (2011), who state that strategic HRM is largely concerned with how HRM influences organizational performance.

Strategic HRM is not any one particular HR strategy, but a framework for shaping and delivering a number of people management strategies, of which performance management could be one. Strategic HRM 'positions' the strategic responsibility for managing performance within HRM. This has influenced the development of the role of HR managers and helped to define the nature of their interaction with other managers. As more and more organizations see their employees as assets which are a source of competitive advantage and contribute value—the concept of human capital—this has signalled the development of a more partnership-based relationship between HRM and business managers. The 'Business Partner' model of HRM described below presents a model proposing how this relationship is structured and operates.

11.3.3 The Business Partner model of HRM

The Business Partner model of HRM first developed by David Ulrich in 1997, and subsequently revised in 2005, proposes a conceptual framework that describes how HRM operates within organizations. Based on strategic and operational perspectives, the model features five areas where HRM can 'partner' with the business in contributing towards achieving its organizational aims: Strategic Partner, Human Capital Developers (strategic), Functional Expert, Employee Advocates (operational), and HR Leader at the centre spanning all areas.

The Business Partner model describes how HR managers can work in partnership with other managers to develop and implement coherent and integrated performance strategies, based on HR policies and practices, to achieve common business goals. This model also supports the concept and application of strategic HRM, but unlike the strategic HRM models we have already met, it identifies functional elements of the HR 'partner' role which impact on strategy and performance. Box 11.2 outlines the role of HR partners in a large public sector organization.

11.3.4 The 'People and Performance' model and high performance work practices

Many definitions of performance management emphasize, either explicitly or implicitly, the significance of individual behaviour in producing outcomes that are to the benefit of both the individual and the organization. John Purcell and his team of researchers at the University of Bath describe in their 'People and Performance' model how employees' discretionary behaviour

Box 11.2 Learning activity
Putting HR at the heart of business leadership

Senior Business Partners Up to £77k + benefits Flexible location with regular travel

A large complex organization, responsible for collecting about £400 billion of UK tax revenue, as well as paying tax credits and child benefits and strengthening UK's frontiers, HMRC is currently engaged in a far-reaching programme of transformational change.

HR is helping drive this agenda, and in these newly created roles you'll 'partner' key business teams and challenge, support and influence the leadership team to deliver excellence.

Acting specifically as the 'intelligent customer' at the HR–business interface, you'll help drive up overall performance by identifying, developing, and delivering initiatives which help align the workforce planning with wider business aims.

Part leader, part interventionist, part 'agent of change', you must be a creative HR professional with superior influencing skills and practical change management experience, together with the credibility to coach at a senior management level. You must be either CIPD qualified or working towards Fellowship.

HM Revenue & Customs welcomes applications from people of every kind of background, so that our workforce reflects the community we serve.

Source: www.hmrc.gov.uk

Activity

1 Identify HRM models that reflect the relationship between HR and performance, as suggested by this advertisement.

2 Based on this description of the 'Senior Business Partner' role, how may this role influence the performance of HMRC?

(how individuals choose to behave) positively influences performance, and how these choices are influenced by people management policies (Purcell et al. 2003). At the heart of the People and Performance model is the fundamental proposition that performance is a function of ability (A), motivation (M), and opportunity (O) (see Boxall and Purcell 2011), expressed as:

$$performance = f(A, M, O).$$

This proposition asserts that for people to perform beyond the minimum requirements, they must be motivated to perform well, have the ability through their knowledge and skills to perform well, and have the opportunity to use their skills in their specific roles and in a wider organizational context.

This model describes how (strategic) HRM works in practice through the implementation of HR strategies as policies and practices which influence these three key variables affecting performance. Purcell describes these practices as 'performance-related HR practices', also known as 'high performance work practices' (HPWPs). His research was based on twelve case study organizations, including Tesco, Jaguar, Nationwide Building Society, Royal Mint, and Siemens Medical. HR strategies and practices are applied in combination, or as 'bundles' of policies and practices, providing an integrated approach that depends on the operational context. Box 11.3 presents the performance-related work practices identified in the 'people performance' research by Purcell et al. (2003).

A study of HPWPs in ten case study organizations and a survey of 294 companies in the UK identified specific HPWPs that are employed in a number of business sectors (Sung and Ashton 2005). The level of HPWP adoption is linked to organizational performance, and high performance work organizations (HPWOs) employ a higher level of HPWPs than other organizations. Specific examples of HR practices in use at some HPWOs include:

- continuous professional development;
- 'back to the floor' managers (managers spending time with employees working in operations);
- profit sharing;
- performance-related pay;
- 360-degree appraisals for all;
- appraisal against attributes for all-round performance;

Box 11.3 Research in focus
Performance-related work practices (high performance work practices)

Professor John Purcell and his research team have examined the HRM policies and practices that are the most universal in influencing the performance of employees (Purcell et al. 2003, 2009). They are:

- careful/sophisticated recruitment and selection;
- job security;
- emphasis on providing career opportunities;
- appraising each individual's performance and development;
- training and learning/development;
- pay satisfaction;
- work–life balance;
- job challenge/job autonomy;
- teamworking;
- involvement in decision-making;
- information sharing and extensive two-way communication.

- recruitment of top candidates exclusively at entry level;
- continuous training for leadership.

Some specific HPWPs have been adopted on a widespread basis; for example, appraisals are used by 95 per cent of the organizations included in the survey. However, the prevalence of other HPWPs, such as share options for all employees (16 per cent of organizations), is substantially lower.

11.3.5 Managing performance: whose responsibility?

Who is ultimately responsible for managing performance in organizations? We have seen how strategic HRM 'makes the case' for HR practitioners as the custodians of managing performance. This is supported by the view that strategic HRM is about implementation of performance strategies that influence organizational performance (Purcell 2001). However, others take a broader perspective on performance management. It 'is about ownership by everyone in the organisation, and especially the line managers—it is emphatically not about guardianship by personnel departments' (CIPD 2006e: 5). According to this view, performance management is a shared responsibility between HR managers, business managers, and employees, but it is HR practitioners, with their expertise in the people and performance relationship, who have a leading role in managing performance at a strategic level.

 Summary and further reading

- The development of HRM has been heavily influenced by organizational performance, with the HRM models of the 1980s being the forerunners of strategic HRM and the Business Partner model.
- Strategic HRM involved the formulation and implementation of high performance work practices (HPWPs) to influence the choices employees make about how they behave (discretionary behaviour) and ultimately perform effectively in their job roles.
- Responsibility for managing performance is shared between HR managers, who have a strategic 'partner' role, line managers, who implement policy at operational level, and employees, in how they contribute towards performance.

Boxall and Purcell (2011) provide the best analysis of business strategy and HRM. For the work of John Purcell and his colleagues on HPWPs, see Purcell et al. (2003), Purcell and Kinnie (2007), and Purcell et al. (2009). For details of the Business Partner concept, see Ulrich and Brockbank (2005).

11.4 Performance management systems

Performance management is about realizing the strategic long-term goals of organizations by providing support mechanisms in the form of systems, policies, and practices which align, enable, and motivate employees to achieve their goals, thus contributing to the performance of the organizations they work for. Performance management systems (PMSs) provide models or frameworks that enable organizations to connect their strategic intention with the aims and activities of groups and individuals in such a way as to align the efforts of all employees with the purpose of their employer.

11.4.1 The nature of performance management systems

There is no single definition of what a PMS is, probably because there are many different systems for managing performance. However, based on the idea of a PMS as a framework or model, the following definition is offered: a PMS is an organizational framework or model that supports the continuous integration and implementation of processes to facilitate the strategic management of performance. All performance management systems incorporate an integrated series of processes based on the management cycle.

Armstrong and Baron (2005) present a description of a PMS based on the aims of such a system, suggesting that a PMS exists when an organization demonstrates the following characteristics:

- it (the organization) communicates a vision of its objectives to all employees;
- it sets departmental and individual performance targets which are related to wider organizational objectives;
- it conducts formal reviews of progress towards these targets;
- it uses the review process to identify training, development, and reward outcomes;
- it evaluates the whole process in order to improve effectiveness;
- it uses formal appraisal procedures as a way of communicating performance requirements that are set on a regular basis.

It is important to recognize the continuous basis of performance management systems, captured by the concept of the performance management cycle (see Figure 11.2). Generally, there are three main stages: performance planning, monitoring progress, and the performance review or appraisal.

11.4.2 Performance planning—setting objectives

Key to performance planning is setting relevant objectives for employees. The traditional emphasis was on quantifiable objectives—those that can be easily measured, such as financial sales. Effective objectives are a good starting point in supporting employees in their efforts to achieve acceptable levels of performance and to facilitate efficacy in the performance management process. When it comes to formulating effective objectives, some variation of the SMART approach is often used by organizations.

S: specific—effective objectives should be clear and precise.

M: measurable—whether or not an employee has attained an objective can be determined.

A: achievable—attaining the objective is within the capability of the employee.

R: relevant—objectives are germane to the role of the individual and the organizational purpose.

T: time-bound—placing a time limit on when the objective should or should not be attained.

The SMART approach helps to define useful employee objectives based on their job role and the employer's strategic aims; individual objectives are translated and cascaded down from the organization's overall aims. Objectives are more specific than goals, which are broader in context and content, and can provide the basis for formulating several SMART objectives. SMART objectives can be used to varying degrees in performance management systems depending on the context of the organization, the job role, and the management approach to reviewing employee performance.

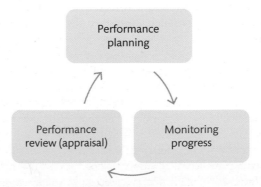

Figure 11.2 The performance management cycle.

The importance of setting clear performance objectives should be evident. Moreover, organizations increasingly use them in ways designed to focus employee activity on achieving organizational goals. For example, the Crown Prosecution Service uses its performance management system to align individual employee objectives with organizational goals (IDS 2009c). Organizations increasingly emphasize not just what objectives are expected of employees, but also how they are to be achieved in the form of particular competences or behaviours. The use of a values, attitudes, and behaviour (VAB) approach is growing in popularity as a method of reviewing employee performance management because it focuses on (discretionary) behaviour and *how* performance is achieved. Many organizations use 'core values' to guide and support the behaviour of employees in achieving their vision and objectives. These values are often incorporated into the performance management process as the basis for reviewing and encouraging the desired behaviours that an organization associates with good performance. For example, the digital media company i-Level uses its five core values of humanity, openness, diligence, enthusiasm, and integrity as the basis for performance objectives. The Big Lottery Fund charity operates a competency framework based on four core behaviours—leadership, working together, customer service and quality, and continuous improvement—supported by relevant behavioural indicators (IDS 2011b). The DVD interview with Tony Peers shows how the National Theatre is attempting to move away from traditional performance measures, and put a greater emphasis on flexibility and risk-taking. One very popular method of deriving performance objectives involves using a methodology derived from the Balanced Scorecard approach, which we discuss in Section 11.4.5.

11.4.3 Monitoring performance

It is important to remember that, unlike the use of backward-looking, one-off, and isolated performance appraisals, performance management is designed to operate as a continuous process (Edwards and Wajcman 2005). In addition to setting objectives, arrangements for monitoring employee performance are often viewed as critical features of effective performance management systems. Clearly, front-line managers play an important part in ensuring that employees work in ways that meet the objectives laid down in performance planning meetings. Often this is done on an informal basis. However, provision is sometimes made for convening formal interim reviews which are used to monitor the performance of employees. For example, the policy of Sony Europe Ltd is for employees in its sales division to have four formal review meetings every year (IDS 2011b). Formal interim reviews can be a useful means of building in some flexibility to the performance management process, helping to accommodate, and responding to, changes in organizational strategy or the focus of an employee's job role, both of which might require some tweaking of objectives.

11.4.4 Performance review (appraisal)

Interim reviews notwithstanding, the appraisal meeting, usually held on an annual basis, is the main tool used to review employee performance in organizations. The appraisal is a formal process that is designed to facilitate the review of employee performance and progress against agreed objectives, and to discuss future performance. The purpose of the appraisal is to provide an opportunity to communicate with employees about all aspects of their individual performance, identify opportunities for training, learning, and development, and motivate them by providing feedback, recognition, and praise, including links to extrinsic reward as appropriate.

Appraisals are usually carried out by line managers, who will need to gather together the appropriate data necessary to provide effective feedback and to determine whether or not employees have met the objectives set for them. One of the main features of the appraisal meeting as part of a system of performance management is that it provides an opportunity for communication between managers and employees that specifically addresses performance issues. Traditionally, this process was a top-down affair involving the manager providing feedback to employees about their performance. The main flaw with relying on top-down feedback is that it is unidirectional and reflects only the view of the manager, which may not be accurate for a variety of reasons. This form of feedback inhibits employees expressing themselves, and does not encourage the sharing of ideas and knowledge. To overcome the problems associated with

top-down feedback, other forms of feedback have been developed and are used by organizations. See Box 11.4 for a skills exercise concerning performance appraisals.

Two trends are particularly evident. First, there is the growing use of multi-rater systems
of feedback, in which multiple sources of evidence are used to inform the process of performance review. Perhaps the most notable approach involves the use of 360-degree feedback.
This incorporates feedback from different individuals associated with the performance of
the employee being assessed, other than just their line-manager (e.g. colleagues, subordinates, suppliers, and customers). The benefit of this form of feedback is that it produces a
more balanced view based on several sources and, in doing so, introduces greater objectivity which one-to-one feedback cannot provide. However, although it is an improvement on
top-down feedback, even 360-degree feedback remains open to bias and false perceptions.
This can create problems when other stakeholders are involved in the performance review
process, where personal agendas, conflict of interests, and loyalties can all distort the feedback provided.

Another popular approach used in combination with other forms of performance assessment
is self-appraisal, which involves individual employees providing their own review of their performance in advance of an appraisal discussion with a manager. This can be a useful process for
engaging employees and encouraging them to take responsibility for their performance. Self-
appraisal can be useful in identifying areas of weak performance and appropriate interventions
to resolve any performance problems, or for personal development. This is valuable information which is relevant to other areas of managing employee performance, for example learning
and development, and it is important that managers capture this during the appraisal process
by using techniques such as self-appraisal. A developmental approach to appraisal focuses on
how performance can be improved through personal development. The role of the manager is
one of providing feedback and supporting employee development plans through HR policies
and practices.

Some kind of method of rating employee performance against the objectives set for them
is an integral feature of most performance management systems, albeit not those designed
mainly for developmental reasons, and the outcome of the performance review is generally
used to inform the rating process. There are two broad approaches to performance measurement which are employed in appraisal. The first is the results-oriented or 'outputs' approach to
performance measurement, where metrics (measures) are used to determine absolute achievement levels by quantifying performance. By using quantifiable measures (e.g. sales turnover
per employee, or the proportion of satisfied customers) the actual performance measured can
be compared with the objective or planned performance as a basis for determining progress.
Secondly, where measures and performance cannot be defined in absolute terms (physical units
such a volume, time, rate, and so on), an alternative approach uses ranking or grading methods
to rate employee performance. This 'pseudo-quantitative' approach to measurement is used for
assessing attitudinal and behavioural aspects of performance, with ranking or rating methods
such as behaviourally anchored rating scales (BARS) commonly being employed.

Organizations often use the outcomes of the performance review meeting to give an
employee a specific overall score. The multinational company Groupe Aeroplan, which runs
the Nectar scheme for supermarkets among other things, uses a seven-point scale, with staff
ranked from 1 (non-performer) to 7 (superstar) (IDS 2009c). While performance reviews can

have a developmental focus, for example helping to establish future training needs and learning opportunities, in a third of workplaces the rating given influences pay outcomes in some way— for example, by determining whether or not someone should be awarded a bonus, progress to a higher salary band, or be entitled to a performance-related element. Of course, operating performance management as an ongoing process means that performance reviews will also be concerned with deriving further objectives in the way described above, thus ensuring that the cycle operates in a continuous manner.

11.4.5 The Balanced Scorecard

The Balanced Scorecard approach developed by Kaplan and Norton (1996) is a very prominent performance management model, and for this reason it is worth looking at in detail. It has gained in popularity to such an extent that it now dominates the field of performance management (Kennerley and Bourne 2003). Nationwide, BP, Ford, and Tesco are among the organizations that use versions of the Balanced Scorecard approach to ensure that, when managing performance, the factors which are critical to the success of the business are taken into account.

Initially described as a strategic management system for communicating an organization's vision and strategy, the Balanced Scorecard model quickly developed from a performance measurement framework into a performance management system. As a strategic management system, the Balanced Scorecard provides a holistic and systematic approach to managing performance, linking vision and strategy with group and individual objectives in all areas of an organization's activities.

The Balanced Scorecard's innovation and strength as a PMS is that it takes into account a number of different perspectives on organizational performance, not just a narrow financial perspective. The traditional view of financial performance being the main measure of organizational performance had disastrous consequences for many organizations, since it led them to chase short-term financial success that could easily be measured and ignore other elements of 'organizational health' necessary to ensure long-term viability (sustainability), such as customer expectations, employee skills, and efficient business processes. The use of the Balanced Scorecard brings a much needed correction to how organizations view performance by focusing on how managers create value. This correction is based on bringing balance to managing performance. Kaplan and Norton (1996) introduced three perspectives to managing performance in addition to the 'traditional' financial view:

- financial—financial viability and prosperity;
- customer—the customer value proposition;
- business processes (operational)—the internal processes and systems;
- innovation and learning (people)—the human contribution through knowledge and skills.

With the vision and strategy at the centre, this drives the Balanced Scorecard as a strategic and performance management system, communicating an organization's aims into specific goals within each perspective (see Figure 11.3).

Goals are defined as strategic goals at the top (corporate) level of an organization, which are then translated into appropriate goals at lower levels, for example business unit, department, team, and individual. The process of translating and cascading strategic aims into goals at every level throughout an organization guides and encourages people to contribute towards the overall performance of the organization. A technique known as 'strategic mapping' is often employed when developing a Balanced Scorecard to help define the strategic aims and relate these to organizational activities as a basis for specifying goals within the different performance perspectives (Kaplan and Norton 1996).

The Balanced Scorecard works in practice by either assigning responsibility to an appropriate functional area of the organization (e.g. sales or production), or assigning responsibility for implementing specific goals to a team. Cascading goals typically means that department or team goals are further translated into appropriate objectives for individuals, which then provide the basis for performance review. In this way, as a PMS the Balanced Scorecard provides a framework that links organizational aims with individual objectives, and the performance appraisal provides the process for reviewing individual performance and progress. Within large

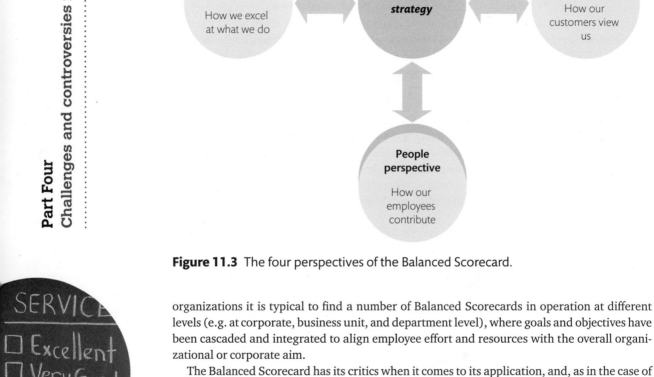

Figure 11.3 The four perspectives of the Balanced Scorecard.

organizations it is typical to find a number of Balanced Scorecards in operation at different levels (e.g. at corporate, business unit, and department level), where goals and objectives have been cascaded and integrated to align employee effort and resources with the overall organizational or corporate aim.

The Balanced Scorecard has its critics when it comes to its application, and, as in the case of MBO, these are mainly to do with how it is interpreted and implemented by managers. Examples include the following: when it is employed only at individual level, when it is deployed primarily as a reporting tool, when it distracts from other business activities, and lack of ownership and accountability. Although unequivocal cause and effect are difficult to demonstrate when multiple variables are involved, there are individual case studies which report a positive improvement in aspects of organizational performance when the Balanced Scorecard has been introduced (Kennerley and Bourne 2003). The problem of causality—distinguishing between cause and effect—and the multiple factors that influence organizational performance remain major challenges in this field of activity, and continue to be a source of contention regarding the validity and reliability of studies in this area.

The four perspectives of performance presented in the Balanced Scorecard are all interrelated and interdependent, but where does HRM feature and what is the relevance for the management of human resources? The innovation and learning domain of the Balanced Scorecard clearly focuses on the people contribution to performance and is relevant to all areas of organizations, impacting on the other three perspectives. Organizations often turn to their HR managers, as business partners, who have the expertise and responsibility for encouraging practice that underpins employee and organizational development, for example high performance work practices based on HR policies. Employees, and the culture they create, are critical to providing the capability for organizations to differentiate themselves and add value. This people or human asset is known as 'human capital advantage' (Boxall and Purcell 2011). Human capital management (HCM) focuses on the strategic management and measurement of an organization's people assets.

11.4.6 HR scorecard

Developed from the Balanced Scorecard, the HR scorecard is a performance management and measurement system specifically designed to support strategic HRM to help determine the contribution of HR policy and practice towards creating shareholder value (Becker, Huselid, and Ulrich 2001). Built on the principles of the HR function, HR systems, and employee behaviours, the HR scorecard provides a systematic approach to performance management of the people asset or 'human capital' within organizations. The use of business-focused metrics in an HR scorecard enables strategic HR 'business partners' to converse in the language of business performance and provide a basis for defining:

- key measures associated with the workforce;
- trends in performance over time as the metrics are tracked;
- measurable workforce outputs and areas of weakness or under performance;
- feedback about measurement methods and the metrics to be tracked;
- appropriate interventions to address deteriorating performance or under-achievement.

The HR scorecard is a 'tool' that facilitates strategic HRM and HCM, combining HRM and performance management methods, whose processes impact on all the performance perspectives described by the Balanced Scorecard. The case study at the end of this chapter describes the design and implementation of an HR scorecard in the form of a 'Workforce Scorecard' within the NHS in the UK.

 Summary and further reading

- Performance management systems comprise arrangements for performance planning, performance monitoring, and performance review, and are increasingly used as a central feature of effective HRM.
- Careful thought needs to go into designing effective and appropriate objectives for employees, with the appraisal meeting often being used to review an individual's performance against the objectives that have been set for them.
- The Balanced Scorecard has become an increasingly popular performance management approach; it takes into account a range of measures of performance, not just narrow financial criteria.

See the case studies of organizational practice published by Incomes Data Services for more details of how organizations operate performance management systems (IDS 2009c, 2011b). For the Balanced Scorecard approach, see Kaplan and Norton (1996).

11.5 Key issues in performance management

There are a number of issues and challenges relating to the process of performance management in organizations. While performance management is often viewed as an integral feature of contemporary HRM, there are a number of reasons why it might not be as effective as managers anticipate.

11.5.1 Key issues and trends in performance management

One of the most important issues relating to performance management in practice concerns arrangements for dealing with poor performance from employees. A leading example concerns excessive absence from work, which we deal with in Section 11.6. Performance reviews provide an opportunity for addressing poor performance as well as supporting effective performance. If a manager believes there are performance issues related to poor performance, the appraisal

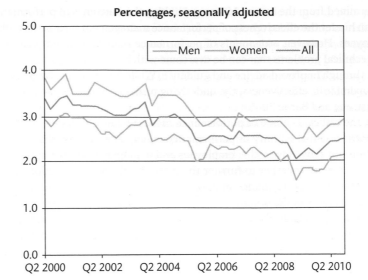

Figure 11.4 Absence trends, 2000–2010.
Source: Office for National Statistics (http://www.ons.gov.uk/ons/dcp171776_223259.pdf).

Absence rates vary by organizational size and industry sector. According to the CIPD's 2010 absence survey (CIPD 2010*a*), organizations with fewer than 50 employees reported an absence rate under half of that reported by organizations with 5000 or more employees—an average of 4.2 days per employee per year compared with 9.9 days per employee per year. See Box 11.5 for international comparisons.

Evidence of consistently higher absence rates in public sector organizations, relative to the private sector, has been a particular source of controversy (see Box 11.6). There is a popular misconception that absence levels are higher on Mondays and Fridays, as a result of workers extending their weekends by taking an extra day or two off work when they are not really unwell. Yet such a claim is not borne out by the evidence, which demonstrates that absence rates vary little across the working week (Barham and Begum 2005; Taylor et al. 2010).

Although absence, and how to reduce it, has been of particular concern in organizations since the 1980s (Edwards and Whitston 1989), in recent years it seems to have become an even more salient issue for managers (Barham and Begum 2005; Taylor et al. 2010). Managing sickness absence, then, is a 'top priority' for employers (IDS 2011*a*). Given the evidence that absence levels have been falling, why is this so?

 Box 11.5 International focus
Sickness absence—international comparisons

International comparisons of sickness absence have to be treated with a certain amount of caution because of variations in how absence is defined, differences in counting measures, and questionable data reliability (Taylor et al. 2010), as is evident from the findings of research by the European Foundation for the Improvement of Living and Working Conditions which compares absence levels between European countries. Their data show that the overall mean average rate of absence among employees was 3.8 per cent; the figure for the UK was 3.3 per cent, suggesting that the level of absence from work there is not particularly high by international standards. The lowest level of absence was found to be in Italy (0.8 per cent); although this finding seems to rest on data which are not very robust. Nordic countries like Norway, whose rate of 7.7 per cent was the highest found in the research, tend to have quite high levels of employee absence, perhaps reflecting the provision of generous welfare support found there (EuroFound 2010).

Box 11.6 Practitioner perspective
Contrasting views of sickness absence in the UK

This practitioner perspective concerns the claims made by the Confederation of British Industry (CBI) that levels of sickness absence are too high, being costly to businesses in the UK and leaving them at a competitive disadvantage relative to foreign firms. The CBI is particularly exercised by the apparently higher absence rates characteristic of public sector organizations. Its 2011 survey of absence (CBI 2011*a*) demonstrates that workers in the public sector take an average of 8.1 days off sick each year compared with an average of 5.9 days for workers in private sector companies.

However, the Trades Union Congress (TUC) argues that overall sickness absence in the UK is relatively low by international standards. The relatively high level of sickness absence in the public sector can be explained by the fact that workers there are often employed in stressful or dangerous jobs. Around a fifth of public sector workers attend work even though they are ill, often because of pressure from managers. According to the TUC's General Secretary, Brendan Barber, many workers 'routinely go into work when they are too ill and should be at home'. Better quality jobs, more opportunities for flexible employment, and healthier working environments would be more effective ways of reducing absence levels than penalizing workers (TUC 2010).

One reason concerns the duty of care that employers owe to their staff, which includes their health, safety, and well-being. Managers are paying greater attention to sickness absence issues out of a concern to avoid litigation by workers who claim that an illness, particularly stress-related conditions, has been caused or exacerbated by their jobs.

More importantly, however, tackling employee absence effectively is often viewed as a key means of generating improved standards of performance by employees (Edwards 2005). Absence, then, is often viewed primarily as a performance issue, not least because controlling it effectively helps to reduce labour costs, particularly in environments where employers are concerned to eliminate slack. 'In highly competitive conditions characterised by intense labour cost pressure, attendance assumes magnified importance precisely because staffing levels have become ever leaner' (Taylor et al. 2010: 284).

The CBI claims that sickness absence costs UK businesses some £17 billion a year and estimates that 16 per cent of absence is not attributable to genuine illness or injury, but is the result of 'skiving' by workers—at a cost of £2.7 billion (CBI 2011*a*). However, some have criticized the 'narrow preoccupation' with the business costs of employee absence, given that employers bear a relatively small proportion of the costs to society of work-related injury and ill-health (Taylor et al. 2010).

In order to understand the financial implications of absence for employers, it is helpful to distinguish between the direct and indirect costs of absence (Bevan et al. 2004). Direct costs include, for example, the salary paid to an employee who is absent, or the wages paid to a temporary worker engaged in the place of the absent member of staff. Indirect costs include, among other things, the management time expended in organizing cover for an absent employee, lower morale among staff expected to cover for absent colleagues, and the detrimental impact on performance of having to substitute absent employees with potentially less experienced replacements (ACAS 2010*c*).

Surprisingly, given the importance attached by managers to controlling employee absence, only a minority of organizations actually evaluate how much it costs them (Bevan et al. 2004; CIPD 2010*a*). As a result, many of the headline figures cited by employers and bodies such as the CBI are simply 'averages of guesses' (Edwards 2005), rather than carefully evaluated sums based on rigorous data collection. Organizations often absorb the 'costs' of absence. For example, on returning from a period of sickness absence, employees may work harder to catch up on what they have missed by being away (Bevan et al. 2004). Thus headline claims about the alleged cost to organizations of sickness absence may be grossly exaggerated. Moreover, the financial impact of absence will vary from organization to organization (Coles et al. 2007). Unplanned absence is particularly disruptive for some firms, such as

those in the transport sector (e.g. airlines). However, call centres often cope relatively easily with high levels of absence by, among other things, adjusting shift patterns at short notice (Hyman, Scholarios, and Baldry 2005). The costs of reducing absence, by improving working conditions or instituting more flexible working arrangements, might outweigh any benefits.

Unsubstantiated allegations about the costs to organizations of sickness absence have to be treated with a considerable amount of caution. Perhaps the main implication of such claims is that a lot of sickness absence is not genuine, but rather can be attributed to the laziness of many workers who are therefore prone to 'absenteeism' (Ackroyd and Thompson 1999). Concerns about the perceived problem of absenteeism have created something of a 'moral panic' about so-called 'sickies' (Edwards 2005; Taylor et al. 2010). In other words, media headlines about the purported cost to businesses of absence, and allegations about workers using the excuse of sickness to absent themselves from work in order to watch sporting events or to recover from a hangover when they are not genuinely unwell, ensure that a relatively minor issue is elevated out of all proportion to its real significance. In fact, as we have seen, overall absence levels are quite stable and may even be falling, and are also relatively low by international standards.

11.6.2 Absence as an organizational issue

What factors influence absence levels in organizations? Clearly, the principal reason for sickness absence is that an employee is unwell. Yet 'the notion that employees take time off work because they are genuinely ill appears not to be universally acknowledged' (Bevan 2003: 19). Psychological studies of absenteeism, for example, tend to focus on the disposition of individual workers to attend work or not (Steers and Rhodes 1978). Among other things, they are concerned with the degree to which individual workers are sufficiently well-suited and adjusted to their job roles, and the extent of their job satisfaction and commitment to the organization. The assumption is that low levels of job satisfaction and organizational commitment are associated with higher absence rates. There is some support for the notion that a propensity for sickness absence is related to the characteristics of particular workers. For example, absence rates for younger and less experienced workers are typically higher than they are for older and more experienced workers (ACAS 2010c). The implication is that organizations can reduce absence levels by instituting more sophisticated induction programmes for new workers, or better training provision, helping them adjust to their jobs and their working environment more effectively and increasing the level of their organizational commitment.

But this approach to understanding and explaining the prevalence of absence has been criticized for concentrating too much on the personality attributes and behavioural characteristics of individual workers, and for paying insufficient attention to the importance of management systems of control and the day-to-day norms and understandings held by the workforce collectively in producing absenteeism (Ackroyd and Thompson 1999). The effect of management control systems can be seen when we observe that absence rates for managers and professional staff are typically lower than for other groups. This is not because seniority necessarily produces a low propensity for sickness absence; rather, the work of managers and professionals is generally less well monitored. Not only is their sickness 'absence' less likely to be recorded, but they are also more opportunities to exercise control over their working arrangements. Workers in jobs that are more tightly controlled may have higher absence rates because, without alternative means of finding some release, sickness absence provides a necessary 'escape valve' from otherwise mundane and restrictive jobs (Edwards and Scullion 1982).

Studies of absence point to the existence of collectively generated day-to-day understanding among staff about acceptable levels of absence (Ackroyd and Thompson 1999). For example, in the case of a call centre located in Northern Ireland the jobs were very intensive and were tightly controlled by managers. For many workers, going off sick was 'a reasonable and collective response to stressful work' (Mulholland 2004: 19). By exacerbating the sense of grievance felt by the workforce, efforts by managers to deal with absenteeism appeared to have little effect.

Rising work pressures are a particular source of stress-related absence from work—see Box 11.7 for a discussion. There is also some evidence that relatively high levels of absence may be linked to the reluctance of firms to develop effective work–life balance arrangements for their staff (Hyman, Scholarios, and Baldry 2005); workers may use sickness absence for the

Box 11.7 Online video link
Tackling the culture of 'presenteeism'

There is some evidence that the adverse economic climate and concerns about job security have produced a climate of 'presenteeism', whereby workers feel under pressure to attend work even though they are genuinely unwell. Go to the Online Resource Centre and follow the link provided for a discussion of the relevant issues.

purpose of attending to their family circumstances. Perhaps surprisingly, then, while absence rates for women are generally higher than for men, the presence of dependent children seems to have little effect, except among women with children aged between 5 and 10 (Barham and Begum 2005).

11.6.3 Managing absence

It is commonly assumed that appropriate interventions by managers can make a significant impact on reducing levels of absence (e.g. Evans and Walters 2003). The formulation and operation of an absence or attendance policy, as a guide for managerial action, is generally considered to be vital to effective absence management. Organizations seem to be paying more attention to ensuring that their absence management policies are relevant and effective (CIPD 2010*a*), although it is important to bear in mind that what is written in the policy does not necessarily describe what happens in organizational practice. ACAS publishes guidance on designing and operating absence policies (ACAS 2010*c*). It covers such matters as appropriate notification arrangements, the operation of return-to-work interviews, the use of 'trigger points' to prompt further managerial investigation of an individual's absence record, and employees' entitlement to sick pay.

One of the main features of absence management policies concerns the rules governing notification of absences. Generally, policies state that staff must directly inform their manager that they will not be able to attend work before the normal start time. For example, accountancy firm KPMG emphasizes that line managers should be the first point of contact for employees who report sickness absence (IDS 2011*a*). Not only are early notification arrangements helpful to managers who may need to arrange cover for an absent employee, but they may also be a useful tool for discouraging unnecessary absence. The obligation on employees to communicate directly with a manager about why they are unfit to attend work may deter them from claiming unwarranted sickness absence. However, practical problems arise with strict notification arrangements; for example, the relevant manager may not be available. This is one of the reasons why some organizations have engaged the services of specialist firms to assist with arrangements for managing absence.

Proper systems for recording and monitoring absence are essential if it is to be managed effectively (Evans and Walters 2003; IDS 2011*a*). The Bradford Index model for calculating absence rates is widely used (see Box 11.8). Evidence from organizational practice suggests that organizations are making more of an effort to record, monitor, and analyse absence data (IDS 2011*a*).

Return-to-work interviews are viewed as a particularly effective absence management tool, and their use has become increasingly widespread (CIPD 2010*a*). They generally involve a meeting between an individual employee and their immediate line manager following every period of absence. Guidance on the conduct of return-to-work interviews suggests that they can be used for a number of reasons, including ensuring an employee's well-being, checking that they are fit to return to work, identifying the causes of their absence, reviewing their absence record, and reminding them of the effects of absence on business operations (e.g. IDS 2011*a*).

Line managers should play a key role in tackling absence issues among their staff, but they are often either insufficiently prepared (CIPD 2010*a*; CBI 2011*a*) or reluctant to become too deeply involved. Return-to-work interviews can become a box-ticking exercise, demonstrating simply that the interview has taken place as dictated by the policy, rather than being used as an effective means of identifying and tackling potential absence problems (Edwards 2005). When

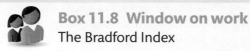

Box 11.8 Window on work
The Bradford Index

The Bradford Index is a widely used model for calculating sickness absence. It weighs the frequency of absence events in any given period, producing an overall score for each employee:

(number of spells of absence × number of spells of absence) × total number of days absent.

The Bradford Index has the advantage of being more a sophisticated approach than a simple tally of days taken sick. It helps managers to identify potential problem areas more easily. In each of the following cases an employee has been absent for a total of 10 days. However, notice the differences in the scores; repeated short-term absences score much higher than isolated long-term absences.

- One spell of absence lasting for ten days: $(1 \times 1) \times 10 = 10$.
- Two spells of absence each lasting for five days $(2 \times 2) \times 10 = 40$.
- Five spells of absence each lasting for two days $(5 \times 5) \times 10 = 250$.

The Bradford Index has been criticized for encouraging managers to view all short-term instances of absences as illegitimate, and for providing managers with a pseudo-scientific rationale for taking disciplinary action against genuinely ill workers (Taylor et al. 2010).

it comes to dealing with absence issues, case studies of organizational practice demonstrate that line managers often attempt to 'pass the baton' back to the human resources function (Dunn and Wilkinson 2002: 238). Line managers may be reticent about involving themselves too closely in the personal, and perhaps sensitive, affairs of their subordinates, and are also perhaps unwilling to apply the rules set out in formal policies when dealing with absence (Dunn and Wilkinson 2002; Edwards 2005).

The use of 'trigger points' is an increasingly popular feature of organizational policy. This is where further managerial investigation of an individual's absence record is prompted by a particular number or pattern of absences, generally within a specific time period. For example, manufacturing company Chep UK operates three trigger points: employees should attend an absence review meeting if they are absent two or more times in a rolling three-month period, three or more times in a rolling six-month period, or four or more times in a rolling twelve-month period (IDS 2011a). However, a problem with using trigger points is that a level of absence below that necessary to initiate them may come to be treated as an acceptable employee entitlement (Dunn and Wilkinson 2002). Moreover, an individual's level of absence may be relatively high, but not be of a pattern which releases the trigger for managerial intervention.

Other approaches to managing absence, such as imposing restrictions on sick pay or awarding staff bonuses for good attendance, have attracted a lot of publicity but are not widely used in organizations. Restricting sick pay could encourage staff who are unwell to attend work, to the detriment of their health and well-being. Attendance bonuses and incentives are often viewed as undesirable by managers since employees are already being paid to attend work. Moreover, workers who are genuinely ill, making them absent through no fault of their own, may end up being unfairly penalized (Dunn and Wilkinson 2002).

Absence is often managed in a punitive way, with the threat of disciplinary sanctions hanging over staff whose attendance levels are deemed unacceptably low. One study found that as a result 'many employees were dragging themselves into work when sick, fearful of disciplinary action or even of losing their job' (Taylor et al. 2010: 282). Studies of airlines, further education colleges, and call centres show how managers put pressure on staff to attend work even when they are genuinely unwell (Boyd 2003; Taylor et al. 2003; Mather 2006). The problem with such a punitive approach, however, is that it can actually exacerbate the problem of absence. Staff may feel obliged to return to work before they are fully recovered from an illness. Not only might this impede their recovery and contribute to further absence, but in cases where the condition is contagious it could also be spread more readily to other workers, making them unwell too (Taylor et al. 2003).

There is a growing awareness that practices which encourage staff to attend work may be more effective at reducing absence levels than conventional approaches to managing absence (Evans and Walters 2003). Greater efforts to promote the health and well-being of staff, particularly inasmuch as they contribute to the reduction of stress, may be an effective way of combating sickness absence (Coats and Max 2005; ACAS 2010c; CIPD 2010a). See Chapter 8 for further information about organizational well-being initiatives. More effective still, it would seem, are efforts to redesign jobs, making them less mundane and repetitive, and changes to the wider working environment. The DVLA, a civil service agency, saw sickness absence rates fall after it instituted improvements to its employees' quality of working life (IDS 2011a).

Much of the managerial concern with tackling absence issues relates to the problem of short-term instances of absence, yet absences from work of four weeks or longer make up a fifth of the days not worked because of sickness absence (CIPD 2010a). Long-term absence raises a number of important issues for organizations, not least whether or not the absent employee will ever be fit enough to resume their job. Managers are encouraged to maintain communication with the absent employee. The involvement of expert occupational health professionals, who can provide advice about the nature and seriousness of an individual employee's condition, and whether or not they are likely to recover sufficiently to resume their work, may also be important. Since April 2010, medical practitioners are required to write 'fit notes' based on what kind of work employees can do, rather than the traditional 'sick notes' which were used to sign them off work entirely.

Although there may be cases where an organization may feel that it is appropriate to dismiss an employee on the grounds of medical incapacity, there are good business reasons for taking action that facilitates the re-entry to the organization of staff who have been absent for a lengthy period, particularly the retention of their skills and expertise. Many organizations operate a system whereby long-term absentees benefit from a staged return to work, involving a partial resumption of their duties initially and building up to their full duties over a period of time. In practice, though, managers can be reluctant to become involved in issues relating to the long-term absence of their employees, especially if work-related stress is a factor. They are often uncomfortable with the notion that such employees can be effectively rehabilitated. As a result, managers may be unwilling to consider the kind of reasonable adjustments that would facilitate the re-entry of staff on long-term sick leave, and may prefer to dismiss them since it seems the less complicated option (James, Cunningham, and Dibben 2002).

 ## Summary and further reading

- The effective management of absence has become an increasingly salient issue for organizations. The increased emphasis on managing absence is linked to a broader concern with tightening performance standards.

- Absence rates vary, by sector, for example, or according to the individual characteristics of employees. But absence is also a product of the work environment. The nature of work, and the way in which jobs are organized, are often sources of poor health. Moreover, collectively generated absence norms are features of some workplaces.

- Key features of absence management policies include appropriate notification and monitoring arrangements, the use of return-to-work interviews, and the establishment of 'trigger points' to prompt further managerial action. Nevertheless, line managers are often reticent about intervening directly in matters related to absence. Moreover, there is often a propensity to deal with absence issues in a punitive, rather than a supportive, way.

For absence data, see the annual surveys produced by the CIPD and the CBI (e.g. CIPD 2010a; CBI 2011a). ACAS (2010c) offers guidance on absence policies. Incomes Data Services provides examples of organizational practice (IDS 2011a). For a good series of case studies, see Dunn and Wilkinson (2002). Taylor et al. (2010) offer some good critical insights.

11.7 Conclusion

The principal concern of this chapter has been to explore the extraordinary phenomenon of performance management, examining the driving forces that have fuelled this growth. We have

seen how this management practice has crossed national and sector boundaries in its proliferation of the management agenda. The development of HRM has been increasingly influenced by performance in this period, as the case for managing people, the human asset of organizations, to create and add value has been crystallized. Organizations increasingly expect HR practitioners to manage their human capital effectively in order to realize the value of this asset. This is particularly evident when we consider the importance of employee absence as a performance issue. The question is will HR managers rise to this challenge and take the opportunity to firmly establish their presence and credibility in the boardroom?

HRM and performance management models and methods have developed in parallel to equip managers to get the best from their people. To do this, HR managers and line managers must work closely together, underpinned by strategic people policies that are aligned with the organization's aims. However, the material on managing absence raises some questions about the extent to which such an approach is capable of being enacted. Although managing performance incorporates systems, processes, and policies, at its very heart are people—the relationship they have with their manager and employer, and ultimately how they choose to behave, influenced by their values and attitudes. Only by understanding this complex relationship between people and performance can organizations and managers effectively intervene to influence employee behaviour that underpins performance. This requires front-line managers with the people skills to encourage and realize high levels of performance from their employees by treating them fairly, and with dignity and respect.

Assignment and discussion questions

1 Why is performance management relevant to employers and employees? How might an employee's perception of performance management differ from that of their employer?

2 What is the purpose of a performance management system? What are its main features?

3 Critically evaluate the role of the performance appraisal as an effective management intervention to improve employee performance.

4 Critically assess the main factors that influence absence levels in organizations.

5 What are the main features of an effective absence management policy?

Online Resource Centre

Test your understanding of this chapter with online questions and answers, keep up to speed with changes to the law through regular updates, and use selected weblinks to quickly access useful resources and further information. Visit the Online Resource Centre at:
www.oxfordtextbooks.co.uk/orc/gilmore_williams2e/

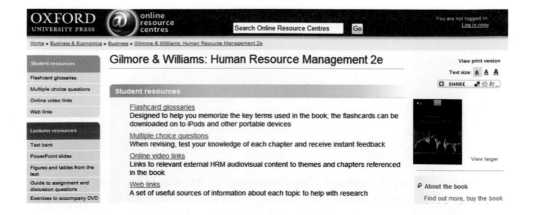

Case study
The development of an HR scorecard at Portsmouth Hospitals NHS Trust

Portsmouth Hospitals NHS Trust (PHT) is a large acute trust with an annual turnover of £400 million and a multi-professional workforce of 7000 employees, which provides emergency, general, and specialist health care to more than 250,000 people each year across three geographically displaced sites.

The requirement to consistently meet national access targets, whilst striving to achieve Foundation Trust status and deliver recurrent financial surpluses, creates a significant challenge for the senior leadership team. For those charged with the effective utilization of the Trust's diverse workforce, this challenge is manifest in the need to establish a business-focused HR performance reporting system.

At PHT, the management concept associated with the Balanced Scorecard methodology is being applied to human resource management, with the development of a 'Workforce Scorecard', with three key aims:

- to align local workforce strategies and HR interventions with organizational goals;
- to measure the contribution of these strategies and interventions to improved organizational performance and patient and staff experience;
- to support efficiency improvements—increased productivity linked with financial improvement.

PHT metrics are associated with four key 'domains'. These domains are directly linked to the delivery of the Workforce Strategy, and all directly influence the Trust's ability to achieve its business objectives; thus all are interdependent. This interdependency, together with the strategic aims associated with measuring each of the four domains, is shown in Figure 11.5.

In determining the individual metrics to be included within each of the four domains, a systematic approach was taken. As an essential first step, it was necessary to revisit the organization's core

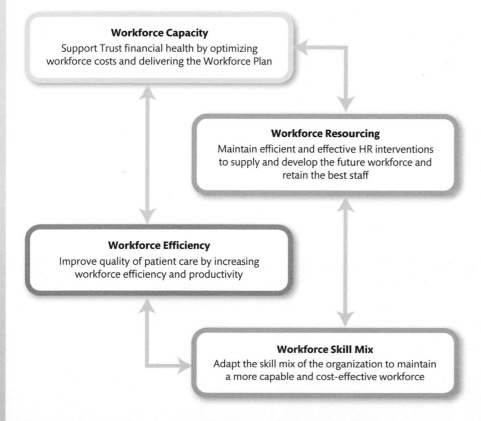

Figure 11.5 The HR scorecard at Portsmouth NHS Hospitals Trust.

business objectives, since these provide the anchor point for any reporting framework that aims to inform and support the process of continuous improvement.

This analysis was conducted in parallel with a review of the Workforce Strategy to ensure synergy between the two. Having established this alignment, the approach taken was 'make it relevant and keep it simple'. This view supported the underpinning principle associated with scorecard methodology, which contends that data should be clearly presented and not overly complex.

In other words, the true value of the data lies in their relative simplicity and ability to focus on key measures that really matter. Therefore, only those measures that could demonstrate alignment with the achievement of the business objectives, and which could be presented in a straightforward manner and effectively benchmarked, were selected.

Applying this testing process eventually reduced the number of key metrics to four within each domain. Broadly, these were as follows: workforce targets (meeting the provision of the corporate workforce plan); temporary workforce; overtime; total workforce capacity; sickness absence; turnover; unit staff costs; workforce productivity; percentage of staff at particular bands/grades, by specialty (i.e. skill mix); percentage of professionally qualified clinical workforce; recruitment effectiveness; workforce stability; diversity profile; essential skills training.

For the first time, this Workforce Scorecard now provides a measure of the overall 'cost-effectiveness' of the workforce through knowledge of unit staff costs and workforce productivity metrics. The real value of these new metrics will be realized as data are compiled and mapped. Current data collation and analysis processes dictate that most metrics are historical, since data are typically collated a month in arrears.

This provides a good indication of overall organizational 'health', but has the disadvantage of potentially delaying timely intervention when problems arise. While likely to increase existing workloads, establishing additional processes to aid the provision and analysis of more real-time data remains a longer-term consideration.

Source: Adapted with permission from Power (2007).

Questions

1 What factors are likely to contribute to the effective implementation of the Workforce Scorecard?

2 What are the implications for managers and employees of the introduction of Workforce Scorecards?

3 What lessons does the experience of Portsmouth Hospitals NHS Trust hold for other organizations?

Employment relations

12

Steve Williams and Iona Byford

Learning objectives

The main objectives of this chapter are:

- to examine the main employment relations features and trends with specific reference to the UK;
- to explain the nature of joint regulation and account for its diminished importance as a means of determining the terms of employment relationships;
- to identify and evaluate critically the principal managerial approaches to employment relations;
- to demonstrate the relevance of conflict and cooperation to understanding the management of employment relations in contemporary organizations.

12.1 Introduction

What is employment relations about? Briefly, it is concerned with understanding the nature of the relationship between employers and employees, and, in particular, how this employment relationship is regulated, experienced, and contested. All employment relationships need to be regulated in some way; in other words, rules have to be set concerning pay rates, hours of work, holiday entitlement, and the pace and organization of work, among other things. In many cases, employers negotiate over such matters with trade unions, organizations of workers concerned with protecting, representing, and improving the pay and conditions of particular groups of workers. The term 'collective bargaining' is used to refer to the way in which the terms of employment relationships are jointly regulated by employers and trade unions in this way. In Section 12.2, we consider the basis of joint regulation as a means of governing employment relationships, demonstrate the extent of its decline, and account for its diminished importance.

The declining significance of joint regulation implies that managers, as the representatives of employers, enjoy a greater degree of control over the regulation of employment relationships. In Section 12.3, we examine the principal managerial approaches to employment relations. While a considerable amount of attention has been directed at how managers can use sophisticated HRM practices to secure greater organizational commitment and engagement from employees, with the aim of improving business performance, the extent to which employment relations has been transformed along cooperative lines as a result is questionable. The material presented in Section 12.4 suggests that a conflict of interest still characterizes the relationship between employers and employees. As well as experiencing employment relations, employees often contest or challenge the terms of their employment relationships. This implies that the job of managing employment relations is concerned with accommodating and managing the disruptive effects of conflict as well as with finding ways of building cooperation.

12.2 Managing through joint regulation

Trade unions have long played an important role in human resource management, mainly by representing workers collectively and bargaining with employers on their behalf. The purpose of this section is to examine the role that unions play in regulating employment relationships, and to account for their declining significance.

12.2.1 The pluralist system of joint regulation

During the course of the twentieth century, joint regulation, based on collective bargaining between employers, or associations of employers, and trade unions, became the dominant means of determining the terms and conditions of employment in many advanced industrialized societies. Employers, such as the car maker Ford, recognized trade unions for collective bargaining purposes primarily because of the pressure that came upon them to do so from their workers. Managers responded to the growing strength of the unions pragmatically, choosing to engage in collective bargaining because it offered them greater opportunities to maintain control over the workplace.

Thus managerial approaches to employment relations were dominated by a pluralist perspective, or 'frame of reference' (Ackers and Wilkinson 2003). Its main elements include a recognition:

- that there is a conflict of interest in the employment relationship;
- that trade unions have a legitimate role in representing the collective interests of the workforce;
- that collective bargaining over the terms and conditions of employment enables conflict to be accommodated and contained within manageable boundaries, making it less likely to be disruptive to business.

Alongside these features, it was assumed that a minimal role for state intervention in employment relations was desirable; the regulation of employment relationships was best managed through the bargaining efforts of employers, or associations of employers, and trade unions, and not by means of legislation. Thus, for a long time, joint regulation was advocated as the most appropriate way of managing employment relations to the overall benefit of the organization.

12.2.2 The erosion of joint regulation

Since the 1980s, the once dominant system of joint regulation has greatly diminished in importance across the industrialized world, particularly in the UK and the USA. This can be illustrated with reference to several developments in particular. First, perhaps the most obvious symbol of the decline of joint regulation has been the fall in trade union membership levels around the world (Frege 2006). In the USA, for example, fewer than one in ten private sector workers are now union members. At the start of the 1980s, there were more than 12 million union members in the UK, over half the employed workforce; by 2010, the figure had fallen to just 6.5 million, barely a quarter of all employees. As can be seen from Table 12.1, aggregate union membership declined substantially during the early 1980s, continued to fall away on a more gradual basis until the late 1990s, and then stabilized somewhat after that, fluctuating around the 7 million mark, before falling away again in the second half of the 2000s.

However, aggregate union membership data fails to capture the extent of variation that exists across industry sectors, as can be seen from Table 12.2 which provides details of sectoral variations in trade union density (the proportion of employees who are union members). Union membership is much higher in some sectors, health and education for example, than it is in others. Fewer than one in 25 employees (3.8 per cent) in hotels and restaurants are trade union members. There is a marked differentiation between the public sector, where over half (56.3 per cent) of employees are union members, and the private sector, where around one in seven employees is a union member. Some unions, particularly those representing professional employees mainly in the public sector, such as the Royal College of Nursing, have increased their membership (Simms and Charlwood 2010). Therefore it is important not to assume that all unions have been equally experiencing decline. See Box 12.1 for links to further information about what unions do, an overview of their role, and details of what has happened to them.

The erosion of joint regulation is also evident from the decline in the proportion of workplaces that recognize a union for collective bargaining purposes, something which has been particularly evident among private sector companies (Blanchflower and Bryson 2009; Simms and Charlwood 2010). In 1980, some two-thirds of workplaces in the UK recognized a union; by 2004, the latest year for which robust data are available, unions were recognized in just 30 per cent of workplaces (Table 12.3). Although the level of union recognition is little changed across the public sector—in schools, central and local government, and the health service for example—where it exists in 90 per cent of workplaces, in the private sector it is much lower, being present in just 16 per cent of workplaces.

Table 12.1 Trade union membership and density, 1980–2010

	Union membership*	Density (%)*§
1980	12,239,000	54.5
1985	10,282,000	49.0
1990	8,835,000	38.1
1995	7,125,000	32.4
2000	7,120,000	29.8
2005	7,056,000	28.6
2010	6,536,000	26.6

*Great Britain (1980–1990), UK (1995–2010).
§Proportion of employees.
Sources: Waddington 2003; Achur 2011.

Table 12.2 Union density by sector and industry sector, UK 2010 (selected industries)

	Union density (%)
All	26.6
Private sector	14.2
Public sector	56.3
Education	52.3
Electricity and gas supply	43.7
Health and social work	41.4
Transport and storage	41.8
Manufacturing	19.8
Financial services	17.4
Construction	14.5
Wholesale, retail, and motor trade	11.8
Hotels and restaurants	3.8

Source: Achur (2011).

One thing to remember is that there is a positive association between workplace size and union recognition, and also between the size of the organization and union recognition—the more people there are employed in the workplace, and in the organization of which it is a part, the more likely it is to have a recognized union. Two-thirds (67 per cent) of workplaces with 500 or more employees have a recognized union, compared with just a fifth (21 per cent) of workplaces with between 10 and 24 employees. Sixty-two per cent of organizations with 10,000 or more employees recognize a union, whereas just 6 per cent of organizations with between 10 and 25 employees do so (Kersley et al. 2006). Half of all employees are in workplaces covered by a union recognition agreement, but just a third of those are in the private sector.

The fall in the coverage of collective bargaining further demonstrates the erosion of joint regulation (Charlwood 2007). In 1980, over two-thirds of employees had their pay set by collective bargaining. By 2004 this had fallen to 35 per cent (Kersley et al. 2006), a decline which persisted in the second half of the 2000s (Achur 2011). Yet collective bargaining coverage remains high in the public sector; some two-thirds of public-sector employees are covered by collective bargaining (Achur 2011). Multi-employer bargaining has disappeared almost entirely from the private sector; where private companies do bargain with trade unions, they now do it themselves, rather than by means of an employers' association. However, it remains relatively common in the public sector, and is the only method of determining pay in over a third (36 per cent) of public sector workplaces (Kersley et al. 2006). For example, most local authorities

Box 12.1 Online video link
Do you know what a trade union is?

Go to the Online Resource Centre for a link to video content on how people respond when they are asked if they know what trade union is, and also a short lecture concerning trade unions in the UK.

The DVD for this book contains an interview with Sarah Veale, head of equality and employment rights for the Trades Union Congress (TUC). She discusses developments in employment relations, and talks about the role of the unions.

Table 12.3 Union recognition, 1980-2004 (percentage of workplaces)

	1980	1990	1998	2004
All workplaces	64	53	42	30
Private sector	50	38	25	16
Public sector	94	87	87	90

Workplaces with 25 or more employees, 1980–1998; workplaces with 10 or more employees, 2004.
Sources: Millward, Bryson, and Forth 2000; Kersley et al. 2006.

negotiate pay agreements with the unions on a national basis. See Box 12.2 for an activity designed to enable you to learn more about the role of trade unions.

12.2.3 Accounting for the decline of joint regulation

Overall, joint regulation is typically present in around a third of workplaces, though it is much more common in public sector organizations than it is in the private sector. The decline of the pluralist system of joint regulation can be attributed to the 'interaction of economic, political, legal and social changes' (Simms and Charlwood 2010: 132). Taking the economy first of all, the high levels of unemployment that characterized periods of economic recession during the 1980s and 1990s had adverse consequences for joint regulation since many of the jobs lost were those in strongly unionized parts of the economy. However, union membership levels failed to recover, and even continued to decline, during periods of economic growth when employment levels rose (Fernie 2005).

Box 12.2 Learning activity
The role of trade unions

The purpose of this activity is to examine the role of trade unions. You should visit the website of at least one trade union and gather information that enables you to address the following questions.

- How many members does the union have?
- In which occupations and industries does the union represent workers?
- What are the main developments and landmarks in the history of the union?
- What are the union's main policy priorities?
- How does the union try and influence government policy?

   A selection of website addresses for some of the major trade unions in Britain is given below. Browse the Trades Union Congress web site (www.tuc.org.uk) for details of many more.

- Unite: unitetheunion.org.uk
- Unison: www.unitetheunion.org.uk
- GMB Union: www.gmb.org.uk
- Communication Workers Union (CWU): www.cwu.org.uk
- Union of Shop Distributive and Allied Workers (USDAW): www.usdaw.org.uk
- Rail Maritime and Transport Union (RMT): www.rmt.org.uk
- National Union of Teachers (NUT): www.teachers.org.uk
- Royal College of Nursing (RCN): www.rcn.org.uk
- Public and Commercial Services Union (PCS): www.pcs.org.uk
- Prospect: www.prospect.org.uk

When thinking about economic change, we also need to be concerned with the impact of broader competitive pressures, particularly those associated with globalization (see Chapter 3). Companies have become more internationally mobile, leading to a weakening in the bargaining power of workers and unions (Anner et al. 2006). Globalization also means that, in advanced capitalist economies like the UK and the USA, there are fewer jobs in sectors that used to be highly unionized, and where joint regulation predominated, such as manufacturing. Moreover, the economic benefits of unions for working people are no longer so evident; while it still exists, the extent of the union wage premium (the extra amount typically earned by unionized workers through collective bargaining compared with non-unionized workers) has considerably narrowed (Metcalf 2005; Blanchflower and Bryson 2009). When it comes to pay, at least, workers do not have the same incentive as they once did to organize in unions and enforce joint regulation.

Still on the subject of economic change, the diminution of joint regulation is often attributed to the changing composition of employment. What this means is that employment levels have been contracting in areas of the economy where unions and collective bargaining are strong, and growing in the areas where they are weak, particularly in private services—for example, leisure and hospitality. Firms in new and growing sectors of the economy are less likely to recognize a union than those in older sectors. These changes have had some important effects on society. It is said that the kind of collective experiences and values that used to bind working people together, and which underpinned unionization and joint regulatory behaviour, have been undermined by changes in the structure of employment (Simms and Charlwood 2010). In the past, workers in large-scale manufacturing enterprises, for example, developed a sense of collective endeavour, based on a strong sense of shared interests. However, workers today tend to be located in relatively small office environments or industrial units, often isolated from others engaged in similar jobs. They are no longer so exposed to unions, and as a consequence are less likely to see their relevance.

However, we need to be careful not to assume that workers in new and growing areas of the economy are incapable of organizing and mobilizing collectively to assert their interests, particularly when faced with poor or deteriorating employment conditions, or the actions of an unreasonable employer. For example, low-paid service workers in many US cities and in London, including cleaners and catering staff, have organized collectively to campaign for a 'living' wage (Luce 2004; Holgate 2009). Moreover, the impact of compositional change should not be exaggerated. Blanchflower and Bryson (2009) assert that it has only been responsible for around a third of the decline of union membership. The decline of joint regulation is evident across all sectors and types of workplaces, indicating that it has largely been caused by 'employers turning their back on trade unions' (Blanchflower and Bryson 2009: 56). Indeed, while union decline has been a feature of many countries, its extent has been especially marked in the UK (Simms and Charlwood 2010). This suggests that, by themselves, broad economic and social factors are inadequate when it comes to accounting for the particularly large extent to which joint regulation has been weakened.

Three other factors explaining the diminution of joint regulation also appear to be relevant. Following on from what has been said about employers 'turning their back' on unions, the first of these concerns the increased reluctance of employers to operate joint regulatory arrangements by means of collective bargaining with trade unions. Much of the decline in the level of union recognition in the private sector was caused by managers de-recognizing unions in some cases, or more commonly not recognizing them in the first place. Some companies, like the fast-food restaurant chain McDonald's, are particularly opposed to union activity (Royle 2000: 110); the airline Ryanair is another employer which is notable for its anti-union stance (see Box 12.4 in Section 12.3.3). Kettle Chips, which makes up market snacks and crisps at its factory near Norwich, England, engaged in an acrimonious but ultimately successful battle to resist union recognition in 2007.

A second relevant factor concerns the failure of unions to organize effectively in new and emerging sectors of the economy, and to gain recognition from employers (Machin 2000). Although some trade unions have made efforts to revitalize themselves by developing new organizing strategies and attempting to expand in new areas (e.g. by attracting young workers), in general the union movement has not been very successful in adapting to changing economic, social, and political circumstances (Simms and Charlwood 2010).

Thirdly, we also need to take into account the political context, which since the 1980s has largely been unsympathetic, and indeed downright hostile at some points, to joint regulation. During the 1980s and 1990s Conservative governments led by Margaret Thatcher and John Major enacted laws regulating the behaviour of unions which had profoundly negative consequences for joint regulation (Simms and Charlwood 2010). While it is difficult to quantify the precise effects of this legislative programme, there can be little doubt that it contributed to a climate which was increasingly antagonistic to joint regulation, for example by giving employers more confidence to challenge and restrict the influence of unions. Under the Labour governments of Tony Blair and Gordon Brown between 1997 and 2010, the diminution of joint regulation slowed somewhat, in part because of the pursuit of a less antagonistic approach to the unions. Nevertheless, Labour retained most of the legislative framework it inherited from its Conservative predecessors, including the bulk of their anti-union laws, and operated an employment relations policy approach which was much more sympathetic to the interests of employers than to trade unions (Smith and Morton 2009).

Labour also accelerated a shift that was already occurring towards the greater legal regulation of employment relationships, instituting a new National Minimum Wage (NMW), for example, and enacting European Union measures in areas such as parental leave, working time, and anti-discrimination. It oversaw the development of a framework of minimum rights underpinning employment relationships. As a result employment protection 'relies increasingly on legal rights not collective organization' (Dickens and Hall 2010: 317). There is a popular misconception that the development of legal regulation has contributed to the declining importance of trade union representation and collective bargaining. Yet, rather than greater legal regulation helping to ease out joint regulation by acting as a substitute for it, there is a symbiotic relationship between the two methods. Trade unions have increasingly focused on using the growing amount of employment law to achieve their objectives of protecting and advancing workers' rights—for example, by representing workers in litigation cases. See the DVD interview with Sarah Veale of the TUC for some of the implications of these developments.

12.2.4 The changing nature of joint regulation

The extent of the decline of joint regulation should not be exaggerated. In many European countries, such as Germany and Sweden, collective bargaining continues to exercise an important influence over the practice of human resource management. Many of the larger private sector employers, such as Honda, BT, and British Airways, operate with recognized unions. The DVD interview with Tony Peers highlights some of the issues and challenges that faced the National Theatre in getting agreement to much needed change from its recognized unions. Public sector organizations are marked by above-average union membership density, recognition levels, and collective bargaining coverage. One of the most interesting features of contemporary human resource management, then, concerns the marked differentiation between how public and private sector organizations manage employment relations.

That said, though, the influence of the trade unions and established collective bargaining arrangements have increasingly been challenged by employers, even in the public sector. While public sector managers seem committed to maintaining relationships with unions, restructuring initiatives and pressures for efficiency savings have contributed to the development of a more forceful managerial approach and greater fragmentation of established regulatory arrangements. At workplace level managers increasingly prefer alternative ways of communicating with their staff directly, rather than through union representatives. Although union membership remains high, and density robust, the ability of the unions to influence managerial decision-making across the public sector seems to have waned (Bach, Kolins Givan, and Forth 2009; Bach 2010).

More generally, the nature of joint regulation appears to have changed; it has taken on a more consultative, rather than confrontational, style. Rather than collective bargaining arrangements being used by unions to secure improvements in pay and conditions to challenge employers, they are increasingly used by companies to facilitate a consensual dialogue about how to achieve greater flexibility and enhance performance (Brown and Nash 2008; Brown, Bryson, and Forth 2009). This is exemplified by the partnership agreements between

unions and employers that exist in many private sector companies, including Barclays, Legal and General, and Tesco. That said, however, the partnership approach is more likely to be found in public sector organizations, particularly in health care (Bacon and Samuel 2009). While the details of partnership agreements vary from organization to organization, generally they comprise a number of key elements:

- the shared commitment of management and unions to improving business performance;

- guarantees from the company about job or employment security;

- union acceptance of more flexible working arrangements;

- new forms of information and consultation provision, sometimes including non-union arrangements for employee representation (e.g. company councils) (Kelly 2004; Terry 2004).

Partnership is based on the assumption that cooperative relations between management and unions can be mutually beneficial to both. For example, it can help to secure support for organizational change initiatives. Barclays initiated a partnership agreement with the finance union Unifi in order to secure its cooperation during a period of extensive organizational restructuring, thus reducing the likelihood of disruptive opposition (Wills 2004).

One interpretation views partnership as helping to resuscitate joint regulation in employment relations; it can be taken as evidence of the ongoing relevance of the pluralist perspective. In some companies, such as the financial services organization 'NatBank', partnership seems to have worked to the advantage of the trade unions, enabling them to secure a presence in the organization, exercise a greater influence over managerial decision-making, increase membership, and extend and strengthen their activist structures (e.g. Johnstone, Wilkinson, and Ackers 2010).

However, an alternative perspective on partnership (Terry 2004) views the emphasis on cooperating with employers, rather than confronting them, as a threat to the trade unions—an initiative designed to undermine the role of joint regulation and to enhance managerial prerogative. From this more critical viewpoint, partnership reflects, and further contributes to, the weakness of the unions (Kelly 2005). Partnership agreements can weaken the role of the unions by eroding their capacity to bargain with managers over employment conditions, or by undermining their organization in the workplace. From the point of view of the employer, the presence of a trade union is acceptable, but only if it helps to contribute to business performance.

 ## Summary and further reading

- During the twentieth century, the joint regulation of the employment relationship, based on collective bargaining with trade unions, became the dominant method of determining terms and conditions of employment, particularly in the UK. The practice of managing employment relations was strongly informed by a pluralist perspective.

- However, between the 1980s and 2000s the significance of joint regulation diminished substantially, as evidenced by the collapse in union membership, the fall in the level of union recognition, the decline in the coverage of collective bargaining, and the diminution in the number of workplace union representatives.

- A number of factors have contributed to the decline of joint regulation, including changes in the economy, the changing composition of employment, the enactment of government policies hostile to unions, and, in particular, the greater unwillingness of managers to support a union presence and collective bargaining in their organizations.

- It is important not to exaggerate the decline of joint regulation. Union recognition and collective bargaining are commonplace across many parts of Europe. They are also present across the public sector, and in many large private sector organizations. The nature of joint regulation has changed, becoming more consensual, as evidenced by the prevalence of partnership agreements.

See Ackers and Wilkinson (2003) for an overview of how employment relations developed as a field of study during the twentieth century. The periodic Workplace Employment Relations Survey (WERS) in the UK contains a mass of relevant information about key aspects of this area of human resource management. The most recent survey was undertaken in 2004, and the results are reported in Kersley et al. (2006). Simms and Charlwood (2010) offer a good explanation of what has happened to the unions. For partnership, see Bacon and Samuel (2009).

12.3 Towards cooperation and commitment?

Clearly, joint regulation is no longer such an important feature of employment relations as it once was, especially in the private sector where only some one in seven employees is a trade union member. While a notable increase in legal regulation has occurred, expanding the framework of minimum employment protection available to workers, it has not been sufficient to compensate for the diminution of joint regulation through trade unions and collective bargaining. Managers enjoy more scope to control how employment relations operates in their organizations, with a greater onus placed on the managerial regulation of employment relationships as a result.

12.3.1 The unitary perspective on employment relations

One implication of the decline of joint regulation, particularly in private sector companies, is that managers have come to expect greater control and authority over employment relations matters. Managerial prerogative—the belief of managers in their sole right to manage—has become a more important influence over the terms of employment relationships. As a result, the management of employment relations has been increasingly influenced by a unitary perspective. In contrast with pluralism, the unitary approach rejects the idea that the employment relationship is marked by a conflict of interests; conflict is the work of external agitators, in particular trade unions, whose activities disrupt the otherwise harmonious relations that would exist within the organization. There is a strong emphasis on the importance of cooperative relations at work.

The unitary label encompasses three broad ways of managing employment relations. First, the 'paternalist' approach involves efforts to secure the loyalty of staff through higher than average rates of pay or non-wage benefits. Managers sometimes refer to the 'family'- or 'team'-based nature of their enterprises and the importance of shared goals; this helps to legitimize their right to manage, and makes trade unionism unnecessary (Fox 1974). The food manufacturing company studied by Wray (1996) enhanced its employees' loyalty and cooperation by offering a range of relatively attractive non-wage benefits, helped by the scarcity of alternative job opportunities in the surrounding area.

Secondly, the 'traditional unitary' approach to managing employment relations is marked by a harsh and authoritarian management style, relatively low pay and poor working conditions, the lack of opportunities for employees to influence decision-making processes, and the reluctance of employers to work with, and sometimes a marked antipathy towards, trade unions (see Box 12.3). It would seem to be rather dated and old-fashioned way of managing employment relations—an assumption one could be forgiven for making given the use of the word 'traditional'. Yet the relevance of the traditional unitary way of managing employment relations is well illustrated by the example of a UK factory making sandwiches for high-street retail outlets. Holgate (2005) found that the largely ethnic minority workforce, many of whom were migrants, had to put up with onerous working conditions and an uncaring management approach. The work was low paid, boring, and hard. There was little, if any, concern on the part of management with securing the commitment of the workforce as a means of improving performance. Rather, workers were given little respect by the company, and sometimes endured treatment that could be construed as racist. For example, members of the mainly black and minority ethnic production workforce were prevented from using the staff car park; the largely white office staff had no such problems.

Thirdly, the neo-unitary approach to managing employment relations is concerned with building strong cooperative relations with employees through the deployment of a range of sophisticated human resource management (HRM) techniques designed to increase their commitment to, and engagement with, the organization. Rather than actively avoiding trade unions, or seeking to suppress them, the neo-unitary approach to managing employment relations holds that union representation is unnecessary, given that employees are already well managed, engaged, and able to influence workplace and organizational decision-making.

Box 12.3 Window on work

Managing employment relations—the Ryanair way

The traditional unitary approach to managing employment relations is exemplified by the approach taken by the self-styled 'low-cost' airline Ryanair. During the 2000s it became the largest operator in Europe, based on an aggressive expansion programme and competitive fares to attract customers. The way in which Ryanair manages its employment relations is consistent with, and indeed exemplifies, the low-cost model on which it has based its business growth. Many of its activities are contracted out to specialist providers, helping to deliver efficiency savings. Cabin crew staff are employed on short-term contracts through agencies, not by the airline itself, with pay and other benefits, like holiday entitlement, that are low by industry standards. They also have to pay for their own training. Ryanair's own staff handbook reveals that workers enjoy few opportunities to be involved in, or to influence, decision-making processes. Rather, the degree of involvement is minimal. The airline has been cited as an example of taking a 'low-road' approach to managing employment relations, where its low-cost efficiency-driven business model 'directly influences its industrial relations approach to the detriment of employees' (O'Sullivan and Gunnigle 2009: 264). Ryanair has also become well known for its prominent anti-trade-union stance. In situations where its workers have asked for union representation, the company has vigorously opposed it. 'Ryanair's policy of vehement opposition to trade unions derives in large measure from its business model, which seeks to establish competitive advantage via extreme cost-cutting measures, going further than other low-cost airlines' (O'Sullivan and Gunnigle 2009: 264).

12.3.2 High commitment management

The neo-unitary perspective and the importance of building cooperative relations at work exercise a strong influence over contemporary approaches to managing employment relations in organizations, particularly where the emphasis is placed on managing staff as if they are assets to be developed, rather than as commodities to be exploited. This involves operating a range of sophisticated HRM techniques, aimed at producing a more highly committed and cooperative workforce who are thereby able to perform their jobs more effectively. The harmonious working environment makes a trade union presence unnecessary. Managers in non-union firms often claim that their staff do not need union representation, because the use of sophisticated HRM practices means that they are well looked after and enjoy plentiful opportunities to influence the decision-making process without it (McLoughlin and Gourlay 1994).

The example of DeliveryCo, the UK operation of a large multinational courier company, illustrates some of the main elements of the sophisticated HRM approach, but also exposes some of its limitations. DeliveryCo espoused a management style that was characterized by the importance of a strong culture. It was supported by a range of sophisticated people management practices, including individual pay reviews, regular appraisals, incentive bonuses, and the presence of extensive communication methods, such as a suggestion scheme. The company's approach to managing its staff was perceived to be a crucial component of its business strategy—for example, by helping to enhance customer service. DeliveryCo did not recognize a trade union. However, the company claimed that this was not because it was against unions; rather, its 'pro-individual' stance, which meant that employees were treated well, made a union presence irrelevant.

This seems to have been acknowledged by some of its staff. According to one of DeliveryCo's call-centre agents: 'I don't think we need a union, you can always go to somebody. If you are not happy with your manager's decision then you can go to the big boss, and they don't mind you doing that' (Dundon and Rollinson 2004: 145). Yet a substantial number of staff were dissatisfied with their inability to influence decisions that affected them at work. Some believed that a union presence would be beneficial, but the possibility of this was seen as unlikely because of management opposition. For all the attractiveness of its employment practices, then, DeliveryCo was not entirely successful in eradicating a perception among its staff that their interests could differ from those of the company (Dundon and Rollinson 2004).

The case of DeliveryCo illustrates the key shift in organizational priorities that has purportedly occurred when it comes to managing employment relations—away from an emphasis on dealing with potential labour conflict and its consequences through joint regulation, to a greater concern with managing for high performance through enhancing the commitment and engagement of employees. There is now a much greater degree of interest in how employers can use sophisticated HRM techniques—'high commitment' or 'high involvement' practices—to improve business performance (Godard 2004; Purcell and Kinnie 2007; Proctor 2008).

The presence of high commitment management practices enhances business performance in two main ways: first, by producing better-quality employees, who are thus more effective in their jobs (Truss 2001), and, secondly, by raising employees' 'discretionary work effort' (Huselid 1995). The theory is that people who are managed well at work, and demonstrate a higher level of organizational commitment as a result, will make more of a contribution to organizational performance. Thus the principal focus of the management of employment relations is held to have shifted away from a concern with managing joint regulation, and accommodating conflict, to a greater emphasis on how employees can be engaged and thus contribute more effectively to the business (Emmott 2005).

One of the main challenges associated with assessing the significance of the high-commitment management approach concerns the problem of defining what in practice constitutes a 'high commitment' practice (Purcell and Kinnie 2007). Some writers use a rather broad definition, including elements of 'best-practice' HRM, such as the use of psychometric tests when selecting employees. However, there appears to be an emerging consensus that the high commitment management approach encompasses four key components. The first is the presence of formal teamworking initiatives, particularly arrangements where members of the team have some responsibility for deciding how work should be done and who should do it. The second component concerns the extent to which members of the workforce are functionally flexible, having the necessary skills to be able to undertake a variety of jobs in their workplace. The third component relates to the degree of employee involvement. In particular, where staff are able to exercise some influence over managerial decision-making, by means of problem-solving and briefing groups, for example, or through the presence of formal consultation arrangements, this is taken as evidence of a high commitment approach. The fourth component concerns the use of sophisticated reward incentives that support high commitment and encourage better performance (White et al. 2004).

Rather than simply using them in isolation, the importance of operating high commitment management practices in a systemic manner, so that they form part of a mutually supportive and interlocking arrangement, has been attested. Originating in the USA, the high performance work system (HPWS) model holds that firms which operate mutually supportive bundles of sophisticated HRM practices, which allow workers to participate in workplace decisions and enhance their skills, and reward them for contributing extra effort, produce a more committed and empowered workforce with positive outcomes for business performance (Appelbaum et al. 2000; Boxall and Macky 2009).

There is some evidence that the use of a sophisticated HRM approach, characterized by practices which enhance the commitment and engagement of employees, has become more prevalent and is present in a substantial number of workplaces, albeit a minority (White et al. 2004; Kersley et al. 2006). While the adoption of the high commitment approach has become less widespread than some had anticipated, its development has nonetheless exercised an important influence on management thinking when it comes to the employment relationship (Wood and Bryson 2009). However, not only does the growth of the high commitment approach seem to have slackened, but it has also been of a rather uneven character, with higher reported usage of some practices, such as those related to teamworking, than of others (Wood and Bryson 2009). In particular, the rather low levels of job discretion experienced by many employees would seem to undermine progress towards greater engagement.

Central to the argument about sophisticated HRM in general, and high commitment practices in particular, is that there is a positive relationship with business performance. Surveys of employers and case studies of organizations indicate that there is an association between the use of high commitment practices and workplace financial performance in private sector companies (e.g. Huselid 1995; Purcell et al. 2003). However, analysis of survey data from the UK suggests that while there is a link between the use of high commitment practices and higher productivity, this is not the case when it comes to financial performance (Wood and

Bryson 2009). There are also some doubts about the survey evidence that underpins claims of a relationship between the use of high commitment practices and performance (Legge 2005). Case study research reveals that the links between business performance and the way in which employees are managed are far from straightforward (Truss 2001; Pass 2005). Moreover, when it comes to the effectiveness of high commitment practices, the behaviour of line managers seems to be of crucial importance; a large part of the success of the high commitment approach depends on how well front-line managers implement and operate it in specific workplaces (Purcell et al. 2009).

12.3.3 Employee engagement

In recent years there has been an increased concern among human resource practitioners and policy-makers with the question of employee engagement, and how employers can engage their staff (MacLeod and Clarke 2009; CIPD 2010*b*). It has been claimed that the principal concern of those responsible for managing employment relations in organizations is with developing and sustaining a climate in which employees will feel valued, and thus be inspired to work effectively and perform better as a result of being more engaged (Emmott 2005). Employee engagement has been defined as: 'being positively present during the performance of work by willingly contributing intellectual effort, experiencing positive emotions and meaningful connections to others.' (CIPD 2010*b*: 5). The three key components of employee engagement are said to be: intellectual engagement, or thinking hard about one's job and how to do it better; affective engagement, or feeling positively about doing a good job; and social engagement, or actively taking opportunities to discuss work-related improvements with others at work (CIPD 2010*b*).

In theory, greater engagement benefits both employers, through enhanced business performance and innovation, and employees, by creating a more positive and stimulating working environment—see Box 12.4 for the case of McDonald's. 'Engagement, going to the heart of the workplace relationship between employee and employer, can be a key to unlocking productivity and to transforming the working lives of many people' (MacLeod and Clarke 2009). The main factors which help to deliver employee engagement are the provision of meaningful work, the commitment of senior management in the organization, the support of front-line managers, and the presence of opportunities for workers to influence workplace and organizational decisions (CIPD 2010*b*). See Box 12.5 for some recommendations on how to improve employee engagement.

In some parts of the economy, companies find it more cost-effective to operate highly efficiency driven approaches to managing employees, viewing them as resources to be exploited, rather than as assets to be nurtured and engaged (Boyd 2003). Performance improvements often come, not from having a more engaged workforce, but as the result of increased work pressures (Danford et al. 2004). Perhaps the most potent sign of the lack of effectiveness of

Box 12.4 Practitioner perspective
Engaging employees at McDonald's

Over the years, the fast-food chain McDonald's developed a reputation as a low-wage employer whose efficiency was predicated upon employing largely young people in boring and monotonous jobs that required low skill levels and offered little autonomy or scope for involvement. However, David Fairhurst, a senior McDonald's executive, claims that the company has transformed the way in which its front-line employees are managed, based on the need to improve customer service and thus deliver better performance. It has tried to increase the engagement of its staff by taking steps to make jobs in the fast-food company more rewarding. Fairhurst claims that 'we have focused our efforts on engaging our people to deliver an outstanding experience for our customers by creating an outstanding employment experience for them' (Fairhurst 2008: 326). Nevertheless, critics of McDonald's question the extent to which employees in the company are genuinely engaged. The pay rates of front-line staff are positioned at or just above the minimum wage, casting doubt upon the company's claim that its employees are valued assets.

Box 12.5 Online video link
What's the secret of engaging employees?

The Chartered Institute of Personnel and Development (CIPD) asked human resource practitioners and other members of the human resources community for their tips on how to engage employees. Go to the Online Resource Centre for a link to a video where their responses are detailed.

efforts to promote engagement is the evidence of high levels of employee disengagement (Coats 2010). Thus we should be wary of claims that the management of employment relations has been transformed along the lines advocated by protagonists of the need to engage with, and secure the commitment of, employees. Maintaining good relationships with employees, and giving them respect and recognition, may be more important than formal HRM practices in building cooperation and commitment (Pass 2005).

12.3.4 Managing employee voice

In the context of the high commitment management approach there has also been a notable increase of interest in methods of managing employee voice (Marchington 2008*a*; Budd, Gollan, and Wilkinson 2010). The concept of employee voice refers to opportunities for employees to have a say over workplace and organizational decisions (Dundon and Rollinson 2004; Wilkinson and Fay 2011). Traditionally, employee voice was associated with trade union representation; voice was expressed through the medium of collective bargaining, based on a pluralist understanding that employees and employers needed to be reconciled. However, much of the growing interest in employee voice reflects the more dominant unitary paradigm. Employee voice arrangements are a central feature of efforts by employers to effect high commitment management and raise levels of employee engagement. For managers, then, voice tends to be viewed as the 'transmission of ideas to managers in order to improve organizational performance' (Dundon et al. 2005: 312) in the absence of, or as a substitute for, trade unions.

Three broad types of employee voice arrangement can be identified. The first concerns the presence of arrangements that enable employers and employees to communicate with one another directly. Direct communication involves the dissemination of information from managers to staff through the use of notice boards, the passing of information down through the management chain, the publication of regular newsletters, and the use of intranet facilities to provide employees with information. It also encompasses face-to-face meetings between managers and staff and team briefings, which give team leaders, supervisors, or junior managers regular opportunities to communicate with their subordinates.

Direct communication also includes practices that enable staff to communicate information to managers. Such upward forms of communication encompass surveys of staff attitudes, the use of electronic mail to convey views and information to managers, and suggestion schemes, which enable employees to propose ways of improving organizational practice. One of the most pronounced trends in employment relations concerns the growth in the prevalence of these direct voice arrangements using one or more of the techniques identified, especially team briefings (Kersley et al. 2006; Willman, Gomez, and Bryson 2009). Table 12.4 highlights the prevalence of these types of direct communication in British workplaces. There is an emerging trend among some companies to encourage the use of social media sites, such as Facebook and Twitter, as mechanisms which can enable employees to be informed about, and discuss, work-related matters (Broughton et al. 2011).

The presence of direct voice arrangements is associated with a more positive climate at work (Willman, Gomez, and Bryson 2009), although there is little evidence that it has much of an effect on employees' commitment or their performance at work. However, managers often favour direct voice arrangements because their prerogatives are left intact. They are used simply to convey information to employees, and to control their behaviour, rather than as mechanisms for allowing employees to exercise genuine voice (Danford et al. 2005).

Table 12.4 Arrangements for direct communications, 2004 (percentage of workplaces)

Communications method	Private sector	Public sector	All workplaces
Meetings between senior managers and the whole workforce	77	89	79
Team briefings	68	81	71
Employee surveys	37	66	42
Email	36	48	38
Suggestion schemes	30	30	30
Notice boards	72	86	84
Systematic use of the management chain	60	81	64
Regular newsletters	41	63	45
Intranet	31	48	34

Source: Kersley et al. (2006: 135).

A second, potentially more potent, type of employee voice concerns mechanisms that enable staff to participate in workplace decisions—in problem-solving groups, for example, or through teamworking arrangements. Problem-solving groups involve bringing managers and staff together to discuss and deal with performance and quality issues. They can be a rather effective way of stimulating employee involvement (Gallie et al. 1998). While the practice of teamworking varies considerably from organization to organization, in its strongest sense it refers to systems which enable workers to organize and manage work processes collectively themselves, without direct supervision by managers. It is often held up as one of the high commitment HRM interventions that can be used to enhance business performance (Marchington and Wilkinson 2005b).

Problem-solving groups and teamworking arrangements are manifestations of 'intelligent flexibility', in the sense that they encourage employees to draw on their knowledge and experience to identify and resolve workplace issues and challenges (White et al. 2004: 46). On the one hand, there is some evidence that 'intelligent flexibility' has become more commonplace; problem-solving groups exist in around a fifth of workplaces. On the other hand, however, its growth seems to have petered out during the 2000s, without it becoming very widespread. Perhaps understandably, then, there is a pervasive feeling among employees in general that they lack genuine scope to participate in, and exercise influence over, workplace decision-making (McGovern et al. 2007).

Whereas communication arrangements and manifestations of 'intelligent flexibility' are forms of direct voice, in the sense that employees are involved directly, the third type of employee voice operates in an indirect manner through union or non-union employee representatives. Traditionally, voice of this kind was dominated by the role of trade unions; employers bargain with union representatives over the terms and conditions of employment relationships, or consult them in advance of making decisions that affect employees. However, with the decline of union representation there has been a growing level of interest in non-union systems of employee representation, particularly arrangements which allow employers to inform and consult with employee representatives (Dundon and Gollan 2007; Gollan 2007; Kaufman and Taras 2010). Companies like Pizza Express and B&Q, which do not recognize unions and are keen to maintain their non-union status, have developed in-house arrangements for informing and consulting staff in the form of 'employee forums' or 'company councils'. EU legislation has also helped to stimulate growing levels of interest in non-union systems of employee representation (see Box 12.6)

While the need to engage employees and secure improvements in business performance through the establishment of voice arrangements has been responsible for encouraging the development of non-union systems of employee representation, perhaps the most important

Box 12.6 Research in focus
The impact of the ICE Regulations

The 2004 Information and Consultation with Employees (ICE) Regulations, which implemented the EU's 2002 Information and Consultation Directive, apply to all firms with 50 or more employees. While managers can take the initiative and establish information and consultation procedures themselves, they are under no obligation to do so unless at least 10 per cent of the workforce submit a written request. There is little evidence that the ICE Regulations have had much of an impact on organizational practice. Where firms do operate information and consultation arrangements, it is generally for internal managerial reasons, such as avoiding trade unions (Hall et al. 2011). In responding to the legislation, many large companies followed a 'risk assessment' rather than a 'compliance' approach (Hall 2006). In other words, they were concerned with reviewing, altering, and strengthening their existing information and consultation practices in the light of the new legislation, rather than with taking action to ensure that their arrangements complied with it. This has been the case with the retail chain B&Q, which revised its 'Grassroots' system of employee consultation partly as a consequence of the ICE Regulations. Grassroots forums, comprising elected employee representatives and managers, exist at store and warehouse level, and also at regional, divisional, and national levels. The arrangements enable 'B&Q employees to pursue a wide range of questions and concerns, suggest ideas for operational improvements and make requests for the development, explanation or clarification of company policy' (Hall 2005: 246–7). The topics covered include queries about pay and conditions, such as maternity benefits, and suggestions for improving in-store equipment.

rationale has been the aim to avoid trade union recognition (Gollan 2007). In the case of a pharmaceutical company, for example, a consultative forum, comprising managers and elected employee representatives who meet on a monthly basis, was established to ensure that employees are informed, and have their views are taken into consideration, about business related matters including major change initiatives. More importantly, perhaps, the presence of the consultative forum helped to keep the plant union free. According to one of the company's managers:

> I think the forum plays a very important role in our ability to remain non-unionised; we've made it quite clear that if ever there was union pressure then we would never consult with a union as much as we do with the forum. (E. Thompson 2011)

Notwithstanding the supposed benefits of non-union systems of employee representation for employers, such arrangements are relatively rare. Indeed, representative forms of voice, both union and non-union, seem to have been in decline (Willman, Gomez, and Bryson 2009). Many workers, especially in the private sector, lack representation of any kind, either union or non-union (Charlwood and Terry 2007). Moreover, non-union arrangements do not seem to be a very effective method of representing employees' interests (Gollan 2007; E. Thompson 2011).

 ## Summary and further reading

- The management of employment relations is increasingly concerned with methods of generating greater organizational commitment and engagement from employees, for example through the use of voice arrangements. Sophisticated HRM, by enhancing employees' organizational commitment, is also held to contribute to improvements in business performance. However, there are doubts about the overall significance of the 'high commitment' paradigm, and also about the nature of the link between HRM and performance.

- The decline of the trade unions would appear to give managers greater power over the way in which employment relationships are regulated. This has enabled them to develop new approaches to managing employment relations, including employee voice arrangements. While there has been a considerable increase in the prevalence of direct communications practices in organizations, such as team briefings and workforce meetings, the resulting degree of employee participation seems rather limited.

- The assumption that a sophisticated HRM approach, based on the use of so-called high commitment practices, is necessarily the only method of managing employment relations in a way that contributes to business performance is questionable. Managers frequently rely on more coercive methods, including resisting trade unions and the use of practices associated with a more traditional unitary style of managing employment relations, in order to realize organizational objectives.

Dundon and Rollinson (2004) provide a good set of case studies of employment relations in non-union firms. Data about the prevalence of high commitment management and voice techniques in the UK are reported in Willman, Gomez, and Bryson (2009). For a discussion of the relationship between HRM and business performance see Purcell and Kinnie (2007) and Proctor (2008). Employee engagement is the focus of reports by MacLeod and Clarke (2009) and the CIPD (2010b). For an introduction to the concept of 'voice' see Budd, Gollan, and Wilkinson (2010) or Wilkinson and Fay (2011). Gollan (2007) is the best study of non-union employee representation.

12.4 Conflict in employment relations

The emphasis on partnership, cooperation, and the importance of securing employee commitment, engagement, and voice is often presented as the predominant feature of employment relations in contemporary organizations. However, in this section we demonstrate that differences of interests between employers and employees continue to feature prominently in human resource management, generating problems, grievances, and, sometimes, instances of conflict that managers must confront. According to a report on conflict management, 'the scale of workplace conflict is remarkable and has increased in the recession' (CIPD 2011a). One illustration of this is the growing number of cases taken by workers to employment tribunals (see Chapter 13).

Moreover, trade unions are often able to mobilize workers with the aim of challenging managerial interests and defending the pay and conditions of the workers they represent. The strike is perhaps the most obvious manifestation of such conflict. A strike can be defined as 'a temporary stoppage of work by a group of employees in order to express a grievance or to enforce a demand' (Griffin 1939, cited in Hyman 1977: 17). While strikes are often taken as a measure of industrial conflict because they are relatively easy to quantify, other types of industrial action can be used by unions to pursue their objectives effectively. For example, a ban on undertaking overtime can be a powerful sanction, as can the work to rule, in which employees refuse to undertake all their usual duties. A good example of the latter occurred in September 2006, when prison officers in part of the UK threatened not to participate in the 'suicide watch' of their charges in a dispute over pay. Effective human resource management relies on recognizing that the employment relationship is marked by both cooperation and the potential for conflict, with the latter being an ever-present feature of working life in organizations. The radical perspective on the employment relationship is particularly important in explaining why conflict at work arises.

12.4.1 The radical perspective on the employment relationship

In contrast to both the unitary and pluralist approaches to employment relations, the radical perspective encompasses a broader and more contextualized view of the nature of the employment relationship. It places employment within the wider economic framework of capitalism with its inevitable cycles of accumulation and crises that create supply and demand issues for both capital (fluctuations in product demand) and labour (fluctuations in the numbers in employment). Based on a Marxist analysis and critique of capitalist society, it incorporates issues such as economic inequality which, it is argued, leads to conflict both in the wider society and at the workplace. This basic inequality is generated through the capitalist system of those who own capital and businesses (employers) and those who can only supply their labour in return for wages or a salary (employees). Therefore their fundamental economic concerns are different and arguably irreconcilable (P. Thompson 2011).

This creates tension through the differential in power relations created by the imbalance in capital resources. However, it should be noted that workers and employers are also dependent on one another in the capitalist system, so issues of power and control and their outcomes are critical in creating consensus or conflict at work. The relevance of the radical perspective is evident when we look at the recessionary economic climate, since there is much discussion around issues of inequality and its detrimental outcomes (Hills 2010; Wilkinson and Pickett 2010).

Although the radical approach may seem somewhat negative, it is argued that pluralism does not address the imbalance in power in a way that acknowledges the real power of employers to control the ownership, production, and delivery of services (Fox 1974). Also, for radical writers the pluralist approach of resolving conflict is essentially one that supports and mimics the capitalist process, thereby not delivering substantive gains for employees, with employers always likely to gain more from negotiations than the employees (Hyman 1975). The system of joint regulation as seen by pluralists reduces the likelihood of conflict, but in so doing it tends to benefit the interests of capital (employers) rather than those of labour (workers). Therefore the radical perspective views the employment relationship as inherently conflictual and antagonistic, something which cannot easily be resolved by negotiations between employers and unions, as under pluralism.

12.4.2 Organizing workers for union recognition

Given the state of the economy, there would seem to be a number of reasons why joining a trade union should benefit workers—for improved protection at work, better pay and conditions, and so on. However, unions find it hard to recruit new members, especially in the private sector (Wright 2011). Some unions have made more of an effort to emphasize the recruitment of new members, including migrant workers (see Box 12.7). The organizing model of trade unionism involves union activists seeking to exploit grievances among workforces as a way of developing union support and building membership. The Trades Union Congress (TUC) established an Organizing Academy which trains union activists in how to recruit new members effectively. During the 2000s the presence of around 270 specialist union organizers helped to recruit some 50,000 new union members and 4500 union activists. An Activist Academy, which is concerned with developing new organizers from among unions' existing activist networks, has also been established (Gall 2009; Nowak 2009).

The organizing unionism model is concerned not simply with recruiting new union members, but also with developing union organization, supporting and involving activists, and deploying a number of distinctive new techniques, such as 'mapping' workforces to determine those who are likely to be supportive of union action, particularly in sectors of the economy where workers have largely been neglected by unions in the past (Heery et al. 2003). For example, efforts have been made to organize the ethnically diverse workforce of London hotels, albeit without much success (Wills 2005). Nevertheless, managers in organizations must consider ways of responding to union activity, and of moderating its effects, particularly in the light of UK legislation that

Box 12.7 Policy example
Organizing migrant workers in unions

The enlargement of the European Union saw an influx of migrant workers, many from Poland, enter the UK during the 2000s. Trade unions were concerned that Polish workers could be exploited by unscrupulous employers who would pay them less than the National Minimum Wage, or fail to respect their employment rights. As a result, the GMB union launched a campaign to help unionize Polish migrant workers. GMB officials were reportedly taken aback by the level of support for the initiative in Southampton, leading to the establishment in the city in 2006 of the UK's first branch dedicated to migrant (mainly Polish) workers. The GMB used its Learning and Organizing Centre in Southampton as a facility to support migrant workers in the city and to develop union organization, including making connections with indigenous workers. It also employed a project worker, whose role involved supporting migrant workers, including organizing and arranging education and training courses. For further information go to the GMB Southern Region's website (www.gmb-southern.org.uk).

may oblige an employer to recognize a trade union for collective bargaining purposes where a majority of the workforce wants it.

The introduction of a statutory union recognition procedure in 2000 seems to have stimulated an increase in the extent of recognition activity, and has provided the unions with a catalyst for organizing workers. Briefly, the procedure, which is overseen by a body called the Central Arbitration Committee (CAC), means that any union, or unions, whose attempt to secure a voluntary recognition agreement with an employer has been rejected can apply to the CAC for recognition and to decide on the bargaining unit to which recognition applies. The bargaining unit is usually decided on the basis of occupational category or location. The procedure does not apply to organizations employing fewer than 21 people. The CAC will investigate the level of support among the workforce for unionization; at least 10 per cent must be union members. While the CAC is empowered to mandate union recognition if 50 per cent or more of the workforce in question are union members, generally it will supervise a ballot to test support for unionization. To secure recognition a union must get the backing of a majority of those voting, as long as at least 40 per cent of the relevant workers support it, including those who do not vote in the ballot.

The procedure encourages unions wishing to secure recognition to build up support in the workplace by organizing new members. What have its effects been? The main outcome has been a notable increase in the number of new recognition agreements (Blanden, Machin, and van Reenen 2006). The period 2000–2005 alone saw over 2000 new recognition cases, although the number fell back markedly during the latter half of the 2000s (Gall 2007, 2010*b*). Among the companies that have signed recognition agreements with unions since the procedure came into effect are Eurotunnel and Honda. However, in most instances they have been voluntary deals, lying outside the statutory procedure itself, but influenced by its presence. Companies such as South-West Water, which have relatively strong support for unions among their staff, chose to recognize a union voluntarily rather than be forced into doing so by the law (Bonner and Gollan 2005). Only a minority of the new recognition deals signed since 2000 have come about directly because of the statutory procedure. By April 2011, it had generated just 225 new agreements, with the CAC receiving just 28 applications from unions for recognition in 2010–2011 (CAC 2011).

The impact of the union recognition legislation should not be exaggerated. Generally, new agreements have tended to come through consolidation in sectors of the economy, like manufacturing, where unions are already relatively strong, rather than in growing areas of the economy, such as services, where their presence is weak (Blanden, Machin, and van Reenen 2006). The slackening pace of new union recognition agreements reflects how difficult it is for unions to make headway, given opposition from employers (Gall 2007, 2010*b*). Moreover, despite the number of new recognition agreements, the proportion of workplaces with union recognition continued to decline in the 2000s, a reflection of ongoing compositional change.

How have companies responded to the more assertive union-organizing campaigns and to the implications of the statutory union recognition procedure? Some seem to have gone about their business virtually unaffected. One of the best-known anti-union companies is the fast-food giant McDonald's. It employs a relatively young workforce, many of whom do not stay in their jobs for very long, and has little concern with the need to consider the implications of trade unionism, largely because of the lack of interest in unions evinced by their staff. They also use each restaurant as a bargaining unit, which frustrates union recognition as it is very resource intensive for unions to have to organize store by store. However, others have been obliged to respond to the prospect of a union presence. Some companies—for example, BMW's Rolls-Royce motor-cars business—realizing that support for unionization among their workforce would make a successful claim for recognition under the statutory procedure likely, have opted to reach their own voluntary agreement with a cooperative union by initiating recognition themselves.

Another response by employers, including well-known companies like the broadcaster BSkyB and the internet retailer Amazon, is to resist union organizing efforts. American-based union-busting firms have often been hired to help companies maintain a union-free environment, marked by the use of intimidatory tactics such as threats to close workplaces or dismiss union activists (Logan 2008). Although some companies do respond positively to the prospect of dealing with unions, hostility from employers is a major obstacle to getting new recognition agreements (Heery and Simms 2010). Clearly, it is mistaken to assume that managing employment relations in contemporary human resource management is solely concerned with finding ways of building cooperative relationships and with working to secure greater employee commitment. Often a key managerial task concerns the obligation to respond to, and deal with the consequences of, pressure from trade unions.

12.4.3 Labour conflict

Strikes and other forms of industrial action are manifestations of labour conflict. During the 1970s there was an average of over 2500 strikes each year, and the number of days not worked as a result amounted to an annual average of over 12 million. During the 1990s and 2000s the incidence of recorded strike activity fell to historically low levels at times (see Table 12.5 for further details). The lowest number of strikes—just 88—was recorded in 2010. While this decline in the incidence of strike activity is a worldwide phenomenon, it is by no means universal (see Box 12.8), but it is particularly acute in the UK. Other forms of industrial action have also become increasingly rare (Kersley et al. 2006).

Despite a reduction in overall strike activity in recent years, we should be wary of claiming that conflict in employment relations has disappeared—for three reasons. First, in some parts of the economy, especially where trade unions are well organized, strikes and other forms of labour conflict still occur and their implications have to be managed. Some sectors, for example the railways, seem to be particularly vulnerable because of their susceptibility to impact. Moreover, unions threaten more strikes than they actually undertake, since this strengthens their bargaining power in negotiations with employers (Darlington 2009).

Secondly, there is evidence that when the issue is important enough, workers readily mobilize for industrial action, particularly in a recessionary economic climate. In his version of mobilization theory, Kelly (1998) theorizes this process from the perspective of how individual workers become a collective actor capable of challenging the interests of the employer. Workers' capacity to mobilize is influenced by having a shared grievance and social identity, good leadership, and the capacity to attribute their problem directly to their employer. While unions enable workers to mobilize effectively against their employer, employers frequently respond to this pressure by taking counter-mobilization measures. An example is the dispute involving British Airways cabin crew between 2009 and 2011, which involved two strikes over pay and terms and conditions. The company tried to prevent the strike by disputing the legality of the strike ballot

Table 12.5 Levels of strike activity, 1974–2010

Year	Number of strikes	Working days lost (000s)	Workers involved (000s)
1974–1979	2412	12,178	1,653
1980–1985	1276	9,806	1,213
1986–1989	893	3,324	781
1990–1994	334	824	223
1995–1999	193	495	180
2000	212	499	183
2002	146	1,323	943
2005	116	157	93
2006	158	755	713
2008	144	756	511
2010	88	365	132

Annual averages 1974–1999.
Sources: Edwards 1995; Office for National Statistics (www.statistics.gov.uk).

Box 12.8 International focus
Workplace conflict around the world

There are signs that a notable upsurge in workplace conflict is occurring around the world. In China, for example, strikes and other forms of labour protests are increasingly commonplace. Multinational automobile firms Honda and Toyota were forced to suspend production in several of their Chinese plants in 2010 after workers walked out in pursuit of higher pay and better working conditions. Moreover, economic recession seems to have accentuated the level of conflict in employment relations, particularly in emerging Latin American economies, such as Argentina, Brazil, and Chile, and in Europe (ILO 2010). Prolonged economic difficulties have stimulated anti-government protests and uprisings by working people in many countries (Mason 2012). During 2010–2011, for example, mass strikes occurred in France, Greece, Italy, Spain, and Portugal as workers took to the streets to protest against government austerity measures, such as cuts in pay and pensions, designed to reduce their budget deficits (Vandeale 2011).

in the courts, disciplining and dismissing union activists, recruiting alternative staff to act as strike-breakers, and creating an anti-strike union (Tuckman 2010; Upchurch 2010).

The adverse economic climate seems to have stimulated growing discontent among workers, exemplified by the strike over proposed cuts to pension entitlements involving up to two million public sector workers which occurred in November 2011. Internationally, there are also signs of an upsurge in labour conflict (see Box 12.8).

The third reason for being careful about assuming that the decline of strike activity means that the significance of conflict in employment relations has now become negligible concerns the various ways in which conflict can be expressed. Strikes are 'the most obvious manifestation' of labour conflict (Hyman 1975: 186), but conflict also takes other forms. In non-union firms, where the organization of strike action is difficult, collective action by workers, such as protests over changes to people's jobs, sometimes encourages managers to revise their proposals, or even to withdraw them entirely (Scott 1994; Dundon and Rollinson 2004). Some studies demonstrate that excessive work pressure or boring jobs can encourage employee sabotage, with adverse consequences for service delivery (e.g. Harris and Ogbonna 2002). Conflict can also be expressed in ways that involve staff withdrawing from work, sometimes by absenting themselves or by quitting. Managers ascribed the high levels of employee turnover in one of the call centres studied by Beynon et al. (2002: 152) to the intolerable working conditions that prevailed—an evident source of 'burn-out'. Thus a variety of worker behaviours are undertaken in order to pursue better employment conditions, to challenge unreasonable management interventions, or to secure some release from harsh and onerous jobs, making them more bearable, that express the antagonistic basis of the employment relationship.

12.4.4 Managing conflict in the employment relationship

One of the most important features of the employment relationship is that it is characterized by the potential for conflict as well as by cooperation. In order to manage their human resources effectively, organizations must consider how they respond to, and manage, the implications of conflict, as well as ways of encouraging commitment and cooperation. This is evident with regard to the use of formal procedures, particularly negotiations, to produce agreements between employers and unions, and the way in which managers, even in non-union firms, must accommodate the interests of their staff by means of tacit and informal understandings.

Many organizations have to respond to, and deal with the implications of, trade unionism. Where there is a recognized union, or unions, formal procedures exist to resolve disputes. Most obviously, arrangements for negotiating agreements are commonplace in organizations that recognize trade unions, but can also encompass consultation processes. Negotiations are an important aspect of the collective bargaining process; by helping to resolve disputes, they ensure that conflict is contained within manageable boundaries,

Box 12.9 Window on work
The 2005 Gate Gourmet dispute

In August 2005, hundreds of Gate Gourmet workers, who produced in-flight meals for British Airways at London's Heathrow Airport, walked off the job in protest at deteriorating working conditions and proposed job cuts, exacerbated by the hiring of temporary agency workers. Gate Gourmet's managers summarily dismissed all those who had taken the action. A large number of BA staff, upset at the way in which their Gate Gourmet colleagues had been treated, many of whom were friends and family members, also stopped work in sympathy. Although the airline was able to persuade its own staff to return to work after just two days, the Gate Gourmet dispute disrupted the airline's catering facilities for months. In September 2005, the Gate Gourmet workers' union, the TGWU, negotiated an agreement with the company whereby some of the sacked workers would be reinstated, while the others would be made redundant with an appropriate pay-off. Gate Gourmet then agreed a new three-year contract with BA to provide in-flight meals. Without the intervention of the TGWU, and the negotiated agreement it was able to facilitate, the ongoing disruption might well have compromised Gate Gourmet's ability to fulfill its new contract with BA.

preventing it from having overly disruptive effects on the organization. See Box 12.9 for an illustrative example of how a negotiated agreement ended a rancorous dispute. What does negotiating involve? It is a process of resolving disputes in which both sides—employer and union—make compromises in order to secure a mutually acceptable agreement. This involves argument between the parties, as they try to convince each other of the merits of their position, and in the process draw closer together, by exchanging compromises and trade-offs, so that a settlement is possible (Torrington 1991; Martin 1992). Box 12.10 features a skills activity around negotiation.

Managers in organizations do not just respond to, and manage, the implications of conflict in the employment relationship by means of formal procedures, such as negotiations. They must also accommodate the interests and concerns of their workforce and secure their tacit acceptance of managerial objectives, even in the absence of unions. In a study of WaterCo, a company supplying drinking-water facilities to offices and other locations, the researchers found that, even though there was no union presence, 'workers were not passive recipients of the conditions they experienced. Rather, they exerted influence in return and, in so doing, partially shaped how management regulated the employment relationship' (Dundon and Rollinson 2004: 91).

Even in small non-union firms, where one might expect managerial authority to be unlimited, managers must accommodate the demands of the workforce. They engage in informal bargaining over such matters as the organization and pace of work. This is best illustrated with reference to Monder Ram's study of employment relations in small Asian-owned clothing factories based in the West Midlands region of the UK (Ram 1994). He found that managerial authority was bounded by the need to bargain with workers over the speed with which work tasks were undertaken, and the appropriate level of wages payable as a result.

Summary and further reading

- Particularly where they act collectively in unions, employees continue to enjoy a degree of power over their employment relationships. They frequently challenge and contest the terms of their employment; as a consequence, managers are obliged to respond to, and accommodate, their interests and concerns.

- Some unions have taken steps to organize workers in a more assertive way, with a view to building membership levels so that they are in a position to make a claim for recognition from an employer.

- While there was a notable increase in union recognition activity during the 2000s, the number of new recognition agreements has markedly diminished. Most of the new recognition agreements have been reached voluntarily between unions and employers, although the statutory union recognition procedure has exercised a notable indirect influence.

Box 12.10 Skills exercise
A negotiating encounter

The purpose of this skills exercise is to give you some insight into the process of negotiation, and the skills and techniques which it involves. Your company operates a chain of bars and restaurants which has experienced a downturn in trade. The management team has published a number of proposals which are designed to reduce employment costs, improve efficiency, and return the company to viability, while avoiding having to make any job losses:

- an 18-month pay freeze, following which there would be an 18-month deal giving all staff a 2.5 per cent pay rise;
- staff will pay an amount (yet to be determined) towards their company uniform;
- a proposed change to the company's sickness absence scheme, so that staff are no longer entitled to sick pay for the first three days of any period of absence;
- to reduce the value of the free meal entitlement by 25 per cent with immediate effect, and by a further 25 per cent in 18 months time;
- to end the current system of waiting staff keeping their own customers' tips; instead they will be collected by the restaurant manager in each establishment and shared between all staff on an equal basis.

The workers' trade union representatives have indicated that they oppose these proposed changes, and have called for an immediate meeting with management. At this meeting the management team and union representatives are due to negotiate over these proposals with a view to achieving an agreement which will satisfy both sides.

One group of students will play the management team, and another group will play the union representatives. In your respective groups you will discuss and plan your approach to the meeting. What would be your ideal outcome from the meeting? What arguments would you use, what arguments are likely to be put forward by the other side? How would you respond to them? Are there any areas where you would be willing to compromise in order to reach an agreement? Having prepared, the management and union groups will then come together to conduct the actual negotiating encounter; perhaps the union group could start things off by setting out their response to the proposals. At the end of the encounter any remaining time can be used to reflect on the key skills needed for effective negotiation in employment relations.

- In order to understand industrial conflict properly, we need to look beyond strikes and consider the range of behaviours expressing the conflict of interest that characterizes employment relationships. Managers in organizations have to deal with, and try to accommodate, the consequences of conflict, either by means of formal procedures, such as negotiating agreements with unions, or informally with employees. The greater emphasis accorded to commitment by no means implies that conflict has ceased to be of importance in employment relations.

The Trades Union Congress (www.tuc.org.uk) and the Central Arbitration Committee (www.cac.gov.uk) publish data on union recognition trends, the latter in its annual report. There are some good case studies of workplace conflict. You can find out more about ACAS from its website (www.acas.gov.uk).

12.5 Conclusion

In this chapter, we have demonstrated that one of the main features of employment relations concerns how employment relationships are regulated. The decline of joint regulation, the determination of terms and conditions by means of collective bargaining between employers and trade unions, is a prominent trend in employment relations. This has been caused by a number of factors, in particular the changing composition of employment and a greater reluctance to deal with unions on the part of employers. Nevertheless, the extent of the diminution of joint regulation should not be exaggerated.

To what extent does the decline of joint regulation signify a shift towards a more cooperative basis for employment relations? Instead of having to bargain over terms and conditions of employment with trade unions, it would seem that managers enjoy greater scope to design and develop practices that help to engage and secure the commitment of employees. Many organizations have developed a sophisticated HRM approach to managing employment relations based on putting in place practices that render a union presence unnecessary. The use of high commitment practices, such as sophisticated forms of employee involvement, is designed not only to win the cooperation of staff, but also, as a consequence, to enhance business performance. But the high commitment management approach seems to be present in a minority of workplaces. A 'traditional unitary' management style, which treats workers as commodities to be exploited rather than as resources to be developed, is a commonplace feature of organizational practice.

Understandably, then, there remains a potential for conflict of interest in employment relationships. Employment relations are concerned not just with how employment relationships are regulated, but also with the experiences of employees and how they challenge and contest the terms of their labour. A key managerial task in organizations is to accommodate conflict, minimizing its potential for disruption. This can involve negotiating agreements with trade unions, for example. But it can also encompass dealing with the complaints of staff, responding to recognition claims from unions, and coping with the high levels of labour turnover and absenteeism, and the instances of sabotage, that result from operating with a badly treated and demotivated workforce. Thus managing employment relations in organizations is concerned not only with engaging employees, securing their commitment to the organization, and realizing their cooperation, but also with accommodating conflict and dealing with its consequences.

 ## Assignment and discussion questions

1 What is meant by the term 'joint regulation' in employment relations?
2 Why has the significance of joint regulation as a means of determining the terms and conditions of employment relationships declined?
3 Critically assess the significance of the high commitment approach to managing employment relations.
4 Why might organizations want to establish employee voice arrangements?
5 To what extent does the level of strike activity provide an effective measure of conflict in employment relations?

 ## Online Resource Centre

Test your understanding of this chapter with online questions and answers, keep up to speed with changes to the law through regular updates, and use selected weblinks to quickly access useful resources and further information. Visit the Online Resource Centre at:
www.oxfordtextbooks.co.uk/orc/gilmore_williams2e/

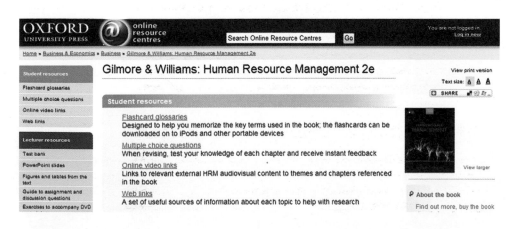

13.1 Introduction

Tackling workplace conflict and resolving problems and disputes at work are integral features of human resource management. The purpose of this chapter is to examine the key mechanisms which organizations use for managing workplace conflict, particularly the use of procedures for dealing with grievance and disciplinary issues. This tends to be an unfashionable aspect of HRM, because of the implication that the relationship between employers and employees is characterized by conflict as well as cooperation (see Chapter 12). Grievances concern complaints by employees that they have been unfairly treated in some way. Discipline involves action taken by managers against staff deemed to be underperforming, or whose conduct violates organizational standards in some way. In theory, grievances and disciplinary matters can be managed in ways that improve organizational performance. Handled effectively, through the use of formal procedures that provide for consistency, fairness, and transparency, these aspects of HRM may enhance the commitment of employees. The extent to which this is the case in practice, though, is an important theme underlying this chapter. In Section 13.2, we examine the nature of formal procedures for handling grievances and disciplinary issues in organizations, the reasons for their existence, and their principal contents. The focus of Section 13.3 is on the issues that relate to the way in which grievances and disciplinary matters are typically dealt with by managers in organizations, and their implications, with reference to some specific topics such as bullying and harassment. It is often believed that workplace conflict is best resolved internally, preventing disputes from escalating and entering the legal system, such as the system of employment tribunals in the UK. In Section 13.4, we examine these tribunals, and also look at the efforts made by governments and agencies to contain workplace conflict, and resolve disputes internally, including by mediation—a means of resolving disputes at work which is becoming increasingly popular.

13.2 Understanding grievance and disciplinary procedures

In order to understand how grievances and discipline are handled in organizations, we must examine the nature of formal procedures for dealing with these issues. Why is there a need for organizations to have formal procedures covering these areas? And what are the main features of grievance and disciplinary procedures? However, before we deal with these questions we first need to consider the nature of rules in organizations.

13.2.1 The nature of organizational rules

Grievance and disciplinary procedures exist to provide a formal means for resolving disputes that have arisen from breaches of organizational rules or acceptable standards of conduct. Disciplinary procedures set out the arrangements for dealing with employees who are suspected of contravening organizational rules in some way—for example, by being persistently late for work. Employees may also have cause to complain about the managerial interpretation of organizational rules, particularly if they feel that they have been treated unfairly in some way—for example, by being denied access to promotion opportunities. Therefore grievance procedures are designed to offer a formal means of resolving a dispute that arises when an individual employee has a complaint regarding his/her treatment at work.

Organizational rules may cover a wide range of topics, everything from arrangements governing access to flexible working arrangements to the appropriate use of email and internet facilities. Why are rules so important in organizations? For one thing, they are crucial to the maintenance of managerial control. Organizational rules prescribe appropriate and acceptable standards of conduct and performance to be followed by employees. Moreover, by providing a defence against arbitrary managerial actions, the existence of organizational rules potentially provides for greater fairness and consistency in managerial decision-making. Therefore rules are also important as a means of securing the motivation, commitment, and loyalty of staff. They can help to ensure that managers comply with their legal obligations when it comes to managing human resources—for example, by proscribing unlawful forms of employment discrimination.

It is important not to see organizational rules purely in a formal sense, as set out in company handbooks and written policies. Informal and tacit understandings that arise among workers, and between workers and managers, are often an important influence on behaviour at work. Thus 'how people behave depends as much on day-to-day understandings as on formal rules. . . . What the rule is cannot be discovered from the rulebook. Day-to-day experience will create standards which may sharply differ from official rules' (Edwards 2005: 377).

In one study, for example, hotel and restaurant staff frequently engaged in practices, such as deliberately compromising hygiene standards, that contravened formal organizational rules. Yet managers seemed to have tacitly accepted such behaviour; they recognized the likely adverse effects on staff motivation and work effort if they were not to do so (Harris and Ogbonna 2002). In some circumstances, then, managers are reluctant to apply the formal rules. In what Gouldner (1954) referred to as an 'indulgency pattern', they tolerate misbehaviour and, in so doing, help to create informal tacit understandings that influence the conduct of staff.

13.2.2 Why have formal grievance and disciplinary procedures?

Before the 1960s few organizations had their own written procedures for dealing with grievances and disciplinary issues (Edwards 2005). However, since then there has been a remarkable increase in the growth of formal grievance and disciplinary procedures. Most large and medium-sized employers operate formal procedures for dealing with individual employee grievances and matters relating to discipline; such procedures tend to be absent only in small firms (Kersley et al. 2006; Suff 2010*a*, *b*).

The growing prevalence of formal procedures for handling grievances and disciplinary issues has come about for three main reasons. First, such arrangements are deemed necessary because of the need to manage workplace conflict which arises between employees, or between employees and their employer. Conflict often arises because of poor working relationships or a breakdown in relations between managers and staff, and its consequences for the organization, whether through undermining employee morale or increasing absence, can be highly damaging (Suff 2011*c*). The economic recession of the late 2000s seems to have stimulated a marked increase in workplace conflict, with managers having to spend more time dealing with grievance and disciplinary matters (CIPD 2011*a*; Suff 2011*c*). Internationally, the importance of workplace conflict, in countries like China for example, is evident in rising numbers of disputes (see Box 13.1).

The second reason for the increasing prevalence of formal procedures for dealing with grievances and disciplinary issues is that they can enable more effective management of this area of human resources (see Box 13.2). Operating a formal grievance procedure, for example, ensures that

Box 13.1 International focus
Workplace conflict and employment disputes in China

Workplace conflict is a global phenomenon. The economic recession of the late 2000s and the austerity policies followed by many governments as a result have generated increases in conflict. For example, many European countries have been affected by an upsurge in workplace conflict because of the adverse economic conditions (ILO 2010). However, perhaps the most notable upsurge in workplace conflict is evident in China, where there has been a significant growth in employment disputes during the 2000s. Economic reforms have generated widespread instances of labour conflict over matters such as unpaid wages and employer violations of labour regulations. China's government has put a great deal of emphasis on developing legal and administrative systems for tackling workers' grievances. The number of officially recorded labour disputes rose from 19,000 in 1994 to over 500,000 in 2007 (Friedman and Lee 2010). However, workers often discover that formal state-run mechanisms for resolving disputes are ineffective; officials tend to be more concerned with upholding the interests of employers and maintaining a business climate which is attractive to foreign investors, than with protecting employment rights.

complaints can be dealt with in a seemingly fair and consistent manner. This can help to enhance among employees a perception of procedural justice, with positive implications for their organizational commitment (Klass 2010). Formal disciplinary procedures have a number of benefits for managers. They can help to define the authority of managers, and thus enhance managerial control; they can also be used to demonstrate that the punishment of an employee (e.g. by dismissal for example) is a fair outcome—the result of following due process—and not an arbitrary decision. Moreover, operating formal procedures for handling disciplinary matters enables managers to establish the standards of performance and conduct expected of their employees, and to change their behaviour where necessary (Klass 2010; ACAS 2011).

Case studies of organizational practice in the hospitality, road transport, and engineering industries demonstrate the benefits of having formal disciplinary procedures. They 'were seen as providing a touchstone in clarifying and articulating the authority of managers in contemplating or in taking disciplinary action' and, moreover, were important in 'setting standards of behaviour or conduct' (Goodman et al. 1998: 544). While having to follow formal procedures might often be perceived as an undesirable impediment to managerial action, their operation may enable more effective human resource management.

The third reason for the increasing use of formal procedures for handling grievances and disciplinary issues concerns the defence they provide when it comes to litigation by current and former employees (Klass 2010). The use of an appropriate formal procedure to discipline or dismiss employees, and a formal grievance procedure to enable staff to raise complaints and then have them resolved, either helps employers to avoid litigation or enables them to defend legal claims by employees more effectively. Consider, for example, the case of a bar worker suspected by his employer of giving drinks away free. The general manager received a report from some investigators. He then called the bar worker into a meeting, informed him that it was a disciplinary hearing, and, on the grounds of the report he had received, told the employee that he was dismissed. However, the absence of a written disciplinary or grievance procedure influenced the decision to adjudge the dismissal as unfair (Earnshaw, Marchington, and Goodman 2000: 66–7).

Employers are under no obligation to operate written grievance and disciplinary procedures. However, as part of their efforts to encourage organizations to resolve workplace conflict without resorting to litigation governments have tried to encourage managers and workers to use internal machinery for resolving grievances or dealing with disciplinary matters. This has prompted organizations to enhance the formality of their procedural arrangements—for example, by specifying that staff must put their grievances in writing (DTI 2007). In the UK, the amount paid in compensation to an aggrieved worker can be adjusted by up to 25 per cent depending on how well the employer has followed an appropriate procedure. The absence of written policies may leave employers in a vulnerable position, particularly if they have to respond to a claim for litigation, since without one it is difficult for them to demonstrate that they have dealt with the grievance or disciplinary issue adequately (Suff 2010a).

13.2.3 The content of disciplinary and grievance procedures

Before we consider the content of disciplinary procedures in detail, it is important to realize that organizations sometimes use separate procedures for dealing with issues of misconduct, poor

Box 13.2 Practitioner perspective
Why are disciplinary and grievance procedures necessary?

The Chartered Institute of Personnel Development (CIPD) offers some interesting insights into why formal grievance and disciplinary procedures are desirable from a practitioner perspective. They provide a clear and transparent framework for dealing with difficulties that may arise out of the employment relationship. They are necessary to ensure that everyone is treated consistently, to enable issues to be dealt with fairly and reasonably, and to comply with the law. The CIPD publishes a fact sheet which explains in more detail why grievance and disciplinary procedures are desirable (http://www.cipd.co.uk/hr-resources/factsheets/discipline-grievances-at-work.aspx).

performance, and sickness absence. For example, Barclays Bank operates a capability procedure, separate from its disciplinary procedure, for employee performance issues (IDS 2009*a*).

Surveys of organizational practice suggest that the content of disciplinary procedures is marked by six key features.

- A statement of principles—something that among other things sets out the purposes for which it will be used and the nature of the approach to be taken. For example, the disciplinary procedure operated by Boots, the retail chemist chain, emphasizes the importance of correcting and improving employees' conduct and performance, rather than just punishing them (IDS 2009*a*).

- Provisions for dealing with instances of minor misconduct informally—for example, occasional poor timekeeping. Employers increasingly seem to prefer using informal methods for tackling minor infractions of organizational rules, with the sanction of a verbal warning for the employee concerned, before instigating formal procedures (IDS 2009*a*).

- A list of behaviours classified as misconduct that would lead to disciplinary procedure being invoked. Instances of misconduct, such as unwarranted absence from work, tend to be distinguished from gross misconduct, which could, among other things, encompass cases of theft or violence at work.

- Provisions for how the alleged misconduct should be investigated, and also for a meeting at which the employee is presented with the case against him/her and given an opportunity to put his/her side of the story.

- Disciplinary procedures provide for the appropriate sanctions to be applied if the case against the employee is upheld following the disciplinary meeting. In most cases the penalty usually takes the form of a written warning placed on an employee's file for a specified period of time. Most disciplinary procedures provide for a series of staged warnings, up to and including the issuing of a final written warning if an employee commits a further offence before the time limit of any existing warnings has expired. The penalty for gross misconduct, or in circumstances where an employee has committed a further offence having already received a final written warning that has yet to expire, is generally summary dismissal, although there may be provision for sanctions short of dismissal, such as a period of suspension without pay.

- Finally, disciplinary procedures almost always make provision for the right of an employee to appeal against the outcome of a disciplinary meeting, commonly to a senior manager who has had no previous involvement in the case.

See Box 13.3 for relevant details of the ACAS code of practice as it applies to handling discipline.

Employee grievances typically tend to be focused on relationships with managers and colleagues, pay and grading, bullying and harassment, and discrimination issues. With regard to the content of grievance procedures, studies of organizational practice highlight five main issues.

- Organizations commonly emphasize the importance of using informal approaches to resolve employee complaints before the formal process is invoked (Suff 2010*a*). For example, in the retail sector the Arcadia Group encourages managers to resolve problems initially 'through open and honest discussion' (IRS 2006: 9).

- If the informal method fails, or where it is not encouraged, the first stage of the grievance procedure generally concerns the employee's statement of grievance. Employers have become more likely to insist on the submission of a written statement from an employee outlining his/her complaint.

- Grievance procedures generally make provision for a meeting to take place between the complainant and a relevant manager in order to discuss the issue, perhaps with the attendance of a representative from the human resources function in larger organizations.

- The right of an employee to appeal against the outcome of a grievance hearing is a feature of most grievance procedures. One level of appeal is the norm, generally to a more senior manager who has not been involved in the case. However, it is not uncommon for larger organizations to have more than one level of appeal. Typically, procedures specify a time limit within which the appeal must be lodged, perhaps five or seven working days from the notification of the outcome of the grievance hearing.

Box 13.3 Policy example
ACAS on disciplinary procedures

The key points of the ACAS Code of Practice on Disciplinary and Grievance Procedures as it applies to discipline include the need to:

- undertake an appropriate investigation to establish the facts of a case;
- notify the employee in writing if it is decided that there is a disciplinary case to answer;
- inform the employee in writing of the details of the disciplinary meeting, which should be convened without unreasonable delay, and of their right to be accompanied by a fellow worker or trade union representative;
- at the disciplinary meeting, allow the employee to set out their case, respond to any allegations, and have a reasonable opportunity to ask questions, present evidence, and call witnesses;
- after the meeting, decide whether or not disciplinary action is justified, and, if it is, impose an appropriate sanction;
- give the employee the opportunity to appeal against the decision, with the appeal to be considered ideally by a manager who has not previously been involved in the case.

Source: www.acas.org.uk/media/pdf/h/m/Acas_Code_of_Practice_1_on_disciplinary_and_grievance_procedures.pdf

- Some grievance procedures provide for external assistance where a dispute cannot be resolved internally to the complainant's satisfaction. Over 40 per cent of the grievance procedures examined in one survey made provision for the intervention of a third party, such as ACAS, to facilitate a resolution (Suff 2010*a*). There is also an increasing tendency for grievance procedures to make reference to mediation as a possible means of resolving conflict (see Section 13.4.3).

Box 13.4 contains relevant details of the ACAS code of practice as it applies to handling grievances.

Box 13.4 Policy example
ACAS on grievance procedures

The key points of the ACAS Code of Practice on Disciplinary and Grievance Procedures as it applies to grievances include:

- the need for an employee to inform a manager who is not the subject of their complaint in writing of their grievance, should it not be possible to resolve the issue informally;
- that a formal meeting should be convened as soon as possible to consider the grievance, at which the employee is entitled to be accompanied by a fellow worker or trade union representative;
- that during the meeting the employee should be allowed to explain their grievance and how they think it should be resolved;
- that following the meeting, management should decide whether any action is appropriate, and inform the employee of the outcome in writing;
- that the employee should be given the opportunity to appeal against the outcome if it is felt that the problem has not been resolved satisfactorily, with the appeal to be heard wherever possible by a manager not previously involved in the case.

Source: www.acas.org.uk/media/pdf/h/m/Acas_Code_of_Practice_1_on_disciplinary_and_grievance_procedures.pdf

A further aspect of both grievance and disciplinary procedures concerns the right of the worker to be accompanied by a companion at a hearing. The Employment Relations Act 1999 stipulates that workers have a right to be accompanied in a grievance or disciplinary meeting, including those concerned with hearing an appeal, by a fellow worker or a trade union representative. The grievance procedure operated by Zurich Financial Services states that companions are entitled to a reasonable amount of paid time off work to discuss the grievance with the complainant, to learn about and ensure that they are familiar with the issue, and to attend the grievance hearing (IDS 2005). While companions are permitted to help in presenting the worker's case, the law does not entitle them to answer questions on the worker's behalf. However, in practice the scope of the companion's contribution often extends more widely than that specified by law. Companions are allowed to answer questions on behalf of the worker in nearly half of all workplaces (Kersley et al. 2006).

 Summary and further reading

- Disciplinary procedures set out the arrangements for dealing with employees who are suspected of contravening organizational rules in some way. Grievance procedures are designed to offer a formal means of resolving the conflict that arises when an individual employee has a complaint regarding his/her treatment at work.

- The existence and use of appropriate procedures can help employers win employment tribunal cases. They can also contribute to more effective human resource management by helping to define managerial authority more clearly, for example, or communicating to employees a sense that they will be treated fairly and consistently—a potential source of organizational commitment.

- Grievance and disciplinary procedures tend to cover such matters as the arrangements for holding the meeting at which the grievance or the alleged offence will be discussed, the nature of the accompanying person's contribution, and the operation of the employee's right to appeal.

For further information and guidance on operating grievance and disciplinary procedures, see the ACAS guide (ACAS 2011). Good case studies and surveys of organizational practice regularly feature in the publications of Incomes Data Services (IDS) and Industrial Relations Services (IRS) (e.g. IDS 2009a; Suff 2010a, b). Edwards (2005) offers some important insights into how to understand the nature of rules and the relevance of discipline in organizations.

13.3 Handling grievances and disciplinary issues

In the previous section, we examined the nature of organizational rules, looked at the reasons why organizations use formal procedures for dealing with disciplinary issues and grievances, and considered the main elements of these procedures. According to the CIPD conflict management survey 2011, managers deal with an average of 16.5 formal disciplinary and 22.3 formal grievance cases per year. This represents a slight decrease in the average number of disciplinary cases, down from 18 in their last survey in 2007, but represents a large increase (up from 8) in the average number of grievances. The majority of both grievance and disciplinary cases are concluded without the employees concerned leaving the organization, but figures fluctuate widely between organizations, with an average of 85 per cent of cases resolved in-house (CIPD 2011a). While there has been no increase in the proportion of cases settled in-house, there has been an increase in the use of mediation practices (see Section 13.4.3), as well as better training for managers in handling difficult conversations, resulting in more matters being resolved internally (CIPD 2011a; Suff 2010a, b). See Box 13.5 for a learning activity concerning grievance and disciplinary issues.

Where procedures for dealing with disciplinary issues and grievances exist, managers have a greater propensity to invoke disciplinary sanctions, and employees are more likely to express a formal grievance, as they will feel more confident that their complaint will be given proper consideration (Earnshaw et al. 1998; Colvin 2003). Thus, an understanding of the issues concerning how grievances and disciplinary issues are handled in organizations, as well as their implications, is essential. We begin by examining the handling of grievances, with a specific focus on the complexities and challenges that exist when dealing with

Box 13.5 Learning activity
Grievances and discipline at work

This learning activity is designed to encourage you to reflect on what gives rise to grievances and disciplinary issues in work organizations. You may like to draw on your experience, or the experiences of people you know, at work in addressing the following two questions.

- What do you think are the main issues that cause grievances in workplaces?
- What do you think are the most common reasons for managers to invoke disciplinary proceedings against employees?

complaints of bullying and harassment. We then move on to look at the handling of discipline in organizations, with specific reference to three topical issues: use of the internet at work, conduct outside work, and poor performance. We finish with a critical assessment of the role of discipline, and of disciplinary procedures, in organizations.

13.3.1 Handling grievances

In recent years there has been a rise in the number of formal grievances being raised in organizations, linked to the increasing presence of procedures. The CIPD suggests that the impact of the recessionary economic climate has also produced a higher volume of complaints by employees over their treatment at work (CIPD 2011a). What, though, do employees complain about? According to survey evidence, the issues that most commonly give rise to grievances are breakdown in relationships between colleagues, or between employees and their line manager, and allegations of bullying or harassment (Suff 2010a).

There are two key features of how organizations deal with grievances: the importance of fairness and the preference for informality. Creating a perception of fairness is essential to the effective handling of grievances. A failure to address the legitimate concerns of staff can leave them feeling angry and may lead to more general unrest and disputes in the workplace. Employees need to know to whom they can turn in the event of a grievance, and the support, such as counselling, that is available to them. Not only do employees need to know how to air grievances, but line managers also need to be familiar with their organization's grievance procedure (CIPD 2011a).

Some employers have introduced 'fair treatment' at work policies in order to instil this concept of fairness, and to aid the quick resolution of grievances. For example, the amount of time spent investigating complaints, and the number of people off sick as a result, under an old time-consuming process has been dramatically reduced since Fife Council introduced its fair treatment policy and appointed two fair treatment advisors (CIPD 2007b).

Most organizations seek to resolve grievances informally; both ACAS (2011) and the CIPD (2011a) recommend taking an informal approach wherever possible. This enables issues and concerns to be raised and dealt with as soon as possible. While pressures for greater formality exist, studies of the experience of employees indicate that there is a tendency to try and resolve grievances informally first (e.g. Abbott 2007: 268). However, Abbott's research among workers who had left their employer as a result of a dispute suggests that both informal attempts to resolve problems and the formal machinery of the grievance procedure had been of little use in dealing with their complaints. Either the procedure was not followed, or managers had made up their minds not to uphold the complaint beforehand. While formal procedures for dealing with employee grievances may exist, this by no means implies that line managers will use them or that they will resolve workplace disputes to the mutual satisfaction of both parties. The limits of grievance procedures in this respect are particularly evident when it comes to dealing with harassment and bullying at work, which we will discuss in the next section. See Box 13.6 for a skills exercise concerning grievance handling.

Box 13.6 Skills exercise
Handling grievance cases

This skills exercise requires you to role play a grievance case. The case concerns Jenny, a long-standing employee with over ten years of service, who works as a clerical assistant in the accounts department of your organization. Jenny has raised a formal grievance, claiming that she has consistently been passed over for promotion to the higher-paid role of accounts officer, despite some of her less experienced colleagues, including Giles and Gary, having been promoted to this position soon after joining the organization. Jenny has been asked to attend a grievance hearing, which will also be attended by appropriate managers.

Working in small groups of four or five, you have 30 minutes to prepare for the grievance hearing role play. Two students should take on the role of Jenny and Nicky, her trade union representative. Separate from the others, you should prepare your grievance case and consider the arguments you want to put forward during the hearing. What points would you want to make? What arguments do you think the managers will put forward, and how will you respond to them? What do you want to get out of the hearing? And what are your options if the outcome is unsatisfactory?

The remaining members of the group should take on the roles of the managers who are due to hear Jenny's grievance claim. You should prepare for the hearing by considering the points that Jenny is likely to make in pursuit of her grievance. How will you respond to them? And what outcome of the hearing do you envisage?

There are ten minutes available for the mock grievance hearing itself, which should commence with the management team welcoming Jenny and Nicky, and asking Jenny to outline her complaint. Following the conclusion of the hearing, you have a further ten minutes as a group to review the overall exercise. What was the outcome of the result? What were the key factors that influenced this result? What lessons are there for effective grievance handling?

13.3.2 Dealing with harassment and bullying at work

Allegations of harassment and bullying constitute a major proportion of the grievances raised by employees in organizations. Although these issues are dealt with at greater length in Chapter 11, we do need to explain what they are here. Harassment can be defined as 'unwanted conduct ... which has the purpose or affect of violating their dignity'. The key is that the actions or comments are viewed as demeaning and unacceptable to the recipient. Bullying is 'offensive, intimidating, malicious or insulting behaviour, an abuse or misuse of power through means intended to undermine, humiliate, denigrate or injure the recipient' (ACAS 2010a: 1). The 2010 Equality Act means that employees are now protected from harassment because of a protected characteristic such as sex or race; although bullying does not have a legal basis, harassment and bullying are closely linked.

Studies continue to demonstrate that harassment and bullying at work are problems that lead to the grievance procedure being invoked (Godwin 2008; CIPD 2011a). Public sector employees are particularly likely to have experienced bullying and harassment; black or disabled employees and women are the most likely victims. One of the main challenges for managers when dealing with such issues is knowing where the line should be drawn between good-natured banter in the workplace and the kind of teasing that could be perceived as, or develop into, bullying behaviour. Ban all teasing, and you take all the fun from the workplace; ignore it, and you risk triggering a formal grievance and a potential employment tribunal claim.

There are good reasons why organizations should take complaints about bullying and harassment seriously. In the UK, managers may be personally liable for harassment where through their actions, or inaction, they allow it to occur to the detriment of an employee. In one case, the Court of Appeal upheld the decision of an employment tribunal that the senior manager of a hair salon was responsible for injuring the feelings of one of her members of staff, having, with other managers under her control, 'consciously fostered and encouraged a discriminatory culture to grow up'. Since 2008, employers who knowingly fail to protect an employee

281

from repeated sexual harassment by third parties, such as clients or customers, may be liable to legal proceedings, and the 2010 Equality Act now makes harassment of 'protected' groups of employees a discriminatory offence.

What use are grievance procedures in dealing with complaints about bullying and harassment at work? Commonly, employees do not take their grievances to their line manager at all. According to Rayner and McIvor (2006), they observe how their manager deals with problems before deciding whether or not to make a complaint themselves. What is the point of complaining if the organization has a track record of not dealing with grievances effectively, or enjoys a reputation for vigorously and successfully defending itself in legal cases?

In their study into workplace bullying and harassment, Rayner and McIvor (2006: 4) found a number of reasons why employees were reluctant to complain. Some thought that there was no point in making or supporting a complaint because nothing would happen as a result. Others stayed silent because they feared retribution. According to one employee, it was 'part of the process of keeping one's nose clean with the boss, otherwise how is one going to get a pay rise or promotion?' People were also reluctant to come forward because they thought that not doing so would protect the organization and thus maintain their job security.

The need to provide evidence of bullying and harassment in order to substantiate a grievance can also be extremely off-putting to complainants. The process of resolving a dispute can be very lengthy; in one case an employee endured seven months of bullying before sufficient evidence to substantiate a complaint could be gathered. It can be one person's word against another's, making it difficult to establish the facts (Rayner and McIvor 2006). For all of these reasons, then, the effectiveness of grievance procedures, and other formal mechanisms for dealing with allegations of bullying and harassment, is frequently limited in practice (Rayner and Lewis 2011). With regard to grievances in general, it would seem that in organizations where unions are not present managers make little effort to resolve them either informally or formally, indicating that grievance procedures often lack teeth and are not effective arrangements for resolving complaints (Abbott 2007).

13.3.3 Handling discipline

According to a prominent survey of employers, the three most common issues that result in disciplinary action are misconduct (90 per cent of respondents), poor timekeeping (73 per cent) and poor performance/capability (87 per cent) (Suff 2010b). In theory, the purpose of a progressive approach to discipline should be to rehabilitate errant employees, using the disciplinary procedure to correct their behaviour, or to improve the performance of employees as opposed to punishing them. Employers are encouraged to use disciplinary arrangements as a means of helping employees to solve their problems; in this way they can contribute more effectively to organizational goals (Christie and Kleiner 2000). In cases of minor misconduct, such as a relatively small amount of poor timekeeping, line managers may prefer to have an informal chat with the employee concerned rather than institute formal disciplinary proceedings. Hillingdon Primary Care Trust encourages a positive approach to discipline, with an emphasis on securing improvements in employees' behaviour through informal resolution methods referred to as 'management counselling' rather than on punishing them. The aim 'is to ensure a fair and effective method of dealing with alleged breaches of standards and professional codes of conduct and should not been seen as a punitive procedure' (IRS 2005).

One of the main principles underlying the effective handling of disciplinary issues in organizations concerns the importance of consistency. Employees generally expect consistent and predictable responses when a rule is violated. This can be achieved by making clear the standards of acceptable performance and conduct required in a job (Falcone 1997). Managers are also encouraged to take into account the circumstances and track record of the individual employee, as well as the nature of the alleged offence, when contemplating disciplinary action or sanctions (Christie and Kleiner 2000). Thus one of the greatest challenges of discipline for line managers concerns the need to balance consistency with the need for appropriate flexibility when dealing with different individuals.

As will already be evident, much of the work involving the handling of grievances and disciplinary proceedings in organizations is undertaken by an employee's immediate line manager.

Box 13.7 Online video link
Handling discipline—Empire HR

You can find information about how to handle disciplinary issues effectively from the website of human resources consultancy Empire HR. A link is provided in the Online Resource Centre.

Line managers seem to be taking on more responsibility for looking after grievance and disciplinary issues (Jones and Saundry 2011). Many large organizations provide training to help line managers in dealing with discipline and grievance handling (CIPD 2011*a*); they often provide training on employment law as well. Line managers tend to know how to operate procedures, but often lack the skills to implement them effectively. Relatively few organizations provide training on the softer skills required to resolve workplace disputes, such as mediation, although more now seem to be doing so (CIPD 2011*a*). Coaching techniques to help managers deal with grievance and disciplinary matters have been developed in some organizations (IRS 2006). Organizations including MFI, the Body Shop, and Cambridgeshire County Council provide training for employee representatives as well as managers. Parceline runs a training session that covers both the legal aspects relating to grievance and disciplinary issues and methods of coping with a wide range of sensitive and complex situations, which is offered to managers, supervisors, and trade union officials alike (Falconer 2004). See Box 13.7 for guidance on handling discipline.

What role do human resources practitioners play in handling grievances and disciplinary issues? Although their specific function will vary from organization to organization, their main concern is with formulating and revising procedures, providing advice and guidance to managers, ensuring fairness and consistency across the organization, and in some cases actually carrying out disciplinary and grievance hearings and imposing sanctions themselves. Often employees expect HR practitioners to act as impartial arbitrators or mediators. There is even some evidence that HR specialists see their role in this way (Rayner and McIvor 2006). Yet their job is primarily to protect and advance the business interests of the organizations for which they work—priorities that may clash with the desirability of seeing that the employee is given adequate justice. For example, an HR manager may choose to support the dismissal of an employee without following the appropriate procedures, weighing up the advantages of getting rid of a perceived troublemaker over the likely costs of a potential tribunal claim. See Box 13.8 for details of some research findings on the relationship between line managers and HR practitioners when it comes to handling discipline. Increasingly, HR practitioners are not only being trained and used as expert mediators to resolve issues on behalf of the business, but are also playing a key role in drawing up so-called 'compromise agreements'. The CIPD (2011*a*) reports that there has been a notable increase in the use of these agreements. They are generally made on termination of someone's employment, with the employer making a payment to an employee in return for the latter agreeing not to pursue legal action arising out of their claim.

13.3.4 Discipline in practice

One way of illustrating the sensitivities and complexities associated with handling discipline in practice is to focus on specific topics. Dealing with unsatisfactory employee performance and misbehaviour outside work are enduring challenges for managers. We begin by examining an increasingly important area of workplace behaviour—that concerning the misuse by employees of internet facilities, including social media sites.

Use of the internet and social media has grown substantially, and the use of new web-based technologies for work-related activities has been a major part of this. One survey reported that around 60 per cent of employees make use of the internet at work, spending an average of seven hours per week online (Dutton, Helsper, and Gerber 2009). Another survey found discovered more extensive use, with 85 per cent of staff being able to access the internet, and 13 per cent able to access to social media sites such as Twitter and Facebook from work (Work Foundation 2009). Therefore the use of organizational internet and email facilities for personal reasons

Managing discipline—HR practitioners and operational managers

Drawing on research in seven case study organizations, Jones and Saundry (2011) investigated the relationship between human resource practitioners and operational managers when it comes to the application of workplace discipline. Operational managers, such as line managers, generally had responsibility for handling disciplinary issues among their staff, although there was some reluctance to get involved in such matters. When they did so, operational managers generally preferred taking a flexible pragmatic approach to tackling disciplinary issues, based on their own sense of fairness and their knowledge of the employee's individual circumstances. However, aware of the possible threat of litigation should disciplinary issues be mishandled, operational managers were sometimes keen for HR practitioners to become more involved. The latter preferred to adopt a more advisory role, acting as 'technical and legal experts' who are mainly concerned with ensuring 'consistency and the robust application of procedure' (Jones and Saundry 2011: 7), especially given their awareness that they would be accountable for any breaches of procedure. Thus 'there is a clear tension between the preference of operational managers for a pragmatic and informal approach to workplace discipline and an ethos of compliance and consistency which underpins HR practice' (Jones and Saundry 2011: 9). One outcome is that operational managers have become more dependent upon HR practitioners, despite viewing them as being wedded to following procedures and thus too risk averse. Moreover, the role of HR practitioners in organizations is increasingly concerned with 'regulating operational managers' (Jones and Saundry 2011: 7).

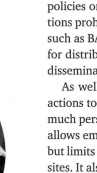

is now commonplace. But what limits should be placed on the personal use of organizational email and internet facilities? How much personal access is legitimate? Many employers have policies defining what is acceptable and unacceptable practice with regard to email and internet use at work; advisory bodies such as the CIPD and ACAS recommend that employers have clear policies on the use of the internet at work. One survey reported that two-thirds of organizations prohibit access to social media sites at work (Charlton 2010*b*). Workers in organizations such as BAE Systems and Swansea College have been disciplined, and even dismissed, either for distributing emails containing sexist and racist material at work or for downloading and disseminating pornographic and other derogatory material (Fuller 2006*a, b*).

As well as establishing rules governing the acceptability of content, and specifying the actions to be taken against those who breach them, organizations also need to consider how much personal IT use is permissible, and when it can occur. For example, BT has a policy that allows employees to use the internet, including social networking sites, during working time, but limits this to 'acceptable use'—for example, blocking access to gambling and pornographic sites. It also conducted some company research into the use of the internet at work and found that, in fact, usage by employees was rather low (Broughton et al. 2011).

Personal web-logs, or 'blogs', and the content of social media pages can also attract the disciplinary attention of employers, particularly when they make potentially disparaging comments about the organization that could arguably undermine its reputation. In many cases, policies on internet use are being extended to cover blogging by staff, setting clear parameters of what is acceptable and classing any breach of the rules as misconduct under the disciplinary procedure (Henders-Green 2007). But how far should this go? Charlton (2010*b*) cites the case of science teacher Kirsty Cook-Bell who was suspended from her job as a teacher because her seemingly harmless holiday photos posted on her Facebook page could be seen by her pupils. This incident illustrates the potential impact that social media are making on the workplace and the challenges employers face in dealing with the ramifications. Virgin Atlantic went one stage further and dismissed 13 staff for bringing the company into disrepute after they had participated in a discussion on Facebook in which passengers were described as 'chavs' and allegations were made that the trains were full of cockroaches (Quinn 2008).

However, employers need to be careful when instigating disciplinary action as a result of the blogging activity of their staff. In 2006, Catherine Sanderson, a British-born secretary working in Paris, won a case for unfair dismissal in France against her employer, the accountants Dixon Wilson, who had sacked her for keeping a personal blog on which she had posted several disparaging comments about her employer (Fox 2006).

This raises the question of the extent to which employers can use rules and discipline to shape or punish behaviour that occurs outside work. Attempts to do so can be rather controversial. In 2007, for example, the Royal Bank of Scotland proposed that staff who did not open one of its accounts, and have their salary paid into it, could face disciplinary action. While the bank claimed that this was common industry practice, the Amicus trade union pointed out that the supermarket chain Tesco does not threaten to discipline its employees for shopping at Sainsbury's (Fuller 2007). In some cases the decision to institute disciplinary action is relatively straightforward. Where an employee whose job involves driving duties is convicted of drink-driving, and thus banned from driving, then the misconduct clearly has obvious adverse consequences for the organization, although a manager might want to consider if there is scope for redeployment. However, it is a much more difficult challenge when an employee has only been accused of a crime. Just because an individual is under investigation by the police, or has been charged with an offence, this is not necessarily grounds for suspension or dismissal. Employers are advised to conduct their own investigation and invoke disciplinary proceedings if appropriate.

Dealing with employees who are perceived to be underperforming is an enduring feature of human resource management in practice. As we have already established, separate capability procedures are sometimes used by organizations to deal with performance issues. However, their effectiveness is open to question. A review of schoolteachers' capability procedures found that their use was generally not associated with satisfactory improvements in performance and even had some adverse consequences, including greater sickness absence. Head teachers were reluctant to tackle performance problems among their staff. Some used alternative strategies, including initiating early retirement or ill-health severance, as a way of dealing with the problem; when they did have to invoke the procedure, they wished they had done so sooner, since it typically took 18 months to complete (Earnshaw et al. 2004). Alternatively, matters relating to capability are often handled on an informal basis, with managers using training interventions, targets, and support mechanisms to induce performance improvements. Only if these fail are managers encouraged to institute more formal disciplinary proceedings (CIPD 2007a). However, survey evidence demonstrates that conventional disciplinary arrangements are still widely used to deal with staff who are perceived to be underperforming (Bentley 2006).

13.3.5 Discipline at work: critical perspectives

We have already suggested that grievance procedures may be of limited effectiveness in resolving workplace disputes satisfactorily. A number of factors inhibit the effective use of disciplinary procedures in resolving disputes at work. For one thing, managers can sometimes be reluctant to take disciplinary action against employees. We have already highlighted the reluctance of head teachers to invoke formal capability procedures in schools. Rayner and McIvor (2006) found that certain 'creative' employees, who were highly valued by the organization, appeared to be protected from formal sanctions altogether. Managers often interpret disciplinary procedures in a 'flexible' manner. Where they have some sympathy with the individual employee concerned, or knowledge of someone's personal affairs, managers may choose to have a private informal conversation and thus resolve the issue without instituting formal proceedings (Earnshaw, Marchington, and Goodman 2000). However, this can give rise to inconsistencies if someone else charged with a similar offence is treated less leniently, something that employees who have been disciplined may realize—and resent (Rollinson et al. 1997).

A second potential problem that inhibits the effectiveness of disciplinary procedures relates to the frequent failure of managers to follow their own procedures. Employers often simply ignore workers' requests to resolve the issue and use their power simply to dismiss people without warning (Abbott 2007). Studies of how disciplinary procedures are used in practice indicate that either the procedure is not used at all or, when it is, there are numerous procedural irregularities, not least a reluctance to allow employees an opportunity to tell their side of the story in advance of the decision to dismiss (Earnshaw et al. 1998). Employees who have been taken through a disciplinary procedure report a strong sense that managers had assumed their guilt

even before the hearing had commenced, and paid little attention to anything said in mitigation (Rollinson et al. 1997).

A third problem undermining the effectiveness of disciplinary procedures as an HRM intervention concerns the tendency for managers to use a punitive approach to workplace discipline. The principal characteristic of the punitive approach is an emphasis on getting workers to obey the rules for fear of the punishment, such as dismissal, that would result from any failure to comply. In theory, discipline, when used in a 'corrective' manner as a means of improving employee performance or correcting employee behaviour, can have obvious organizational benefits. The 'consensus' approach holds that there has been a shift over time from a generally punitive style of discipline towards a more corrective style evident in contemporary organizational practice (Henry 1982).

However, there is strong evidence for the persistence of a punitive approach to discipline in contemporary organizations. Capability procedures, for example, may be applied in a way that punishes staff who appear to be underperforming (Earnshaw et al. 2004). Managers are sometimes too hasty when it comes to instigating disciplinary proceedings. See, for example, the 2004 case of the brain surgeon who was suspended from work for allegedly not paying for a second portion of soup in the staff canteen (Carvel 2004). The study by Rollinson et al. (1997: 298) of workers who had experienced being disciplined found that, for many of them, 'the process was not seen as a persuasive one designed to get them to observe rules, but as an event which gave the manager an opportunity to take retribution, or administer a deterrent to limit future transgressions'. A study of disciplinary processes in nursing shows that, while the overall approach was one of correction, managers frequently took punitive measures, such as in the case of drug errors, and demotion was a common punishment (Cooke 2006). Therefore it is mistaken to assume that a punitive approach to discipline has been superseded by a corrective one.

 ## Summary and further reading

- The most frequent reasons for grievances by employees are their relationship with their manager or colleagues, bullying and harassment, and pay and grading issues. Disciplinary matters tend to fall into the two areas of conduct and capability, with attendance, timekeeping, and performance matters arising most frequently as disciplinary issues.

- The effective handling of grievances and discipline in organizations involves ensuring fairness and consistency in the treatment of employees. However, because of the need for managerial flexibility, efforts to resolve workplace disputes are often marked by inconsistent and arbitrary management approaches, undermining the potential contribution of procedures to enhance organizational effectiveness.

- In theory, the use of a corrective approach to dealing with allegations of employee misconduct or perceived poor performance, focusing on stimulating improvements in employee performance and conduct, is the most effective way of managing discipline at work. In practice, however, a punitive approach characterizes this area of human resource management, symbolizing the exercise of managerial power.

For further information and guidance on operating grievance and disciplinary procedures, see the ACAS guide (ACAS 2011). Good case studies and surveys of organizational practice regularly feature in the publications of Incomes Data Services and XpertHR. The CIPD produces a number of relevant fact sheets and guidance notes on topics including discipline, grievance, and performance management.

13.4 Resolving workplace disputes

The purpose of this section is to examine what happens when disputes arise out of unsettled grievances, or as the result of the application of disciplinary sanctions. While the system of employment tribunals is designed to handle claims for redress from aggrieved workers, a strong emphasis is often placed on trying to settle disputes without recourse to litigation. This is where the intervention of agencies like ACAS, whose role is concerned with resolving workplace conflict, is important—something that encompasses promoting mediation services.

13.4.1 The system of employment tribunals

What happens when conflicts at work cannot be resolved internally? What do workers do if they consider that they have been disciplined or dismissed without good reason, or that their grievance has not been handled to their satisfaction? The purpose of this section is to examine the external mechanisms that aim to resolve workplace disputes and give workers redress. Many countries operate specialist arms of the legal apparatus to handle disputes between workers and their employers, or dedicated sections of the civil court system to deal with labour issues. In Germany, for example, there is a system of labour courts. France operates a system of 'industrial tribunals' which typically adjudicate claims over matters such as unjustified dismissal, non-payment of wages, and allegations of discrimination. In the UK, employment tribunals, independent judicial bodies which comprise a legally qualified chair and two lay representatives, adjudicate claims brought by workers against their current or former employers.

The tribunal system has developed since the 1960s; tribunals were originally conceived as relatively informal forums within which employers and employees could resolve disputes cheaply and quickly without the formalities associated with traditional courts of law. They deal with a large and expanding number of jurisdictions, including complaints about sex, race, and disability discrimination, disputes over alleged failures to pay the National Minimum Wage, and, most commonly, unfair dismissal claims. Partly because of the increasing number of jurisdictions over which they can adjudicate, during the 1990s and 2000s the number of claims submitted to tribunals rose substantially (Pollert 2007). In 1980, there were 41,000 tribunal claims; by 2000–2001 the number had risen to over 100,000, and by 2009–2010 to nearly 240,000. Redress is generally in the form of compensation; it is extremely rare for workers judged to have been unfairly dismissed to get their jobs back.

Many employers are troubled by what they see as the increasingly burdensome nature of the tribunal system. It is said to impose substantial costs on businesses, not just in potentially having to engage lawyers, but also in the amount of management time and resources expended in responding to, and contesting claims from, former or current employees. Often employers prefer to reach a financial settlement before a claim reaches a tribunal hearing in order to prevent costs from escalating; although an alternative interpretation of such behaviour is that it signals the weakness of the employer's case. There is also some evidence that tribunals may not sufficiently take into account the circumstances of small firms, and the more informal flexible approaches they take to managing staff (Earnshaw, Marchington, and Goodman 2000).

Successive governments have been sympathetic to complaints from employers and pro-business lobbyists that the growth in the number of claims to tribunals is the product of a 'compensation culture' in which employees are increasingly prone to make spurious claims against their employer in the hope of gaining some generally undeserved financial recompense. A number of measures designed to reduce the supposed crisis of the tribunal system and the burdens it imposed on businesses have been enacted as a result. During the 2000s efforts were made to weed out supposedly weak claims, disposing of supposedly 'misconceived' cases before a tribunal hearing is convened (Colling 2004, 2010). There has also been an emphasis on reducing the number of tribunal claims arising in the first place through the provision of incentives to encourage greater internal resolution of claims. Amidst business concerns that employees now have too many rights at work, something which is said to discourage hiring new staff and to be an impediment to job growth, since 2010 the coalition government has accelerated efforts to reform the system of employment tribunals with the aim of ensuring that businesses feel more confident about hiring staff, and putting an increased emphasis on resolving disputes within the workplace, and at an earlier stage, thus reducing the burden on employment tribunals (BIS 2011b; Tailby et al. 2011). See Box 13.9 for details of the government's measures.

However, such policy objectives rest on some questionable assumptions, not least that the rise in the number of tribunal claims is linked to the growth of a compensation culture in which workers are increasingly keen to pursue unwarranted claims against employers for financial redress. Much of the increase in the number of tribunal claims has come about because of a growth in the coverage of individual legal employment rights, particularly with respect to equality and discrimination issues, where the law tends to be rather complex. Those relating to equal pay, in particular, are often submitted on a multiple basis, further increasing the number of

Box 13.9 Window on work
Tribunal reform

The UK coalition government has been particularly keen to respond to business concerns that having to respond to employment tribunal claims has become too burdensome for employers. Two specific policy changes are especially noteworthy. First, in April 2012 the government raised the qualifying period for unfair dismissal, so that instead of workers being able to submit a claim after one year in a job, they now have to wait for two years. Secondly, the government also plans to introduce a system of fees under which workers may have to pay up to £1500 for taking a claim to an employment tribunal hearing, refundable only if they are successful. It is anticipated that such measures will reduce the number of employment tribunal claims, reducing the burden on business, and, because employers will be less anxious about hiring new employees, help to stimulate job growth (BIS 2011c). However, critics question their likely effectiveness. The measures may have unintended consequences; dismissed workers who are not eligible to claim unfair dismissal may look to make a claim on the grounds of discrimination, for which there is no qualifying period. Legal protections for workers are already weak, especially compared with other countries; further restricting the ability of aggrieved workers to gain redress for workplace problems may shift the balance of power in the employment relationship too far in favour of employers. The likely result is the development of a 'hire and fire' culture in workplaces, encouraging bad employers who exploit their staff rather than making the effort to secure their commitment and engagement.

registered claims (Dix, Sisson, and Forth 2009). Moreover, the expansion of the private services sector, where the management of employment relations is often undertaken in an arbitrary manner and where unions are weak, may also have helped to encourage a greater number of tribunal claims (Dickens 2000). For example, in the largely non-union hotel industry the unilateral exercise of managerial prerogative is the cause of numerous complaints to tribunals from employees who feel that they have been treated harshly (Head and Lucas 2004). The rise in tribunal claims reflects a climate of growing discontent at work, with workplace conflict on the increase, rather than the somewhat nebulous notion of a compensation culture—see Section 13.2.2 (Tailby et al. 2011).

This relates to another area of criticism, which is the assertion that employees have too many rights relative to employers. Evidently, growing numbers of often complex claims have led to delays in hearing cases (Colling 2010). Given the magnitude of workplace conflict, though, perhaps the most surprising thing is not that there are too many tribunal claims, but so few. Unorganized workers, those who do not enjoy union representation, face particular problems in trying to bring claims to tribunals. For one thing, the high cost of legal representation is a disincentive. Moreover, such workers may lack awareness of their employment rights or be insufficiently confident about asserting them (TUC 2008; Pollert 2009). Changes to the tribunal system, supposedly designed to reduce the burden on tribunals, may reduce still further the ability of many workers to assert their statutory rights. Only around a sixth of tribunal claims get as far as a hearing anyway, with most being either withdrawn or settled beforehand (Tailby et al. 2011).

The main problem with the system of employment tribunals is not that it is too burdensome for employers, but that it does not deliver effective justice to workers who have grievances at work or are treated in a harsh and arbitrary manner by their employers. Workers are rarely in a position to assert their legal employment rights effectively, and their chances of success are low even if they do embark on litigation (Colling 2010). Policies which place a greater emphasis on resolving disputes internally, within the workplace, potentially restrict workers' access to justice (Colling 2004; Pollert 2007), as do increases in the qualifying period for being able to claim unfair dismissal and fee arrangements. While workers who are trade union members can call upon their union for advice and guidance, for the majority of (non-union) workers alternative sources of support are scarce with voluntary and community legal services often highly stretched and significantly resource constrained (Tailby et al. 2011). The DVD interview with Sarah Veale of the TUC highlights some of the obstacles facing workers who want to assert their legal rights. There have been calls for more effective methods of ensuring that employers comply with employment legislation to be instituted. This could encompass a proactive system of labour inspection, instead of the current arrangements which depend upon workers themselves registering complaints with an employment tribunal (Citizens' Advice 2011).

13.4.2 The role of ACAS

Where can workers and employers get advice, and any help needed to resolve disputes satisfactorily? Employers needing external advice can use their employers' association, if they are a member, or perhaps specialist lawyers. Workers in trade unions can call upon their union for support. Given that legal representation is often too expensive, non-unionized workers may have to rely on voluntary sector bodies and community organizations for help. In the USA, for example, grassroots workers' centres offer advice and support to working people in local communities (Fine 2006). There are also legal advocacy organizations which represent workers in litigation against employers (Jolls 2005). In the UK, the network of local Citizens' Advice Bureaux provides working people in dispute with their employer with advice, and in some cases representation at a tribunal hearing (Abbott 2007). However, the resources of voluntary sector bodies and community organizations are often stretched, limiting the amount of support they are able to offer. Funding cuts, arising out of the austerity measures put in place by the government to tackle the budget deficit, have exacerbated the situation (Tailby et al. 2011).

In many countries the state operates machinery for helping to settle workplace disputes. In the UK, for example, ACAS undertakes a range of HRM functions, including helping to resolve workplace disputes. Traditionally, the role of ACAS was dominated by the task of resolving collective disputes between unions and employers (see Chapter 12) by offering conciliation, helping the parties to reach their own agreement, or providing access to arbitration, where a settlement is proposed by an independent expert after weighing up the evidence supplied by the parties and taking into account any other relevant factors. While this remains an important area of activity for ACAS, a large part of its role is now concerned with attempting to settle individual disputes—those arising between an individual worker and their current or former employer (Sisson and Taylor 2006). In particular, once a worker has submitted an employment tribunal claim, ACAS is obliged to offer conciliation in an effort to reach a resolution before the dispute reaches a tribunal hearing. ACAS conciliation helps to filter out cases by highlighting their weaknesses, communicating an offer from an employer to settle, and clarifying expectations by indicating how similar cases have fared. In aiming to resolve a dispute before it gets as far as a tribunal hearing, ACAS conciliation is concerned with producing a compromise agreement. However, the work of ACAS in this area has raised the concern that search for compromise may have the effect of preventing workers from exercising their rights (Dickens 2000).

Since 2009, ACAS has also offered a voluntary pre-claim conciliation service, providing parties with the opportunity to resolve a dispute without resorting to a tribunal claim. This is part of an increasing emphasis on avoiding litigation as a means of settling workplace disputes, something which includes the promotion of mediation as an additional form of alternative dispute resolution in addition to arbitration and conciliation (see Section 13.4.3). ACAS is an important source of advice and guidance for workers and employers. For example, it operates a telephone helpline service which had some 950,000 users in 2010–2011. ACAS also publishes advisory handbooks and codes of practice designed to help managers, unions, and workers deal with workplace issues, including grievance and discipline handling.

While much of the work of ACAS is devoted to resolving workplace disputes, it has become increasingly concerned with helping employers, employees, and unions improve working relationships. The principal aim is to prevent disputes from arising in the first place (Dix and Oxenbridge 2004). ACAS interventions are also dedicated to improving workforce effectiveness. It demonstrates how promoting 'good' relations at work can help to enhance business performance; for example, carefully designed attendance management policies can reduce absence levels (ACAS 2010c). ACAS has also encouraged the greater use of mediation arrangements to resolve workplace disputes.

13.4.3 Mediation

Mediation is becoming an increasingly popular mechanism for resolving workplace conflicts. Like conciliation and arbitration, it is viewed as a form of alternative dispute resolution (ADR),

in the sense of being a non-legalistic route to settling disputes. Mediation involves a non-judgemental approach whereby an 'impartial third party, the mediator, helps two or more people in dispute to attempt to reach an agreement. Any agreement comes from those in dispute, not from the mediator' (CIPD/ACAS 2008: 8). Mediation differs from other forms of ADR in one major respect; whereas with arbitration and conciliation the main concern is on resolving disputes that arise from people's behaviour in the past, with mediation there is a greater emphasis on trying to influence future behaviour by tackling potential sources of conflict (Ridley-Duff and Bennett 2011).

Mediation embodies a number of key principles, namely flexibility, informality, confidentiality, and that it is entered into on a voluntary basis (see Latreille 2011). The flexible nature of mediation means that it is adaptable and can be modified as the circumstances dictate. Informality is also an advantage, because it means that problems can be tackled in an appropriate matter, on their own terms, rather than according to some predetermined format. However, it is the confidential and voluntary nature of mediation that is considered critical to its effectiveness. Participants should feel able to contribute fully, without having to be suspicious about how their interventions are used or interpreted. Moreover, mediation will not work if the parties to a dispute are compelled to participate.

Mediation is used to resolve workplace disputes in a number of countries, including the USA where there has been increasing interest in the use of ADR in general (Lipsky, Seeber, and Fincher 2003). For example, the REDRESS programme operated by the US Postal Service has generated a lot of attention. Moreover, during the 2000s greater use of mediation came to be advocated by policy-makers (e.g. DTI 2007). Why, then, has mediation become more popular? It is thought that mediation can help to resolve conflict at an early stage, before its effects become too damaging. It is particularly 'effective when used at the initial phase of any disagreement, before conflict escalates in the workplace. An early intervention can prevent both sides from becoming entrenched and the difference turning into a full-blown dispute' (CIPD/ACAS 2008: 3). Linked to this, the government has been keen to promote mediation as part of its broader approach to resolving workplace disputes, which entails easing the burden on employers by reducing the number of potentially costly claims heard by employment tribunals (BIS 2011b; Latreille 2011; Suff 2011d).

While the incidence of mediation remains relatively uncommon, it is becoming increasingly used by employers (CIPD 2008c; Latreille 2011). For example, in 2009 the retail company Arcadia Group developed a pilot mediation scheme in its TopShop and TopMan stores, before deciding to extend it to all its businesses during 2011 (CIPD 2011a). Mediation has a number of advantages for employers wishing to improve the efficiency and effectiveness of their dispute resolution machinery. The business benefits of mediation include improved working relationships and avoiding the costs associated with taking workplace conflict through formal procedures, particularly if they get as far as a tribunal claim (IDS 2009a; CIPD 2011a). There are some issues that are viewed as particularly suitable for mediation, such as grievances, especially those arising from working relationships between employees or between employees and managers (CIPD 2008c; IDS 2009a). However, disciplinary matters may be less appropriate for resolving by mediation, particularly when they involve relatively serious allegations of misconduct.

How does mediation operate in practice? Some organizations develop an in-house function. Julie Connah, of Derbyshire County Council, which has taken such an approach, calls mediation 'quick, future-focused and positive' and 'a very productive approach to conflict resolution' (Suff 2011d). Organizations which do operate in-house mediation arrangements, such as Arcadia Group and East Lancashire Primary Care Trust, invest in the training of appropriate staff, including HR practitioners and union representatives, in mediation skills (CIPD 2011a; Saundry, McArdle, and Thomas 2011). Alternatively, mediation can be outsourced to a specialist external provider (see Box 13.10). Typically, a single mediation event will take place over a single day, with the mediator hosting separate sessions with the respective parties to the dispute in the morning, before convening a joint meeting with all the parties in the afternoon (Latreille 2011). Generally, the mediator takes the role of a facilitator, prompting 'a constructive discussion of the issues so that the parties can themselves find a mutually acceptable resolution' (IDS 2009a: 26). Maintaining impartiality and being non-judgemental are key features of the mediator's role, if mediation is to function effectively (Latreille 2011).

Box 13.10 Online video link
TCM mediation

Established in 2001, the TCM Group is a leading specialist provider of workplace mediation services. Go to the Online Resource Centre for a link to video content where David Liddle of the TCM Group explains how mediation was undertaken in the National Health Service. You can find out more about the work of the TCM Group from its website (www.thetcmgroup.com/).

Some clear benefits of mediation have been identified. Although convening mediation events can be costly, they may in fact end up by being cost-effective by obviating the need for formal procedures. For example, the pilot mediation scheme operated by Arcadia Group not only saw a substantial reduction in the number of cases being taken through the formal grievance procedure, but also a diminution in the number of grievances being raised in the first place (CIPD 2011a). This highlights the positive contribution that mediation can make, not just to the organizational bottom line, but also to the workplace climate, by improving employee morale and building good working relationships (Suff 2011d). In the case of East Lancashire Primary Care Trust, the introduction of mediation helped to prompt, and also reflected, a shift from an adversarial 'grievance culture' to a more partnership-based approach marked by more cooperative relations with the trade union representatives (Saundry, McArdle, and Thomas 2011).

A number of challenges have to be overcome before mediation becomes a more commonplace arrangement for resolving workplace disputes. In particular, the suspicions of unions and managers have to be allayed. For example, managers may be concerned that mediation weakens their authority when it comes to workplace decision-making (IDS 2009a). There are also reservations about the costs of implementing and operating a mediation scheme. For this reason, advocates of mediation may need to demonstrate its value against a financial 'bottom line' (Latreille 2011: 63), highlighting any cost savings from its use. Unions may be concerned that mediation undermines the capacity of workers to secure access to justice, reducing the extent to which they can gain redress for problems experienced at work. The rationale for mediation is based on a unitary perspective (see Chapter 12), in which its business benefits are emphasized; workers may not benefit to the same degree, particularly where mediation arrangements are controlled by management. That said, the potentially transformative nature of mediation has been recognized, since it has the latent capacity to challenge established structures of managerial authority, ceding power to workers (Ridley-Duff and Bennett (2011).

Summary and further reading

- Legal arrangements exist for the purposes of settling workplace disputes and allowing aggrieved workers to pursue redress for their complaints. The system of employment tribunals in the UK has become increasingly controversial, as it handles an increasing number of claims from workers. Although the government and business groups assert that tribunals have become too much of a burden for employers, and that action is needed to reduce the number of claims, there is a concern that this would restrict workers' access to justice.

- Employers and workers can draw on a number of sources of advice and support when it comes to pursuing a dispute. ACAS is a particularly useful source of information when help with workplace issues or problems is required. Much of the activity of ACAS is concerned with helping to resolve workplace disputes, although there is a growing emphasis on encouraging interventions that prevent disputes from arising in the first place.

- Mediation is an alternative form of dispute resolution, designed to avoid litigation, which has become increasingly popular. Particularly appropriate for resolving conflict which arises from a breakdown of relationships, mediation can be a cost-effective way of tackling disputes and contribute to a less adversarial workplace climate.

See Colling (2010: 336–8) for the system of employment tribunals. You can find out more about ACAS and how the system of employment tribunals operates from the following websites:

www.acas.org.uk

www.justice.gov.uk/guidance/courts-and-tribunals/tribunals/employment/index.htm

With regard to the case for mediation, how it operates, and organizational practice, see ACAS/ CIPD (2008), CIPD (2008c), IDS (2009a), and Suff (2011d).

13.5 Conclusion

The principal contribution of this chapter has been to demonstrate the importance of grievances and disciplinary issues to HRM in contemporary organizations. Formal procedures are used for the purposes of handling grievances raised by employees, dealing with staff misconduct, and poor performance at work. The development of formal procedures for dealing with grievances and discipline has been stimulated by the need to accommodate workplace conflict, by changes in the legislative framework governing dispute resolution at work, and because they have organizational benefits by, for example, influencing employees' standards of behaviour or supporting managerial authority.

What about the view that, by promoting consistency, fairness, and transparency in managerial decision-making, the use of formal procedures for handling grievances and disciplinary issues can enhance employee commitment and contribute to organizational performance? A number of important factors act to inhibit the use of procedures in this way. If we take grievances, for example, how effective are relevant procedures at bringing problems out into the open, getting them discussed, and then resolved, to the mutual benefit of the organization and its staff? People can be reluctant to express a grievance, either because they perceive that it would not have any effect, or from a fear that it might prompt management hostility. The presence of formal procedures for handling discipline may have reduced, but not eradicated, arbitrary managerial action.

Moreover, the exercise of discipline in organizations is often characterized by a punitive approach, with the emphasis on punishing poor performance or misconduct, rather than on developing ways of helping the employee to improve, or correct, his/her behaviour. Dealing with grievances, performance problems, and employee misconduct is one of the most challenging and time-consuming aspects of managers' work. Organizations have been encouraged to deal with these matters in a more resolute and strategic way, based on the need to stimulate greater employee commitment and performance improvements. This includes using mediation arrangements to reduce levels of conflict. However, the management of grievances and disciplinary issues is marked by considerable complexities and challenges, implying the need for an approach that avoids over-simplistic prescriptions for change.

 Assignment and discussion questions

1 What are the main reasons why organizations use formal written procedures for dealing with grievances and disciplinary issues?

2 What are the main issues that managers need to take into account when handling disciplinary matters in organizations?

3 To what extent does the use of grievance and disciplinary procedures help to resolve workplace disputes in a way that gives justice to workers?

4 How far do you agree with the view that the rise in the number of employment tribunal cases is the effect of an increasingly litigious culture?

5 Assess the effectiveness of mediation as a mechanism for resolving workplace conflict.

 Online Resource Centre

Test your understanding of this chapter with online questions and answers, keep up to speed with changes to the law through regular updates, and use selected weblinks to quickly access useful resources and further information. Visit the Online Resource Centre at:
www.oxfordtextbooks.co.uk/orc/gilmore_williams2e/

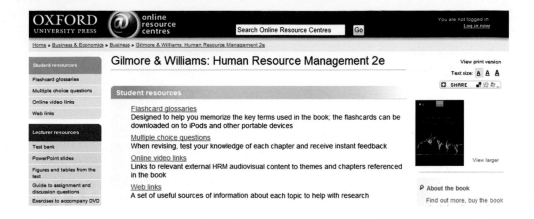

Case study
Dealing with staff problems in S&W Engineering

S&W Engineering is a medium-sized engineering firm that employs some 500 people making electronic components for the auto industry. Nine months ago, Gary was appointed to the position of manager in S&W Engineering's busy purchasing department. He had already worked for the company for five years and was delighted to be appointed to the position of manager. He has nine staff working for him directly: two administrators, three senior buyers, and seven buyers.

Following his Christmas vacation, Gary returned to work on 2 January. He remembers that, just before Christmas, Jan, one of his senior buyers, had come to see him to complain that Larry, one of the buyers, had not been pulling his weight and had made a number of errors that needed to be rectified. Gary already knew that Larry's performance was not as strong as that of the rest of the team. What made things worse was that another buyer, Pete, was off work sick following major surgery. He had been due to come back to work in early December, but had still not returned. Pete's absence had put added pressure on the whole buying team. Gary had tried to have a word with Larry about his performance before Christmas. Larry responded in quite an aggressive manner, complaining that, in Pete's absence, his workload was unmanageable, that he had never been given any proper training on the new computer system for handling purchasing, and that no one had mentioned that he was underperforming before. With Pete off sick and with no date set for his return, Gary realizes that he needs to address the matter of Larry's poor performance. The difficulty is that Larry is a long-serving and well-liked member of staff.

While Gary is pondering on how to deal with Larry, and also manage the department's workload in the continuing absence of Pete, Kim, one of his buyers, comes into his office. She wants to talk to him about the behaviour of one of the firm's sales managers, John, at the company's Christmas party held just ten days previously. Kim alleges that John had made some rather lewd and sexually explicit comments to her, which in retrospect she finds quite insulting. While she is willing to forget about the matter, given that John had clearly consumed far too much alcohol, Kim has been told informally that John has made inappropriate advances to one of the junior administrators who is too scared to take the matter further herself.

Gary agrees to look into the matter. Just after Kim leaves, though, Gill, one of his other buyers, telephones to report that she is unwell and will not be able to come to work that day. Gary remembers that, just before Christmas, the firm's human resources manager had sent him a note about Gill's attendance and punctuality record. In the last two months, she has been late for work on seven occasions; and in the last year, she has been absent for 12 days because of sickness. Gill's persistent tardiness and absence are putting additional pressure on the rest of the buying team. Yet she often stays quite late in the evening to catch up with any outstanding work. Gary knows Gill quite well, and is aware that she has three school-age children to look after. For these reasons, he has not yet spoken to Gill about her attendance and punctuality record. Along with Larry's underperformance, Pete's absence from work, and Kim's allegations concerning the sales manager's behaviour, it is something that will have to be dealt with if the purchasing department is to function effectively.

Questions

1 If you were Gary, how would you approach these issues in a way that gave you sufficient flexibility while also ensuring that the commitment of the staff to the organization was not compromised?

2 What actions would you take?

3 What further information would you require?

Ethics and human resource management

Richard Christy and Gill Christy

Learning objectives

The main objectives of this chapter are:

- to identify the major approaches to ethics in Western philosophy, distinguishing between deontological, consequentialist, and virtue-based approaches;
- to apply these approaches to the consideration of ethical behaviour by organizations;
- to analyse the human resource management aspects of organizational strategy, policy, and practice in ethical terms;
- to demonstrate in a structured way some particular ethical dilemmas or questions facing both generalist managers and HRM specialists.

14.1 Introduction

There is a growing interest in the way that organizations behave. Much of the recent commentary focuses on their allegedly bad behaviour—exploitative employment practices in a globalized labour market, major frauds and deceptions, or the environmental impact of their activities. There seems to be less interest in the positive achievements of businesses, such as providing affordable food or transporting people safely around the country. Very few of these outcomes are provided without the organized efforts of people whose very employment is also an important benefit both to them as individuals and to society at large. The management of people is at the heart of all organizational activity, and good or bad approaches to human resource management (HRM) are closely linked to the ethical behaviour of the organization as a whole.

The chapter is discursive rather than prescriptive in tone. We aim to present some basic frameworks and concepts that can help to structure thinking and debate, not to provide model or 'right' answers to HRM questions. It is also selective; all HRM questions should be the subject of structured 'ethical' thinking, and we can only hope to give a few examples within the scope of this text. The important thing is to be able to make choices and decisions that are ethically explicit and coherent, not to achieve some kind of uniformity of action or standardized behaviour.

In Section 14.2, we review the main approaches to ethics in Western philosophy, discussing their strengths and weaknesses as guides to 'good' action. We then consider how these approaches can be applied to the human activity of business, with particular reference to the notion of organizational purpose in determining ethical requirements. In Section 14.3, we turn to the special features of the employment relationship as an important starting point for considering the ethics of HRM. In Section 14.4, we examine the concept of whistle-blowing, and investigate the ethical questions and problems posed when engaging in two core HRM activities, employee reward and the management of equality and diversity issues. The concluding section highlights the role of HRM specialists with respect to organizational ethics and asks if they have a potential role as 'ethical stewards' or the 'conscience' of the organization.

14.2 The meaning of ethics

In Western philosophy and culture, we find a wide range of views of what makes good things good and bad things bad. The problem is not so much a shortage of theories as an abundance of contrasting explanations, most of which make some intuitive sense but often lead to contradictory conclusions. This becomes even more evident as the focus is extended to other cultural traditions—at a fundamental level, it is hardly surprising that there is general agreement about what types of behaviour are seen as very bad, but there are important differences in how these things are discussed and explained, and this become relevant when human resources are managed internationally.

Ethics and law are separate, but strongly interrelated. For example, the law can be used to reinforce behaviours that are thought to be ethically desirable, or to deter individuals from unethical acts. However, the law does not cover every situation in which ethical choices may arise. Furthermore, in some places and at some points in history, there have been laws that have upheld ethically unacceptable social arrangements and even obliged citizens and companies to behave in unethical ways. As De George (2010) describes, the experience of American multinational companies in apartheid South Africa (where racial segregation was legally enforced) led to the drawing-up of principles regarding the treatment of employees which were in direct conflict with the apartheid laws.

One perspective on good and bad is that of ethical relativism—that good and bad are determined by the conventions of the time and place where one finds oneself. Taken to an extreme, this stance may lead to a bleak view of human prospects. However, there is undoubtedly some truth in the more general proposition that values and conventions change. For example, in the UK we no longer regard it as acceptable for children to work in factories, or for women to be dismissed from employment on marriage, and no doubt there are some aspects of what we regard as normal employment practice today that will be seen as unacceptable in a hundred years' time.

An important test of an ethical proposition is that of universalization—to ask whether the proposer would apply the same principle or rule not just to the case in hand, but to all similar cases. The aim is to remove the influence of selfishness, which might otherwise lead to ethical propositions that are unfair and unacceptable.

14.2.1 Approaches to ethics

Philosophers have argued about the nature of good and bad for many centuries. In Western ethical philosophy, there has been a key distinction between approaches that see ethics as *principles, duties, and rights*, on the one hand, and those that see ethics as *consequences*, on the other. Both approaches seem to correspond to some of the ways that we think about ethics in daily life—there are things that we feel uncomfortable about doing, whether or not there is a real prospect of being found out.

Yet it is also true that we naturally attempt to think about the consequences of different courses of action when trying to decide the best way forward. Unfortunately, however, each approach on its own is subject to real practical problems, and hybrid approaches usually become snagged on questions about which approach should be given priority, and why. These are some of the main reasons why the subject of ethics remains very much open, despite the exertion of much intellectual effort over the centuries.

14.2.2 Deontology

An approach to ethics that emphasizes duties, rights, and principles is known as deontological (from the Greek word for duty). In deontological ethics, good or bad is evident in the act itself, irrespective of the consequences of the act. What is bad about lying is lying itself, without consideration of the effects of the lie. The same would be true of other unethical acts, such as stealing, cheating, or killing. Deontological propositions often take the form of lists of types of action that should be encouraged or refrained from. The German philosopher Kant (1724–1804) was a leading voice in deontological ethics; his idea of the 'categorical imperative' remains influential. An *imperative* is a command—for instance, 'study hard'. In ethical reasoning this command could be expressed in relation to the end in view, such as 'study hard in order to get a good degree'. This type of command is called a *hypothetical* imperative—it is a reasonable hypothesis to believe that by studying hard you will get a good degree. But some acts should be done *anyway*, regardless of the end in view. These are called *categorical* imperatives; they are *always* and absolutely the right thing to do. Kant proposed three forms of the categorical imperative, two of which are important for this chapter. The first is about universalization (see above)—we should follow only rules that could be universalized. The second form requires that we should not treat other people *only* as a means to some desired end, but *also* as an end in themselves.

What are the implications of this requirement for HRM? The second form of the categorical imperative does not mean that employing someone is an unethical act. If we pay a plumber to fix a leaking tap, our main interest may well be fixing the leak, but the plumber has the opportunity to decline our offer and so no ethical objection arises. To put it another way, our duty is to behave in a way that respects his/her moral agency—his/her ability to make choices of his/her own volition. The same can be said of normal mainstream employment; if those who work for an organization are free to leave at any time, then the employing organization is respecting their moral agency. Naturally, if an employer uses the threat of violence or other degrading treatment to persuade employees to obey instructions, or introduces other elements into the employment circumstances that effectively enslave the employee, the employee's rights are violated and the arrangement is clearly unethical.

In advanced economies, our normal expectation is for employment circumstances that will satisfy the second form of the categorical imperative—exceptions to this rule are not unknown, of course, but would generate considerable public disapproval and possible legal sanctions. Historically, for example, the practice of paying workers part of their wages in tokens that could be spent only in company-owned shops—known as the 'truck' system, and sometimes called 'debt bondage'—resulted in conditions of employment that bound workers to the employer and limited their freedom to leave. Although such arrangements have been outlawed, the reported experience of some migrant workers in the UK suggests that this type of behaviour by employers remains a problem. It is also common in some developing countries, and was the issue that inspired 2006 Nobel Peace Prize winner Muhammad Yunus to found the Grameen Banks.

14.2.3 Libertarianism

For libertarians, the preservation of an individual's freedom to choose is the most important criterion in ethical analysis—the life worth living is one in which we are able, and in most cases obliged, to make choices for ourselves and live with the consequences, good or bad. From this point of view, the role of government should be minimal—to do with national defence, the protection of property rights, and the enforcement of contracts. Individual freedom offers no guarantee of happiness and well-being—liberty is desirable in its own right. As the philosopher Isaiah Berlin (1969: 125) put it: 'Liberty is liberty, not equality or fairness or justice or culture, or human happiness or a quiet conscience'.

A fully libertarian society would oblige its members to learn to get along with each other, each enjoying his/her freedom without compromising the liberty of others. We highlight libertarianism not just for historical reasons, but because it remains an important intellectual foundation of a capitalist society in which the distribution of many products and services is left to more or less free markets. In Adam Smith's notion of the 'invisible hand' of the free market, individuals pursuing their own interest are guided to do good for others even if they do not intend to do so. As a result, a free market automatically and efficiently creates prosperity. The Chicago economist Milton Friedman was a fierce advocate of the effectiveness of free markets throughout his career. He would still have advocated free markets, even if it could be shown that an alternative economic system was more efficient, because they embody the human values of 'choice, challenge, and risk'. For Friedman, the preservation of liberty is deontologically desirable.

Both libertarianism in particular and deontology in general identify things that are held to be desirable or undesirable *in their own right.* These ideas of duties, principles, and rights are intuitively important in everyday ethical decision-making, even if they are not always explicitly recognized as such. But an exclusively deontological approach to ethics entails significant problems that have been discussed by moral philosophers for a long time. For example, there is the problem of absolutism—can it *never* be all right to say something that we know to be untrue? The alternative approach of carefully defining exceptions to the rule as they arise in real life quickly becomes very complex. There can also be a problem of priorities: if both lying and killing are wrong, is it right to lie in order to prevent a killing? And, whatever the answer to that question, how do we know? What new principle reveals the one as being more undesirable than the other?

14.2.4 Consequentialism

An alternative would be to abandon the search for a comprehensive and workable list of duties, and to declare instead that a good act is one that leads to good outcomes and a bad one is one that has bad outcomes. This is the consequentialist approach to ethics: goodness or badness is not determined by the act in general, but by what happens as a result of this act. Thus there can be good and bad lies and, while stealing will usually lead to bad outcomes, a 'good' theft could be imagined. More controversially, consequentialist arguments are sometimes made for 'good' acts of killing.

If good and bad are to be judged by the consequences of the act in question, then two questions pop up immediately: *which* consequences and consequences *for whom*? The idea of utilitarianism helps to define these terms: it considers changes in happiness for all who may be affected by the act being contemplated, and looks for the act that will result in the greatest good for the greatest number. This approach to ethics was strongly associated with the English philosopher Jeremy Bentham (1748–1832), who proposed the method of listing all who might be affected by the proposed act and then considering for each their likely change in happiness (positive or negative) as a result of the act. If the net change in happiness was positive, then the proposed act was likely to be good.

There is a natural appeal in the simplicity of this system; it obliges us to give others equal weight in our calculations and it centres on something that sounds right—happiness. Who could be against the greatest good for the greatest number? In practice, however, there are difficulties; the method is far less simple than it looks. But these difficulties are relatively minor compared with the problems that utilitarianism can cause in terms of justice—loosely, our sense of 'fairness'. A utilitarian calculation might well justify undeserved and very bad treatment of employees if many others (customers, shareholders, taxpayers) were to benefit as a result.

14.2.5 'Act' and 'rule' utilitarianism

The idea of 'rule' utilitarianism goes some way towards addressing this problem. Simple *act* utilitarianism tries to assess the changes in net happiness for the specific act being contemplated, and only this act. In contrast, *rule* utilitarianism applies a more demanding test—what would the changes to net happiness be if acts of this type became the rule in all similar circumstances? This helps to reveal a consequential objection to the routine bad treatment of employees; ultimately, nobody would wish to be employed, and businesses or other employing organizations would cease to exist, thus resulting in bad consequences for everyone.

However, injustice remains a significant problem for utilitarianism, and even for rule utilitarianism; as John Mackie (1980) suggests, the difficulty is that this approach encourages and perhaps even requires that the happiness of some can, and should, be offset by the underserved misery of others, as long as the net effect is to increase the sum of net happiness. This is, of course, of no comfort to those who are doing the offsetting. For example, some argue that the process of globalization is a good thing because it promotes faster economic growth, which alleviates poverty. However, this argument does not mean that the difficulties suffered by those whose lives are being seriously disrupted by the process are of no ethical significance.

We should also return to the question discussed earlier in this chapter—can the act of employment be regarded as ethical? A deontological analysis suggests that employment is normally perfectly compatible with the requirement to respect the moral agency of the employee and is for that reason acceptable in principle. What tests would consequentialist ethics apply to this question? The answer is clear enough: employment is ethically justifiable if it results in a set of consequences that are good. This outlook might take account of the superior material well-being for the employee that can be taken to result from employment (compared with the alternative), allowing for the costs in terms of time, effort, stress, and so on that also result from the employment. A utilitarian analysis might also consider the more general benefits and costs of a society in which employment is commonplace—for example, compared with a hypothetical society in which employment is unknown or uncommon. Such a society might consist of a mass of individuals trading with each other, without the benefit of employing institutions. In such a world, the authors of this chapter might find themselves forlornly wandering the streets, trying to exchange a series of lectures for a new pair of shoes.

14.2.6 Cultural traditions and ethics

This chapter has an explicit focus on approaches to ethics found in Western philosophy. Any review of approaches to ethics in Western philosophy should also mention ethics as virtues (see Box 14.1).

We make no attempt to encompass the great diversity of ethical ideas that come from non-Western cultural traditions. However, before closing this section, it is important to highlight that Western thinking about right and wrong is itself strongly influenced by the cultural context(s) in which these ideas were formed over the centuries. It would be quite wrong, for example, to see Western ideas on ethics as being in some way uniquely separate from European and North American cultural traditions, and still less as having some extra quality of objectivity or universality compared with ideas that have their origins in other traditions. For example, the teachings of Confucius are a strong influence on Chinese culture and thus on relationships and practices in Chinese organizations.

Influences from different traditions can make themselves felt in the workplace. For example, Geert Hofstede (1991: 164) proposed 'Confucian dynamism', which embodied a long-term rather than a short-term orientation to work, based on values such as perseverance and thrift as

Box 14.1 Window on work
Virtue ethics

The classical Greek philosopher Aristotle (384–322 BC) is associated with the concept of virtue ethics. Virtues are desirable character traits that lie between undesirable extremes: 'courage', for example, is a virtue that lies between cowardice, at one end of the scale, and foolhardiness, at the other. Virtues are linked to purpose: someone who embodies virtues is more able to fulfil his/her purpose as a human being and to live a life that is worth living (sometimes referred to as a 'good life', without any necessary connection to particular levels of material well-being). How does one acquire virtues? The answer is simple and pragmatic—by studying the lives of those who are good and admirable and seeking to emulate them. This approach has some points of potential interest for HRM. For example, how might we define the virtues of a leader, a supervisor, an employee, or an entrepreneur? How can those virtues be inculcated, for instance, through training and development?

a separate dimension in understanding the differences between national cultures. These values, together with the familiar Confucian emphasis on hierarchy, will influence the behaviours and attitudes that are accepted and admired at work. In an increasingly global economy, understanding the influence of cultural difference is becoming very important in managing business relationships across national boundaries. Whilst basic ideas about good and bad behaviour may not differ very much from one culture to another, the way in which those ideas are discussed, understood, and lived will have important implications for organizations that seek to do business ethically outside their home environment.

 ## Summary and further reading

- Ethics is the study of right and wrong, in this case the right and wrong ways to treat employees.

- Ethics has an important relationship with law, and also with convention or culture.

- In Western philosophy, the main approaches to ethics have been those of deontology (in which goodness or badness is evident in the act itself), consequentialism (in which goodness or badness is evident in the results of the act), and virtue (the desirable character traits that lie between undesirable extremes.

- Cultural differences may require further and more detailed consideration of questions of what can be defined as 'good' and 'bad' in HRM practice for organizations that operate across national boundaries.

Business Ethics (Crane and Matten 2010) is a detailed introduction to the application of ethical ideas to the world of business. It includes specific chapters on ethics in relation to employees, governments, and civil society organizations, including trade unions, as well as considering the ethics of globalization.

14.3 Ethics and organizations

So far, the ethical ideas we have considered in this chapter have been mainly aimed at people—how we should behave as individuals. To deal with the question of the ethical aspects of HRM, we also need to consider the ethics of the conduct of organizations. Organizations are impersonal entities, but they do act with intent and their actions can have major impacts (good and bad) on people, other organizations, and society as a whole. What is good and bad conduct by an organization, and how do we know? This question is very much bound up with the question about the role and nature of HRM. If it is concerned with helping an organization to achieve its objectives, an ethical analysis of HRM must at least touch on the ethical desirability of those objectives themselves.

14.3.1 Business ethics: the shareholder view

Much of the discussion in the literature focuses on the ethics of a particular type of employing organization—a business. Many of the arguments about how businesses should behave revolve around what a business is *for*—its purpose. At one end of the spectrum are those who agree with Milton Friedman (1970) that a business has the purpose of making as much money as possible for its shareholders, within the rules of law, competition, and ordinary decency. The basis of this argument is that the company is owned by the shareholders, who appoint directors whose duty to the shareholders is to find profitable opportunities to exploit in competition with other shareholder-owned firms. From this point of view, actions by a business that serve this purpose (and comply with the constraints of lawfulness and free and fair competition) are ethical, while other types of action by a business are not.

In the shareholder view of business, an employer has contractual duties towards its employees and must treat its employees (and all others with whom it comes into contact) with common decency. The reason for employing someone is to serve the central business purpose—to make money for the owners. This apparently hard-hearted view of employment need not be associated with low pay and poor working conditions—employers are in competition with each other in the marketplace for customers for their products and services, and must also compete with each other for the human resources they need to pursue their competitive strategies. This competitive process may lead a business to offer very attractive salaries and other benefits where a particular type of human resource is scarce, as is often (and not always persuasively) argued in the case of senior executives.

14.3.2 Business ethics: the stakeholder view

In contrast, a stakeholder view of employment might recognize a separate set of duties towards employees that are *additional* to the contractual and legal obligations. What these extra duties are may vary from one employer to another, but in virtually every case competitive pressures will place a real limit on the extent and duration of any voluntary generosity on the part of employers. As Sternberg (2000) observes, it is unethical for firms to promise things that they cannot guarantee, such as lifetime employment; ethically, it is far more preferable for any promises to be realistic and serious.

The desirability of the corporate social responsibility (CSR) approach to business holds that business has a broader set of responsibilities than just making money for the owners, and argues that it also owes duties to the different parts of the society in which it operates. This has remained a lively topic of discussion in the academic and professional press since the 1960s (e.g. *Economist* 2005). A public commitment to CSR seems to be required of major corporations today, although the depth of that commitment may vary. A review of the websites of most prominent multinational corporations will show significant amounts of space devoted to social and environmental initiatives, as seen in Box 14.2

In this emerging corporate consensus, CSR initiatives are to be seen as good business, rather than acts of selfless generosity. To be effective in competing for customers, a company must be seen to be responsible and concerned. Porter and Kramer (2006) suggest that effective CSR initiatives in this sense are likely to be those that are related to the company's sustainable competitive advantage. In terms of HRM, the implication may be that a company that manages to project a credible image as a good employer (perhaps an 'employer of choice') is likely to benefit in terms of not just the productivity of its human resources, but also customer preference, particularly if its competitors are seen as less desirable.

The ethics of employment depend to some extent on the purpose of the employing organization; the debate over CSR is mainly about the definition of the business purpose. However, not all employing organizations are businesses—in modern economies, many large employers have no shareholders to enrich, serve several different 'publics', are subject to little or no external competitive pressure, and work to a complex set of aims and objectives. These organizations may be modelled on an alternative principle, such as the cooperative model, or they may be parts of the public sector. In a non-business employing organization (e.g. a government organization) it can be much more difficult to know what the organization's purpose requires. However, 'difficult' is not the same as impossible; most people have no problem in recognizing a good hospital, school, or university. HRM practices may differ in detail from one organization to another, but in each case HRM is about finding, developing, and looking after people who can produce the 'outputs' of the organization, whether or not those outputs are

Box 14.2 Policy example
Corporate social responsibility

Corporate social responsibility is now a very common and prominent feature of corporate communications. Governments are generally supportive of moves by companies to apply corporate resources to projects and activities that are not directly connected to the company's main business: see, for example, the European Commission's website (at http://ec.europa.eu/enterprise/policies/sustainable-business/corporate-social-responsibility).

For example, the UK's major supermarkets, seem to vie with each other not just in terms of business variables, such as value for money, service, and quality, but also in terms of their positive impact on society and the environment. Their motivation for making these investments is likely to be a mixture of a number of factors. Commercial common sense will usually be part of that mix; we are more likely to continue to use a company whose behaviour we approve of (as long as the basic offering is still seen as good value for money). CSR commitment may also be a matter of deliberately starting to work to higher (say) environmental standards, quite possibly because the company feels that it is the right thing to do, but reinforced by the sense that future regulations may require the new standards before too long anyway, leaving laggard competitors at a possible disadvantage. Airlines are similarly keen to proclaim their commitments to CSR and sustainability. Even low-cost carrier RyanAir, whose management has been famously combative towards environmentalists for years, now includes a report on its website showing the basis for their claim to be 'Europe's greenest airline'.

sold in a competitive market. The video link in Box 14.3 provides a discussion of shareholder and stakeholder approaches.

14.3.3 Ethics and HRM

An important starting point for a more specific consideration of the ethics of employment and HRM might be to examine those special features of the employment relationship and the contract of employment that differentiate them from other business relationships and contracts, such as those with customers, suppliers, other businesses, and so on. After all, if labour is a commodity much like any other, it becomes difficult to see what ethical principle prevents employees from being treated in the same way as these other assets—acquired, used, and disposed of as the business purpose determines. In deontological terms, we might consider the Kantian point about treating people not *solely* as a means to an end, but always at the same time as an end in themselves. Thus there is an important difference between employees and other company assets, requiring employers to show respect for persons and to recognize an individual's independence of action. We should, perhaps, be cautious about describing people as 'assets' or 'resources'—terms which might lead managers to think of them in this way.

Alternatively, we could examine the employment relationship from a consequentialist perspective and identify the net benefits that accrue from certain employment practices—for example, the notion of the open-ended employment contract. Historically, the notion of regular and continuing employment was the exception rather than the rule; the practice of hiring labourers by the day from amongst those who presented themselves at the factory gates in the morning

Box 14.3 Online video link
Stakeholder theory

The Online Resource Centre contains a link to video content published by the Darden Business School at the University of Virginia. The material shows prominent business academic R. Edward Freeman discussing stakeholder theory. It includes a discussion of the shareholder and stakeholder views mentioned in this chapter, and provides an even-handed discussion, leading to an understanding in greater depth of this important topic.

was common. This system certainly had some benefits. Employers could choose the best workers and avoid the unreliable or weak ones, and all applicants might be treated on the basis of availability and merit in a crude form of daily equal opportunity (if you weren't picked one day, you could try again the next). The notion persists, albeit in a more organized form, in the normal practices of many temporary employment agencies, particularly in the hospitality sector.

In contrast, the consequences of a system of regular and continuing employment contracts might well be preferable for both workers and businesses. There is likely to be a positive change in net happiness for workers, resulting from reduced uncertainty as well as the social benefits that flow from having a predictable and regular income—for instance, access to mortgages. For employers, the benefits include reliable levels of regular labour supply together with reduced transaction costs such as recruitment and training. The mutual trust engendered by a continuing relationship also provides the basis for employers to invest in such things as training and development activities which should both improve the skills of workers (making them more valuable) and enhance the performance of the organization, which can then apply those skills profitably. This increases economic productivity and ultimately national prosperity, which is one reason why governments are so keen to encourage employers to 'invest in people' (despite the risks of losing the benefit of such 'investment' to another employer) and workers to become 'lifelong learners'.

From a libertarian point of view, we might consider employment an important means by which an employer and a worker can freely exchange labour for reward. However, we also need to recognize that such an exchange is subject to significant inequalities in power between the two parties. In the vast majority of cases, the employer enjoys greater power in the labour market and more opportunity to exercise choice. In a democratic society, it is not surprising that people vote for governments who promise to redress some of these inequalities by legislating to protect employees from the arbitrary exercise of such power. Hence, we generally accept the need for legislation relating to such things as minimum wages, maximum working hours, unjust sackings, and unfair discrimination. However, the greater the constraints on employers, the more reluctant they might be to actually employ people, especially if it becomes expensive or difficult to do so.

Governments clearly need to engage in a form of utilitarian assessment when deciding both the nature and the extent of desirable interventions in the labour market. The UK's attitude towards the EU's Working Time Directive provides one example. Clearly, any legal restriction on working hours is one that inhibits the freedom of both workers and employers to exchange work for reward, so the government has to estimate the nature and extent of the net benefit of such restrictions to be sure that the overall result will be 'good' in utilitarian terms. The estimate of the balance between good and bad consequences might be contested; for instance, the continuing use in the UK of a clause that enables workers to 'opt out' of the 48-hour maximum working week, something many EU member states oppose, has been defended by successive UK governments on the basis that it provides much needed flexibility for employers, and enables workers to increase their earnings by working additional hours if they wish. Similar issues are raised by the 2011 Agency Workers Directive, which gives agency workers rights (after 12 weeks) to the same basic employment and working conditions as directly recruited staff in an organization. This change aims to address the unsatisfactory treatment of some agency workers in the past, but necessarily does away with some of the flexibility of the agency option, which has been attractive to both employers and agency staff.

14.3.4 Ethics, HRM, and the law

This leads us to give some further thought to the relationship between ethics, HRM, and the law. If we consider the type of employment-related legislation that has been enacted over the past two centuries, we can see that much of it had the purpose of redressing the balance in an unequal power relationship between employers and workers. Early legislation was often humanitarian in its intent; aiming to offer some basic protection to workers, particularly women and children, from the worst of contemporary employment conditions. This, and more recent legislation about health and safety, clearly derive from an ethical consideration which believes that some poor working conditions, bad practices, or mistakes have possible results that are far too damaging to permit them to be left to the free market.

More recently, legislation has concerned itself with different ethical considerations, mostly relating to ideas of social justice or fairness. The ever-increasing scope of 'equal opportunity' or 'anti-discrimination' legislation has the ethical purpose of requiring employers to behave in ways that help to redress the social disadvantage historically experienced by certain groups (e.g. people with disabilities) arising from prejudice, or from historical practices that denied them certain types of education or training (Goss 1994). In the UK, the 1970 Equal Pay Act (which came into effect in 1975) outlawed an unjust practice, previously supported by employers and many trade unionists alike, whereby a man was routinely paid more for carrying out the same job as a woman on the grounds that he needed to support a family whereas a woman did not (the so-called family wage). This problem was addressed through the simultaneous introduction of the Sex Discrimination Act in 1975, which made such decisions unlawful, and went further to give protection from sexual harassment, to ensure equality of access to the type of vocational training usually reserved for men, and to enable women to retain jobs once they had them. Legislation that gives women the right to take up to a year's paid maternity leave, together with regulations about paternity and parental leave, go further towards ensuring that women are helped to stay in work whilst raising a family.

A libertarian might argue that much of this amounts to the transfer of responsibility for some of the costs of child-rearing from individual families to employers and the state, and thus undermines one important aspect of freedom—that which emphazises the importance of taking responsibility for your own choices. A consequentialist might respond that the net benefit to women and their families, as well as to the economy as a whole, outweighs the disadvantage to employers and taxpayers of the extra costs they now incur. Here we can see a good example of a clash of values; the arguments on each side are strong, but the two positions contradict each other, and a choice has to be made between two sets of values.

As we can see, the approach taken by governments with respect to HRM practices is in most respects one of rule utilitarianism, although health and safety legislation is clearly deontological in origin. Minimum wage legislation might be viewed as stemming from a Kantian notion of respect. However, one significant reason for its introduction was that of preventing bad employers from exploiting the system of income support by paying low wages, safe in the knowledge that the state would pick up part of the bill—a utilitarian assessment of consequences.

 ## Summary and further reading

- The ethics of employing people is influenced by the strategic orientation of the employing organization. The view of the business purpose will clearly affect one's view about how employees should be treated.

- The employment relationship is unlike other buyer–seller relationships from an ethical point of view. First, it differs with respect to the duties owed to individual people in their own right; people are not, in fact, assets. Secondly, there is also an unequal power relationship between an employer and employee.

- This second point is perhaps the main factor driving the growth of employment law, which has the effect of converting ethical choices into legal obligations.

For a review of some of the significant approaches to the ethics of business in general, and the shareholder approach as championed by Friedman (1970), see Sternberg (2000). This text contains an interesting chapter on ethics and personnel, which challenges many of the accepted norms associated with the HRM role. Hutton's (1995) book *The State We're In* remains an accessible argument for the stakeholder approach. A more recent contribution in this area is Wilkinson and Pickett's (2010) book *The Spirit Level*, which examines the links between high levels of income and wealth inequality in societies and a surprisingly wide range of social problems.

14.4 The ethical aspects of HRM activities

The ethical principles and considerations discussed above can be applied to any of the activities that are characteristic of organizational HRM. Here we illustrate the process by discussing two such activities in depth, employee reward and the management of equality and diversity issues. Before we do so, though, we consider some of the issues that arise when individuals seek to draw attention to something bad that is being done by their organization, or 'whistle-blowing' as it is often called.

14.4.1 Ethical behaviour and whistle-blowing

If we accept that individuals work for organizations whose purpose they believe to be legitimate, what should happen if an employee becomes concerned about the conduct of his/her employer, or possibly the conduct of colleagues? We might begin to answer this question by making a deontological point and suggest that employers should respect an employee's right, as a fellow member of the rational community, to express an opinion and to criticize what he/she views as bad behaviour by the organization. We could also argue from a utilitarian perspective that society at large, not to mention fellow employees, will be better off if bad and potentially dangerous practices by employers can be identified and then put right before they cause real damage. From a business value perspective we might consider that a whistle-blower is in fact a valuable source of information about malpractices that could seriously harm the value of a business to its owners (Sternberg 2000). Managers should be interested in collecting such information so that they can address the problem. Theoretically, therefore, there seems to be a strong case that whistle-blowing should be seen as a good thing.

Yet there are significant problems with this view, mainly for potential whistle-blowers who may seem to be breaching a duty of loyalty to management, colleagues, and the organization, and may even be subject to victimization as a result, despite legislation designed to protect genuine legitimate complainants. What can organizations do to encourage reporting of unethical behaviour? One key aspect could be the development of an organizational culture where potential problem areas can be explored and resolved in a way which ensures that employees know that their concerns have, at least, been heard. Systems for reporting potentially unethical behaviour to appropriate senior managers, so that cases can be investigated and handled by those with the power to do so, can also be developed, as illustrated in Box 14.4. Such measures

Box 14.4 Policy example
Code of Business Conduct at Tesco (extract)

The Code seeks to set out how we should act on behalf of the business. If you suspect that the Code, or the laws that underpin it, are not being followed, you have an obligation to report it. Anyone who acts in good faith to raise a concern about a possible breach will be supported by the business.

Who should I contact if I consider that the Code may have been breached?

In the first instance, you should contact your Line Manager unless you suspect that they have breached the Code. If you cannot speak to your Line Manager, you should contact your Personnel Manager. Alternatively, you can contact your local Protector Line on the numbers/email addresses listed.

About Protector Line

Protector Line allows you to report real concerns regarding misconduct at work. You must speak out if you:

- have concerns at work about anything you think may be unlawful, breaches the Code or company policy;
- think there are unreported dangers to staff, customers or the general public;
- or think that information about these things is being deliberately concealed.

Protector Line is completely confidential and offers callers total anonymity. You will not be required to give your name in order to raise a concern. But, if you do leave your name, we will be able to report back to you the results of any investigations or contact you to request further information (if necessary). As a business, we support the UK Public Interest Disclosure Act 1998 (and its foreign law equivalents), which protects the confidentiality of complaints. This means that as long as you are acting in good faith and your concerns are genuine, you are legally protected from victimization and will not be at risk of losing your job or suffering any form of retribution as a result of raising a concern, even if you are mistaken.

Source: Tesco corporate website (www.tescoplc.com/our-people).

would be classed as internal whistle-blowing, and, if operating successfully, should encourage self-regulating behaviour by employees and managers alike.

But what if no such system exists, or it fails or becomes corrupt? Would it then be ethically justifiable to go outside the organization, to blow the whistle externally by alerting the media, regulators, or governments? De George (2010) provides a framework that can be used as the basis both for understanding the significance of whistle-blowing, and for training in the ethical questions thus raised. For external whistle-blowing to be permissible, he suggests that three criteria have to be met. In summary they are:

1. that the firm, through its product or policy, will do serious and considerable harm to employees or to the public;

2. that once employees identify a serious threat, they should report it to their immediate superior and make their moral concern known;

3. that if his/her immediate superior does nothing effective about the concern, the employee should exhaust the internal procedures and possibilities within the firm.

If these three steps have been taken and the company does not take any action to prevent the harm, there is sufficient justification for the employee to turn to external whistle-blowing. For De George (2010), external whistle-blowing becomes morally *obligatory* when two further conditions are met. These are:

4. that the whistle-blower must have documented evidence that would convince a reasonable impartial observer that the company's product or practice poses a serious and likely danger to the public or the user;

5. that the employee must have good reasons to believe that, by going public, he/she will ensure that the necessary changes will be brought about.

14.4.2 Employee reward

The management of reward is potentially one of the most contentious aspects of HRM practice (see Chapter 7). Much revolves around issues that are at the core of ethical thinking, such as fairness and justice. What do we actually mean by these terms, and how can we structure our consideration of reward systems to enlighten the debate?

The idea of fairness (a fair day's work for a fair day's pay) might appear simple on the surface, but how do we actually define fair? One way of determining a fair reward might be one based on *merit*; reward is consistent with what an employee brings to the organization in terms of such things as expertise, knowledge, or skills. It appears fair that an individual who has superior capabilities, or who has expended time and effort in obtaining complex skills, should be rewarded more than one who lacks them. This notion is built into many organizational pay structures, and is additionally used as a basis for hiring and promoting. It also appears strongly consistent with notions of equality of opportunity. However, is it still fair if someone fails to use his/her skills properly on behalf of the organization, or is appointed to a job that does not actually require them? Furthermore, simple possession of a qualification may not guarantee superior levels of performance. This leads us to think of a slightly different definition of fairness—one that is based on *contribution*. For example, Sternberg (2000) suggests that fairness in this aspect of business ethics means offering rewards that are proportional to an individual's contribution to the output of the organization. This is how she defines 'distributive justice', and it is clearly consistent with the principle of performance-related pay—if not always with the actual practice of it. Identifying the precise nature and degree of individual performance as separate from other influences is often very difficult, as well as being open to subjective interpretation and personal bias. Some see possible offences against distributive justice in the high rewards obtained by very senior managers and chief executives.

A related question is whether it can be ethical for an organization to benefit from work done by people who are engaged on an unpaid basis, particularly since the introduction of the National Minimum Wage in the UK. The special case of voluntary work for charitable causes is generally agreed to be a desirable exception in this area, but there has recently been media discussion of the increasing prevalence of unpaid internships for young people (in which interns

Box 14.5 Research in focus
Unpaid internships

In Spring 2011, the Low Pay Commission's annual report highlighted the particularly difficult position of young people, including graduates, in the labour market. It identified three groups who are not classed as workers for the purposes of National Minimum Wage (NMW) legislation and whose employers are thus exempt from its provisions:

- voluntary workers, i.e. those working for specific organizations (a charity, voluntary organization, associated fund-raising body, or statutory body) and receiving only very specific payments and benefits in kind;

- volunteers, who can volunteer for anybody and not just for organizations in the not-for-profit sector;

- students on work placement which lasts for less than a year as part of a UK-based higher or further education course.

However, people on unpaid work experience are in a more ambiguous position. The terms 'intern' and 'internship' are not recognised in the NMW legislation, and there is strong governmental encouragement for employers to offer such opportunities, particularly in the professions, as part of its attempt to tackle youth unemployment and to encourage greater social mobility. The Graduate Talent Pool website advises that an intern should not be under an obligation to work and should not do work that is normally done by someone who would be covered by the NMW legislation. It is here that the Commission identifies increasing abuse. In evidence taken from trade unions (Equity, NUJ, BECTU), as well as the TUC, it found that not only have some employers built unpaid work placements into their business model, but that it is becoming increasingly common for them to demand a period of unpaid work as an entry ticket to an industry or job, thus both exploiting young people and putting those from poorer backgrounds at a disadvantage. Some employers' associations were also concerned about this trend, as it undermines fair employers, and called for a new category of worker to be created; the CIPD suggested that internships be incorporated into apprenticeship wage structures. In the event, the Commission recommended that HM Revenue & Customs should enforce the current law more strongly; and a task force to crack down on the abuse of internships began its operations in November 2011.

Sources: The National Minimum Wage, Low Pay Commission (2010): http://www.lowpay.gov.uk
The National Minimum Wage, Low Pay Commission (2011): http://www.lowpay.gov.uk
Graduate Talent Pool website: http://graduatetalentpool.bis.gov.uk

gain experience of the work of the organization without being paid, and without any firm promise of a paid post at the end of the arrangement) suggesting that this practice is ethically controversial, as illustrated in Box 14.5.

14.4.3 Fairness and 'fat-cat' pay

Accusations about the unethical nature of 'fat-cat' salaries may take one of several forms: the absolute level of the pay ('nobody should be paid that much'); the relative level of the pay ('she earns twenty times the pay of those at the bottom and that can't be right'); the value for money that the pay represents ('what exactly did he do to justify that salary/bonus?'); and sometimes to the process through which the package is determined ('they all look after each other in boardrooms'). But are huge pay differentials between the lowest- and highest-paid employees in an organization automatically unfair or unethical? How far should we tolerate or even encourage such differences? A utilitarian approach might attempt to identify how much net benefit is achieved as the result of arrangements that contain significant inequalities. If the employees, customers, and shareholders of a business can be seen to benefit as the result of paying a chief executive at a level that means he/she continues to perform well for the business, then it could be seen as the right thing to do. On the other hand, if this level of pay is achieved at the expense of other stakeholders, the majority of whom are worse off as a result, then it is not so easy to justify.

Questions of inequality and distributive justice can also be addressed using a device called the 'veil of ignorance' (Rawls 1973). In *A Theory of Justice*, Rawls attempts to construct the rules of a society or other system from a position behind a 'veil of ignorance', which means that, whilst you are perfectly capable of rational thought, you have no knowledge of who you are. You do not know your ethnicity, if you are rich or poor, old or young, physically strong or disabled, or male or female. The purpose of this thought experiment was to try to identify the principles of a social system that would be rationally acceptable when the veil was lifted and you took your place within it. Rawls's view was that two important principles would probably emerge from such an exercise. First, each person would have an equal right to the most extensive basic liberty, which was compatible with similar liberty for others. Secondly, social and economic inequalities would be arranged, as far as possible, to everyone's advantage and should be attached to positions and offices that were open to all. The implication of this for pay and reward would be to suggest that any degree of inequality is tolerable as long as *everyone* is better off to some extent, including the poorest. Whilst it could be argued that the equal opportunity conditions may be more or less met in today's market for senior executive talent, it is much less easy to be sure that the very high rewards for chief executives really are to the benefit of all.

Another way of considering fairness might be in relation to *need*. While this has evident currency in some aspects of life (it is the cornerstone for the provision of accident and emergency services by the UK's National Health Service, for example), it does not play a major part in organizational reward systems today, partly because it appears *unfair* to differentiate between the rewards offered to employees on the basis that they have a larger family or some other significant personal responsibility. Finally, we could take an egalitarian approach and suggest that a fair approach would be one that offers *equal* rewards to every employee. Few organizations in Western capitalist systems retain such an approach to the payment of basic wages and salaries, although some cooperative ventures might still find it an important principle. However, it might well form the basis for a one-off 'all-staff' bonus, when the management of an organization wishes to make a standard token payment to everyone without reference to individual contribution.

14.4.4 Implications of fairness in reward

What can we take from these discussions to help human resource managers identify ethically justifiable methods of rewarding employees? First, the transparency of any reward system is important. If those to whom it applies can understand the rules and see that they are being applied evenly, the system is more likely to be accepted as fair—the more so if the rules relate to values that are acknowledged as reasonable. A reward system that is so complex as to be incomprehensible is a potential breeding ground for exploitative behaviour, injustice, or suspicion. Secondly, managers should ensure that the system is also true to its purpose. If the purpose of the organization is clearly understood, reward should follow behaviour and activity that is consistent with that purpose. If the purpose of the business is the maximization of shareholder value, then behaviour that damages that value (for example, flouting health and safety regulations and thereby exposing the business to significant financial and other risks as a result) should not be rewarded, even if it results in short-term increases in output. Finally, managers might need to ensure that employees accept whichever principles (merit, contribution, egalitarianism) are applied, and this means clear communication of these principles when recruiting. Making such information clear during the recruitment and induction process both respects individual moral agency and allows potential recruits to make an informed choice. The activity in Box 14.6 uses some of the ethical frameworks discussed so far to explore the issue of unpaid work.

A prominent example of the need to align reward structures to organizational objectives is associated with the 2007–2008 global financial crisis and the effects of 'moral hazard'—the way in which an inappropriately designed system can actually encourage destructive behaviour. At the macro-scale, banks had evolved over a number of decades into large, interconnected, and powerful entities that were increasingly seen as 'too big to fail'. Once it became generally assumed that governments would step in to rescue a failing bank, the incentives for banks changed and the problem of moral hazard became dangerously significant. Knowing

Box 14.6 Skills exercise
Ethical analysis

This exercise involves using some of the ideas discussed in this chapter to carry out an ethical analysis of a current issue for many HR departments—the question of whether or not to offer unpaid internships, in which those taking part can gain experience of the work of your organization for a period, but will not be paid and cannot be given any promise of paid employment at the end of the internship. In small groups, choose one of the following, draw up a summary of your discussion, and report back to the full class.

- Carry out an ethical analysis from a deontological, or duty-based, point of view. What duties seem to be owed to those who would be involved in such a scheme? Would any rights be violated by the scheme? And whatever the answer to these questions, does it feel like the *right* answer?

- Carry out an ethical analysis from a consequentialist point of view. What good and bad consequences might flow from the adoption of such a scheme? What seems to be the balance of advantage? And whatever the answer to these questions, does it feel like the *right* answer?

Following a report back to the whole group, you may wish to continue the discussion by exploring what sort of regulation (either self-regulation, or imposed by government) of unpaid internships might help individual companies to make ethical decisions in this area.

that governments would bail out catastrophic failure, banks had every incentive to take higher risks in order to earn higher profits and thus higher bonuses. At the micro-level, this moral hazard influenced the design of individual incentive schemes, with very large rewards available for those who took high risks and won. The scale of the problems that built up became shockingly evident in 2008 as large numbers of well-known banks teetered and in some cases fell. As former US Federal Reserve Chairman Alan Greenspan ruefully observed, bank managements failed to protect shareholder value—the problem of moral hazard was a significant factor in the disaster that ensued.

14.4.5 Equality of opportunity: fairness and justice

Another area of HRM activity that is open to frequent debate on ethical grounds is the process of selection. This is usually linked with the recruitment of employees, but it is also highly significant in relation to training, promotion, and redundancy decisions. Questions about who should be chosen, and how these choices can be defensibly made, are inextricably bound up with both legal and ethical considerations, most of which are found under the more general heading of 'equality of opportunity'.

As we saw earlier, a potentially important principle for a just society is that of equal access to positions that might offer high rewards. The concept is strongly ingrained in contemporary HRM thinking in Western culture, and acts as a guiding principle for most of the HRM tasks that involve selection. The use of application systems based around clear job descriptions and person specifications is a means of taking conscious and unconscious bias out of the selection process. It serves the needs of the organization by ensuring the widest possible choice, and at the same time seeks to treat individuals properly by avoiding unfair discrimination based on prejudice. From a Kantian perspective, Boatright (2000) observes that it is an offence against respect for persons to treat an individual with contempt or enmity because he/she happens to be a member of a group about which negative stereotypes may be held, rather than as a person in his/her own right.

The important point here is not about avoiding 'discrimination' per se, which properly means 'to distinguish or differentiate' and is clearly the essence of any selection decision. What *is* important, however, is to ensure that selection decisions are relevant, fair, and justifiable. There may be an ethical case for the adoption of *positive* discrimination (such as is common in the USA but unlawful in the UK) if the level of historical disadvantage is so great or prejudice is so ingrained that there is little prospect of justice and fairness being achieved other than by compulsion. A notable contemporary example of positive discrimination is the Norwegian law that obliged all listed companies on the Oslo Stock Exchange to fill 40 per cent of their Board places with women from 2008, following a six-year transition period. On the other hand, positive discrimination is arguably just as unethical as negative discrimination, since it also fails to treat individuals as persons. An intelligent and serious approach to the question of equal opportunities might involve thinking more broadly about how to access and appeal to under-represented groups in order to ensure that they know about the opportunities on offer, or to engage in 'positive-action' training schemes that aim to level the playing field for people from disadvantaged groups by offering them the chance to acquire skills that in turn enable them to compete for jobs more effectively, as seen in the example in Box 14.7.

We often read about the perceived unfairness that results in fewer women holding senior positions in business and other organizations, or earning less on average than men (Women and Work Commission 2006). Implicit in these discussions is the notion that there is some 'fair' or more just pattern of distribution that *ought* to be achieved, and that specific action should be taken to move towards this pattern. Equality of opportunity is a very different thing from equality of outcome, but is it ethically defensible to aim for such a pattern? Nozick (1974) makes a potentially relevant point about distributive justice that can be applied to jobs, salary levels, or any other benefit. He proposes that, if the *process* of distribution (for example, by which employees are recruited and promoted) is just, then the end result, *whatever it may look like*, must also be just. Interfering with a just process in order to achieve some more pleasing outcome can be done only by inflicting injustice on others. Of course, utilitarians could argue that the undeserved unfairness inflicted on some is offset by the superior benefit to others, but this risks offending against distributive justice, which is likely to cause resentment, some of which may be felt against those who are supposed to be the beneficiaries. This type of consideration is important when considering any organizational interventions intended to achieve 'social justice' objectives. Statistical patterns within the workforce may be important indicators of problems in terms of equality of opportunity or injustice, but, on the other hand, they may simply indicate the exercise of informed choice by individuals (Hakim 2004; Shackleton 2008). A firm concentration on ensuring the fairness of the *process* may be more important than generating unfocused anxiety about the resulting pattern.

Box 14.7 Research in focus
The effects of positive action training

In the mid-1980s, Positive Action on Training in Housing (PATH) schemes were developed to address the under-representation of managers from black and minority ethnic communities in social housing (Joseph Rowntree Foundation 2001; Julienne 2001). Ten schemes trained people full time for between one and three years through placements with housing associations and local authority housing departments, supplemented by day-release college attendance and short training courses. Fifteen years later, over 80 per cent of the more than 1000 participants had obtained the jobs they were trained for. A study of the experience of former PATH trainees found the following:

- The majority of respondents had remained in employment since leaving PATH, most working in social housing management. More than half had been out of the labour market on joining PATH and, of those who had been in employment, most had been in unskilled or semi-skilled jobs.

- Most respondents had obtained formal qualifications during and since PATH. When converted into NVQ equivalents, these qualifications added an average of almost three NVQ points to each respondent.

- The overwhelming majority of respondents were very positive about their experience of PATH. Many cited PATH as the most important contributor to their career development.

- Other factors perceived as helping career development included respondents' personalities, particularly their 'determination to succeed', a commitment to address discrimination and disadvantage by working with/for people from black and minority ethnic communities, and key individuals at work who acted as a supporter/mentor. However, racial discrimination and stereotyping were still perceived to be obstructing the development of people's careers.

14.4.6 Equal opportunity: the shareholder value perspective

As was seen in Chapter 11, employment law has a great deal to say about questions of equality of opportunity, mostly on the basis of the need to achieve social justice and to prevent employing organizations of all types from behaving badly towards groups of people identified as disadvantaged. From a shareholder value perspective it might be expected that fair and open recruitment, training, and promotion practices would make good sense from a business point of view; by discriminating against talented individuals on some irrelevant grounds, such as sex or race, an organization is likely to find itself outperformed in a truly competitive market by organizations that employ diverse talent. As Friedman and Friedman (1990) suggest, the most reliable and effective protection for most workers is provided by the existence of many employers who compete with each other for staff. It might appear to be both a smart and a moral choice. So why do most advanced economies find it necessary to legislate rather than allow employers to self-regulate? The reason often relates back to the asymmetry of power in the employment relationship.

It might be because many employing organizations do not work within a competitive market system and thus no evident penalty is incurred by continuing to employ in a prejudiced manner. This could be argued for the public sector, for instance, where instances of poor levels of organizational performance do not generally result in bankruptcy or closure. It is also possible that, whilst the self-regulating theory might work in the long run, the process might take longer than a government might wish, or that the market penalties for unfair discrimination are not damaging enough to be taken seriously by prejudiced employers. The legislative approach might also be more clearly necessary in the case of disability, where the employment of individuals with some types of disability, whilst morally desirable, could result in real costs for an employer, such as building adaptations or special equipment. There seems to be a legitimate case for legal compulsion that would prevent 'fair' employers being put at a disadvantage by less scrupulous ones. See Box 14.8 for an activity in which you are expected to examine organizational equality/diversity policies with reference to the main ethical approaches discussed in Section 14.3.

14.4.7 The law of unintended consequences

This is not to suggest that the legislative approach is problem free. From an ethical perspective, being forced to behave in a certain way means that the subsequent act is no longer one of ethical choice; moral agency has been largely removed from the equation. There are practical problems associated with the legislative approach as well. For a small business, for instance, the potential costs associated with legal compliance could threaten its very survival. We might also see the law of unintended consequences beginning to operate here; what was supposed to protect and enhance women's employment could be having the reverse effect in some parts of the market. For example, Smith, Smith, and Verne (2011) reported on a study of women in senior roles in Denmark and suggested that the generous family-friendly schemes (such as maternity leave and day-care allowances) in that country may have had unintentionally negative effects on the careers of all women, whether or not they choose to become mothers. If some employers develop an unspoken assumption about the likelihood that family-friendly rights will be taken up by any woman within a certain age range, then a so-called statistical discrimination effect

Box 14.8 Learning activity
Ethics and equality/diversity policies

This learning activity is designed to enable you to learn about the ethical perspectives covered in this chapter by applying them to equality and diversity policies. Using the internet or other published material, research the equality/diversity policies of three different organizations: one commercial organization, one public sector organization, and one not-for-profit organization. Analyse the explanations and justifications for these policies in terms of the ethical frameworks discussed in Section 14.3.

Box 14.9 International focus
Equality of opportunity—a cultural phenomenon?

It may be useful to think about the equality legislation described in this chapter in relation to the idea of ethical relativism. In many Western developed economies, such as the USA and the UK, the notion of equality of opportunity and the removal of prejudice is a component of 'good' behaviour, and not only in employment. As businesses extend their operations into new and developing parts of the world, they often take this philosophy of 'good' employment with them. However, equal opportunity in these terms is not a universally accepted principle. In some societies, an important guiding principle of good behaviour is that of looking after one's own (family, kin, members of the immediate community). There is a deontological argument here—care of one's family is an important duty, so how can it be good to favour strangers over those to whom we owe a greater duty of care? There may also be consequentialist arguments; for a small business, a reasonably competent family member may be seen as a better bet than a more highly qualified stranger because the risk may be seen as smaller. Family members may be seen as less likely to behave badly towards their employer because of the social sanctions available; indeed, they may be motivated to work harder or better because of the kinship ties. The reason for raising this point is that it would be a mistake to assume that equal opportunity (whatever its business benefits) is taken for granted as a good thing in every country around the world—globally, equality of opportunity considerations may not even characterize the majority of employment decisions.

may start to play a part, to the detriment of any woman candidate for appointment or promotion. The authors also suggest that this effect may be more important for women aiming at the top jobs. Hakim makes a similar point about family-friendly policies and gender equality across a broader range of countries:

> all the evidence shows family-friendly policies generally reduce gender equality in the workforce, rather than raising it, as everyone has assumed until now. This conclusion has now been drawn simultaneously by several scholars working independently using data for a variety of countries: the US, Sweden, Denmark and Germany. In particular, Sweden's generous family-friendly policies have created a larger glass ceiling problem than exists in the US, where there is a general lack of such policies. (Hakim 2011: 25)

Additionally, notions of equality of opportunity are not universally accepted, as illustrated in Box 14.9.

Perhaps the key message for HR practitioners from this research is that it is simplistic and possibly misleading to see the existence of a gender pay gap and/or a glass ceiling (i.e. a barrier that keeps women from the top jobs) as evidence of something unethical in the organization's practices. An organization that complies with equal pay legislation and applies equal opportunities principles in its recruitment and selection should not necessarily be dismayed by the persistence of gender pay gaps. These gaps need not reflect anything more than the effects of individual men and women making their own life and career choices from the options available to them. But organizations might be well-advised to ensure that this is, in fact, the case.

Summary and further reading

- Revealing unethical behaviour by individuals or organizations is known as whistle-blowing. Internal systems for reporting unethical activity are important, but external whistle-blowing can be justified under certain circumstances.

- Ethical considerations bear upon all the main HRM tasks; central policies such as equal opportunities are founded on strong ethical justifications from both a deontological and a consequentialist point of view.

- Ethical analysis can also be applied to understand some of the contemporary issues for HRM.

See Winstanley and Woodall (2000) and Pinnington, Macklin, and Campbell (2007) for up-to-date commentaries on ethics and HRM from a variety of perspectives, with contributors who cover most of the major HRM activities and present thoughts on the ethical content of mainstream HRM functions in a variety of national contexts. Concerning the issue of moral hazard and the 2007–2008 financial crisis, those wishing to explore in more detail could start with the interview given by Bank of England Governor Sir Mervyn King to Charles Moore in the Daily Telegraph on 4 March 2011 (http://www.telegraph.co.uk/finance/economics). Speeches given by Bank of England officials go into more technical and analytical detail: the talk 'Control Rights and Wrongs' by Bank of England Executive Director Andrew Haldane in October 2011 is a very useful review of the way in which the distribution of risks and returns in financial services has developed over the years. The text of this speech is available via the Bank of England website (www.bankofengland.co.uk). Also, Roubini and Mihm (2010) take an accessible global and historical perspective on the crisis.

14.5 Conclusion

Ethical analysis is complex. At several points in this chapter we have considered points of view that are both very well founded and yet largely contradictory. However, 'complex' is not the same as impossible, and the ethics of HRM can be seen to incorporate both deontological and consequentialist considerations. There are strong deontological requirements to treat people with respect, and not to abuse the unequal power that an employment situation usually represents. However, alongside these requirements, good and bad treatment of employees must also consider the effect of particular policies on the organization's ability to fulfil its purpose. It is both required and advisable to treat employees ethically, but this ethical duty is limited to that which arises from the employment relationship.

We conclude by touching on the suggestion that specialist HR managers have a special role as the 'conscience' of an organization—that they are, or should act as, 'ethical stewards' (e.g. Winstanley and Woodall 2000). It is obviously desirable that HR managers should behave ethically at work. There is also much that they can and should do in the way of training and internal communications to make it possible for others to do their job ethically (see Box 14.6 for an example of a training intervention). However, there seem to be three important reasons why an organization should not rely solely on its HRM department if it wishes to behave well. First, the main concern of the HRM department is with managing employees, but organizations can also behave well or badly towards other categories of people—customers, suppliers, competitors, and so on. Secondly, it would be very much a second-best option to have ethics regarded as the responsibility of the HRM department, thus allowing others to avoid thinking about what they are doing in ethical terms. Finally, there is the pragmatic reason that ethical problems often have their origin in the detail of work done at a junior level, which may be completely off the radar as far as even the most conscientious HRM department is concerned. An effective organization needs to have ethical considerations interwoven into all its systems and strategies. See the DVD interview with Richard Solly for an illustration of how organizations can be inspired by ethical values. However, HR practitioners can have a dominant influence on the way that employees are treated, and can also assist in the ethical development of the organization by designing and providing suitable training and creating channels of communication that can help ethical problems to be identified and addressed.

 Assignment and discussion questions

1 What are the main implications for HRM of the approaches to ethics discussed in Section 14.3?

2 What would you include in a 'code of practice' for human resource managers? Try to identify and explain four or five main items for your code, and explain the ethical principles behind them.

3 This chapter concentrates on the ethical treatment of employees by employers through HRM practices. But do employees have any ethical duties towards their employers? If so, what are they? If not, why not? Use the concepts outlined in Section 14.3 to frame your answer.

4 Read the two articles by Richard Reeves and Alex Wilson in *People Management*, 3 October 2002, under the heading 'Do the business or do the right thing?' (available online at www.peoplemanagement.co.uk). Analyse and identify the types of ethical arguments made by each of the writers.

5 Read the material in Chapter 10 about workplace bullying and harassment. Use the ethical frameworks discussed in this chapter to identify exactly what is objectionable about bullying in the workplace, and to evaluate the policy measures that have been proposed to deal with it.

 Online Resource Centre

Test your understanding of this chapter with online questions and answers, keep up to speed with changes to the law through regular updates, and use selected weblinks to quickly access useful resources and further information. Visit the Online Resource Centre at:
www.oxfordtextbooks.co.uk/orc/gilmore_williams2e/

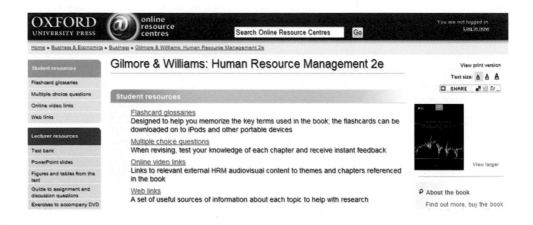

 Case study
Olympus: whistle-blowing in the executive suite?

This case is about whistle-blowing—action taken by an employee to expose perceived wrongdoing by an employing organization, in the hope of bringing about a resolution to the problem. Most of the well-reported whistle-blowing cases involve a middle-rank or junior employee faced with an anguished decision about an issue that is causing concern; however, in this one the whistle-blower was the boss himself. In October 2011, British press reports began to emerge about the abrupt departure of the recently appointed CEO of Olympus, the global camera, electronics, and medical equipment corporation. The CEO was Michael Woodford, a 51-year-old Briton who had worked for Olympus for 30 years. Until his appointment to the top job, he had worked mostly in Europe.

The contentious issue in this case centred on unusual payments made in the course of Olympus's takeover of Gyrus, a UK medical equipment company, in 2008, well before Michael Woodford's appointment as CEO. As Iain Dey and Oliver Shah reported in the *Sunday Times Business News* of 23 October 2011, the newly appointed Woodford first became aware of the issue when his attention was drawn to an article in a Japanese investigative magazine. The article was critical of Woodford's predecessor Tsuyoshi Kikukawa, who remained President (Chairman) of the company, and alluded to unexplained payments and accounting at the time of the Gyrus acquisition. Woodford held a series of meetings with Kikukawa and Executive Vice-President Hisashi Mori to gather information about what had happened, and as a result decided to commission his own investigation. Three months later, he concluded that there were grounds for serious concern; for example, advisory fees equivalent to about 35 per cent of the Gyrus acquisition price (much higher than the normal 1–2 per cent) had been paid to an unfamiliar company in the Cayman Islands. Woodford raised these concerns with Kikukawa and Mori clearly, and in writing: the *Sunday Times* article quotes from the final letter as follows:

> It is truly extraordinary and frankly unbelievable that Olympus, a major Nikkei-listed public company, made a series of payments approaching $700m in fees to a company in the Cayman Islands whose ultimate ownership is still unknown to us.

Shortly afterwards, Woodford was unceremoniously sacked by the company because of 'differences in management direction and methods'. He left Japan and briefed the Serious Fraud Office in London, as well as its Japanese equivalent and the largest shareholders in Olympus. As the abrupt dismissal became known, the Olympus share price fell sharply, despite the attempts by the company to publicly dismiss the allegations. On 25 October 2011, Olympus President Kikukawa accused Woodford of deliberately seeking to damage the company's reputation by making the payments public. He repeated the complaint about Woodford's management style, suggested that Woodford did not like Japan, and alleged that Woodford and a 'gang' of sympathisers at Olympus were trying to drive him from the company. On the following day, Kikukawa resigned. The company said that this was in response to the trouble caused to customers, business partners, and investors. The new President, Shuichi Takayama, promised to investigate the matter thoroughly, although Woodford was quick to point out that a past internal investigation in Olympus had found that there had been no wrongdoing by management. On 8 November 2011, the BBC reported the dismissal of Executive Vice-President Mori from the Board, following the shocking news that the unusual payments had been part of an attempt by the company to hide losses made in earlier acquisitions. By mid-November, discontent among major shareholders was continuing and the Japanese Prime Minister had expressed concern about the implications of the affair for investment in Japanese companies.

As Sternberg (2000) observes, the things that worry potential whistle-blowers will often be damaging to shareholder value, once known more widely. Therefore good companies will treat whistle-blowers as a valuable resource and ensure that their concerns are addressed before the damage is done. The rapid decline in the Olympus share price in the immediate aftermath of the revelations demonstrates this point dramatically: markets are easily spooked by allegations of irregularity, and attempts blandly to brush them aside may increase that unease. Reputations in business are immensely valuable—they are unique to the company and very difficult for competitors to copy. However, they usually take years to build up and can be seriously damaged in a matter of days or weeks.

Questions

1 Compare the action taken by Michael Woodford with the advice provided by De George's whistle-blowing code in Section 14.5.1. On the basis of the evidence in the case, was Woodford justified in taking his concerns outside the company?

2 What are the key implications for the company and its owners of the allegations made by Michael Woodford in this case?

3 What should be the short- and medium-term priorities of the new Olympus board with respect to the ethical concerns raised by Woodford?

News Online 2010). Equally importantly, sometimes the mere threat of moving production may be sufficient to extract desired concessions from a workforce. Particularly in 'high-cost' countries with established labour protection, such as Germany and Sweden, negotiations between firms and unions to achieve cost-cutting or flexibility-enhancing measures have often been accompanied by management comparisons with other possible employment locations and threats to move to them (Marginson and Meardi 2009).

However, matters are not quite this simple. It would be an exaggeration to claim that multinational firms, intent on fashioning their own internal HR systems, are trampling underfoot the employment traditions and systems built up over generations in countries around the world. A number of commentators have tried to distinguish between different factors that may influence the precise conjunction of HR policies adopted in particular firms in individual countries. Smith and Meiksins (1995) identify *societal* influences on national employment systems, *dominance* effects, through transfer of employment policies and practices characteristic of whichever nations are politically or economically dominant at any given time, and *system* effects resulting from the structural imperatives of capitalist forms of industrial organization. Delbridge, Hauptmeier, and Sengupta (2011) propose adding *corporate* effects to this influential schema, concerned with the nature of relations between corporate headquarters in MNCs and their local, often overseas, subsidiaries (see below).

The implications of globalization for HRM are further complicated by the advent of a more multipolar world, as evidenced by the rise of nations like China and India. Not only do Western-owned MNCs operate in these markets, but multinationals based in emerging countries are increasingly acquiring Western 'brands', as shown by Indian MNC Tata's takeover of Corus Steel and the Tetley marque, for example. Several writers argue that it is extremely difficult to predict the outcomes for HRM practices, given the extreme cultural diversities between 'Western' and 'Eastern' business heritages (Chen and Miller 2010; Budhwar and Varma 2011).

15.2.2 Convergence of HRM?

The globalization of HRM implies that, to some extent, certain HR policies are deemed particularly efficient or effective and are—indeed, should be—capable of use, regardless of any particular national context. The previous discussion has indicated that globalization has produced certain *pressures* for convergence and conformity in national employment systems, although this does not mean that the *policies* pursued in particular countries or policy *outcomes* will converge (Hay 2000: 514). The country that has institutions or laws providing unusually high degrees of reward or protection for its workers is unlikely to retain its relative attractiveness as a place in which firms will wish to invest indefinitely. The literature currently assumes convergence towards the Anglo-American model, and views the firm, and particularly the multinational company, as the primary agent of the transmission of innovative policies. As we will discuss further below, such changes will be easier to achieve in countries that are relatively weak in independent 'intermediate' labour market institutions that might be able to obstruct, delay, or derail new initiatives. Such intermediate institutions might include trade unions, works councils, training organizations, and so on, which will be especially powerful if firms are required to engage with, or obtain approval from, such bodies for their plans. Innovative HR policies are more likely to be transferred within less distinctive 'institution-poor' countries.

However, even those countries that are generally agreed to possess relatively stable and unique employment systems, such as Germany and Japan, are not totally immune from Anglo-American employment practices, with convergence evident in certain areas. One common trend noted in Europe is decentralization of the typical level at which bargaining between employers and employees over pay and conditions takes place. In much of Europe most of this bargaining has traditionally taken place at the level of the individual industry, or sector, such as metalworking, banking, and printing. Increasingly, however, agreements are now being struck between employer and trade union at the level of the individual firm (Traxler, Blaschke, and Kittel 2001; Eurofound 2011). Some of these firm-level agreements are perfectly compatible with the continuation of bargaining at the level of the industry sector. In other cases they could be interpreted as a 'Trojan horse'—agreements within one firm that have the potential to undermine previously agreed conditions for other firms in the same industry. An example is the 2004 deal between Siemens and the metalworkers' union IG Metall in Germany, where the union agreed to longer working hours to prevent the threatened transfer of production to Hungary (EIRO 2004).

As was discussed in Chapter 2, a number of largely American authors have made claims for the universal potential of certain human resource techniques and practices that have been combined under the generic labels of 'high-commitment or 'best-practice' management (e.g. Huselid 1995). Although their emphases vary, the kinds of HR practices they believe to be generalizible show some remarkable overlaps. The most commonly cited techniques include extensive in-company training, decentralized teamworking, sophisticated recruitment practices, extensive communication with employees, and relatively high pay, albeit contingent on individual performance. Such views have attracted widespread criticism (see Marchington and Grugulis 2000). Some firms compete through lowering costs, including labour costs, to the bare minimum and largely eschew positive HR policies, something that can be just as economically successful (see Box 15.1). Firms may be better advised to 'pick and mix' the 'best-fit' individual combination of HR policies that matches their business model most closely rather than to cling to the full menu of policies recommended by the 'best-practice' theorists. Indeed, as we suggested above, evidence suggests that, in non-Western contexts, some MNCs have found that an idiosyncratic mixture of Western 'best practice' and more indigenous HR techniques seems to be more appropriate (Som 2006, 2008; Pereira and Anderson 2011).

15.2.3 Explanations for the diversity in national HRM practices

An alternative explanation of contemporary developments in comparative HRM is to reject notions of convergence around some form of global 'best practice'. Instead, some stress the significance of factors that help to entrench the rather obvious differences between national employment systems and practices. Thus HR practices in different countries will remain nationally distinctive and diverse, and possibly even grow more divergent. Two strands to this form of analysis are noteworthy, each of which originates from different intellectual disciplinary roots. First, there is what can be termed an 'institutionalist' approach, rooted mainly in the academic disciplines of politics, sociology, or international relations. This school argues broadly that dissimilarity between distinctive *institutional frameworks*, such as political, legal, educational, and business systems, in different countries leads to national variations in norms and values,

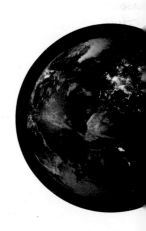

 Box 15.1 International focus
Walmart across the world

The US retailer Walmart provides a useful example of some of the possibilities and limits of pursuing a relatively uniform corporate approach to aspects of international HR policies. An epitome of small-town American values, the firm has expanded to become one of the largest corporations in the world (Moreton 2009). Walmart's growth within the USA and beyond has been achieved largely through a 'low-cost operator' business model, focusing on continuously reducing business costs, including labour costs, and passing the resultant savings on to the consumer in the form of lower prices (Fishman 2006; O'Toole and Lawler 2006: 11–12, 27, 241).

Walmart prefers a paternalist individualistic approach to labour relations with its employees that eschews trade unions in favour of direct forms of communication (Rosen 2005). Walmart has managed to defeat all attempts at trade union organization within its stores on the North American continent, including the closure in 2005 of a store in Jonquière, Quebec, shortly after a successful ballot in favour of union recognition there (Krauss 2005). Outside North America, however, this approach to workers has sometimes run into problems, as has its business model more generally (Halapete, Seshradi Iyer, and Park 2008). In 2006 its Asda subsidiary in the UK made concessions to the GMB union in the face of a threatened strike at its delivery depots. Walmart has pulled out of Germany, partly because of employment relations difficulties (Knorr and Arndt 2003). In China, Japan, and Brazil, Walmart has had to concede union organization within its stores (Bibby 2005: 2; Union Network International 2006).

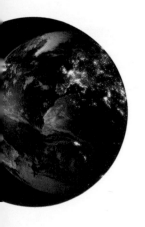

and therefore in employment systems, organizational expectations, policies, and practices, including HRM practices. By contrast, another view, based more in psychology, holds that deep-rooted national cultural differences in norms influence the institutional and employment frameworks that arise, and workers' expectations and values in an organizational context. Let us examine each of these in turn.

The institutionalist position rejects the hypothesis that employment systems in capitalist societies will gradually converge on one most 'efficient' model—specifically now the Anglo-American model. Rather, it sees this as just one possible model, whose economic 'success' is contingent on factors such as weak formal labour market institutions and trade unions, and relatively little regulation of firms. It cannot 'work' and its 'success' cannot be replicated outside this institutional context. However, argue the institutionalists, the economic strength of other countries is based on other conjunctions of forces that have developed over time. In Germany, for instance, a strong network of labour market rules and institutions, such as employers' associations, vocational training bodies, and labour unions, complement and interlock with each other and provide other possible routes to economic success. Once such a nationally specific complex has been formed, the argument goes, it will become self-reinforcing.

While a number of strands to the institutional school of thought have developed since the 1980s, the so-called 'varieties of capitalism' approach (e.g. Hall and Soskice 2001) has been extremely influential as an explanation for the synchronization of elements of national employment systems and their durability in the face of global business, political, and economic pressures. Just two 'ideal types' of capitalism are distinguished: liberal market economies, best represented by the UK and the USA, and coordinated market economies, of which Germany represents the prime example. This could fairly be regarded as rather a short list. Others expand the typology, such as Amable's (2003) differentiation between five types of capitalism. These add an 'Asian' type, a 'Nordic' model, encompassing the Scandinavian countries, and a 'southern European' model, into which most of the Latin countries bordering the Mediterranean are placed.

Certain shortcomings of the 'varieties' approach must be noted. First, in stressing the roles of institutions, labour market rules, and stability, it could be seen as unduly determinist, failing to allow for the possibility of change or the pursuit alternative policies (Crouch 2005; Streeck and Thelen 2005; Allen 2006; Almond and Gonzalez Menendez 2006; Black 2011; Howell and Kolin Givan 2011). Possible solutions to this drawback will be discussed further below. Secondly, once one accepts that there is more than one variety of capitalism, one must then ask how many different 'types' can be classified, without either lapsing into treating each country as a unique special case or over-generalizing.

An alternative explanation of national business diversity has come from those who see it as rooted in entrenched cultural attitudes that remain extremely resistant to change. While the best-known explanation is that of Hofstede's multinational surveys of employees within the US conglomerate IBM (Hofstede 2001), other authors have also enquired about the weight placed in different national cultures on factors such as respect for authority and rules, formality, individualism, the importance of hierarchy, equality between individuals, and so on (Laurent 1983; Trompenaars and Hampden-Turner 1997). As with some of the institutional approaches discussed above, the 'culturalist' studies often also try to group nations according to similar characteristics, and therefore are equally vulnerable to charges of simplification and stereotyping, as well as methodological and other criticisms (McSweeney 2002, 2009). Such studies may have some value in identifying in which national cultures the various high-performance techniques identified earlier in this section may be likely to succeed or fail. For example, teamworking is unlikely to work in cultures placing a high regard on formal authority and hierarchy, and performance-related pay may fall on stony ground in egalitarian cultures.

15.2.4 Going beyond 'convergence' and 'diversity' approaches

As we have seen above, it is relatively easy to find evidence that most employment practices and systems remain nationally based, and also that the growing influence of multinational firms and international pressures for convergence are causing greater cross-national transparency and transferability of HR practices. This does not really help us to understand more precisely the unevenness and complexity of the interplay between these two trends. Luckily, a number of studies provide a more nuanced view on the nature of developments in comparative HRM practices and suggest that sectoral differences may be increasingly supplanting national similarities (Katz and Darbishire 2000; Marginson and Sisson 2004; Bechter, Brandl, and Meardi 2011).

To illustrate two of these cross-national and cross-sectoral comparative studies, Katz and Darbishire (2000) investigated the telecommunications and motor industries across seven nations, while Marginson and Sisson (2004) studied the metalworking and banking sectors in four EU countries. Importantly, Marginson and Sisson (2004) found that greater convergence is detectable in employment practices across countries in those sectors more open to the international economy and to the penetration of multinational companies. In other respects, and especially outside such sectors, considerable national differences are more noticeable.

Katz and Darbishire (2000) detected similar cross-national similarities emerging in the sectors they investigated, both of which are now strongly internationalized. They argued that, regardless of country, four main patterns of work are emerging, ushered in especially by major firms, which are increasingly dictating the particular strategic work pattern they wish to pursue. Katz and Darbishire termed these patterns low-wage, Japanese-oriented, HRM, and joint team-working, each with a different value attached to sophisticated labour-management policies, innovative work organization, and so on. Such findings suggest that the main focus of activity in employment systems is becoming transformed in more internationalized sectors (Spicer 2006). Many multinational companies in internationalized economic sectors wish to coordinate their HR practices, regardless of country of operation. For example, the Ford Motor Company has one operating division for the whole of Europe. In more protected sectors, the national level remains the main scale of action.

 ## Summary and further reading

- Globalization is affecting HRM and employment systems through the activities of multinational firms and the dominance of particular political philosophies and economic policies, notably the spread of the Anglo-American neoliberal model. The decentralization of collective bargaining in some countries from industrial or sector level to the individual firm itself is one of the main examples of how globalization is affecting HR policies.

- In opposition to theories of convergence, national institutional and cultural factors have been identified by research as important reasons for the persistence of differences in employment systems between nations. These differences are becoming more extreme and significant as emerging nations, and their MNCs, become more active in the world economy. 'Institutionalist' and 'culturalist' theories have certain drawbacks, including stereotyping and generalizing, and are having difficulty in accounting for change.

- Recent research has identified uneven changes cross-nationally in the convergence of HRM practices, depending on the extent to which different firms and sectors are internationalized.

Philips and Eamets (2007) provide a broad account of the impact of globalization on HRM and industrial relations developments in major economies, taking the impact of the global recession into account. Hancké, Rhodes, and Thatcher (2007) provide a good summary of debates about the 'varieties of capitalism' approach.

15.3 Multinational companies and HRM

One of the main features of IHRM is a concern with understanding the human resource practices of MNCs—for example, how they manage staff undertaking international assignments (see Section 15.4). But we also need to examine how MNCs attempt to transfer HR practices on an international basis, from their corporate headquarters to subsidiaries in foreign countries and vice versa, and the factors that influence this process of diffusion.

15.3.1 Multinationals in the global economy

For our purposes, a key feature of multinational companies concerns their role as international employers (Kidger 2002). Since the 1980s there has been a marked increase in the scale and scope of MNC activity. By 2008, there were some 82,000 MNCs in existence, responsible for hundreds of thousands of affiliates around the world (UNCTAD 2010). While firms operating in the vehicle manufacturing, oil, telecommunications, and information technology sectors, including companies such as Toyota, BP, Vodafone, and Siemens, dominate the list of largest MNCs, the presence of multinationals has become a feature of most industrial sectors. In the service sector the French Accor group operates hotels in over 140 countries worldwide.

MNCs can be viewed as the 'primary movers and shapers' of the global economy (Dicken 2007: 106). In particular, rising levels of foreign direct investment (FDI) by multinationals have been a major contribution to economic globalization. While the economic crisis of the late 2000s produced a substantial decline in the amount of FDI, such that by 2010 it was over a third less than the peak level attained in 2007, it was still responsible for more than a quarter of global GDP (UNCTAD 2011c). Much FDI is manifest in the internationalization of production activity, through the operation of cross-border production networks by MNCs and the development of 'offshore' sites, such as call-centre facilities in India (Dicken 2007). In Asia, for example, the Philippines is a major location for the production of electronic goods, particularly semiconductors, by multinational firms (McKay 2006). FDI increasingly takes the form of cross-border mergers and acquisitions (UNCTAD 2011c), such as in the case of the merger of British Airways and Spanish operator Iberia to form the International Airlines Group in 2010.

Most FDI flows occur between advanced economies, especially within the so-called triad of the USA, Western Europe, and Japan. The UK is a particularly attractive location for multinational investment, with many industry sectors, including financial services, retail, and hotels, dominated by foreign-owned enterprises (Marginson and Meardi 2010). However, there is a growing trend for investment to go to emerging economies such as China (UNCTAD 2011c), which has become a prominent location for the production of manufactured goods. In 2010 China attracted record levels of FDI, with a value of $106 billion. Moreover, firms originating from emerging economies like India increasingly act as a source of FDI, reflecting their growing international presence (Ramamurti and Singh 2009; Sauvant, Prakash Pradhan, and Chatterjee 2010). Latin American companies, such as the Mexican cement producer Cemex and the Brazilian oil company Petrobas, have expanded their international presence, becoming major multinational firms in the process (Casanova 2009). As China has become more integrated into the international economy, some of its enterprises have also developed a more substantial multinational character (Shen and Edwards 2006).

15.3.2 Approaches to HRM in multinationals

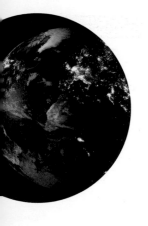

A key feature of the management of human resources in multinationals concerns the approach taken to staffing policy across the organization (Scullion and Collings 2006; Collings, Scullion, and Dowling 2009). The concept of 'global staffing', as applied to MNCs, concerns the 'critical issues faced by multinational corporations with regard to the employment of home, host and third country nationals to fill key positions in their headquarter and subsidiary operations' (Collings and Scullion 2009: 1249).

Perlmutter's (1969) distinction between three broad approaches to staffing policy is the most useful starting point for assessing the nature of HRM in multinationals. He outlined the main characteristics of a polycentric, an ethnocentric, and a geocentric approach to staffing policy. In MNCs favouring a polycentric approach, the emphasis is on recruiting local staff, or host country nationals (HCNs), to operate and manage subsidiary operations. The ethnocentric approach is characterized by a reliance on expatriate staff transferred from an MNC's home country—parent country nationals (PCNs)—to manage overseas subsidiaries. However, multinationals employing a geocentric staffing policy operate subsidiaries with an appropriate mix of HCNs, PCNs, and third country nationals (TCNs), people who come from a location other than the home and host countries. An example of a TCN would be an American manager working in the German subsidiary of a UK multinational. Perlmutter subsequently developed a fourth type of staffing policy in multinationals—the regiocentric approach. MNCs following a regiocentric staffing policy tend to transfer managers between operations within particular regions of the world (e.g. Western Europe).

The use of HCNs, PCNs, and TCNs varies considerably, according to both the country of origin of the multinational in question and the sector in which it operates. For example, German and Japanese MNCs use a relatively high proportion of PCNs compared with UK and US MNCs, who generally rely more on HCNs to manage subsidiaries. In sectors where companies have increasingly been able to develop a globally integrated dimension to their activities, such as the automobile and consumer electronics sectors, the use of expatriate PCNs and TCNs is more commonplace than in, say, the food and beverages sector, where subsidiaries are often relatively autonomous and less subject to central control from corporate headquarters (Harzing 1999).

It is better to see polycentricism, ethnocentrism, and geocentricism as competing influences on the practice of HRM in multinationals, rather than more narrowly simply as approaches to staffing policy. However, before we go on to assess the appropriateness of the polycentric, ethnocentric, and geocentric influences on the management of human resources in multinationals, we need to address a number of issues arising from Perlmutter's classification. For one thing, MNCs often take a somewhat reactive and unsystematic approach to staffing policy (Borg and Harzing 1995, cited by Harzing 1999) that is not characterized by any great deal of coherence or consistency. However, a growing amount of attention is being directed at the important role played by TCNs in multinationals, particularly the contribution they make to promoting organizational learning and innovation (Collings, Scullion, and Dowling 2009). A further issue concerns the growing recognition given to the dynamic and complex set of factors that influence staffing policy in multinationals, including the structure of the firm and the nature of its strategy (Tarique, Schuler, and Gong 2006).

With the increasing internationalization of economic activity, one would expect geocentric tendencies to exercise a more profound effect on the practice of HRM in multinationals. MNCs supposedly enjoy greater scope to develop and disseminate organization-based approaches to managing human resources across national borders in a way that transcends cross-national cultural and institutional influences. This is evident in the growing interest evinced by MNCs in operating global talent management arrangements (Tarique and Schuler 2010), although actual practice in many firms is still rather unsystematic (McDonnell et al. 2010).

15.3.3 The home country effect on the practice of HRM in multinationals

There are limits to the influence of geocentricism over HRM in multinationals. The characteristics of national business systems, both that of an MNC's home country and those of the host countries in which its subsidiaries operate, exercise an important influence over the practice of human resource management in multinationals; consistent with both the ethnocentric and polycentric approaches. We consider the host country influence in Section 15.3.4. In this section our concern is with the persistent ethnocentric, or home country, effect on the practice of HRM in multinationals.

MNCs are far from being stateless actors; generally they have strong ties to, and are embedded within, their national country of origin (Dicken 2007; Hirst, Thompson, and Bromley 2009). Even a major US multinational like Walmart has most of its operations in its home country (Edwards 2011). The implication is that a multinational's business practices, including the approach taken to the management of human resources, is strongly influenced by the features of its home country's national business system.

There is clear evidence of a notable home country, or 'country of origin', effect on HRM in multinationals (Ferner 1997), linked to the transfer of HR practices to foreign subsidiaries, a process which is called 'forward diffusion'. For example, Walsh and Zhu's (2007) study of MNCs operating in China found that US-owned firms were more likely to have established individualized incentive pay arrangements than Japanese-owned firms. Group-based incentives were more popular among the latter, reflecting differences in the dominant approaches in their home countries.

However, we need to be careful when evaluating the extent of the home country influence on the practice of HRM. Some national business systems, like that of the USA for example, may be more dominant in the global economy than others. This would imply that the home country effect is a more important influence on HRM in US multinationals than it is for, say, French or

German firms. Moreover, the characteristics of a home country's national business system may change over time (Tempel, Wächter, and Walgenbach 2006), meaning that the ethnocentric influence will vary, rather than being permanently fixed. One source of change may relate to the way in which MNCs transfer HR policies developed in their foreign subsidiaries back to their home base, thus influencing practice in their home country. This suggests the presence of an important host country influence on the practice of HRM in multinationals.

15.3.4 The host country effect

MNCs often have to adapt HR practices to reflect the cultural and institutional characteristics of the host country locations in which their subsidiaries are based. This suggests that HRM in multinationals is marked by a polycentric tendency; they adapt their practices to reflect local laws, norms, and values, something that constrains the extent to which they can effect the forward diffusion of HR practices from corporate headquarters to host country locations.

There are two main ways in which the host country environment influences management of HR in multinationals. First, national culture may influence the practice of HRM. We examined the question of cross-cultural diversity in Section 15.2.3. A study of MNCs in Greece found that the presence of 'strong and persistent national cultural norms and values meant that there was a notable 'tendency for MNCs to adapt to local practices', limiting the extent to which they could implement corporate HR policies (Myloni, Harzing, and Mirza 2004: 71). Secondly, institutional factors may have a powerful effect on HRM arrangements, linked to the characteristics of the host country's national business system, such as its legal framework, and the nature and structure of its labour market institutions, including trade unions and works councils (Edwards 2011).

To what extent do the institutional characteristics of the host country environment influence the practice of HRM in multinationals? For one thing, they can inform a process of 'reverse diffusion' (see Box 15.2). Moreover, practices not subject to national level legal regulation, such as management development arrangements, are more likely to be diffused successfully to host country locations (Ferner 2010). The extent to which forward diffusion is possible varies according to the strength of institutional regulation in the host country, and therefore how far it permits the successful transfer or HRM practices (Ferner 2010). Kostova's (1999) concept of 'institutional distance' implies that MNCs should find it easier to diffuse practices between home and host countries that have relatively similar institutional frameworks. Some host countries, such as the UK with its lightly regulated labour market, offer environments which are more amenable to transfer than others (Edwards and Ferner 2002; Marginson and Meardi 2010).

Box 15.2 Research in focus
The reverse diffusion of HR practices in multinationals

While we have been mainly concerned with the way in which multinationals attempt to transfer HR practices to subsidiaries in foreign locations through forward diffusion, they may be transferred in any direction, including from subsidiaries to corporate headquarters (Ferner 2010). The concept of 'reverse diffusion' refers to the way in which multinationals transfer HR practices from subsidiaries in foreign locations back to their home country base, or throughout the firm as a whole. MNCs may be able to draw on the advantages of the host country environments of their foreign subsidiaries to experiment with innovative HR practices, perhaps with the intention of using them more widely. Case study evidence from the UK and German subsidiaries of US multinationals indicates that the incidence of reverse diffusion can vary widely from one company to another, and indeed even between subsidiaries of the same company (Edwards and Tempel 2010). For example, a leadership development programme originated in a German subsidiary of a business services firm was taken up as the basis for overall company policy. In the case of a manufacturing firm, which operated a highly standardized corporate management approach, no successful reverse diffusion was evident despite some efforts to promote it. Among the factors that influence the presence of reverse diffusion is the nature of the host country's business system. For example, UK subsidiaries were better placed to promote innovative HR practices than German subsidiaries because the characteristics of their host country environment were more closely aligned with those of the US firm's home country base.

Although the characteristics of the host country environment exercise an important influence over the way in which HR is managed in multinational subsidiaries, firms enjoy some room for manoeuvre when it comes to diffusing practices. In China, for example, the increasing presence of multinationals appears to have eroded the constraints imposed by the host country environment, contributing to the wider diffusion of Western HR practices (Cooke 2005). There is often a process of adaptation, whereby practices are transferred, but in a way that is moderated by aspects of to the host country context (Edwards 2011). Like the home country effect, then, the host country influence on HRM is subject to change, and evolves over time, rather than being permanently fixed.

15.3.5 Power, politics, and the management of HRM in multinationals

How far do structural factors, such as home and host country effects and corporate systems of control and coordination, influence the practice of human resource management within multinationals? What about the role of managers who, as key actors within MNCs, may be able to draw on sources of power to resist the diffusion of HR practices? Multinational firms are political entities, which are characterized by struggles for power, and bargaining between, managers in different parts of the organization (Ferner and Edwards 1995; Dörrenbächer and Geppert 2011). Transferring HR practices is an 'essentially *political* process' (Ferner 2010: 549). Managers in subsidiaries of multinational firms use the characteristics of their host country's institutional environment as a source of power—something that enables them to facilitate, amend, or resist the diffusion of practices as appropriate (Geppert and Williams 2006; Ferner 2010; Edwards 2011).

Thus there is strong support for an actor-centred approach to understanding the practice of HRM in multinationals, one that captures the important way in which the activities of managers themselves influence the diffusion of HR initiatives, albeit within particular institutional contexts (Geppert and Mayer 2006). Local actors, particularly the managers of subsidiary operations, draw on elements of their host country environment to influence the extent to which, and also how, corporate practices are implemented in their sites (Edwards, Colling, and Ferner 2007).

Perhaps the most useful insights into how subsidiary managers resist unwelcome or inappropriate parent country HR initiatives come from a study of diversity policy in US multinationals with subsidiaries in the UK (Ferner, Almond, and Colling 2005). The MNCs studied had all instituted robust policies for managing diversity on a global basis, based on practice in their home country base. However, managers in the UK subsidiaries were concerned that the diffusion of diversity policy had been attempted in a way that was incommensurate with the host country environment. Thus there was a complex process of negotiation between home and host country managers to ensure that the diversity policies were applied to the subsidiaries appropriately. Managers in the UK were able to draw upon aspects of the legal framework governing diversity issues to modify the corporate policy, rendering it more appropriate in the British context. While geocentric, polycentric, and ethnocentric influences on the management of human resources in subsidiaries of multinationals undoubtedly have important effects, the extent of diffusion is also marked by the outcomes of power struggles between organizational actors.

 Summary and further reading

- Understanding the factors that influence HR practices in MNCs is one of the key features of IHRM as a topic of enquiry. The transfer, or diffusion, of best-practice HRM across national borders reflects the globally integrated approach that multinationals increasingly use to manage their human resources.

- The diffusion of HR practices across national borders is influenced by both the characteristics of the national business system in which the MNC originates, and those of the countries where its subsidiaries are located.

- The diffusion of HR practices is also influenced by political factors relating to organizational decision-making within MNCs. An actor-centred approach which captures the important way in which the activities of managers themselves influence the diffusion of HR initiatives, albeit within particular institutional contexts, may be desirable. This is a further constraint on the power of multinationals to transfer HRM across national borders.

See Collings and Scullion (2009) for the influences on staffing arrangements in multinationals. Marginson and Meardi (2010) examine multinationals in the UK. For a good overview of the influences on HRM in multinationals, particularly the transfer of HR practices, see Edwards (2011).

15.4 Managing international assignments and assignees

Organizations increasingly function in an international working environment as their operations expand into more countries. Establishing a new subsidiary in a foreign location may require a firm's existing staff to spend some time working in a new country. An alternative resourcing option is to employ self-initiated expatriates (SIEs). SIEs can be defined as 'employees who decided to migrate to another country for work' (Howe-Walsh and Schyns 2010: 262). How people who are working in a foreign location—or expatriates, as they are known—are managed may have a crucial effect on the success of the new operation. Around 40 per cent of staff who return from an international assignment subsequently leave the organization within 12 months of coming back (Brookfield 2011), resulting in significant additional costs, including loss of knowledge. Given the extensive use of international assignments globally (Mercer 2011; PricewaterhouseCoopers 2011), the importance of managing the expatriate process effectively acquires greater importance. The purpose of this section is to investigate the HRM issues concerning the management of international assignees that organizations face within an increasingly globalized environment.

15.4.1 Why use international assignments?

International assignments are used for three key reasons. First, companies may need to fill a vacant position in a subsidiary, and sending an international assignee is a means of filling that vacancy. A second purpose of international assignments is to develop global competencies in the management team. Creating in-house globally competent employees can enhance a firm's global competitive advantage. Providing opportunities to develop global competencies could form part of an organization's development strategy. International assignments enhance an individual's career prospects, as well as supporting organizational goals (Stahl et al. 2009). By helping to nurture its internal talent, through opportunities to develop international careers, firms can also retain key staff (see Box 15.3). International assignments may be required as part of career progression in multinationals (Suutari and Burch 2001; Vance 2005; Kraimer, Shaffer, and Bolino 2009).

Thirdly, international assignments aid the process of knowledge transfer within a company (Vance 2005). The transfer of knowledge is twofold: from the assignee to the foreign subsidiary, and, via the assignee, from the subsidiary to the home organization. In order to maximize the

Box 15.3 Practitioner perspective
Promoting international assignments at Hewlett Packard

International assignments are often used by multinationals to enable staff to develop organizational careers across national borders (Vance 2005; Kraimer, Shaffer, and Bolino 2009). This is evident from the case of IT firm Hewlett Packard (HP), according to Jane Keith, its people development director for Europe, the Middle East, and Africa. Increasing the mobility of key staff should produce more talented employees, enhance the diffusion of organizational knowledge across national borders, and also encourage people to stay with the firm. For Keith, the 'key thing is to move people around geographically and across business units'. She aims to develop an environment in which people 'know that to move up the chain, they need to experience working across geographical and business boundaries' (Pitcher 2008).

extent of knowledge transfer, rather than lose it to a competitor, organizations try to ensure that opportunities which can enable the employee's career needs to be aligned with the firm's interest in supporting his/her retention are available within the home organization (Lazarova and Tarique 2005).

15.4.2 Types of international assignments

Four types of international assignment can be identified. First, with 'traditional' assignments staff are often deployed to a foreign location on a long-term basis; anything over 12 months would fall into this category. Typically, a partner/partner and family would accompany the expatriate. Secondly, short-term assignments continue to grow in popularity (PricewaterhouseCoopers 2011). They entail a reduced overall package of compensation in order to accommodate the shorter assignment. Thirdly, 'virtual' or 'commuter' assignments involve regular travel to a foreign location on a weekly or bi-weekly basis, while the assignee's family remains at home. Fourthly, there are also frequent business fliers: staff are based at home, but travel frequently for business purposes (Collings, Scullion, and Morley 2007; Welch, Welch, and Worm 2007).

One of the HRM challenges facing firms that operate international assignments concerns tracking the type of assignment an employee is undertaking. Keeping track of the number of assignees can also become difficult when the company does not have a clear international policy. A frequent issue for multinationals is the need to determine the assignment population—those employees who are thought to be on a business trip or commuting assignment, or are undertaking in effect a short- or long-term assignment. The implications of not categorizing assignees is often an issue that remains undiscovered until a compliance problem has arisen—an issue that will be addressed below.

15.4.3 Selecting assignees

Selecting an international assignee is not always given the same due care and attention as the organization's domestic selection procedures. It often takes place informally during discussions based on chance conversations within the office. The main problem with this informal 'coffee machine' approach to selecting assignees is the lack of consideration given to the candidate's overall suitability for an international assignment (Harris and Brewster 1999; Brookfield 2011). Does the person have the right sets of competencies, such as adaptability, flexibility, conflict-resolution skills, questioning and listening skills, cross-cultural awareness, communicative ability, influencing skills, emotional maturity, self-motivation, and resilience, needed as an international assignee (Moore 2011)?

In addition to this well-used list, how receptive will the employee be to an international assignment? What are the key drivers to accepting the assignment, and what are the potential barriers? Some studies (e.g. Black, Mendenhall, and Oddou 1991) focus on the issue of expatriate adjustment—how likely is it that an individual will be receptive to an international career and cope with the resulting uncertainty (Tharenou 2002)? Other important factors that influence individual decision-making concern the potential of relocating abroad to generate lifestyle changes, disruption to the family, and potential dual-career issues if the potential assignee's partner is in employment. Moore (2011: 189) believes that one or more of the following reasons are likely to lead to an employee wanting to undertake an international assignment.

- Career advancement: this may be either within the employee's current organization or in a future organization.
- Financial incentives: the package provided by the company may enhance the overall compensation that the employee currently receives.
- Interest in the destination: the assignee may have a link to the assignment location.
- Interest in travel: this is especially pertinent for those without family commitments who may be at a relatively early stage in their careers.

Generally, organizations use internal candidates to fill assignments. Maintaining control of operations, and the interest of corporate headquarters in the assignment location, requires

Box 15.4 Learning activity
Selecting staff for international assignments

The purpose of this activity is to encourage you to consider arrangements for selecting staff for international assignments in more detail. There are three tasks.

1 List the main attributes you think are required by staff who are going to be working in an international environment.

2 Based on the list you have compiled, consider the methods you would use to select appropriate staff to work in an international environment.

3 What are the problems you may encounter when attempting to put your selection exercise into practice, and how would you try to overcome them?

internal candidates who have a proven track record and are trusted by the organization. Expatriates may also perform a strategic role (Torbiorn 1997; Bonache and Fernandez 2007). If an internal candidate is not found, the need to recruit externally provides additional challenges. External recruitment can bring new knowledge and skills that will benefit the organization. Nevertheless, external candidates are unlikely to be imbued with its cultural ethos.

The pool of internal candidates from which to select could potentially be rather small, reflecting changes in organizations, particularly the shift towards operating with a narrower core of staff (Beynon et al. 2002). Recruitment difficulties at home may also be reflected in the international assignment arena, given a limited potential pool of talent. See Box 15.4 for a learning activity about selecting staff for international assignments.

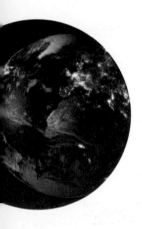

The number of female expatriates is very low relative to males. According to PricewaterhouseCoopers (2005), the proportion of females undertaking international assignments is under 10 per cent of the total, although some surveys offer a slightly brighter picture (Brookfield 2011). Whilst there is a debate regarding whether this is solely the result of biased selection processes, linked to the informal nature of selection (Harris and Brewster 1999), female self-perception may play a part in the low take-up of international assignments. Fischlmayr (2002: 780–1) cites some of the reasons for the low female take-up of international assignments.

- Women have a tendency to adjust their lives to their people: their partner, their children, their superiors, etc.

- Women have internalized their roles, behave according to them, and do not attempt to change the status quo.

- Women believe that age is a prohibitive factor.

- Women are conscious of the stereotype they continue to perpetuate.

Nevertheless, some authors have been sharply critical of the 'myth' of female lack of motivation for undertaking international assignments. A more important factor concerns the assumptions of senior male managers in multinationals that women are unsuitable as expatriates (Adler 1994). Extending the debate, an exploratory study of female expatriates considered female expatriates as active agents, capable of producing effective professional identities when interacting with men which enhanced their success on assignment (Janssens, Cappellen, and Zanoni 2006).

15.4.4 Support for international assignees

From an assignee's point of view, one of the greatest concerns and potential barriers to undertaking an international assignment is the effect that it will have on his/her family. According to practitioner studies, nearly half of all potential assignments are turned down on this basis (PricewaterhouseCoopers 2005; Brookfield 2011). An organization's ability to recognize the importance of providing partner assistance, as well as considering the children who may accompany the assignee, is crucial. The education of children is a key concern to a parent; it is vital to recognize that continuity of schooling needs to be top of the list of discussions regarding the assignment. Providing support to the partner in terms of job hunting, recruitment services, work permit assistance, training and development, and additional allowances can all enhance the chances of a successful assignment.

There are many support mechanisms that can be utilized for both the assignee and his/her family. Effective HRM can provide invaluable assistance in establishing home and host links for the assignee, which should commence before the assignment begins. Pre-assignment trips (known as 'look–see trips') to properties, schools, and local amenities play an important role is establishing initial support. If the assignee is accompanied, it is important that the partner participates in the trip. Furthermore, providing assistance to help working partners find suitable employment, or to provide additional allowance for training, can encourage women to undertake assignments.

Other activities include the provision of cultural briefings, language lessons, and assistance with payroll arrangements. Cultural briefings help to focus on some of the key cultural differences faced by the assignee. It is worth noting that assignments to countries that are perceived to be relatively close in culture to that of the home country still require briefing sessions. Tung (1987:120) suggests that cross-cultural training offered across Europe results in lower cases of assignment failure.

Additional training and support for an expatriate's family could be considered. Again, pre-assignment training has focused on cross-cultural and language issues; however, people can benefit from training interventions whilst they are on assignment and adjusting to the new environment. Indeed, Suutari and Burch (2001: 308) argue that the adjustment of the family appears to be far more difficult than that of the assignee. They note that the key areas experienced were with local interaction, often caused by language problems, and a general lack of local or expatriate contacts. Additional support mechanisms could include extending mentoring programmes to families.

Providing advice on coping strategies can lessen or shorten the effects of culture shock. Stahl and Caliguri (2005: 611) suggest that coping strategies are influenced by various factors, such as the nature of the host country environment, the position, and the time spent on assignment. Abbott, Stening, and Atkins (2006) argue that a systematic approach to coaching can aid the acculturation of expatriates, enabling them to cope more effectively. Providing an external focus by means of a coach can assist with non-work aspects of the assignment, such as family issues. Internal coaching undertaken by a mentor may well be another legitimate form of support (Reiche, Kraimer, and Harzing 2011). Mezias and Scandura (2005: 519) advocate the use of a multi-mentor approach before, during, and after an assignment. Adopting multiple mentoring, both formal and informal, undertaken by peers and managers can improve the management of expatriation. The link to the home organization forms part of the mentoring relationship. However, the role of a sponsor should be undertaken by a specific person of senior standing within the business area. The activities undertaken by the sponsor could, for example, include agreeing the terms of the assignment (PricewaterhouseCoopers 2005).

With regard to international reward arrangements, there are a number of approaches that an organization can adopt. The most common is known as the balance sheet/build-up approach (PricewaterhouseCoopers 2005). While this is simple in theory, ensuring that the expatriate is no worse or no better off than if he/she had stayed at home, the actual calculations can be rather difficult. There is also the option of retaining the assignee on home country terms, but providing protection against additional tax liabilities, or of moving his/her package to host country pay, perhaps involving the reduction of the actual taxes paid by the assignee (see Box 15.5). Provision of additional allowances such as goods and services, or hardship allowances, also needs to be taken into account. Salary payments either remain in the home country or take the form of split payments, some to the host country and the remainder to the home country. Reward arrangements for expatriates are among the aspects of managing international assignments that firms often outsource to external providers (see Box 15.6).

Box 15.5 Online video link
Expatriate remuneration

Go to the Online Resource Centre for a link to video content in which Lee Quane, Regional Director Asia for global human resources consultancy firm ECA International, outlines the main approaches to reward for employees undertaking international assignments.

15.4.5 Repatriation issues

Much of the literature on the return, or repatriation, of staff to the home country suggests that it is at this time that an expatriate is most likely to leave the organization (Baruch, Steele, and Quantrill 2002; O'Sullivan 2002; Paik, Segaud, and Malinowski 2002; Brookfield 2011). The first 12 months after returning from an assignment are the most crucial stage of managing the expectations of the employee (PriceWaterhouseCoopers 2005). Linehan and Scullion (2002) propose that repatriation is more stressful than the initial expatriation event. Furthermore, for female international managers this is compounded by the pioneering nature of their senior roles and the lack of established career paths, which result in difficulties in finding a suitable position upon repatriation. The lack of career advancement upon return undoubtedly contributes to retention (Kraimer, Shaffer, and Bolino 2009). Differences between the management of the repatriation process appear to vary according to the country

Box 15.6 Policy example
Outsourcing expatriate management

Outsourcing HR functions to external suppliers has become an increasingly commonplace feature of HRM in organizations (Gospel and Sako 2010). Some multinationals outsource elements of the management of expatriates. Companies such as BT and the Royal Bank of Scotland (RBS) have outsourced aspects of how they manage international assignments. Outsourcing provides particular specialist services that may not be readily available within the organization, such as securing work permits through an immigration provider, or advice and costings from tax specialists and social security authorities. It is also possible to secure recruitment and selection, on-assignment, and repatriation services from external providers. They also help with establishing international policies, processes, and procedures, which are then managed internally within the organization. RBS believes that running a partially outsourced HR service provides many benefits to the organization (IRS 2000). For example, standardized processes are adopted and a more consistent approach to delivery is pursued. In addition, the costs to the business are more transparent. Management information is provided, enabling enhanced decisions to add value to the business. Human resource practitioners are then able to concentrate on other matters—see Figure 15.1 for the options that may be incorporated within an outsourced HR administration.

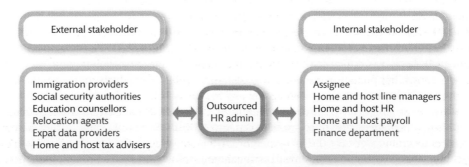

Figure 15.1 An outsourced HR administration for international assignments.

of origin of the company; European MNCs are often better at retaining expatriates than their American counterparts.

Does it matter if expatriates leave the organization following their repatriation? If the object of the assignment was to fill a vacancy, perhaps the position is longer required. However, if either of the other two reasons for the assignment applies—developing global competencies and transferring knowledge (Oddou, Osland, and Blakeney 2009)—it really is worth trying to retain expatriates when they return from an assignment. After all, the cost of an international assignment can be up to five times an employee's salary. Suutari and Valimaa (2002) suggest that the repatriation process should consist of varying adjustments that cover the expatriate's age, the length of the assignment, the timing of the negotiations, any adjustment problems, the extent of contact with home, and the presence of role conflict.

Whilst the literature points to the need for a clear process for managing repatriation, the assignee and the organization may have differing expectations. Paik, Segaud, and Malinowski (2002) explain that discrepancies often exist between the motivations and expectations of managers and of assignees. The timing of a repatriated assignee's new role, and negotiations over it, mark the adjustment process. Line managers have an important role (Harris, Brewster, and Sparrow 2003: 74). The multinational bank HSBC has formalized the continuing link between the international assignee and the home country by ensuring that there is a home business sponsor who is responsible for monitoring the assignee. In addition, the home sponsor ensures that the assignee forms part of the bank's talent pool. The sponsor becomes key to managing the assignee's career throughout the assignment, including involvement in annual reviews, and also ensuring that a suitable role is found upon repatriation (Brookfield 2011).

 ## Summary and further reading

- Managing international assignments is a key feature of IHRM. If done effectively, it can contribute to improved performance. Assignments can take a number of forms, but the traditional long-term assignment poses some particular HRM challenges for organizations in the areas of selection, training, support, reward, and repatriation.

- The selection of staff to undertake international assignments is marked by a considerable degree of informality since organizations have to be concerned with both the availability and the willingness of an employee to take up a post in a foreign location.

- Effective support for staff undertaking international assignments, and also their families where necessary, is a major contribution to the effectiveness of expatriation and also aids the process of repatriating the assignee.

For further information on the HRM issues concerning the management of staff on international assignments, Dowling, Festing, and Engle (2008) and Edwards and Rees (2011) are particularly recommended. See Harris and Brewster (1999) for a discussion of the informal basis of expatriate selection arrangements.

15.5 Towards strategic international HRM?

There is an increasing amount of interest in the relationship between the human resources policies and practices of MNCs and their business strategies (Brewster, Sparrow, and Harris 2005). The management of human resources on an international basis is seen as a crucial factor underpinning the global effectiveness of multinational firms (Schuler and Tarique 2007). Strategic IHRM is concerned with how the management of human resources in multinationals supports, and is itself influenced by, their overall business objectives which, by definition, have an international dimension (Taylor, Beechler, and Napier 1996).

At an international level the principal strategic challenge for MNCs concerns the need to reconcile pressures for global coordination with the desirability of being responsive to the different circumstances that prevail in the various countries where they have operations (Hall and Wailes 2010). We consider the main theoretical approaches that have been applied to strategic IHRM, examine the main ways in which MNCs have attempted to realize it in practice, and highlight some relevant developments concerning the HR function in multinationals.

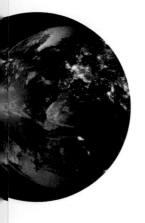

operates a 'Talent Pipeline' initiative, designed to identify, develop, and nurture potential global leaders (Sparrow, Brewster, and Harris 2004).

The scarcity of international managerial talent and heightened competition for that talent, as greater numbers of firms develop an international presence and managers become more internationally mobile, have been major drivers of the global talent management approach (McDonnell et al. 2010; Scullion and Collings 2010). Typically, this encompasses global succession planning arrangements, although these are not always formalized, and global management development schemes (McDonnell and Collings 2010). However, the presence of an integrated strategic approach to global talent management may not be all that common in practice (Collings, Scullion, and Morley 2007; Schuler, Jackson, and Tarique 2011). Moreover, obstacles often prevent it from achieving its potential, such as a paucity of senior management commitment, a lack of relevant knowledge and expertise, and the presence of organizational structures that obstruct cross-border learning and collaboration (Mellahi and Collings 2010; Schuler, Jackson, and Tarique 2011).

Ensuring that cross-border alliances between firms function effectively would seem to demand the enactment of a strategic IHRM capability. Such alliances arise when two or more firms with headquarters in different countries agree to work with each other, sharing resources and expertise, for a specific purpose (Schuler, Jackson, and Luo 2004). A potential role for IHRM is particularly evident in those forms of cross-border alliances where ownership implications arise. Mergers between firms involve the formation of a separate entity with each of its predecessors having an equal stake in the new company. Acquisitions occur when a firm buys a full or controlling stake in another one. International joint ventures (IJVs) can be an effective way for firms to break into new markets, helping to spread the risks associated with operating in territories where institutional and cultural norms are unfamiliar. For example, alliances between multinationals and indigenous firms are a commonplace investment vehicle in China.

Strategic IHRM can support the process of building successful cross-border alliances in a number of ways, by working to ensure that IJVs are staffed by high quality managers, for example, or by helping to ensure that cultural diversity is managed effectively in mergers and acquisitions (Schuler, Jackson, and Luo 2004). 'There is no shortage of evidence that attention to people and to cultural issues is one of the most critical elements in achieving the cross-border acquisition strategy' (Pucik et al. 2011: 130). Yet in practice the involvement of HRM in such alliances is often limited, particularly in the early planning stages. HRM issues tend to be operated in a non-strategic fashion, restricted to the implementation stage (Pucik et al. 2011)—reacting to the issues and problems generated by the merger and acquisition process, such as how to retain key staff and handling any associated redundancies.

Two further areas where multinationals look to operate IHRM in a strategic manner concern arrangements for transferring knowledge between sites in different countries and the management of diversity issues. Effective knowledge sharing can be a crucial source of improved organizational effectiveness. Firms such as the steel manufacturer ArcelorMittal and the oil company BP have established formal programmes which bring together managers from different business units around the world to discuss performance issues and share ideas about how to resolve common problems (Björkman, Evans, and Pucik 2011). Managing diversity issues on a global basis is also increasingly seen as an important element of strategic IHRM (Nishii and Özbilgin 2007). The key challenge for multinationals concerns the need to balance the imperative for a globally integrated corporate approach with sensitivity to the demands of diverse cultural and institutional national contexts (Sippola and Smale 2007)—see Box 15.7.

 Box 15.7 Skills exercise
Reflecting on your cross-cultural skills

Watch the short video of Professor Denis Leclerc of the Thunderbird School of Global Management speaking about the skills that form part of a manager's global mindset (at www.youtube.com/watch?v=f2F6LRBfPy4).

Then, working in small groups, think about and discuss the skills that are necessary to be effective as a manager in a global context, particularly when it comes to managing human resources.

Finally, we need to recognize the important role played by the corporate HR function in facilitating strategic IHRM in multinational firms. Studies of the role of the corporate HR function suggest that it plays an increasingly prominent part in coordinating HRM activities by, for example, building and enhancing a strong corporate culture, which helps to support the emergence of a 'global' approach to managing human resources in some leading multinationals, and supporting the development of global talent initiatives (Brewster, Sparrow, and Harris 2005; Farndale, Scullion, and Sparrow 2010; Farndale, Paauwe, et al. 2010). Multinationals have sought to enhance the contribution made by their corporate HR function to supporting business goals and, in particular, to enhancing their ability to reconcile pressures for global integration with the need to recognize local differences. This can encompass a wide variety of approaches. For example the 'shared services' model is becoming more popular (see Box 15.8). The study of sixteen MNCs, including Siemens, IKEA, and Samsung, by Farndale, Paauwe, et al. (2010) examines the respective roles of the corporate HR function. Samsung, for example, looks to control key new HR practices, especially those relating to cultural integration, from the centre, but also allows national level subsidiaries some scope for HR differentiation. However, one of the priorities of IKEA's corporate HR function is to sustain and disseminate a set of core principles, designed to guide HRM policies in subsidiaries, rather than prescribe a set of practices which they are expected to enact.

15.5.3 Strategic international HRM: a critical summary

How easily can multinational firms effect the strategic management of their human resources across national borders in the way we have outlined? The main problem with theoretical approaches to understanding strategic IHRM is that they present an idealized, over-rational, and thus simplistic picture of the strategy process, paying insufficient heed to the messy and often highly politicized way in which firms attempt to develop and realize their strategic objectives. See Section 15.3.5 for evidence of the importance of power relations in multinational firms. It is important to recognize that balancing global integration and local responsiveness is a process, rather than an outcome, which is subject to, and influenced by, a range of factors including internal political struggles.

While it may have garnered a growing amount of attention as a concept, there is a lack of actual evidence concerning how strategic IHRM operates in practice (Hall and Wailes 2010). Moreover, the extent of HR influence over business objectives in multinationals is often rather limited, as is evident when it comes to planning and developing cross-border alliances. In practice, while multinationals are urged to make more effective use of staff on international assignments, there are few signs that they are doing so to any great degree, notwithstanding those initiatives instituted by high-profile case study firms. Despite suggestions to the contrary, there is often little evidence to support the existence of a demonstrable link between HRM and business performance in multinational firms.

Box 15.8 Window on work
Restructuring the HR function in multinational firms—the 'shared services' approach

One of the ways in which multinational firms have been restructuring their HR functions concerns the development of the so-called 'shared services' model. The idea is that routine administrative HRM queries are directed to a central service centre shared by operations in a number of countries, often on a regional basis (e.g. Europe), leaving specialist HR practitioners to focus on broader strategic-level issues. The shared services approach seems to be a particularly efficient and cost-effective means of delivering HR support to line managers across the various sites operated by a multinational. They benefit from the same source of advice and expertise about HRM matters. Using shared services enables multinational firms to avoid duplicating HRM activities by obviating the need for a fully staffed dedicated HR function in each country where they operate. For insights into the working of the shared services approach in practice, see the case of the US multinational ITCO (a pseudonym). Its European service centre could deal with the majority of the HR issues and queries, covering matters such as pay and maternity entitlements, raised by line and functional managers across a range of different countries (Wächter et al. 2006).

Summary and further reading

- Strategic IHRM is concerned with the relationship between the HRM activities, the structure, and the overall business objectives of multinational companies. The main strategic challenge facing multinationals is to reconcile pressures for global integration with the need for local responsiveness.

- A number of different theoretical approaches are used to understand the concept of strategic IHRM—the life-cycle, organizational design and change, and contingency models. The main problem with theories of strategic IHRM is that they tend to offer a highly idealized view of the strategy formulation process.

- Multinationals attempt to realize strategic IHRM in practice in a number of ways, for example by establishing arrangements to identify and develop global leadership cadres, and by reorganizing the HR function so that it supports the firm's overall strategic objectives more effectively.

See Sparrow and Braun (2007) for an overview of the main theoretical approaches to strategic IHRM. Ferner (2010) and Hall and Wailes (2010) also contain useful material. For the topic of global talent management, Schuler, Jackson, and Tarique (2011) is recommended. For the role of the corporate HR function in multinationals, see the study by Farndale, Paauwe, et al. (2010).

15.6 Conclusion

In this chapter we have reviewed the increasingly important international dimension of HRM activities. IHRM encompasses a concern with identifying and understanding differences in the management of people across national borders, and with accounting for the ease, or otherwise, with which MNCs are able to transfer HR practices between sites in different countries. While there are global pressures for convergence around a model of best practice, HRM is still marked by a considerable amount of national level diversity. We highlighted the complex and uneven process of convergence, and the resilience of diversity. The transfer of HRM practices from an MNC's home base to its foreign subsidiaries, through forward diffusion, is an important lever for disseminating global best practice in HRM. However, this process is constrained by a number of factors that inhibit the extent to which it can facilitate global integration. For example, the way in which human resources are managed in the subsidiaries of MNCs is often marked by a polycentric tendency, with the result that it has to be adapted and made responsive to national level cultural and institutional characteristics.

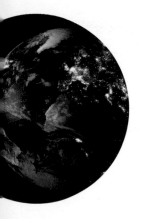

Staff undertaking international assignments, or expatriates, play a key role in the transfer of HRM practices across national borders. Thus one of the key features of IHRM as a topic concerns the people management interventions that can render international assignments effective. Appropriate selection, preparation, support, reward, and repatriation arrangements increase the likelihood that an international assignment will be successful for a company. In theory, IHRM has the potential to make a strong contribution to the effectiveness of multinational companies, for example by ensuring that global managerial talent is nurtured and nourished. In practice, however, HRM often lacks influence over the strategic business objectives of multinationals. Moreover, the strategic realization of IHRM across national borders is constrained by the persistence of national diversity and the power struggles that impede the diffusion of employment practices. In most multinationals, strategic IHRM remains more an aspiration than an achievement.

 ## Assignment and discussion questions

1 Critically assess the main implications of globalization for HRM.

2 What is meant by the concept of 'convergence'? To what extent is the practice of HRM in an international context marked by increasing convergence?

3 Evaluate the main factors that influence the diffusion of HRM practices between the headquarters of multinational companies and their foreign subsidiaries.

4 What are the main ways in which HRM interventions can enhance the effectiveness of international assignments?

5 How are multinational companies attempting to institute a strategic approach to their international human resource management activities?

 # Online Resource Centre

Test your understanding of this chapter with online questions and answers, keep up to speed with changes to the law through regular updates, and use selected weblinks to quickly access useful resources and further information. Visit the Online Resource Centre at:

www.oxfordtextbooks.co.uk/orc/gilmore_williams2e/

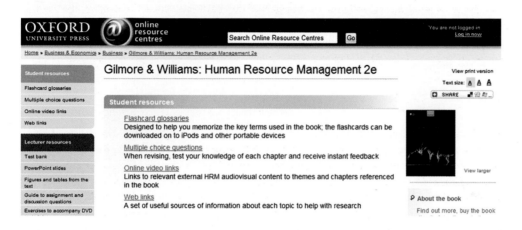

 # Case study
Regulating international labour standards

One of the most controversial areas of IHRM in practice concerns the issue of international labour standards. Increasing globalization means that the products enjoyed by consumers in Western markets are manufactured in countries such as China, Bangladesh, and Indonesia, where costs, particularly labour costs, are much cheaper than they are in developed countries. However, retailers frequently face allegations of exploitative and degrading working conditions in the factories that supply them with goods. For example, in 2010 fashion chain Monsoon's own internal checks revealed that some of its goods were being sourced from factories in India which made use of child labour and paid workers less than the legal minimum.

There are three broad positions in the debate over international labour standards. One holds that working conditions in supply chains are best improved through the voluntary efforts of MNCs themselves. MNCs such as Nike publish corporate codes of conduct which it expects supplier firms to abide by. In the UK, the Ethical Trading Initiative (ETI), which comprises major companies like Marks and Spencer, Monsoon, and Asda, non-governmental organizations (NGOs), and the Trades Union Congress (TUC), publishes a base code covering such matters as child labour and the freedom of workers to associate in trade unions. There is evidence that voluntary corporate codes, which have no power in law, can be an effective means of producing improvements in labour standards, particularly the reduction of child labour. In other areas, such as the protection of workers' rights to join trade unions, codes seem to be less successful. Perhaps the main criticism of voluntary efforts by companies to encourage improvements in labour standards is that they lack teeth and are largely public relations exercises.

A second position holds that the threat of legal sanctions is necessary to promote improvements in labour standards. Trade unions in developed countries and campaigning NGOs sometimes call for penalties, in the form of trade sanctions, to be imposed on countries that allow companies to operate factories with exploitative and degrading working conditions. A potential global legal framework already exists in the form of International Labour Organization (ILO) conventions. A tripartite body, with representatives of

339

governments, unions, and employers' bodies among its membership, the ILO has existed since 1919. It produces conventions that member countries are invited to ratify, and then follow. These conventions cover, among other things, the eradication of child labour and respect of the right of workers freely to associate in trade unions. However, not all member countries ratify ILO conventions, and even those that do are under no obligation to put them into practice. The ILO has limited powers to enforce compliance with its sanctions; instead it relies on voluntary efforts, such as through publicity, discussion, and technical assistance.

People who hold the third broad position vigorously oppose the notion that international labour standards should be subject to a greater amount of legal regulation. Liberal economists, in particular, highlight the comparative advantages that accrue to developing countries as a result of the low cost of their labour. It helps them to attract foreign investment and, as such, is an important source of economic growth and prosperity. MNC suppliers and subsidiaries generally offer higher rates of pay and better working conditions than firms that service local markets. Attempts to impose labour standards on developing countries would increase costs, drive out investment, and reduce employment opportunities, to the detriment of workers in the countries concerned. Calls for greater international labour standards tend to come from trade unions in developed countries who want to protect unfairly the jobs of their own members. Free trade, not fair trade, is the most effective way of ensuring that economic opportunities, and therefore wealth, become more widely diffused around the world.

Question

1 Which of the three broad positions on international labour standards do you tend to support, and why?

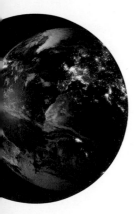

Conclusions

Sarah Gilmore

16.1 The 'promise' of HRM

Chapter 1 showed that the term 'human resource management' (HRM) can have multiple meanings. The ways in which HRM has been used in the book have largely seen it as referring to anything and everything associated with the management of a company's employees without any tie to a particular orientation towards people management, managerial philosophy, or style (Boxall and Purcell 2011). It was also acknowledged that HRM can be seen as 'a distinctive approach to employment management which seeks to achieve competitive advantage through the strategic deployment of a highly committed and capable workforce using an array of cultural, structural and personnel techniques' (Storey 2001: 6).

For Storey, the distinctiveness of HRM lies in four key elements. The first concerns beliefs and assumptions, and sees the human resource as the one element amongst all the factors of production that really makes the difference, with human capability and commitment marking out successful organizations from their competitors. The second key element is allied to the first and concerns the issue of strategy. If employees are a key strategic lever and a source of innovation and survival, then HRM is too important to be left to the HR function alone and requires the full attention of senior managers. An associated prescription made here is that HR policies and practices should be explicitly aligned with the organization's business strategy, even contributing to it, because performance improvements are argued to be more likely to occur when this takes place.

The third element of this approach concerns the role of line managers and the crucial role they play in the effective delivery of HRM policies and practice, with much greater attention needing to be paid to the management of managers themselves. The fourth distinguishing feature of HRM relates to the key levers used to implement this approach, and in particular to the shift away from the use of rules and procedures as the basis of good practice in favour of an accent on the management of the organization's culture. This has generated additional interest because it is seen to offer a key to the attainment of flexibility and commitment—inherently prized objectives. Commitment is seen as key to carrying labour performance to an even higher level because committed employees are seen to be more willing to 'go the extra mile' in pursuit of organizational goals. Hence, commitment becomes more than simply a willingness to work flexibly and is seen as being key to unlocking discretionary effort.

This particular view of HRM sees it as having the potential to operate as an influential and persuasive narrative that helps in giving some shape, direction, and meaning to a complex world, its accompanying business challenges, and concomitant ways of managing people (Storey 2001). However, as noted in Chapter 1, the rhetoric of such approaches towards people management does not seem to have been matched by related practice in the UK, with many organizations preferring to use 'low-road' HR practices. Six broad themes have emerged from this book—strategy, performance, commitment, flexibility, culture, and power—all being concerned with the kinds of debates and activities outlined in this book's chapters, exploring and illustrating the tensions and difficulties inherent in managing people. Therefore it is appropriate to review what can be learned from the exploration of the book through these themes before moving on to consider, in the light of this review, what the future of HRM might be.

16.2 HRM themes: an assessment

These themes are important in understanding the practice of HRM in contemporary organizations and the relationships they might possess (or not) with relevant theory. Their individual importance and inclusion has varied according to the subject matter of the chapter under consideration, but their operation has often highlighted areas of conflict and debate within HRM, and in particular the discrepancies existing between the articulation of 'best practice' promulgated by academics, practitioners, and their representatives, and organizational activity.

16.2.1 Strategy

As previously stated, one of the major arguments used by proponents of softer high-performance working practices models of HRM is that sustained organizational performance is more likely to occur if HR policies and practices are aligned to the organization's business strategy. As illustrated in Chapters 2 and 3, such a view sees an organization's strategy as being based on formal considered methods of formulation, and, as such, is capable of being explained and communicated to others. But, as these chapters showed, organizational strategy is often shaped and driven by the external environment, or it emerges within the organization in response to change. Emergent approaches towards strategy showed that companies have to cope with environmental volatility, and that this can militate against rational planning, making forms of HR alignment difficult to achieve. Therefore HR policies and practices become more pragmatic, contingent, and reactive, making it difficult (but not impossible) to achieve this close alignment between strategy and HR practices seen to be a prerequisite for sustained organizational performance.

The challenges of managing strategically were also highlighted in the coverage of employment relations in Chapter 12. It shows that the sophisticated 'best-practice' HRM approach, based on the use of high-commitment practices, seems to be present in only a minority of organizations. But, whilst a 'best-fit' approach might be more appropriate, helping to explain the situation in a company like Ryanair which takes a low-cost approach to managing its staff that is consistent with its overall business model, we should not exaggerate the degree to which employment relations are amenable to being managed strategically. The need to control employees and ensure that they comply with organizational rules, as well as gaining their cooperation and commitment, and accommodating their interests and concerns, means that managers are generally required to be pragmatic in the way in which they approach employment relations (Hyman 1987).

16.2.2 Performance

Concerns with improving and sustaining performance seem to lie at the heart of many of the HRM activities outlined in this book. This is explicitly outlined in the coverage of performance management in Chapter 11. With pressure to increase competitiveness in the private sector to improve shareholder return on investment, deliver better 'value for money' to the taxpayer in the public sector, and meet customer expectations in both, managing performance through improving effectiveness and efficiency has become a strategic activity for many organizations. Chapter 7 shows that pay and reward activities are increasingly being used as sophisticated levers to encourage business performance, with 'old-pay' approaches of reward for longevity of service being replaced by alternatives that link rewards (financial or otherwise) to the attainment of individually and collectively determined performance goals, linked to corporate strategy and business outcomes. This concern with ensuring an alignment between HRM activities and performance is evident in Chapter 6. Companies use training and development to leverage performance improvements, with some organizations being prepared to reward employees for competence upgrading.

Set against this imperative for performance improvements, Chapter 4 illustrates that, whilst the need to enhance corporate performance often underpins many organizational change initiatives, in practice managers are not necessarily free to act as they wish. Chapters 7 and 10 also highlight the circumscribed nature of managerial action here, showing that, in areas such as pay and workforce diversity, managerial actions are limited by legislation aimed at securing equity of treatment. As shown in Chapter 8, this is also true with regard to health and safety at work, with managers being legally required to ensure certain standards. Employee representatives may be willing to issue legal challenges to employers when heightened demands for performance cause physical and mental harm to staff. Hence, whilst the imperatives for performance continue, managers do not necessarily have the freedom to act as they wish.

16.2.3 Flexibility

The theme of flexibility permeates issues of employment and labour utilization, as well as the concept of post-bureaucratic organization outlined in Chapter 4. It also shows that managers have to manage difficult tensions occurring within the employment relationship. The 'soft' commitment-based models of HRM saw flexibility being achieved through enlarged roles, giving employees a variety of different jobs and thus utilizing a range of skills in enlarged roles, often

companies operating internationally, whilst the management of HRM across national borders is often influenced by the national cultures of the countries concerned, national level institutional frameworks are even more important, with the characteristics of a country's political, legal, and business system often exercising more of an influence over HRM than culture.

16.2.6 Commitment

Many authors have identified that one of the defining characteristics of HRM is the fostering of employee commitment (e.g. Guest 1995). This is rooted in a human relations approach towards the management of employees, with its focus on how managers can secure increased levels of motivation and organizational commitment from workers by recognizing the social needs of employees at work, such as the desire to influence how work is carried out. Those stressing the importance of teamwork claim that this approach gives employees greater autonomy and discretion and can heighten performance, as well as strengthen employee commitment to the team and to the firm. The discussion of the learning organization in Chapter 6 asks whether the use of learning to sustain performance is seeing a resurgence of interest in commitment models or 'soft' approaches towards HRM. However, Chapter 4 illustrates that the take-up of such initiatives seems limited, and Chapter 7's coverage of pay and reward shows that organizations are reluctant to reward commitment as marked by longevity of service, and are increasingly seeking evidence of commitment as witnessed in focused performance geared towards the achievement of strategic goals, or are more prepared to reward those possessing rare and important skills or knowledge.

Whilst commitment is often seen as being manifest by certain employee and employer practices, it is also an emotional state. As such, it is volatile, fragile, and capable of being enhanced or damaged by unequal treatment, redundancies, and the ways in which discipline and grievance cases are handled. Therefore the ability to enhance employee commitment will depend on managerial capabilities in such instances.

To conclude this discussion of the HRM themes, the ways in which they operate in practice are often removed from the ways in which they are seen to connect and interrelate with each other and with HR practices in models such as that of Storey (2001). In many instances, the operation of the themes illustrates where managers seem able to exert latitude in relation to HRM and where they face restrictions, either from other institutional forces, such as legislation, or from the collective organization and representation of employees. Additionally, the scope of managerial action in relation to the themes might be affected by individual preference for some ways of managing employees over others but, again, this might be limited by such factors as organizational culture and history, or environmental change, militating against the operation of best-practice HRM and illustrating its contingent nature.

16.3 The future of HRM

To close this book, it is pertinent to ask what the future holds for HRM. Discussion of the six HRM themes has illustrated just a few of the tensions and complexities of managing people: the fragility of sustaining employee commitment, the tensions witnessed in relation to flexibility, and the extent to which managers can exert authority and power. Does the future hold anything different for the operation of HRM, or is it a case of (literally) business as usual?

In exploring this issue, it might be helpful to frame the discussion by considering the nature of change. As witnessed in the first segment of the book, the ways in which change has been presented within the HRM literature and practice have focused on its rapid, discontinuous nature, as well as on the scope of change occurring within organizations. Whilst Chapters 1, 3, and 4 highlight the extent of change witnessed in the business environment and ongoing volatility in the wake of the economic downturn, it is also possible to find areas of continuity within even the most fast-paced instances of change. Therefore, in terms of assessing the future of HRM, it might be helpful to identify areas where the rapidity and scope of change issue a challenge to the practice of people management, as well as the areas of relative stability.

All organizations are facing the impact of changes in workforce demography, with increasing numbers of employees aged 45 and over and a declining number of those entering organizations

who are of school-leaving age. Organizations are adjusting to this demographic downturn in a number of ways. These involve schemes to recruit and retain older employees, as well as incentives to persuade older employers to put off retirement, or at least to mentor or engage in knowledge-sharing so that the organization retains elements of their experience and skills.

Alongside this challenge to the organization's recruitment, selection, retention, and development activities comes an additional test: how to improve employee work–life balance and to respond to a workforce that is becoming increasingly diverse, not just in terms of age, gender, sexual orientation, and disability, but also in terms of nationality, as migration and immigration flows are becoming more fluid, and the ways in which growing numbers of people are seeking a different balance between employment and life outside the workplace. How well managers handle these pressures for diversity might well be the hallmark of successful HRM, particularly where a company operates on a global or international basis within volatile markets, where speedy delivery of new products or services is crucial to survival, and how it responds to economic developments—be they positive or negative.

This book has charted profound change in other areas of HRM, such as the ways in which people are now paid and rewarded, the ways in which performance itself is assessed, and the imperative now placed on workforce skills and inimitable knowledge. It could be stated that these specific changes share a joint concern with leveraging improved and sustained performance at the individual and corporate level, and it is likely that HR practices in this area will continue to seek new ways of instigating performance improvements in line with business objectives. Although this could be perceived as an example of HR continuity, it could be argued that the sheer nature of change witnessed in these areas heightens the likelihood that this will continue into the future as organizations, through their focus on these activities, seem to perceive them as key HRM levers. One note of caution needs to be raised in terms of developments in the wider economy and the extent to which the HRM function has the ability to enact these kinds of 'enlightened' HR practices during economically difficult times.

Set alongside these areas of rapid change, this book has identified areas of HR practice where there has been less volatility and where we might witness less volatility in the future. Whilst there has been a shift in power away from the collective power of trade unions, as noted in the themes, the collective representation of employee concerns is one of the limits placed on managerial authority and power. Many organizations, especially larger employers, continue to recognize trade unions, seeing this as an efficient and effective method of managing the employment relationship. This continuity of practice has also been witnessed in other aspects of HRM, such as the ways in which managers conduct disciplinary and grievance cases, as well as the ways in which employees are made redundant. This could also be said of recruitment and selection in that, whilst some of the methods used to employ staff have become more complex and multiple, organizations still regularly engage in this activity with little sign of it diminishing. So, whilst aspects of the specific ways in which these activities are carried out might have undergone alteration, the broad contours of these processes remain broadly intact.

Finally, all organizations face the fundamental problem of securing and retaining viability—in buoyant economic times and in more challenging ones. As the example of Saatchi & Saatchi in Chapter 2 illustrates, in order to talk about the operation and existence of HRM we have to have a viable organization, with an appropriate set of goals and a relevant set of staff and other resources, as well as systems that will help it to survive in its sector. These systems also need to be acceptable and 'fit' that sector as well as the society in which the organization operates (Boxall and Purcell 2011). The discussion of how Saatchi & Saatchi overcame their problem of viability not only illustrates the need to find an appropriate method of restoring this, but also shows the ways in which this depended upon its key resource—its employees.

Glossary

360-degree feedback: feedback from superiors, subordinates, peers, and customers that provides a 'rounded' impression of performance.

Appraisal: a formal communication process to evaluate performance and plan how to proceed.

Assessment centre: this selection method usually involves some simulation of the main tasks involved with the job, thus giving candidates a degree of insight as to what a post involves. They can vary in length from half a day to three or more days and can take place at an external centre or be run by the prospective employer.

Best fit: these models are based on the idea that different kinds of people management are needed for different kinds of business conditions. Therefore competitive advantage is gained when HRM policies and practices 'fit' the organization's strategy, labour market, and other factors such as company structure and size.

Best practice: a particular set of HRM practices that engender improved performance for all organizations. These are sometimes referred to as high-commitment HRM, high-involvement HRM, or high performance work systems. They can take a universalistic approach or focus on the ways in which HRM practices are bundled together.

Broadbanding: compressing the number of grades in a graded pay strategy into a smaller number of bands in order to increase pay flexibility and managerial discretion.

Bureaucracy: a way of coordinating organizational activities based on formal rules and procedures, rigid managerial hierarchies, and the specialization of job roles.

Bureaucratic dysfunctionalism: the adverse consequences of bureaucratic organization, particularly where it is applied zealously.

Business process re-engineering (BPR): an approach to organizational change based on re-designing processes in a way that adds value to the business, particularly by eschewing rigid and unwieldy bureaucracy.

Capability procedure: a formal procedure for managing and supporting employees who are under-performing.

Categorical imperative: in Kantian ethics, a behavioural requirement that must be followed for its own sake. In contrast, a 'hypothetical imperative' is one that should be followed if a particular outcome is desired.

Collective bargaining: this term is used to refer to the process by which pay, and other conditions of employment, are negotiated by an employer, or employers' association, and one or more trade unions.

Communities of practice: these are formed by people who engage in a process of collective learning in a shared endeavour such as a workplace.

Consequentialist: a view of ethics that considers the consequences of the proposed act.

Consultation: a form of workplace and organizational decision-making under which managers submit their proposals to employees, or their representatives, to gauge their views, but retain the right to make the final decision.

Contestable market: normally applied to product markets and relates to the ease with which new firms can enter, and existing firms exit, a market or industry.

Continuous professional development (CPD): a process whereby skills and knowledge are continuously updated and extended.

Convergence: the growing degree of uniformity in HRM practices across national borders, as stimulated by globalization.

Corporate social responsibility (CSR): the study of the responsibilities of a business towards the society in which it operates.

Democracy: a system of government, normally based on elections, with virtually all adults having the right to influence government policy, including the laws that are passed.

Deontological: a view of ethics that is related to duties, rights, and principles.

Direct discrimination: refers to situations where an employer treats an employee less favourably than others on account of some aspect of their social characteristics, such as age or gender.

Disciplinary procedure: a formal arrangement that enables managers to deal with alleged poor performance or misconduct of their staff.

Discretionary effort: the additional effort employees will go to on behalf of the organization to solve problems, take ownership of them, invest in their ideas, and go beyond contractual terms and conditions of employment.

Diversity management: an approach to dealing with workplace inequality which emphasizes how organizations can recognize, and benefit from, individual differences among their staff.

Downsizing: the reduction of organizational levels, functions, and job roles with the aim of streamlining operations and realizing efficiency savings.

Delayering: the reduction of layers of management and management reporting within an organization, leading to flatter organizational structures.

Early retirement: a method of making workforce reductions whereby older employees are encouraged to retire earlier than planned with the offer of an appropriate financial incentive.

E-learning: the delivery of training, learning, or development programmes by a range of electronic media such as CD-ROM, DVD, the internet, or company intranets.

Emotional labour: a term used to describe a form of work that requires the employee to suppress or stimulate emotions to suit the organization's ends—as witnessed in jobs such as nursing or in flight attendants. It is increasingly built into the design of many jobs and job training, and can also involve the employee proving their worth, loyalty, and commitment by engaging continuously and successfully in such emotional performances.

Employee Assistance Programmes (EAPs): counselling and assistance interventions provided by a third party and directed at staff in an organization.

Employee engagement: a positive attitude held by an employee towards the organization and its values. An engaged employee is aware of the organization's business context and works with staff to improve performance within the job for the benefit of the organization as well as for him/herself. Such a relationship requires nurture on behalf of the organization to secure and maintain it, as it is a two-way process.

Employee involvement: managerial interventions, such as direct communications techniques, that are designed to encourage greater organizational commitment from employees.

Employee referral scheme: these schemes usually involve existing staff being offered a cash incentive to recommend contacts to fill vacancies within the company.

Employee voice: opportunities for employees to have a say over workplace and organizational decisions.

Employment benefits: financial rewards other than pay, such as holidays, pensions, staff discounts, and pensions.

Employment tribunal: a body that adjudicates upon disputes between individual employees and employers.

Empowerment: the devolution of some supervisory tasks from managers to workers, with the latter given more discretion over their jobs.

Equal opportunity: the provision of a level organizational playing field on which all staff are treated the same, regardless of their social characteristics, with regard to recruitment, selection, and promotion decisions, etc.

Ethical relativism: the view that the definitions of good and bad depend strongly upon the time and place where the judgement is being made. In the extreme form of this version of ethics, there are no universal ethical truths—everything depends upon the local convention at the time.

Ethnocentric: an approach to HRM in multinational companies that focuses on the dominance of home country practices throughout their foreign subsidiaries.

Evolutionary approaches: these approaches toward strategy formation argue that markets will ensure that only the best performers will survive, whatever methods managers adopt in developing strategy. It is often likened to Darwinian ideas of survival of the fittest.

Expatriate: an employee, generally a manager, who is assigned, usually on a temporary basis, to work in a foreign location.

Extrinsic reward: bestowed on the employee and normally tangible, such as pay, holidays, and pensions.

Final salary pension: a pension which has defined benefits and is calculated using years of service and final pay.

Financial reward: pay and employment benefits.

Financialization: a term used to describe the dominance of profit-making mechanisms that rely on financial transactions in the global finance markets rather than on trading and commodity/service production.

Fiscal policy: a government's policies on its taxation, expenditure, and overall budget with the aim of managing economic activity.

Flexible benefits: an arrangement whereby employees can select from a portfolio of employment benefits according to personal need.

Forward diffusion: the transfer of HRM practices from the home base of a multinational company to its subsidiaries in foreign locations.

Functional flexibility: the work tasks, skills, and job requirements of the workforces are managed to ensure that workers are more effective in a range of different job roles.

Geocentric: an approach to HRM in multinational companies that focuses on the dissemination of best practice on a global basis.

Globalization: a set of processes (economic, financial, political, and social) which are causing countries of the world to be increasingly integrated and interdependent.

Goal displacement: a form of bureaucratic dysfunctionalism which refers to situations where an excessive concern with complying with formal rules directs managerial attention away from the activities that advance the interests of the organization.

Graded pay: a pay strategy where jobs are ranked according to an evaluation of their relative worth to the organization and employees are paid at the rate for the job following a process of job evaluation.

Grievance procedure: a formal arrangement for handling complaints from employees concerning their treatment at work.

Harassment: unwanted conduct that violates a person's dignity or creates an intimidating, hostile, degrading, humiliating, or offensive environment.

High-commitment/high-road HRM: the idea that a particular set or number of HR practices has the ability to bring about improved organizational performance, often through the unlocking of discretionary effort and securing employee identification with and commitment to the goals and values of the organization.

High-performance work practices (HPWPs): work practices associated with increasing effectiveness and efficiency, resulting in increased performance and productivity.

Hot-desking: an arrangement whereby workers use shared facilities, rather than having their own dedicated work spaces.

Human capital: the stock of skills, knowledge, and personal attributes embodied in an organization's workforce to perform work that produces economic value.

Human relations: an approach to managing people at work which holds that increased levels of employee motivation and commitment are best secured by recognizing their social needs.

Human resource management (HRM): can refer to all the varied activities involved in managing people in organizations. It also denotes a specific approach towards this activity, seeing it as operating from a managerial perspective, and often argues for the need to establish a series of integrated personnel policies designed to achieve the organization's strategic goals.

Hybridization of pay strategies: the design of a pay strategy which incorporates elements of graded pay, market-related pay, and performance-related pay.

Indirect discrimination: the use of apparently neutral criteria or practices which mean that people with particular social characteristics are treated less favourably than others, and which cannot be justified on objective grounds.

Inflation: continuous rise in the general level of prices in an economy.

Institutional framework: the political, legal, educational, and business systems of a country.

Intrinsic reward: a 'feel-good' reward such as praise and recognition, challenging work, and a degree of empowerment.

Job description: written statement that describes job duties, the most important contributions and outcomes needed from a position, and the required qualifications, as well as the post's reporting relationships.

Job evaluation: a systematic process whereby jobs in an organization are ranked according to their relevant importance.

Joint regulation: term used to refer to the process by which terms and conditions of employment are determined jointly as a result of bargaining between employers, or employers' associations, and one or more trade unions.

Knowledge management: the process of systematically and actively managing and leveraging the stores of knowledge in an organization.

Labour market: where organizations that wish to hire (or 'demand') a particular type of labour meet with individuals who wish to supply the particular type of labour service, normally for financial gain.

Learning organization: '. . . an organization which facilitates the learning of all its members and continuously transforms itself' (Pedler et al. 1991: 3).

Libertarianism: the philosophy that takes the main aim of preserving as much individual freedom of choice as possible.

Line manager: a manager who has direct responsibility for employees and their work.

Macro-economy: normally applied to the study of the total economic activity that occurs within a country's boundaries plus the involvement of a country's organizations and citizens overseas.

Managerial prerogative: the right of managers to exercise unilateral control over workplace relations.

Market-related pay: a pay strategy where the 'going rate' for a job within the labour market is established following the gathering of labour market intelligence. It rewards employees according to their commercial worth.

Mediation: a non-judgemental approach whereby an impartial third party helps two or more people in a dispute to attempt to reach an agreement.

Migration: the geographical movement of people from one area to another where they settle permanently.

Monetary policy: money supply or interest rate policies normally carried out by a central bank on behalf of government with the aim of managing economic activity.

Money purchase pensions: a pension which has defined contributions, but where the pension itself will be dependent on level of investment, investment performance, and annuity rates at the time of retirement.

Moral hazard: a problem in which the design of a system may provide an incentive to someone to behave inappropriately (for example, taking a higher risk than can safely be managed).

Multinational company (MNC): a firm that operates in more than one country, particularly as an employer.

Multi-employer bargaining: situations where collective bargaining takes place between a group of employers, usually in the form of an employers' association, and one or more trade unions.

Natural wastage: a method of making workforce reductions that involves not replacing staff when their positions become vacant.

Negotiation: a process of resolving disputes in which both sides argue and are required to make compromises in order to secure a mutually acceptable agreement.

New pay: a term which describes contemporary emphasis on reward strategy in relation to aligning organizational strategy with pay strategy.

Non-financial rewards: intrinsic rewards relating to self-actualization, desirable work, and work–life balance opportunities.

Occupational health and safety: a term that is used to refer to the health and safety issues that affect people in their jobs.

Off-the-job learning: this form of learning takes place away from the workplace and is often associated with internally or externally provided courses but can also refer to other modes of learning such as planned experiences with suppliers, competitors, or collaborators.

Off-shoring: the relocation of production facilities and service provision to foreign locations.

On-the-job learning: refers to processes of training and development that occur through doing aspects of the job the trainee holds. This can involve a wide range of methods from observation to workplace-based assignments.

Organizational culture: the unwritten symbols, values, and beliefs that exist within organizations.

Organizational misbehaviour: behaviour in organizations that does not correspond to managerial expectations or standards.

Organizational structure: formal arrangements for dividing up job roles and other organizational activities vertically, through managerial hierarchies for example, and also horizontally, according to function, business orientation, or territory.

Organizational wellness: a phrase that is used to capture the notion that employee well-being and organizational success complement each other.

Outplacement services: external firms that specialize in providing advice and support to workers affected by redundancy.

Partnership agreement: a term used to describe a formal relationship between an employer and a union that is based on the importance of cooperation and shared interests, rather than conflict.

Performance: a combination of effectiveness and efficiency in changing from an initial state to another state, or in completing a specified action or task.

Performance management: methods or interventions utilized to improve individual and organization performance.

Performance-related pay: a pay strategy where an assessment of individual employee performance determines the level of pay for a job. It rewards employees according to their individual worth.

Person specification: this is derived from the job description and translates the components of it into the skills and abilities needed to perform the job effectively.

351

Personnel management: a term used with reference to a specialist organizational function or department responsible for determining and enacting all policies and procedures that determine the various aspects of employment from recruitment and selection through to termination of employment. It is also a term used to describe a particular approach to people management prior to and coexisting with the arrival of HRM.

Pluralism: a perspective on employment relations that recognizes that employers and employees may have conflicting interests, but that these can be resolved to the mutual benefit of both by means of formal procedures, particularly bargaining relationships with trade unions.

Polycentric: an approach to HRM in multinational companies that focuses on the way in which their subsidiaries adapt their practices to respond to national level circumstances.

Positive action: the use of measures, such as targets, designed to improve the employment and organizational prospects of people from disadvantaged social groups.

Positive discrimination: actions taken by organizations whereby people who belong to disadvantaged social groups are given preference over others in relation to recruitment, selection, promotion, etc.

Post-bureaucracy: an approach to understanding organizations which emphasizes the greater flexibility and decentralization that marks their activities, and the more limited role for formal rules, procedures, and managerial hierarchies.

Privatization: the complete or partial sale of publicly (i.e. government) owned organizations to private sector individuals or companies.

Processual approach: sees strategy as emerging in incremental steps over time. It acknowledges the bounded rationality involved in decision-making and therefore sees strategy formation as the product of political compromise.

Product market: the coming together of sellers and buyers of goods or services with the aim of completing the sale of the item from a supplier to a purchaser.

Psychometric tests: standardized procedures that attempt to quantify some psychological attribute or attributes of an individual, such as sensitivity, memory, intelligence, aptitude, or personality.

Rational planning approaches: usually depicted as occurring at corporate, strategic business unit, and operational level, using a range of assessments to arrive at objectives.

Recruitment: a process aiming to attract a pool of suitably qualified candidates for a given position. Successful recruitment will result in the possibility of selecting and appointing a candidate to a post.

Redeployment: a method of effecting workforce reductions in one part of an organization by transferring staff elsewhere in the same organization, often with appropriate retraining.

Redundancy: a method used by employers to dismiss employees in circumstances where fewer staff are needed to undertake a particular set of work activities.

Repatriation: the process of returning a member of staff undertaking an international assignment to their home country environment.

Repetitive strain injury (RSI): a term used to refer to a range of different upper-limb disorders often, but not always, caused by fast or repetitive finger, hand, or arm movements.

Resource-based view: holds that organizations have unique bundles of assets, and that access to these, coupled with the company's ability to make effective use of them, provides the source of competitive advantage within the marketplace. The resource in question must add value, be unique or rare, be inimitable, and not be capable of substitution by another resource by competing firms.

Return-to-work interview: a meeting between an individual employee and a manager following every instance of absence

Reverse diffusion: the transfer of HRM practices from the subsidiary of a multinational company to its home base and throughout the firm as a whole.

Reward: a contemporary HR term which signals that employees come to work for more than just pay.

Reward strategy: the alignment of reward policies and practices with the strategic direction of the organization in order to elicit managerially desired behaviours and performance from employees.

Scientific management: an approach to managing work in organizations which holds that efficiency is best gained by dividing up jobs into narrow tasks and getting appropriately trained workers to do them under a regime of strict managerial control, with the prospect of financial reward as the main motivation to work hard.

Selection: applying appropriate techniques and methods with the view to select, appoint, and then induct a competent person or persons into a job.

Statistical discrimination: unfavourable treatment of an individual based on stereotypical behaviours believed to apply to the group to which that individual belongs.

Strategy: the simplest definition of strategy sees it as the characteristic way a company copes with engaging in business. The more complex view sees strategy as being concerned with the long-term direction and scope of an organization, and how it secures competitive advantage and fulfils stakeholder expectations by the way it configures resources at its disposal.

Strike: the temporary withdrawal of labour by a group of workers, undertaken in order to express a grievance or to enforce a demand.

Survivor syndrome: a term used to describe the negative consequences of redundancy exercises on the motivation, morale, commitment, and performance of remaining staff.

Systemic approaches: highlight the importance of national, regional, and local factors such as culture, legislation, etc. to strategy formation.

Systematic training cycle: describes a means of structuring training and development activity through engagement in four interrelated activities: needs analysis, design, delivery, and evaluation.

Talent management: refers to the ability of an organization to attract, retain, and integrate workers as well as developing existing employees in order to meet current and future business goals. Talent management activities might relate to the whole of an organization's workforce, or be viewed more narrowly and focus on a more elite segment of employees or roles.

Teamworking: arrangements that allow workers to organize collectively and operate their work activities themselves.

Technology: the use of knowledge, particularly scientific knowledge, in the design and/or production of goods and services.

Teleworking: applies to situations where workers operate outside of their employers' premises, at home or on the move, facilitated by developments in information and communication technologies.

Total quality management (TQM): a method of manufacturing a product or delivering a service in which quality is built in at all stages, and responsibility for quality is shared by all staff.

Total reward: a holistic term to describe a combination of pay, employment benefits, and non-financial (intrinsic) rewards.

Trade union: a membership organization comprised mainly of workers which is principally concerned with representing their interests at work and in society at large.

Unemployment: often measured as a percentage of the labour force, it is the number of people who are not in work but are actively seeking work.

Union recognition: the act of an employer who agrees to enter into a formal relationship, usually involving collective bargaining, with a trade union.

Unitary: a perspective on employment relations that emphasizes the harmony of interests that exists between employers and their employees.

Universalization: the principle that ethical propositions should be capable of being applied to any similar case (in an attempt to exclude the influence of self-interest).

Utilitarianism: a form of consequentialist ethics that seeks to achieve the greatest good for the greatest number: *act utilitarianism* considers the consequences of the proposed act only, while *rule utilitarianism* considers the consequences if the proposed act were to become commonplace.

Validity: selection methods possess face validity if, on the face of it, they seem to assess the areas that the test purports to measure and are relevant to the job. A selection method has a high construct validity if it is based on sound evidence or underpinning theory.

Victimization: unfavourable treatment experienced by an employee, or a group of employees, as a result of their making a complaint at work.

Vocational education and training (VET): this is concerned with ensuring that the nation achieves the levels of skills it needs. Therefore VET policies and practices are focused on facilitating their development.

Voluntarism: in the training and development context, voluntarism refers to government approaches which let employers decide the degree of investment they want to make in this domain.

Voluntary redundancy: a method of effecting redundancies in which staff are encouraged to leave employment with an organization of their own accord, with the promise of an attractive financial settlement.

Work-related stress: physical and psychological ill-health caused or exacerbated by the characteristics and pressures of jobs.

353

References

Abbott, B. (2007). 'Workplace and employment characteristics of the Citizens' Advice Bureau clients'. *Employee Relations*, 29/3, 262–79.

Abbott, G., Stening, B., and Atkins, P. (2006). 'Coaching expatriate managers for success: adding value beyond training and mentoring'. *Asia–Pacific Journal of Human Resources*, 44/3: 295–316.

ACAS (Advisory, Conciliation, and Arbitration Service) (2010a). *Advisory Booklet—Redundancy Handling*. London: ACAS.

ACAS (Advisory, Conciliation and Arbitration Service) (2010b). *Bullying and Harassment at Work: Guidance for Employees*. London: ACAS

ACAS (Advisory, Conciliation, and Arbitration Service) (2010c). *Managing Attendance and Employee Turnover*. London: ACAS.

ACAS (Advisory, Conciliation, and Arbitration Service) (2010d). *Recruitment and Induction*. London: ACAS.

ACAS (Advisory, Conciliation, and Arbitration Service) (2011). *Discipline and Grievances at Work: the ACAS Guide*. London: ACAS.

Achur, J. (2011). *Trade Union Membership 2010*. London: BIS/ONS.

Ackers, P. and Wilkinson, A. (2003). 'Introduction: the British industrial relations tradition— formation, breakdown and salvage', in P. Ackers and A. Wilkinson, A. (eds), *Understanding Work and Employment: Industrial Relations in Transition*. Oxford: Oxford University Press, 1–27.

Ackroyd, S. (2002). *The Organization of Business*. Oxford: Oxford University Press.

Ackroyd, S. and Thompson, P. (1999). *Organizational Misbehaviour*. London: Sage.

Adams, L., Gore, K., and Shury, J. (2010). *Gender Pay Gap Reporting Survey 2009*. Manchester: Equality and Human Rights Commission.

Adler, N. (1994). 'Competitive frontiers: women managing across borders'. *Journal of Management Development,* 13/2: 24–41.

Adler, N. and Ghadar, F. (1990). 'Strategic human resource management: a global perspective', in R. Pieper (ed.), *Human Resource Management in International Comparison*. Berlin: De Gruyter, 235–60.

Adler, P. (1999). 'Building better bureaucracies'. *Academy of Management Executive*, 13/4: 36–47.

African Development Bank (2011). *Infrastructure and growth in Sierra Leone: summary report*. Tunisia: African Development Bank Group. http://reliefweb.int/sites/reliefweb.int/files/resources/Full_Report_2891.pdf

Aggett, M. (2007). 'What has influenced growth in the UK's boutique hotel sector?' *International Journal of Contemporary Hospitality Management*, 12/2: 169–77.

Allen, D., Bryant, P., and Vardaman, J. (2010). 'Retaining talent: replacing misconceptions with evidence-based strategies'. *Academy of Management Perspectives*, 24: 48–64.

Allen, M. (2006). *The Varieties of Capitalism Paradigm: Explaining Germany's Comparative Advantage?* Basingstoke: Palgrave Macmillan.

Alli, B. (2008). *Fundamental Principles of Occupational Health and Safety*. New York: International Labour Office.

Almond, P. and Gonzalez Menendez, M. (2006). 'Varieties of capitalism: the importance of political and social choices'. *Transfer*, 12/3: 407–25.

Alvesson, M. and Sveningsson, S. (2008). *Changing Organizational Culture*. Abingdon: Routledge.

Alvesson, M. and Thompson, P. (2005). 'Post-bureaucracy?', in S. Ackroyd, R. Batt, P. Thompson, and P. Tolbert (eds), *Oxford Handbook of Work Organization*. Oxford: Oxford University Press, 485–507.

Amable, B. (2003). *The Diversity of Modern Capitalism*. Oxford: Oxford University Press.

Anderson, V. (2007). *The Value of Learning: From Return on Investment to Return on Expectation*. London: CIPD.

Andreasen, A. and Kotler, P. (2008). *Strategic Marketing for Nonprofit Organizations* (7th edn). Upper Saddle River, NJ: Pearson– Prentice Hall.

Anner, M., Greer, I., Hauptmeier, M., Lillie, N., and Winchester, N. (2006). 'The industrial determinants of transnational solidarity: global interunion politics in three sectors'. *European Journal of Industrial Relations*, 12/7, 7–27.

Appelbaum, E., Bailey, T., Berg, P., and Kallenberg, A. (2000). *Manufacturing Advantage: Why High-Performance Work Systems Pay Off*. Ithaca, NY: Cornell University Press.

Appelbaum, S., Delage, C. Labib, N., and Gault, G. (1997). 'The survivor syndrome: aftermath of downsizing'. *Career Development International*, 2/6: 278–86.

Archer, D. (1999). 'Exploring "bullying" culture in the paramilitary organisation'. *International Journal of Manpower,* 20/1–2: 94–105.

Armstrong, M. (2000). 'Feel the width', *People Management*, 3 February: 34–8.

Armstrong, M. (2005). *Employee Reward*. London: CIPD.

Armstrong, M. (2006). *Performance Management* (3rd edn). London: Kogan Page.

Armstrong, M. (2012). *Handbook of Reward Management Practice: Improving Performance Through Reward*. London: Kogan Page.

Armstrong, M. and Baron, A. (2005). *Managing Performance*. London: CIPD

Armstrong, M. and Brown, D. (2001). *New Dimensions in Pay Management*. London: CIPD.

Armstrong, M. and Brown, D. (2005). 'Reward strategies and trends in the UK: the land of diverse and pragmatic dreams'. *Compensation Benefits Review*, 37/4: 41–53.

Armstrong, S. (2010). 'Saatchi brothers mark 40 years since the foundation of their ad agency'. *Guardian*, 6 September. www.guardianonline.co.uk

Arnold, H. (2008). 'Time is running out'. *Occupational Health*, 60/2: 14–16.

Arthur, C. (2011). 'Microsoft said to be preparing bid for Yahoo as AOl and Alibaba circle'. *Guardian*, 20 October. www.guardianonline.co.uk

Arthur, M. and Rousseau, D. (1996). *The Boundaryless Career*. Oxford: Oxford University Press.

Arulampalam, A., Booth, A., and Bryan, M. (2007). 'Is there a glass ceiling over Europe? Exploring the gender pay gap across the wage distribution'. *Industrial and Labor Relations Review*, 60/2: 163–86.

Ashton, C. (1998). *Managing Best Practices— Transforming Business Performance by Identifying, Disseminating, and Managing Best Practice*. London: Business Intelligence.

Ashton, C. and Morton, L. (2005). 'Managing talent for competitive advantage'. *Strategic Human Resources Review*, 4/5: 28–31.

Asteris, M. and Thomas, R. (2009). 'Boxing clever: containerisation and globalisation'. *Teaching Business & Economics*, 13/1: 21–3.

Atkinson, J. (1984). 'Manpower strategies for flexible organizations'. *Personnel Management*. August: 28–31.

Bach, S. (2005a). 'Personnel management in transition', in S. Bach (ed.), *Managing Human Resources*. Oxford: Blackwell, 3–44.

Bach, S. (2005b). 'New directions in performance management', in S. Bach (ed.), *Managing Human Resources*. Oxford: Blackwell, 289–316.

Bach, S. (2010). 'Public sector industrial relations: the challenge of modernization', in T. Colling and M. Terry (eds), *Industrial Relations: Theory and Practice*, Chichester: John Wiley, 151–77.

Bach, S., Kolins Givan, R., and Forth, J. (2009). 'The public sector in transition', in W. Brown, A. Bryson, J. Forth, and K. Whitfield (eds), *The Evolution of the Modern Workplace*. Cambridge: Cambridge University Press, 307–31.

Bacon, N. and Samuel, P. (2009). 'Partnership agreement adoption and survival in the British private and public sectors'. *Work, Employment and Society*, 23/2, 231–48.

Baines, D. and Cunningham, I. (2011). '"White knuckle care work": violence, gender and new public management in the public sector'. *Work, Employment, and Society*, 25/4: 760–76.

Baker, K. (2009) 'Aviva HR chief calls on firms to develop in-house talent'. *Personnel Today*, 18 March. www.personneltoday.com

Balekjian, C. and Sarheim, L. (2011). *The Boutique Hotels Segment: Standing Out from the Crowd*. London: HVS.

Balmer, J. and Gray, E. (2004). 'Corporate brands: what are they? What of them?' *European Journal of Marketing*, 37/7–8: 972–97.

Barham, C. and Begum, N. (2005). 'Sickness absence from work in the UK'. *Labour Market Trends*, April: 149–58.

Barker, J. (1993). 'Tightening the iron cage: concertive control in self-managing teams'. *Administrative Science Quarterly*, 38: 408–37.

Barley, S. and Kunda, G. (2004). *Gurus, Hired Guns, and Warm Bodies: Itinerant Experts in a Knowledge Economy*. Princeton, NJ: Princeton University Press.

Barney, J. (1995). Looking inside for competitive advantage. *Academy of Management Executive*, 9/4: 49–61.

Bartlett, C. and Ghoshal, S. (1989). *Managing Across Borders*. London: Hutchinson.

Baruch, Y. and Hind, P. (2000). '"Survivor syndrome"—a management myth?'. *Journal of Managerial Psychology*, 15/1: 29–45.

Baruch, Y., Steele, D., and Quantrill, G. (2002). 'Management of expatriation and repatriation for novice global players'. *International Journal of Manpower*, 23/7: 659–71.

BBC News Online (2010). 'Cadbury factory closure by Kraft "despicable"'. *BBC News Online*, 10 February. http://news.bbc.co.uk/1/hi/8507780.stm

BBC News Online (2011a). 'Jaguar Land Rover creates more than 1000 Solihull jobs'. 10 November. www.bbc.co.uk

BBC News Online (2011b). 'Why can't everyone telework?'. 2 June. http://www.bbc.co.uk/news/magazine-11879241

BBC News Online (2012). 'Primark owner AB Foods sees strong sales'. 19 January. www.bbc.co.uk

Beardwell, I. (ed.) (1996). *Contemporary Industrial Relations*. Oxford: Oxford University Press.

Bechter, B., Brandl, B., and Meardi, G. (2011). *From National to Sectoral Industrial Relations: Developments in Sectoral Industrial Relations in the EU*. Dublin: European Foundation for the Improvement of Living and Working Conditions.

Becker, B. and Gerhart, B. (1996). 'The impact of human resource management on organizational performance: progress and prospects'. *Academy of Management Journal*, 39/4: 779–801.

Becker, B. and Huselid, M. (1998). 'High performance work systems and firm performance: a synthesis of research and managerial implications'. *Research in Personnel and Human Resources Management*, 16: 53–101.

Becker, B. and and Huselid, M. (2006). 'Strategic human resource management. Where do we go from here?' *Journal of Management*, 32/6: 898–925.

Becker, B., Huselid, M., and Beatty, R. (2009). *The Differentiated Workforce: Transforming Talent into Strategic Impact*. Boston, MA: Harvard Business Press.

Becker, B., Huselid, M., and Ulrich, D. (2001). *The HR Scorecard: Linking People, Strategy, and Performance*. Boston, MA: Harvard Business School Press.

Becker, G. (1994). *Human Capital: A Theoretical and Empirical Analysis*. Chicago, IL: Chicago University Press.

Beer, M. and Ruh, R. (1976). 'Employee growth through performance monitoring: a review of human resource issues'. *Human Resource Management Review*, Winter: 267–88.

Beer, M., Spencer, P., Lawrence, D., Quinn Mills, D., and Walton, R. (1984). *Managing Human Assets*. New York: Free Press.

Begg, D., Fischer, S., and Dornbusch, R. (2008). *Economics* (8th edn). London: McGraw-Hill.

Belbin, M. (1993). *Team Roles at Work*. Oxford: Butterworth–Heinemann.

Bell, E., Taylor, S., and Thorpe, R. (2002). 'A step in the right direction? Investors in People and the learning organization'. *British Journal of Management*, 13/2: 161–71.

Bennett, R. and Sargeant, A. (2005). 'The nonprofit marketing landscape'. *Journal of Business Research*, 58/6: 797–805.

Bentley, R. (2006). 'The price of a poor performer'. *Employers' Law*, 1 March. http://xperthr

Berg, A. (2006). 'Transforming public services—transforming the public servant?' *International Journal of Public Sector Management*, 19/4: 293–315.

Berlin, I. (1969). *Four Essays on Liberty*. Oxford: Oxford University Press.

BERR (Department for Business, Enterprise, and Regulatory Reform) (2008). *Agency Working in the UK: A Review of the Evidence*. Employment Relations Research Series No.93. London: Department for Business, Enterprise, and Regulatory Reform.

BIS (Department for Business, Innovation and Skills) (2011a). *Agency Workers Regulations: Guidance*. London: BIS.

BIS (Department for Business, Innovation and Skills) (2011b). *Resolving Workplace Disputes: A Consultation*. London: BIS/Tribunals Service.

BIS (Department for Business, Innovation and Skills) (2011c). *Low Carbon and Environmental Goods and Services (LCEGS): Report for 2009/10*. London: BIS.

Berridge, J. and Cooper, C. (1994). 'The employee assistance programme: its role in organizational coping and excellence'. *Personnel Review,* 23/7: 4–20.

Berry, L., Mirabito, A., and Baun, W. (2010). 'What's the hard return on employee wellness programs?'. *Harvard Business Review*, 88/3: 104–12.

Bevan, S. (2003). *Attendance Management*. London: Work Foundation.

Bevan, S. (2010). *The Business Case for Employees Health and Well-being*. London: Work Foundation.

Bevan, S., Dench, S., Harper, H., and Hayday, S. (2004). *How Employers Manage Absence*. Employment Relations Research Series, No.25. London: Department of Trade and Industry.

Beynon, H., Grimshaw, D., Rubery, J., and Ward, K. (2002). *Managing Employment Change: The New Realities of Work*. Oxford: Oxford University Press.

Bibby, A. (2005). *Die Wal-Martiesierung der Welt: Globale Reaktion von UNI*. Nyon: Union Network International.

Bird, J. and Lawton, K. (2009). *The Future's Green: Jobs and the UK Low-Carbon Transition*. London: Institute for Public Policy Research.

Birdi, K., Clegg, C., Patterson, C., Robinson, A., Stride, C.B., Wall, T.D., and Wood, S.J. (2008). 'The impact of human resource and operational management practices on company productivity: a longitudinal study'. *Personnel Psychology*, 61/3: 467–501.

Björkman, I., Evans, P., and Pucik, V. (2011). 'Managing knowledge in multinational firms', in A.-W. Harzing and A. Pinnington (eds), *International Human Resource Management* (3rd edn). London: Sage, 345–76.

Black, B. (2011). 'Partisan politics and the varieties of employment relations and HRM'. *International Journal of Human Resource Management*, 22/18: 3672–91.

Black, C. (2008). *Working for a Healthier Tomorrow*. London: TSO

Black, J., Mendenhall, M., and Oddou, G. (1991). 'Toward a model of international adjustment'. *Academy of Management Review*, 16/2: 291–317.

Blaine, B. (2007). *Understanding the Psychology of Diversity*. London: Sage.

Blanchflower, D. and Bryson, A. (2009). 'Trade union decline and the economics of the workplace', in W. Brown, A. Bryson, J. Forth, and K. Whitfield (eds), *The Evolution of the Modern Workplace*. Cambridge: Cambridge University Press, 48–73.

Blanden, J., Machin, S. and van Reenen, J. (2006). 'Have unions turned the corner? New evidence on recent trends in union recognition in UK firms'. *British Journal of Industrial Relations*, 44/2, 169–90.

Blase, J. (1991). *The Politics of Life in Schools: Power, Conflict, and Cooperation*. Newbury Park, CA: Sage.

Blass, E. (2009). *Talent Management: Cases and Commentary*. Basingstoke: Palgrave Macmillan.

Blinder, A. (2006). 'Offshoring: The next industrial revolution?' *Foreign Affairs*, 85/2: 113–28.

Bloom, D., Canning, D., and Fink, G. (2010). 'Implications of population ageing for economic growth'. *Oxford Review of Economic Policy*, 26/4: 583–612.

Blyton, P. and Turnbull, P. (2004). *The Dynamics of Employee Relations* (3rd edn). Basingstoke: Palgrave Macmillan.

Boatright, J. (2000). *Ethics and the Conduct of Business*. London: Prentice Hall.

Bolton, S. (ed.) (2007). *Dimensions in Dignity at Work*. Oxford: Butterworth–Heinemann.

Bonache, J. and Fernandez, Z. (2007). 'Strategic staffing in multinational companies', in M. Mendenhall, G. Oddou, and G. Stahl (eds), *Readings and Cases in International Human Resource Management* (4th edn). Oxford: Routledge, 99–118.

Bonini, S., Mendonca, L., and Oppenheim, J. (2006). 'When social issues become strategic'. *McKinsey Quarterly*, 2006/2: 20–32.

Bonner, C. and Gollan, P. (2005). 'A bridge over troubled water: a decade of representation at South West Water'. *Employee Relations*, 27/3, 238–58.

Borg, M. and Harzing, A.-W. (1995). 'Composing an international staff', in A.-W. Harzing and J. Van Ruysseveldt (eds), *International Human Resource Management*. London: Sage, 179–204.

Borjas, G. (2010). *Labor Economics* (5th edn). London: McGraw-Hill Irwin.

Boselie, P., Dietz, G., and Boon, C. (2005). 'Commonalities and contradictions in HRM and performance research'. *Human Resource Management Journal*, 15/1: 67–94.

Bourne, M. and Franco-Santos, M. (2010). *Investors in People, Managerial Capabilities and Performance*. Cranfield: Cranfield University: School of Management.

Bourne, M., Franco-Santos, M., Pavlov, A., Lucianetti, L., Martinez, V., and Mura, M. (2008). *The Impact of Investors in People on People Management Practices and Firm Performance*. Cranfield: Cranfield University School of Management.

Bouverie, J. (2010) 'Macmillan cancer support—emerging strategy'. http://www.knowhownonprofit.org/

Boxall, P. (1996). 'The strategic human resource management debate and the resource-based view of the firm.' *Human Resource Management Journal*, 6/1: 59–77.

Boxall, P. and Macky, K. (2009). 'Research and theory on high-performance work systems: progressing the high-involvement stream'. *Human Resource Management Journal*, 19/1: 3–23.

Boxall, P. and Purcell, J. (2011). *Strategy and Human Resource Management* (3rd edn). Basingstoke: Palgrave Macmillan.

Boxall, J. and Steeneveld, M. (1999). 'Human resource strategy and competitive advantage: a longitudinal study of engineering consultancies'. *Journal of Management*, 36/4: 443–63.

Boxall, P., Purcell, J., and Wright, P. (2007). 'Human resource management: scope, analysis and significance', in P. Boxall, J. Purcell, and P. Wright (eds), *Oxford Handbook of Human Resource Management*. Oxford: Oxford University Press, 1–18.

Boyd, C. (2003). *Human Resource Management and Occupational Health and Safety*. London: Routledge.

Boydell, T. (1976). *Guide to the Identification of Training Needs*. London: BACIE.

Bradley, Q. (2008). 'Capturing the castle: tenant governance in social housing companies'. *Housing Studies*, 23/6: 879–97.

Bradshaw, T. (2011). '"Silicon roundabout" ready to ignite'. *Financial Times*, 4 February. www.ft.com

Braverman, H. (1974). *Labor and Monopoly Capital: The Degradation of Work in the Twentieth Century*. New York: Monthly Review Press.

Brewster, C. (2004). 'European perspectives on human resource management'. *Human Resource Management Review*, 14/4: 365–82.

Brewster, C., Sparrow, P., and Harris, H. (2005). 'Towards a new model of globalizing HRM'. *International Journal of Human Resource Management*, 16/6: 949–70.

Brewster, C., Carey, L., Dowling, P., Grobler, P., Holland, P., and Warnick, S. (2003). *Contemporary Issues in Human Resource Management*. Oxford: Oxford University Press.

Brockett, J. (2009). 'Waitrose uses psychometric tests to filter graduates'. *People Management,* 30 November. www.peoplemanagement.co.uk

Brockett, J. (2011). 'KPMG launches "immersive" graduate assessment centre'. *People Management*, 14 October. www.peoplemanagement.co.uk

Brookfield GRS (2011). *Global Relocation Trends Survey Report 2011*. www.brookfieldgrs.com

Broughton, A., Higgins, T., Hicks, B., and Cox, A. (2011). *Workplaces and Social Networking: the Implications for Employment Relations*. ACAS Research Paper 11/11. London: ACAS.

Brown, A. (1998). *Organisational Culture* (2nd edn). London: Financial Times–Prentice Hall.

Brown, N. (2011). 'Jackson v Liverpool City Council'. *People Management*, 12 October. www.peoplemanagement.co.uk

Brown, W. and Nash, D. (2008). 'What has been happening to collective bargaining under New Labour?'. *Industrial Relations Journal*, 39/2, 91–103.

Brown, W., Bryson, A., and Forth, J. (2009). 'Competition and the retreat from collective bargaining', in W. Brown, A. Bryson, J. Forth, and K. Whitfield (eds), *The Evolution of the Modern Workplace*. Cambridge: Cambridge University Press, 22–47.

Brooks, I., Weatherston, J., and Wilkinson, G. (2011). *The International Business Environment: Challenges and Changes* (2nd edn). Harlow: Financial Times–Prentice Hall.

Buchan, J. (2006). *From Boom to Bust? The UK Nursing Labour Market Review 2005/6*. London: Royal College of Nursing.

Buchan, J. (2007). *Nurse Workforce Planning in the UK: A Report for the Royal College of Nursing*. London: Royal College of Nursing.

Buchan, J. and Seccombe, I. (2011). *A Decisive Decade: The 2011 UK Nursing Labour Market Review*. London: Royal College of Nursing.

Buchanan, D. and Badham, R. (2008). *Power, Politics, and Organizational Change* (2nd edn). London: Sage.

Buckley, R. and Caple, J. (2009). *The Theory and Practice of Training*. London: Kogan Page.

Budd, J., Gollan, P. and Wilkinson, A. (2010). 'New approaches to employee voice and participation'. *Human Relations*, 63/3: 1–8.

Budhwar, P. (2000). 'Evaluating levels of strategic integration and devolvement of human resource management in the UK'. *Personnel Review*, 29/1: 141–57.

Budhwar, P. and Varma, A. (2011). 'Emerging HR management trends in India and the way forward'. *Organizational Dynamics*, 40/4: 317–25.

Bui, H.T.M. and Baruch, Y. (2011) 'Learning organizations in higher education: an empirical evaluation within an international context'. *Management Learning*. doi: 10.1177/1350507611431212

Burchell, B., Day, D., Hudson, M., Lapido, D., Mankelow, R., Nolan, J., Reed, H., Wichert, I., and Wilkinson, D. (1999). *Job Insecurity and Work Intensification: Flexibility and the Changing Boundaries of Work*. York: York Publishing Services for the Joseph Rowntree Foundation.

Burgess, J. and Connell, J. (eds) (2006). *Developments in the Call Centre Industry; Analysis, Changes and Challenges*. Abingdon: Routledge.

Burns, T. and Stalker, G. (1961). *The Management of Innovation*. London: Tavistock.

Cabinet Office (2003). *Ethnic Minorities in the Labour Market*. London: Cabinet Office.

CAC (Central Arbitration Committee) (2011). *Annual Report 2010–2011*. London: CAC

Canaan, J. (1999). 'In the hand or in the head? Contextualizing the debate about repetitive strain injury (RSI)', in N. Daykin and L. Doyal (eds), *Health at Work: Critical Perspectives*. Basingstoke: Macmillan, 143–60.

Caldwell, R. (2001). 'Champions, adaptors, consultants and synergists: the new change agents in HRM.' *Human Resource Management Journal*, 11/1: 39–52.

Callaghan, G. and Thompson, P. (2002). ' "We recruit attitude": the selection and shaping of routine call centre work'. *Journal of Management Studies*, 39/2: 233–53.

Cambridge University Hospitals NHS Foundation Trust (2011). *Dignity at Work Policy*. Cambridge: Cambridge University Hospitals NHS Foundation Trust.

Cannell, M. (1997). 'Practice makes perfect.' *People Management*, 6 March: 26–33.

Carless, S.A. (2009). 'Psychological testing for selection purposes: a guide to evidence-based practice for human resource professionals.' *International Journal of Human Resource Management*, 20/12: 2517–32.

Carley, M (2011). 'Europe-wide competence profiles agreed in chemicals industry'. IRS: *European Employment Review*. http://www.xperthr

Carroll, A. and Buchholtz, A. (2009). *Business and Society: Ethics and Stakeholder Management* (7th edn). Mason, OH: South-Western Cengage Learning.

Cartwright, S. and Cooper, C. (2011). 'The role of organizations in promoting health and well-being', in S. Cartwright and C. Cooper (eds), *Innovations in Stress and Health*. Basingstoke: Palgrave Macmillan, 153–72.

Carvel, J. (2004). 'NHS Trust reinstates crouton surgeon'. *Guardian*, 25 March.

Casanova, L. (2009). *Global Latinas: Latin America's Emerging Multinationals*. Basingstoke: Palgrave Macmillan.

Cascio, W. (1993). 'Downsizing: what do we know, what have we learned?'. *Academy of Management Executive*, 7/1: 95–104.

Cascio, W. (2010). 'Downsizing and redundancy', in A. Wilkinson, N. Bacon, T. Redman, and S. Snell (eds), *Sage Handbook of Human Resource Management*. London: Sage, 337–348.

Cascio, W. and Boudreau, J. (2011). *Investing in People: Financial Impact of Human Resource Initiatives*. Harlow: Financial Times–Pearson.

Castells, M. (2000). *The Information Age: Economy, Society and Culture. Volume 1: The Rise of Network Society* (2nd edn). Oxford: Blackwell.

CBI (Confederation of British Industry) (2009). *Jobs for the Future: The Business Vision for Sustainable Employment in the UK*. London: CBI

CBI (Confederation of British Industry) (2011*a*). *Healthy Returns? Absence and Workplace Health Survey 2011*. London: CBI.

CBI (Confederation of British Industry) (2011*b*). 'Urgent action needed to meet creative industries demand'. 22 September. www.cbi.org.uk

CEDEFOP (2010). *Skill Needs in Europe: Focus on 2020*. Luxembourg: Office for Official Publications of the European Communities.

Chandler, A. (1962). *Strategy and Structure: Chapters in the History of the American Industrial Enterprise*. Cambridge, MA: MIT Press.

Charlton, J. (2010*a*). 'Tackling stress using pay and benefits'. *Personnel Today*, 13 April. www.xperthr.co.uk

Charlton, J. (2010*b*). 'Ten social media legal risks for employers'. *Employers' Law*, 1 November.

Charlwood, A. (2007). 'The de–collectivisation of pay setting in Britain 1990–98: incidence, determinants and impact'. *Industrial Relations Journal*, 38/1, 33–50.

Charlwood, A. and Terry, M. (2007). 21st-century models of employee representation: structures, processes and outcomes. *Industrial Relations Journal*, 38, 320–37.

Chase, R. (1997). 'The knowledge-based organization: an international study'. *Journal of Knowledge Management*, 6/March: 38–49.

Chen, M.-J. and Miller, D. (2010) 'West meets East: toward an ambicultural approach to management'. *Academy of Management Perspective*, 24/4: 17–24.

Child, J. (2005). *Organization: Contemporary Principles and Practice*. Oxford: Blackwell.

Child, J. and McGrath, R. (2001). 'Organizations unfettered: organizational form in an information-intensive economy'. *Academy of Management Journal,* 44/6: 1135–48.

Christie, B. and Kleiner, B (2000). 'When is an employee unsalvageable?'. *Equal Opportunities International,* 19/6–7: 40–4.

Churchard, C. (2010). 'Life sciences employers lack talent management at the top'. *People Management*, 3 March. www.peoplemanagement.co.uk

Churchard, C. (2011). 'Emergency services staff to be given Olympics e-learning'. *People Management Online*, 27 July. www.peoplemanagement.co.uk

CIA (Central Intelligence Agency) (n.d.*a*). *The World Factbook*. www.cia.gov

CIA (Central Intelligence Agency) (n.d.*b*). *The World Factbook: Sierra Leone*. www.cia.gov

CIPD (Chartered Institute of Personnel Development) (2002). *Work, Parenting, and Careers: Survey Report*. London: CIPD.

CIPD (Chartered Institute of Personnel Development) (2006*a*). *Diversity—an Overview: Factsheet*. London: CIPD.

CIPD (Chartered Institute of Personnel Development) (2006*b*). *Market Pricing: Approaches and Considerations: Factsheet*. London: CIPD.

CIPD (Chartered Institute of Personnel Development) (2006*c*). *Matching Training Interventions with Organizational Needs at Infosys: International Dimension Case Studies*. London: CIPD.

CIPD (Chartered Institute of Personnel Development) (2006*d*). *Measuring True Employee Engagement*. London: CIPD.

CIPD (Chartered Institute of Personnel Development) (2006*e*). *Performance Management: Survey Report*. London: CIPD.

CIPD (Chartered Institute of Personnel Development) (2007*a*). *Discipline and Grievance at Work: Factsheet 2007*. London: CIPD.

CIPD (Chartered Institute of Personnel Development) (2007*b*). *Managing Conflict at Work: Survey Report*. London: CIPD.

CIPD (Chartered Institute of Personnel Development) (2007*c*). *Redundancy Factsheet*. London: CIPD.

CIPD (Chartered Institute of Personnel Development) (2007*d*). *Talent: Strategy, Management, Measurement*. London: CIPD.

CIPD (Chartered Institute of Personnel Development) (2008*a*). *Building the Business Case for Managing Stress in the Workplace*. London: CIPD.

CIPD (Chartered Institute of Personnel Development) (2008*b*). *Recruitment, Retention, and Turnover: Annual Survey Report*. London: CIPD.

CIPD (Chartered Institute of Personnel Development) (2008*c*). *Workplace Mediation: How Employers Do It*. London: CIPD.

CIPD (Chartered Institute of Personnel Development) (2009). *Talent Management: Factsheet*. London: CIPD.

CIPD (Chartered Institute of Personnel Development) (2010*a*). *Absence Management. Annual Survey Report 2010*. London: CIPD.

CIPD (Chartered Institute of Personnel Development) (2010b). *Creating an Engaged Workforce*. London: CIPD.

CIPD (Chartered Institute of Personnel Development) (2010c). *Evaluating Learning and Talent Development: Resource Summary*. London: CIPD.

CIPD (Chartered Institute of Personnel Development) (2010d). *Internships: To Pay or Not to Pay?* London: CIPD.

CIPD (Chartered Institute of Personnel and Development) (2010e). *Resourcing and Talent Planning: Annual Survey Report*. London: CIPD.

CIPD (Chartered Institute of Personnel and Development) (2010f). *Workforce Planning: Right People, Right Time, Right Skills*. London: CIPD.

CIPD (Chartered Institute of Personnel and Development) (2010g). *The Talent Perspective: What Does it Feel Like to be Talent-Managed? Annual Survey*. London: CIPD.

CIPD (Chartered Institute of Personnel Development) (2011a). *Conflict Management*. London: CIPD.

CIPD (Chartered Institute of Personnel and Development) (2011b). *Diversity in the Workplace: An Overview*. London: CIPD.

CIPD (Chartered Institute of Personnel Development) (2011c). *Employee Engagement: Factsheet*. London: CIPD.

CIPD (Chartered Institute of Personnel and Development) (2011d). *Competence and Competency Frameworks: Factsheet*. London: CIPD.

CIPD (Chartered Institute of Personnel Development) (2011e). *Human Capital: Factsheet*. London: CIPD.

CIPD (Chartered Institute of Personnel Development) (2011f). *Labour Market Outlook*. London: CIPD.

CIPD (Chartered Institute of Personnel Development) (2011g). *Learning and Talent Development Report*. London: CIPD

CIPD (Chartered Institute of Personnel and Development) (2011h). *Resourcing and Talent Planning: Annual Survey Report*. London: CIPD.

CIPD (Chartered Institute of Personnel Development) (2011i). *Reward Management Survey*. London: CIPD.

CIPD (Chartered Institute of Personnel Development) (2011j). *Shaping the Future: Sustainable Organization Performance—What Really Makes the Difference?* London: CIPD.

CIPD (Chartered Institute of Personnel Development) (2011k). *Learning and Talent Development: Annual Survey*. London: CIPD.

CIPD (Chartered Institute of Personnel Development) (2011l). *Absence Management 2011: Survey Report*. London: CIPD.

CIPD (Chartered Institute of Personnel Development) (2012). *The Rise in Self-Employment*. London: CIPD.

CIPD/ACAS (Chartered Institute of Personnel and Development/Advisory, Conciliation, and Arbitration Service) (2008). *Mediation: An Employer's Guide*, London: CIPD.

Citizens' Advice (2011). *Give us a Break! The CAB Service's Case for a Fair Employment Agency*. London: Citizens' Advice.

Clarke, M. (2005). 'The voluntary redundancy option: carrot or stick?'. *British Journal of Management*, 16: 245–51.

Clarke, M. (2007). 'Choices and constraints: individual perceptions of the voluntary redundancy experience'. *Human Resource Management Journal*, 17/1: 76–93.

Clarke, S. and Cooper, C. (2000). 'The risk management of occupational stress'. *Health, Risk, and Society*, 2/2: 173–87.

Clegg, S., Kornberger, M., and Pitsis, T. (2008). *Managing and Organizations. An Introduction to Theory and Practice*. London: Sage.

Clifford, J. and De Chickera, A. (2010). 'Comparative perspectives on equality law—a view from the United States and the European Union'. *Equal Rights Review*, 5: 101–4.

CMI (Chartered Management Institute) (2011). *National Management Salary Survey*. www.xperthr.co.uk

Coats, D. (2010). *Time to Cut the Gordian Knot: The Case for Consensus and Reform of the UK's Employment Relations System*. London: Smith Institute.

Coats, D. and Max, C. (2005). *Healthy Work: Productive Workplaces*. London: Work Foundation.

Coles, M., Lanfranchi, J., Skalli, A., and Treble, J. (2007). 'Pay, technology, and the cost of worker absence'. *Economic Inquiry*, 45/2, 268–85.

Collier, P. (2005). 'Governance and the quasi–public organization: a case study of social housing'. *Critical Perspectives on Accounting*, 16/7: 929–49.

Collinder, A. (2011). 'At 30, Sandals unveils $multibillion growth plan'. *The Gleaner*, 29 July.

Colling, T. (2004). 'No claim, no pain? The privatization of dispute resolution in Britain'. *Economic and Industrial Democracy*, 25/4, 555–79.

Colling, T. (2010). 'Legal institutions and the regulation of workplaces', in T. Colling and M. Terry (eds), *Industrial Relations: Theory and Practice*. Chichester: John Wiley, 323–46.

Collings, D. and Scullion, H. (2009). 'Global staffing'. *International Journal of Human Resource Management*, 20/6: 1249–52.

Collings, D., Scullion, H., and Dowling, P. (2009). 'Global staffing: a review and thematic research agenda'. *International Journal of Human Resource Management*, 20/6: 1253–72.

Collings, D., Scullion, H., and Morley, M. (2007). 'Changing patterns of global staffing in the multinational enterprise: challenges to the conventional expatriate assignment and emerging alternatives'. *Journal of World Business*, 42/4: 198–213.

Collins, D. (1998). *Organizational Change: Sociological Perspectives*. London: Routledge.

Collins, L. and Smith, J. (2004). 'Understanding the new Investors in People standard—lessons from experience'. *Personnel Review*, 33/5: 583–604.

Collins, M. (2005). 'The (not so simple) case for teleworking: a study at Lloyd's of London'. *New Technology, Work, and Employment*, 20/2: 115–32.

Collinson, D. (2003). 'Identities and insecurities: selves at work'. *Organization*, 10/3: 385–409.

Colquitt, J., Conlon, D., Wesson, M., Porter, C., and Ng, K. (2001). 'Justice at the millennium: a meta-analytic review of 25 years of organizational justice research'. *Journal of Applied Psychology,* 86/3: 425–45.

Colvin, A. (2003). 'Institutional pressures, human resource strategies, and the rise of non-union dispute resolution procedures'. *Industrial and Labour Relations Review,* 56/3, 375–92.

Combs, J., Liu, Y., Hall, A., and Ketchen, D. (2006). 'Do high performance work practices matter? A meta-analysis of their effects on organizational performance'. *Personnel Psychology,* 59/4: 501–28.

Competition Commission (n.d.). *About us.* www.competition-commission.org.uk

Cooke, F.-L. (2005). *HRM, Work, and Employment in China.* London: Routledge.

Cooke, H. (2006). 'Examining the disciplinary process in nursing: a case study approach'. *Work, Employment and Society,* 20/4, 687–707.

Corby, S. and White, G. (1999). *Employee Relations in the Public Services: Themes and Issues.* London: Routledge.

Cörvers, F. and Meriküll, J. (2008). *Occupational Structures across 25 EU Countries: The Importance of Industry Structure and Technology in Old and New EU Countries.* Maastricht: Research Centre for Education and the Labour Market.

Costa, J. (1995). 'An empirically-based review of the concept of environmental scanning'. *International Journal of Contemporary Hospitality Management,* 7/7: 4–9.

Countouris, N. and Horton, R. (2009). 'The Temporary Agency Work Directive: another broken promise?'. *Industrial Law Journal,* 38/3: 329–38.

Cousins, J., Mackay, R., Clarke, S., Kelly, C., Kelly, P., and McCaig, R. (2004). 'Management standards and work-related stress in the UK: practical developments'. *Work and Stress,* 18/2: 113–36.

Cox, A. (2007). *Re-visiting the NVQ Debate: 'Bad' Qualifications, Expansive Learning Environments and Prospects for Upskilling Workers.* ESRC Centre on Skills, Knowledge and Organizational Performance, SKOPE Research Paper No. 71. Oxford: University of Oxford

Cox, A., Higgins, T., and Speckesser, S. (2011). *Management Practices and Sustainable Organisational Performance: An Analysis of the European Company Survey 2009.* Dublin: Eurofound.

Craig, T. (2009). 'Older workers adding value—four case studies'. *Personnel Today,* 20 March.

Crane, A. and Matten, D. (2010). *Business Ethics.* Oxford: Oxford University Press.

Crompton, R. (1997). *Women and Work in Modern Britain.* Oxford: Oxford University Press.

Cropanano R., Bowen D., and Gilliland, S. (2007). 'The management of organizational justice'. *Academy of Management Review,* 34/1: 34–49

Crouch, C. (2005). *Capitalist Diversity and Change.* Oxford: Oxford University Press.

Cudahy, B. (2006). 'The container ship revolution: Malcolm McLean's 1956 innovation goes global'. *TR News,* 246: 5–9.

Cully, M., Woodland, S., O'Reilly, A., and Dix, G. (1999). *Britain at Work.* London: Routledge.

Cunningham, I. and Hyman, J. (1999). 'The poverty of empowerment? A critical case study', *Personnel Review,* 28/3: 192–207.

Cushen, J., and Thompson, P. (2011). 'Doing it by the textbook. Liberal markets, HRM and the angry, insecure high performer'. Presented at: SASE Conference, Madrid.

Cuthbert, G. and Ward, C. (2010). 'G.E.M—journey to performance excellence'. Presented at: 11th International Conference on Human Resource Development Research and Practice across Europe, University of Pecs, Hungary, 2–4 June.

Dahl, R. (1957). 'The concept of power'. *Behavioural Science,* 2: 201–15.

Dale, M. (2001). 'Organizational design', in E. Wilson (ed.), *Organizational Behaviour Reassessed.* London: Sage, 149–67.

Daniel, W. (1968). *Racial Discrimination in England.* Harmondsworth: Penguin Books.

Danford, A., Richardson, M., Stewart, P., Tailby, S., and Upchurch, M. (2004). 'Partnership, mutuality and the high-performance workplace: a case study of union strategy and worker experience in the aircraft industry', in G. Healy, E. Heery, P. Taylor, and W. Brown (eds), *The Future of Worker Representation,* Basingstoke: Palgrave Macmillan, 167–86.

Danford, A., Richardson, M., Stewart, P., Tailby, S., and Upchurch, M. (2005). *Partnership and the High Performance Workplace.* Basingstoke: Palgrave Macmillan.

Darlington, R (2009). 'Organising, militancy and revitalisation: the case of the RMT union', in G. Gall (ed.), *Union Revitalisation in Advanced Economies.* Basingstoke: Palgrave Macmillan, 83–106.

Datta, D., Guthrie, J., Basuil, D., and Pandey, A. (2010). 'Causes and effects of employee downsizing: a review and synthesis'. *Journal of Management,* 36/1, 281–348.

Dawson, P. (2003). *Reshaping Change: A Processual Perspective.* London: Routledge.

Dawson, S., Willman, P., Clinton, A., and Bamfield, M. (1988). *Safety at Work: The Limits of Self-Regulation.* Cambridge: Cambridge University Press.

De Cieri, H. and Dowling, P. (1999). 'Strategic human resource management in multinational enterprises: theoretical and empirical developments', in P. Wright, L. Dyer, J. Boudreau, and G. Milkovich (eds), *Strategic Human Resource Management: An Agenda for the 21st Century.* Stamford, CT: JAI Press, 305–27.

De George, R. (2010). *Business Ethics* (7th edn). Boston, MA: Prentice Hall.

Deal, T. and Kennedy, A. (1982). *Organization Cultures: the Rites and Rituals of Organization Life.* Reading, MA: Addison-Wesley.

Deery, S. and Kinnie, N. (2004). 'Introduction: the nature and management of call centre work', in S. Deery and N. Kinnie (eds), *Call Centres and Human Resource Management: A Cross-national Perspective.* Basingstoke: Palgrave Macmillan, 1–22.

Delbridge, R., Hauptmeier, M., and Sengupta, S. (2011). 'Beyond the enterprise: broadening the horizons of international HRM'. *Human Relations,* 64/4: 483–505.

Delery, J. and Doty, D. (1996). 'Modes of theorizing in strategic human resource management: tests of universalistic, contingency, and configurational performance predictions'. *Academy of Management Journal*, 39/4: 802–35.

Dempsey, K. (2007). 'Employers ignore the social stigma on obesity'. *Personnel Today*, 9 March. www.personneltoday.com

DeNavas Walt, C., Proctor, B., and Smith, J. (2010). Income, Poverty, and Health Insurance Coverage in the United States: 2009. US Census Bureau, Current Population Reports, P60–238. Washington, DC: US Government Printing Office.

Derbyshire, E. (2010). 'An exploration of the importance of trust in the post-acquisition integration context in high-technology industry'. Unpublished DBA thesis, University of Portsmouth.

de Ruyter, A., Bailey, D., and Mahdon, M. (2010). 'Changing lanes or stuck in the slow lane? Employment precariousness and labour market status of MG Rover workers four years after closure', in C. Thornley, S. Jeffreys, and B. Appay (eds), *Globalization and Precarious Forms of Production and Employment: Challenges for Workers and Unions*. Cheltenham: Edward Elgar, 214–29.

Dewhurst, M., Gutridge, M., and Mohr, E. (2009). 'Motivating people: getting beyond money'. *McKinsey Quarterly*. www.mckinseyquarterly.com

DfEE (Department for Education and Employment) (1998). *The Learning Age: A Renaissance for a New Britain*. Green Paper. Sheffield: DfEE.

DfES (Department for Education and Skills) (2004). *Further Education and Work-Based Learning for Young People: Learner Outcomes 2002/03*. Sheffield: Department for Education and Skills.

Dicken, P. (2007). *Global Shift: Mapping the Contours of the World Economy* (5th edn). London: Sage.

Dickens, L. (2000). 'Doing more with less: ACAS and individual conciliation', in B. Towers and W. Brown (eds), *Employment Relations in Britain: 25 Years of the Advisory, Conciliation and Arbitration Service*. Oxford: Blackwell, 67–91.

Dickens, L. and Hall, M. (2010). 'The changing legal framework of employment relations', in T. Colling and M. Terry (eds), *Industrial Relations: Theory and Practice*. Chichester: John Wiley, 298–322.

Dickmann, M. and Harris, H. (2005). 'Developing career capital for global careers: the role of international assignments'. *Journal of World Business*, 40/4: 399–408.

Directgov (2011). *Qualifications: What the Different Levels Mean*. http://www.direct.gov.uk

Dix, G. and Oxenbridge, S. (2004). 'Coming to the table with ACAS: from conflict to co-operation'. *Employee Relations*, 26/5: 510–30.

Dix, G., Sisson, K., and Forth, J. (2009). 'Conflict at work: the changing pattern of disputes', in W. Brown, A. Bryson, J. Forth, and K. Whitfield (eds), *The Evolution of the Modern Workplace*. Cambridge: Cambridge University Press, 176–200.

Doherty, L. (2004). 'Work–life balance initiatives: implications for women'. *Employee Relations*, 26/4: 433–52.

Doherty, N. (1997). 'The role of outplacement in redundancy management'. *Personnel Review*, 27/4: 343–53.

Doherty, N. and Tyson, S. (1993). *Executive Redundancy and Outplacement*. London: Kogan Page.

Doherty, N., Bank, J., and Vinnicombe, S. (1996). 'Managing survivors: the experience of survivors in British Telecom and the British financial services sector'. *Journal of Managerial Psychology*, 11/7: 51–60.

Donnelly, E. (1987). 'The training model: time for a change'. *Industrial and Commercial Training*, May/June: 6–8.

Donnelly, M. and Scholarios, D. (1998). 'Workers' experiences of redundancy: evidence from Scottish defence-dependent companies'. *Personnel Review*, 27/4: 325–42.

Dörrenbächer, C. and Geppert, M. (eds) (2011). *Politics and Power in the Multinational Corporation*. Cambridge: Cambridge University Press.

Dowglass, M. (2011). *Cancer Workforce Development Strategy 2010–15*. London: Macmillan.

Dowling, P., Festing, M. and Engle, A. (2008). *International Human Resource Management* (5th edn). London: Thomson Learning.

Doyle, J. and Reeves, R. (2003). *Time Out: the Case for Time Sovereignty*. London: Work Foundation.

Drejer, A. (2002). *Strategic Management and Core Competencies: Theory and Application*. Westport, CT: Quorum Books.

Drucker, P. (1955). *The Practice of Management*. London: Heinemann.

DTI (Department of Trade and Industry) (2005). *High Performance Work Practices: Linking Strategy and Skills to Performance Outcomes*. London: DTI in association with the CIPD.

DTI (Department of Trade and Industry) (2007). *Better Dispute Resolution: A Review of Employment Dispute Resolution in Great Britain*. London: DTI.

du Gay, P. (2000). *In Praise of Bureaucracy: Weber, Organization, Ethics*. London: Sage.

Dundon, T. and Rollinson, D. (2004). *Employment Relations in Non-Union Firms*. London: Routledge.

Dundon, T. and Gollan, P. (2007). 'Re-conceptualizing voice in the non-union workplace'. *International Journal of Human Resource Management*, 18/7: 1182–98.

Dundon, T., Wilkinson, A., Marchington, M., and Ackers, P. (2005). 'The management of voice in non-union organisations: managers' perspectives'. *Employee Relations*, 27/3: 307–19.

Dunleavy, P. and Hood, C. (1994). 'From old public administration to new public management'. *Public Money and Management*, 14/3: 34–43.

Dunn, C. and Wilkinson, A. (2002). 'Wish you were here: managing absence'. *Personnel Review*, 31/2: 228–46.

Dutton, W., Helsper, E., and Gerber, M. (2009). *The Internet in Britain 2009*. Oxford: Institute for the Internet.

DWP (Department for Work and Pensions) (2011a). *Good Health and Safety for Everyone*. London: DWP.

DWP (Department for Work and Pensions) (2011*b*). *The Work Programme*. www.dwp. gov.uk

Dyson, J. (2007). 'A move in the right direction'. *The Engineer Online*. www.theengineer.co.uk

Earnshaw, J Goodman, J. Harrison R., and Marchington, M. (1998). *Industrial Tribunals, Workplace Disciplinary Procedures and Employment Practices*. Employment Relations Research Series No. 2. London: DTI.

Earnshaw, J., Marchington, M., and Goodman, J. (2000). 'Unfair to whom? Discipline and dismissal in small establishments', *Industrial Relations Journal*, 31/1: 62–73.

Earnshaw, J., Marchington, L., Ritchie, E., and Torrington. D. (2004). 'Neither fish nor fowl? An assessment of teacher capability procedures'. *Industrial Relations Journal*, 35/2: 139–52.

Easterby–Smith, M. and Mikhailava, I. (2011). *The Knowledge Management Challenge: Mastering the Softer Side of Knowledge Management*. London: Advanced Institute of Management Research.

Economist (2005). 'The good company—a survey of corporate social responsibility', *Economist*, 22 January.

Economist (2008). 'Special report: migration. Open up'. *Economist*, 3 January.

Economist (2009). 'Government debt: the big sweat'. *Economist*, 11 June.

Edelenbos, J. and van Buuren, R. (2005). 'The learning evaluation: a theoretical and empirical exploration'. *Evaluation Review*, 29: 591–612.

Edward, P. (2006). 'Examining inequality: who really benefits from global growth?' *World Development*, 34/10: 1667–95.

Edwards, P. (1995). 'Strikes and industrial conflict', in P. Edwards (ed.), *Industrial Relations: Theory and Practice in Britain*. Oxford: Blackwell, 434–60.

Edwards, P. (2005). 'Discipline and attendance: a murky aspect of people management', in S. Bach (ed.), *Managing Human Resources* (4th edn). Oxford: Blackwell, 375–97.

Edwards, P. and Scullion, H. (1982). *The Social Organisation of Industrial Conflict*. Oxford: Basil Blackwell.

Edwards, P. and Wajcman, J. (2005). *The Politics of Working Life*. Oxford: Oxford University Press.

Edwards, T. (2011). 'The transfer of employment practices across borders in multinational companies', in A.W. Harzing and A. Pinnington (eds), *International Human Resource Management* (3rd edn). London: Sage, 267–90.

Edwards, T. and Ferner, A. (2002). 'The renewed "American challenge": a review of employment practice in US multinationals'. *Industrial Relations Journal*, 33/2: 94–111.

Edwards, T. and Rees, C. (eds) (2011). *International Human Resource Management: Globalization, National Systems and Multinational Companies* (2nd edn). Harlow: Financial Times–Prentice Hall.

Edwards, T. and Tempel, A. (2010). 'Explaining variation in reverse diffusion of HR practices: evidence from the German and British subsidiaries of American multinationals'. *Journal of World Business*, 45: 19–28.

Edwards, T., Colling, T., and Ferner, A. (2007). 'Conceptual approaches to the transfer of employment practices in multinational companies: an integrated approach'. *Human Resource Management Journal*, 17/3: 201–17.

EHRC (Equality and Human Rights Commission) (2009). *Gender Pay Activity in Large Non-Public Sector Organisations: Baseline Report*. Manchester: EHRC.

EHRC (Equality and Human Rights Commission) (2011). *Financial Services Inquiry: Follow Up Report*. www.equalityhumanrights.com

EIRO (European Industrial Relations Observatory) (2004). 'Siemens deal launches debate on longer working hours', *EIROnline*, July. www.eurofound. europa.eu/eiro/2004/07/feature/de0407106f. html

Emmott, M. (2005). *What is Employee Relations?* London: CIPD.

EOC (Equal Opportunities Commission) (2007*a*). *Sex and Power: Who Runs Britain?: Annual Survey Report*. Manchester: EOC.

EOC (Equal Opportunities Commission) (2007*b*). *Working Outside the Box: Survey Report*. Manchester: EOC.

Eurofound (European Foundation for the Improvement of Living and Working Conditions) (2010). *Absence from Work*. http://www. eurofound.europa.eu/docs/ewco/tn0911039s/ tn0911039s.pdf

Eurofound (European Foundation for the Improvement of Living and Working Conditions) (2011). *Recent Developments in Wage Setting and Collective Bargaining in the Wake of the Global Economic Crisis*. Dublin: Eurofound.

European Commission (2010). *The Lifelong Learning Programme: Education and Training Opportunities for All*. http://ec.europa.eu.

European Commission Competition (2011). *Delivering for Consumers*. ec.europa.eu/ competition/consumers/index_en.html

Evans, A. and Walters, M. (2003). *From Absence to Attendance* (2nd edn). London: CIPD.

Fairhurst, D. (2008). 'Am I "bovvered?" Driving a performance culture through to the front line'. *Human Resource Management Journal*, 18/4: 321–6.

Fairtrade Foundation (2011). *Facts and Figures on Fairtrade*. www.fairtrade.org.uk

Falcone, P. (1997). 'The fundamentals of progressive discipline'. *HR Magazine*, 42/2: 82–94.

Falconer, H. (2004). *Managing Disputes: Case Studies*. Personnel Today Management Resources: One-stop Guide on Managing Disputes. www.xperthr.co.uk

Faragher, J. (2011). 'Agency Workers Regulations not hitting use of temporary staff'. *Personnel Today*, 22 December. http://www.personneltoday. com/articles/2011/12/22/58247/agency-workers-regulations-not-hitting-use-of-temporary-staff.html

Farndale, E. (2005). 'HR department professionalism: a comparison between the UK and other European countries'. *International Journal of Human Resource Management*, 16: 660–75.

Farndale, E., Scullion, H., and Sparrow, P. (2010). 'The role of the corporate HR function in global talent management'. *Journal of World Business*, 45: 161–8.

Farndale, E., Paauwe, J., Morris, S., Stahl, G., Stiles, P., Trevor, J., and Wright, M. (2010).

'Context-bound configurations of corporate HR functions in multinational corporations'. *Human Resource Management*, 49/1: 45–66.

Farnham, D. (2006). 'Human resource strategy: perspectives and theories', in S. Pilbeam and M. Corbridge (eds), *People Resourcing: Contemporary HRM in Practice*. Harlow: Prentice Hall, 40–60.

Farnham, D. (2010). *Human Resource Management in Context: Strategy, Insights, and Solutions* (3rd edn). London: CIPD.

Farrell, D., Ghai, S., and Shavers, T. (2005). 'The demographic deficit: how aging will reduce global wealth'. www.mckinseyquarterly.com

Farrell, G. (1999). 'Aggression in clinical settings: nurses' views'. *Journal of Advanced Nursing*, 29/3: 532–41.

Fawcett Society (2010). *Equal Pay: Where Next?* London: Fawcett Society.

Fenn, P. and Ashby, S. (2004). 'Workplace risk, establishment size and union density'. *British Journal of Industrial Relations*, 42/3: 461–80.

Fernandez, R., Taylor, S., and Bell, E. (2005). *How Long Until We Get There? A Survival Analysis of the Investors in People Initiative 1991–2001*. SKOPE Research Paper No. 56, University of Oxford.

Ferner, A. (1997). 'Country of origin effects and HRM in multinational companies'. *Human Resource Management Journal*, 7/1: 19–37.

Ferner, A. (2010). 'HRM in multinational companies', in A. Wilkinson, N. Bacon, T. Redman, and S. Snell (eds), *Sage Handbook of Human Resource Management*, London: Sage, 541–60.

Ferner, A. and Edwards, P. (1995). 'Power and the diffusion of organizational change within multinational corporations'. *European Journal of Industrial Relations*, 1/2: 229–57.

Ferner, A., Almond, P., and Colling, T. (2005). 'Institutional theory and the cross-national transfer of employment policy: the case of "workforce diversity" in US multinationals'. *Journal of International Business Studies*, 36: 304–21.

Fernie, S. (2005). 'The future of British unions: introduction and conclusions', in S. Fernie and D. Metcalf (eds), *Trade Unions: Resurgence or Demise?* London: Routledge, 1–18.

Fine, J. (2006). *Worker Centers: Organizing Communities at the Edge of the Dream*. Ithaca, NY: ILR Press.

Fineman, S. (1993). 'Organizations as emotional arenas', in S. Fineman (ed.), *Emotion in Organizations*. London: Sage.

Fineman, S. (1997). 'Emotion and management learning'. *Management Learning*, 28/1: 13–25.

Finlay, P. (2000). *Strategic Management: An Introduction to Business and Corporate Strategy*. Harlow: Financial Times–Prentice Hall.

Fischlmayr, I. (2002). 'Female self–perception as a barrier to international careers?'. *International Journal of Human Resource Management*, 13/5: 773–83.

Fisher, C. and Lovell, A. (2006). *Business Ethics and Values: Individual, Corporate, and International Perspectives* (2nd edn). Harlow: Financial Times–Prentice Hall.

Fishman, C. (2006). *The Wal-mart Effect*. New York: Penguin.

Flood, P., Guthrie, J., Liu, W., O'Regan, C., Armstrong, A., MacCurtain, S., and Mkamwa, T. (2008). *New Models of High Performance Work Systems: The Business Case for Strategic HRM, Partnership and Diversity and Equality Systems*. Dublin: National Centre for Partnership Performance and the Equality Authority.

Flynn, M. (2010). 'The United Kingdom government's "business case" approach to the regulation of retirement'. *Ageing and Society*, 30/3: 421–43.

Fogarty, H., Scott, P., and Williams, S. (2011). 'The half-empty office: dilemmas in managing locational flexibility'. *New Technology, Work and Employment*, 26/3: 183–95.

Fombrun, C., Tichy, N., and Devanna, M. (1984). *Strategic Human Resource Management*. New York: John Wiley.

Forde, C. and Slater, G. (2006). 'The nature and experience of agency working in Britain. What are the challenges for human resource management?'. *Personnel Review*, 35/2: 141–57.

Forde, C., MacKenzie, R., and Robinson, A. (2008). ' "Help wanted". Employers' use of temporary agencies in the UK construction industry'. *Employee Relations*, 30/6: 679–98.

Forde, C., Stuart, M., Gardiner, J., Greenwood, I., MacKenzie, R. and Perrett, R. (2009). *Socially Responsible Restructuring in an Era of Mass Redundancy*. Working Paper No.5, Leeds University Centre for Employment Relations Innovation and Change.

Foreign and Commonwealth Office (2011). *Travel and Living Abroad: Sierra Leone*. www.fco.gov. uk/en/travel-and-living-abroad/travel-advice-by-country/sub-saharan-africa/sierra-leone

Fortin, N. (2005). 'Gender role attitudes and the labour-market outcomes of women across OECD countries'. *Oxford Review of Economic Policy*, 21/3: 416–38.

Fotheringham, W. (2011). 'Mark Cavendish confirms he will join Team Sky for 2012'. *Guardian,* 11 October. www.guardian.co.uk

Fotheringham, W. (2012). 'Mark Cavendish and Bradley Wiggins can take Team Sky to new heights'. *Guardian*, 1 March. www.guardian. co.uk

Foucault, M. (1972). *The Archaeology of Knowledge*. London: Tavistock.

Foucault, M. (1977). *Discipline and Punish: The Birth of the Prison*. Harmondsworth: Penguin.

Fox, A. (1974). *Beyond Contract: Work, Power, and Trust Relations*. London: Faber.

Fox, R. (2006). 'Legal Q&A: blogging'. *Personnel Today*, 22 August. www.personneltoday.com

Francis, H. and Keegan, A. (2006). 'The changing face of HRM: in search of balance'. *Human Resource Management Journal*, 16/3: 231–49.

Frank, J. (2006). 'Gay glass ceilings'. *Economica*, 73/291: 485–508

Fraser, J. and Gold, M. (2001). 'Portfolio workers: autonomy and control amongst freelance translators'. *Work, Employment and Society*, 15/4: 679–97.

Fredman, S. and Szyszczak, E. (1992). 'The interaction of race and gender', in B. Hepple and E. Szyszczak (eds), *Discrimination and the Limits of the Law*. London: Mansell, 214–27.

Frege, C. (2006). 'International trends in unionisation', in M. Morley, P. Gunnigle, and D. Collings (eds), *Global Industrial Relations*. London: Routledge, 221–38.

Friedman, E. and Lee, C.K. (2010). 'Remaking the world of Chinese labour: a 30-year retrospective'. *British Journal of Industrial Relations*, 48/3, 507–33.

Friedman, M. (1970). 'The social responsibility of business is to increase its profits'. *New York Times Magazine*, 13 September.

Friedman, M. and Friedman, R. (1990). *Free To Choose*. London: Thomson Learning.

Frogner, M.L. (2002). 'Skills shortages'. *Labour Market Trends*. January: 17–27.

Fryer, R. (1973). 'Redundancy, values and public policy'. *Industrial Relations Journal*, 4/2: 2–19.

Fuller, A. and Unwin, L. (2003). 'Fostering workplace learning: looking through the lens of apprenticeship'. *European Educational Research Journal*, 2/1: 41–55.

Fuller, G. (2006a). 'BAE systems investigates 100 employees for e-mail misuse'. *Personnel Today*, 4 August. www.personneltoday.com

Fuller, G. (2006b). 'Swansea College sacks five staff and disciplines 70 more for misusing e-mail systems'. *Personnel Today*, 10 October. www.personneltoday.com

Fuller, G. (2007). 'RBS threatens staff with disciplinary action for refusing to open an account at the bank'. *Personnel Today*, 23 March. www.personneltoday.com

Furnham, A. (2005). *The Psychology of Behaviour at Work*. London: Routledge.

Furnham, A. and Chaudhuri, A. (2001). 'The truth will out'. *Guardian*, 24 April. www.guardian.co.uk

Gabriel, Y., Fineman, S., and Sims, D. (2000). *Organizing and Organizations* (2nd edn) London: Sage.

Gall, G. (2007). 'Trade union recognition in Britain: an emerging crisis for trade unions?' *Economic and Industrial Democracy*, 28/1, 78–109.

Gall, G. (2009). 'Union organising—past, present and future', in G. Gall (ed.), *The Future of Union Organising*, Basingstoke: Palgrave Macmillan, 1–9.

Gall, G. (2010a). 'Resisting recession and redundancy: contemporary worker occupations in Britain'. *Working USA*, 13/1, 107–32.

Gall, G. (2010b). 'The first ten years of the third statutory union recognition procedure in Britain'. *Industrial Law Journal*, 39/4, 444–8.

Gall, G. (2011). 'Contemporary workplace occupations in Britain: motivations, stimuli, dynamics and outcomes'. *Employee Relations*, 33/6, 607–23.

Gallie, D. (2005). 'Work pressure in Europe 1996–2001: trends and determinants'. *British Journal of Industrial Relations*, 43/3: 351–75.

Gallie, D., White, M., Cheng, Y., and Tomlinson, M. (1998). *Restructuring the Employment Relationship*. Oxford: Clarendon Press.

Gamble, A. (1988). *The Free Economy and the Strong State: The Politics of Thatcherism*. Basingstoke: Macmillan Education.

Garavan, T. (1997). 'The learning organization: a review and evaluation'. *Learning Organization*, 4/1: 18–29.

Garavan, T., Heraty, N., and Barnicle, B. (1999). 'Human resource development: current issues, priorities and dilemmas'. *Journal of European Industrial Training*, 23/4–5: 169–79.

Garvin, D. (1993). 'Building a learning organization'. *Harvard Business Review*, 71/4: 78–91.

Garvin, D., Edmondson, A., and Gino, F. (2008). 'Is yours a learning organization?' *Harvard Business Review*, 86/3: 2–10.

Gatrell, C. (2005). *Hard Labour: The Sociology of Parenthood*. Maidenhead: Open University Press.

Geiger, A. (2006). *EU Lobbying Hand Book: A Guide to Modern Participation in Brussels*. Berlin: Helios Media.

Geppert, M. and Mayer, M. (eds) (2006). *Global, National, and Local Practices in Multinational Companies*. Basingstoke: Palgrave Macmillan.

Geppert, M. and Williams, K. (2006). 'Global, national, and local practices in multinational corporations: towards a sociopolitical framework'. *International Journal of Human Resource Management*, 17/1: 49–69.

Gerhart, B. (2005). 'Human resources and business performance: findings, unanswered questions, and an alternative approach'. *Management Revue*, 16/2: 174–85.

Gerhart, B. (2007). Modeling HRM and performance linkages. In P. Boxall, J. Purcell, and P. Wright (eds), *Oxford Handbook of Human Resource Management*. Oxford: Oxford University Press, 252–80.

Gibb, S. (2002). *Learning and Development: Processes, Practices and Perspectives at Work*. Basingstoke: Palgrave Macmillan.

Gibb, S. and Megginson, D. (2005). 'Training and development', in T. Redman and A. Wilkinson (eds), *Contemporary Human Resource Management: Text and Cases*. Harlow: Financial Times–Prentice Hall, 128–67.

Giddens, A. (2009). *Sociology* (6th edn). Cambridge: Polity Press.

Gielen, A., Kerkhofs, M., and van Ours, J. (2009). 'How performance related pay affects productivity and employment'. *Journal of Population Economics*, 23/1: 291–301.

Gilmore, S. and Williams, S. (2007). 'Conceptualising the personnel professional: a critical analysis of the Chartered Institute of Personnel and Development's Professional Qualification Scheme'. *Personnel Review*, 36/4: 398–414.

Gilson, C., Hurd, F., and Wagar, T. (2004). 'Creating a concession climate: the case of the serial downsizers'. *International Journal of Human Resource Management*, 15/6: 1056–68.

Gittell, J. and Bamber, G. (2010). 'High- and low-road strategies for competing on costs and their implications for employment relations: international studies in the airline industry'. *International Journal of Human Resource Management*, 21/2: 165–79.

Glaso, L., Nielsen, M., and Einarsen, S. (2009). 'Interpersonal problems amongst perpetrators and targets of workplace bullying'. *Journal of Applied Social Psychology*, 39/6: 1316–33.

Glyn, A. (2004). 'The assessment: how far has globalization gone?' *Oxford Review of Economic Policy*, 20/1: 1–14.

Godard, J. (2004). 'A critical assessment of the high performance paradigm'. *British Journal of Industrial Relations*, 42/2: 349–78.

Godfrey, H. (2011). 'UK women top of obesity league, and men are second—EU survey'. *Guardian*, 26 November. www.guardian.co.uk

Godwin, K. (2008). 'Bullying and harassment: EOR Survey 2008'. *Equal Opportunities Review*, 176, May.

Gold, J. (2007). 'Human resource development', in J. Bratton and J. Gold (eds), *Human Resource Management: Theory and Practice* (4th edn). Basingstoke: Macmillan, 306–57.

Golden, T. (2007). 'Co-workers who telework and the impact on those in the office: understanding the implications of virtual work for co-worker satisfaction and turnover intentions'. *Human Relations*, 60/11: 1641–67.

Goldfinch, S., Gauld, R., and Baldwin, N. (2011). 'Information and communications technology use, e-government, pain and stress amongst public servants'. *New Technology, Work, and Employment*, 26/1: 39–53.

Gollan, P. (2007). *Employee Representation in Non-union Firms*. London: Sage.

Gooderham, P., Parry, E., and Ringdal, K. (2008). 'The impact of bundles on strategic human resource management practices on the performance of European firms'. *International Journal of Human Resource Management*, 19/12: 2041–56.

Goodman, J., Earnshaw, J., Marchington, M., and Harrison, R. (1998). 'Unfair dismissal cases, disciplinary procedures, recruitment methods and management style: case study evidence from three industrial sectors'. *Employee Relations*, 20/6: 536–50.

Gospel, H. and Sako, M. (2010). 'The unbundling of corporate practices: the evolution of shared services and outsourcing in human resource management'. *Industrial and Corporate Change*, 19/5: 1367–96.

Goss, D. (1994). *Principles of Human Resource Management*. London: Routledge.

Gould, A. (2010). 'Working at McDonalds: some redeeming features of McJobs'. *Work, Employment, and Society*, 24/4: 780–802.

Gouldner, A. (1954). *Patterns of Industrial Bureaucracy*. New York: Free Press.

Government Equalities Office (2011). *Think, Act, Report—Framework*. London: Home Office.

Grainger, J., Clark, D., and Asteris, M. (2007). *Socio-economic impact assessment of Portsmouth Naval Base*. Portsmouth: Centre for Local and Regional Economic Analysis, University of Portsmouth Business School.

Green, F. (2004). 'Why has work become more intense?'. *Industrial Relations*, 43/4: 709–41.

Green, F. (2006). *Demanding Work*. Princeton, NJ: Princeton University Press.

Greenberg, J. (1990). 'Looking fair vs being fair: managing impressions of organizational justice', in B. Staw and L. Cummings (eds), *Research in Organizational Behavior*. Greenwich, CT: JAI Press, 111–57.

Griffin, J. (1939). *Strikes: A Study in Quantitative Economics*. New York: Columbia University Press.

Griffiths, L. (2009). 'Obesity: The big issue'. *Personnel Today*, 1 May. www.personneltoday.com

Griffiths, A. and Wall, S. (eds) (2012). *Applied Economics* (12th edn). Harlow: Financial Times–Prentice Hall.

Grimshaw, D. and Rubery, J. (2010). 'Pay and working time: shifting contours of the employment relationship', in T. Colling and M. Terry (eds), *Industrial Relations: Theory and Practice*. Chichester: John Wiley, 349–77.

Grugulis, I. and Bevitt, S. (2002). 'The impact of Investors in People: a case study of a hospital trust'. *Human Resource Management Journal*, 12/3: 44–60.

Guardian (2011). 'ABCs: national daily newspaper circulation'. June 2011. www.guardian.co.uk

Guerci, M. and Vinante, M. (2011). 'Training evaluation: an analysis of the stakeholders' evaluation needs'. *Journal of European Industrial Training*, 35/4: 385–410.

Guest, D. (1987). 'Human resource management and industrial relations'. *Journal of Management Studies*, 24/5: 503–21.

Guest, D. (1989). 'Personnel and HRM: can you tell the difference?'. *Personnel Management*, January: 49.

Guest, D. (1995). 'Human resource management, trade unions and industrial relations', in J. Storey (ed.), *Human Resource Management: A Critical Text*. London: Thomson, 110–41.

Guest, D. and King, Z. (2004). 'Power, innovation and problem-solving: the personnel managers' three steps to heaven?' *Journal of Management Studies*, 41/3: 401–23.

Haines, R. (2009). 'Organizational outsourcing and the implication for HRM', in D. Collings and G. Wood (eds), *Human Resource Management: A Critical Guide*. Abingdon: Routledge, 92–112.

Hakim, C. (1995). *Key Issues in Women's Work*. London: Athlone Press.

Hakim, C. (2004). *Key Issues in Women's Work* (2nd edn). London: Glasshouse Press.

Hakim, C. (2011). *Feminist Myths and Magic Medicine: The Flawed Thinking Behind Calls for Further Equality Legislation*. London: Centre for Policy Studies.

Halapete, J., Seshradi Iyer, K., and Park, S.C. (2008). 'Wal-Mart in India: a success or failure?'. *International Journal of Retail and Distribution Management*, 36/9: 701–13.

Hale, B. (2010). 'Obesity and the workforce'. *Personnel Today*, 9 July. www.personneltoday.com

Hales, C. (2002). ' "Bureaucracy-lite" and continuities in managerial work'. *British Journal of Management*, 13/1: 51–66.

Hall, D., Pilbeam, S., and Corbridge, M. (2012). *Strategic People Management: A Case Based Approach*. Basingstoke: Palgrave Macmillan.

Hall, M. (2005). 'Using a multi-level consultation framework: the case of B&Q', in J. Storey (ed.), *Adding Value through Information and Consultation*. Basingstoke: Palgrave Macmillan, 240–53.

Hall, M. (2006). 'A cool response to the ICE Regulations? Employer and trade union approaches to the new legal framework for information and consultation'. *Industrial Relations Journal*, 37/5: 456–72.

Hall, M. and Edwards, P. (1999). 'Reforming the statutory redundancy consultation procedure'. *Industrial Law Journal*, 28/4: 299–318.

Hall, M., Hutchinson, S., Purcell, J., Terry, M., and Parker, J. (2011). 'Promoting effective consultation? Assessing the impact of the ICE Regulations'. *British Journal of Industrial Relations*, doi: 10.1111/j.1467–8543.2011.00870.x

Hall, P. and Soskice, D. (2001). *Varieties of Capitalism: The Institutional Foundations of Comparative Advantage*. Oxford: Oxford University Press.

Hall, R. and Wailes, N. (2010). 'International and comparative human resource management', in A. Wilkinson, N. Bacon, T. Redman, and S. Snell (eds), *Sage Handbook of Human Resource Management*. London: Sage, 115–32.

Hammer, M. and Champy, J. (1993). *Reengineering the Corporation: A Manifesto for Business Revolution*. London: Nicholas Brealey.

Hampshire Fire and Rescue Service (2007). *The Service: Corporate Planning Process*. Hampshire Fire and Rescue Service. www.hantsfire.gov.uk

Hancké, B., Rhodes, M., and Thatcher, M. (eds) (2007). *Beyond Varieties of Capitalism*. Oxford: Oxford University Press.

Harford, T. (2006). *The Undercover Economist*. London: Little Brown.

Harford, T. (2008). *The Logic of Life: Uncovering The New Economics of Everything*. London: Little Brown.

Harker, R. (2011). *NHS Funding and Expenditure*. www.parliament.uk/briefing–papers/SN00724

Harmer, J. (2010). 'Firmdale holds strong during recession'. *Caterer and HotelKeeper*, 13 July. www.catersearch.com

Harrington, J. (2001). 'Health effects of shift work and extended hours of work'. *Occupational Environmental Medicine*, 58/1: 68–72.

Harris, C. (1987). *Redundancy and Recession*. Oxford: Basil Blackwell.

Harris, H. and Brewster, C. (1999). 'The coffee-machine system: how international selection really works'. *International Journal of Human Resource Management*, 10/3: 488–500.

Harris, H., Brewster, C., and Sparrow, P. (2003). *International Human Resource Management*. London: CIPD.

Harris, L. and Ogbonna, E. (2002). 'Exploring service sabotage: the antecedents, types and consequences of frontline, deviant, antiservice behaviors'. *Journal of Service Research*, 4/3: 163–83.

Harris, P. (2007). *An Introduction to Law* (7th edn). Cambridge: Cambridge University Press.

Harrison, A. (2010). *Business Environment in a Global Context*. Oxford: Oxford University Press.

Harrison, D. and Klein, K. (2007). 'What's the difference? Diversity constructs as separation, variety, or disparity in organizations'. *Academy of Management Review*, 32/4: 1199–1228.

Harzing, A.-W. (1999). *Managing the Multinationals*. Cheltenham: Edward Elgar.

Harzing, A.-W. and Pinnington, A. (2011). *International Human Resource Management*. London: Sage.

Hay, C. (2000). 'Contemporary capitalism, globalization, regionalization and the persistence of national variation'. *Review of International Studies*, 26/4: 509–31.

Head, J. and Lucas, R. (2004). 'Employee relations in the non-union hotel industry: a case of "determined opportunism"?'. *Personnel Review*, 33/6: 693–710.

Heather, K. (2004). *Economics: Theory in Action* (4th edn). Harlow: Financial Times–Prentice Hall.

Heckscher, C. (1994). 'Defining the post-bureaucratic type', in C. Heckscher and A. Donnellon (eds), *The Post-bureaucratic Organization—New Perspectives on Organizational Change*. London: Sage, 14–62.

Heery, E. and Simms, M. (2010). 'Employer responses to union organising: patterns and effects'. *Human Resource Management Journal*, 20/1: 3–22.

Heery, E., Simms, M., Delbridge, R., Salmon, J., and Simpson, D. (2003). 'Trade union recruitment policy in Britain: form and effects', in G. Gall (ed.), *Union Organizing: Campaigning for Union Recognition*. London: Routledge, 56–78.

Hella, S. and Moll, S. (2009). 'E-recruitment: a study into applicant perceptions of an online application system'. *International Journal of Selection and Assessment*, 17/3: 311–23.

Henders-Green, A. (2007). 'Blogging'. *Personnel Today*, 17 April. http://www.personneltoday.com

Henry, S. (1982). 'Factory law: the changing disciplinary technology of industrial social control'. *International Journal of the Sociology of Law*, 10: 365–83.

Herzberg, F. (1959). *The Motivation to Work*. New York: John Wiley.

Hewlett, S. and Rashid, R. (2011). *Winning the War for Talent in Emerging Markets: Why Women are the Answer*. Boston, MA: Harvard Business Press.

Hills, J. (2010). *An Anatomy of Economic Inequality in the UK: Report of the National Equality Panel*. London: Government Equalities Office.

Hirst, A. (2011). 'Settlers, vagrants, and mutual indifference: unintended consequences of hot-desking'. *Journal of Organizational Change Management*, 24/6: 767–88.

Hirst, P., Thompson, G., and Bromley, S. (2009). *Globalization in Question* (3rd edn). Cambridge: Polity.

HM Government (2011). *Consultation on Modern Workplaces*. www.bis.gov.uk/assets/biscore/employment-matters/docs/c/11-699-consultation-modern-workplaces.pdf

Ho, C.-L. and Dzeng, R. (2010). 'Construction safety via e-learning: learning effectiveness and user safety'. *Computers and Education*, 55/2: 858–67.

Hochschild, A. (1983). *The Managed Heart*. Berkeley, CA: University of California Press.

Hoel, H. and Cooper, C, (2000). *Destructive Conflict and Bullying at Work*. London: British Occupational Health Foundation.

Hofstede, G. (1991). *Cultures and Organizations*. London: Profile Books.

Hofstede, G. (2001). *Culture's Consequences: Comparing Values, Behaviors, Attitudes, and Organizations across Nations*. London: Sage.

Holdsworth, A. (1988). *Out of the Dolls House*. London: BBC Books.

Holgate, J. (2005). 'Organizing migrant workers: a case study of working conditions and unionization in a London sandwich factory'. *Work, Employment and Society*, 19/3, 463–80.

Holgate, J. (2009). 'Contested terrain: London's living wage campaign and the tensions between community and union organising', in J. McBride and I. Greenwood (eds), *Community Unionism: A Comparative Analysis of Concepts and Contexts*. Basingstoke: Palgrave Macmillan, 49–74.

Hooker, H., Neathey, F., Casebourne, J., and Munro, M. (2007). *The Third Work–Life Balance Employees' Survey: Main Findings*. Employment Relations Research Series No. 58. London: Department for Trade and Industry.

House of Commons Trade and Industry Committee (2007). *Success and Failure in the UK Car Manufacturing Industry*. London: Stationery Office.

House of Lords (2008). *The Economic Impact of Immigration. Volume I: Report*. London: Stationery Office.

Howe-Walsh, L. and Schyns, B. (2010). 'Self-initiated expatriation: implications for HRM'. *International Journal of Human Resource Management*, 21/2: 260–73.

Howell, C. and Kolin Givan, R. (2011). 'Rethinking institutions and institutional change in European industrial relations'. *British Journal of Industrial Relations*, 49/2: 231–55.

HSE (Health and Safety Executive) (2006). *Managing Shift Work: Health and Safety Guidance*. London: HSE.

HSE (Health and Safety Executive) (2008). *Working Together to Reduce Stress at Work: A Guide for Employees*. London: HSE.

HSE (Health and Safety Executive) (2011*a*). *Annual Statistics Report*. London: HSE.

HSE (Health and Safety Executive) (2011*b*). *Violence at Work: Statistics from the 2010/11 British Crime Survey & RIDDOR*. London: HSE.

Hudson, M. (2002). 'Flexibility and the reorganisation of work', in B. Burchell, D. Ladipo, and F. Wilkinson (eds), *Job Insecurity and Work Intensification*. London: Routledge, 39–60.

Hughes, G. (2011). *The Myth of Green Jobs*. London: Global Warming Policy Foundation.

Hughes, M. (2006). *Change Management: A Critical Perspective*. London: CIPD.

Human Rights Watch (2011). *Country Summary: Sierra Leone*. www.hrw.org

Huselid, M. (1995). 'The impact of human resource management practices on turnover, productivity and corporate financial performance'. *Academy of Management Journal*, 38/3: 635–72.

Huselid, M. and Becker, B. (1996). 'Methodological issues in cross-sectional and panel estimates of the HRM–firm performance link'. *Industrial Relations*, 35/3: 400–22.

Huselid, M., Beatty, R., and Becker, B. (2005). 'A players or A positions? The strategic logic of workforce management'. *Harvard Business Review*, 83/12: 110–17.

Hutton, W. (1995). *The State We're In*. London: Jonathan Cape.

Hyman, J., Scholarios, D., and Baldry, C. (2005). ' "Daddy, I don't like these shifts you're working because I never see you": coping strategies for home and work', in D. Houston (ed), *Work–Life Balance in the 21st Century*. Basingstoke: Palgrave Macmillan, 122–46.

Hyman, R. (1975). *Industrial Relations: A Marxist Introduction*. London: Macmillan.

Hyman, R. (1977). *Strikes* (2nd edn). Glasgow: Fontana–Collins.

Hyman, R. (1987). 'Strategy or structure? Capital, labour, and control'. *Work, Employment, and Society*, 1/1: 25–55.

IDS (Incomes Data Services) (2005). 'Grievance procedures'. *IDS HR Study*, 801.

IDS (Incomes Data Services) (2007). 'Managing redundancy'. *IDS HR Study Plus*, 860.

IDS (Incomes Data Services) (2009*a*). 'Discipline, grievance, and mediation'. *IDS HR Studies*, 906.

IDS (Incomes Data Services) (2009*b*). 'Managing redundancy'. *IDS HR Studies*, 902.

IDS (Incomes Data Services) (2009*c*). 'Performance management'. *IDS HR Studies*, 886.

IDS (Incomes Data Services) (2011*a*). 'Absence management'. *IDS HR Studies*, 936.

IDS (Incomes Data Services) (2011*b*). 'Performance management'. *IDS HR Studies*, 938.

Iles, P. (2001). 'Employee resourcing', in J. Storey (ed.) *Human Resource Management: A Critical Text* (2nd edn). London: Thomson Business Press, 203–33.

Iles, P. and Salaman, G. (1995). 'Recruitment, selection, and assessment', in J. Storey (ed.), *Human Resource Management: A Critical Text*. London: Thomson Business Press, 203–33.

Iles, P., Chuai, X., and Preece, D. (2010). 'Talent management and HRM in multinational companies in Beijing: definitions, differences and drivers'. *Journal of World Business*, 45/2: 179–89.

Iles, P., Preece, D., and Chuai, X. (2010). 'Talent management as a management fashion in HRD: towards a research agenda'. *Human Resource Development International*, 13/2: 125–45.

ILO (International Labour Organization) (2006). *Offshoring and Job Losses: Is the Rising International Integration of Products and Services Good for Labour Markets in the Developed World?* Geneva: ILO.

ILO (International Labour Organization) (2010). *World of Work Report 2010: From One Crisis to the Next?* Geneva: ILO and International Institute for Labour Standards.

Innovas Solutions (2009). *Low Carbon and Environmental Goods and Services: An Industry Analysis*. London: Department for Business, Innovation, and Skills.

Innovation, Universities, Science and Skills Committee (2009). *Re-skilling for Recovery: After Leitch, Implementing Skills and Training Policies*. London: Stationery Office.

Investors in People (2011). *Investors in People Standard*. http://www.investorsinpeople.co.uk

IPM (Institute of Personnel Management) (1992). *Performance Management in the UK: An Analysis of the Issues*. London: IPM.

IRS (Industrial Relations Services) (2000). 'Using outsourcing to reposition HR at the Royal Bank of Scotland'. *Employment Trends*, 714.

IRS (Industrial Relations Services) (2002). 'Focus of attention'. *IRS Employment Review*. www.xperthr.co.uk

IRS (Industrial Relations Services) (2005). 'Hillingdon PCT encourages informal dispute resolution'. *Employment Review*, 837, www.xperthr.co.uk

IRS (Industrial Relations Services) (2006). 'Grievances and discipline: taking a proactive approach'. *Employment Trends*, 849, www.xperthr.co.uk

IRS (Industrial Relations Services) (2009). 'Using corporate websites for recruitment: the 2009 survey' *IRS Employment Review*. www.xperthr.co.uk

Jacobs, T., Shepherd, J., and Johnson, G. (1998). 'Strengths, weaknesses, opportunities and threats (SWOT) analysis', in V. Ambrosini, G. Johnson, and K. Scholes (eds), *Exploring Techniques of Analysis and Evaluation in Strategic Management*. London: Prentice Hall, 122–33.

James, P., Cunningham, I., and Dibben, P. (2002). 'Absence management and the issues of job retention and return to work'. *Human Resource Management Journal*, 12/2: 82–94.

James, S. (2006). *Adding New Ingredients to an Old Recipe: NVQs and the Influence of CATERBASE*. Issue Paper No. 13, ESRC Centre on Skills, Knowledge, and Organizational Performance. Oxford: SKOPE.

James, S. and Lloyd, C. (2008). 'Too much pressure? Retailer power and occupational health and safety in the food processing industry'. *Work, Employment, and Society*, 22/4: 713–30.

Janssens, M., Cappellen T., and Zanoni, P. (2006). 'Successful female expatriates as agents: positioning oneself through gender, hierarchy, and culture'. *Journal of World Business*, 41: 133–48.

Johnson, G., Whittington, R., and Scholes, K. (2011). *Exploring Strategy: Texts and Cases* (11th edn). Harlow: Financial Times–Prentice Hall.

Johnson, R. (2007). 'Can you feel it?' *People Management*, 23 August: 34–7.

Johnston, R., Poulsen, M., and Forrest, J. (2010). 'Moving on from indices, refocusing on mix: on measuring and understanding ethnic patterns of residential segregation'. *Journal of Ethnic and Migration Studies*, 36/4: 697–706.

Johnstone, S. (2010). *Labour and Management Co-operation. Workplace Partnership in UK Financial Services*. Farnham: Gower.

Johnstone, S., Wilkinson, A., and Ackers, P. (2010). 'Critical incidents of partnership: five years' experience at NatBank'. *Industrial Relations Journal*, 41/4: 382–98.

Jolls, C. (2005). 'The role and functioning of public-interest legal organisations in the enforcement of the employment laws', in R. Freeman, J. Hersch, and L. Mishel (eds), *Emerging Labor Market Institutions for the Twenty-First Century*. Chicago, IL: University of Chicago Press, 141–77.

Jones, B. and Norton, P. (eds) (2010). *Politics UK* (7th edn). Harlow: Pearson Education.

Jones, C. and Saundry, R. (2011). 'The practice of discipline: evaluating the roles and relationship between managers and HR professionals'. *Human Resource Management Journal*, doi: 10.1111/j.1748–8583.2011.00175.x

Jorgensen, B. and Taylor, P. (2008). 'Older workers, government and business: implications for ageing populations of a globalizing economy'. *Economic Affairs*, 28/1: 17–22.

Joseph Rowntree Foundation (2001). *Examining the Experience of Positive Action Training in Housing*. www.jrf.org.uk/knowledge/findings/housing/331.asp

Julienne, L. (2001). *The Root to my Tree: Examining the Experience of Positive Action Training in Housing*. Ruislip: LJ8 Publications.

Kalmi, P. and Kauhanen, A. (2008). 'Workplace innovations and employee outcomes: evidence from Finland'. *Industrial Relations*, 47/3: 430–59.

Kamenou, N. and Fearful, A. (2006). 'Ethnic minority women: a lost voice in HRM'. *Human Resource Management Journal*, 16/2: 154–72.

Kandola, B. and Fullerton, J. (1994). *Managing the Mosaic: Diversity in Action*. London: IPD.

Kaplan R. and Norton D. (1996). *The Balanced Scorecard—Translating Strategy into Action*. Boston, MA: Harvard Business School Press.

Katz, H. and Darbishire, O. (2000). *Converging Divergences: Worldwide Changes in Employment Systems*. Ithaca: ILR Press.

Kaufman, B. (2010*a*). 'SHRM theory in the post-Huselid era. Why it is fundamentally misspecified?'. *Industrial Relations*, 49/2: 286–313.

Kaufman, B. (2010*b*). 'A theory of the firm's demand for HRM practices'. *International Journal of Human Resource Management*, 21/5: 615–36.

Kaufman, B. and Taras, D. (2010). 'Employee participation through non-union forms of employee representation', in A. Wilkinson, P. Gollan, M. Marchington, and D. Lewin (eds), *Oxford Handbook of Participation in Organizations*. Oxford: Oxford University Press, 258–85.

Kaufman, D., Kraay, A., and Mastruzzi, M. (2009). *Governance Matters VIII: Aggregate and Individual Governance Indicators, 1996–2008*. World Bank Policy Research Working Paper No. 4978. www-wds.worldbank.org

Kauhanen, A. (2009). 'The incidence of high-performance work systems: evidence from a nationally representative employee survey'. *Economic and Industrial Democracy,* 30/3: 454–80.

Keenoy, T. (1990). 'Human resource management: rhetoric, reality, and contradiction'. *International Journal of Human Resource Management*, 1/3: 363–84.

Keep, E. (2007). *The Multiple Paradoxes of State Power in the English Education and Training System*. Abingdon: Routledge.

Kelly, J. (1998). *Rethinking Industrial Relations*. London: Routledge.

Kelly, J. (2004). 'Social partnership agreements in Britain: labor cooperation and compliance'. *Industrial Relations*, 43/1: 267–92.

Kelly, J. (2005). 'Social partnership agreements in Britain', in M. Stuart and M. Martinez Lucio (eds), *Partnership and Modernisation in Employment Relations*. London: Routledge, 188–209.

Kelly R (2007). 'Changing skill intensity in Australian industry'. *Australian Economic Review*, 40/1: 62–79.

Kennerley, M. and Bourne, M. (2003). *Assessing and Maximizing the Impact of Measuring Business Performance.* Cranfield: Centre for Business Performance, Cranfield School of Management.

Kersley, B., Alpin, C., Forth, J., Bryson, A., Bewley, H., Dix, G., and Oxenbridge, S. (2006). *Inside the Workplace: Findings from the 2004 Workplace Employment Relations Survey.* London: Routledge.

Kew, J. and Stredwick, J. (2010). *Human Resource Management in a Business Context*. London: CIPD.

Kidger, P. (2002). 'Human resource management responses to global strategy in multinational enterprises', in Y. Debrah and I. Smith (eds), *Globalization, Employment, and the Workplace: Diverse Impacts*. London: Routledge, 170–90.

Kinnie, N., Swart, J., Rayton, B., Hutchinson, S., and Purcell, J. (2004). 'HRM policy and performance: an occupational analysis'. Presented at the Conference of the International Industrial Relations Association, Lisbon.

Kirkpatrick, I., de Ruyter, A., Hoque, K., and Lonsdale, C. (2011). ' "Practising what they preach"? The disconnect between the state as regulator and user of employment agencies'. *International Journal of Human Resource Management*, 22/18: 3711–26.

Kirton, G. and Healy, G. (2009). 'Using competency-based assessment centres to select judges—implications for equality and diversity'. *Human Resource Management Journal*, 19/3: 302–18.

Kitson, M., Martin, R., and Wilkinson, F. (2000). 'Labour markets, social justice, and economic efficiency'. *Cambridge Journal of Economics,* 24/6: 631–41.

Klass, B. (2010). 'Discipline and grievances', in A. Wilkinson, N. Bacon, T. Redman, and S. Snell (eds), *Sage Handbook of Human Resource Management*. London: Sage, 322–35.

Kline, R. (2006). 'Performance related pay is not the silver bullet we need'. *Education Guardian,* 14 November. http://education.guardian.co.ukegweekly/story/0194659700.html

Knorr, A. and Arndt, A. (2003). *Why did Wal-Mart Fail in Germany?* Bremen: Institut für Welwirtschaft und Internationales Management.

Knox, A. (2010). ' "Lost in translation": an analysis of temporary work agency employment in hotels'. *Work, Employment, and Society*, 24/3: 449–67.

Kochan, T. and Barrocci, T. (1985). *Human Resource Management and Industrial Relations*. Boston, MA: Little Brown.

Konrad, A., Prasad, P., and Pringle, J. (eds) (2005). *Handbook of Workplace Diversity*. London: Sage.

Korczynski, M. (2002). *Human Resource Management in Service Work*. Basingstoke: Palgrave.

Kostova, T. (1999). 'Transnational transfer of strategic organizational practices: a contextual perspective'. *Academy of Management Review*, 24/2: 308–24.

Kotler, P. and Keller, K. (2012). *Marketing Management* (14th edn). Boston, MA: Pearson Education.

Kraimer, M., Shaffer, M., and Bolino, M. (2009). 'The influence of expatriate and repatriate experiences on career advancement and repatriate retention'. *Human Resource Management*, 4/1: 27–47.

Krauss, C. (2005), 'Wal-Mart battle puts Quebec on edge', *International Herald Tribune*, 11 March. www.iht.com/articles/2005/03/10/business.walmart.php

Krug, J. (2003). 'Why do they keep leaving?' *Harvard Business Review*, 18/2: 14–15.

LaMontagne A. (2004). 'Integrating health promotion and health protection in the workplace', in R. Moodie and A. Hulme (eds), *Hands on Health Promotion*. Melbourne: IP Communications, 285–98.

LaMontagne, A., Keegel, T., Amber, M., and Landsbergis, P. (2007). 'A systematic review of the job-stress intervention evaluation literature, 1990–2005'. *International Journal of Occupational and Environmental Health*, 13/2: 268–80.

Lashley, C. (2000). 'Empowerment through involvement: a case study of TGI Friday's restaurants'. *Personnel Review*, 29/6: 799–815.

Latreille, P. (2011). 'Mediation: a thematic review of the ACAS/CIPD evidence', *ACAS Research Paper 13/11*. London: ACAS.

Laurent, A. (1983). 'The cultural diversity of Western conceptions of management'. *International Studies of Management and Organization*, 13/1–2: 75–96.

Lave, J. and Wenger, E. (1991). *Situated Learning: Legitimate Peripheral Participation*. Cambridge: Cambridge University Press.

Lawler, E., Cohen, S., and Chang, L. (1993). 'Strategic human resource management', in P. Mirvis (ed.), *Building the Competitive Workforce*. New York: John Wiley, 31–59.

Lawton, K. and Potter, D. (2010). *Why Interns Need a Fair Wage*. London: Institute for Public Policy Research.

Lazarova, M. and Tarique, I. (2005). 'Knowledge transfer upon repatriation'. *Journal of World Business*, 40/4: 361–73.

Le Fevre, M., Kolt, G., and Matheny, J. (2006). 'Eustress, distress and their interpretation in primary and secondary occupational stress management interventions: which way first?' *Journal of Managerial Psychology*, 21/6: 547–65.

Leadbeater, C. (1999). *Living on Thin Air*. London: Viking.

Ledford, G. and Kochanski, J. (2004). 'Allocating training and development resources based on contribution', in L. Berger and D. Berger (eds), *The Talent Management Handbook*. New York: McGraw-Hill, 218–29.

Lee, S. and Blake, H. (2010). 'The price is right: making workplace wellness financially sustainable'. *International Journal of Workplace Health Management*, 3/1: 58–69.

Legge, K. (1995). 'Rhetoric, reality, and hidden agendas', in J. Storey (ed.), *Human Resource Management: A Critical Text*. London: Routledge.

Legge, K. (2005). *Human Resource Management: Rhetoric and Realities* (2nd edn). Basingstoke: Palgrave Macmillan.

Leitch, S. (2006). *Leitch Review of Skills: Prosperity for All in the Global Economy*. London: TSO.

Leopold, J. and Harris, L. (2009). *The Strategic Managing of Human Resources* (2nd edn). Harlow: Financial Times–Prentice Hall.

Levitt, S. and Dubner, S. (2006). *Freakonomics: A Rogue Economist Explores The Hidden Side of Everything*. Harmondsworth: Penguin.

Levitt, S. and Dubner, S. (2009). *Superfreakonomics: Global Cooling, Patriotic Prostitutes, and Why Suicide Bombers Should Buy Life Insurance*. New York: HarperCollins.

Lewin, K. (1951). *Field Theory in Social Science*. New York: Harper and Row.

Lewis, P. (1993). *The Successful Management of Redundancy*. Oxford: Blackwell.

Lim, W. and Endean, M. (2009). 'Elucidating the aesthetic and operational characteristics of UK boutique hotels'. *International Journal of Contemporary Hospitality Management*, 21/1: 38–51.

Linehan, M. and Scullion, H. (2002). 'Repatriation of European female corporate executives: an empirical study'. *International Human Resource Management Journal*, 13/2: 254–67.

Linehan, M. and Scullion, H. (2008). 'The development of female global managers: the role of mentoring and networking'. *Journal of Business Ethics*, 83: 29–40.

Linstead, S. (1985). 'Jokers wild: the importance of humour and the maintenance of organisational culture'. *Sociological Review*, 33/4: 741–67.

Lipsky, D., Seeber, R., and Fincher, R. (2003). *Emerging Systems for Managing Workplace Conflict*. San Francisco, CA: Jossey–Bass.

Littler, C. (1982). *The Development of the Labour Process in Capitalist Societies*. London: Heinemann.

Loch, C., Sting, F., Bauer, N., and Mauermann, H. (2010). 'How BMW is defusing the demographic time bomb'. *Harvard Business Review*, 88/3: 99–102.

Locke, E. (1968). 'Towards a theory of task and incentives'. *Organizational Behavior and Human Performance*, 3: 157–89.

Lockwood, N. (2005). *Talent Management Overview*. Alexandria, VA: Society for Human Resource Management.

Logan, J. (2008). *US Anti-Union Consultants: A Threat to the Rights of British Workers*. London: Trades Union Congress.

Löfstedt, R. (2011). *Reclaiming Health and Safety for All: An Independent Review of Health and Safety Legislation*. London: Department of Work and Pensions.

Lord Young (2010). *Common Sense, Common Safety*. London: HM Government.

Luce, S. (2004). *Fighting for a Living Wage*. New York: Cornell University Press.

Lukes, S. (1974). *Power: A Radical View*. London: Macmillan.

Lukes, S. (2005). *Power: A Radical View* (2nd edn). Basingstoke: Palgrave Macmillan.

McCarthy, D. and Mayhew, C. (2004). *Safeguarding the Organization Against Violence and Bullying: An International Perspective*. Basingstoke: Palgrave Macmillan.

MacDonald, L. (2005). *Wellness at Work*. London: CIPD.

McDonnell, A. and Collings, D. (2010). 'The identification and evaluation of talent in MNEs', in H. Scullion and D. Collings (eds), *Global Talent Management*, Abingdon: Routledge, 56–73.

McDonnell, A., Lamare, R., Gunnigle, P., and Lavelle, J. (2010). 'Developing tomorrow's leaders—evidence of global talent management in multinational enterprises'. *Journal of World Business*, 45: 150–60.

MacDuffie, J. (1995). 'Human resource bundles and manufacturing performance: organizational logic and flexible production systems in the world auto industry'. *Industrial and Labor Relations Review*, 48/2: 197–221.

McElroy, J. and Morrow, P. (2010). 'Employee reactions to office redesign: a naturally occurring quasi-field experiment in a multi-generational setting'. *Human Relations*, 63/5: 609–36.

McGovern, P., Hill, S., Mills, C., and White, M. (2007). *Market, Class, and Employment*. Oxford: Oxford University Press.

McKay, S. and Markova, E. (2010). 'The operation and management of agency workers in conditions of vulnerability'. *Industrial Relations Journal*, 41/5: 446–60.

McKellar, R. (2010). *A Short Guide to Political Risk*. Farnham: Gower.

MacLeod, D. and Clarke, N. (2009). *Engaging for Success: Enhancing Performance Through Employee Engagement*. London: Department for Business, Innovation and Skills.

McLoughlin. I. and Gourlay, S. (1994). *Enterprise without Unions*. Buckingham: Open University Press.

McRae, D. (2011). 'Dave Brailsford: the full transcript'. *Guardian*, 15 February. www.guardian.co.uk

McSweeney, B. (2002). 'Hofstede's model of national cultural differences and their consequences: a triumph of faith—a failure of analysis'. *Human Relations*, 55/1: 89–117.

McSweeney, B. (2009). 'Dynamic diversity: variety and variation within countries.' *Organization Studies*, 30/9: 933–57.

Machin, S. (2000). 'Union decline in Britain'. *British Journal of Industrial Relations*, 38/4: 631–45.

Machin, S. and Manning, A. (2004). 'A test of the competitive labor market theory: the wage structure among elder care assistants in the South of England'. *Industrial and Labor Relations Review*, 57/3: 371–85.

Mackie, J (1980). *Ethics—Inventing Right and Wrong*. Harmondsworth: Penguin.

Maertz, C., Wiley, J., LeRouge, C., and Campion, M. (2010). 'Downsizing effects on survivors: layoffs, offshoring, and outsourcing'. *Industrial Relations*, 49/2: 275–85.

Makinson, J. (2000). *Incentives for Change*. London: HM Treasury.

Malik, F., McKie, L., Beattie, R., and Hogg, G. (2010). 'A toolkit to support human resource practice'. *Personnel Review*, 39/3: 287–307.

Malik, S. and Ball, J. (2011). 'Interns work— and should be paid, lawyers warn ministers', *Guardian*, 4 November. www.guardianonline.co.uk

Mankin, D. (2009). *Human Resource Development*. Oxford: Oxford University Press.

Manning, A. (2006). *The Gender Pay Gap*. London: EOC.

Manning, A. and Petrongolo, B. (2005). *The Part-time Pay Penalty*. Centre for Economic Performance Discussion Paper. London: London School of Economics.

Marchington, M. (2008*a*). 'Employee voice systems', in P. Boxall, J. Purcell, and P. Wright (eds), *Oxford Handbook of Human Resource Management*. Oxford: Oxford University Press, 231–50.

Marchington, M. (2008*b*). *Where Next for HRM? Rediscovering the Heart and Soul of People Management*. IES Working Paper WP20. London: Institute for Employment Studies.

Marchington, M. and Grugulis, I. (2000). ' "Best practice" human resource management: perfect opportunity or dangerous illusion?' *International Journal of Human Resource Management*, 11/6: 1104–24.

Marchington, M. and Wilkinson, A. (2005*a*). *Human Resource Management at Work: People Management and Development*. London: CIPD.

Marchington, M. and Wilkinson, A. (2005*b*). 'Direct participation and involvement', in S. Bach (ed.), *Managing Human Resources*. Oxford: Blackwell, 398–423.

Marchington, M., Cooke, F.-L., and Hebson, G. (2010). 'Human resource management across organizational boundaries', in A. Wilkinson, N. Bacon, T. Redman, and S. Snell (eds), *Sage Handbook of Human Resource Management*. London: Sage, 460–74.

Marchington, M., Grimshaw, D., Rubery, J., and Willmott, H. (2005). *Fragmenting Work*. Oxford: Oxford University Press.

Marginson, P. and Meardi, G. (2009). *Multinational Companies and Collective Bargaining*. Dublin: European Foundation for the Improvement of Living and Working Conditions. http://www.eurofound.europa.eu/docs/eiro/tn0904049s/tn0904049s.pdf

Marginson, P. and Meardi, G. (2010). 'Multinational companies: transforming national industrial relations?', in T. Colling and M. Terry (eds), *Industrial Relations: Theory and Practice* (2nd edn). Chichester: John Wiley, 207–30.

Marginson, P. and Sisson, K. (2004). *European Integration and Industrial Relations*. Basingstoke: Palgrave Macmillan.

Mars, G. (1982). *Cheats at Work*. London: Allen and Unwin.

Marsden, D (2004). *Unions and Procedural Justice: An Alternative to the 'Common Rule'*. London: Centre for Economic Performance, London School of Economics.

Martin, B. (1999). 'The transmission of monetary policy'. *Economic Review*, November, 20–4.

Martin, L. and Elwes, R. (2008). *Investors in People: Realising Business Ambitions through People in Times of Change*. London: COI Strategic Consultancy.

Martin, R. (1992). *Bargaining Power*. Oxford: Clarendon Press.

Maslow, A. (1987). *Motivation and Personality* (3rd edn). New York: Harper and Row.

Mason, C., Carter S., and Tagg, S. (2011). 'Invisible businesses: the characteristics of home-based businesses in the United Kingdom'. *Regional Studies*, 45/5: 625–39.

Mason, P. (2012). *Why it's Kicking Off Everywhere: The New Global Revolutions*. London: Verso.

Mather, K. (2006). 'Learning to lecture: a study of the changes in the labour management and labour process of further education lecturers'. Unpublished PhD thesis, Keele University.

Matthews, V. (2007). 'Mother of all problems'. *Personnel Today*, 10 April. www.personneltoday.com

Matthews, V. (2011). 'Social media background checks—a minefield for recruiters.' *Personnel Today*, 15 September. www.personneltoday.com

Mayo, A. (1998). 'Memory bankers'. *People Management*, 22 January: 34–8.

Mellahi, K. and Collings, D. (2010). 'The barriers to effective global talent management: the example of corporate elites in MNEs'. *Journal of World Business*, 45: 143–9.

Mercer (2011). Mercer podcast 15.9.11. 'Why auditing your global mobility program is a must do'. www.mercer.com/webcasts?EventID=4234287&FirstName=Anonymous&LastName=Anonymous&Email=&RET=1319200964725

Merton, R. (1940). 'Bureaucratic structure and personality'. *Social Forces*, May: 560–8.

Metcalf, D. (2005). 'Trade unions: resurgence or perdition? An economic analysis?', in S. Fernie and D. Metcalf (eds), *Trade Unions: Resurgence or Demise?* London: Routledge, 83–117.

Mezias, J. and Scandura, T. (2005). 'Approaches to expatriate adjustment and development'. *Journal of International Business Studies*, 36/5: 519–38.

Michaels, E., Handfield-Jones, H., and Axelrod, B. (2001). *The War for Talent*. Boston, MA: McKinsey.

Milburn, A. (2009). *Unleashing Aspiration: The Final Report of the Panel on Fair Access to the Professions*. London: Cabinet Office.

Millward, L., Haslam, S., and Postmes, T. (2007). 'Putting employees in their place: the impact of hot desking on organizational and team identification'. *Organizational Science*, 18/4: 547–59.

Millward, N., Bryson, A., and Forth, J. (2000). *All Change at Work*. London: Routledge.

Mintzberg, H. (1978). 'Patterns in strategy formation'. *Management Science*, 24/9: 934–48.

Mintzberg, H. (1987). 'Crafting strategy'. *Harvard Business Review*, July/August: 65–75.

Mintzberg, H. (1994). *The Rise and Fall of Strategic Planning*. London: Basic Books.

Mohrman, A. and Mohrman, S. (1995). 'Performance management is "running the business"'. *Compensation and Benefits Review*, July–August: 69–75.

Moore, F. (2011). 'Recruitment and selection of international managers', in T. Edwards and C. Rees (eds), *International Human Resource Management: Globalization, National Systems and Multinational Companies* (2nd edn). Harlow: Financial Times–Prentice Hall, 184–205.

Moreton, B. (2009). *To Serve God and Wal-mart: the Making of Christian Free Enterprise*. Cambridge, MA: Harvard University Press.

Morgan, G. (1997). *Images of Organization* (2nd edn). London: Sage.

Morris, H., Willey, B., and Sachdev, S. (2002). *Managing in a Business Context: An HR Approach*. Harlow: Pearson Education.

Morrison, J. (2011). *The Global Business Environment: Meeting the Challenges* (3rd edn). Basingstoke: Palgrave Macmillan.

Mueller, F. (1996). 'Human resources as strategic assets; an evolutionary resource-based theory'. *Journal of Management Studies*, 33/6: 757–86.

Mulholland, K. (2004). 'Workplace resistance in an Irish call centre: slammin', scammin' smokin' an' leavin''. *Work, Employment and Society*, 18/4: 709–24.

Mullins, D. and Craig, L. (2005) *Testing the Climate: Mergers and Alliances in the Housing Association Sector*. National Housing Federation. www.curs.bham.ac.uk

Myloni, B., Harzing, A.-W., and Mirza, H. (2004). 'Human resource management in Greece: have the colours of culture faded away?'. *International Journal of Cross Cultural Management*, 59/4: 59–76.

National Theatre (2011). *National Theatre Annual Report*. London: National Theatre.

NCVO (National Council for Voluntary Organisations) (2011). 'International campaigns and movements'. *Third Sector Foresight*. www.3s4.org.uk

Needle, D. (2010). *Business in Context: An Introduction to Business and its Environment* (5th edn). Andover: Cengage Learning EMEA.

NESS (National Employers Skills Survey) (2010). http://nessdata.ukces.org.uk

Newell, S. (2005). 'Recruitment and selection', in S. Bach (ed.), *Managing Human Resources: Personnel Management in Transition* (4th edn). Oxford: Blackwell, 114–47.

Newell, S. (2006). 'Selection and assessment', in T. Redman and A. Wilkinson (eds), *Contemporary Human Resource Management: Text and Cases* (2nd edn). Harlow: Financial Times–Prentice Hall, 65–98.

Newell, S. and Shackleton, V. (2000). 'Recruitment and selection', in S. Bach and K. Sisson (eds), *Personnel Management: A Comprehensive Guide to Theory and Practice* (3rd edn). Oxford: Blackwell, 111–36.

Newell, S. and Shackleton, V. (2001). 'Selection and assessment as an interactive decision–action process', in T. Redman and A. Wilkinson (eds), *Contemporary Human Resource Management: Text and Cases*. Harlow: Financial Times–Prentice Hall, 24–56.

NHS Wales (2006). *Designed to Work: A Workforce Strategy to Deliver Designed for Life*. Cardiff: NHS Wales.

Nichols, T. (1997). *The Sociology of Industrial Injury*. London: Mansell.

Nickson, D., Warhurst, C., Dutton, E., and Hurrell, S. (2008). 'A job to believe in: recruitment in the Scottish voluntary sector'. *Human Resource Management Journal*, 18/1: 20–35.

Nishii, L. and Özbilgin, M. (2007). 'Global diversity management: towards a conceptual framework'. *International Journal of Human Resource Management,* 18/11: 1883–94.

Noblet, A. and LaMontagne, A. (2006). 'The role of workplace health promotion in addressing job stress'. *Health Promotion International*, 21/4: 346–53.

Nonaka, I. (1991). 'The knowledge creating company'. *Harvard Business Review*, November–December: 97–104.

Nonaka, I. and Takeuchi, H. (1995). *The Knowledge Creating Company*. New York: Oxford University Press.

Nowak, P. (2009). 'Building stronger unions' in G. Gall (ed.), *Union Revitalisation in Advanced Economies*. Basingstoke: Palgrave Macmillan, 131–53.

Nozick, R. (1974). *Anarchy, State, and Utopia*. Oxford: Blackwell.

Oates, T. (2004). 'The role and outcomes-based national qualifications in the development of an effective vocational education and training system: the case of England and Wales'. *Policy Futures in Education*, 2/1: 53–71.

Oddou, G., Osland, J., and Blakeney, R. (2009). 'Repatriating knowledge: variables influencing the "transfer" process'. *Journal of International Business Studies*, 40/2: 181–99.

OECD (Organization for Economic Cooperation and Development) (2004). *The Significance of Knowledge Management in the Business Sector: Policy Brief*. www.oecd.org

Ogbonna, E. and Wilkinson, B. (1990). 'Corporate strategy and corporate culture: the view from the checkout'. *Personnel Review*, 19/1: 9–15.

Ogbonna, E. and Wilkinson, B. (2003). 'The false promise of organizational culture change: a case study of middle managers in grocery retailing'. *Journal of Management Studies*, 40/5: 1151–78.

ONS (Office for National Statistics) (2005). *Labour Force Survey Spring 2005* www.statistics.gov.uk

ONS (Office for National Statistics) (2011). *Annual Survey of Hours and Earnings*. http://www.ons. gov.uk/ons/dcp171778_241497.pdf

ONS (Office for National Statistics) (2012). *Labour Market Statistics*, April 2012. http://www.ons. gov.uk/ons/dcp171778_260957.pdf

Ordanini, A. and Silvestri, G. (2008). 'Recruitment and selection services: efficiency and competitive reasons in the outsourcing of HR practices'. *International Journal of Human Resource Management*, 19/2: 372–91.

Orey, M. (2006). 'White men can't help it'. *Business Week,* 3984: 55.

Orlitzky, M. and Frenkel, S. J. (2005). 'Alternative pathways to high performance workplaces'. *International Journal of Human Resource Management*, 16/8: 1325–48.

O'Sullivan, S. (2002). 'The protean approach to managing repatriation transitions'. *International Journal of Manpower*, 23/7: 597–616.

O'Sullivan, M. and Gunnigle, P. (2009). 'Bearing all the hallmarks of oppression—union avoidance in Europe's largest low-cost airline'. *Labor Studies Journal*, 34/2: 252–70.

O'Toole, J. and Lawler, E. (2006). *The New American Workplace*. New York: Palgrave Macmillan.

Ovide, S. (2011). 'Who needs banks? In Yahoo takeover Google and Microsoft play banker'. *Wall Street Journal*, 24 October.

Paauwe, J. and Boselie, P. (2007). 'HRM and social embeddedness' in P. Boxall, J. Purcell, and P. Wright (eds), *Oxford Handbook of Human Resource Management*. Oxford: Oxford University Press, 166–86.

Paik, Y., Segaud, B., and Malinowski, C. (2002). 'How to improve repatriation management: motivations and expectations congruent between the company and expatriates'. *International Journal of Manpower*, 23/7: 635–48.

Panagiotou, G. and van Wijnen, R. (2005). 'The "telescopic observations" framework: an attainable strategic tool'. *Marketing Intelligence and Planning*, 23/2: 155–71.

Parry, E., Kelliher, C., Mills, T., and Tyson, S. (2005). 'Comparing HRM in the voluntary and public sectors'. *Personnel Review*, 34/5: 588–602.

Parvin, P. (2007). *Friend or Foe? Lobbying in British Democracy. A Discussion Paper*. London: The Hansard Society.

Pass, S. (2005). 'On the line'. *People Management*, 15 September: 38–40.

Patterson, M., West M., Lawthom, R., and Nickell, S. (1998). *Impact of People Management Practices on Business Performance*. London: Institute of Personnel and Development.

Pawson, H. and Mullins, D. (2010). *After Council Housing: Britain's New Social Landlords*. Basingstoke: Palgrave Macmillan.

Peacock, L. (2011). '8000 apply for 1000 new Jaguar Land Rover jobs within seven days'. *The Telegraph*, 17 November. www.telegraph.co.uk

Peacock, M. and Kubler, M. (2001). 'The failure of "control" in the hospitality industry'. *International Journal of Hospitality Management*, 20/4: 353–65.

Pedler, M., Burgoyne, J., and Boydell, T. (eds) (1991). *The Learning Company: A Strategy for Sustainable Development*. London: McGraw-Hill.

People Management (2005). 'Psychometric testing for parking wardens'. *People Management Online*. www.peoplemanagement.co.uk

People Management (2008). 'Bricking up the skills gap'. *People Management Online*. ww.peoplemanagement.co.uk

Pereira, V. and Anderson, V. (2011). 'A longitudinal examination of HRM in a human resources outsourcing (HRO) organization operating from India'. *Journal of World Business*, doi.org/10.1016/j.jwb.2011.04.009

Perkins, S. and Vartiainen, M. (2010). 'European reward management? Introducing the special issue'. *Thunderbird International Business Review*, 52/3: 175–87.

Perkins, S. and White, G. (2010). 'Modernising pay in the UK public services: trends and implications'. *Human Resource Management Journal*, 20/3: 244–57.

Perkins, S. and White, G. (2011). *Employee Reward: Alternatives, Consequences, and Contexts*. London: CIPD.

Perlin, R. (2011). *Intern Nation: How to Earn Nothing and Earn Little in the Brave New Economy*. London: Verso.

Perlmutter, H. (1969). 'The tortuous evolution of the multinational corporation'. *Columbia Journal of World Business*, January/February: 9–18.

Peters, T. and Waterman, R. (1982). *In Search of Excellence: Lessons from America's Best-Run Companies*. New York: Harper and Row.

Pettigrew, A. (1973). *The Politics of Organizational Decision-Making*. London: Tavistock.

Pettigrew, A. (1985). *The Awakening Giant: Continuity and Change in ICI*. Oxford: Blackwell.

Pfeffer, J. (1994). *Competitive Advantage Through People*. Boston, MA: Harvard Business School Press.

Pfeffer, J. (1998). *The Human Equation: Building Profits by Putting People First*. Boston, MA: Harvard Business School Press.

Pffeffer, J. (2007). 'Human resources from an organizational behaviour perspective: some paradoxes explained'. *Journal of Economic Perspectives*, 21/1: 115–34.

Philips, K. and Eamets, R. (2007). *Impact of Globalisation on Industrial Relations in the EU and other Major Economies*. Luxembourg: Office for Official Publications of the European Communities.

Phillips, L. (2008a). 'Google concentrates on the right recruitment' *People Management Online*. www.peoplemanagement.co.uk

Phillips, L. (2008b). 'Travelodge WLTM new managers', *People Management Online*. www.peoplemanagement.co.uk

Phillips, L. (2009). 'Aviva widen definition of talent'. *People Management*, 22 April. www.peoplemanagement.co.uk

Pilbeam, S. (1998). 'Individual performance related pay: believers and sceptics'. *Employee Relations Review*, 5: 9–16.

Pilbeam, S. and Corbridge, M. (2010). *People Resourcing and Talent Planning: HRM in Practice* (4th edn). Harlow: Financial Times–Prentice Hall.

Pinch, S. and Mason, C. (1991). 'Redundancy in an expanding labour market: a case-study of displaced workers from two manufacturing plants in Southampton'. *Urban Studies*, 28/5: 735–57.

Pinnington, A., Macklin, R., and Campbell, T. (eds) (2007). *Human Resource Management: Ethics and Employment*. Oxford: Oxford University Press.

Pitcher, G. (2008). 'HP top talent encouraged to work abroad'. *Personnel Today*: 13 March.

Plantenga, J. and Remery, C. (2010). *Flexible Working Time Arrangements and Gender Equality: A Comparative Review of 30 European Countries*. Luxembourg: Publications Office of the European Union.

Platman, K. (2004). ' "Portfolio careers" and the search for flexibility in later life'. *Work, Employment, and Society*, 18/3: 573–99.

Pollard, R. (2011). 'The genesis of leadership'. *Accountancy Age*, 20 April. www.accountancyage.com

Pollert, A. (2007). 'Individual employment rights: paper tigers—fierce in appearance but missing in tooth and claw'. *Economic and Industrial Democracy*, 28/1, 110–39.

Pollert, A. (2009). 'The reality of vulnerability amongst Britain's non-unionised workers with problems at work', in S. Bolton and M. Houlihan (eds), *Work Matters: Critical Reflections on Contemporary Work*. Basingstoke: Palgrave Macmillan.

Pollitt, C. (2006). 'Performance management in practice: a comparative study of executive agencies'. *Journal of Public Administration Research and Theory*, 16/1: 25–44.

Porter, M. (1985). *Competitive Strategy: Creating and Sustaining Superior Performance*. New York: Free Press.

Porter, M. (1998). *The Competitive Advantage of Nations*. Basingstoke: Macmillan.

Porter, M. and Kramer, M. (2006). 'Strategy and society: the link between competitive advantage and corporate social responsibility'. *Harvard Business Review*, December: 78–92.

Power, M. (2007). 'Workforce scorecard metrics for business focused HR performance reporting'. *HR Bulletin—Research and Practice*, CIPD Portsmouth Group.

Prahalad, C. and Hamel, G. (1990). 'The core competence of the corporation'. *Harvard Business Review*, May/June: 79–91.

Preece, D. (2008). 'Change and continuity in UK public house retailing'. *Services Industries Journal*, 28/7–8: 1107–24.

Preece, D. and Iles, P. (2009). 'Executive development: assuaging uncertainties through joining a leadership academy'. *Personnel Review*, 38/3: 286–306.

Preece, D., Iles, P., and Chuai, X. (2011). 'Talent management and management fashion in Chinese enterprises: exploring case studies in Beijing'. *International Journal of Human Resource Management*, 22/16: 3413–28.

Preece, D., Steven, G., and Steven, V. (1999). *Work, Change, and Competition: Managing for Bass*. London: Routledge.

Press Association (2010) 'Primark profits soar 35%'. *Guardian*, 9 November. www.guardianonline.co.uk

PricewaterhouseCoopers (2005). *International Assignment: Global Policy and Practice. Key Trends 2005*. London: PricewaterhouseCoopers.

PricewaterhouseCoopers (PwC) (2011). *Securing the Talent to Succeed*. www.pwc.be/en/hr–management/assets/International–mobility–FS.pdf

Pringle, T. (2011). *Trade Unions in China: the Challenge of Labour Unrest*. Abingdon: Routledge.

Proctor, S. (2008). 'New forms of work and the high performance paradigm', in P. Blyton, N. Bacon, J. Fiorito, and E. Heery (eds), *Sage Handbook of Industrial Relations*. London: Sage, 149–69.

Procter, S. and Mueller, F. (eds) (2000). *Teamworking*. Basingstoke: Macmillan.

Pucik, V., Björkman, I., Evans, P., and Stahl, G. (2011). 'Human resource management in cross-border mergers and acquisitions', in A.-W. Harzing and A. Pinnington (eds), *International Human Resource Management* (3rd edn). London: Sage, 119–52.

Pugh, D. and Hickson, D. (1976). *Organization Structure in its Context: the Aston Programme 1*. London: Saxon House.

Purcell, J. (1999). 'The search for 'best practice' and 'best fit': chimera or cul-de-sac?' *Human Resource Management Journal*, 9/3: 26–41.

Purcell, J. (2001). 'The meaning of strategy in human resource management', in J. Storey (ed.), *Human Resource Management: A Critical Text* (2nd edn). London: Thomson Learning, 59–77.

Purcell, J. and Hutchinson, S. (2007). 'Front line managers as agents in the HRM–performance causal chain: theory, analysis and evidence'. *Human Resource Management Journal*, 17/1: 3–20.

Purcell, J. and Kinnie, N. (2007). 'Human resource management and business performance'. In P. Boxall, J. Purcell, and P. Wright (eds), *Oxford Handbook of Human Resource Management*. Oxford: Oxford University Press, 533–51.

Purcell, J., Purcell, K., and Tailby, S. (2004). 'Temporary work agencies: here today, gone tomorrow?'. *British Journal of Industrial Relations*, 42/4: 705–25.

Purcell, J., Kinnie, N., Hutchinson, S., Rayton, B., and Swart, J. (2003). *Understanding the People and Performance Link: Unlocking the Black Box*. London: CIPD.

Purcell, J., Kinnie, N., Swart, J., Rayton, B., and Hutchinson, S. (2009). *People Management and Performance*. Abingdon: Routledge.

Quinn, B. (2008). 'Virgin sacks 13 over Facebook "chav remarks"'. *Guardian*, 1 November. http://www.guardian.co.uk

Ram, M. (1994). *Managing to Survive*. Oxford: Blackwell.

Ramamurti, R. and Singh, J.V. (eds) (2009). *Emerging Multinationals in Emerging Markets*. Cambridge: Cambridge University Press.

Rankin, N. (2007). 'Employee Assistance Programmes: the IRS report', *IRS Employment Review*, XpertHR.

Rawls, J. (1973). *A Theory of Justice*. London: Oxford University Press.

Rayner, C. (1997). 'Incidence of workplace bullying'. *Journal of Community and Applied Social Psychology*, 7/3: 199–208.

Rayner, C. (2009). *Workplace Bullying and Harassment*. London: UNISON.

Rayner, C. and Keashly, L. (2005). 'Bullying at work: a perspective from Britain and North America', in S. Fox and P. Spector, (eds), *Counterproductive Work Behavior: Investigations of Actors and Targets*. Washington, DC: American Psychological Association Publishers, 271–96.

Rayner, C. and Lewis, D. (2011). 'Managing workplace bullying: the role of policies', in S. Einarsen, H. Hoel, D. Zapf, and C. Cooper (eds), *Bullying and Harassment in the Workplace: Developments in Theory, Research and Practice*. Boca Raton, FL: Taylor & Francis, 327–40.

Rayner, C. and McIvor, K. (2006). *Dignity at Work: Report to the Project Steering Committee*. London: Amicus/DTI.

Rayner, C., Hoel, H., and Cooper, C. (2002). *Workplace Bullying: What We Know, Who is to Blame, and What Can We Do?*. London: Taylor & Francis.

Ready, D., Hill, L., Conger, J. (2008). 'Winning the race for talent in emerging markets'. *Harvard Business Review*, November: 63–70

Reiche, S., Kraimer, M., and Harzing, A.-W. (2011). 'Why do international assignees stay? An organizational embeddedness perspective'. *Journal of International Business Studies*, 42/4: 521–44.

Reid, M., Barrington, H., and Brown, M. (2004). *Human Resource Development: Beyond Training Interventions*. London: CIPD.

Ridley-Duff, R. and Bennett, A. (2011). 'Towards mediation: developing a theoretical framework to understand alternative dispute resolution'. *Industrial Relations Journal*, 42/2: 106–23.

Ritzer, G. (2004). *The McDonaldization of Society* (rev. edn). Thousand Oaks, CA: Pine Forge Press.

Roberts, K. (2005). *Lovemarks: The Future Beyond Brands*. New York: Power House Books.

Robinson, A. and Smallman, C. (2006). 'The contemporary British workplace: a safer and healthier place?'. *Work, Employment and Society*, 20/1: 87–101.

Roe, P., Wiseman, J., and Costello, M. (2006): *Perceptions and Use of NVQs: A Survey of Employers in England*. Research Report 714. London: Department for Education and Skills.

Rogers, S. (2011). 'The public sector employment map of the UK: the full data'. *Guardian*, 21 November. www.guardian.co.uk

Rollinson, D., Handley, J., Hook, C., and Foot, M. (1997). 'The disciplinary experience and its effects on behaviour'. *Work, Employment and Society*, 11/2: 281–311.

Rose, M. (1975). *Industrial Behaviour*. London: Allen Lane.

Rosen, E. (2005). 'Life inside America's largest dysfunctional family: working for Wal-mart'. *New Labor Forum*, 14/1: 31–9.

Roth, R. (2010). 'How BMW deals with an aging workforce'. www.cbsnews.com

Roubini, N. and Mihm, S. (2010). *Crisis Economics: A Crash Course in the Future of Finance*. London: Allen Lane.

Royle, T. (2000). *Working for McDonalds in Europe: the Unequal Struggle?* London: Routledge.

RSA (2010). 'Talent lifecycle management in today's life sciences sector'. http://www.thersagroup.com/talent/latest-tls-survey-results.shtml

Rugman, A. and Collinson, S. (2009). *International Business* (5th edn). Harlow: Financial Times–Prentice Hall.

Ruiz, Y and Walling, A. (2005). 'Home-based working using communications technologies'. *Labour Market Trends*, 113/10: 417–26.

Rushton, S. (2008). 'Minimising reference risks'. *People Management Online*. www.peoplemanagement.co.uk

Russell, B. and Thite, M. (2008). 'The next division of labour: work skills in Australian and Indian call centres'. *Work, Employment and Society*, 22/4: 615–34.

Ryan, M. and Haslam, S. (2007). *Women in the Boardroom: the Risks of Being at the Top*. London: CIPD.

Ryan, P., Gospel, H., and Lewis, P. (2007). 'Large employers and apprentice training in Britain'. *British Journal of Industrial Relations*, 45/1: 127–53.

Saam, N. (2010). 'Interventions in workplace bullying: a multilevel approach'. *European Journal of Work and Organizational Psychology*, 19/1: 51–75.

Sackmann, S., Eggenhofer-Rehart, P., and Friesl, M. (2009). 'Sustainable change: long-term efforts toward developing a learning organization'. *Journal of Applied Behavioral Science,* 45/4: 521–49.

Salin, D. (2003). 'Ways of explaining workplace bullying: a review of enabling, motivating, and precipitating structures and process in the work environment'. *Human Relations*, 56/10: 1222–32.

Sargeant, A. (2009). *Marketing Management for Nonprofit Organizations* (3rd edn). Oxford: Oxford University Press.

Saundry, R., McArdle, L., and Thomas, P. (2011). *Transforming Conflict Management in the Public Sector? Mediation, Trade Unions and Partnerships in a Primary Care Trust*. ACAS Research Paper 01/11. London: ACAS.

Sauvant, K., Prakash Pradhan, J., Chatterjee, A., and Harley, B. (2010). *The Rise of Indian Multinationals*. Basingstoke: Palgrave Macmillan.

Scarbrough, H. and Swan, J. (2001). 'Explaining the diffusion of knowledge management: the role of fashion'. *British Journal of Management*, 12/1: 3–12.

Schein, E. (1992). *Organizational Culture and Leadership*. San Francisco, CA: Jossey Bass.

Schorr Hirsch, M (2007). 'Getting to the truth of the matter'. *People Management Online*. www.peoplemanagement.co.uk

Schuler, R. and Jackson, S. (1987). 'Linking competitive strategies with human resource management practices'. *Academy of Management Executive*, 1/3: 207–19.

Schuler, R. and Jackson, S. (2007). *Strategic Human Resource Management*. Malden, MA: Blackwell.

Schuler, R. and Tarique, I. (2007). 'International human resource management: a North American perspective, a thematic update and suggestions for future research'. *International Journal of Human Resource Management*, 18/5: 717–44.

Schuler, R., Dowling, P., and De Cieri, H. (1993). 'An integrative framework for strategic international human resource management'. *Journal of Management*, 19/2: 419–59.

Schuler, R., Jackson, S., and Luo, Y. (2004). *Managing Human Resources in Cross-Border Alliances*. London: Routledge.

Schuler, R., Jackson, S., and Tarique, I. (2011). 'Global talent management and global talent challenges: strategic opportunities for IHRM'. *Journal of World Business*, 46: 506–16.

Scott, A. (1994). *Willing Slaves? British Workers under Human Resource Management*. Cambridge: Cambridge University Press.

Scott, A. (2006). 'NHS automates management training assessment'. *People Management Online*. www.peoplemanagement.co.uk

Scullion, H. and Collings, D. (eds) (2006). *Global Staffing*. London: Routledge.

Scullion, H. and Collings, D. (2010). 'Global talent management: introduction', in H. Scullion and D. Collings (eds), *Global Talent Management*. Abingdon: Routledge, 3–16.

Scullion, H. and Paauwe, J. (2004). 'International human resource management: recent developments in theory and empirical research', in A.W. Harzing and J. van Ruysseveldt (eds), *International Human Resource Management: Managing People Across Borders* (2nd edn). London: Sage, 65–88.

Senge, P. (1990). *The Fifth Discipline*. New York: Doubleday.

Sennett, R. (1998). *The Corrosion of Character: The Personal Consequences of Work in New Capitalism*. London: Norton.

Sewell, G. (1998). 'The discipline of teams: the control of team-based industrial work through electronic and peer surveillance'. *Administrative Science Quarterly*, 43: 406–69.

Shackleton, J. (2008). *Should We Mind the Gap? Gender Pay Differentials and Public Policy*. London: IEA Publications

Sheehan, J., Morris, J., and Hassard, J. (2000). 'Redundancies in Chinese state enterprises: a research report'. *Industrial Relations*, 39/3: 486–501.

Shen, J. and Edwards, V. (2006). *International Human Resource Management in Chinese Multinationals*. London: Routledge.

Sherwood, B. (2007). Business gets a taste for Eastern appetites. *Financial Times*, 24 April.

Shipping and World Trade (n.d). *The Low Cost of Transporting Goods by Sea*. The Round Table of International Shipping Associations. www.marisec.org

Simms, M. and Charlwood, A. (2010). 'Trade unions: power and influence in a changed context', in

T. Colling and M. Terry (eds), *Industrial Relations: Theory and Practice*. Chichester: John Wiley, 125–48.

Singh, J. (2001). 'McKinsey's managing director Rajat Gupta on leading a knowledge-based global consulting organization'. *Academy of Management Executive*, 15/1: 34–44.

Sippola, A. and Smale, A. (2007). 'The global integration of diversity management: a longitudinal case study'. *International Journal of Human Resource Management*, 18/11: 1183–94.

Sisson, K. and Taylor, J. (2006). 'The Advisory, Conciliation, and Arbitration Service', in L. Dickens and A. Neal (eds), *The Changing Institutional Face of British Employment Relations*, Alphen aan den Rign: Kluwer Law International, 25–36.

Skingle, Y. (2006). *Achieving Success Together: The Essex Authorities*. London: IDeA.

Skinner, W. (1981). 'Big hat, no cattle: managing human resources'. *Harvard Business Review*, 59/5: 106–14.

Sloman, M. (2007). *The Changing World of the Trainer*. Oxford: Butterworth–Heinemann.

Sloman, J. and Jones, E. (2011). *Economics and the Business Environment* (3rd edn). Harlow: Financial Times–Prentice Hall.

Sloman, J. and Wride, A. (2009). *Economics* (7th edn). Harlow: Financial Times–Prentice Hall.

Smedley, T. (2012). 'Obesity: bad for the bottom line?' *People Management*, 31 January. www.peoplemanagement.co.uk

Smircich, L. (1983). 'Concepts of culture and organisational analysis'. *Administrative Science Quarterly*, 23/2: 339–58.

Smith, C. and Meiksins, P. (1995). 'System, societal and dominance effects in cross-national organisational analysis'. *Work, Employment, and Society*, 9/2: 241–68.

Smith, D. (2003). *Free Lunch: Easily Digestible Economics, Served on a Plate*. London: Profile Books.

Smith, R. (2009). 'Greed is good'. *Wall Street Journal*, 7 February. www.wsj.com

Smith, P. and Morton, G. (2009). 'Employment legislation: New Labour's neoliberal legal project to subordinate trade unions', in G. Daniels and J. McIlroy (eds), *Trade Unions in a Neoliberal World: British Trade Unions under New Labour*. Abingdon: Routledge, 205–29.

Smith, N., Smith, V., and Verne, M. (2011). 'The gender pay gap in top corporate jobs in Denmark'. *International Journal of Manpower*, 32/2: 156–77.

Solon, O. (2011). 'Silicon roundabout hiring talent away from Silicon Valley'. *Wired*, 26 October, www.wired.co.uk

Som, A. (2006). 'Bracing for MNC competition through innovative HRM practices: the way ahead for Indian firms'. *Thunderbird International Business Review*, 48/2: 207–37.

Som, A. (2008). 'Innovative human resource management and corporate performance in the context of economic liberalization in India'. *International Journal of Human Resource Management*, 19/7: 1278–97.

Sparrow, P. (2009). 'International reward management', in G. White and J. Druker (eds), *Reward Management: A Critical Text*. London: Routledge, 233–57.

Sparrow, P. and Braun, W. (2007). 'Human resource strategy in international context', in R. Schuler and S. Jackson (eds), *Strategic Human Resource Management* (2nd edn). Oxford: Blackwell, 162–99.

Sparrow, P., Brewster, C., and Harris, H. (2004). *Globalizing Human Resource Management*. London: Routledge.

Spence Laschinger, H., Grau, A., Finegan, J., and Wilk, P. (2010). 'New graduate nurses' experiences of bullying and burnout in hospital settings'. *Journal of Advanced Nursing*, 66/12: 2732–42.

Spicer, A. (2006). 'Beyond the convergence–divergence debate: the role of spatial scales in transforming organizational logic'. *Organization Studies*, 27/10: 1467–83.

Spinwatch (2008). *Spinning the Wheels: A Guide to the PR and Lobbying Industry in the UK*. London: Spinwatch.

Stahl, G. and Caligiuri, P. (2005). 'The effectiveness of expatriate coping strategies: the moderating role of cultural distance, position level, and time on international assignment'. *Journal of Applied Psychology*, 90/4: 603–15.

Stahl, G., Chua, C., Caligiuri, P., Cerdin, J.-L., and Taniguchi, M. (2009). 'Predictors of turnover intentions in learning-driven and demand-driven international assignments: The role of repatriation concerns, satisfaction with company support, and perceived career advancement opportunities'. *Human Resource Management*, 48/1: 91–111.

Stainton, A. (2005). 'Talent management: Latest buzzword or refocusing existing processes?' *Competency and Emotional Intelligence*, 12/4: 39–43.

Steers, R. and Rhodes, S. (1978). 'Major influences on employee attendance: a process model'. *Journal of Applied Psychology*, 63/4, 391–407.

Steger, M. (2003). *Globalization: A Very Short Introduction*. Oxford: Oxford University Press.

Stephens, N. (2010). 'Talent management: ensuring your people give you the competitive edge'. *Strategic Direction*, 26/7: 3–5.

Sternberg, E. (2000). *Just Business: Business Ethics in Action* (2nd edn). Oxford: Oxford University Press.

Stewart, H. (2011). 'Chancellor will use budget to create 50,000 apprenticeships'. *Guardian*, 29 March. www.guardianonline.co.uk

Storey, J. (1992). *Developments in the Management of Human Resources: An Analytical Review*. London: Blackwell.

Storey, J. (2001). *Human Resource Management: A Critical Text* (2nd edn). London: Routledge.

Storrie, D. with Ward, T. (2007). *ERM Report 2007: Restructuring and Employment in the EU: the Impact of Globalisation*. Luxembourg: Office for Official Publications of the European Communities.

Stredwick, J. (2000). 'Aligning rewards to organisational goals—a multinational's experience'. *European Business Review*, 12/1: 9–18.

Streeck, W. and Thelen, K. (eds) (2005). *Beyond Continuity: Institutional Change in Advanced Political Economies*. Oxford: Oxford University Press.

Suff, R. (2005). 'Centres of attention'. *IRS Employment Review*. www.xperthr.co.uk

Suff, R. (2006). 'The right person for the right role: using competencies in recruitment and selection'. *Competency and Emotional Intelligence*. www.xperthr.co.uk

Suff, R. (2008). 'Background checks in recruitment: employers' current methods'. *IRS Employment Review*, 17 April. www.xperthr.co.uk

Suff, R. (2010*a*). 'IRS dispute resolution survey: grievances and the new ACAS code of conduct'. *IRS Employment Review*, 12 April. www.xperthr.co.uk

Suff, R. (2010*b*). 'IRS dispute resolution survey: managing discipline'. *IRS Employment Review*, 26 April. www.xperthr.co.uk

Suff, R. (2010*c*). 'Getting the most out of employee assistance programmes'. *IRS Employment Review*, 31 August. www.xperthr.co.uk

Suff, R. (2011*a*). 'Assessment centres 2011 survey: the process and employer practice, *IRS Employment Review*, 14 September. www.xperthr.co.uk

Suff, R. (2011*b*). 'Employers' use of employment agencies and recruitment agencies', *IRS Employment Review*. 25 May. www.xperthr.co.uk

Suff, R. (2011*c*). 'Workplace conflict survey 2011: levels and causes'. *IRS Employment Review*, 9 May. www.xperthr.co.uk

Suff, R. (2011*d*). 'Workplace conflict survey 2011: mediation practices'. *IRS Employment Review*, 23 May. www.xperthr.co.uk

Suff, R. (2012). 'Recruitment trends survey 2012: activity picks up'. *IRS Employment Review*, 21 March. www.xperthr.co.uk

Sunday Times (2011). 'Travel: fair trade holiday is here'. *Sunday Times Travel*, 13 November.

Sung, J. and Ashton, D. (2005). *High Performance Work Practices: Linking Strategy and Skills to Performance Outcomes*. London: DTI/CIPD.

Sussex, J. and Towse, A. (2000) 'Getting EU expenditure up to the EU mean. What does that mean?' *British Medical Journal*, 320: 640–2.

Suutari, V. and Burch, D. (2001). 'The role of on-site training and support in expatriation: existing and necessary host-company practices'. *Career Development International*, 6/6: 298–311.

Suutari, V. and Valimaa, K. (2002). 'Antecedents of repatriation adjustment: new evidence from Finnish expatriates'. *International Journal of Manpower*, 23/7: 617–34.

Swailes, S. and Roodhouse, S. (2003). 'Structural barriers to the take up of higher level NVQs', *Journal of Vocational Education and Training*, 55/1: 85–110.

Syal, R. (2012). 'Government's employment scheme faces stinging criticism from auditors'. *Guardian*, 24 January. www.guardianonline.co.uk

Tailby, S., Pollert, A., Warren, S., Danford, A., and Wilton, N. (2011). 'Under-funded and overwhelmed: the voluntary sector as worker representation in Britain's individualised industrial relations system'. *Industrial Relations Journal*, 42: 273–92.

Tamkin, P., Cowling, M., and Hunt, W. (2008). *People and the Bottom Line*. Brighton: Institute for Employment Studies.

Tarique, I. and Schuler, R. (2010). 'Global talent management: literature review, integrative framework, and suggestions for further research'. *Journal of World Business*, 45: 122–33.

Tarique, I., Schuler, R., and Gong, Y. (2006). 'A model of multinational enterprise subsidiary staffing composition'. *International Journal of Human Resource Management*, 17/2: 207–24.

Taylor, M. (2011). 'Anti-cuts campaigners plan "carnival of civil disobedience"'. *Guardian*, 14 March.

Taylor, P. and Bain, P. (1999). ' "An assembly line in the head": work and employee relations in the call centre'. *Industrial Relations Journal*, 30/2: 101–17.

Taylor, P. and Bain, P. (2005). ' "India calling to the far away towns": the call centre labour process and globalization'. *Work, Employment, and Society*, 19/2: 261–82.

Taylor, P., Baldry, C., Bain, P., and Ellis, V. (2003). ' "A unique working environment": health, sickness and absence management in UK call centres'. *Work, Employment, and Society*, 17/3: 435–58.

Taylor, P., Cunningham, I., Newsome, K., and Scholarios, D. (2010). ' "Too scared to go sick"— reformulating the research agenda on sickness absence'. *Industrial Relations Journal*, 41/4: 270–88.

Taylor, S. (2007). 'Creating social capital in MNCs: the international human resource management challenge'. *Human Resource Management Journal*, 17/4: 336–54.

Taylor, S., Beechler, S., and Napier, N. (1996). 'Toward an integrative model of strategic international human resource management'. *Academy of Management Review*, 21/4: 959–85.

Telegraph (2011). 'London 2012 Olympics: games organisers preparing to recruit 100,000 volunteers'. www.telegraph.co.uk

Tempel, A., Wächter, H., and Walgenbach, P. (2006). 'The comparative institutional approach to human resource management in multinational companies', in M. Geppert and M. Mayer (eds), *Global, National, and Local Practices in Multinational Companies*. Basingstoke: Palgrave Macmillan, 17–37.

Terry, M. (2004). ' "Partnership": a serious strategy for the UK trade unions?', in A. Verma and T. Kochan (eds), *Unions in the 21st Century: An International Perspective*. Basingstoke: Palgrave Macmillan, 205–19.

Tharenou, P. (2002). 'Receptivity to careers in international work—abroad and at home'. *Australian Journal of Management*, 27/special issue: 129–36.

Thomas, D. (2005). 'HR challenges... I'm lovin' it'. *Personnel Today*, 6 September. http://www.personneltoday.com/articles/2005/09/06/31465/hr-challenges-im–lovin-it.html

Thomas, R. (2007). 'Britain's national daily newspaper industry'. *Teaching Business and Economics*, 11/1: 5–7.

Thompson, E. (2011). 'Employee voice in a non-union firm'. BA Human Resource Management dissertation, University of Portsmouth Business School.

Thompson, P. (2003). Disconnected capitalism: or why employers can't keep their side of the bargain'. *Work, Employment, and Society*, 17/2: 359–78.

Thompson, P. (2011). 'The trouble with HRM'. *Human Resource Management Journal*, 21/4: 355–67.

Thompson, P. and McHugh, D. (2009). *Work Organizations: A Critical Approach* (4th edn). Basingstoke: Palgrave Macmillan.

Thorndike, E. (1920). 'A constant error on psychological rating'. *Journal of Applied Psychology*, 4/1: 25–29.

Thornhill, A. and Gibbons, A. (1995). 'The positive management of redundancy survivors: issues and lessons'. *Employee Counselling Today*, 7/3: 5–12.

Thornhill, A. and Saunders, M. (1998). 'The meanings, consequences and implications of the management of downsizing and redundancy: a review'. *Personnel Review*, 27/4: 271–95.

Tompkins, P. and Cheney, G. (1985). 'Communication and unobtrusive control in contemporary organizations', in R. McPhee and P. Tompkins (eds), *Organizational Communication: Traditional Themes and New Directions.* Beverly Hills, CA: Sage.

Torbiorn, I. (1997). 'Staffing for international operations'. *Human Resource Management Journal*, 7/3: 42–57.

Torrington, D. (1991). *Management Face to Face.* Hemel Hempstead: Prentice Hall.

Transparency International (2011). *Corruption Perceptions Index 2011.* cpi.transparency.org

Traxler, F., Blaschke, S., and Kittel, B. (2001). *National Labour Relations in Internationalized Markets.* Oxford: Oxford University Press.

Treanor, J. (2012*a*). 'Boardroom pay needs overhaul say leading pension funds'. *Guardian*, 27 March. www.guardian.co.uk

Treanor, J. (2012*b*). 'UK 'bad' bank boss takes 5% pay cut'. *Guardian*, 28 March. www.guardian.co.uk

Tremblay, D.-G. and Genin, E. (2010). 'IT self-employed workers between constraint and flexibility', *New Technology, Work, and Employment*, 25/1: 34–48.

Trevino, L. and Nelson K. (2011). *Managing Business Ethics: Straight Talk about how to do it Right* (5th edn). Hoboken, NJ: Wiley.

Trevor, C. (2001). 'Interactions among actual ease of movement determinants and job satisfaction in the prediction of voluntary turnover'. *Academy of Management Journal*, 44: 621–38.

Trompenaars, F. and Hampden-Turner, C. (1997). *Riding the Waves of Culture.* London: Nicholas Brealey.

Truss, C. (2001). 'Complexities and controversies in linking HRM with organizational outcomes'. *Journal of Management Studies*, 38/8: 1121–49.

TUC (Trades Union Congress) (2007). *Migrant Agency Workers in the UK.* London: TUC.

TUC (Trades Union Congress) (2008). *Hard Work, Hidden Lives. Report of the Commission on Vulnerable Employment.* London: TUC.

TUC (Trades Union Congress) (2010). *The Truth About Sickness Absence.* London: TUC.

Tuckman, A. (2010). 'Defying extinction? The revival of the strike in UK employment relations'. *Working USA*, 13: 325–42.

Tung, R. (1987). 'Expatriate assignments: enhancing success and minimizing failure'. *Academy of Management Executive*, 1/2: 117–26.

Turnbull, P. (1988). 'Leaner and possibly fitter: the management of redundancy in Britain'. *Industrial Relations Journal*, 19/3: 201–13.

Turnbull, P. and Wass, V. (1994). 'The greatest game no more—redundant dockers and the demise of "dock work"'. *Work, Employment and Society*, 8/4: 487–506.

Turnbull, P. and Wass, V. (1997). 'Job insecurity and labour market lemons: the (mis) management of redundancy in steel making, coal mining and port transport'. *Journal of Management Studies*, 34/1: 27–51.

Turnbull, P. and Wass, V. (2000). 'Redundancy and the paradox of job insecurity', in E. Heery and J. Salmon (eds), *The Insecure Workforce.* London: Routledge, 57–77.

Twentyman, J. (2010). 'The potential of social media in HR'. *Personnel Today*, 20 April, www.xperthr.co.uk

Tyler, M. and Abbot, P. (1998). 'Chocs away: weight watching in the contemporary airline industry'. *Sociology*, 32/3: 433–50.

UK Border Agency. (n.d.). *Working in the UK.* www.ukba.homeoffice.gov.uk

UKCES (UK Commission for Employment and Skills) (2009). *Towards Ambition 2020: Skills, Jobs, Growth.* London: UKCES.

UKCES (UK Commission for Employment and Skills) (2010). *High Performance Working: A Policy Review.* London: UKCES.

Ulrich, D. (1997). *Human Resource Champions: The Next Agenda for Adding Value and Delivering Results.* Boston, MA: Harvard Business School Press.

Ulrich, D. and Brockbank, W. (2005). *The HR Value Proposition.* Boston, MA: Harvard Business School Press.

Ulrich, D., Brockbank, W., Johnson, D., and Younger, J. (2009). *Human Resource Competencies: Rising to Meet the Business Challenge.* Provo, UT: RBL Group.

UNCTAD (United Nations Conference on Trade and Development) (2010). *World Investment Report 2010. Non-equity Modes of International Production and Development.* New York and Geneva: United Nations.

UNCTAD (United Nations Conference on Trade and Development) (2011*a*). *Review of Maritime Transport 2010.* New York and Geneva: United Nations.

UNCTAD (United Nations Conference on Trade and Development) (2011*b*). *UNCTADSTAT: Inward and Outward Foreign Direct Investment Stock 1980–2010.* New York and Geneva: United Nations.

UNCTAD (United Nations Conference on Trade and Development) (2011*c*). *World Investment Report 2011. Investing in a Low-Carbon Economy.* New York and Geneva: United Nations.

UNDP (United Nations Development Programme) (2011). *Human Development Reports: Sierra Leone Country Profile.* http://hdrstats.undp.org/en/countries/profiles/SLE.html

Union Network International (2006). 'Wal-Mart will Gespräche mit dem Allchinesischen Gewerkschaftsbund (ACFTU) aufnehmen: Wie ware es nun mit einem Sozialdialog in Amerika?', 10 August. www.union-network.org/UNIsite/Commerce/Deutsch/Wal-mart_China_Chance_auf_Sozialdialog_in_USA.htm

United Nations (1948). *Universal Declaration of Human Rights*. New York: United Nations.

United Nations (2011*a*). *Global Compact*. www.unglobalcompact.org

United Nations (2011*b*). *World Population Prospects: The 2010 Revision Population Database. Country Profiles*. www.un.org

Upchurch, M. (2010). *Creating a Sustainable Work Environment in British Airways: Implications of the 2010 Cabin Crew Dispute*. London: Global, Work and Employment Project, Middlesex University.

Uren, L., King, V., Fawcett, R., and Huestis, G. (2004). *Look Closer: Managing Today's Talent to Create Tomorrow's Leaders*. London: Towers Perrin.

van den Brink, M., Benschop, Y., and Jansen, W. (2010). 'Transparency in academic recruitment: a problematic tool for gender equality?' *Organization Studies*, 31/11: 1459–83.

Vance, C. (2005). 'The personal quest for building global competence: a taxonomy of self-initiating career path strategies for gaining business experience abroad'. *Journal of World Business,* 40/4: 374–85.

Vandeale, K. (2011). *Sustaining or Abandoning 'Social Peace'? Strike Developments and Trends in Europe since the 1990s*. European Trade Union Institute Working Paper 2011.05. Brussels: ETUI.

Vidal, J. (2006). 'How the world's biggest ship is delivering our Christmas—all the way from China'. *Guardian,* 30 October. www.guardian.co.uk

Virtanen, M., Ferrie, J., Singh-Manoux, A., Shipley, M., Vahtera, J., Marmot, M., and Kivmäki, M. (2010). 'Overtime work and incident coronary heart disease: the Whitehall II participative cohort study'. *European Heart Journal*, 31/14: 1737–44.

Wächter, H., Peters, R., Ferner, A., Gunnigle, P., and Quintanilla, J. (2006). 'The role of the international personnel function', in P. Almond and A. Ferner (eds), *American Multinationals in Europe.* Oxford: Oxford University Press, 248–70.

Waddington, J. (2003). 'Trade union organization', in P. Edwards (ed.), *Industrial Relations* (2nd edn). Oxford: Blackwell, 214–56.

Wade, R. (2007). 'Should we worry about income inequality?', in D. Held and A. Kaya (eds), *Global Inequality: Patterns and Explanations*. Cambridge: Polity Press, 104–31.

Walker, J. (2002). 'Perspectives. Talent pools: the best and the rest'. *Human Resource Planning*, 25/3: 12–14.

Wall, S., Minocha, S., and Rees, B. (2010). *International Business* (3rd edn). Harlow: Pearson Education.

Wallace, C., Eagleson, G., and Waldersee, R. (2000). 'The sacrificial HR strategy in call centres'. *International Journal of Service Industry Management*, 11/2: 174–84.

Wallace, J., Tiernan, S., and White, L. (2007). 'Industrial adaptation in Aer Lingus: the path from legacy to low fares carrier', unpublished case study.

Walsh, J. (2010). 'Working time and work–life balance', in A. Wilkinson, N. Bacon, T. Redman, and S. Snell (eds), *Sage Handbook of Human Resource Management*. London: Sage, 491–506.

Walsh, J. and Zhu, Y. (2007). 'Local complexities and global uncertainties: a study of foreign ownership and human resource management in China'. *International Journal of Human Resource Management*, 18/2: 249–67.

Walters, D. and Nichols, T. (2007). *Worker Representation and Workplace Health and Safety*. Basingstoke: Palgrave Macmillan.

Walters, D., Nichols, T., Connor, J., Tasiran, A., and Cam, S. (2005). *The Role and Effectiveness of Safety Representatives in Influencing Workplace Health and Safety*. HSE Research Report 363. London: Health and Safety Executive.

Walton, R. (1985). 'From control to commitment in the workplace'. *Harvard Business Review*, 63/2: 77–84.

Wang, G. and Swanson, R. (2008). 'The idea of national HRD: an analysis based on economics and theory development methodology'. *Advances in Developing Human Resources*, 7/1: 79–103.

Ward, C. and Preece, D. (2010). 'Managership development?' Presented at 11th International Conference on Human Resource Development Research and Practice across Europe, University of Pecs, Hungary, June.

Waters, C. (2008). 'Carers: many of your best staff will have caring responsibilities'. *Personnel Today*, 14 August. http://www.personneltoday.com

Watkins, J. (2003). 'Tests cut EA turnover'. *People Management*, 25 September: 7.

Watson, T. (2002). *Organizing and Managing Work*. Harlow: Financial Times–Prentice Hall.

Weber, M. (1947). *The Theory of Social and Economic Organization* (transl. A. Henderson and T. Parsons, ed. T. Parsons). New York: Free Press.

Weick, K. (1995). *Sensemaking in Organizations*. London: Sage.

Welch, D., Welch, L., and Worm, V. (2007). 'The international business traveller: a neglected but strategic human resource'. *International Journal of Human Resource Management,* 18/2: 173–83.

Welfare, S. (2011). 'Benefits and allowances survey 2011: no decline in popularity'. *IRS Employment Review*, 10 June. www.xperthr.co.uk

Wenger, E. and Snyder, W. (2000). 'Communities of practice: the organizational frontier'. *Harvard Business Review*, January/February: 139–45.

Westman, M. (2007). 'Survivors' syndrome', in S. Rogelberg (ed.), *Encyclopaedia of Industrial and Organizational Psychology*, Vol. 2. Thousand Oaks, CA: Sage, 782–4.

White, G. and Druker, J. (2000). *Reward Management: A Critical Text*. London: Routledge.

White, M., Hill, S., Mills, C., and Smeaton, D. (2004). *Managing to Change?* Basingstoke: Palgrave Macmillan.

White, P. (1983). 'The management of redundancy'. *Industrial Relations Journal*, 14/1: 32–40.

Whittington, R. (2001). *What is Strategy and Does it Matter?* London: Routledge.

Wilkinson, A. and Fay, C. (2011). 'New times for employee voice?' *Human Resource Management*, 50/1: 65–74.

Wilkinson, R. and Pickett, K. (2010). *The Spirit Level: Why More Equal Societies Almost Always do Better*. London: Penguin.

Willey, B. (2003). *Employment Law in Context: An Introduction for HR Professionals* (2nd edn). London: Financial Times–Prentice Hall.

379

Williams, C. (2007). *Rethinking the Future of Work: Directions and Visions*. Basingstoke: Palgrave Macmillan.

Williamson, O. (1991). 'Strategizing, economizing, and economic organizations'. *Strategic Management Journal*, 12/2: 75–94.

Williams, S., Bradley, H., Erickson, M., and Devadason, R. (2013). *Globalization and Work*. Cambridge: Polity Press.

Willman, P., Gomez, R., and Bryson, A. (2009). 'Voice at the workplace: where do we find it, why is it there and where is it going?', in W. Brown, A. Bryson, J. Forth, and K. Whitfield (eds), *The Evolution of the Modern Workplace*. Cambridge: Cambridge University Press, 97–119.

Willmott, H. (1993). 'Strength is ignorance; slavery is freedom: managing culture in modern organizations'. *Journal of Management Studies*, 30/4: 515–52.

Wills, J. (2004). 'Trade unionism and partnership in practice: evidence from the Barclays–Unifi agreement'. *Industrial Relations Journal*, 35/4: 329–43.

Wills, J. (2005). 'The geography of union organising in low-paid service industries in the UK: lessons from the T&G's campaign to unionise the Dorchester Hotel, London'. *Antipode*, 37/1: 139–59.

Wilson, J. (2005). *Human Resource Development: Learning and Training for Individuals and Organizations*. London: Kogan Page.

Winstanley, D. and Woodall, J. (eds) (2000). *Ethical Issues in Contemporary Human Resource Management*. Basingstoke: Macmillan.

Wolf, A. and Jenkins, A. (2006). 'Explaining greater test use for selection: the role of HR professionals in a world of expanding regulation.' *Human Resource Management Journal*, 16/2: 193–213.

Womack, J., Jones, D., and Roos, D. (1990). *The Machine that Changed the World*. New York: Rawson Associates.

Women and Work Commission (2006) *Shaping a Fairer Future*. www.womenandequalityunit. gov.uk

Wood, S. and Albanese, M. (1995). 'Can we speak of a high commitment management on the shop-floor?' *Journal of Management Studies*, 32/2: 215–47.

Wood, S. and Bryson, A. (2009). 'High involvement management', in W. Brown, A. Bryson, J. Forth, and K. Whitfield (eds), *The Evolution of the Modern Workplace*. Cambridge: Cambridge University Press, 151–75.

Work Foundation (2009). *Changing Relationships at Work*. London: Work Foundation.

World Bank (2011a). *Data: GDP Growth (annual %)*. data.worldbank.org

World Bank (2011b). *Sierra Leone: Country Brief*. web.worldbank.org

World Bank (2011c). *Doing Business: Measuring Business Regulations*. www.doingbusiness.org

World Bank Institute (2011). *Worldwide Governance Indicators: Country Data Report for Sierra Leone, 1996–2010*. info. worldbank.org

World Fair Trade Association (2011). *10 Principles of Fair Trade*. www.wfto.com

Wornham, D. (2003). 'A descriptive investigation of morality and victimisation at work'. *Journal of Business Ethics*, 45/1: 29–40.

Worrall, L., Cooper, C., and Campbell, F. (2000). 'The new reality for UK managers: perpetual change and employment instability'. *Work, Employment, and Society*, 14/4: 647–68.

Worthington, I. and Britton, C. (2009). *The Business Environment* (6th edn). Harlow: Financial Times–Prentice Hall.

Wray, D. (1996). 'Paternalism and its discontents'. *Work, Employment, and Society*, 10/4: 701–15.

Wright, C. (2011). *What Role for Trade Unions in Future Workplace Relations?* Future of Workplace Relations Discussion Paper Series. London: ACAS.

Wyatt, M., Pathak, S., and Zibarras, L. (2010). 'Advancing selection in an SME: is best practice methodology applicable?' *International Small Business Journal*, 28/3: 258–73.

Yamada, D. (2011). 'Workplace bullying and the law: emerging global responses', in S. Einarsen, H. Hoel, D. Zapf, and C. Cooper (eds), *Bullying and Harassment in the Workplace: Developments in Theory, Research, and Practice*. Boca Raton, FL: Taylor & Francis, 469–84.

Young, M. (2011). 'National vocational qualifications in the United Kingdom: their origins and legacy'. *Journal of Education and Work*, 24/3–4: 259–78.

Zaidi, A. (2009). *Welfare to Work Programmes in the UK and Lessons for Other Countries*. Vienna: European Centre for Social Welfare Policy and Research.

References

Index

Page references in italics indicate figures or tables. HRM stands for 'human resource management'.